The Gigantic Book
of
Fishing Stories

The Gigantic Book
of
Fishing Stories

Edited and with an Introduction by

NICK LYONS

Foreword by

DAVID HALBERSTAM

SKYHORSE PUBLISHING

www.skyhorsepublishing.com

10 9 8 7 6 5 4 3 2 1

ISBN-13: 978-1-60239-013-3
ISBN-10: 1-60239-013-4

Library of Congress Cataloging-in-Publication-Data is available on file.

Part of the proceeds of this book will go to support the FishAmerica Foundation, which annually provides over $1 million for projects that help keep our fish and waters healthy in all fifty states and along every American coastline and the Future Fisherman Foundation, which annually reaches hundreds of thousands of new anglers with extensive education programs, including "Physh Ed," which has been embraced by schools in more than thirty states.

Jacket artwork, "Bluegill Sunfish," "Brown Trout," "Smallmouth Bass," and "Yellowfin Tuna" © 2006 by Flick Ford, from Fish: 77 Great North American Fishing, published by The Greenwich Workshop Press, 2006.

Printed in China

CONTENTS

Foreword by David Halberstam xiii
Introduction by Nick Lyons xix

PART I
Early Days—of It and Us

"The Primitive Fish-Hook"
Barnet Phillips 3

"Ælian—The Macedonian Invention, or the First Mention of an Artificial Fly"
William Radcliffe 13

"The Compleat Angler" (selections)
Izaak Walton and Charles Cotton 20

"Ktaadn Trout" and "The Ponds" (selections)
Henry David Thoreau 42

"Trout: Meeting Them on the 'June Rise'"
"Nessmuk" 52

"Trout Fishing on Long Island"
Frank Forester 57

"Reuben Wood: My First Fish"
Fred Mather 69

"Trouting Along the Catasauqua"
Frank Forester 75

"The Boy and the Angle"
Rowland E. Robinson 81

"The Boy and the Brook"
Lathan A. Crandall 84

"A Little Miss and a Big Fish"
Ruth Mae Lawrence 89

"Little Bob's First Bass"
H. C. Mahin 93

"Some Memories of Early Days"
Lord Grey of Falloden 95

"Fishing with My Daddy"
Jimmy Carter 105

"The River God"
Roland Pertwee 109

Part II
The Warm Water Mix

"They're in the River"
John McPhee 125

"The Black Bass as a Game Fish"
James A. Henshall 128

"Red, White, and Bluegill"
Ted Leeson 142

"Among the Northern Pines"
Lathan A. Crandall 145

"Sacred Eels"
James Prosek 150

"Colors that Attract Bass"
Ozark Ripley 162

"A Dive for a Big Fellow"
Edward C. Kemper 165

"A Wise Ol' Cat"
George V. Triplett 168

"The Leopard of the Lake"
Leonard Hulit 171

"A Big Fish, S-o-o-o-o Long"
W. N. Hull 177

"The 'Lunge"
Stewart Edward White 179

"Slasher and the Shad"
Hart Stilwell 185

"Carp Fishing"
Frank Forester 191

"Bow-fin Fishing in the South Slang"
Rowland E. Robinson 194

"The Mascalonge"
James A. Henshall 200

"A Pickerel Yarn"
Fred Mather 207

"A Big Muskellunge"
W. N. Hull 211

"The Shanty"
Jerry Gibbs 215

"Fishing in the Ohio"
John James Audubon 221

Part III
A Touch of Salt

"Down to the Sea!"
Charles Kingsley 229

"On Sea and Shore"
Lathan A. Crandall 235

"Tale of a Bonefish"
C. Blackburn Miller 240

"The Angler and the Weakfish"
Charles Bradford 246

"Sea-Fishing in Simon's Bay"
Sir George Aston 251

"Sharks on the Shell Bars"
Vereen Bell 255

"The Saga of the Yellowfin"
Mark Sosin 262

"Keeping Busy When Not on the Casting Deck"
Lefty Kreh 266

"The Angler's Battle Royal: The Taking of the Tarpon"
Charles F. W. Mielatz 269

"The Tarpon of Turner's River"
A. W. Dimock 276

"The King of the Mackerel"
Charles F. Holder 286

"The Island"
Margot Page 292

"Trailing the Sea-Bat"
Charles F. Holder 300

"Byme-by-Tarpon"
Zane Grey 311

"Skelton's Party" (selection)
Thomas McGuane 315

Part IV
Trout and the Lure of Feathers

"The Lakes at Inhluzane"
Tom Sutcliffe 321

"2000 Words of Heartfelt Advice"
Verlyn Klinkenborg 326

"About the Brown Trout"
Samuel G. Camp 330

"The Trout and the Indian"
General John McNulta 333

"First of April"
William Senior 337

"Practical Dry-Fly Fishing for Beginners"
Emlyn M. Gill 342

"The Evolution of a Flyfisher"
Joan Salvato Wulff 349

"Pied Beauty"
Gerard Manley Hopkins 353

"A Bit of Luck"
Harry Plunket-Greene 354

"Fishing with a Worm"
Bliss Perry 357

"Nuptial Dress and Etiquette"
O. W. Smith 366

"The Value of Observation"
George M. L. LaBranche 369

"The Demon of the Foam"
H. Prescott Beach 378

"Salmon-Fishing"
A. G. Wilkinson 383

"Empty Baskets Change the Tune"
Alexander Mackie 410

"Two Old Trout of the Pools, and the Little Dry-Fly that
Finally Accomplished Their Ruin"
Emlyn Gill 411

"The Big Trout of the Hog-Back"
O. W. Smith 416

"The Finest Trout in the World"
Harry Plunket-Greene 423

"Winter Angling"
Frank S. Pinckney 426

"Nothing Fishy About Trout"
Dave Barry 433

"In Praise of Trout—And Also Me"
Paul O'Neil 435

Part V
Some Adventures on Water

"The Miramichi it ain't, so all right, it's 116th St."
John Bryan 453

"An Exploring Expedition"
W. C. Prime 458

"A Furcoated Fish"
B. F. Wilder 466

"The Sportsman Tourist"
John A. Lant 472

"Memories of Mahseer"
P. R. Bairnsfather 474

"The One That Got Away" (selection)
Howell Raines 482

Part VI
Anglers All—and Matters Philosophic

"The Man Who Lived Two Lives in One: Zane Grey"
Robert H. Boyle 487

"Thaddeus Norris"
Fred Mather 498

"The Angler"
Washington Irving 506

"What and Who Is an Angler?"
Thaddeus Norris 513

"The Fisherman's Song"
Thomas D'Urfey 520

"The Devout Angler"
Collin D. B. Ellis 523

"Observations on the Practice of Angling"
American Angler's Guide 525

"Note to *Don Juan* Canto XIII"
Lord Byron 529

"Fishin' Jimmy"
Annie Trumbull Slosson 530

"A Painter, an Angler, and Some Others"
William Scrope 542

"Fishing"
Reverend Thomas Bastard 551

"Crazy for Rivers"
Bill Barich 552

"A River Runs Through It" (selection)
Norman Maclean 556

"On Norman Maclean"
John Maclean 570

"George Croonenberghs"
John Maclean 572

"A Worm's-Eye View of Fishermen"
Beatrice Cook 577

"A Defense of Fishermen"
Grover Cleveland 583

"A Single Step"
George Reiger 589

"The Even-Tempered Angler" (selection)
Louis Rubin 591

"What's in a Name?"
Howard Frank Mosher 594

"The Solitary and Friendly Sport"
R. Palmer Baker, Jr. 597

"Midstream Crisis"
Lamar Underwood 602

"Blue Dun"
Frank Mele 608

Part VII
Classic Fishing Stories

"Storytelling on the Thames"
Jerome K. Jerome 623

"On the Loch"
William Black 629

"Three Bottles of Claret"
W. C. Prime 639

"Ol' Settler of Deep Hole"
Irving Bacheller 654

"The Lucy Coffin"
W. D. Wetherell 660

"Crocker's Hole"
R. D. Blackmore 671

"Plain Fishing"
Frank R. Stockton 684

"Owen's Adventure"
Robert Allen 696

"A Fatal Salmon"
Frank Forester 705

"A Gallant Poacher"
John Buchan 713

"Brannigan's Trout"
Nick Lyons 720

"A Fatal Success"
Henry van Dyke 732

"On Dry-Cow Fishing as a Fine Art"
Rudyard Kipling 739

"The Hole"
Guy de Maupassant 744

"The Lady or the Salmon?"
Andrew Lang 750

"Fish Are Such Liars!"
Roland Pertwee 755

"A Wedding Gift"
John Taintor Foote 769

"Mr. Theodore Castwell"
G. E. M. Skues 790

Acknowledgments 793

FOREWORD—A MEMOIR

David Halberstam

I am a fisherman and thus a dreamer of a certain quite precise kind, almost always when I am on the water; in my day job I am the most skeptical of men in one of the most skeptical of professions in a world which regrettably holds out fewer and fewer dreams the older I get. But on the water, fly rod in hand, my dreams never desert me; I can look out and even when the river water is murky and deep and running too fast, I can visualize a trout, always of a goodly size, rising to my fly, or if it's a clear day in the Caribbean, I can see a handsome bonefish moving steadily on its anointed course toward our boat, at the last second breaking off the requisite two feet to hit my fly. On the water, as I am never without dreams, I am never without hope.

The dreams began long ago, in 1940, when I was a boy, and I worked our old family row boat, caulked and recaulked as it was (mostly by me), and dreamed of what seemed back then like the rarest of rewards, a legal-sized bass (that is one at least ten inches long). And now that I am a man and a septuagenarian to boot, I still dream many of the same dreams, changed little over the years in subject matter, albeit expanded greatly in scope. Highland Lake, where the dreams began, was just two miles from downtown Winsted, Connecticut, a mill town where I spent the best part of my boyhood. It was in truth a terrible fished-out lake, but who dares tell a young and eager boy that, that his passion to fish might be at this moment ill-considered and more or less hopeless and that he would be better off concentrating on his swimming? To the contrary, my dreams were all the more important, my hopes for what would happen each time I fished inevitably greater than the reality of what did happen. I fished Highland Lake almost every day of every summer from roughly 1940 to 1948, starting when I was six, and ending when I was fourteen. I fished it mostly with worms which I dug myself; on occasion, after it had rained, with night crawlers; sometimes with crawfish (almost as much fun to catch in their rock-covered hideaways as the fish themselves); and on rare occasion, when either my uncle or my father was with my brother and me and we were being rather fancy, with live bait.

More often than not, I fished with a clunky old metal telescopic rod—the promise had been made (but no exact date set) that when I got older there would be a bamboo rod for me. In addition, I had an old casting rod and reel; this was the era just before the arrival of spinning gear when you could still get a world class back-lash—an entire morning often devoted to the untangling—with the wrong kind of cast. In those days, I could cast, with surprising distance for someone so young, a red-headed white-bodied Jitterbug, and sometimes a black skeletal Heddon River Runt, and occasionally a Hawaiian Wiggler (you could easily change the rubber skirt on the Wiggler), or, most simple of all, a red and white spoon. I have not touched a casting rod in sixty years, and sitting here writing about those days, I am stunned that I still remember the names of the different plugs, and can still see myself casting with that surprisingly short and stiff rod, and can even remember the rare strike of a bass or pickerel on the surface with the Jitterbug.

I was a fully committed fisherman as a boy. I read *Field & Stream* faithfully—I loved the byline of Ted Trueblood (was there ever a sportsman more appropriately named?), a man always, it seemed, on the case of some giant lunker that lurked in the most inaccessible of places. I admired as well the sketches that came with the articles, depicting huge record-breaking bass or muskie exploding out of deep weed patches, and dreamt that one day I too would catch my own lunkers. In those days, my brother and I—he was two years older and an accomplice in all this, though I do not think quite as passionate as I—not only fished every day, but we lingered in Mr. Rank's store in downtown Winsted, a place where fishing and hunting gear was sold. I loved Rank's—I did not then and do not now know his first name, for he was always Mr. Rank to us—and I loved the sense that, unlike any other store in Winsted, his had been designed for someone like me, a store stocked for a boy's fantasy world, stacks of rods, some of them bamboo, perhaps one of them one day mine, and dif-ferent reels, all carefully set out, row on row of them, and a vast variety of lures, surely all of them magical, sure to find the hidden lunkers of that world. In addition, Mr. Rank was the local tobacconist, and there was a marvelous smell of pipe tobacco in that shop. On those days when my brother and I missed the school bus because we were playing baseball or football after school and walked the two miles back to our house on the lake, we almost always stopped at Rank's, lingering as long as we dared, the time passed there in inverse proportion I am sure to the tiny scale of our pur-chases (a few Eagle Claw hooks perhaps). I liked everything about the store, except for the fact that Mr. Rank called me Sonny; I did not then, and do not now, think of myself as a Sonny, and I felt it demeaned me as a serious customer.

Highland Lake had three bays and we lived right on the lake in my uncle's house on First Bay—my father was off in the war—and I fished the lake every day. Each summer my hands were quickly hardened with the calluses that came from rowing our boat. Highland Lake was, truth to be told, rarely if ever restocked, and I was lucky if I caught two or three legal-sized bass a year. I think in all those years I caught one truly large bass, perhaps two or three pounds, but I can remember my father's warning when it struck—one of those warnings you hear and never forget, good for all occasions and all kinds of larger fish still to come—Never horse a bass! Up in Third Bay—I could row there, although in time we were given what I remember as a five-horsepower, extremely temperamental Evinrude motor, which started almost as often as it did not—there was an area filled with lilies which we called the Pickerel Grounds, which somehow promised (though rarely produced) more big fish, and I would row there, perhaps two miles each way, with higher hopes than when I fished First Bay.

I did not realize this at the time, but from the start, I was always at peace with myself when I fished. Back then, I loved every moment on the water, the days when I caught nothing, and the days when we caught the rare bass and perch, and the days when we caught rock bass and pumpkinseed, some of them surely for the umpteenth time that summer. I am sure as well that from the start, fishing gave me a wonderful sense of expectation, the belief that the next cast will be the best, and the fact that the last cast of the day is surely going to be the best one. I think back now, so many years later, and I cannot think of myself ever returning to our house and being unhappy—rather simply more determined than ever to do it again the next day.

The promised bamboo rods never materialized in my childhood. My father died when I was young, and as such I moved away from fishing for a long time. My career took over my life; journalists when they are young do not control their itineraries—they go where they are sent, to places like the Congo and Vietnam where even Ted Trueblood had probably never fished. But then in my mid-Thirties I bought a house in Nantucket, and came back to fishing. My friend Dick Steadman and I bought a twenty-foot Mako, and there were years when he and I and our friend David Fine fished two and three times a week, using very light spinning tackle and going after blues, the most savage of predators, and stripers, usually one hook, no barb. Though I had not fished in twenty years, it was as if I had never been away, the pleasure was so acute. Often there were days when I caught more big fish—ferocious ones; if they shook the hook during the struggle, they would often strike again—in one afternoon than I had caught in an entire summer as a boy. It was as if all those boyhood hopes and dreams had finally been fulfilled, or at least partially fulfilled.

And so I had, without consciously seeking to, come back to fishing and returned as well to a critical part of my boyhood. Now as I get older it has become an ever more important part of my life. The truth is, I suppose, that the thrill of it, that great sense of anticipation for every cast, the belief that this is the day that it will all happen, never went away. Late in life, a little restless with the self-imposed limits of fishing on

Nantucket, I started to fly fish. We all, I suspect, need enablers in life to push us to do the things we want and need to do, and when I was in my sixties I found my enabler, a friend named Richard Berlin—we became connected through our daughters, who were pals at boarding school. He is the most serious of fishermen. He had asked me when we first met, because of my Nantucket connection, if I was a fisherman, and with that the connection was made. His boyhood as a fisherman was as different from mine as it possibly could have been: it was spent with gifted guides at some of the world's great fishing lodges, significant skills honed long before there was a chance to learn how to do things the wrong way. When I was catching and recatching the same sunfish throughout the long summers of my boyhood, he was working great Canadian rivers like the Miramichi, catching monster Atlantic salmon.

He is not merely a very gifted fisherman, but even more important, he has impeccable fishing manners: he is generous, tuned to how other, less skilled friends are doing and how much fun they are having, and never worried about his own success; he is good enough to know that he will get his rightful share of big fish. And in time—for it was never deliberate, just something that happened—he started putting together a group of us, drawn from different parts of his life, unlikely friendships for all of us on our normal scale of palship, our politics and professions as different as it is possible to be, but joined by one thing, the sheer madness or the sheer logic of fishing, whichever it really is, the easy camaraderie that comes with unhurried time on the water, all of us with very different stories of how we got to be there, and always the sweetness of going off some great distance to fish together, with nothing else on the agenda, the comforting days on the water blended as it were with the occasional raucous noise of the lodge at the end of the day. Some of the men I fish with are truly gifted; they started young, had a natural grace and never stopped getting better. They cast with a certain artistry and there are moments when I am fishing that I stop for a time and steal a glance, admiring the skill in the way they cast, and admiring as well their modesty when we are back at the lodge, the fact they never boast about how well they have done, their awareness that it is all in the doing, and if they do it well there is no need to tell someone else that they have done it well. The trips we have made, aided by so many accumulated airline miles, strike me in retrospect as beyond exotic: the Rio Grande in Tierra del Fuego, the Zhupanova in Kamchatka, and a number of islands in the Caribbean, places I suspect beyond the reach of even the mighty Ted Trueblood. Sometimes now when I try to understand the passion I retain for fishing, my willingness to go halfway around the world, I trace it back to Highland Lake, to the fact that fishing there was so hard, that I am still, late in life looking for the rewards denied me when I was a boy; some of my friends, I think, still fish because of what they caught when they were boys—I fish, in no small part, because of what I didn't catch as a boy.

I was not good with a fly rod in the beginning and it was frustrating at first, but year after year, the more I practice, the better I've become, and I like that—it's a rare thing, to feel that you're getting better at something in your sixties and even in your seventies; mostly the opposite is true, the things you did so easily when you were young fade from your mastery. My equipment has gotten better, lighter and whippier. The telescopic rods of my childhood are but a distant memory (I do remember, as I write this, oiling those rods with three-in-one oil, so that they would not rust) relegated to an imaginary place that all of us have, the museum of childhood things, a place of memories rather than objects, and a reminder of how lucky I've been and how far I've come and how I do things now that once seemed so far out of reach. The venues, even as I visit them, stagger me, for their geographic reach—I who read *Field & Stream* faithfully as a boy, and thought that anyone who fished in Canada for salmon or in northern Minnesota for musky was blessed, now fly halfway around the world to fish. But the pleasures, I think, are much the same as the pleasures first discovered by that boy in Winsted more than sixty years ago. I remain forever a dreamer on the water, believing still, often against impressive evidence, that on the last cast of the day I will beget my best strike, and even when that does not happen, that tomorrow will always be better than today.

David Halberstam is a writer in New York and the winner of the 1964 Pulitzer Prize for international reporting. In the fall of 2007, his twenty-first book, *The Coldest Winter*, about the Chinese entry into the Korean War, will be published by Hyperion. His last fourteen books, starting with *The Best and the Brightest*, have been national bestsellers. Halberstam is convinced that he is becoming a more skillful fly fisherman with each year. He is delighted that a portion of the proceeds for this book are going to conservation and education via the good work of the FishAmerica and Future Fisherman Foundations.

INTRODUCTION

What a lot of fun I've had collecting the stories, memoirs, articles, and poems in this "gigantic" book. It is probably the largest, fullest, and most diverse collection of this sort ever compiled. And its very diversity and fullness are what excite me most—and what I predict will appeal to the vast number of people who share a love of fishing.

Surely there is a bond—too little acknowledged, I fear—between the catfish angler and the fly fisher. Both pursue a creature from that mysterious element, water, with some sort of bait, lure, or feathered thing. People have been fishing for a long time and parts of the practice have changed radically. Still, the early fish-hook (about which you can read an excellent essay in this book) persists, albeit in subtle new variations. The fishing done by a boy sometimes remains the same or sometimes evolves into one of many new forms. In this anthology, you will find both tradition and change—and some wonderful surprises, too.

There are selections from and about the earliest days of angling. There is a long section on warm-water fishing that includes some of James Henshall's classic writing about the small and largemouth basses and has John McPhee on shad, "the founding fish"; Ted Leeson on bluegill; James Prosek on eels; and John James Audubon on fishing for catfish in the Ohio River. Muskies, pike, bow-fin, pickerel, and carp are not wanting here, either.

A special section on salt-water angling includes writing about fishing for bonefish, sharks, tuna, weakfish, and the great tarpon. A longer section covers the trout and the variety of ways we fish for it (a good deal of the time with flies). Paul O'Neil's brilliant, often overlooked, essay "In Praise of Trout—And Also Me," caps this section. It was originally published in *Life* Magazine and is surely one of the best modern pieces of its kind; I'm proud to include it.

Howell Raines contributes a wonderful adventure narrative from his new book, *The One That Got Away*, and John Bryan's "The Miramichi it ain't"—which takes place much closer to home, in New York's Hudson River—is a wonderful example of how exciting and adventuresome fishing nearby can be. You don't have to go to the Himalayas for mahseer for real adventure—though that's here too.

There is much here about the variety of folks who fish—the famous (like Zane Grey, various presidents, and the great Norman Maclean) and the not-so-famous (but perhaps more addicted) people who bottom fish, fish with worms or fish with flies—and their passions, foibles and ways of doing this thing so many of us love.

And at the end I've included over twenty of my favorite stories, by de Maupassant, Kipling, John Taintor Foote, G. E. M. Skues and others. Forgive me if I've slipped in one I wrote, which rarely gets republished.

I hope you have as much fun reading this collection as I had bringing its pieces together from the vast world of writing about fishing. I hope you will be inspired to find more writings by the authors you most enjoy here, a good number of whom you'll probably be reading for the first time.

We spend more time off the water than on it. I hope you'll find those days at home a bit more enjoyable in the company of these memorable authors, anglers all.

Nick Lyons
November 2006

PART I

Early Days—
of
It and Us

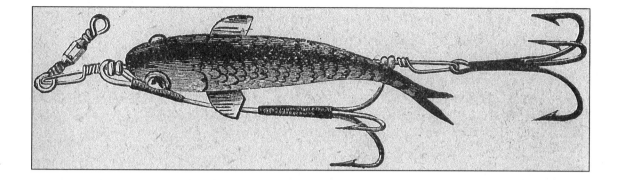

The Primitive Fish-Hook

BARNET PHILLIPS

I have before me an illustrated catalogue of modern fish-hooks and angling implements, and in looking over its pages I find an *embarrass de choix*. I have no need for rods, for mine, like well-kept violins, have rather improved by age. A lashing may be frayed, or a ferrule loose, but fifteen minutes' pleasant work will make my rods all right again. Lines are sound, for I have carefully stretched them after use. But my hooks! They are certainly the worse for wear. I began my season's fishing with a meager stock. Friends borrowed from me, and in replenishing my fly-book in an out-of-the-way place, the purchase was unsatisfactory. As I lost more than one fish from badly tempered or worse fashioned hooks, I recalled a delightful paper by Mr. Froude. Rod in hand, he was whipping some pleasant trout stream, near an historic site, the home of the Russells, and, breaking his hooks, commenced from that very moment to indulge in the gloomiest forebodings as to the future of England.

Fairly familiar with the general character of fishing-gear, either for business or amusement, I see in my book, Kirby, Limerick, Dublin, O'Shaughnessy, Kinsey, Carlisle, Harrison, Central Draught, as somewhat distant families of hooks, used for sea or river fishing, and from these main stocks there grow many varieties, with all conceivable twists, quirls, and crookednesses. I discard all trap-hooks, infernal machines working with springs, as only adapted for the capture of land animals. Somehow I remember an aggressive book, given to me at an early age, which, containing more than one depressing passage, had one of extraordinary malevolence. This was couched nearly as follows: "Suppose you were translated only some seven hundred years back, then, pray, what would you be good for? Could you make gunpowder? You have, perhaps, a vague idea that sulfur, saltpeter, and charcoal are the component parts, but do you know where or how they are procured?" I forget whether this dispiriting author was not equally harrowing in regard to the youthful reader's turning off a spectroscope at a minute's notice, or wound up with the modest request that you should try your hand among the Crusaders with an aneroid barometer of your own special manufacture.

Still this question arises: Suppose you were famishing, though fish were plenty in a stream, and you had neither line nor hook, What would you do? Now, has a condition of this kind ever occurred? Yes, it has, and certainly thousands of times. Not so many years ago, the early surveyors of the Panama route suffered terrible privations from the want of fishing implements. The rains had rendered their powder worthless; they could not use their guns. Had they only been provided with hooks and lines, they could have subsisted on fish. Then there are circumstances under which it would be really necessary for a man to be somewhat of a Jack-of-all-trades, and to be able to fashion the implements he might require, and so this crabbed old book might, after all, act in the guise of a useful reminder. There was certainly a period, when every man was in a condition of comparative helplessness, when his existence depended on his proficiency in making such implements as would catch fish or kill animals. He must fashion hooks or something else to take fish with, or die.

Probably man, in the first stage of his existence, took much of his food from the water, although whether he did or not might depend upon locality. If on certain portions of the earth's surface there were stretches of land intersected by rivers, dotted by lakes, or bordering on the seas, the presence of shell-fish, the invertebrates or the vertebrates, cetaceans and fish, to the exclusion of land animals, might have rendered primitive man icthyophagous, or dependent for subsistence upon the art of fishing. But herein we grapple at once with that most abstruse of all problems, the procession of life. Still, it is natural to suppose, so far as the study of man goes, when considered in relation to his pursuits, that in the early dawn of humanity, mammals, birds, and fish must have been synchronous.

After brute instinct, which is imitativeness, then came shiftiness and adaptiveness. The rapid stride of civilization, considered in its material sense, is due solely to the use of such implements as are specially adapted for a particular kind of work. With primitive man, this could never have been the case. Tools of the Paleolithic or Neolithic age (which terms indicate stages of civilization, but are not chronological), whether they were axes, hammers, or arrows, must have served river-drift or cave-men for more than a single purpose. People with few tools do manage by skill alone to adapt these to a variety of ends. The Fijian and the Russian peasant, one with a stone adze, the other with a hatchet, bring to their trades the minimum of tools. The Kafir, with his assegai, fights his battles, kills cattle, carves his spoons, and shaves himself. It was only as man advanced that he devised special tools for different purposes.

According to our present acquaintance with primitive habits, if man existed in the later Miocene age, and used a lance or spear for the killing of land animals, he probably employed the same weapons for the destruction of the creatures—possibly of gigantic form—inhabiting the seas, lakes, and rivers. The presence of harpoons made of bone, found in so many localities, belonging to a later period, may not in all cases point to the existence of animals, but to the presence of large fish.

Following, then, closely the advance of man, when his fishing implements are particularly considered, we are inclined to believe that he first used the spear for taking fish; next, the hook and line; and, lastly, the net. There might have been an intermediate stage between the spear and the hook, when the bow and arrow were used.

Interesting as is the whole subject of primitive fishing, we are, however, to occupy ourselves principally with the form of the primitive fish-hook. To-day there are some careful archaeologists who are not willing to accept that particular form which is presented below. I believe, from the many reasons which can be advanced, that this simple form was the first device used by man in taking fish with a line. The argument I shall use is in some respects a novel one.

These illustrations, exactly copied to size, represent a small piece of dark, polished stone. It was found in the valley of the Somme, in France, and was dug out of a peat-bed twenty-two feet below the surface. The age of this peat-bed has been variously estimated. M. Boucher de Perthes thought that thirty thousand years must have elapsed since the lowest layer of peat was formed. The late Sir Charles Lyell and Sir John Lubbock, without too strict an adher-

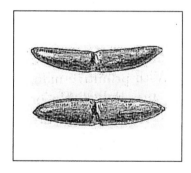

ence to date, believed that this peat-bed represented in its formation "that vast lapse of time which began with the commencement of the Neolithic period." Later authorities deem it not older than seven thousand years B. C.

Wonderful changes have come to pass since this bit of polished stone was lost in what must have been a lake. Examining this piece of worked stone, which once belonged to a prehistoric man living in that valley, we find it fairly well polished, though the action of countless years has slightly "weathered" or disintegrated its once smooth surface. In the center, a groove has been cut, and the ends of the stone rise slightly from the middle. It is rather crescent-shaped. It must have been tied to a line, and this stone gorge was covered with a bait; the fish swallowed it, and, the gorge coming crosswise with the gullet, the fish was captured.

The evolution of any present form of implement from an older one is often more cleverly specious than logically conclusive; nevertheless, I believe that, in this case, starting with the crude fish-gorge, I can show, step by step, the complete sequence of the fish-hook, until it ends with the perfected hook of to-day. It can be insisted upon even that there is persistence of form in the descendants of this fish-gorge, for, as Professor Mitchell writes in his "Past in the Present," "an old art may long refuse to disappear wholly, even in the midst of conditions which seem to be necessarily fatal to its continued existence."

In the Swiss lakes are found the remains of the Lacustrine dwellers. Among the many implements discovered are fish-gorges made of bronze wire. When these forms are studied, the fact must be recognized at once that they follow, in shape and principle of construction, the stone gorges of the Neolithic period. Now, it is perfectly

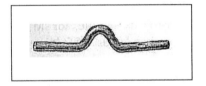

well known that the early bronze-worker invariably followed the stone patterns. The Lacustrine gorges have had the name of *bricole* given them. This is a faithful copy of a bronze bricole found in the Lake of Neufchatel. It is made of bronze wire, and is bent in the simplest way, with an open curve allowing the line to be fastened to it. The ends of the gorge are very slightly bent, but they were probably sharpened when first made.

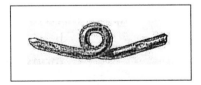

This bricole varies from the rather straight one found in the Lake of Neufchatel, and belongs to a later period. It is possible to imagine that the lake-dweller, according to his pleasure, made one or the other of these two forms of fishing implements. As the double hook required more bronze, and bronze at first was very precious, he might not have had material enough in the early period to make it. This device is, however, a clever one, for a fisherman of to-day who had lost his hook might imitate it with a bit of wire. Had any member of the hungry Isthmus party before mentioned known this form of Lacustrine hook, he might have twisted some part of a suspender buckle, providing there were no thorny plants at hand, and have caught fish.

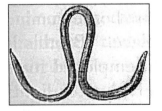

When we compare the four forms, showing only their outlines, the evolution of the fish-hook can be better appreciated. Returning to the stone fish-gorge, the work of the Neolithic period, it is evident that the man of that time followed the shape handed down to him by his ancestors; and as this fashioned stone from the valley of the Somme is of a most remote period, how much older must have been the Paleolithic fish-gorge of rough stone. It might have been with a splinter of flint attached to some tendril, in lieu of a line, that the first fish was taken.

It is very curious to learn that in France a modification of this gorge-hook is in use to-day for catching eels. A needle is sharpened at its eye-end, a slight groove is made in the middle of it, and around this some shreds of flax are attached. A worm is spitted, a little of the line being covered with the bait.

Not eels alone are taken with this needle, for M. de la Blanchere informs us that many kinds of fish are caught with it in France.

Any doubts as to the use of the Neolithic form of fish-gorge must be removed when it can be insisted upon that precisely this form of implement was in use by our Indians not more than forty years ago. In 1878, when studying this question of the primitive hook, I was fortunate enough to receive direct testimony on the subject. My informant, who in his younger days had lived among the Indians at the headwaters of Lake Superior, said that in 1846 the Indians used a gorge made of bone to catch their fish. My authority, who had never seen a prehistoric fish-gorge, save the drawing of one, said that the Indian form was precisely like the early shape, and that the Chippewas fished some with the hook of civilization, others with bone gorges of a primitive period.

In tracing the history of the fish-hook, it should be borne in mind that an overlapping of periods must have taken place. By this is meant, that at one and the same time an individual employed tools or weapons of various periods. To-day, the Western hunter lights his fire with a match. This splinter of wood, tipped with phosphorus, the chlorates, sulfur, or paraffin, represents the progress made in chemistry from the time of the alchemists. But this trapper is sure to have stowed away in his pouch, ready for an emergency, his flint and steel. The Esquimau, the Alaskan, shoots his seal with an American repeating rifle, and, in lieu of a knife, flays the creature with a flint splinter. The net of the Norseman is to-day sunk with stones or buoyed with wood,—certainly the same devices as were used by the early Scandinavian,—while the net, so far as the making of the thread goes, is due to the best modern mechanical appliances. Survival of forms requires some consideration apart from that of material, the first having the much stronger reasons for persistence. It is, then, very curious to note that hooks not made of iron and steel, but of bronze, or alloys of copper, are still in use on the coast of Finland, as I have quite recently obtained brass hooks from Northern Europe such as are commonly in use by fishermen there.

The origin of the double hook having been, I believe, satisfactorily explained, to make the barb on it was readily suggested to primitive man, as he had used the same device on fish-spears and harpoons.

This double-barbed hook from the Swiss lakes is quite common. Then, from the double to the single hook the transition was rapid. Single bronze hooks of the Lacustrine period sometimes have no barb. Such differences as exist are due to the various methods of attaching the line.

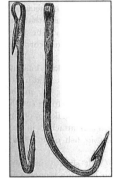

In Professor A. M. Mayer's collection there is a Lacustrine bronze hook, the shank of which is bent over parallel with the stem of the hook. This hook is a large one, and must have been used for big fish—probably the trout of the Swiss lakes.

Hooks made of stone are exceedingly rare, and though it is barely possible that they might have been used for fish, I think this has not been conclusively shown. Wilson gives, in his work, drawings of two stone hooks which were found in Scandinavia. Though the theory that these stone objects were fashioned for fishing is supported by so good an authority as Mr. Charles Rau, the archaeologist of the United States National Museum at Washington, it does not seem to me possible that these hooks could have been made for fishing. Such forms, from the nature of the material, would have been exceedingly difficult to fashion, and, even if made, would have presented few advantages over the primitive gorge.

This, however, must be borne in mind: in catching fish, primitive man could have had no inkling of the present curved form of fish-hook, which, with its barb, secures the fish by penetration. A large proportion of sea-fish, and many river-fish, swallow the hook, and are caught, not by the hook entering the jaws of the fish, but because it is fastened in their stomachs. In the Gloucester fisherman's language of to-day, a fish so captured is called "poke-hooked"; and accordingly, when the representative of the Neolithic period fished in that lake in the valley of the Somme, all the fish he took must have been poke-hooked. A bone hook, excellent in form, has been found near the remains of a huge species of pike (*Esox*). Hooks made of the tusks of the wild boar have also been discovered with Lacustrine remains.

In commenting on the large size of the bone hook figured in Wilson's work, its proximity to the remains of large fish was noticed. When the endless varieties of hooks belonging to savage races are subjects of discussion, the kind of fish they serve for catching should always be cited. In the examples of hooks which illustrate works of travel, a good many errors arise from the simple fact that the writers are not fish-

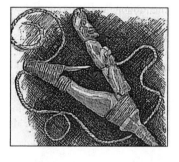

ermen. Although the outline of a hook be accurately given, the method of securing it to the line is often incorrectly drawn.

In the engraving on this page, an Alaskan halibut-hook is represented. The form is a common one, and is used by all the savage races of the Pacific; but the main interest lay in the manner of tying the line to this hook. Since the fish to be caught was the halibut, the form was the best adapted to the taking of

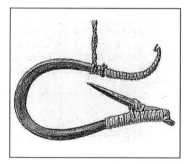

the *Hippoglossus Americanus*; but had the line been attached in any other way than exactly as represented, this big fish could hardly have been caught with such a hook.

In the drawing, the halibut-hook hangs but slightly inclining toward the sea-bottom, the weight of the bait having a tendency to lower it. In this position it can be readily taken by the fish; but should it be suspended in a dif-

ferent way, it must be at once seen how difficult it would be for the fish to swallow it. In this Alaskan hook must be recognized the very first idea of what we call to-day the center-draught hook. A drawing is also given of a steel hook of a peculiar form coming from Northern Russia. The resemblance between the Alaskan and this

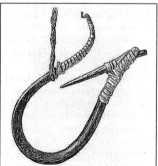

Russian hook is at first apparently slight, but they both are, nevertheless, constructed on the same principle. When this Russian hook is seized by the fish, and force is applied to the line by the fisherman, the point of the barb and the line are almost in one and the same direction. Almost the same may be said of the Alaskan hook. Desirous of testing the capabilities of this hook, I

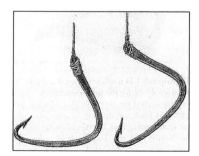

had a gross made after the Russian model, and sent them to Captain J. W. Collins, of the United States Fish Commission, stationed at Gloucester, requesting him to distribute them among the fishermen. While writing this article, I am in receipt of a letter from Captain Collins, informing me that these hooks are excellent, the captains of fishing-smacks reporting that a great many deep-sea fish were taken with them.

A study of these hooks—the Alaskan and the Russian—with reference to the method of attaching the line, explains, I think, the peculiarity of certain shell-hooks of great antiquity found in California which have puzzled archaeologists. These hooks, the originals of which are to be found in the National Museum at Washington, are shown in the following engravings. The notch cut in one of the hooks seems to show that the line was attached at that place. Hang the hooks in any other position and they would catch no fish, for one could hardly suppose that the blunt barb could penetrate the mouth of the fish.

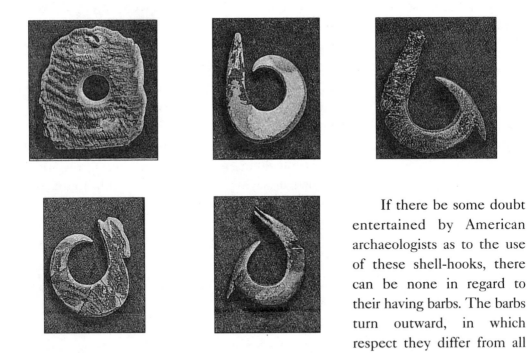

If there be some doubt entertained by American archaeologists as to the use of these shell-hooks, there can be none in regard to their having barbs. The barbs turn outward, in which respect they differ from all the primitive European hooks I have seen. In confirmation of the idea advanced as to the proper place of attaching the line, Professors C. C. Abbott and F. W. Putnam, in a chapter entitled "Implements and Weapons made of Bone and Wood," in the United States Geographical Survey, west of the hundredth meridian, write, referring to these hooks: "These hooks are flattened and are longer than wide . . . The barbs in these specimens are judged by fishermen of to-day to be on the wrong side of a good fish-hook, and the point is too near the shank. By having the line so fastened that the point of tension is at the notch at the base of the shank, instead of at the extreme end of the stem, the defect of the design of the hook would be somewhat remedied, as the barb would be forced down, so that it might possibly catch itself in the lower jaw of the fish that had taken the hook." The summing up of this is, I think, that in an imperfect way the maker of this Santa Barbara hook had some idea of the efficiency of a center-draught hook. As the first step in manufacturing this hook, a hole was drilled in the shell, and the hook finished up afterward by rounding the outside. Dr. West, of Brooklyn, has a series of such primitive work in his collection.

To advance the idea that in all cases hooks have been improved by slightly increased culture among semi-civilized races would be a source of error. It is quite possible that in many instances there has been retrogression from the better forms of fishing implements once in use. This relapse might have been brought about, not so much by a decrease of intelligence, as changes due to fortuitous causes. A fishing race might have been driven away from a shore or a river-bank and replaced by an inland people.

Some primitive races still use a hook made from a thorn, and in this practice we find to-day a most wonderful survival. On the coast of France, hooks made of thorns are still used to catch fish, the fishermen representing that they possess the great advantage of costing nothing and of not fouling on the sea-bottom. The Piutes take the spine of a cactus, bending it to suit their purpose, and very simple barbless hooks of this kind may be seen in the collections of the National Museum at Washington.

Undoubtedly, in primitive times, hooks of a compound character were used. Just as men tipped a deer's antler with a flint, they combined more than one material in the making of their hooks, lashing together a shank of bone or wood with a bronze barb. It would be almost impossible in a single article to follow all the varieties of hooks used and the ingenuity displayed in their manufacture. Occasionally, a savage will construct a lure for fish which rivals the daintiest fly ever made by the most fastidious of anglers. In Professor Mayer's collection there is an exceedingly clever hook, coming from the North-western coast, which shows very fine lapidary work. A small red quartoze pebble of great hardness has been rounded, polished, and joined to a piece of bone. The piece is small, not more than an inch and three-quarters in length, and might weigh an ounce and a half. In the shank of bone a small hook is hidden. It somewhat imitates a shrimp. The parts are joined together by lashings of tendon, and these are laid in grooves cut into the stone. It must have taken much toil to perfect this clever artificial bait, and, as it is to-day, it might be used with success by a clever striped-bass fisherman at Newport.

In this necessarily brief study of primitive fishing, I have endeavored to show the genesis of the fish-hook, from the stone gorge to the more perfected implement of to-day. Simple as it may seem, it is a subject on which a good deal of research is still requisite. "It is not an acquaintance with a single series of things which can throw light on any subject, but a thorough comparison of the whole of them." If in the Swiss lakes there are found bronze hooks of a very large size, out of proportion to the fish which swim there to-day, it is but just to suppose that, many thousands of years ago, long before history had its dawn, the aquatic fauna were then of greater bulk than in 1883. Considerations of the primitive form of the fish-hook must even comprehend examination of prior geological conditions, differences of land and water, or such geographical changes as may have taken place. Then ichthyology becomes an important factor, for by the character of the hook, the kind of fish taken, in some instances, may be understood. We are fast coming to this conclusion: that, putting aside what can only be the merest speculations as to the condition of man when he is said to have first diverged from the brute, he was soon endowed with a wonderful degree of intelligence. And, if I am not mistaken, primitive man did not confine himself in his fishing to the rivers and lakes alone, but went out boldly to sea after the cod.

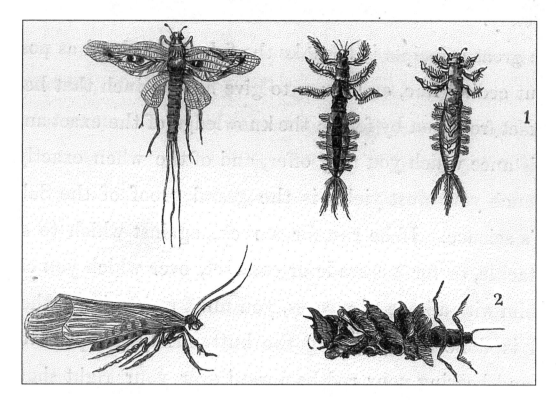

Ælian—The Macedonian Invention, or the First Mention of an Artificial Fly

WILLIAM RADCLIFFE

"They knew 'e stole; 'e knew they knowed;
They did not tell, or make a fuss,
But winked at Ælian down the road,
And 'e winked back—the same as us!"[1]

Ælian (170–230 A. D.), who, though born in Italy and brought up in the Latin tongue, acquired so complete a command of Greek that he could speak it as well as an Athenian gentleman (hence his sobriquet μείγλωττος), composed his works in Greek.

His *Natural History*[2] soon became a standard work on Zoology, although in arrangement it is very defective: for instance, he skips from elephants (XI. 15) to dragons in the very next chapter, and from the livers of mice in II. 56 to the uses of oxen in II. 57. This treatment of things, ποικίλα ποικίλως, is asserted by the author to be intentional, so as to avoid boring the

---

[1]After Kipling.
[2]Περί Ζώων ἰοιότηος.

reader. For his part he avows that he prefers observing the habits of animals and fish, listening to the nightingale, or studying the migration of cranes, to heaping up riches![3]

Whether as a naturalist Ælian possesses any value, whether his work is "scrappy and gossiping, and largely collected from older and more logical writers,"[4] or "from the industry displayed, despite deficiency in arrangement, a valuable collection in Natural History," to us fishermen matters little, for unto him has been ascribed the great glory of being the first author of all ages and of all countries specially to mention and roughly describe an Artificial Fly.

And not only is he the first, but also (with possibly one exception) the only author during fourteen hundred years, who makes any reference to any such fly.[5] From Ælian until the *Treatyse of Fysshynge with an Angle* we find no mention of, or allusion to, the Artifical Fly, but that it was well known as a method of angling is easily deduced from the authoress's abrupt introduction of the subject, "These ben the xij flies or dubbes with which ye shall angle."[6]

The usually accurate *Bibliotheca Piscatoria* of Westwood and Satchell states under heading of 'Ælian,' that Stephen Oliver (Mr. Chatto), in his *Scenes and Recollections of Fly Fishing*, first pointed out this remarkable passage. Now the first edition of Oliver's book is dated 1834; so, if the *Bibliotheca Piscatoria* be correct, Ælian's statement apparently remained unknown to Anglers for nearly eighteen centuries.

I purposely set out a translation of the whole passage in Ælian, XV. 1, because short extracts are usually given, and because these vary greatly on a very important point. I adopt with some alterations the translation by Mr. O. Lambert in his *Angling Literature in England* (1881).

"I have heard of a Macedonian way of catching fish, and it is this: between Beroea and Thessalonica runs a river called the Astraeus, and in it there are fish with speckled skins; what the natives of the country call them you had better ask the Macedonians. These fish feed on a fly peculiar to the country, which hovers on

---

[3]See Smith's *Dict. Gk. And Rom. Biog. And Myth.*, *s.v.* 'Aelian.'

[4]Perizonius has proved that Aelian transferred large portions of the *Deipnosophistæ* of Athenaeus to his *Varia Historia*, a robbery which must have been committed almost in the lifetime of the pillaged author: that Aelian extended such transference to his *Natural History* also, his story of the *Pinna*, and others would seemingly demonstrate. Sir J. E. Sandys, *A History of Classical Scholarship*, ed. 2 (Cambridge, 1906), i. 336, goes so far as to say: "He is the author of seventeen books *On Animals*, mainly borrowed from Alexander of Myndos (first century A.D.)."

[5]Dr. W. J. Turrell, *op. cit.*, XI., states that a Latin poem written by Richard de Fournival, about the thirteenth century, alludes incidentally to fishing, and from this it appears that the *fly* and the worm were among the lures then used by anglers, but does not state expressly whether Fournival's fly was natural or artificial.

[6]Cf. H. Mayer, *Sport with Rod and Line*, Barnet and Phillips, New York.

the river. It is not like flies found elsewhere, nor does it resemble a wasp in appearance, nor in shape would one justly describe it as a midge or a bee, yet it has something of each of these. In boldness it is like a fly, in size you might call it a midge, it imitates the color of a wasp, and it hums like a bee. The natives generally call it the *Hipporous*.

"These flies seek their food over the river, but do not escape the observation of the fish swimming below. When then the fish observes a fly on the surface, it swims quietly up, afraid to stir the water above, lest it should scare away its prey; then coming up by its shadow, it opens its mouth gently and gulps down the fly, like a wolf carrying off a sheep from the fold or an eagle a goose from the farmyard; having done this it goes below the rippling water.

"Now though the fishermen know of this, they do not use these flies at all for bait for fish; for if a man's hand touch them, they lose their natural color, their wings wither, and they become unfit food for the fish. For this reason they have nothing to do with them, hating them for their bad character; but they have planned a snare for the fish, and get the better of them by their fisherman's craft.

"They fasten red (crimson red) wool round a hook, and fix on to the wool two feathers which grow under a cock's wattles, and which in color are like wax. Their rod is six feet long, and their line is the same length. Then they throw their snare, and the fish, attracted and maddened by the color, comes straight at it, thinking from the pretty sight to get a dainty mouthful; when, however, it opens its jaws, it is caught by the hook and enjoys a bitter repast, a captive."

The lines which describe the making up of the fly—τῶ ἀγκίστρω περιβάλλουσιν ἔριον φοινικοῦν, ἥρμοσταί τε τῶ ἐρίω δύο πτερὰ ἀλεκτρυόνος ὑπό τοίς καλλαίσις πεφυκότα καί κηρῶ τήν χρύαν προσεικασμένα[7] are translated in Westwood and Satchell's *Bibl. Pisc.*, and by Mr. Lambert quite differently.

In the *Bibl. Pisc.*:

"Round the hook they twist scarlet wool, and two wings are secured on this wool from the feathers which grow under the wattles of a cock, brought up to the proper color with wax."

In Lambert:

"They fasten red wool round a hook and fit on the wool two feathers which grow under a cock's wattles, and which in color are like wax."

---

[7]Jacobs adopts κηρῶ, instead of Gesner's χρυσῶ, chiefly because it is written thus quite clearly in the Codex Augustanus. It also seems to fit the context better.

It is asserted in the *Bibl. Pisc.* that the whole passage is therein "for the first time, accurately, translated," but this proud boast must take a back seat, for Mr. Lambert translates with far nearer accuracy. One grave error springs from mistranslation in the former of προσεικασμένα as "brought up to," instead of "like," a meaning very common in Greek writers in the second and third century.

But, apart from the question which of the two be better rendering, no doubt whatever can exist which of the flies described would be found the better, if not the only, killer. Application of wax to the hackles of a cock would certainly cause the fiber to stick together, entirely destroy their free play in the water, and render them useless as wings.

This passage, ever since its rediscovery by Oliver in 1834, has been acclaimed by most writers on Fishing as (A) being the first instance in literature, or for that matter in art, of the Artificial Fly, and as (B) ascribing to the Macedonians the credit of a "new invention" in Angling.

It is undoubtedly the first and only express mention of a specially made-up Artificial Fly down to 500 A.D., and probably even down to Dame Juliana's Book (*c.* 1500). But I suggest and believe that this passage is intended, not as a description of a "new invention," or of a striking departure from old methods of Angling. It merely instances the Macedonian's adaptability to his environment, and his imitative skill in dressing from his wools and feathers a fly to resemble as closely as possible the natural fly on which the fish were feeding, a practice very common among anglers of the present day.

So far from the Artificial Fly being a "new invention," it seems to me to have been for a long time in more or less regular use. The materials necessary or employed for dressing flies are set forth in two other places by Ælian in this same work. The Macedonian fly is described at length and in special detail, probably because it marked an advance in making up a fly.

I have not been able so far to find the passages in Bk. III. 43, and Bk. XV. 10, mentioned (except in Blümner's general list of fishing weapons under "*Fischfang*"[8]) or alluded to in connection with fly-making, much less brought into the prominence which their special pertinence of a surety deserves and demands.

This omission may be due to previous writers being content with the authority and researches of Oliver and of Westwood and Satchell, and on the line of least exertion not pursuing the subject any further even in the pages of Ælian himself. If they had so pursued, they would have discovered in the first passage in Bk. XII. 43, which is separated by only three books, and in the second passage in Bk. XV. 10, which is

---

[8]*Die römischen Privataltertümer* (Munich, 1911), pp. 529–530.

separated by only nine chapters from the *locus classicus* in Bk. XV. I, strong inventions for qualifying their statement as to the Macedonian "invention."

In Bk. XII. 43, Fishing is divided into four kinds—by Nets, Spears, Weels, and Hooks; that by hooks (αγκιστρεία) is adjudged "the most skilful, and most becoming for free men," that by Weels (κυρτεία) the least so. In each class Ælian carefully enumerates the articles necessary or generally used.

The list of those necessary for fishing with hooks, or Angling, recounts "natural horsehair, white, and black, and flame-colored, and half-grey; but of the dyed hair, they select only those that are grey, or of true sea-purple, for the rest, they say, are pretty poor. They use, too, the straight bristles of swine, and thread, and much copper and lead, and cords." Now follow the important words—"and feathers, chiefly white or black, or various. They use two wools, red and blue."[9]

Further requirements are "corks, and wood, and iron, and of things they need, are reeds well-grown, and nets, and soaked rushes, a shaved wand, and a dog-wood Rod, and the horns and hide of a she-goat." The equipment is as ample as amazing. What use, in the name of every fishing Deity, unless the author is referring to Oppian's method, did the *Angler* make of the "horns and hide of a she-goat"?

Ælian concludes with ἀλλος δέ ἀλλω τούτων ιχθύς αιρεί ται, which antedates the tale of the millionaire, who, reproached with having brought a thousand times too many flies, ejaculated, "With some of these, if I can't get a salmon, maybe I'll strike a sucker!"

In XV. 10, which deals with the capture of pelamyde or young tunny fish, one of the crew sitting at the stern lets down on either side of the ship lines with hooks. On each hook he ties a bait (perhaps not a bait in our modern technical sense, but rather a lure) wrapped in wool of Laconian red, and to each hook attaches the feather of a seamew.[10]

Let us set aside, because of Ælian's haphazard method of arrangement, any argument which might otherwise fairly be adduced from the following facts. (A) He expressly sets forth in XII. 43 (three books before he mentions the Macedonian device) *red and other wools and feathers* as part of the *ordinary tackle* of an Angler—most probably in river or lake, for here, unlike XV. 10, where the prey is a sea-fish, we have no mention of a ship, oars, etc. (B) When he does mention the Macedonian device, he does not announce it in any way as a new invention or a striking departure from the old methods of fishing, but quite simply, in the words: "I have heard of the Macedonian way of fishing, and it is this."

---

[9]Καί πτεροις, μάλιστα μέν λευκοις καί ποικίλοις. Χρῶνταί γε μήν οἱ ἁλιεις καί φοινικοίς ἐρίοις καί αλουργέσι, κ.τ.λ.

[10]καί πτερόν ἑκάσν λαρον ἑκάστω ἀγκίστ ρω προσήρτηται.

Setting aside, I repeat, any arguments thus to be deduced, we are face to face with the hard and curious fact, that in all three passages the materials, out of which the lures are constructed, *are the same*; they are wools of various colors, and feathers taken from birds, in XV. I, from a cock, in XV. 10, from a seamew.

Any assertion or suggestion that these wools and feathers were used, and are specially stated to have been used for tying only the Macedonian fly, and that this special statement of such uses is meant expressly to differentiate the Macedonian from all other ways of fishing, and thus constitutes the first mention of an Artificial Fly, I counter by a couple of queries.

Why in XII. 43, and XV. 10, are these self-same wools and feathers set out among the necessary ordinary requisite tackle of a fisherman, if they were not used for dressing a fly, perhaps more primitive but still Artificial? And, if they were not so used, to what other fishing purpose can they be fairly applied?

Again, let us for a moment grant that the Macedonian device was the absolutely new invention or the striking departure from all preceding angling methods, which, had artificial flies not previously been well known, it most certainly would have been. In this case, surely Ælian, meticulous in his examination and classification of the tackle, etc., needed for each of the four stated kinds of fishing, would have employed, when about to tell of this invention, words calling more instant attention to and far worthier of this great revolution than the simple, "I have heard of the Macedonian way of fishing, and it is this!"

As supporting my contention, a further point must be noted. In the list of tackle in XII. 43, wools and feathers are mentioned in a general manner, but in XV. 1, their use is particularized and elaborated. Similarly in the first passage the making and material of Rods are given, but in the second (and here only) the particular length of rod is stated.

It is on these passages (XII. 43, and XV. 10) and on their natural implication, that I chiefly found my conclusion that (A) the practice of making up and fishing with some kind of artificial fly had been in more or less general use for a long time previous to the Macedonian device, and (B) that the device is quoted merely as an instance of a special, local, and improved adaptation of such usage—in a word as *le dernier cri* in flies![11]

If in Martial (*Ep.*, V. 18. 8) *musco*, not *musca*, should be read, then to Ælian would belong the credit of being the first to mention not only the use of the artificial fly, but also the use of the natural fly.

---

[11]If Sandys (*antea*, 185, note 4) be right about Ælian's work being "mainly borrowed from Alexander of Myndos," first century A.D., the artificial fly was probably well known in Martial's time.

In XIV. 22, we read of the *Thymalus* (a kind of grayling), which alone of all fishes gives out after capture no fishy smell, but rather so fragrant an odor that one would almost swear that in his hand he held a freshly gathered bunch of thyme ("that herb so beloved by bees"), instead of a fish. Ælian then lays down that, while it is easy to catch this fish in nets, it is impossible to do so with a hook baited with *anything* except the κώνωψ, *i.e.* the gnat, or more probably from the vivid description by one who has evidently suffered, the mosquito, "that horrid insect, a foe to man, both day and night, alike with his bite and his buzz."[12]

Here then, in XIV. 22, we get, if the conjecture *musco* should be held to deprive Martial of his priority, the first mention of angling with a *natural* fly.

The difficulty, obvious at once to the practical angler, of how the ancients (or even the moderns with all the elaborate perfections of Redditch) could manufacture a hook little enough to impale a mosquito did not escape Aldrovandi.[13] But the κώνωψ, said to spring from the σκώληκες, *i.e.*, *larvæ* found in the sediment of vinegar, was apparently even smaller than his brother mosquito, the ἐμπίς.[14]

As not only with great care, and even then only on very fine wire, can the smallest modern hook, No. 000, be coaxed to impale a big gnat, the problem before the Ancients of impaling with a hook one, and this not even the largest, of the mosquito tribe seems insoluble. But perhaps Ælian?s κώνωψ (as probably also his ἵππουρος) was far larger than its descendant of the present day, or perhaps our author has substituted by mistake the mosquito for some larger but similar gnat.

---

[12]πονηρῶ μέν ζώῳ καί μεθ ἡμέραν καί νύκτωρ ἀνθρώποις καί δακείν καί βοῆσαι.

[13]For size of hooks, see *antea*, p. 157 and note 1.

[14]Cf. Arist., *N. H.*, V. 19. The σκώληξ of Aristotle is an immature product of generation which grows and finally becomes a pupa, or (so Aristotle believed) an egg giving birth to the perfect animal.

The Compleat Angler (selections)

IZAAK WALTON AND CHARLES COTTON

Now for the art of catching fish, that is to say, how to make a man that was none to be an angler by a book, he that undertakes it shall undertake a harder task than Mr. Hales, a most valiant and excellent fencer, who, in a printed book called "A Private School of Defence" undertook by it to teach that art or science, and was laughed at for his labor. Not but many useful things might be learnt by that book, but he was laughed at because that art was not to be taught by words, but practice: and so must angling. And in this discourse I do not undertake to say all that is known or may be said of it, but I undertake to acquaint the reader with many things that are not usually known to every angler; and I shall leave gleanings and observations enough to be made out of the experience of all that love and practice this recreation, to which I shall encourage them. For angling may be said to be so like the mathematics that it can never be fully learnt; at least not so fully, but that there will still be more new experiments left for the trial of other men that succeed us.

But I think all that love this game may here learn something that may be worth their money, if they be not poor and needy men: and in case they be, I then wish them to forbear to buy it; for I write not to get money, but for pleasure, and this discourse boasts of no more; for I hate to promise much, and deceive the reader.

And however it proves to him, yet I am sure I have found a high content in the search and conference of what is here offered to the reader's view and censure. I wish him as much in the perusal of it. And so I might here take my leave, but will stay a little and tell him that whereas it is said by many that in fly-fishing for a trout, the angler must observe his twelve several flies for the twelve months of the year; I say he that follows that rule shall be sure to catch fish and be as wise as he that makes hay by the fair days in an almanac, and no surer; for those very flies that use to appear about and on the water in one month of the year may the following year come almost a month sooner or later, as the same year proves colder or hotter; and yet in the following discourse I have set down the twelve flies that are in reputation with many anglers, and they may serve to give him some light concerning them. And he may note that there are in Wales and other countries peculiar flies, proper to the particular place or country; and doubtless, unless a man makes a fly to counterfeit that very fly in that place, he is like to lose his labor, or much of it; but for the generality, three or four flies neat and rightly made, and not too big, serve for a trout in most rivers all the summer. And for winter fly-fishing it is as useful as an almanac out of date. And of these (because as no man is born an artist, so no man is born an angler) I thought fit to give thee this notice.

***

And for you that have heard many grave, serious men pity anglers; let me tell you, Sir, there be many men that are by others taken to be serious and grave men which we condemn and pity. Men that are taken to be grave, because nature hath made them of a sour complexion, money-getting men, men that spend all their time first in getting, and next in anxious care to keep it, men that are condemned to be rich, and then always busy or discontented. For these poor-rich-men, we anglers pity them perfectly, and stand in no need to borrow their thoughts to think ourselves happy. No, no, Sir, we enjoy a contentedness above the reach of such dispositions, and as the learned and ingenuous Montaigne says, like himself freely, "When my cat and I entertain each other with mutual apish tricks, as playing with a garter, who knows but that I make my cat more sport than she makes me? Shall I conclude her to be simple, that has her time to begin or refuse sportiveness as freely as I myself have? Nay, who knows but that it is a defect of my not understanding her language (for doubtless cats talk and reason with one another) that we agree no better? and who knows but that she pities me for being no wiser, and laughs and censures my folly for making sport for her when we two play together?"

Thus freely speaks Montaigne concerning cats, and I hope I may take as great a liberty to blame any man, and laugh at him too, let him be never so serious, that hath not heard what anglers can say in the justification of their art and recreation. Which I may again tell you is so full of pleasure that we need not borrow their thoughts, to think ourselves happy.

***

PISCATOR. O, sir, doubt not but that angling is an art! Is it not an art to deceive a trout with an artificial fly? a trout! that is more sharp-sighted than any hawk you have named and more watchful and timorous than your high-mettled merlin is bold! And yet I doubt not to catch a brace or two tomorrow, for a friend's breakfast. Doubt not, therefore, Sir, but that angling is an art and an art worth your learning. The question is rather whether you be capable of learning it! for angling is somewhat like poetry, men are to be born so. I mean, with inclinations to it, though both may be heightened by practice and experience; but he that hopes to be a good angler must not only bring an inquiring, searching, observing wit, but he must bring a large measure of hope and patience and a love and propensity to the art itself; but having once got and practiced it, then doubt not but angling will prove to be so pleasant that it will prove to be, like virtue, a reward to itself.

VENATOR. Sir, I am now become so full of expectation, that I long much to have you proceed and in the order that you propose.

PISCATOR. Then first, for the antiquity of angling, of which I shall not say much but only this: some say it is as ancient as Deucalion's Flood; others, that Belus, who was the first inventor of godly and virtuous recreations, was the first inventor of angling; and some others say, for former times have had their disquisitions about the antiquity of it, that Seth, one of the sons of Adam, taught it to his sons, and that by them it was derived to posterity; others say that he left it engraven on those pillars which he erected and trusted to preserve the knowledge of mathematics, music, and the rest of that precious knowledge and those useful arts, which by God's appointment or allowance and his noble industry were thereby preserved from perishing in Noah's Flood.

These, sir, have been the opinions of several men, that have possibly endeavored to make angling more ancient than is needful or may well be warranted; but for my part, I shall content myself in telling you, that angling is much more ancient than the incarnation of our Savior; for in the Prophet Amos mention is made of fish-hooks; and in the Book of Job—which was long before the days of Amos, for that book is said to have been writ by Moses—mention is made also of fish-hooks, which must imply anglers in those times.

But, my worthy friend, as I would rather prove myself a gentleman, by being learned and humble, valiant and inoffensive, virtuous and communicable, than by any fond ostentation of riches, or, wanting those virtues myself, boast that these were in my ancestors—and yet I grant that where a noble and ancient descent and such merit meet in any man it is a double dignification of that person—so if this antiquity of angling—which for my part I have not forced—shall, like an ancient family, be either an honor or an ornament to this virtuous art which I profess to love and practice, I shall be the gladder that I made an accidental mention of the antiquity of it; of which I shall say no more, but proceed to that just commendation which I think it deserves.

And for that I shall tell you that in ancient times a debate hath risen, and it remains yet unresolved—whether the happiness of man in this world doth consist more in contemplation or action.

Concerning which some have endeavored to maintain their opinion of the first, by saying, "that the nearer we mortals come to God by way of imitation the more happy we are." And they say, "that God enjoys himself only by a contemplation of his own infiniteness, eternity, power, and goodness," and the like. And upon this ground many cloisteral men of great learning and devotion prefer contemplation before action. And many of the fathers seem to approve this opinion, as may appear in their commentaries upon the words of our Savior to Martha, Luke 10:41, 42.

And on the contrary there want not men of equal authority and credit that prefer action to be the more excellent, as namely "experiments in physic and the application of it, both for the ease and prolongation of man's life"; by which each man is enabled to act and do good to others, either to serve his country or do good to particular persons; and they say also "that action is doctrinal and teaches both art and virtue and is a maintainer of human society"; and for these and other like reasons to be preferred before contemplation.

Concerning which two opinions I shall forbear to add a third by declaring my own, and rest myself contented in telling you, my very worthy friend, that both these meet together, and do most properly belong to the most honest, ingenuous, quiet, and harmless art of angling.

And first, I shall tell you what some have observed, and I have found to be a real truth, that the very sitting by the river's side, is not only the quietest and fittest place for contemplation but will invite an angler to it. And this seems to be maintained by the learned Pet. du Moulin, who, in his discourse of the Fulfilling of Prophecies, observes that when God intended to reveal any future event or high notions to his prophets, he then carried them either to the deserts or the sea-shore, that having so separated them from amidst the press of people and business and the cares of the world he might settle their mind in a quiet repose, and make them fit for revelation.

***

And for the lawfulness of fishing, it may very well be maintained by our Savior's bidding St. Peter cast his hook into the water and catch a fish for money to pay tribute to Caesar. And let me tell you that angling is of high esteem and of much use in other nations. He that reads the voyages of Ferdinand Mendez Pinto shall find that there he declares to have found a king and several priests a-fishing.

And he that reads Plutarch shall find that angling was not contemptible in the days of Marc Antony and Cleopatra and that they in the midst of their wonderful glory used angling as a principal recreation. And let me tell you that in the Scripture angling is always taken in the best sense and that though hunting may be sometimes so taken, yet it is but seldom to be so understood. And let me add this more. He that views the ancient ecclesiastical canons shall find hunting to be forbidden to churchmen, as being a toilsome, perplexing recreation; and shall find angling allowed to clergymen, as being a harmless recreation, a recreation that invites them to contemplation and quietness.

***

My next and last example shall be that undervaluer of money, the late Provost of Eton College, Sir Henry Wotton, a man with whom I have often fished and conversed, a man whose foreign employments in the service of this nation and whose experience, learning, wit, and cheerfulness made his company to be esteemed one of the delights of mankind. This man, whose very approbation of angling were sufficient to convince any modest censurer of it, this man was also a most dear lover and a frequent practice of the art of angling; of which he would say, " 'Twas an employment for his idle time, which was not then idly spent"; for angling was, after tedious study, "a rest to his mind, a cheerer of his spirits, a diverter of sadness, a calmer of unquiet thoughts, a moderator of passions, a procurer of contentedness; and that it begot habits of peace and patience in those that professed and practiced it." Indeed, my friend, you will find angling to be like the virtue of humility, which has a calmness of spirit and a world of other blessings attending upon it.

Sir, this was the saying of that learned man, and I do easily believe, that peace and patience and a calm content did cohabit in the cheerful heart of Sir Henry Wotton, because I know that when he was beyond seventy years of age, he made this description of a part of the present pleasure that possessed him, as he sat quietly in a summer's evening on a bank a-fishing. It is a description of the spring, which, because it glides as soft and sweetly from his pen as that river does at this time, by which it was then made, I shall repeat it unto you:

> This day Dame Nature seemed in love;
> The lusty sap began to move;
> Fresh juice did stir th' embracing vines,
> And birds had drawn their valentines.

The jealous trout, that low did lie,
Rose at a well-dissembled fly;
There stood my friend with patient skill
Attending of his trembling quill.

Already were the eaves possessed
With the swift pilgrim's daubed nest;
The groves already did rejoice,
In Philomel's triumphing voice,
The showers were short, the weather mild,
The morning fresh, the evening smiled.
Joan takes her neat-rubbed pail, and now
She trips to milk the sand-red cow;

Where, for some sturdy foot-ball swain,
Joan strokes a syllabub or twain;
The fields and gardens were beset
With tulips, crocus, violet;

And now, though late, the modest rose
Did more than half a blush disclose.
Thus all looks gay, and full of cheer,
To welcome the new-liveried year.

These were the thoughts that then possessed the undisturbed mind of Sir Henry
Wotton. Will you hear the wish of another angler, and the commendation of his happy
life, which he also sings in verse; *viz.* Jo. Davors, Esq.?

Let me live harmlessly; and near the brink
Of Trent or Avon have a dwelling place,
Where I may see my quill or cork down sink
With eager bite of perch, or bleak, or dace;
And on the world and my Creator think;
Whilst some men strive ill-gotten goods t'embrace;
And others spend their time in base excess
Of wine or worse, in war and wantonness:

Let them that list these pastimes still pursue,
And on such pleasing fancies feed their fill,

So I the fields and meadows green may view,
And daily by fresh rivers walk at will
Among the daisies and the violets blue,
Red hyacinth, and yellow daffodil,
Purple Narcissus like the morning rays,
Pale gander-grass, and azure culver-keys.

I count it higher pleasure to behold
The stately compass of the lofty sky;
And in the midst thereof, like burning gold,
The flaming chariot of the world's great eye;
The watery clouds that in the air up-rolled,
With sundry kinds of painted colors fly;
And fair Aurora, lifting up her head,
Still blushing rise from old Tithonus' bed;

The hills and mountains raisèd from the plains,
The plains extended level with the ground,
The grounds divided into sundry veins,
The veins enclosed with rivers running round;
These rivers making way through nature's chains,
With headlong course into the sea profound;
The raging sea, beneath the valleys low,
Where lakes and rills and rivulets do flow;

The lofty woods, the forests wide and long,
Adorned with leaves, and branches fresh and green,
In whose cool bowers the birds with many a song
Do welcome with their quire the summer's queen;
The meadows fair where Flora's gifts among
Are intermixed with verdant grass between;
The silver-scalèd fish that softly swim
Within the sweet brook's crystal watery stream.

All these, and many more, of his creation
That made the heavens, the angler oft doth see,
Taking therein no little delectation,
To think how strange, how wonderful they be,
Framing thereof an inward contemplation,

To set his heart from other fancies free;
And whilst he looks on these with joyful eye,
His mind is rapt above the starry sky.

***

PISCATOR. The Trout is a fish highly valued, both in this and foreign nations. He may be justly said, as the old poet said of wine and we English say of venison, to be a generous fish; a fish that is so like the buck, that he also has his seasons; for it is observed that he comes in and goes out of season with the stag and buck. Gesner says his name is of a German offspring, and says he is a fish that feeds clean and purely, in the swiftest streams, and on the hardest gravel, and that he may justly contend with all fresh water fish, as the mullet may with all sea fish, for precedency and daintiness of taste; and that being in right season, the most dainty palates have allowed precedency to him.

And before I go farther in my discourse, let me tell you that you are to observe that as there be some barren does that are good in summer, so there be some barren trouts that are good in winter; but there are not many that are so; for usually they be in their perfection in the month of May and decline with the buck. Now you are to take notice that in several countries, as in Germany and in other parts, compared to ours, fish do differ much in their bigness and shape, and other ways; and so do trouts. It is well known that in the Lake Leman, the Lake of Geneva, there are trouts taken of three cubits long, as is affirmed by Gesner, a writer of good credit, and Mercator says the trouts that are taken in the Lake of Geneva are a great part of the merchandise of that famous city. And you are further to know that there be certain waters that breed trouts remarkable both for their number and smallness. I know a little brook in Kent that breeds them to a number incredible, and you may take them twenty or forty in an hour, but none greater than about the size of a gudgeon. There are also in divers rivers, especially that relate to, or be near to the sea, as Winchester or the Thames about Windsor, a little trout called a samlet or skegger Trout, in both which places I have caught twenty or forty at a standing, that will bite as fast and as freely as minnows; these be by some taken to be young salmons, but in those waters they never grow to be bigger than a herring.

There is also in Kent, near to Canterbury, a trout called there a Fordidge trout, a Trout that bears the name of the town where it is usually caught, that is accounted the rarest of fish, many of them near the bigness of a salmon, but known by their different color, and in their best season they cut very white; and none of these have been known to be caught with an angle, unless it were one that was caught by Sir George Hastings, an excellent angler, and now with God; and he hath told me, he thought that trout bit not for hunger but wantonness; and it is the rather to be believed, because both he then and many others before him have been curious to search into their bellies, what the food was by which they lived; and have found out nothing by which they might satisfy their curiosity.

Concerning which you are to take notice that it is reported by good authors that grasshoppers and some fish have no mouths, but are nourished and take breath by the porousness of their gills, man knows not how; and this may be believed, if we consider that when the raven hath hatched her eggs, she takes no further care, but leaves her young ones to the care of the God of nature, who is said, in the Psalms, "to feed the young ravens that call upon him." And they be kept alive and fed by a dew, or worms that breed in their nests, or some other ways that we mortals know not. And this may be believed of the Fordidge Trout which, as it is said of the stork that he knows his season, so he knows his times, I think almost his day, of coming into that river out of the sea, where he lives, and, it is like, feeds, nine months of the year, and fasts three in the River of Fordidge. And you are to note that those townsmen are very punctual in observing the time of beginning to fish for them; and boast much that their river affords a trout that exceeds all others. And just so does Sussex boast of several fish, as namely a Shelsey cockle, a Chichester lobster, an Arundel mullet, and an Amerly trout.

And now, for some confirmation of the Fordidge trout, you are to know that this Trout is thought to eat nothing in the fresh water; and it may be the better believed because it is well known that swallows, which are not seen to fly in England for six months in the year but about Michelmas leave us for a hotter climate, yet some of them that have been left behind their fellows have been found many thousands at a time in hollow trees, where they have been observed to live and sleep out the whole winter without meat; and so Albertus observes that there is one kind of frog that hath her mouth naturally shut up about the end of August and that she lives so all the winter; and though it be strange to some, yet it is known to too many among us to be doubted.

And so much for these Fordidge trouts, which never afford an angler sport, but either live their time of being in the fresh water by their meat formerly gotten in the sea, not unlike the swallow or frog, or by the virtue of the fresh water only; or as the birds of paradise and the chameleon are said to live, by the sun and the air.

There is also in Northumberland a trout called a bull-trout, of a much greater length and bigness than any in these southern parts; and there is in many rivers that relate to the sea salmon-trouts, as much different from others both in shape and in their spots, as we see sheep in some countries differ one from another in their shape and bigness, and in the fineness of the wool; and, certainly, as some pastures breed larger sheep; so do some rivers by reason of the ground over which they run breed larger trouts.

Now the next thing that I will commend to your consideration is that the trout is of a more sudden growth than other fish. Concerning which you are also to take notice that he lives not so long as the perch and divers other fishes do, as Sir Francis Bacon hath observed in his History of Life and Death.

And next you are to take notice that he is not like the crocodile, which if he lives never so long, yet always thrives till his death; but 'tis not so with the trout, for after he is come to his full growth, he declines in his body, and keeps his bigness or thrives only in his head till his death. And you are to know that he will about (especially before), the time of his spawning get almost miraculously through weirs and flood-gates against the stream, even through such high and swift places as is almost incredible. Next, that the trout usually spawns about October or November, but in some rivers a little sooner or later. Which is the more observable because most other fish spawn in the spring or summer when the sun hath warmed both the earth and water and made it fit for generation. And you are to note that he continues many months out of season; for it may be observed of the trout that he is like the buck or the ox that will not be fat in many months, though he go in the very same pastures that horses do which will be fat in one month; and so you may observe that most other fishes recover strength and grow sooner fat and in season than the trout doth.

And next you are to note that till the sun gets to such a height as to warm the earth and the water the trout is sick and lean and lousy and unwholesome; for you shall in winter find him to have a big head and then to be lank and thin and lean; at which time many of them have sticking on them sugs, or trout-lice, which is a kind of worm in shape like a clove or pin with a big head, and sticks close to him and sucks his moisture; these, I think, the trout breeds himself, and never thrives till he free himself from them, which is till warm weather comes; and then, as he grows stronger, he gets from the dead, still water into the sharp streams and the gravel and there rubs off these worms or lice, and then as he grows stronger, so he gets him into swifter and swifter streams, and there lies at the watch for any fly or minnow that comes near to him; and he especially loves the May-fly, which is bred of the cod-worm or caddis; and these make the trout bold and lusty, and he is usually fatter and better meat at the end of that month than at any time of the year.

Now you are to know that it is observed that usually the best trouts are either red or yellow, though some, as the Fordidge trout, be white and yet good; but that is not usual. And it is a note observable that the female trout hath usually a less head and a deeper body than the male trout, and is usually the better meat. And note that a hog-back and a little head to any fish, either trout, salmon, or other fish, is a sign that that fish is in season.

But yet you are to note that as you see some willows or palm-trees bud and blossom sooner than others do, as some trouts be in some rivers sooner in season; and as some hollies or oaks are longer before they cast their leaves, so are some trouts in some rivers longer before they go out of season.

And you are to note that there are several kinds of trouts. But these several kinds are not considered but by very few men; for they go under the general name of trouts; just as pigeons do in most places, though it is certain there are tame and wild pigeons; and of the tame there be helmits and runts and carriers and croppers, and indeed too many to name. Nay, the Royal Society have found and published lately that there be thirty and three kinds of spiders; and yet all, for aught I know, go under that one general name of spider. And it is so with many kinds of fish, and of trouts especially, which differ in their bigness and shapes and spots and color. The great Kentish hens may be an instance, compared to other hens; and doubtless there is a kind of small trout which will never thrive to be big that breeds very many more than others do that be of a larger size. Which you may rather believe, if you consider that the little wren and titmouse will have twenty young ones at a time, when usually the noble hawk or the musical throstle or blackbird shall exceed not four or five.

And now you shall see me try my skill to catch a trout; and at my next walking, either this evening or tomorrow morning, I will give you directions how you yourself shall fish for him.

VENATOR. Trust me, master, I see now it is a harder matter to catch a trout than a chub; for I have put on patience and followed you these two hours and not seen a fish stir, neither at your minnow nor your worm.

PISCATOR. Well, scholar, you must endure worse luck sometime, or you will never make a good angler. But what say you now? There is a trout now, and a good one too, if I can but hold him; and two or three turns more will tire him. Now you see he lies still, and the sleight is to land him. Reach me that landing-net. So, Sir, now he is mine own. What say you now? is this not worth all my labor and your patience?

VENATOR. On my word, master, this is a gallant trout; what shall we do with him?

PISCATOR. Marry, e'en eat him to supper. We'll go to my hostess from whence we came; she told me, as I was going out of door, that my brother Peter, a good angler and a cheerful companion, had sent word he would lodge there tonight and bring a friend with him. My hostess has two beds, and I know you and I may have the best. We'll rejoice with my brother Peter and his friend, tell tales, or sing ballads, or make a catch, or find some harmless sport to content us, and pass away a little time without offence to God or man.

VENATOR. A match, good master, let's go to that house, for the linen looks white and smells of lavender, and I long to lie in a pair of sheets that smell so. Let's be going, good master, for I am hungry again with fishing.

PISCATOR. Nay, stay a little, good scholar. I caught my last trout with a worm, now I will put on a minnow and try a quarter of an hour about yonder tree for another, and so walk towards our lodging. Look you, scholar, thereabout we shall have a bite presently, or not at all. Have with you, Sir! On my word, I have hold of him. Oh, it is a great logger-headed chub! Come, hang him upon that willow twig, and let's be going.

***

VENATOR. Well now, good master, as we walk toward the river, give me direction, according to your promise, how I shall fish for a trout.

PISCATOR. My honest scholar, I will take this very convenient opportunity to do it.

The trout is usually caught with a worm or a minnow, which some call a penk, or with a fly, *viz.* either a natural or an artificial fly. Concerning which three I will give you some observations and directions.

And, first, for worms. Of these there be very many sorts, some bred only in the earth, as the earth-worm, others of or amongst plants, as the dug-worm, and others bred either out of excrements or in the bodies of living creatures, as in the horns of sheep or deer, or some of dead flesh, as the maggot or gentle, and others.

Now these be most of them particularly good for particular fishes. But for the trout the dew-worm, which some also call the lob-worm, and the brandling are the chief; and especially the first for a great trout, and the latter for a less. There be also of lob-worms some called squirrel-tails, a worm that has a red head, a streak down the back, and a broad tail, which are noted to be the best because they are the toughest and most lively and live longest in the water; for you are to know that a dead worm is but a dead bait and like to catch nothing, compared to a lively, quick, stirring worm. And for a brandling he is usually found in an old dunghill or some very rotten place near to it, but most usually in cow-dung or hog's-dung, rather than horse-dung, which is somewhat too hot and dry for that worm. But the best of them are to be found in the bark of the tanners which they have cast up in heaps after they have used it about their leather.

There are also divers other kinds of worms which for color and shape alter even as the ground out of which they are got; as the marsh-worm, the tag-tail, the flag-worm, the dock-worm, the oak-worm, the gilt-tail, the twachel or lob-worm, which of all others is the most excellent bait for a salmon, and too many to name, even as many sorts as some think there be of several herbs or shrubs or of several kinds of birds in the air. Of which I shall say no more but tell you that what worms so ever you fish with are the better for being long kept before they are used. And in case you have not been so provident, then the way to cleanse and scour them quickly is to put them all night in water if they be lob-worms, and then put them into your bag with fennel. But you must not put your brandlings above an hour in water and then put them into fennel, for sudden use; but if you have time and purpose to keep them long, then they be best preserved in an earthen pot, with good store of moss, which is to be fresh every three or four days in summer and every week or eight days in winter; or at least the moss taken from them and clean washed and wrung betwixt your hands till it be dry, and then put it to them again. And when your worms, especially the brandling, begins to be sick and lose of his bigness, then you may recover him by putting a little milk or cream, about a spoonful in a day, into them by drops on the moss; and if there be added to the cream an egg beaten and boiled in it, then it will both fatten and preserve them long. And note that when the knot which is near to the middle of the brandling begins to swell, then he is sick; and if he be not well looked to, is near dying. And for moss you are to note that there be divers kinds of it which I could name to you, but I will only tell you that which is likest; a buck's-horn is the best, except it be soft white moss that grows on some heaths and is hard to be found. And note that in a very dry time when you are put to an extremity for worms walnut-tree leaves squeezed into water, or salt in water to make it bitter or salt, and then that water poured on the ground where you shall see worms are used to rise in the night will make them to appear above ground presently.

And now, I shall show you how to bait your hook with a worm so as shall prevent you from much trouble and the loss of many a hook too, when you fish for a trout with a running line, that is to say, when you fish for him by hand at the ground. I will direct you in this as plainly as I can, that you may not mistake.

Suppose it be a big lob-worm. Put your hook into him somewhat above the middle and out again a little below the middle. Having so done, draw your worm above the arming of your hook; but note that at the entering of your hook it must not be at the head-end of the worm but at the tail-end of him, that the point of your hook may come out toward the head-end. And having drawn him above the arming of your hook, then put the point of your hook again into the very head of the worm till it come near to the place where the point of the hook first came out. And then draw back that part of the worm that was above the shank or arming of your hook, and so fish with it. And if you mean to fish with two worms, then put the second on before you turn back the hook's-head of the first worm. You cannot lose above two or three worms before you attain to what I direct you; and having attained it, you will find it very useful, and thank me for it. For you will run on the ground without tangling.

Now for the minnow, or penk, he is not easily found and caught till March, or in April, for then he appears first in the river, nature having taught him to shelter and hide himself in the winter in ditches that be near to the river, and there both to hide and keep himself warm in the mud or in the weeds, which rot not so soon as in a running river, in which place if he were in winter, the distempered floods that are usually in that season would suffer him to take no rest, but carry him headlong to mills and weirs to his confusion. And of these minnows, first, you are to know that the biggest size is not the best; and next, that the middle size and the whitest are the best; and then you are to know that your minnow must be so put on your hook that it must turn round when 'tis drawn against the stream, and, that it may turn nimbly, you must put it on a big-sized hook, as I shall now direct you, which is thus: put your hook in at his mouth, and out at his gill; then, having drawn your hook two or three inches beyond or through his gill, put it again into his mouth, and the point and beard out at his tail; and then tie the hook and his tail about very neatly with a white thread, which will make it the apter to turn quick in the water; that done, pull back that part of your line which was slack when you did put your hook into the minnow the second time; I say, pull that part of it back so that it shall fasten the head so that the body of the minnow shall be almost straight on your hook; this done, try how it will turn, by drawing it across the water or against a stream; and if it do not turn nimbly, then turn the tail a little to the right or left hand, and try again till it turn quick; for if not, you are in danger to catch nothing; for know, that it is impossible that it should turn too quick. And you are yet to know that in case you want a minnow, then a small loach, or a stickleback, or any other small fish will serve as well. And you are yet to know that you may salt them and by that means keep them fit for use three or four days or longer; and that of salt, bay-salt is the best.

And here let me tell you, what many old anglers know right well, that at some times and in some waters a minnow is not to be got; and therefore let me tell you I have (which I will show to you) an artificial minnow that will catch a trout as well as an artificial fly. And it was made by a handsome woman that had a fine hand, and a live minnow lying by her: the mould or body of the minnow was cloth and wrought upon or over it thus with a needle; the back of it with very sad French green silk, and paler green silk towards the belly, shadowed as perfectly as you can imagine, just as you see a minnow; the belly was wrought also with a needle, and it was, a part of it, white silk; and another part of it with silver thread; the tail and fins were of a quill which was shaven thin; the eyes were of two little black beads; and the head was so shadowed and all of it so curiously wrought and so exactly dissembled that it would beguile any sharp-sighted trout in a swift stream. And this minnow I will now show you, and if you like it, lend it you to have two or three made by it; for they be easily carried about an angler, and be of excellent use; for note that a large trout will come as fiercely at a minnow as the highest-mettled hawk doth seize on a partridge, or a greyhound on a hare. I have been told that one hundred sixty minnows have been found in a trout's belly. Either the Trout had devoured so many, or the miller that gave it a friend of mine had forced them down his throat after he had taken him.

Now for flies, which is the third bait wherewith trouts are usually taken. You are to know that there are so many sorts of flies as there be of fruits. I will name you but some of them: as the dun-fly, the stone-fly, the red-fly, the moor-fly, the tawny-fly, the shell-fly, the cloudy or blackish-fly, the flag-fly, the vine-fly; there be of flies, cater-pillars and canker-flies, and bear-flies; and indeed too many either for me to name, or for you to remember. And their breeding is so various and wonderful that I might easily amaze myself and tire you in a relation of them.

And yet I will exercise your promised patience by saying a little of the caterpillar, or the palmer-fly or worm, that by them you may guess what a work it were in a dis-course but to run over those very many flies, worms, and little living creatures with which the sun and summer adorn and beautify the river-banks and meadows, both for the recreation and contemplation of us anglers, and which, I think, myself enjoy more than any other man that is not of my profession.

Pliny holds an opinion that many have their birth or being from a dew that in the spring falls upon the leaves of trees, and that some kinds of them are from a dew left upon herbs or flowers; and others from a dew left upon coleworts or cabbages. All which kinds of dews, being thickened and condensed, are by the sun's generative heat most of them hatched and in three days made living creatures; and these of sev-eral shapes and colors; some being hard and tough; some smooth and soft; some are horned in their head, some in their tail, some have none; some have hair, some none; some have sixteen feet, some less, and some have none, but (as our Topsel hath with great diligence observed) those which have none move upon the earth or upon broad leaves, their motion being not unlike to the waves of the sea. Some of them he also observes to be bred of the eggs of other caterpillars and that those in their time turn to be butterflies; and again that their eggs turn the following year to be caterpillars. And some affirm that every plant has its particular fly or caterpillar which it breeds and feeds. I have seen, and may therefore affirm it, a green caterpillar, or worm, as big as a small peascod, which had fourteen legs, eight on the belly, four under the neck, and two near the tail. It was found on a hedge of privet, and was taken thence and put into a large box and a little branch or two of privet put to it, on which I saw it feed as sharply as a dog gnaws a bone. It lived thus five or six days and thrived and changed the color two or three times, but by some neglect in the keeper of it, it then died and did not turn to a fly. But if it had lived, it had doubtless turned to one of those flies that some call flies of prey, which those that walk by the rivers may in summer see fasten on smaller flies and I think make them their food. And 'tis observ-able that as there be these flies of prey which be very large, so there be others, very little, created I think only to feed them, and bred out of I know not what; whose life, they say, nature intended not to exceed an hour, and yet that life is thus made shorter by other flies, or accident.

'Tis endless to tell you what the curious searchers into nature's productions have observed of these worms and flies. But yet I shall tell you what Aldrovandus, our Topsel, and others say of the palmer-worm or caterpillar: that whereas others content themselves to feed on particular herbs or leaves (for most think those very leaves that gave them life and shape give them a particular feeding and nourishment and that upon them they usually abide), yet he observes that this is called a pilgrim or palmer-worm for his very wandering life and various food; not contenting himself, as others do, with any one certain place for his abode nor any certain kind of herb or flower for his feeding, but will boldly and disorderly wander up and down and not endure to be kept to a diet or fixed to a particular place.

Nay, the very colors of caterpillars are, as one has observed, very elegant and beautiful. I shall, for a taste of the rest, describe one of them which I will some time the next month show you feeding on a willow-tree, and you shall find him punctually to answer this very description: his lips and mouth somewhat yellow, his eyes black as jet, his forehead purple, his feet and hinder parts green, his tail two-forked and black, the whole body stained with a kind of red spots which run along the neck and shoulder-blade, not unlike the form of St. Andrew's cross or the letter X made thus crosswise, and a white line drawn down his back to his tail; all which add much beauty to his whole body. And it is to me observable that at a fixed age this caterpillar gives over to eat, and towards winter comes to be covered over with a strange shell or crust called an aurelia, and so lives a kind of dead life without eating all the winter. And as others of several kinds turn to be several kinds of flies and vermin the spring following, so this caterpillar then turns to be a painted butterfly.

***

VENATOR. Master, I can neither catch with the first nor second angle. I have no fortune.

PISCATOR. Look you, scholar, I have yet another. And now, having caught three brace of trouts, I will tell you a short tale as we walk towards our breakfast: a scholar—a preacher I should say—that was to preach to procure the approbation of a parish that he might be their lecturer had got from his fellow-pupil the copy of a sermon that was first preached with great commendation by him that composed and preached it; and though the borrower of it preached it word for word as it was at first, yet it was utterly disliked as it was preached by the second. Which the sermon-borrower complained of to the lender of it; and was thus answered: "I lent you, indeed, my fiddle, but not my fiddle-stick; for you are to know that everyone cannot make music with my words, which are fitted for my own mouth." And so, my scholar, you are to know that as the ill pronunciation or ill accenting of words in a sermon spoils it, so the ill carriage of your line or not fishing even to a foot in a right place makes you lose your labor. And you are to know that though you have my fiddle, that is, my very rod and tacklings with which you see I catch fish, yet you have not my fiddle-stick, that is, you yet have not skill to know how to carry your hand and line nor how to guide it to a right place. And this must be taught you—for you are to remember I told you angling is an art—either by practice or a long observation or both. But take this for a rule: when you fish for a trout with a worm, let your line have so much and not more lead than will fit the stream in which you fish; that is to say, more in a great troublesome stream than in a smaller that is quieter; as near as may be, so much as will sink the bait to the bottom and keep it still in motion, and not more.

But now, let's say grace, and fall to breakfast. What say you, scholar, to the providence of an old angler? Does not this meat taste well? and was not this place well chosen to eat it? for this sycamore-tree will shade us from the sun's heat.

VENATOR. All excellent good, and my stomach excellent too. And now I remember and find that true which devout Lessius says, "That poor men and those that fast often have much more pleasure in eating than rich men and gluttons, that always feed before their stomachs are empty of their last meat and so rob themselves of that pleasure that hunger brings to poor men." And I do seriously approve of that saying of yours, "That you had rather be a civil, well-grounded, temperate, poor angler than a drunken lord." But I hope there is none such. However, I am certain of this, that I have been at many very costly dinners that have not afforded me half the content that this has done, for which I thank God and you.

And now, good master, proceed to your promised direction for making and ordering my artificial fly.

PISCATOR. My honest scholar, I will do it, for it is a debt due unto you by my promise. And because you shall not think yourself more engaged to me than indeed you really are, I will freely give you such directions as were lately given to me by an ingenious brother of the angle, an honest man, and a most excellent fly-fisher.

You are to note that there are twelve kinds of artificial-made flies to angle with upon the top of the water. Note, by the way, that the fittest season of using these is in a blustering windy day, when the waters are so troubled that the natural fly cannot be seen, or rest upon them. The first is the dun-fly in March; the body is made of dun wool, the wings, of the partridge's feathers. The second is another dun-fly; the body of black wool, and the wings made of the black drake's feathers and of the feathers under his tail. The third is the stone-fly in April; the body is made of black wool made yellow under the wings and under the tail and so made with wings of the drake. The fourth is the ruddy-fly in the beginning of May; the body made of red wool, wrapt about with black silk, and the feathers are the wings of the drake, with the feathers of a red capon also, which hang dangling on his sides next to the tail. The fifth is the yellow or greenish fly, in May likewise; the body made of yellow wool; and the wings made of the red cock's hackle or tail. The sixth is the black-fly, in May also; the body made of black wool, and lapt about with the herle of a peacock's tail, the wings are made of the wings of a brown capon, with his blue feathers in his head. The seventh is the sad yellow-fly in June; the body is made of black wool, with a yellow list on either side, and the wings taken off the wings of a buzzard, bound with black braked hemp. The eighth is the moorish-fly; made with the body of duskish wool, and the wings made of the blackish mail of the drake. The ninth is the tawny-fly, good until the middle of June; the body made of tawny wool, the wings made contrary one against the other, made of the whitish mail of the wild drake. The tenth is the wasp-fly in July; the body made of black wool, lapt about with yellow silk, the wings made of the feathers of the drake or of the buzzard. The eleventh is the shell-fly, good in mid-July; the body made of greenish wool, lapt about with the herle of a peacock's tail, and the wings made of the wings of the buzzard. The twelfth is the dark drake-fly, good in August; the body made with black wool, lapt about with black silk, his wings are made with the mail of the black drake, with a black head. Thus have you a jury of flies likely to betray and condemn all the trouts in the river.

I shall next give you some other directions for fly-fishing such as are given by Mr. Thomas Barker, a gentleman that hath spent much time in fishing; but I shall do it with a little variation.

First, let your rod be light, and very gentle. I take the best to be of two pieces. And let not your line exceed, especially for three or four links next to the hook, I say, not exceed three or four hairs at the most, though you may fish a little stronger above, in the upper part of your line. But if you can attain to angle with one hair, you shall have more rises, and catch more fish. Now you must be sure not to cumber yourself with too long a line, as most do. And before you begin to angle, cast to have the wind on your back; and the sun, if it shines, to be before you, and to fish down the stream; and carry the point or top of your rod downward, by which means the shadow of yourself and rod too will be the least offensive to the fish; for the sight of any shade amazes the fish and spoils your sport, of which you must take great care.

In the middle of March—till which time a man should not in honesty catch a trout—or in April, if the weather be dark or a little windy or cloudy, the best fishing is with the palmer-worm, of which I last spoke to you; but of these there be divers kinds, or at least of divers colors. These and the May-fly are the ground of all fly-angling. Which are to be thus made:

First, you must arm your hook with the line in the inside of it; then take your scissors and cut so much of a brown mallard's feather as in your own reason, will make the wings of it, you having withal regard to the bigness or littleness of your hook; then lay the outmost part of your feather next to your hook; then the point of your feather next the shank of your hook; and having so done, whip it three or four times about the hook with the same silk with which your hook was armed; and having made the silk fast, take the hackle of a cock or capon's neck or a plover's top, which is usually better; take off the one side of the feather, and then take the hackle, silk, or crewel, gold or silver thread; make these fast at the bent of the hook, that is to say, below your arming; then you must take the hackle, the silver or gold thread, and work it up to the wings, shifting or still removing your finger as you turn the silk about the hook and still looking at every stop or turn that your gold or what materials soever you make your fly of do lie right and neatly; and if you find they do so, then when you have made the head, make all fast; and then work your hackle up to the head, and make that fast; and then with a needle or pin divide the wing into two; and then with the arming silk whip it about cross-ways betwixt the wings; and then with your thumb you must turn the point of the feather towards the bent of the hook; and then work three or four times about the shank of the hook; and then view the proportion; and if all be neat and to your liking, fasten.

I confess no direction can be given to make a man of a dull capacity able to make a fly well. And yet I know this, with a little practice, will help an ingenious angler in a good degree. But to see a fly made by an artist in that kind is the best teaching to make it. And then an ingenious angler may walk by the river and mark what flies fall on the water that day, and catch one of them, if he sees the trouts leap at a fly of that kind: and then having always hooks ready-hung with him and having a bag always with him with bear's hair or the hair of a brown or sad-colored heifer, hackles of a cock or capon, several colored silk and crewel to make the body of the fly, the feathers of a drake's head, black or brown sheep's wool, or hog's wool, or hair, thread of gold and of silver; silk of several colors, especially sad-colored, to make the fly's head; and there be also other colored feathers, both of little birds and of speckled fowl—I say, having those with him in a bag and trying to make a fly, though he miss at first, yet shall he at last hit it better even to such a perfection as none can well teach him. And if he hit to make his fly right and have the luck to hit also where there is store of trouts, a dark day, and a right wind, he will catch such store of them as will encourage him to grow more and more in love with the art of fly-making.

VENATOR. But, my loving master, if any wind will not serve, then I wish I were in Lapland, to buy a good wind of one of the honest witches that sell so many winds there and so cheap.

PISCATOR. Marry, scholar, but I would not be there, nor indeed from under this tree. For look how it begins to rain, and by the clouds, if I mistake not, we shall presently have a smoking shower, and therefore sit close. This sycamore-tree will shelter us. And I will tell you, as they shall come into my mind, more observations of fly-fishing for a trout.

But first for the wind, you are to take notice that of the winds the south wind is said to be best. One observes that

when the wind is south,
It blows your bait into a fish's mouth.

Next to that the west wind is believed to be the best. And having told you that the east wind is the worst, I need not tell you which wind is the best in the third degree. And yet, as Solomon observes, that "he that considers the wind shall never sow"; so he that busies his head too much about them, if the weather be not made extreme cold by an east wind, shall be a little superstitious. For as it is observed by some that "There is no good horse of a bad color"; so I have observed that if it be a cloudy day and not extreme cold, let the wind sit in what corner it will and do its worst. And yet take this for a rule, that I would willingly fish standing on the lee-shore. And you are to take notice that the fish lies or swims nearer the bottom and in deeper water in winter than in summer; and also nearer the bottom in any cold day, and then gets nearest the lee-side of the water.

But I promised to tell you more of the fly-fishing for a trout; which I may have time enough to do, for you see it rains May butter. First for a May-fly, you may make his body with greenish-colored crewel, or willowish color, darkening it in most places with waxed silk, or ribbed with black hair, or some of them ribbed with silver thread, and such wings for the color as you see the fly to have at that season, nay, at that very day on the water. Or you may make the oak-fly, with an orange-tawny and black ground, and the brown of a mallard's feather for the wings. And you are to know that these two are most excellent flies, that is, the May-fly and the oak-fly. And let me again tell you that you keep as far from the water as you can possibly, whether you fish with a fly or worm, and fish down the stream. And when you fish with a fly, if it be possible, let no part of your line touch the water, but your fly only; and be still moving your fly upon the water, or casting it into the water, you yourself being also always moving down the stream. Mr. Barker commends several sorts of the palmer-flies, not only those ribbed with silver and gold, but others that have their bodies all made of black, or some with red, and a red hackle. You may also make the hawthorn-fly, which is all black, and not big, but very small, the smaller the better. Or the oak-fly, the body of which is orange color and black crewel, with a brown wing. Or a fly made with a peacock's feather is excellent in a bright day. You must be sure you want not in your magazine-bag the peacock's feather and grounds of such wool and crewel as will make the grasshopper. And note that usually the smallest flies are the best; and note also that the light fly does usually make most sport in a dark day, and the darkest and least fly in a bright or clear day; and lastly note that you are to repair upon any occasion to your magazine-bag: and upon any occasion vary and make them lighter or sadder according to your fancy or the day.

And now I shall tell you that the fishing with a natural fly is excellent, and affords much pleasure. They may be found thus: the May-fly usually in and about that month near to the river-side, especially against rain; the oak-fly on the butt or body of an oak or ash from the beginning of May to the end of August; it is a brownish fly and easy to be so found, and stands usually with his head downward, that is to say, towards the root of the tree; the small black-fly, or hawthorn-fly, is to be had on any hawthorn bush after the leaves be come forth. With these and a short line, as I showed to angle for a chub, you may dape or dop, and also with a grasshopper, behind a tree or in any deep hole; still making it to move on the top of the water as if it were alive and still keeping yourself out of sight, you shall certainly have sport if there be trouts; yea, in a hot day, but especially in the evening of a hot day.

And now, scholar, my direction for fly-fishing is ended with this shower, for it has done raining. And now look about you, and see how pleasantly that meadow looks; nay, and the earth smells so sweetly too. Come let me tell you what holy Mr. Herbert says of such days and flowers as these, and then we will thank God that we enjoy them, and walk to the river and sit down quietly, and try to catch the other place of trouts.

> Sweet day, so cool, so calm, so bright,
> The bridal of the earth and sky,
> Sweet dews shall weep thy fall tonight,
> For thou must die.
>
> Sweet rose, whose hue, angry and brave,
> Bids the rash gazer wipe his eye,
> Thy root is ever in its grave,
> And thus must die.
>
> Sweet spring, full of sweet days and roses,
> A box where sweets compacted lie;
> My music shows you have your closes,
> And all must die.
>
> Only a sweet and virtuous soul
> Like seasoned timber never gives,
> But when the whole world turns to coal,
> Then chiefly lives.

VENATOR. I thank you, good master, for your good direction for fly-fishing and for the sweet enjoyment of the pleasant day, which is so far spent without offence to God or man; and I thank you for the sweet close of your discourse with Mr. Herbert's verses, which, I have heard, loved angling; and I do the rather believe it, because he had a spirit suitable to anglers and to those primitive Christians that you love and have so much commended.

***

No life, my honest scholar, no life so happy and so pleasant as the life of a well-governed angler; for when the lawyer is swallowed up with business and the statesman is preventing or contriving plots, then we sit on cowslip-banks, hear the birds sing, and possess ourselves in as much quietness as these silent silver streams which we now see glide so quietly by us. Indeed, my good scholar, we may say of angling as Dr. Boteler said of strawberries, "Doubtless God could have made a better berry, but doubtless God never did"; and if so I might be judge, God never did make a more calm, quiet, innocent recreation than angling.

"Ktaadn Trout" and "The Ponds" (selections)

HENRY DAVID THOREAU

"KTAADN TROUT"

The last half mile carried us to the Sowadnehunk dead-water, so called from the stream of the same name, signifying "running between mountains," an important tributary which comes in a mile above. Here we decided to camp, about twenty miles from the Dam, at the mouth of Murch Brook and the Aboljacknagesic, mountain streams, broad off from Ktaadn, and about a dozen miles from its summit, having made fifteen miles this day.

We had been told by McCauslin that we should here find trout enough; so, while some prepared the camp, the rest fell to fishing. Seizing the birch-poles which some party of Indians, or white hunters, had left on the shore, and baiting our hooks with pork, and with trout, as soon as they were caught, we cast our lines into the mouth of the Aboljacknagesic, a clear, swift, shallow stream, which came in from Ktaadn. Instantly a shoal of white chivin (*Leucisci pulchelli*), silvery roaches, cousin-trout, or what not, large and small, prowling there-abouts, fell upon our bait, and one after another were landed amidst the bushes. Anon their cousins, the true trout, took their turn, and alternately the speckled trout, and the silvery roaches, swallowed the bait as fast as we could throw in; and the finest specimens of both that I have ever seen, the largest one weighing three pounds, were heaved upon the shore, though at first in vain, to wriggle down into the water again, for we stood in the boat; but soon we learned to remedy this evil; for one, who had lost his hook, stood on shore to catch them as they fell in a perfect shower around him—sometimes, wet and slippery, full in his face and bosom, as his arms were outstretched to receive them. While yet alive, before their tints had faded, they glistened like the fairest flowers, the product of primitive rivers; and he could hardly trust his senses, as he stood over them, that these jewels should have swam away in that Aboljacknagesic water for so long, so many dark ages— these bright fluviatile flowers, seen of Indians only, made beautiful, the Lord only knows why, to swim there! I could understand better, for this, the truth of mythology, the fables of Proteus, and all those beautiful sea-monsters—how all history, indeed, put to a terrestrial use, is mere history; but put to a celestial, is mythology always.

But there is the rough voice of Uncle George, who commands at the frying-pan, to send over what you've got, and then you may stay till morning. The pork sizzles and cries for fish. Luckily for the foolish race, and this particularly foolish generation of trout, the night shut down at last, not a little deepened by the dark side of Ktaadn, which, like a permanent shadow, reared itself from the eastern bank. Lescarbot, writing in 1609, tells us that the Sieur Champdorée, who, with one of the people of the Sieur de Monts, ascended some fifty leagues up the St. John in 1608, found the fish so plenty, *"qu'en mettant la chaudière sur le feu ils en avoient pris suffisamment pour eux disner avant que l'eau fust chaude."* Their descendants here are no less numerous. So we accompanied Tom into the woods to cut cedar-twigs for our bed. While he went ahead with the axe and lopped off the smallest twigs of the flat-leaved cedar, the arbor-vitæ of the gardens, we gathered them up, and returned with them to the boat, until it was loaded. Our bed was made with as much care and skill as a roof is shingled; beginning at the foot, and laying the twig end of the cedar upward, we advanced to the head, a course at a time, thus successively covering the stub-ends, and producing a soft and level bed. For us six it was about ten feet long by six in breadth. This time we lay under our tent, having pitched it more prudently with reference to the wind and the flame, and the usual huge fire blazed in front. Supper was eaten off a large log, which some freshet had thrown up. This night we had a dish of arbor-vitæ, or cedar-tea, which the lumberer sometimes uses when other herbs fail,

A quart of arbor-vitæ,
To make him strong and mighty,

but I had no wish to repeat the experiment. It had too medicinal a taste for my palate. There was the skeleton of a moose here, whose bones some Indian hunters had picked on this very spot.

In the night I dreamed of trout-fishing; and, when at length I awoke, it seemed a fable that this painted fish swam there so near my couch, and rose to our hooks the last evening, and I doubted if I had not dreamed it all. So I arose before dawn to test its truth, while my companions were still sleeping. There stood Ktaadn with distinct and cloudless outline in the moonlight; and the rippling of the rapids was the only sound to break the stillness. Standing on the shore, I once more cast my line into the stream, and found the dream to be real and the fable true. The speckled trout and silvery roach, like flying-fish, sped swiftly through the moonlight air, describing bright arcs on the dark side of Ktaadn, until moonlight, now fading into daylight, brought satiety to my mind, and the minds of my companions, who had joined me.

"THE PONDS" (FROM *WALDEN*)

Occasionally, after my hoeing was done for the day, I joined some impatient companion who had been fishing on the pond since morning, as silent and motionless as a duck or a floating leaf, and, after practicing various kinds of philosophy, had concluded commonly, by the time I arrived, that he belonged to the ancient sect of Coenobites. There was one older man, an excellent fisher and skilled in all kinds of woodcraft, who was pleased to look upon my house as a building erected for the convenience of fishermen; and I was equally pleased when he sat in my doorway to arrange his lines. Once in a while we sat together on the pond, he at one end of the boat, and I at the other; but not many words passed between us, for he had grown deaf in his later years, but he occasionally hummed a psalm, which harmonized well enough with my philosophy. Our intercourse was thus altogether one of unbroken harmony, far more pleasing to remember than if it had been carried on by speech. When, as was commonly the case, I had none to commune with, I used to raise the echoes by striking with a paddle on the side of my boat, filling the surrounding woods with circling and dilating sound, stirring them up as the keeper of a menagerie his wild beasts, until I elicited a growl from every wooded vale and hill-side.

In warm evenings I frequently sat in the boat playing the flute, and saw the perch, which I seem to have charmed, hovering around me, and the moon traveling over the ribbed bottom, which was strewed with the wrecks of the forest. Formerly I had come to this pond adventurously, from time to time, in dark summer nights, with a companion, and, making a fire close to the water's edge, which we thought attracted the fishes, we caught pouts with a bunch of worms strung on a thread, and when we had done, far in the night, threw the burning brands high into the air like skyrockets, which, coming down into the pond, were quenched with a loud hissing, and we were suddenly groping in total darkness. Through this, whistling a tune, we took our way to the haunts of men again. But now I had made my home by the shore.

Sometimes, after staying in a village parlor till the family had all retired, I have returned to the woods, and, partly with a view to the next day's dinner, spent the hours of midnight fishing from a boat by moonlight, serenaded by owls and foxes, and hearing, from time to time, the creaking note of some unknown bird close at hand. These experiences were very memorable and valuable to me—anchored in forty feet of water, and twenty or thirty rods from the shore, surrounded sometimes by thousands of small perch and shiners, dimpling the surface with their tails in the moonlight, and communicating by a long flaxen line with mysterious nocturnal fishes which had their dwelling forty feet below, or sometimes dragging sixty feet of line about the pond as I drifted in the gentle night breeze, now and then feeling a slight vibration along it, indicative of some life prowling about its extremity, of dull uncertain blundering purpose there, and slow to make up its mind. At length you slowly raise, pulling hand over hand, some horned pout squeaking and squirming to the upper air. It was very queer, especially in dark nights, when your thoughts had wandered to vast and cosmogonal themes in other spheres, to feel this faint jerk, which came to interrupt your dreams and link you to Nature again. It seemed as if I might next cast my line upward into the air, as well as downward into this element, which was scarcely more dense. Thus I caught two fishes as it were with one hook.

The scenery of Walden is on a humble scale, and, though very beautiful, does not approach to grandeur, nor can it much concern one who has not long frequented it or lived by its shore; yet this pond is so remarkable for its depth and purity as to merit a particular description. It is a clear and deep green well, half a mile long and a mile and three quarters in circumference, and contains about sixty-one and a half acres; a perennial spring in the midst of pine and oak woods, without any visible inlet or outlet except by the clouds and evaporation. The surrounding hills rise abruptly from the water to the height of forty to eighty feet, though on the south-east and east they attain to about one hundred and one hundred and fifty feet respectively, within a quarter and a third of a mile. They are exclusively woodland. All our Concord waters have two colors at least; one when viewed at a distance, and another, more proper, close at hand. The first depends more on the light, and follows the sky. In clear weather, in summer, they appear blue at a little distance, especially if agitated, and at a great distance all appear alike. In stormy weather they are sometimes of a dark slate color. The sea, however, is said to be blue one day and green another without any perceptible change in the atmosphere. I have seen our river, when, the landscape being covered with snow, both water and ice were almost as green as grass. Some consider blue "to be the color of pure water, whether liquid or solid." But, looking directly down into our waters from a boat, they are seen to be of very different colors. Walden is blue at one time and green at another, even from the same point of view. Lying between the earth and the heavens, it partakes of the color of both. Viewed from a hilltop it reflects the color of the sky; but near at hand it is of a yellowish tint next the shore where you can see the sand, then a light green, which gradually deepens to a uniform dark green in the body of the pond. In some lights, viewed even from a hilltop, it is of a vivid green next the shore. Some have referred this to the reflection of the verdure; but it is equally green there against the railroad sandbank, and in the spring, before the leaves are expanded, and it may be simply the result of the prevailing blue mixed with the yellow of the sand. Such is the color of its iris. This is that portion, also, where in the spring, the ice being warmed by the heat of the sun reflected from the bottom, and also transmitted through the earth, melts first and forms a narrow canal about the still frozen middle. Like the rest of our waters, when much agitated, in clear weather, so that the surface of the waves may reflect the sky at the right angle, or because there is more light mixed with it, it appears at a little distance of a darker blue than the sky itself; and at such a time, being on its surface, and looking with divided vision, so as to see the reflection, I have discerned a matchless and indescribable light blue, such as watered or change-able silks and sword blades suggest, more cerulean than the sky itself, alternating with the original dark green on the opposite sides of the waves, which last appeared but muddy in comparison. It is a vitreous greenish blue, as I remember it, like those patches of the winter sky seen through cloud vistas in the west before sundown. Yet a single glass of its water held up to the light is as colorless as an equal quantity of air. It is well known that a large plate of glass will have a green tint, owing, as the makers say, to its "body," but a small piece of the same will be colorless. How large a body of Walden water would be required to reflect a green tint I have never proved. The water of our river is black or a very dark brown to one looking directly down on it, and, like that of most ponds, imparts to the body of one bathing in it a yellowish tinge; but this water is of such crystalline purity that the body of the bather appears of an alabaster whiteness, still more unnatural, which, as the limbs are magnified and distorted withal, produces a monstrous effect, making fit studies for a Michael Angelo.

The water is so transparent that the bottom can easily be discerned at the depth of twenty-five or thirty feet. Paddling over it, you may see, many feet beneath the surface, the schools of perch and shiners, perhaps only an inch long, yet the former easily distinguished by their transverse bars, and you think that they must be ascetic fish that find a subsistence there. Once, in the winter, many years ago, when I had been cutting holes through the ice in order to catch pickerel, as I stepped ashore I tossed my axe back on to the ice, but, as if some evil genius had directed it, it slid four or five rods directly into one of the holes, where the water was twenty-five feet deep. Out of curiosity, I lay down on the ice and looked through the hole, until I saw the axe a little on one side, standing on its head, with its helve erect and gently swaying to and fro with the pulse of the pond; and there it might have stood erect and swaying till in the course of time the handle rotted off, if I had not disturbed it.

Making another hole directly over it with an ice chisel which I had, and cutting down the longest birch which I could find in the neighborhood with my knife, I made a slip-noose, which I attached to its end, and, letting it down carefully, passed it over the knob of the handle, and drew it by a line along the birch, and so pulled the axe out again.

The shore is composed of a belt of smooth rounded white stones like paving-stones, excepting one or two short sand beaches, and is so steep that in many places a single leap will carry you into water over your head; and were it not for its remarkable transparency, that would be the last to be seen of its bottom till it rose on the opposite side. Some think it is bottomless. It is nowhere muddy, and a casual observer would say that there were no weeds at all in it; and of noticeable plants, except in the little meadows recently overflowed, which do not properly belong to it, a closer scrutiny does not detect a flag nor a bulrush, nor even a lily, yellow or white, but only a few small heart-leaves and potamogetons, and perhaps a water-target or two; all which however a bather might not perceive; and these plants are clean and bright like the element they grow in. The stones extend a rod or two into the water, and then the bottom is pure sand, except in the deepest parts, where there is usually a little sediment, probably from the decay of the leaves which have been wafted on to it so many successive falls, and a bright green weed is brought up on anchors even in midwinter.

We have one other pond just like this, White Pond, in Nine Acre Corner, about two and a half miles westerly; but, though I am acquainted with most of the ponds within a dozen miles of this centre, I do not know a third of this pure and well-like character. Successive nations perchance have drank at, admired, and fathomed it, and passed away, and still its water is green and pellucid as ever. Not an intermitting spring! Perhaps on that spring morning when Adam and Eve were driven out of Eden Walden Pond was already in existence, and even then breaking up in a gentle spring rain accompanied with mist and a southerly wind, and covered with myriads of ducks and geese, which had not heard of the fall, when still such pure lakes sufficed them. Even then it had commenced to rise and fall, and had clarified its waters and colored them of the hue they now wear, and obtained a patent of Heaven to be the only Walden Pond in the world and distiller of celestial dews. Who knows in how many unremembered nations' literatures this has been the Castalian Fountain? or what nymphs presided over it in the Golden Age? It is a gem of the first water which Concord wears in her coronet.

Yet perchance the first who came to this well have left some trace of their foot-steps. I have been surprised to detect encircling the pond, even where a thick wood has just been cut down on the shore, a narrow shelf-like path in the steep hillside, alternately rising and falling, approaching and receding from the water's edge, as old probably as the race of man here, worn by the feet of aboriginal hunters, and still from time to time unwittingly trodden by the present occupants of the land. This is particularly distinct to one standing on the middle of the pond in winter, just after a light snow has fallen, appearing as a clear undulating white line, unobscured by weeds and twigs, and very obvious a quarter of a mile off in many places where in summer it is hardly distinguishable close at hand. The snow reprints it, as it were, in clear white type alto-relievo. The ornamented grounds of villas which will one day be built here may still preserve some trace of this.

The pond rises and falls, but whether regularly or not, and within what period, nobody knows, though, as usual, many pretend to know. It is commonly higher in the winter and lower in the summer, though not corresponding to the general wet and dryness. I can remember when it was a foot or two lower, and also when it was at least five feet higher, than when I lived by it. There is a narrow sand-bar running into it, with very deep water on one side, on which I helped boil a kettle of chowder, some six rods from the main shore, about the year 1824, which it has not been possible to do for twenty-five years; and, on the other hand, my friends used to listen with incredulity when I told them, that a few years later I was accustomed to fish from a boat in a secluded cove in the woods, fifteen rods from the only shore they knew, which place was long since converted into a meadow. But the pond has risen steadily for two years, and now, in the summer of '52, is just five feet higher than when I lived there, or as high as it was thirty years ago, and fishing goes on again in the meadow. This makes a difference of level, at the outside, of six or seven feet; and yet the water shed by the surrounding hills is insignificant in amount, and this overflow must be referred to causes which affect the deep springs. This same summer the pond has begun to fall again. It is remarkable that this fluctuation, whether periodical or not, appears thus to require many years for its accomplishment. I have observed one rise and a part of two falls, and I expect that a dozen or fifteen years hence the water will again be as low as I have ever known it. Flints' Pond, a mile eastward, allowing for the disturbance occasioned by its inlets and outlets, and the smaller intermediate ponds also, sympathize with Walden, and recently attained their greatest height at the same time with the latter. The same is true, as far as my observation goes, of White Pond.

This rise and fall of Walden at long intervals serves this use at least; the water standing at this great height for a year or more, though it makes it difficult to walk round it, kills the shrubs and trees which have sprung up about its edge since the last rise—pitch-pines, birches, alders, aspens, and others—and, falling again, leaves an unobstructed shore; for, unlike many ponds and all waters which are subject to a daily tide, its shore is cleanest when the water is lowest. On the side of the pond next my house a row of pitch-pines, fifteen feet high, has been killed and tipped over as if by a lever, and thus a stop put to their encroachments; and their size indicates how many years have elapsed since the last rise to this height. By this fluctuation the pond asserts its title to a shore, and thus the *shore* is *shorn*, and the trees cannot hold it by right of possession. These are the lips of the lake, on which no beard grows. It licks its chaps from time to time. When the water is at its height, the alders, willows, and maples send forth a mass of fibrous red roots several feet long from all sides of their stems in the water, and to the height of three or four feet from the ground, in the effort to maintain themselves; and I have known the high-blueberry bushes about the shore, which commonly produce no fruit, bear an abundant crop under these circumstances.

Some have been puzzled to tell how the shore became so regularly paved. My townsmen have all heard the tradition, the oldest people tell me that they heard it in their youth, that anciently the Indians were holding a pow-wow upon a hill here, which rose as high into the heavens as the pond now sinks deep into the earth, and they used much profanity, as the story goes, though this vice is one of which the Indians were never guilty, and while they were thus engaged the hill shook and suddenly sank, and only one old squaw, named Walden, escaped, and from her the pond was named. It has been conjectured that when the hill shook these stones rolled down its side and became the present shore. It is very certain, at any rate, that once there was no pond here, and now there is one; and this Indian fable does not in any respect conflict with the account of that ancient settler whom I have mentioned, who remembers so well when he first came here with his divining-rod, saw a thin vapor rising from the sward, and the hazel pointed steadily downward, and he concluded to dig a well here. As for the stones, many still think that they are hardly to be accounted for by the action of the waves on these hills; but I observe that the surrounding hills are remarkably full of the same kind of stones, so that they have been obliged to pile them up in walls on both sides of the railroad cut nearest the pond; and, moreover, there are most stones where the shore is most abrupt; so that, unfortunately, it is no longer a mystery to me. I detect the paver. If the name was not derived from that of some English locality—Saffron Walden, for instance—one might suppose that it was called originally *Walled-in* Pond.

The pond was my well ready dug. For four months in the year its water is as cold as it is pure at all times; and I think that it is then as good as any, if not the best, in the town. In the winter, all water which is exposed to the air is colder than springs and wells which are protected from it. The temperature of the pond water which had stood in the room where I sat from five o'clock in the afternoon till noon the next day, the sixth of March, 1846, the thermometer having been up to 65° or 70° some of the time, owing partly to the sun on the roof, was 42°, or one degree colder than the water of one of the coldest wells in the village just drawn. The temperature of the Boiling

Spring the same day was 45°, or the warmest of any water tried, though it is the coldest that I know of in summer, when, beside, shallow and stagnant surface water is not mingled with it. Moreover, in summer, Walden never becomes so warm as most water which is exposed to the sun, on account of its depth. In the warmest weather I usually placed a pailful in my cellar, where it became cool in the night, and remained so during the day; though I also resorted to a spring in the neighborhood. It was as good when a week old as the day it was dipped, and had no taste of the pump. Whoever camps for a week in summer by the shore of a pond, needs only bury a pail of water a few feet deep in the shade of his camp to be independent of the luxury of ice.

There have been caught in Walden pickerel, one weighing seven pounds,—to say nothing of another which carried off a reel with great velocity, which the fisherman safely set down at eight pounds because he did not see him—perch and pouts, some of each weighing over two pounds, shiners, chivins or roach (*Leuciscus pulchellus*), a very few breams (*Pomotis obesus*), and a couple of eels, one weighing four pounds—I am thus particular because the weight of a fish is commonly its only title to fame, and these are the only eels I have heard of here; also, I have a faint recollection of a little fish some five inches long, with silvery sides and a greenish back, somewhat dace-like in its character, which I mention here chiefly to link my facts to fable. Nevertheless, this pond is not very fertile in fish. Its pickerel, though not abundant, are its chief boast. I have seen at one time lying on the ice pickerel of at least three different kinds: a long and shallow one, steel-colored, most like those caught in the river; a bright golden kind, with greenish reflections and remarkably deep, which is the most common here; and another, golden-colored, and shaped like the last, but peppered on the sides with small dark brown or black spots, intermixed with a few faint blood-red ones, very much like a trout. The specific name *reticulatus* would not apply to this; it should be *guttatus* rather. These are all very firm fish, and weigh more than their size promises. The shiners, pouts, and perch also, and indeed all the fishes which inhabit this pond, are much cleaner, handsomer, and firmer-fleshed than those in the river and most other ponds, as the water is purer, and they can easily be distinguished from them. Probably many ichthyologists would make new varieties of some of them. There are also a clean race of frogs and tortoises, and a few mussels in it; muskrats and minks leave their traces about it, and occasionally a traveling mud-turtle visits it. Sometimes, when I pushed off my boat in the morning, I disturbed a great mud-turtle which had secreted himself under the boat in the night. Ducks and geese frequent it in the spring and fall, the white-bellied swallows (*Hirundo bicolor*) skim over it, and the peet-weets (*Totanus macularius*) "teeter" along its stony shores all summer. I have sometimes disturbed a fish hawk sitting on a white pine over the water; but I doubt if it is ever profaned by the wing of a gull, like Fair Haven. At most, it tolerates one annual loon. These are all the animals of consequence which frequent it now.

You may see from a boat, in calm weather, near the sandy eastern shore, where the water is eight or ten feet deep, and also in some other parts of the pond, some circular heaps half a dozen feet in diameter by a foot in height, consisting of small stones less than a hen's egg in size, where all around is bare sand. At first you wonder if the Indians could have formed them on the ice for any purpose, and so, when the ice melted, they sank to the bottom; but they are too regular and some of them plainly too fresh for that. They are similar to those found in rivers; but as there are no suckers nor lampreys here, I know not by what fish they could be made. Perhaps they are the nests of the chivin. These lend a pleasing mystery to the bottom.

The shore is irregular enough not to be monotonous. I have in my mind's eye the western, indented with deep bays, the bolder northern, and the beautifully scalloped southern shore, where successive capes overlap each other and suggest unexplored coves between. The forest has never so good a setting, nor is so distinctly beautiful, as when seen from the middle of a small lake amid hills which rise from the water's edge; for the water in which it is reflected not only makes the best foreground in such a case, but, with its winding shore, the most natural and agreeable boundary to it. There is no rawness nor imperfection in its edge there, as where the axe has cleared a part, or a cultivated field abuts on it. The trees have ample room to expand on the water side, and each sends forth its most vigorous branch in that direction. There Nature has woven a natural selvage, and the eye rises by just gradations from the low shrubs of the shore to the highest trees. There are few traces of man's hand to be seen. The water laves the shore as it did a thousand years ago.

A lake is the landscape's most beautiful and expressive feature. It is earth's eye; looking into which the beholder measures the depth of his own nature.

Trout: Meeting Them on the "June Rise"

"NESSMUK"

There is a spot where plumy pines
O'erhang the sylvan banks of Otter;
Where wood-ducks build among the vines
That bend above the crystal water.

And there the blue-jay makes her nest
In thickest shade of water beeches;
The fish-hawk, statuesque in rest,
Keeps guard o'er glassy pools and reaches.

'Tis there the deer come down to drink,
From laurel brakes and wooded ridges;
The trout, beneath the sedgy brink,
Are sharp on ship-wrecked flies and midges.

And of the scores of mountain trout-streams that I have fished, the Otter is associated with the most pleasant memories.

It is, or was, a model trout-stream; a thing to dream of. Having its rise within three miles of the village, it meandered southward for ten miles through a mountain valley to its confluence with the second fork of Pine Creek, six miles of the distance being through a forest without settler or clearing.

The stream was swift, stony, and exceptionally free of brush, fallen timber and the usual *debris* that is so trying to the angler on most wooded streams. Then, it was just the right distance from town. It was so handy to start from the village in the middle of an afternoon in early summer, walk an hour and a half at a leisurely pace, and find one's self on a brawling brook where speckled trout were plenty as a reasonable man could wish.

Fishing only the most promising places for a couple of miles always gave trout enough for supper and breakfast, and brought the angler to the "Trout-House," as a modest cottage of squared logs was called, it being the last house in the clearings and owned by good-natured Charley Davis, who never refused to entertain fishermen with the best his little house afforded. His accommodations were of the narrowest, but also of the neatest, and few women could fry trout so nicely as Mrs. Davis. True, there was only one spare bed, and, if more than two anglers desired lodgings, they were relegated to the barn, with a supply of buffalo skins and blankets. On a soft bed of sweet hay this was all that could be desired by way of lodgings, with the advantage of being free from mosquitoes and punkies. The best of rich, yellow butter with good bread were always to be had at Charley's, and his charges were 12½ cents for meals, and the same for lodgings.

The two miles of fishing above the "Trout-House" led through clearings, and the banks were much overgrown with willows, making it expedient to use bait, or a single fly. I chose the latter; my favorite bug for such fishing being the red hackle, though I am obliged to confess that the fellow who used a white grub generally beat me.

But the evening episode was only preliminary; it meant a pleasant walk, thirty or forty brook-trout for supper and breakfast, and a quiet night's rest. The real angling commenced the next morning at the bridge, with a six-mile stretch of clear, cold, rushing water to fish. My old-fashioned creel held an honest twelve pounds of dressed trout, and I do not recollect that I ever missed filling it, with time to spare, on that stretch of water. Nor, though I could sometimes fill it in a forenoon, did I ever continue to fish after it *was* full. Twelve pounds of trout is enough for any but a trout-hog.

But the peculiar phase of trout lore that most interested me, was the "run" of trout that were sure to find their way up stream whenever we had a flood late in May or the first half of June. They were distinct and different from the trout that came up with the early spring freshets. Lighter in color, deeper in body, with smaller heads, and better conditioned altogether. They could be distinguished at a glance; the individuals of any school were as like as peas in color and size, and we never saw them except on a summer flood. The natives called them river trout. They came in schools of one hundred to five times as many, just as the flood was subsiding, and they had a way of halting to rest at the deep pools and spring-holes along their route. Lucky was the angler who could find them at rest in a deep pool, under a scooped out bank, or at the foot of a rushing cascade. At such times they seemed to lose their usual shyness, and would take the fly or worm indifferently, until their numbers were reduced more than one-half. To "meet them on the June rise" was the ardent desire of every angler who fished the streams which they were accustomed to ascend. These streams were not numerous. The First, Second, and Third Forks of Pine Creek, with the Otter, comprised the list so far as I know. And no man could be certain of striking a school at any time; it depended somewhat on judgment, but more on luck. Two or three times I tried it on the Otter and missed; while a friend who had the pluck and muscle to make a ten-mile tramp over the mountain to Second Fork took forty pounds of fine trout from a single school. It was a hoggish thing to do; but he was a native and knew no reason for letting up.

At length my white day came around. There was a fierce rain for three days, and the raging waters took mills, fences and lumber down stream in a way to be remembered. Luckily it also took the lumbermen the same way, and left few native anglers at home. When the waters had subsided to a fair volume, and the streams had still a suspicion of milkiness, I started at 3 P.M. of a lovely June afternoon for the Trout-House. An easy two hours walk, an hour of delightful angling, and I reached the little hostelry with three dozen brook trout, averaging about seven inches in length only, but fresh and sweet, all caught on a single red hackle, which will probably remain my favorite bug until I go over the last carry (though I notice it has gone well out of fashion with modern anglers).

A supper of trout; an evening such as must be seen and felt to be appreciated; trout again for breakfast, with a dozen packed for lunch, and I struck in at the bridge before sunrise for an all day bout, "to meet 'em on the June rise." I didn't do it. I took the entire day to whip that six miles of bright, dashing water. I filled a twelve-pound creel with trout, putting back everything under eight inches. I put back more than I kept. I had one of the most enjoyable days of my life; I came out at the lower bridge after sundown—and I had not seen or caught one fresh-run river trout. They were all the slender, large-mouthed, dark-mottled fish of the gloomy forest, with crimson spots like fresh drops of blood. But I was not discouraged. Had the trout been there I should have met them. I walked half a mile to the little inn at Babb's, selected a dozen of my best fish for supper and breakfast, gave away the rest, and, tired as a hound, slept the sleep of the just man.

At 4 o'clock the next morning I was on the stream again, feeling my way carefully down, catching a trout at every cast, and putting them mostly back with care, that they might live; but for an hour no sign of a fresh-run river trout.

Below the bridge there is a meadow, the oldest clearing on the creek; there are trees scattered about this meadow that are models of arborial beauty, black walnut, elm, ash, birch, hickory, maple, etc. Most of them grand, spreading trees. One of them, a large, umbrageous yellow-birch, stood on the left bank of the stream, and was already in danger of a fall by

"The swifter current that mined its roots."

It was here that I met them on the June rise.

I dropped my cast of two flies just above the roots of the birch, and on the instant, two fresh-run, silver-sided, red-spotted trout immolated themselves, with a generous self-abnegation that I shall never forget.

Standing there on that glorious June morning, I made cast after cast, taking, usually, two at each cast. I made no boyish "show" of playing them. They were lifted out as soon as struck. To have fooled with them would have tangled me, and very likely have scattered the school.

It was old-time angling; I shall not see it again.

My cast was a red hackle for tail-fly, with something like the brown hen for hand-fly. I only used two, with four-foot leader; and I was about the only angler who used a fly at all in those days, on these waters.

I fished about one hour. I caught sixty-four trout, weighing thirteen and three quarter pounds. I caught too many. I was obliged to *string* some of them, as the creel would not hold them all. But my head was moderately level. When I had caught as many as I thought right I held up; and I said, if any of these natives get on to this school, they will take the last trout, if it be a hundred pounds. And they will *salt them down*. So when I was done, and the fishing was as good as the start, I cut a long "staddle," with a bush at the top, and I just went for that school of trout. I chevied, harried and scattered them, up stream and down, until I could not see a fish. Then I packed my duffle and went to the little inn for breakfast. Of course every male biped was anxious to know "where I met 'em." I told them truly; and they started, man and boy, for the "Big Birch," with beech rods, stiff linen lines, and a full stock of white grubs.

I was credibly informed afterwards, that these backwoods cherubs did not succeed in "Meeting 'em on the June rise." I have a word to add, which is not important though it may be novel.

There is a roaring, impetuous brook emptying into Second Fork, called "Rock Run." It heads in a level swamp, near the summit of the mountain. The swamp contains about forty acres, and is simply a level bed of loose stones, completely overgrown with bright green moss.

"Rock Run" heads in a strong, ice-cold spring, but is soon sunken and lost among the loose stones of the swamp. Just where the immense hemlocks, that make the swamp a sunless gloom, get their foothold, is one of the things I shall never find out. But, all the same, they are *there*. And "Rock Run" finds its way underground for 80 rods with never a ray of sunlight to illuminate its course. Not once in its swamp course does it break out to daylight. You may follow it by its heavy gurgling, going by ear; but you cannot see the water. Now remove the heavy coating of moss here and there, and you may see glimpses of dark, cold water, three or four feet beneath the surface. Drop a hook, baited with angle-worm down these dark watery holes, and it will be instantly taken by a dark, crimson-spotted specimen of simon pure *Salmo fontinalis*. They are small, four to six inches in length, hard, sweet; the *beau ideal* of mountain trout. Follow this subterranean brook for eighty rods, and you find it gushing over the mountain's brink in a cascade that no fish could or would attempt to ascend. Follow the roaring brook down to its confluence with Second Fork, and you will not find one trout in the course of a mile. The stream is simply a succession of falls, cascades, and rapids, up which no fish can beat its way for one hundred yards. And yet at the head of this stream is a subterranean brook stocked with the finest specimens of *Salmo fontinalis*. They did not breed on the mountain top. They *cannot* ascend the stream. Where did they originate? When, and how did they manage to get there? I leave the questions to *savants* and *naturalists*. As for myself, I state the fact— still demonstrable—for the trout are yet there. But I take it to be one of the conundrums "no fellah can ever find out."

P.S.—A word as to bugs, lures, flies, etc. Now I have no criticism to offer as regards flies or lures. I saw a Gotham banker in 1880, making a cast on Third lake, with a leader that carried *twelve flies*. Why not? He enjoyed it; and he caught some trout. Even the guides laughed at him. I did not: he rode his hobby, and he rode it well. Fishing beside him, with a five-dollar rod, I caught two to his one. What did he care? He came out to enjoy himself after his own fashion, and he did it. Like myself, he only cared for the sport—the recreation and enough trout for supper. (I cannot cast twelve flies.)

Now my favorite lures—with forty years' experience—stand about thus. Tail fly, red hackle; second, brown hen; third, Romeyn. Or, tail fly, red ibis; second, brown hackle; third, queen of the waters. Or, red hackle, queen, royal coachman. Sometimes trout will *not* rise to the fly. I respect their tastes. I use then—tail fly, an angle worm, with a bit of clear pork for the head, and a white miller for second. If this fails I go to camp and sleep. I am not above worms and grubs, but prefer the fly. *And I take but what I need for present use.* Can all brother anglers say the same?

Trout Fishing on Long Island

FRANK FORESTER

Long Island has been, for many years, the Utopia of New York sportsmen, and still continues, although many of its attractions have been lost, owing to the extinction of several species of game which formerly abounded there, to be the favorite resort of all who can pitch up a heavy gun with accuracy upon a team of wild fowl, or cast a long line lightly for the speckled trout.

It is with this last branch of the sport that I have now to do; and it is in this precisely that the Long Island sporting has the least deteriorated.

It is true that the noble heath-fowl, the pinnated grouse of North America, crows no more in her scrub oaks, and brushplains; that his congener the ruffled grouse drums less frequently than of old; that the incessant and merciless warfare waged on them from sunken batteries, is fast banishing the wild fowl from her bays and inlets; but, thanks to the enforcement of good and judicious laws, trout fishing still flourishes and is likely to flourish, so long as grass grows and water runs.

The natural formation of Long Island is not indeed such, that we should look to it, if strangers to its qualities in this respect, with any high degree of expectation as a mother of trout streams; and yet it is probably surpassed in this particular by no region in the world.

It is, as most of our readers of course well know, a long, narrow, and, for the most part, sandy strip of land, running nearly from east to west, the eastern part being the bolder and more rocky, between the Sound and the Atlantic Ocean.

It has no mountains, scarce indeed anything that can be called hills, if you except a line of low-irregular elevations running nearly midway its whole length, of altitude little more than sufficing to shed its waters, this way and that, to the Sound and to the ocean.

With few large streams, no river worthy of the name, and scarcely anything that, in the incorrect phraseology of the country, would be called a *creek*, it abounds in small crystal rivulets, which, rising in the elevations above mentioned, take their way, for the most part directly, and without receiving any tributary waters, into their respective seas.

It is in these rivulets, and in the ponds, which have been formed along their courses, either for the erection of grist and saw mills, or for the sake of the fish themselves, that the brook trout are found in abundance; and in a degree of perfection, which I, at least, have seen equaled in no other waters, either American or British.

In all the waters of the island, this noble and delicious fish is taken readily by a skilful fisherman, both on the north or Sound, and the south or Atlantic side; but it is with the latter district that I am the most familiar; and it is conceded that its fish are superior in shape, color, flavor, and number, though perhaps not in size, to those of some of the northern waters.

It is to the south side that I shall, therefore, principally confine my remarks; although there is one pond on the northern side which must on no account be passed over, as the run of fish in it is larger probably than in any other on the island, perhaps on the continent.

To proceed, however, the ponds and streams of the south side present a general resemblance so strong that a brief description of one will suffice to make the stranger acquainted with the prevalent character of all.

The rivulet rising, we will suppose, at some four or five miles distance from the bays into which it falls at last, creeps along during the earlier two-thirds of its career, among thickets and tangled coverts, which it is by no means an easy task to penetrate, and among which, if it were desirable, it would be hardly possible to throw a fly, or wield so much even as an eight foot rod. In this part of their courses, however, though trout are to be found, they are so diminutive as to offer no reward or excitement to the angler.

After a while, following the waters down from their head, we come upon a clear bright pond, of various size, from one or two to many acres in extent, surrounded on three sides by the same sort of tangled swampy woodland, as that through which the brook has passed in its downward course, and on the fourth, or seaward side, by the dam which supports its waters.

This dam is, for the most part, planted with willows, in order to render it firmer against the wear and tear of floods and freshets; and, therefore, it is difficult to throw a line from the shore at this point, the others being from the nature of the soil and underwood entirely impracticable. In consequence of this, the angling in these ponds is carried on almost entirely from boats, which can readily be obtained everywhere, for a moderate compensation.

Pouring down clear and copious from the sluice or floodgate of the first pond, the brook rushes away, now through cleared fields, now among brakes and thickets, until it again expands into a second, and probably a larger sheet of water, the character of which is precisely the same with that above.

Thus, in proportion to the fall and volume of these streams, they form a series of pools, more or less in number; the last of which almost invariably lies close to the upper side of the excellent road which runs along the south shore of the island, dividing more or less accurately the uplands from the salt meadows.

Thence, changing its character altogether, the stream flows gently, in a deeper channel, ebbing and flowing with the tide, which, for the most part, runs quite up to the floodgates of the last pond, through the level oozy salt marshes; and here it is, in my opinion, that the finest and most highly flavored fish are to be taken.

This brief description thus concluded, I shall proceed, after a few words on what I consider the peculiarities of the Long Island trout, and the distinctions between it and the fish of the British waters, to review the different streams and ponds, as we travel eastward; and shall conclude with a brief summary of the times, the seasons, the bait, and the tackle, which, from my own experience and the information of others, I deem the most likely to insure sport.

The principal distinctions that strike the careful observer between the trout of Long Island, or, indeed, I might say North America in general, and those of the British Isles, is, first, the great uniformity of size on the part of the former, which rarely exceed two or three pounds in weight and *never*, so far as I have been able to ascertain, five or six—and, secondly, the fact that in the United States trout are never taken in the large rivers, or, if ever, so rarely as to prove the rule by the wonder arising from the exception.

On Long Island, there are some half dozen instances on record, within three times as many years, of fish varying in weight from four to six pounds, taken with the rod and line. Two of these instances occur to me, as connected with circumstances which may render the relation acceptable, as of anecdotes very unusual, and almost, but that they are proved beyond the possibility of doubt, incredible.

Both these instances occurred at Stump-pond, on the north side; one in the pond itself, the other in the mill-pond, at the outlet.

A gentleman from New York, thus runs the story, who had never thrown a line, or taken a trout in his life, and who had come out lately equipped with a complete outfit of Conroy's best and strongest tackle, all spick-and-span new, and point device, on throwing his hook, baited with a common-lob worm, into the water, was greeted with an immediate bite, and bob of the float, which incontinently disappeared beneath the surface, carried away by the hard pull of a heavy fish. The novice, ignorant of all the soft and shrewd seductions of the angler's art, hauled in his prize, main force, and actually, without the aid of gaff or landing net, brought to basket a five-pounder!

The fact is remarkable; the example decidedly unworthy of imitation!

The other instance to which I have referred is, in all respects, except the size of the fish, the very opposite of the former; as, in it, the success of the fortunate fisherman is due as much to superior science in his craft, as *his*, in the former, is attributable to blind and unmerited good luck.

The hero of this anecdote is a gentleman, known by the *nom de guerre* of Commodore Limbrick, a character in which he has figured many a day in the columns of the Spirit of the Times, and who is universally allowed to be one of the best and most experienced, as well as the oldest fisherman in the city.

After having fished all the morning with various success in the pond, he ascertained, it seems, that in the pool below the mill there was a fish of extraordinary size, which had been observed repeatedly, and fished for constantly, at all hours of the day and evening, with every variety of bait, to no purpose. Hearing this, he betook himself to the miller, and there having verified the information which he had received, and having satisfied himself that neither fly nor minnow, gentle nor red-worm, would attract the great trout, he procured, *horesco referens*, a *mouse* from the miller's trap, and proceeding to troll therewith, took at the first cast of that inordinate dainty, a fish that weighed four pounds and three-quarters.

Another fish or two of the like dimensions have been taken in Liff. Snedecor's and in Carman's streams; and it is on record that at Fireplace, many years since, a trout was taken of eleven pounds. A rough drawing of this fish is still to be seen on the wall of the tavern bar-room, but it has every appearance of being the sketch of a salmon; and I am informed by a thorough sportsman, who remembers the time and the occurrence, although he did not see the fish, that no doubt was entertained by experienced anglers who did see it, of its being in truth a salmon.

In the double-pond among the Musconetcong Hills, on the confines of New York and New Jersey, in the Greenwood Lake of the same region, and in some other ponds of Orange County, brook trout have been occasionally taken of the same unusual size—one fish I saw myself on last New Year's Day, which, shameful to tell! had been caught through the ice, near Newburgh. This fish weighed an ounce or two above five pounds, and was well fed, and apparently in good condition—but, as I said before, all these must be taken as exceptions proving the rule, that trout in American waters rarely exceed two or three pounds in weight, and never compare in size with the fish taken in England, and still less with those of the Scottish and Irish waters, in all of which, the regular, red-spotted, yellow-finned, brook trout are constantly taken, with the fly, of ten pounds of weight and upward; and sometimes, in the lakes of Ireland and Cumberland, in the Blackwater, Coquet, and Stour rivers, attain to the enormous bulk of twenty-six and thirty pounds.

With regard to the second point of distinction, I have never heard of a trout being taken in the Hudson; never in the Delaware, even so far up as Milford, where the tributaries of the river abound in large and well fed fish; never in the lower waters of the Connecticut, or any Eastern river so far as the Penobscot, although the head waters of all these fine and limpid rivers teem with fish of high color and flavor. In Great Britain, on the contrary, it is to the larger, if not to the largest, rivers that the angler looks altogether for good sport and large fish; and it is there as rare a thing to take a fish a pound weight in a rivulet or brook, as it is here to catch a trout at all in a large river.

In Canada, and in the British provinces to the eastward of Maine, it is true that sea trout, or salmon peel, are taken of large size in the St. Lawrence, and in the rivers falling into the bays of Gaspé and Chaleurs, but although occasionally confounded with the trout proper, this is in truth a totally different fish, and one, so far as I know, which is never taken in any of the waters of the United States.

In appearance, the brook trout of America and Great Britain are to my eye identical; both presenting, in well fed and well conditioned fish, the same smallness of head, depth of belly, and breadth of back; the same silvery luster of the scales, the same bright crimson spots, and the same yellow fins. The flesh of the American fish, when in prime order, and taken in the best waters, is, I must confess, of a deep red hue, and of a higher flavor, than that of any which it has been my fortune to taste at home—and I have often eaten the Thames trout, which, rarely taken below ten pounds in weight are esteemed by epicures the very best of the species.

We travel now, be it observed, by railroad to our fishing stations, but for the convenience of reviewing the country, and scanning the waters, in regular succession as we pass onward, I will suppose that, as in the pleasant days of old, we are rolling along in our light wagon, over the level roads, on a mild afternoon in the latter days of March, or the first of April.

We have started from Williamsburg or Brooklyn, after an early dinner; passed through Jamaica; rolled over the plains toward Hempstead; and, passing through it without stoppage, have turned suddenly to the right toward the bays, beyond which lies the beach, with the incessant surge of the Atlantic moaning in the deep monotony of its calm, or thundering in the hoarse fury of its storm, against its pebbly barrier.

Now we are in the land of trout streams, baymen, and wild fowl.

The rippling dash of falling waters catches our ear, at every half mile as we roll along, and every here and there, the raised bank on our left hand with its line of stunted willows bent landward by the strong sea-breeze, the sluice-gate, and the little bridge, with the clear stream rushing seaweed under it, tell us that we are passing a trout pond.

On the right hand, the salt meadows stretch away, a wide, waste, desolate expanse, to the bays which glitter afar off under the declining sun, whence you can hear at times the bellowing roar of a heavy gun, telling of decimated flocks of brant and broadbill.

Now we pass by a larger pond than any we have yet seen, with a mill at its outlet, and in a mile further, pull up at the door of Jem Smith's tavern.

And there we will halt tonight, although it be a better station for fowling than for fishing, for we are sure of neat though homely accommodation, and of a kindly welcome; and here it is that the first essay is to be made of Long Island waters.

On this stream there are two ponds, both of which were formerly private property and closed against all persons except those who were furnished and with a permit; they are now open to all persons indiscriminately, and I believe without restriction as to the number that may be taken by each individual, or by a party. The consequence of this is that these ponds have deteriorated very rapidly, and that although they are well stocked with fish of fair flavor and quality, trout are rarely taken of such a size as to remunerate the exertions of a good fisherman. Half a pound may be taken as a *good* average of the fish killed here. In the creek below, where the tide makes, there are of course fish, but I never have heard of much work being done in it; and in truth, except that this is the first southern pond of any note, I would hardly advise the angler to pause here.

About a mile and a half further eastward is a large pond, and a fine house, both recently constructed at a great expense by Judge Jones—the former exclusively designed as a fish-pond. The place has, however, passed out of his hands, and the house is now kept as a hotel by one of the Snedecors. The pond has hitherto been private, but is now open, though with a limitation. It is well stocked with fish of a fair size. When I was last there, a fortnight since, a gentleman had taken eight fish, weighing as many pounds, with a fly that morning. The larger did not exceed a pound and a half, but they were handsome, clean, well fed fish, and, as the day was anything but propitious, easterly wind, and very raw and cold, I considered it fair sport. He had not been fishing above a couple of hours. I understand, however, that there are many pike in this pond, and the stream that supplies it; and I much fear that this must ultimately prove destructive to all the fish in the water, although those residents on the spot assert that the pike never grows in that region to above half a pound, and rarely to that weight, and that little if any detriment is observed to arise from his presence.

This, however, I cannot believe, for the growth of the pike is usually almost as rapid as his voracity is excessive; and I am aware of many instances, both in the United States and in England, where ponds and streams, excellently stocked with trout, have been utterly devastated and rendered worthless by the introduction of this shark of the fresh waters.

The house is well kept, as is almost invariably the case on Long Island; and I have no doubt that the angler may pass some days here with pleasure.

Some miles beyond this, still keeping the southside road, we come to Babylon, where there is an excellent house under the management of Mr. Concklin, of whom all accommodation may be obtained, both as regards fowl shooting in the bays and trout fishing in the neighborhood. There are several ponds and streams more or less well stocked in this vicinity, but none of any particular note, either for the size or flavor of the fish.

Such, however, is not the case with the next station at which we arrive, Liff. Snedecor's; in whose pond the fish run to a larger size than in any water we have yet noted. The trout here, both in the pond and in the stream below, are noted for their great beauty both of form and color; and although there is some debate among connoisseurs as to the comparative flavor of Snedecor's fish and those taken at Carman's, eighteen miles further east, the judgment of the best sportsmen inclines to the former.

The pond is of the same character with those which I have described heretofore, and can be fished only from boats. It is open to all anglers, but the number of fish to be basketed by each person in one day is limited to a dozen. In the stream there is no limit, nor indeed can there be, as the tide-waters cannot be preserved, or the free right of fishing them prohibited. The trout here are not only very numerous and of the first quality of excellence—their flesh being redder than that of the salmon—but very large; the average probably exceeds a pound, and fish of two and two and a half pounds' weight are taken so frequently as to be no rarity.

The outlet of this pond, after running a few hundred yards, opens upon the salt meadows, where there is no obstacle whatever to throwing a long line. It is broader and longer than any stream we have hitherto encountered, and is incomparably the best, containing fish even larger than those of the pond above, and in my opinion of a finer flavor. I believe it, indeed, to be an indisputable fact, that trout, which have access to salt water, are invariably more highly colored and flavored than those which are confined to fresh streams by natural or artificial obstacles.

There is no distinction, of which I am aware, in favor of pond or stream, for the use of the fly, the fish taking it readily in either, although as a general rule they will rise to it earlier in the fresh, than in the tide water.

At some distance down this stream there is a range of willows on the bank, nearly opposite to a place owned by Mrs. Ludlow, and under the trees are some holes famous for being the resorts of the largest fish, which affect here the deepest water and the principal channel. Here, as in the pond, fish of two and a half pounds are no rarity, and, in fact, such are taken here more frequently than above. I should say that one would rarely hook a trout in this stream under one and a half pounds; and the true angler well knows that a well conditioned fresh-run fish, from this size to a pound larger, on the finest and most delicate tackle, will give him nothing of which to complain in the way of exercise or excitement.

At a short distance from Snedecor's is another stream, known as Green's Creek, which contains a peculiar and distinct variety of trout, which is called in that district the silver trout. I have not seen this fish, but learn from good sportsmen that it is of a much lighter and more pearly hue than the common trout, the bright and silvery luster of the scales prevailing over the back and shoulders. It is crimson spotted, but the fins are less strongly yellow, and it is perhaps a slenderer fish in form. The flesh is said to be firm and well flavored. The silver trout is rarely taken much over or much under a pound in weight, and rises to the fly or takes the bait indiscriminately. This stream has, I know not wherefore, of late years lost much of its celebrity, and is rarely visited by the best sportsmen.

At Patchogue, yet a few miles further, there is a very large pond, which was formerly perhaps the most famous on the island, both for the abundance and the size of the fish which it contained. They have, however, become latterly so scarce, that few persons from a distance think it worth their while to pause there, but proceed at once to Sam Carman's, at Fireplace, eighteen miles eastward from Liff. Snedecor's; these two being in fact the *par excellence* fishing grounds of the Island, and the difference between the two rather a matter of individual prejudice and fancy, than of any real or well grounded opinion.

The character of the fishing at Fireplace is nearly similar to that at Islip; the stream flowing from the pond is larger, and contains much larger fish, the most beautiful, both in shape and brightness of color, of any on the island. In this stream two pounds is a very common size; perhaps fish are as frequently taken of this weight as under it, and upwards to four pounds. Their flesh is very highly colored, and their flavor, as I have observed before, second to none. Indeed, it is but a few years since Carman's fish were estimated by old sportsmen the *only* fish worth eating; of late, however, fashion—which rules in gastronomic tastes as otherwise—has veered a little in favor of the Islip trout, and it remains at present a debatable point between the two. The course of Carman's stream lies chiefly through open salt meadows, and the banks are entirely destitute of covert, so that very careful and delicate fishing is necessary in order to fill a basket. Even with ground bait it is desirable to keep completely out of sight, walking as far from the bank as possible, and to avoid jarring the water, so wary and shy are the larger fish. It is also advisable to fish down wind.

Trolling is very successful in this water, the same precautions being taken, and the bait-fish being dropped as lightly on the surface as if it were a fly, so as to create neither splash nor sound. The pond above is likewise deservedly celebrated, the fish *averaging* at least a pound in weight, and equal in all respects to any pond trout in this or any other region. The fly fishing here in season is probably the best on Long Island, although of late, here as everywhere else, trout are becoming comparatively few in number; so that it has been found necessary to impose a limit on sportsmen.

Not many years ago, a celebrated English shot and angler, who has since left this country, and who, I believe, was among the first, if not the very first, to use the fly on Long Island waters, took between forty and fifty good fish in this pond before dinner, and in the afternoon basketed above a dozen of yet larger size in the stream below.

This feat, the like of which will not, I fear, be heard of again, was performed with a fly, the body of which was composed of hare's ear fur, and the hackle of a woodcock's wings—a very killing fly, be it observed, for all waters, especially early in the season.

On the same stream with Carman's pond, and but a short distance above it, is another called Middle Island Pond, with a saw and flour mill at the outlet, which contains a great number of fish, of very large and very uniform size, running from one and a half to two pounds weight. It is remarkable, however, that the trout in the lower pond being esteemed the best, those in the upper should be the worst of any taken on the south side of the Island. Such, notwithstanding, is the case; they are long, shallow, ill fed fish, dingy colored and woody flavored. They are not, however, blackmouthed, as are the fish of a pond which I shall have occasion to mention hereafter.

I remember that a fact of the same sort is recorded of two lakes, I think in the *north* of Ireland, connected by a short stream running through a bog meadow. In the upper of these lakes the fish, as here, are worthless—in the lower superlative; and they are never known to intermingle. How this should be, cannot well be explained; for granting that the excellence of the fish arises from the soil and food, and that the inferior fish improves on coming into the superior water, still there must be a transition state.

With this pond I shall close my notice of the south side waters, merely adding that at Moriches, and yet further east, there are many streams and lakelets abounding in fish, though inferior to those of the waters I have enumerated, both in size and quality; and these are, I believe, all open without limit to all persons who desire to fish them.

It may be worth while here to mention, for the benefit of strangers, that the houses kept by Snedecor and Carman are by no means country taverns, at which nothing can be obtained, as is often the case in the interior, but hard salt ham and tough hens just slaughtered. Being frequented by gentlemen only, they are admirable hotels in every respect.

I will now turn, for a moment, to the north side, on which there are also many streams containing trout, but none, with a single exception, which can show size or numbers against the southern waters. That exception is Stump Pond, near Smithtown, now rented to a company of gentlemen, and of course shut to the public in general. The fish in this large sheet of water are very numerous and very large, but are for the most part ill-shaped, ill-conditioned, and inferior in flavor—long, lank fish with very large black mouths. I have been informed that in latter years the fish in this water have been gradually improving, but of this I cannot speak from personal experience; it is, however, notorious, that occasionally trout of very fine quality, both in appearance and flavor, have been caught here; which is somewhat remarkable, inasmuch as the same feeding grounds rarely produce two different qualities of fish.

I shall take leave of the waters of Long Island for the present, having briefly but fairly enumerated them with their merits and defects; and before taking leave of the reader also, shall proceed to state a few facts and opinions relative to the best methods of taking this king of fish on these waters, and to the differences I have observed in the habits and feeding of the trout here and in England.

In the first place, I would remark that the season of trout fishing on the Island commences, as defined by law and sanctioned by all true brothers of the angle, on the first of March; and if the month be genial and the spring gentle, the earlier after that date the angler is abroad, the better his chances of success; the waters being so continually whipped that ere long many of the best fish are taken, and the others pricked and teased by bad fishermen till they become so shy that they can hardly be tempted to rise to fish or fly.

With regard to weather, a darkish day with a moderately brisk breeze, sufficient to make a strong ripple on the water, is the most favorable. It is somewhat singular, that in spite of the generally received opinion that southerly or south-westerly weather is the *only* weather for trout fishing, few old Long Island anglers are to be found who cannot state that they have taken as many, some say *more*, fish during the prevalence of easterly winds, as in any weather. A friend of mine, on whose authority I can perfectly rely, and to whom I gladly record my indebtedness for many facts stated in this paper, assures me that he has never known trout to take the fly more freely than during a northeasterly snow storm. Still, I must consider these as exceptions to the general rule; and I at least would select, if I had my choice, "a southerly wind and a cloudy sky"—always barring thunder—and no objection to a slight sprinkling of warm rain.

There is another peculiarity to observe in the Long Island waters—and, so far as I know, in them only—that trout bite decidedly better and more freely, when the water is very fine and clear, than when it is in flood and turbid. Indeed, if there be a good ripple on the surface, the water can hardly be too transparent.

It has been suggested to me that this may be accounted for by the fact that in flood the waters are so well filled with natural bait that the fish become gorged and lazy. I cannot say, however, that this is perfectly satisfactory to me; as the same must be the case, more or less, in all waters; whereas it is unquestionably the case, wherever I have fished, except on Long Island, that trout are more easily taken in turbid than in fine water.

As connected with the foregoing remarks I will add here that, as a general rule, the minnow, with spinning or trolling tackle, is found to be more killing than ground bait in the ponds, and *vice versa*, in the tide streams—probably from the mere fact that the minnow is the rarer in the one water, the red-worm in the other, and that each in its rarity becomes the greater dainty.

For myself, I would not give sixpence to kill the finest trout that ever ran a line off a reel, with a ground-bait, and even spinning a minnow I hold to be ignoble sport, as compared with throwing the fly; and, so far as I have myself observed, and have heard from others, the same flies which are the most killing in England, as a general rule, take the most and best fish here—I mean the different shades of hackle, from dun and bright red, to partridge, woodcock, and dark grey or black.

The darker flies I consider to be the most killing early in the season; and, very late, I have seen extremely bright flies, with bodies of silk and tinsel, do considerable execution.

It is worthy of remark, though it is quite unaccountable to me why it should be so, that the English imported flies fail altogether, from being tied on hooks many times *too small*; the trout in all American waters, so far as I have seen, rising more readily, and being more easily taken with a very large fly, which no English fish would look at. This is the more remarkable because, as I have observed, the trout in the English rivers run to six or eight times the size of the average fish of this country; yet these monsters are taken with a hook which would be properly rejected as too small by every experienced angler in the United States.

Beyond this, there is little difference in the mode of taking trout here or there, with this sole exception, that—from being comparatively less harassed—the fish here are much bolder, and can be taken with much heavier tackle, and with much less skill, than in any British waters. This distinction is, however, growing smaller every day, especially on Long Island; where, from the same causes, the fish are becoming shier and more difficult every year, and where, in consequence, finer tackle and greater skill are constantly coming into requisition. Perhaps, even at this moment, there is a broader difference in this respect between the trout of Long Island and those of the interior of Pennsylvania, where I have taken very large fish in very large numbers with ridiculously coarse tackle, than there is between the fish of the United States, and of the British islands.

And here I will bring this over-long paper to a close. No one can be more fully aware of its deficiencies than I am myself; the only apology I can offer is that it has been thrown in haste, at moments snatched from severer labors; and the only hope in which I do offer it is that it may contain some hint which may prove not wholly unworthy of better brothers of the angle than myself, and that it may be regarded as a tribute of my affection to what has been well termed the *gentle art*.

The Cedars, April 15, 1847

Reuben Wood: My First Fish

FRED MATHER

This noted sportsman, who for nearly half a century made his home in Syracuse, N. Y., was well known throughout the State, and it was my good fortune to have him as an instructor in the art of angling in earliest boyhood. We were born in the then small village of Greenbush (opposite Albany), he in December, 1822, and I eleven years later.

Almost every man who has passed the half-century milestone on life's journey loves to imitate Lot's wife and look over his shoulder, and usually the retrospect is pleasant because we do not remember clearly; we conjure up the roses in the pathway, and the small thorns are indistinct in the distance; a faint humming of the bees whose honey we stole brings no remembrance of the penalty paid for it; the wound of the sting is cured by the honey—in memory, at least. Poor indeed is the man of fifty who has no wealth of retrospect and who thinks the punishment of Lot's wife was fitted to the crime! It was cruelly unjust, and in compensation at this late date she should be sainted perhaps with the name and title of Saint Salina. Here I pause to ask if there is really any such thing as an occult celebration which caused my pen to turn to thoughts of Lot's wife while writing an apology for looking back at the boyhood of a citizen of Syracuse, N. Y., the great salt-producing city of the State?

There are men who never could have been boys—engaged in boyish sports and had a boy's thoughts. Everyone has known such men. Men who must have been at least fifty years old when they were born—if that event ever happened to them—and have no sort of sympathy for a boy nor his ways; crusty old curmudgeons who never burned their fingers with a firecracker or played hookey from school to go a-fishing. They may be very endurable in a business way, but are of no possible use as fishing companions. I speak by the card, for I've been in the woods with them.

Reuben Wood was a boy, and was one to me as long as he lived. We were boys together, he being a big boy when I was but a little one; he was at our house a great deal, and is among the earliest of memories. He was "Reub" all through life to all his familiars, and they were many.

It was a summer day, and I was some six or eight summers old, when Reub came down the street with some fish that he had caught in a stream then the northern boundary of the village, but now in it and fishless. After much solicitation he agreed to let me in the party next day—Bruin and me. Now, Bruin was a big Newfoundland dog belonging to my father which Reub had taught to pick me up whenever he said, "Bruin, go fetch Fred," no matter what screams, kicks and protests his burden made, and this was one of Reub's jokes which I failed to appreciate. We started, Bruin and I, in high glee. Reub cut some poles, rigged the lines, floats and hooks and put on the worms, and he soon had a perch, a monster it seemed then and does yet, while the sunfish that tried to run away with my float and which Reub helped to land probably weighed more than the grocer's scales could tell; it must have been as big as 100 modern ones, and Reub said "it was as big as a piece of chalk." Such was my first experience in angling, as clear in memory as if only a week ago.

A little pond turtle stuck his head up near the float, looked at it and us, and paddled to the bottom in the funniest way. Reub called it a "skillypot," but he had funny names for everything. Then I caught a perch, actually bigger than the sunfish, and a new world seemed to open; but the spines of the fish cut my hand and the world was not so bright. Five fish came to my lot in all, but Reub had about twenty—some perch, sunfish, two bullheads and an eel. He said that I let the fish eat the worms off. I saw a turtle climb on a log while Reub was up the bank after more worms, and I went out on the log to get it, but the turtle slid into the water, and so did I. A scream brought Reub, who whistled for Bruin and ordered him to "Fetch Fred," and he did. Oh, the dripping of clothes and the splashing of shoes as we went home, and the fearful tale of a turtle who wouldn't wait to be caught! This last seemed the greatest cause of grief and afforded Reub and the other boys a text for teasing, which they worked to an annoying extent, and it was long before he would take me fishing again, saying, "No, you'll go diving for turtles." This occurred about 1840, and Reub referred to it the last time I saw him, in 1883.

At this time Greenbush was a very quaint little village on the upper Hudson, whose connection with the outside world was by the Albany stage to Boston and by ferry to Albany. No railroad entered it, and in fact the only one at that time in the whole State of New York ran from Albany to Schenectady, and hauled its cars to the top of the hill by a stationary engine before hooking on the light locomotive. The place was favorable for the development of character, unhampered by the conventionalities which come from contact with outside people, and Reuben grew to manhood there and retained a quiet simplicity all his life, a rugged, honest nature, whom it was refreshing to know, and was a lovable man to meet. If, as a boy, he ever indulged in forays on the fruit and melon patches of the farmers, the fact is unknown to me. That I did is certain, but the disparity of years forbade comradeship in such nocturnal pleasures. He was large, strong and heavy of movement, with a deep chest voice, even when he was a boy, that was remarkable. His brother Ira, nearer my age, resembled him in this and other particulars, and in both there was an air of honesty and truthfulness, not so frequent in boys, which was fully borne out in their characters as men.

In after years I had a joke on Reub which was originally on me as a boy, but later knowledge reversed it. With some other boys I had been fishing away up the hill in the pond of the locally famous "red mill," and had seen a pair of wood ducks alight upon a tree. We somehow knew that they were wild ducks, but had no idea that the term included more than one kind, for at that day we only knew one sort of tame ducks. To see a duck alight on a tree was strange, and I told Reub of it; and he spread the incredible story, for he knew nothing of wood ducks, and the laugh was on me. "Seen any ducks lightin' on trees lately?" was a common question and annoying salutation, and years later the question was turned on Reub. I fished with him many times as a boy, never after he left Greenbush for Syracuse, in 1852; but we met occasionally after 1876, when thrown together at fairs and fly-casting tournaments, and he seemed to be the same boy that somehow had gray hair.

The picture of him gives an excellent idea of his manly face, but the cigar I do not recognize. This is not remarkable, because he used from a dozen to twenty each day, and there are people who might not recognize his picture without a cigar of some kind. The badge upon his corduroy coat is a certificate that he is a member of the Onondaga Fishing Club, of Syracuse, which was always represented at the State Sportsmen's tournaments. Take a good look at him! That kind, honest face would be a passport anywhere. To me he was always the same lovable boy to whom I looked up as guide, philosopher and friend on my first fishing trip away back in the forties. I think I am a better man for knowing Reub Wood when he was a big boy and I a child. From him I learned that the world was round—"rounder than a marble," he said—and I saw that the sky was the upper half and that we were inside the world; if he knew better he never explained the matter.

Reuben's humor was manifested in the use of strange words, which he probably manufactured, as I never heard them from any other person. A bad knot in a fish line was a "wrinkle-hawk," an excellent thing was "just exebogenus," a big fish was "an old codwalloper," and a long-stemmed pipe was "a flugemocker." What a blank page is a boy's memory that such things written on it remain indelible for over half a century when more important ones have faded! The name of Reub Wood conjures up these trifling things, which, if heard ten years ago, would have been forgotten. But he had such a strong individuality that a person who only met him for ten minutes would be impressed by it, and would know him in after years; what wonder that he should carve his personality on the mind of a child? Impressions of other men and boys in that small village are also quite distinct, and, as is usual in such places, there is more profanity and obscenity heard by a boy than in cities, for the tough boy in small places excels in such things, and it seems to me that he was worse then than now. But the worst that I ever heard Reub say was "Gosh hang it," under the provocation of having to cut a fish hook out of his thumb. His mind was as pure as his life, and that is more than can be said of many who live straight enough, but have to resist temptation frequently. A man is not so much to be judged by his actions as by his thoughts, if you only knew them, and Reub's thoughts were his spoken words.

In Greenbush he was employed in the bakery of Jonas Whiting, where he learned the mysteries of bread and cakes, and when he went to Syracuse he blossomed out as a caterer for balls and parties, and then established a business in fishing tackle, now carried on under the name of "Reuben Wood's Sons." His old cash book is still extant, and was not only what its name implied, but was day book, journal and ledger all in one, with a margin for a weather record which contained such items as "Gone hunting," "Went after ducks," "Gone a-fishing," etc. This is indefinite, and one wonders what the result may have been until we strike the entry: "Wood returned from Piseco with 250 lbs. of trout."

In that early day, in the fifties, Onondaga Lake abounded in pickerel and eels, and Reub and his companions often made a night of it, taking them with torch and spear, as was the custom of the time, and the catch went to their friends and the poor. When this mode of fishing became unpopular and unlawful, in later years, Reuben was one of the foremost in suppressing all kinds of fishing that the law forbade; but at the time of which we speak there was neither law on the subject nor public sentiment against spearing. He followed the custom of the day, merely drawing the line at fishing on Sunday.

A chum of Reub's was Mr. Charles Wells, of Wells, Fargo & Co.'s Express, and they went shooting and fishing when the spirit moved. Mr. Wells had not only all the railroad transportation necessary, but could have trains stopped anywhere in the woods if necessary, night or day, by flag or fire signal. This brings a sigh, not of envy, but merely a wish that such conditions existed today and I was "in it," as the saying goes.

One day in the fall of 1857 a report came to Mr. Wells that there were "rafts of ducks" on Cayuga Lake, one of those numerous large lakes of Western New York lying some thirty miles west of Syracuse, and a famous one for ducks. He told Reub just in time for him to gather his muzzle-loader and ammunition and get the next train going to Cayuga, at the foot of the lake via the "old road" of the New York Central R. R., a road then so slow that it took the best part of a day to get there. Wells had his camping outfit, and they camped for the night. As Reub told me the story years afterward, daylight found him in an old dugout, the only semblance of a boat at hand, while Wells had a good place on the shore. The ducks were flying down the lake and Wells had killed several, and was signaling him to come and pick them up, when a great flock of bluebills came up the stream and turned directly over Reub's head. As he let both barrels go the dugout somehow let him go into ice-cold water, but he hung on to his gun and got ashore chilled to the bone, and took the first train for Syracuse, where he traded his gun and equipments for a Knight's Templar badge and other things, and from that day foreswore the gun and devoted his energies to wielding the rod.

About this time Mr. Wells learned to fish with the fly and taught Reuben the art, to which he became devoted. It was long after this that I met Reuben, the occasion being the tournaments of the New York State Association for the Protection of Fish and Game, where he was a frequent competitor in the fly-casting tournaments, but never would allow himself or his brother Ira to win first prize because of a chivalric idea that another competitor—to whom he always deferred—should not be beaten. Either of them could outcast the other man, whose hoggish nature never allowed him to acknowledge the knightly courtesy—if he had the capacity to appreciate the sacrifice. Not until the State Association held its tournament at Brighton Beach, Coney Island, in June, 1881, did Reuben Wood ever have a chance to cast unhampered by his sentiment. Here he had a new competitor with a great local reputation, who had never cast in a State tournament before. This was in the two-handed salmon rod contest, and Reuben won the first prize, valued at $50, with a cast of 110ft. His brother Ira came second, with 101ft. Harry Prichard cast 91ft., and F. P. Dennison 94ft. All but Prichard were members of the Onondaga Fishing Club, of Syracuse, and cast with the same rod—a split-bamboo, won by Reuben in the tournament at Buffalo in 1878; length, 17ft. 1 in. As there was an allowance of 5ft. for every foot of rod in length, Mr. Prichard was allowed 9ft. 10 in. because his green-heart rod (made by himself) was 1ft. 10in. shorter than the one used by the others; hence his amended record of 91ft. had an allowance of 9ft. 10in., making it 100ft. 10in., giving him third prize over Dennison.

In 1883 Prof. Spencer F. Baird appointed Reuben to take charge of the angling department of the American display at the International Fisheries Exposition in

London, an appointment of which he was justly proud, as he wrote me in a farewell letter, and on June 11 he took part in the English fly-casting tournament at the Welch Harp, where he won first in salmon casting with an 18ft. split-bamboo rod, scoring 108ft., Mr. Mallock casting 105ft. with an 18ft. greenheart rod. In the single-handed trout contest he won first with 82½ft. over four competitors. In a contest with two-handed trout rods, a thing unknown in America, Mr. Mallock won first with 105ft., and Mr. Wood took second prize with 102ft. 9in. His many trophies in the tournaments of Central Park, New York City, are familiar to readers of *Forest and Stream.*

He died at his home in Syracuse on Feb. 16, 1884, in his sixty-second year. Mr. R. B. Marston, editor of the English *Fishing Gazette*, said of him: "I know many an angler in this country will feel sad at hearing genial, jolly, lovable 'Uncle Reub' has gone to his long rest. During his stay in this country he never failed to make friends of all who came in contact with him. I shall never forget the enthusiasm and almost boy-like glee with which he enjoyed a fishing trip with me to the Kennet, at Hungerford. He would stand for hours on the old bridge watching the trout and marveling at their cuteness. The system of dry-fly fishing pleased and astonished him greatly, and he told me he meant to try it on some wary old American trout he was acquainted with. Then he would show us some of his long casting with a split-cane rod. If we in this country, who only knew him so short a time, feel his loss so keenly, what must those home friends of his feel—his family and that wide circle of acquaintances who were proud to call him friend?"

His death was very sudden—he fell dead while entering his dining room. In addition to his love of the rod he was for many years an active member of the Syracuse Citizens' Corps, and later of the Sumner Corps, two well-known military organizations. He was also a member of the Baptist Church, and his name was a synonym for all that was honest and manly. The last time I met him he referred to our first fishing experience by saying, "Fred, are you catching many turtles now?" And the answer was, "No, Reub, it keeps me busy watching wood ducks light upon trees."

Trouting Along the Catasauqua

FRANK FORESTER

"And this 'clattering creek,' what sort of water is it?" asked Frank; "that I may learn at once the whole lay of the land."

"A real mountain burn."

"I'm thinking of trying it myself tomorrow," said Robins. "Mr. Langdale tells me it can only be fished with bait, and that's what I'm best at. Besides, there are bigger fish in it."

"But fewer," answered Langdale. "No, Robins, I'd advise you to stick to the 'Stony,' unless you'll try a cast of the fly with us over the pool and down the Catasauqua."

"No, no," replied St. Clair, half indignantly, "none of your flies for me, and no canoe-work. But why do you advise me against it? You said there were no trees, bait-fishing and big fish. What is there against it?"

"The toughest crag-climbing and the most difficult fishing you ever tried."

"What like fishing is it, Lancelot?" asked Frank.

"Exactly what that capital sportsman, Colquhoon of Luss, describes in his excellent book, the 'Moor and Loch,' under the title of 'Moorburn'."

"I remember," replied Frank. "Is it as bad as that?"

"Worse; but the fish much larger. I have caught them up to two pounds."

"I should like to hear about that. Can't you read it to me?" asked the Wall-street man, eager for information.

"I've no objection," said Langdale, "if Frank has not. HE has read it fifty times already."

"I'm convenient," answered Frank, laying down his knife and fork, the last duck having disappeared.

"Well, then, here goes. Now, Scipio, look alive and clear away the table; bring us our pipes and our coffee; and then we'll to bed, for we must be afoot by day-break."

And with the word he rose, and, after turning over a few volumes on his crowded shelves, brought down the volume in question, with its pages underlined, and inter-lined, and filled with marginal notes and references. This done, he ensconced him-self in the chimney corner, threw on a fresh log, and read as follows:

" 'In most of the small Highland burns, there is a succession of cataracts and pools, with a parapet of rock rising perpendicularly on each side, and often scarcely footing enough for a dog to pass. The greater proportion of picturesque-looking brethren of the angle would almost start at the idea of continuing their pastime under such disadvantages. They therefore make a circuit, and come down again upon the burn, where it is more easy to fish, and the ground less rugged. The trout in these places are thus left until many of them grow large, and each taking possession of a favorite nook, drives all the smaller fry away. The difficulty of reaching these places is, I admit, often great, the angler having sometimes to scramble up on his hands and knees, covered with wet moss or gravel, and then drag his fishing-rod after him. These lyns should always be fished up-stream, otherwise the moment you appear at the top of the waterfall or rock, the trout are very like to see you, and slink into their hiding-place. The burn, however, must always be low, as at no other time can you dis-tinguish the snug retreat of these little tyrants, which, indeed, they often leave, during the slightest flood, in search of prey. By fishing up the stream, your head will be on a level with the different eddies and pools, as they successively present them-selves, and the rest of your person out of sight. Hold the baited hook with the left hand, jerking out the rod, underhanded, with your right, so as to make the bait fall softly at the lower end of the pool. The trout always take their station either there or at the top where the water flows in, ready to pounce on worms, snails, slugs, etc., as they enter or leave the pool. Should a trout seize the bait, a little time may be given to allow it to gorge, which it will most likely do without much ceremony. If large, care must be taken to prevent it from getting to the top of the lyn, which may probably harbor another expectant. The best plan is, if possible, to persuade it to descend into the pool below. Having deposited the half-pounder in your creel, you will now crawl upon hands and knees, just so near the top of the lyn as will enable you to drop the bait immediately below the bubbling foam, nearly as favorite a station for an over-grown, monopolizing trout as the other. Except in such situations, the burn trout seldom exceeds a quarter of a pound, and may be pulled out with single gut, without much risk of breaking it. In these lyns, however, I have occasionally taken them upward of a pound, which is easily accounted for. As soon as the trout grows to a sufficient size to intimidate his pigmy neighbors, he falls back into the best pool for feeding, not occupied by a greater giant than himself, and as these lyns are almost always in precipices very difficult of access, he remains undisturbed and alone, or with a single companion, driving all others away, until he may at last attain to a pound weight.'

"Now, I fear, brother angler, that you are in some respects what the indefatigable Gael would call a 'picturesque angler'; so I advise you in good faith, stick to the 'Stony Brook'; fish it from the long fall carefully down. Scipio shall attend you with the landing-net and plenty of worms and minnows; the last, hooked through the lip and back fin, will do you yeoman service in the lower pools; and Frank and I will join you in the afternoon."

"Agreed," said Mr. Robins; "I'll take your advice, I believe; and now I guess I'll turn in. Good night."

"Time, too," said Frank, laughing. "He was beginning to get a little white about the gills. Could that be his old Otard; he did not drink so much of it."

"Lord help you, no! he'd drink a gallon of it and no hurt. No! But he will persist in smoking Cavendish tobacco and kinnikinnic, because he has seen me do it, and, I believe, imagines that it confers some special powers of trout-catching. But come, suppose we turn in, too; you'll be tired after your journey, and a good night's rest will give a steady hand and clear eye tomorrow."

"*Volontiers.*"

So they incontinently joined the Wall-street man, who declared, half asleep, that the bed was not so very bad, after all; while Frank, once ensconced in the fragrant sheets, swore, by the great god Pan, patron of hunters, that never had bed so sweet, so soft, so warm, in every way so excellent, received the limbs of weary hunter. And so, indeed, it proved; for, until Scipio made his entree, with his announcement that breakfast was ready, no one stirred or spoke during the livelong night.

Thereon they all turned, like the Iron Duke, not over, but out. Their sporting toilets were soon made; but Frank and Lancelot, in their old shepherd's plaid jackets and trews and hob-nailed fishing shoes, could not but exchange glances and smiles at the elaborate rig of their friend, which some Broadway artist had, it was evident, elaborated from a Parisian fashion-plate, the high boots of exquisitely enameled leather, the fine doeskin trousers, the many-pocketed, pearl-buttoned shooting jacket of fawn-colored silk plush, the batiste neckerchief and waistcoat, point device, with green and silver fishes embroidered on a blue ground, and, to complete the whole, a cavalier hat, in which, but that it lacked the king's black feather, Rupert might well have charged at Marston Moor or Naseby. He seemed, however, so happy, that it would have been as useless as ill-natured to indoctrinate him; for evidently, as an angler, the man was hopelessly incurable, though, as Frank observed, for Wall-street, he was wonderfully decent.

His weapon was a right good Conroy's general-fishing rod, but without reel, and having its line, an unusually stout silk one, with a superb salmon-gut bottom, which, in good hands, would have held a twenty-pounder, made carefully fast to the top funnel; eschewing all use of the ring and destroying all chance of the rod's regularly bending to its work. But again, to counsel would have been to offend; so our friends held their peace.

The smoked venison ham, broiled troutlings, dry toast and black tea, which furnished their morning meal, were soon finished; and forth they went into the delicious, breezy air of the quiet summer morning, not a sound disturbing the solitude, except the plash and rippling of the rapid waters, the low voices of the never-silent pine-tops, and the twittering of the swallows, as they skimmed the limpid pool.

Up the gorge of the Stony Brook, followed by Scipio, with bait of all kinds enough to have kept the kraten fat for one day at least, a large creel at his back, and gaff and landing-net in hand, away went St. Clair Robins, gay and joyous and confident; and then, but not till then quoth Forester—

"And whither we?"

"To the other side of the pool. You may see the big fish rising under the alders, there, in the shadow of the big hill, from this distance. That shadow will hang there until noon, while all this side of the basin will be in blazing sunshine. Not a fish will bite here, I warrant me, until three o'clock, while we'll fill our basket there with good ones, certain. The best fish in the pool lies under that round-headed stone, just in the tail of the strong eddy, where the 'Clattering Creek' comes in, in the broken water. I rate him a six-pounder, and have saved him for you all the spring. As soon as the sun turns westward, and the hemlocks' shadows cross the white water, you shall kill him, and then we'll away to the Wall-street man"; and therewith the larger birch canoe was manned, paddled gently over to the shady side of the pool and moored in about twenty-foot water, and then, the rods being put together, the reels secured and the lines carried duly through the rings, the following colloquy followed:

"What flies do you most affect here, Lancelot?" asked Frank.

"Any, at times, and almost all," answered Langdale. "In some weather I have killed well with middle-sized gaudy lake flies; but my favorites, on the whole, are all the red, brown, orange, and yellow hackles, and the blue and yellow duns. And yours?"

"My favorite of all is a snipe feather and mouse body; next to that the black and the furnace hackles."

"And will you use them today?"

"I will; the snipe wing for my stretcher. I mean to kill the big chap with him this evening."

"Be it so! to work."

And to work they went; but, though most glorious the sport to enjoy, or even to see performed gnostically, to read of it described, is as little interesting as to describe it is difficult. Suffice it to say, that before the sun had begun to turn westward, sixteen brace and a half were fairly brought to basket by our anglers, one a three-pound-and-a-halfer, three two-pounders, there or there about; not a fish under a pound, all smaller were thrown back unscathed, and very few so small as that, all beautifully fed fish, big-bellied, small-headed, high in color, prime in condition. At one o'clock, they paddled leisurely back to the cabin, lunched frugally on a crust of bread and a glass of sherry, and awaited the hour when the hemlock's shadow should be on the white water.

At the moment they were there; and lo! the big trout was feeding fiercely on the natural fly.

"Be ready, Frank, and when next he rises drop your fly right in the middle of his bell."

"Be easy, I mean it." His line, as he spoke, was describing an easy circle around his head; the fish rose not. The second revolution succeeded; the great trout rose, missed his object, disappeared; and, on the instant, right in the centre of the bell, ere the inmost circle had subsided, the snipe feather fell and fluttered. With an arrowy rush, the monster rose, and as his broad tail showed above the surface, the merry music of the resonant click-reel told that Frank had him. Well struck, he was better played, killed unexceptionably; in thirteen minutes he lay fluttering on the greensward, lacking four ounces of a six-pounder. The snipe feather and mouse body won the day in a canter. So off they started up the Stony Brook, to admire the feats of P. St. Clair Robins. It was not long ere they found him; he had reached the lower waters of the brook, full of beautiful scours, eddies, whirlpools and basins, and was fishing quietly down it, wading about knee deep with his bait, he was roving with a minnow, some ten yards down the stream, playing naturally enough in the clear, swirling waters. Some trees on the bank hung thickly over his head; a few yards behind him was a pretty rocky cascade, and above that an open upland glade, lighted up by a gleam of the westering sun; and, altogether, with his gay garb, he presented quite a picturesque, if not a very sportsmanly appearance.

"After all," said Frank, as unseen themselves, they stood observing him, "he does not do it so very badly as one might have expected."

But before the words had passed his lips, a good fish, at least a pounder, threw itself clear out of the water and seized his minnow. In a second, in the twinkling of an eye, by a movement never before seen or contemplated by mortal angler, he ran his right hand up to the top of the third joint of his rod, which he held perpendicu-larly aloft, and with his left grasped his line, mid length, and essayed to drag the trout by main force out of his element. The tackle was stout, the stream strong, the bottom slippery, the fish active, and, before any one could see how it was done, hand and foot both slipped, the line parted, the rod crashed in the middle, the fish went over the next fall with a joyous flirt of his tail, and the fisherman, hapless fisherman, measured his own length in the deepest pool of the Stony Brook.

He was soon fished out, equipped in dry rigging, comforted with a hot glass of his favorite cognac; but he would not be consoled. He was off at daylight the following morning, and, for aught that I have heard, Cotton's Cabin beheld him nevermore.

The Boy and the Angle

ROWLAND E. ROBINSON

Not solely for the scientific angler with his eight-ounce rod, silken line, and flies cunningly fashioned to resemble no living thing, are all and the chiefest delights of the gentle pastime. There is one of humble estate in the brotherhood of the angle who makes no pretensions to skill, and uses the most uncouth and coarsest tackle, to whom it yields supremest enjoyment. He never cast a fly, and knows no "green drake" but him of the duck pond, no "doctor" but the village practitioner who gives him an occasional nauseous dose, no "processor" but the "deestrict" schoolmaster, and if he ever heard of a split bamboo, thinks a split pole must be a poor stick to fish with. He wants no reel to wind in his fish with, but "yanks" them out and lands them high and dry and safe from return to the flood, casting them the length of pole and line behind him. This is, of course, our young and unsophisticated friend, the boy of the country, he who remains a boy till he has grown big enough to go a-fishing, and perhaps never becomes a young gentleman, but keeps a boy's heart within him, and a boy's ways until he becomes a man. He does not always wear a torn hat, nor always trousers in which he feels most at ease if sitting down when big girls are about, nor does he always go barefoot from spring till fall, though he likes to give his naked soles a taste of the soil for a few days when he has seen the necessary seventeen butterflies.

Furthermore, we do not claim for him, nor does he for himself, that he can catch more fish that the scientific angler; but how he loves to go a-fishin', and how he enjoys it all, from the preparative beginning to the very end! What happiness is his in the cutting of the pole in the always-pleasant woods, where many a sapling is critically scanned and many a one laid low before the right and foreordained one is found; and in the buying of the ten-cent line and half dozen beautiful blue fish-hooks, selected with much deliberation from the tempting array in the showcase of the country store. How continually is he full of anticipation of sport from the moment he begins digging his bait; each big worm unearthed and going into the leaky coffee-pot promises a fish, and as he hurries across the fields to the stream he cannot stop even to look for a bird's nest, though sparrow, bobolink, and meadow lark start from almost at his feet. Nor hardly can he halt to disentangle his hook and line from the fence or bush they are seen to catch in, for he knows the fish are waiting for him. Then out of breath beside the stream he impales a lively worm, spits on it, not so much for luck as in deference to time-honored usage, gets his line straight out behind him, and sends it with a whiz and a resounding "plung!" of the two-ounce sinker far out into the waters, and waits for a bite with what patience a boy can muster. Presently perhaps the expected thrill runs up his angle to his hands and through all his nerves, the tip of the pole nods, then bows low to the flood, and by no "turn of the wrist," but by main strength and by one and the same motion he hooks his victim and tears it from its watery hold. So swiftly has it made its curved flight over its head, unseen but as a dissolving streak, that he knows not till he has rushed to where it is kicking the grass whether his prize is a green-and-golden-barred perch, a gaudy-mottled pumpkin-seed, a silvery shiner or an ugly but toothsome bullpout, gritting his wide jaws when his horns do him no good, though they may yet do his captor a mischief.

Whatever it may be, he gloats over it as much as any man over his well-fought trout or bass, and straightway runs to cut a forked wand whereon to string it, and takes care that it be long enough to hold many another. If the fish do not bite he sets his pole in a crotched stick and lets it fish for itself while he explores the shore and catches a "mud turcle," "almost" kills a "mush rat" or scares himself with a big water snake.

Returning to his pole, perhaps he finds the tip under water and tugs out a writhing eel, the wild fun and horror, and the abominable, all-pervading sliminess of whose final capture makes memorable the hour and the day thereof. Perhaps a hungry and not too fastidious pickerel or pike-perch or bass may gorge the worm-indued hook and be hauled ashore, and then the measure of the boy's glory is filled and the capacity of his trousers to contain him tried to the utmost.

Though he goes home with a beggarly account of small fry dangling at the end of his writhe, he is unabashed, if not proud, and hopeful for another day. But if it is strung so full that his arms ache with lugging it, what pride fills his heart as he displays his fish! Till they are eaten and digested he ceases to be a "no-account" boy. He cleans them and enjoys it. Every scale is a cent, bright from the mint, and he catches each fish over again as he takes it up. He recognizes his worms in their maws. When they are cooked, whoever tasted fish so good?

The boy is no more a contemplative angler than he is a gentle one, and he does not of choice go fishing alone. He would rather go with the renowned old fisherman of the neighborhood and learn something of the mysteries of his art, but that worthy does not overmuch desire the companionship of youthful anglers. So perforce the young fisherman goes with another boy and has some one to "holler" to, compare notes with, and enter into rivalry with, and he can say with truth, when he gets home, "Me and Jim ketched twenty!" though he forgets to add that Jim caught nineteen of them. Wherefore not? Do not his biggers and betters brag of scores which would not have been made if their guides and oarsmen had not fished?

Alack, for the bygone days! When May comes with south winds and soft skies and the green fields are dotted with the gold of dandelions and patched with the blue of violets, and the bobolinks are riotous with song over them, who would not be a boy again just for one day to go a-fishing?

The Boy and the Brook

LATHAN A. CRANDALL

"Ma, may I go fishing?"

That the boy should use the homely "Ma," rather than "Mamma," makes it clear that he is not of our generation, although his generous crop of freckles looks familiar, and his blue jumper, coming down to the knees, and that battered straw hat, are sometimes duplicated in our own day. It is fifty years across which we look, even if he does stand out so clearly. The question is one that he asks daily, if not oftener, from the time when the pussy-willows begin to swell in the spring-time, to the season for comforters and woolen mittens in the late fall.

Hark! Do you hear the voice that is calling the boy? It comes distinctly across the long stretch of years, and is as sweet and compelling now as when it pulled at the heart of the lad on that long-ago summer day. It is the voice of the brook. It gurgles and laughs and pleads. It says, "Ha! ha! ha! Isn't this a beautiful world, and this the finest day ever? Come on, little boy, and play in my ripples. I've some nice peppermint growing on my banks, and all sorts of pretty pebbles that I have washed for you. Look sharp, now! Do you see that trout lying at the head of the riffle? Do you know that I counted thirty-seven as big as he is between the bridge and the Deer Pond? Come and catch 'em!"

That brook was a part, and a large one, of the first permanent impressions made upon the boy's mind. It had its rise in a little pond, concerning which there was the usual dark legend that it had no bottom. Just what held up the water was a mystery, but the boy never doubted the legend. It was fed by numerous springs. Vigorous and noisy from the moment when it broke forth from its source, the brook was ten miles of silvery laughter.

"If you'll not go out of sight of the house you may go for an hour," says the mother, for she too has ears to hear the call of the brook and can understand its charm for her lad. "Just up in the pasture-lot above the bridge," calls back the boy, and starts off with his pole and a supply of angleworms wrapped up in paper. Take special notice of that pole, for it is the joy of the boy's heart. He had thought that a cedar sapling, peeled and thoroughly dried, made an ideal outfit, until a friend gave him a straight cane-pole painted a brilliant blue. In after years he owned not a few jointed rods, made by hand of split bamboo; but the tide of joy and pride has never risen higher in his heart than the day when he became the possessor of the blue cane-pole.

There is a place in the pasture-lot where the brook stretches itself out in a long reach of still water. Above and below are rippling shallows. Wary as is his approach, the boy sees the shy trout darting from the riffles into the darker water. Patiently he dangles his baited hook by the side of a sunken log, and trails it temptingly back and forth before the coverts where the cunning fish lie hidden, but all in vain. They have learned by experience that the presence of a blue jumper and a blue pole spells out danger for them, and refuse to take any risks. Is this, like so many other fishing trips, to end in failure? Watch the boy! Laying the blue pole carefully on the ground, he rolls his sleeves to his shoulders and, lying on his stomach on the bank of the brook, thrusts one hand very gently into the water. With the utmost caution he feels here and there under the overhanging sods until at last his fingers touch something that sends an electric thrill tingling through the length of his little body. He feels a trout, and strangely enough it does not stir. The little fingers gently tickle the belly of the trout as they work their way toward its head, and when they have encircled the body at the gills they suddenly contract and the fish is thrown far back upon the grass. This performance is repeated three or four times, and then the trophies are gathered up in the jumper and with blue pole over his shoulder the boy goes proudly homeward.

Many years after the boy had grown to manhood he was riding with a friend on their way to a famous trout preserve. Naturally, the conversation turned to fishing experiences, and he told the story of the brook and of catching trout with his hands. The friend looked a whole volume of incredulity and exclaimed, "Well, of all the fish-lies I ever heard that takes the cake." When the clubhouse was reached the keeper, a canny Scotchman, was interviewed. "Andrew, did you ever hear of catching trout with the hands?" "Is it guddlin' you mean? Mony a time. I've caught plenty of 'em in the burns when a boy." The skeptic was silent if not convinced. Since that time a heated discussion of this mooted question has appeared in a prominent sporting journal, and able arguments have been adduced to prove the impossibility of any such feat as that ascribed to the boy. But he knows, and the brook knows, and the blue pole knows; and those may doubt who will.

"May I go fishin' down in the woods?" The question came from an anxious heart, and the boy proceeded to support his request with reasons. "The biggest trout are down there. Edwin Crumb caught one that weighed 'most a pound down there last week. There are no big ones in the pasture-lot. I'll be careful, and I'm 'most seven now, you know." It was a momentous question. For two miles after leaving the bridge the brook ran through the woods, and the mother fancied all manner of possible and impossible dangers to her boy lurking among those trees. But then, the lad must be allowed to go out of her sight sometime, and the day was full of sunshine.

"If you'll be very careful, and not go far, and be back early, you may go." "Whoop!" and a small boy has disappeared from view before the permission is fairly spoken. No blue pole this time. The brush and alders are too thick and the pole too long. It is only a small birch limb, six feet long, possibly, that he pulls out from under the barn as he rushes to get out of hearing before his mother repents her rashness.

What a day that was! He has not gone far before, alongside the alders in the swift water, he captures a larger trout than any ever granted him by the pasture-lot. He cuts a stringer from the over-hanging alders, and with fish in one hand and pole in the other proceeds on his adventurous way. For some time he steals along the gravelly bed of the brook, eagerly expectant but without getting even a bite. Certainly this is not very exciting and his gaze begins to wander to the woods. Is that crinkle-root? Investigation yields a plentiful supply of the peppery plant and also three or four ground-nuts. Then the brook pulls him back to itself and a few rods farther on he comes to a log across the stream and partly under water. His heart gives a thump, for this must be the place where Edwin Crumb caught his big trout. It exactly fits the oft-repeated description. He leaves the bed of the brook, fetches a circuit through the brush and comes out just where he can drop his hook by the upper side of the log in the still water. The answer to his invitation is prompt, but the captive is not as large as was anticipated. Again and yet again he returns his lure only to meet a cordial reception, until five fair-sized trout have been added to the alder stringer; then activities cease.

We cannot follow him all through his eventful pilgrimage, but there is one experience that must not go unrecorded. In a tangle of brush formed by a tree-top which has fallen into a deep place in the stream he spies an open space, possibly eighteen inches in diameter, where the water is covered with scum and foam. Just the place for a big trout, but there is no way of getting even his short pole through the brush. The line is untied, and he goes crawling out on a limb that hangs over the brook, and sits, at last, astride it and directly above the enticing spot. A fresh and exceedingly fat angleworm is looped upon the hook and the wriggling mass is cautiously dropped into the middle of the scum. It has no sooner touched the water than there is a sharp tug and a mighty swirl, but only the hook and the remainders of the worm come back in answer to his pull. Another bait, and again the hook is lowered into the pool. No, the old fellow was not pricked the first time, for here he is again and this time firmly hooked. To balance the body on the limb when both hands are employed in tugging on the line, is no easy task, but at least the trout is in his hands and hugged to his breast. With the fingers of one hand through the gills and the thumb among the sharp teeth of the fish's mouth, the slow journey is made back to the shore. Glory enough for one day! The prize measures about twelve inches and is thick through. Edwin Crumb's trout is beaten with room to spare.

But now it dawns upon the boy that he has been gone a long time, and if he hopes to be permitted to repeat this trip he must hurry home. He also becomes acutely aware of an awful vacuum in his stomach which even crinkle-root and ground-nuts will not fill. He reasons with himself that he can reach home more quickly by striking through the woods to the road than by retracing his way along the brook. He is very sure that he knows the way, but his certitude evaporates steadily as he plunges his way through the woods. Just when he admits to himself that he has no idea in which direction the road lies, he emerges into a clearing and sees before him a group of farm buildings. They are certainly unfamiliar; but some one must live here and he can get directions as to his shortest way home. Who is that in the doorway? It cannot be Mrs. Woodman whose home is only a short half-mile from his own? But it is, and, to make his joy complete, this is baking day and the good woman hands him out an apple turnover. All turnovers are good, but that one was far and away the best ever baked. A hungry boy and an apple turnover form a great combination.

It would not do to say that the boy and the brook were inseparable companions, for there were long months when the Frost King had everything his own way and the merry stream found it hard work to maintain its appearance even on the shallow riffles. Then there were swift flights down the hillsides for the boy, and long journeys up again dragging his sled. Often in the long winter nights he heard the half-smothered gurgle of the near-by brook, and wondered where the trout lived when the thermometer was below zero.

Even in the summer days the two friends could not be together all the time. A mile or so over the hill was the brown school-house to which the boy must make his pilgrimages five days each week for three months at a time, and where he learned, helped by the pictures, that three cherries and two cherries make five cherries, and wrestled more or less successfully with the multiplication table. The old meadow just above the orchard was a famous place for strawberries, and many hours the boy spent in gathering the luscious fruit while the bobolinks, perched on swaying mullein stalks or the old rail-fence, engaged in a vocal contest of riotous and maudlin song. Then a robin had built its nest on one of the big beams under the meetinghouse shed on the top of the hill, and the eggs must needs be watched and the young birds looked after. Sometimes the children strayed into the burial ground adjoining the church and pushed aside the myrtle to read on the little head-stone the name of a child that had died long, long ago.

If anything could make the boy forget the brook it was his dog. Very likely the dog had a pedigree, but it had not been recorded, and he was as dear to the heart of the child as if his ancestors had all been decorated with blue ribbons. Pedro and the lad knew where the woodchucks lived on the side of the hill above the pond, and it was a red-letter day when one of them was cut off from his hole by the two hunters and Pedro vanquished him in a pitched battle.

The brook has run through the years and its laughter sounds now in the ears of the writer. Somehow he hopes that the River of Life will be like the brook, larger grown. And ever as its murmur is heard a vision of the mother is seen. The two grew into the boy's heart together. In the last days when that mother had grown weary and was waiting for rest, the son sat by her bedside and they talked together of the long past days, the silence, and of the brook with its sun-painted trout. She has been sleeping for many years on the banks of the Susquehanna, lulled by the ceaseless flow of the noble river with whose waters the waters of the brook are mingled.

A Little Miss and a Big Fish

RUTH MAE LAWRENCE

Gentlemen, allow me to introduce you to the Royal Chinook. To shake his hand, you must have strength, courage, endurance, and adaptability, for no two of these gallant fish fight the same. I have seen one leap eight times out of the water, each leap higher than a man's head, and again have never seen them until they were dragged dead to the boat, and lifted gently in with the gaff, while the perspiring victor received his congratulations with beaming face.

When the waters of the mighty Columbia are in flood, they back up into the Willamette through the city of Portland, making dock owners hastily move their shipping goods to higher levels and fishermen resignedly remove the miscellaneous floatage of two great rivers from their hooks and lines or not so resignedly lose their tackle on some hidden snag. At a bend of the Willamette in the Rose City lies Swan Island, with graceful trees on its high banks in the drowsy summer time, but covered with water in many places when the freshets sweep down the river in the Spring. It is the Mecca of the still-water trollers who court the lordly Royal Chinook during his invasion of these waters during the months of April, May, and June.

One Decoration Day, five years ago, my father, my sister, and I sallied forth in our row-boat, the *Raft*, fully determined to bring home with us all the salmon which would deign to strike our hooks. I was then fourteen years old, small and slight for my age, and with no great strength. Despite my stature, I was born with the love of solemn forests, inaccessible mountains, rushing brooks, and wide rivers. There was something about the ride on the river, the cool breezes, and the sweet excitement of the fight with one of those kings of the deep that filled me with an ecstatic happiness I have never found duplicated in any other way.

As befitted my strength, I was given a trout rod, with a three-ounce tip, a small trout reel, a twenty-pound test line, and a light lead to hold the No. 3 or 4 salmon spinner to the bottom of the river. Even the slow strain of trolling in a gentle current with this light tackle made my arms and shoulders tired. My father and sister both had sturdier tackle, of course.

We were trolling as near the island as we could and yet not snag our hooks, when there came a swift jerk at my sister's line. The reel sang its deliriously happy song, and the rod bent lower and lower.

"Hang on to him, Laura," yelled Daddy, as he and I feverishly drew in our lines and laid the rods and tackle in the bottom of the boat. He picked up the gaff and an oar to guide the boat, while I made myself as small and out-of-the-way as I could in a dinky rowboat. Laura reeled in madly. Then the fish turned around and raced across the river. Down she pressed on the line, making the fish fight for every inch he took. Finally he turned back slowly, and then it was her turn to fight for every inch of the line she could get.

Slower and slower he came, with little jerks to the line, until we could see the top of the leader through the water. What luck to bring him so close with the first breaking of water! Then we saw the finny monster, his eyes gleaming, his sides the color of the rainbow, opalescent blue shading into green, with glitterings here of silver, there of gold, his graceful proportion swayed by his dorsal fin. Oh, but he was fighting! Laura could not hold him long while there was so much life in him. Now he jerked his head back again. Why didn't she give him some line?

Daddy leaned over the side with his gaff, and then I saw him shake his head just a little. I turned to look at Laura impatiently, for the fish was jerking fiercely at the line, and I was afraid he would break it. She had frozen on the reel. Her eyes were staring fixedly at the fish, as though she were hypnotized by those glittering eyes, and her knuckles were white with the cords of her hands standing out as though they would come through the flesh. Her thumb was locked around the reel-handle so that the only force able to move it would be a charge of dynamite. There was a great splash. The rod bent and bent, and bent, and then came back with a snap, while the line hung limp. Laura looked at her line dazedly, as though she had just awakened from a deep sleep, and blinked her eyes. Daddy's face was a picture of disappointment and wrath. He put down the gaff, and picked up his oars. Let us pass over what was said.

We now knew there were fish running that day, so we kept pulling our lines anxiously and holding the rods instead of putting them in their holders as they had been previously. Daddy swept back and forth, time and time again, over the spot where we had come across Laura's fish. The forenoon was rapidly passing away, and my brother, who would be home for the afternoon, would take our place in the boat with Daddy.

Finally Daddy said it was time to go home. I think my face must have mirrored my dejection, for he stopped and looked at me, and then kindly said we would go up to the head of the island and down its side once more. I brightened immediately and started to sing my war song to the tune of "Floating Down the Old Green River" and had just reached the last two lines, "and I had to drink the whole Willamette dry to bring a salmon home to you," when we came around the head of the island.

Just at that moment my trout rod began to bend, oh, so slowly, quietly, with never a jerk or tremor. It was a fish—a big fish! I, who had so successfully caught a nine-pounder, knew that while this one felt like a block of granite, it was yet a fish, for there was a gentle vibration to the line that only a whirling propeller at the end of some huge fish could give.

Daddy was busy with his oars, but he came to his feet with a jump when I said very calmly and solemnly: "I've got a fish." He looked a little bit disgusted as he saw the bent rod without a single thrill of life in it, and said, "Oh, no, it's just a snag," and came forward to rid the line of it. He gave the line a test jerk. Then a shock of electricity ran down his whole frame, and his face looked like the sun coming from behind a rain cloud, as he shouted to Laura to get her line in as fast as she could, and not to mind about the speed records. He said many words in the next half minute, which translated very elegantly would run something like this: "Great heavens above and earth below! Ye sun, and stars, and moon! Yes, my darling daughter, you have a fish, but he is as big as the whole bottom of the river, and as strong as ten elephants. Now you follow your father's instructions implicitly and you will land this Goliath even as a David." I hope you admire my translation, for it is hard to find words dramatic enough to supplant: "Goshamighty! Yep, you have a fish! He's a whale, the granddaddy of all rod-busters that ever swam with fins. He's a gewholicker! We'll get him if you keep a stiff upper lip, and a good bend to that toothpick of yours."

In the meantime the fish, not at all abashed by the commotion he was creating above him, was returning to his native haunts via Astoria, as that was the only way he could reach the ocean. He needed company, so he was taking us along, too. We were halfway down the island. Don't blame it on the current, for whatever current there was was upstream, due to the backing up of the floods. My rod was bending nicely; the line was departing from the reel with little staccato yelps; and I was nursing my strength for the fray which would soon be more exciting. I could feel the mighty throb of the fish as he swam smoothly on, with scarcely a twinge to make me believe he was at all bothered about towing a rowboat with three people around.

Now the boat was trimmed for action. The rods and lines were neatly placed in the bottom, Laura was crouched in the stern. The gaff hook was by Daddy's side, and he sat down in his seat with the oars in his hands.

"Ready," he commanded, and he pulled the oars back with all his strength, while I pressed heavily on the reel with both thumbs. Then the curtain rose. Daddy turned to me and said, "Now Ruth, you've had him up three times, and no matter if he knocks the boat over the next time he comes up, if you bring him as close as you did this last time, I'll gaff him."

I nodded my head, but I was so tired the words irritated me. Why couldn't that miserable fish behave and be caught this last time? Oh, I was so tired! Who said this was sport? As this last thought struck me, I drew a deep breath of fatigue, and loosened the bend of my pole for a second.

Daddy called, "Look out, Ruth! Hold up your pole and keep a tight line!" The fish was coming up again, slower and slower. Then came the leader! I reeled in as fast as I could, but my instant of slack line came to punish me. As slowly as the fish had struck I felt him leave. One second of slack line had loosened the hook enough so that he had shaken it out. I drew the leader up. It came so easily. There was something heart-breaking in its very easiness, and the reel sobbed over the wet line. I picked it up, laid the rod and tackle in the boat, felt for a seat, and gazed at those inscrutable waters that harbored my desire. Daddy picked up the oars. There was a huge lump in my throat, so I turned from the river to look at my hands lying inertly in my lap. My fingers were covered with blood where I had knocked my knuckles on the reel. I had never noticed it until this second.

Daddy said with a forced cheerfulness, "Well, girls, it is time to go home." He looked at the clock, and then we discovered that I had played that fish, or that fish had played me, whichever you think more suitable, more than forty-five minutes.

Little Bob's First Bass

H. C. MAHIN

The profession of being Daddy to a small boy is a more or less serious calling, for, to use a contemporary idiom, we have to watch our step pretty carefully. As the tree is bent, so is the twig inclined; and our kids are inclined to follow in our footsteps pretty closely, sometimes.

Last year I became enthused over bass fishing in the Wabash, Tippecanoe, and tributary waters near Lafayette, and of course Bob, at four, absorbed spirit purely by emulation. His favorite bed-time story was one concerning "Billy Bass," which had a close second a little later in the year in the tale of "Daddy Duck, Mummer Duck and Tommy Duck!" His one absorbing ambition was to get a little bigger and a little bigger, until he would be big enough to really catch a bass for himself. His mother knew not whether to second this ambition very strongly, and mustered as Exhibit A all the village ne'er-do-wells as a dire illustration of the fate that overtakes those who spend any portion at all of their time in hunting and fishing. The defense had to name all the illustrious Teddies and Grovers to prove that in rare instances the sportsman is not preordained to ignominy, and womanlike, she was still unconvinced. But Bob's bent was not thereby reduced to the extent of a single little kink. He still dreamed of catching a bass.

Since the opening of the Tragic Moments the tubers in the Murphy barrel ran low, and Dad was called upon to replenish the supply. Far be it from me to pursue the lowly garden hackle in his hidden ways, but when pursuing potatoes one comes across him in considerable numbers, may it not be that the powers intend for him to make use thereof? Be that as it may, I was tempted, and forthwith gathered several of him into one old tomato can with intent.

The next day being Sunday, to make good matters bad, I gathered up the family, Mother and all, and we betook ourselves into our canoe and up the river to a quiet little cove, seeking sunfish. Mother sat in the bow of the canoe, reading a magazine, while Bob and I performed the ceremony of wetting the line. Bob's tackle consisted of a stout linen carpet thread, small hook, and a float made of a large cork suspended from his dad's lancewood pole.

All was quiet along the Wabash for the space of half an hour, the Biblical limit for a woman to keep quiet, when we suddenly discovered that Bob was busy, very busy in fact. For before we could get to him he had raised a bass, a real *bass*, out of the water and had him dangling in the air. Now all of you hardened sinners must not believe that the fish has to get away to make a tragedy of the affair—not in the least. In another moment Bob had swung the pole in my direction and the fish was safely in the boat.

But some unregenerate legislators in Indiana had made and provided a statute to the purpose and effect that a fish of this particular breed must attain a length of ten inches in order to be considered legitimate treasure trove, and this "little whale," to use Bob's expression for it, could only muster a paltry seven. *Tragedy?* You who have seen your five to seven-pounder vanish in the swirling water, taking with him your best fly, have no common measure of despair and grief with the youngster who, by reason of a law, recognizing no difference in attendant circumstances, must see his first bass, caught with his own hands, disappear over the side of the canoe.

Some Memories of Early Days

LORD GREY OF FALLODEN

Every angler must have some account to give of the beginning of his keenness for angling. Some of us remember it as the great excitement of our boyhood, whilst others have only discovered its existence in later years of life. I think, however, that the keenest anglers are born and not made; that the passion is latent in them from the beginning, and is revealed sooner or later according to opportunity. In some cases it may be that the passion perishes unsuspected and unrevealed, because there is no opportunity of indulging or discovering it, till too late in life. The longer we live the deeper becomes the groove or the rut in which our life moves, and the more difficult it becomes to go outside it. To me the opportunity for fishing came early, and the passion for it awoke suddenly. I was about seven years old, and was riding on a Shetland pony by the side of a very small burn. A mill was working higher up the stream, and the water was full of life and agitation, caused by the opening of the sluice of the mill pond above. I had seen small trout caught in the burn before, but now, for the first time and suddenly, came an overpowering desire to fish, which gave no rest till some very primitive tackle was given me. With this and some worms, many afternoons were spent in vain. The impulse to see the trout destroyed all chance of success. It did not suit me to believe that it was fatal to look into the water before dropping a worm over the bank, or that I could not see the trout first and catch them afterwards, and I preferred to learn by experience and disappointment rather than the short, but unconvincing, method of believing what I was told.

For some years this burn fishing was all that I knew. It was very fascinating, though the trout were so small that one of four ounces was considered a good one, whilst the very largest ran to six ounces. These larger trout taught me a second lesson—self-restraint. The first lesson was, as has been said, to learn to refrain from looking into the water before I fished it: all the trout of every size combined to teach this. The second difficulty was to restrain the excitement when I had a bite. The natural impulse then was to strike so hard as to hurl the fish into the air overhead: this answered very well with trout of two or three ounces, though once a small one came unfastened in the air, flew off at a tangent into the hay behind, and could not be found. But with six ounce trout this violent method did not answer so well; neither the angler, nor the rod, nor the tackle, was always strong enough to deal with them so summarily. Catastrophes occurred, and by slow degrees and painful losses I learnt the necessity of getting keenness under control. After I had improved in these matters there still remained the hardest trial of all, which has to be undergone by all anglers, namely, how to face the disappointment of losing a fish. Many of us must have known what it is in boyhood to suffer anguish after losing an unexpectedly large fish. The whole of life then seems laid waste by despair; the memory of past joys counts for nothing; one is sure that no future success can ever compensate for the present loss; and one rails against the established order of everything, and is indignant that any human being should ever have been born to undergo such intolerable misery. Even in later years we cannot hope to face the loss of very large fish with equanimity. Nobody can become perfect in bearing what is unbearable, and it may be counted to our credit if in these very bitter moments silence descends upon us, and we preserve outward appearances. Here is a saying that is very relevant: "When things can neither be cured nor endured, one has to pretend."

Burn fishing is not without its charm even in later years, and is a peculiar form of angling separate from all others. I am thinking now of those north country burns too small for fly fishing, which run in narrow stony channels between overgrown banks. Here one must fish with a worm and a short line, and the difficulty consists in getting the worm into the water without any part of oneself being seen by the trout. The usual method is to advance stealthily, sometimes stooping, sometimes on one's knees, sometimes at full length, according to the necessities of the case, pushing the rod in front, and at last swinging the worm gently on a short line over the edge of the bank and lowering it into the water. When the angler knows the burn well he goes at once from place to place, approaching the bank afresh at each spot which he knows to be suitable. If he does not know the burn he most reconnoiter from a distance to see the sort of water that is before him. It does not do to drop a worm blindly over the bank without knowing where it will fall, as the hooks are sure in this case to become mixed up sooner or later with a bush or a heap of sticks.

One burn I used to fish flowed through a wood of high trees down a steep rocky channel. Here it was possible, at least for a small boy, to keep out of sight by walking up the bed of the burn itself, stooping low, jerking the worm up into little pools and cascades above, and lifting the trout out down stream on to the bank. This was very pretty work. I remember once getting several trout quickly one after the other in this place, and then they suddenly stopped taking. One little favorite pool after another produced nothing, and a fear of something unknown came over me; the gloom and stillness of the wood made me uneasy, everything about me seemed to know something, to have a meaning, which was hidden from me; and I felt as if my fishing was out of place. At last I could resist the feeling of apprehension no longer; I left the rod with the line in a pool to fish for itself, and went up to the edge of the wood to see what was happening in the open world outside. There was a great storm coming up full of awful menace, as thunderclouds often are. It filled me with terror. I hurried back for my rod, left the burn and the wood, and fled before the storm, going slow to get breath now and then, and continually urged to running again by the sound of thunder behind me.

Burn trout are wayward little things. Sometimes they take a worm greedily on the brightest days in low clear water, rushing to it directly it falls into the pool, or seizing it as it travels down the stream, and being hooked without trouble. On these days all the angler need do is wait for four or five seconds after he knows, by the stopping or the trembling of the line, that the worm has been taken, and then strike sharply but not violently. If the trout is very small it may be lifted out at once, but if it is four ounces' weight or heavier it is safer to let it do some splashing and struggling in the water, to wait till it is still, and then to lift it out with an even movement, quickly but without any sudden jerk. If there is a clear space without branches or bushes in the way, this can be done without the trout struggling in the air. It is always unsafe to lift a fish which is in the act of struggling, for the jerks of the fish, added to the dead weight of its body in the air, greatly increase the risk either of the line breaking or of the hooks coming out. If the trout exceeds six ounces, I play it with as much respect as if it were a salmon, and choose a shallow landing-place, and draw it on to that without lifting it at all. The feeling of losing a trout in the air is familiar to burn anglers. The fish falls back into the water with a splash, the line flies up into the air, often becoming hopelessly entangled in a tree; and before it is extricated the angler has frightened all the other fish in the pool, and is convinced that the trout and the branches and the rod and line and hooks are all in a conspiracy against him. I use the word "hooks," as I have found small Stewart or Pennell worm tackle much the best for trout fishing: it is easily baited, and with it the angler can, if he likes, strike directly the worm is taken, though it is better to wait just long enough to let the trout get all the worm well into its mouth, and not long enough to let the worm be swallowed.

On some days burn trout are very aggravating, and will take the worm and chew it without being hooked. The angler waits and then strikes, and feels that he has just touched a fish and no more, and this happens time after time. He tries the effect of waiting longer before striking, and then finds either that he still just misses the fish, or else that the fish has taken the worm off the hooks or left the worm altogether; or that a very small trout not worth killing has swallowed the hooks, and wasted its own life and his time and trouble. I suppose on these days the trout are not really hungry, and begin to chew the worm instead of trying to swallow it at once. They then discover the presence of the hooks, and either reject the whole thing, or try to separate the worm from the hooks with their lips, which results in the angler's touching without hooking them when he strikes. There are other days when burn trout dash at the worm and endeavor to make off with it immediately at speed. On these occasions the angler feels a quick tug and all is over before he can strike; he probably does strike too late, and his line having no resistance at the end is jerked out of the water into a bush, if there is one near.

Three other moods are common to burn trout; they are those of indifference, suspicion, and abnormal fright. When the trout are indifferent, they simply ignore the worm, and appear not to notice its presence: one might think from their behavior either that they were blind, or that they habitually lived with worms before their eyes. When they are suspicious, they will, on the contrary, swim up to the worm and investigate it as if they had never seen such a thing before, or dash about it as if its presence excited them. On other days, and these are not necessarily the brightest, it is almost impossible to keep out of sight of the trout, which seem to be watching for the least hint of the approach of an angler; and even when the angler succeeds in concealing himself, they fly from the sight of the rod, or the gut, however quietly it is put before them. All these things make burn fishing an interesting and delicate sport. The drawback to it is that the constant stooping and crawling become so much harder as years go on. Joints ache and crack, and the continual effort of keeping a stiff and full-grown body out of sight is difficult and painful. Some of the crouching may be avoided by using a long rod, but among bushes and trees a long rod is an awkward instrument, and one cannot guide the line so accurately among the branches. To dodge bushes and leaves and twigs successfully, the angler must use a short stiff rod and a short line. He can then not only guide the line and drop the worm more accurately with the rod, but after fishing each place can catch the end of the short line with one hand, while still holding the rod with the other, and so make his way through the trees to the next pool, without having to put the rod down and alter the length of the line. A well wooded burn is the nicest of all. It has places where the angler can watch the trout and see his worm taken, while he is hidden behind leaves, or lying in tall meadow-sweet or some such undergrowth of herbs. Even if he does not feel the thrill and the rapt excitement, which he felt as a boy when his line stopped and trembled in the stream with a bite, or when he saw a trout open its mouth and take his worm, he can still remember what he used to feel in those early days, and "beget that golden time again." He can enjoy, too, more than he ever did before, the light playing through the leaves upon the still water of a clear pool, the running water sparkling in the sun, the tinkling sound of little streams, and the shade and the hot summer's day. And even yet there is some satisfaction, when the burn is low and clear, in outwitting the trout, small as they are, for it is not to be done without care, difficulty, and effort.

I need hardly add that fine drawn gut is proper for burn fishing: in small burns two or three feet of gut is enough, as the water is shallow, the line is kept more perpendicular than horizontal, and but little of it falls into the water. The special merits of brandling worms were so impressed upon me from the first that I have never been content to use any other kind. They are certainly good both in color and size. The objection to them is that they are rather soft, but for burn fishing, where the worm is dropped rather than cast into the water, this does not matter so much. Brandling worms, however, are not to be found in common earth, nor in every heap of decaying manure or rubbish. Kitchen garden refuse is a valuable ingredient, but it is not the only one, and the heaps must be of the right material in the right stage of decay; young anglers of intelligence and observation make it their business to know the best places for brandling worms, so that they may be sure of getting a good supply whenever they want it. The brandlings are best after being kept for a day or two in clean moss, but trout take them well enough when they are fresh.

Very wonderful is the perspective of childhood, which can make a small burn seem greater than rivers in after life. There was one burn which I knew intimately from its source to the sea. Much of the upper part was wooded, and it was stony and shallow, till within two miles of its mouth. Here there was for a child another world. There were no trees, the bottom of the burn was of mud or sand, and the channel was full of rustling reeds, with open pools of some depth at intervals. These pools had a fascination for me, there was something about them which kept me excited with expectation of great events, as I lay behind the reeds, peering through them, and watching the line intently. The result of much waiting was generally an eel, or a small flat fish up from the sea; or now and then a small trout, but never for many years one of the monsters which I was sure must inhabit such mysterious pools. At last one evening something heavy really did take the worm. The fish kept deep, played round and round the pool and could not be seen, but I remember shouting to a companion at a little distance, that I had hooked a trout of one pound, and being conscious from the tone of his reply that he didn't in the least believe me, for a trout of one pound was in those days our very utmost limit of legitimate expectation. There was a mill pond higher up in which such a weight had been attained, and we who fished the burn could talk of trout of that size, and yet feel that we were speaking like anglers of this world. But this fish turned out to be heavier even than one pound, and when at last it came up from the depth into my view, I felt that the great moment had come which was to make or mar my happiness for ever. I got into the shallow water below the fish, and after great anxieties secured with the help of my hand a fresh run sea trout of three pounds. Never was a dead fish treated with more care and honor. It had swallowed the hooks, and rather than risk spoiling its appearance in getting them out, the gut was cut and they were left inside. The small trout and eels and flounders were turned out of my basket and put into my companion's, so that the great sea trout might lie in state. It was felt that the expectation of years was justified, that the marvelous had become real, that the glory which had been unseen was revealed, and that after the present moment the hope of great things in the future would live for ever. A few years ago there was published a delightful book called *The Golden Age* in which the author describes the world of childhood as it has been to all of us—a world whose boundaries are unknown, where everything is at the same time more wonderful and more real than it seems afterwards, and where mystery is our most constant companion. So it was with me, especially in the places where I fished. I used to go to the lower part of this burn in the charge of an old gamekeeper, and after a long journey through pathless open fields, we seemed to reach a distant land where things happened otherwise than in the world nearer home. At the end of the walk it was as if we had reached another country, and were living in another day under a different sky. The gamekeeper fished more leisurely than I, and sometimes he would be lost among the windings of the burn, to be found again by the sight of the smoke from his pipe rising gently from behind a whin bush. When I now recall that distant land, I see always somewhere among the whin bushes a little curl of thin smoke, and no other sign of an inhabitant.

In course of time there came experience of a fine Highland river, and lochs near it and of fly fishing in them in August. The trout did not always rise very well in August, but many of them were three-quarters of a pound in weight, a few were even larger, and the sport seemed to me magnificent. Three great days happened all in different years on this river and its lochs. Once the trout took exceptionally well in the loch, and instead of the usual number of twenty or less I landed forty-eight, averaging about three to the pound. Another day there was a little fresh water in the river, and I tried an artificial minnow. First a trout of about two pounds, larger than any trout ever hooked by me before, was lost. While I was still in the agony of disappointment, a second weighing three pounds and a quarter was hooked and eventually landed, and directly after that a third trout of about the same size was hooked and lost, when it was in full view and half in the landing net. Then nothing more would take, and I spent the rest of the day without further incident, trying to think of the fish landed and not of the ones lost.

But the greatest day of all was the third. I was standing at the end of a pier built for salmon fishing, casting out into the smooth strong stream, when a sort of wave seemed to come suddenly and swallow the top fly, and a large heavy body went down stream pulling out the line. I shouted, "A salmon!" and the old gillie came hurrying to my side. His first words were, "We shall never get him," against which I protested with rage, and he partially retracted and set to work to advise me. We could not follow the fish downward, but it hove to about twenty years below us and hung steady in the stream. We turned the trout rod up stream and held it still, keeping a steady strain upon the fish, and waited for what seemed an age without result; but the good old man encouraged me when I grew faint-hearted, and kept me patient. Eventually the fish began to yield. We gained line foot by foot, and more than once got the fish up stream nearly opposite the pier, but it saw us and dropped back each time to the old place down stream. At last amid great excitement it was coaxed past the pier, in a moment was in the backwater above, and to my astonishment was then almost at once exhausted and landed. It was a grilse of about six pounds, and rather red, but the distinction between grilse and salmon, between red fish and fresh run fish, was nothing to me. That same day another grilse of about four pounds took the same fly. This second fish took with a splash, ran freely and was landed without difficulty. In the course of many seasons I must have had dozens of days' trout fishing in that same river at the same time of year, but never on any other day did I hook or even rise a grilse or salmon with a trout fly.

These were the triumphs of luck, but they came at an age when youth, not from conceit, but from sheer gladness and simplicity, does not discriminate between luck and skill. The first temptation to become proud of possessing skill came later, and after the use of the dry fly had been learnt at Winchester. It was not on the Itchen that any pride was felt, for I was only a learner there, improving year by year, but with examples of greater skill and success than mine constantly before me. In the holidays, however, I took away with me from the Itchen to distant rivers the art of the dry fly, which was then not nearly so widely known as it has come to be in the last twenty years. So it happened that on west or north country streams, or in Ireland, or on dark smooth water in the Highlands, I was sometimes the first to introduce the dry fly, with results which astonished the trout and the local anglers, and were very gratifying to myself. In the Highland river spoken of above there was a long dark stretch, bordered by rocks and trees, where the river flowed with a deep even stream, carrying a few thin flecks of slow-moving foam upon its surface, but without a ripple. Here, especially in the evening, some of the best trout used to rise. You might fish every day for a week in the rougher water and never hook a trout of one pound weight with a fly and be very grateful for half-pounders, but in this smooth deep part many of the trout were upwards of one pound; and the average weight was about three-quarters of a pound. Often had I tried them with March-browns, and small Heckum Peckums and the various patterns which are attractive in the Highlands, but not one of these particular trout would stand the sight of my flies. I continued to visit that river in my summer holidays, and the time came when I brought with me some drawn gut, some small olive and red quills, and a single-handed rod with which to cast them lightly. A pupil on the Itchen was a master among these Highland trout, and in the still hour of sunset on many an August evening I used to endure the torment of the midges and find a rich reward. A struggle with a trout of one pound and a half hooked on Itchen tackle in that fine flow of deep water, among the rocks and trees, was no mean affair.

In the Easter holidays I went alone once or twice to the Dart. I do not know how the Dart fares now, for it is nearly twenty years since I have seen it; but in those days there was beautiful trout water between Staverton and Buckfastleigh, which could be fished by ticket, and if one was not disappointed with trout of less than half a pound, there was very good sport to be had. I remember once fishing a part of the river where there was a succession of streams, which towards the middle of the day seemed alive with little trout, rising actively all over the water at natural flies. It was one of those maddening days when the trout rise in quantities and take no notice of artificial flies. I could do nothing, and the other anglers above and below me, of whom two or three were in sight, were not doing very much better. At last in despair I waded to the bank, and went down to a smooth piece of the river between wooded banks. In this place the water was clear, and varied from a foot to perhaps three feet in depth. No one was fishing, and there were trout rising in shoals and very quietly. A stout March-brown, such as I had been using above, would have put them all to flight, but the trouble of using a dry fly for such separate trout seemed out of proportion to the size of the fish. Yet as I wanted very much to save an empty basket, I gave up the hope of counting trout that day by the dozen, put on one small olive quill and waded in quietly below the rising fish. They took the little dry fly as if they were pleased to see it, and when the rise was over I waded out with thirty-one trout in my basket. The old angling diary to which I have referred gives the weight of the largest as eight ounces. It does not give the total weight, but I remember congratulating myself on the fact that the average size of my trout was at least equal to the size of those generally caught with fly in April in the more favorite streams above. As I emerged from the trees on the bank, I met one of the best of the local anglers returning from above with a lighter basket than usual. He stopped me and asked what I had done. I opened my basket. "You can't have caught those to-day with fly," he said. "Yes," I replied; "I caught them with a dry fly." "Dry fly," he said very sternly, "we know nothing about a dry fly here." Then he went on his way, with thoughts, I fear, that were not very kind.

The next reminiscence goes back to about 1880, and has to do with a river in Ireland. The first time I saw this river was late in August. There were said to be trout, and good ones, and it was believed to be possible to catch some with fly earlier in the season, when the water was in order. The river had in parts a very wide bed, which when low it did not nearly fill. The water ran in all sorts of channels between beds of bright green weeds. Here and there was a long stream with a stony bottom, free from weeds, and now and then there would be a huge pool, full of peaty-colored water of unknown depth, in which one or two salmon lay. One could wander for miles all day about the most extraordinary variety of water. The river was full of pike, and it was said, probably with truth, that the inhabitants of the district forked trout out of the weeds in low water with various agricultural implements. But there were trout enough for dry fly fishing. Half a dozen or so might be found rising near together, and then perhaps one would have to go several hundred yards before another one was found; a little sound would be heard presently, as if a small pebble had dropped in somewhere without a splash, and heard perhaps two or three times before the rise could be seen in such a large and curious river. Then there was a different stalk, probably through water and weeds, with the chance of going overhead into a big hole unawares.

I was warned that at this season of the year, when the water was low, I must not expect to catch any of these fish, but I cared nothing for warnings. The trout were there, and were rising, and though I saw at once that it was a case for dry fly and for that only, I had by this time been taught to believe that any one, who could catch Winchester trout, could catch rising trout anywhere. These trout, however, at first upset my calculations. They brought me face to face with a difficulty which did not exist on the ticket water at Winchester—they were unapproachable. Never was an angler more put upon his mettle. There were trout visibly and audibly rising, which had never seen an artificial dry fly, and would probably take it at once. They were evidently also big trout. There was splendid sport to be had, and reputation and glory to be won in catching even one of them, and yet so shy were they, that I could not get my dry fly to them.

For two days they defeated me utterly. I walked and knelt and waded and labored and perspired under an August sun without success. Some of the trout were put down by my approach, some were scared by the first waving of the rod, and some, which had been successfully stalked, turned tail and fled when the gut floated over them without even the last drag; at last, on the second evening in a fading light, I hooked a fish which went off up stream at once with a mighty rush, and came to rest somewhere out of sight at the end of a lot of line. I waded carefully up in the twilight, keeping a tight line by reeling up as I went till I was over a great bed of strong weeds.

Into this one hand carefully felt its way along the casting line, and touched at last the side of a great fish. Nothing could be seen for it was getting dark, and the weeds were too thick for a landing net to be used in them. I tried with one hand to arrange a grip on the trout, and very broad and hard he felt; but at the critical moment he made the most violent commotion in the weeds and dashed of somewhere. When all was still I felt again and found in the weeds only the end of broken gut. There was nothing more to be done that evening, and I waded out and lay on the bank in the dusk. On the whole, I think that was the bitterest moment I have ever known in angling. To have come so near to success, and to have it snatched from me at the last moment, after keenness and effort had been sustained at the very highest pitch for two whole days, was more than could be borne.

But success did come afterwards, and in broad daylight; I found a place where, by wading and kneeling in the river on the shallow side, it was possible to get within reach of and *opposite* to rising trout without frightening them. Then the fly could be thrown some way above them with an underhand cast, so as not to show the rod; and being opposite and not below, I could let the fly float down a few inches on the near side of a rising trout, so that only the fly and none of the gut was seen. In this way I at last caught one or two trout, and then somehow, when the frost of failure had once broken up, it seemed more easy to succeed all over the river.

These trout were the shyest I have ever known. They were more difficult to approach and more easily scared by rod or gut than any others I ever fished for; but if the fly could be floated to a rising fish without frightening it, the fly was generally taken. On the best day that I had there I caught eleven fish. None of these weighed three pounds, but the first two were each over two pounds and three-quarters. For such shy fish really fine gut had to be used, and there were many disasters in the weeds, but also many splendid struggles fought out in pools which were far too deep for any vegetation. It was the wildest and most exciting and most fascinating dry fly fishing that I have ever had. My experience of it has only been during late August or early September, but I can imagine that in May and in June it might be the finest dry fly fishing in the United Kingdom.[1]

---

[1]The river was the Suir, and the part of it described was at Graiguenoe, not far from Thurles. Before 1880 I do not think any one had ever fished it with a dry fly. I was never there after 1886, but I heard that the merits of the water for dry fly fishing were afterwards much appreciated by many anglers.

Fishing with My Daddy

JIMMY CARTER

A few miles north of the Okefenokee was the small village of Hortense, not far from where the Little Satilla River joins the Big Satilla. This was one of my father's favorite fishing spots; he tried to go there every year with some of his associates in the farming, peanut, and fertilizer business. On two occasions he took me with him, when I was about ten or twelve years old.

We stayed in a big and somewhat dilapidated wood-frame house, on a small farm near the banks of the Little Satilla. The house had been built to accommodate at least three generations of a family, but now there was just a man named Joe Strickland, his wife, Shug, and two daughters, one a pretty girl in her teens named Jessie. Joe was the guide for our group of about six people. The women cooked our meals and plowed mules in the small fields during the day while we were fishing. It was the first time I had seen women plowing, which I found quite surprising, but they all seemed to take it as a matter of course.

The Little Satilla is a serpentine stream in the flattest part of Georgia's coastal plain, weaving back and forth from one bend to another. A number of oxbow lakes had been left behind when the river changed its course. We fished in the area of what was called Ludie's Lake. On the outside of almost every bend of the stream there was a deep hole, often cut into a steep bank, and on the opposite side of the river was usually a sand bar. There were not as many bushes and snags in the water as we had around Plains, and the bottom was sandy and firm.

I had never done this kind of fishing before. We spent our time in the stream, wading halfway across it to fish in the deep water under the overhanging banks, using the longest cane poles we could handle. I wore cutoff overall pants with no shirt, and tied my fish stringer to one of the belt loops. Joe and I were the only ones barefoot; all the other men had on old tennis shoes or brogans to protect their tender feet. We fished with large pond worms and caught mostly "copperheads," which were very large bluegill bream whose heads, when mature, assumed a bronze color, perhaps from the tannin stain in the water.

The group of us would string out along the river, my daddy and I usually fishing within sight of each other. We always had a fairly good idea of what luck each fisherman was having. For some reason I never understood, the men would shout "Billy McKay!" when they had on a nice fish. The words would roll through the woods as all of us smiled; the enthusiasm of the voices was contagious. Each night after supper I went to bed early, but the men stayed up to play poker and to have a few drinks. Sometimes they made enough noise to wake me up, but I didn't mind. It seemed to make me more a member of the party if they weren't trying to stay quiet just for me. Most often I was tired enough to go right back to sleep.

While we were in the river Joe moved quietly from one of us to another, just to make sure we were properly spaced and to give advice about the water and some of the bypasses we had to take around obstacles. He tried—successfully—to build up a reputation as something of a character and always gave the group something to talk about during the months between our visits to Hortense.

Once we were walking single file along a path toward the river and Joe called, "Watch out for the barbed wire!"

One of the men said, "Joe, you didn't look down. How do you know wire's there?"

Joe said, "My feet will flatten briers or thorns, but I can feel barbed wire when I step on it."

Another time, when we had to cross the river, Joe walked down the bank, entered the water with his pole and lunch over his head, and moved smoothly across toward the other side with the water never higher than his armpits. The next man, whom I called Mr. Charlie, was the oldest in the group, and he stepped off in the water and immediately went down out of sight. He came up sputtering, and shouted, "Joe, how deep is it here?"

Joe replied, "Oh, I reckon it's about fifteen foot." Joe could tread water like a duck, and just wanted to demonstrate his prowess so that none of us would forget.

Then came my most memorable day. Late one afternoon, after a good day of fishing, Daddy called me over and asked me to keep his string of fish while he went up the river to talk to one of his friends. I tied it on with mine on the downstream side of me while I kept fishing, enjoying the steady pull of the current on our day's catch. It wasn't long before I watched my cork begin to move slowly and steadily up under a snag and knew I had hooked a big one. After a few minutes I had a large copperhead bream in my hands, but as I struggled with it and wondered how I was going to hold the fish while untying the stringer, a cold chill went down my spine. I realized that the tugging of the current on the stringers was gone, as were all our fish! My belt loop had broken.

I threw my pole up on the nearest sandbar and began to dive madly into the river below where I had been standing.

Then I heard Daddy's voice calling my nickname. "Hot," he said, "what's wrong?"

"I've lost the fish, Daddy."

"All of them? Mine too?"

"Yes, sir." I began to cry, and the tears and water ran down my face together each time I came up for breath.

Daddy was rarely patient with foolishness or mistakes. But after a long silence, he said, "Let them go." I stumbled out on the bank, and he put his arms around me. It seems foolish now, but at that time it was a great tragedy for me. We stood there for a while, and he said, "There are a lot more fish in the river. We'll get them tomorrow." He knew how I felt and was especially nice to me for the next couple of days. I worshipped him.

At Joe's home we ate fish and whatever was in season. Both times I went, our breakfasts consisted of biscuits, grits, green beans, and fried fish. It was the first time I had eaten green beans early in the morning, but soon it seemed like a normal thing to do. With plenty of butter and sugar-cane syrup to go with the piles of hot biscuits, we never got up from the table hungry.

When I left Joe's place to come home, his daughter Jessie told me that she had brought me a going-away present. She then handed me a baby alligator about a foot long, whom I immediately named Mickey Mouse. When I returned to our house I installed him inside a large truck tire, partially buried in the ground and covered with boards. For a number of weeks I fed him earthworms, crickets, wasp larvae, and anything else he would eat. My friends were quite envious of my new pet. Unfortunately, the cats and dogs around the farm were also interested. One morning I went out to feed Mickey and found the boards pushed aside and the little alligator missing. Daddy was very considerate and said he was sure the 'gator had escaped into the nearest swamp. I was not quite naïve enough to believe him, but from then on I stayed on the lookout for my 'gator whenever I was fishing or exploring along the neighborhood creeks.

Almost fifty years later, after I left the White House, I stopped by Hortense, Georgia to try to find the place we used to visit. I couldn't remember the roads or even Joe's last name when I inquired of some folks in the service station. I did recall the pretty daughter, but one of the men told me, "We had a lot of pretty daughters around here." At least I remembered the bare feet, barbed wire, good catches, lost fish, Mickey Mouse, and green beans for breakfast. When I described some of these things to the postmistress, she said, "You must mean Joe Strickland. Miss Jessie still lives at the same place, but in a new house." I followed her directions and found the cottage in what had been the large yard of the old house, just a few steps from the Little Satilla River.

Miss Jessie responded to our knock on her door, saying, "Won't y'all come in!" even before she knew who we were. We had a good time reminiscing about old times. Both her parents had died long ago, and she was intrigued that I remembered so much about them. She said that she remembered my visits: "I told a lot of people while you were in the White House that the President had fished with my daddy."

To which I replied, "When I was in the White House, I told several people the same thing about yours. Many of the most highly publicized events of my presidency are not nearly as memorable or significant in my life as fishing with my daddy or yours when I was a boy. Certainly, almost none of them was as enjoyable!"

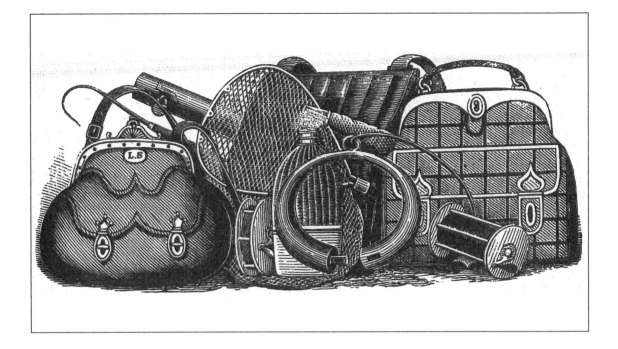

The River God

ROLAND PERTWEE

When I was a little boy I had a friend who was a colonel. He was not the kind of colonel you meet nowadays, who manages a motor showroom in the West End of London and wears crocodile shoes and a small mustache and who calls you "old man" and slaps your back, independent of the fact that you may have been no more than a private in the war. My colonel was of the older order that takes a third of a century and a lot of Indian sun and Madras curry in the making. A veteran of the Mutiny he was, and wore side whiskers to prove it. Once he came upon a number of Sepoys conspiring mischief in a byre with a barrel of gunpowder. So he put the butt of his cheroot into the barrel and presently they all went to hell. That was the kind of man he was in the way of business.

In the way of pleasure he was very different. In the way of pleasure he wore an old Norfolk coat that smelt of heather and brine, and which had no elbows to speak of. And he wore a Sherlock Holmesy kind of cap with a swarm of salmon flies upon it, that to my boyish fancy was more splendid than a crown. I cannot remember his legs, because they were nearly always under water, hidden in great canvas waders. But once he sent me a photograph of himself riding on a tricycle, so I expect he had some knickerbockers, too, which would have been that tight kind, with box cloth under the knees. Boys don't take much stock of clothes. His head occupied my imagination. A big, brave, white-haired head with cherry-red rugose cheeks and honest, laughing, puckered eyes, with gunpowder marks in their corners.

People at the little Welsh fishing inn where we met said he was a bore; but I knew him to be a god and shall prove it.

I was ten years old and his best friend.

He was seventy something and my hero.

Properly I should not have mentioned my hero so soon in this narrative. He belongs to a later epoch, but sometimes it is forgivable to start with a boast, and now that I have committed myself I lack the courage to call upon my colonel to fall back two paces to the rear, quick march, and wait until he is wanted.

The real beginning takes place, as I remember, somewhere in Hampshire on the Grayshott Road, among sandy banks, sentinel firs and plum-colored wastes of heather. Summer-holiday time it was, and I was among folks whose names have since vanished like lizards under the stones of forgetfulness. Perhaps it was a picnic walk; perhaps I carried a basket and was told not to swing it for fear of bursting its cargo of ginger beer. In those days ginger beer had big bulgy corks held down with a string. In a hot sun or under stress of too much agitation the string would break and the corks fly. Then there would be a merry foaming fountain and someone would get reproached.

One of our company had a fishing rod. He was a young man who, one day, was to be an uncle of mine. But that didn't concern me. What concerned me was the fishing rod and presently—perhaps because he felt he must keep in with the family—he let me carry it. To the fisherman born there is nothing so provoking of curiosity as a fishing rod in a case.

Surreptitiously I opened the flap, which contained a small grass spear in a wee pocket, and, pulling down the case a little, I admired the beauties of the cork butt, with its gun-metal ferrule and reel rings and the exquisite frail slenderness of the two top joints.

"It's got two top joints—two!" I exclaimed ecstatically.

"Of course," said he. "All good trout rods have two."

I marveled in silence at what seemed to me then a combination of extravagance and excellent precaution.

There must have been something inherently understanding and noble about that young man who would one day be my uncle, for, taking me by the arm, he sat me down on a tuft of heather and took the pieces of rod from the case and fitted them together. The rest of the company moved on and left me in Paradise.

It is thirty-five years ago since that moment and not one detail of it is forgotten. There sounds in my ears today as clearly as then, the faint, clear pop made by the little cork stoppers with their boxwood tops as they were withdrawn. I remember how, before fitting the pieces together, he rubbed the ferrules against the side of his nose to prevent them from sticking. I remember looking up the length of it through a tunnel of sneck rings to the eyelet at the end. Not until he had fixed a reel and passed a line through the rings did he put the lovely thing into my hand. So light it was, so firm, so persuasive; such a thing alive—a scepter. I could do no more than say "Oo!" and again, "Oo!"

"A thrill, ain't it?" said he.

I had no need to answer that. In my new-found rapture was only one sorrow—the knowledge that such happiness would not endure and that, all too soon, a blank and rodless future awaited me.

"They must be awfully—awfully 'spensive," I said.

"Couple of guineas," he replied offhandedly.

A couple of guineas! And we were poor folk and the future was more rodless than ever.

"Then I shall save and save and save," I said.

And my imagination started to add up twopence a week into guineas. Two hundred and forty pennies to the pound, multiplied by two—four hundred and eighty—and then another twenty-four pennies—five hundred and four. Why, it would take a lifetime, and no sweets, no elastic for catapults, no penny novelty boxes or air-gun bullets or ices or anything. Tragedy must have been writ large upon my face, for he said suddenly, "When's your birthday?"

I was almost ashamed to tell him how soon it was. Perhaps he, too, was a little taken aback by its proximity, for that future uncle of mine was not so rich as uncles should be.

"We must see about it."

"But it wouldn't—it couldn't be one like that," I said.

I must have touched his pride, for he answered loftily, "Certainly it will."

In the fortnight that followed I walked on air and told everybody I had as good as got a couple-of-guineas rod.

No one can deceive a child, save the child himself, and when my birthday came and with it a long brown paper parcel, I knew, even before I had removed the wrappers, that this two-guinea rod was not worth the money. There was a brown linen case, it is true, but it was not a case with a neat compartment for each joint, nor was there a spear in the flap. There was only one top instead of two, and there were no popping little stoppers to protect the ferrules from dust and injury. The lower joint boasted no elegant cork hand piece, but was a tapered affair coarsely made and rudely varnished. When I fitted the pieces together, what I balanced in my hand was tough and stodgy, rather than limber. The reel, which had come in a different parcel, was of wood. It had neither check nor brake, the line overran and backwound itself with distressing frequency.

I had not read and reread Gamages' price list without knowing something of rods, and I did not need to look long at this rod before realizing that it was no match to the one I had handled on the Grayshott Road.

I believe at first a great sadness possessed me, but very presently imagination came to the rescue. For I told myself that I had only to think that this was the rod of all other rods that I desired most and it would be so. And it was so.

Furthermore, I told myself that, in this great wide ignorant world, but few people existed with such expert knowledge of rods as I possessed. That I had but to say, "Here is the final word in good rods," and they would accept it as such.

Very confidently I tried the experiment on my mother, with inevitable success. From the depths of her affection and her ignorance on all such matters, she produced:

"It's a magnificent rod."

I went my way, knowing full well that she knew not what she said, but that she was kind.

With rather less confidence I approached my father, saying, "Look, father! It cost two guineas. It's absolutely the best sort you can get."

And he, after waggling it a few moments in silence, quoted cryptically:

"There is nothing either good or bad but thinking makes it so."

Young as I was, I had some curiosity about words, and on any other occasion I would have called on him to explain. But this I did not do, but left hurriedly for fear that he should explain.

In the two years that followed I fished every day in the slip of a back garden of our tiny London house. And, having regard to the fact that this rod was never fashioned to throw a fly, I acquired a pretty knack in the fullness of time and performed some glib casting at the nasturtiums and marigolds that flourished by the back wall.

My parents' fortunes must have been in the ascendant, I suppose, for a call to mind an unforgettable breakfast when my mother told me that father had decided we should spend our summer holiday at a Welsh hotel on the river Lledr. The place was called Pont-y-pant, and she showed me a picture of the hotel with a great knock-me-down river creaming past the front of it.

Although in my dreams I had heard fast water often enough, I had never seen it, and the knowledge that in a month's time I should wake with the music of a cataract in my ears was almost more than patience could endure.

In that exquisite, intolerable period of suspense I suffered as only childish longing and enthusiasm can suffer. Even the hank of guilt that I bought and bent into innumerable casts failed to alleviate that suffering. I would walk for miles in a moment's delight captured in gluing my nose to the windows of tackleists' shops in the West End. I learned from my grandmother—a wise and calm old lady—how to make nets and, having mastered the art, I made myself a landing net. This I set up on a frame fashioned from a penny schoolmaster's cane bound to an old walking stick. It would be pleasant to record that this was a good and serviceable net, but it was not. It flopped over in a very distressing fashion when called upon to lift the lightest weight. I had to confess to myself that I had more enthusiasm than skill in the manufacture of such articles.

At school there was a boy who had a fishing creel, which he swapped with me for a Swedish knife, a copy of the *Rogues of the Fiery Cross*, and an Easter egg which I had kept on account of its rare beauty. He had forced a hard bargain and was sure he had the best of it, but I knew otherwise.

At last the great day dawned, and after infinite travel by train we reached our destination as the glow of sunset was graying into dark. The river was in spate, and as we crossed a tall stone bridge on our way to the hotel I heard it below me, barking and grumbling among great rocks. I was pretty far gone in tiredness, for I remember little else that night but a rod rack in the hall—a dozen rods of different sorts and sizes, with gaudy salmon flies, some nets, a gaff and an oak coffer upon which lay a freshly caught salmon on a blue ashet. Then supper by candlelight, bed, a glitter of stars through the open window, and the ceaseless drumming of water.

By six o'clock next morning I was on the river bank, fitting my rod together and watching in awe the great brown ribbon of water go fleetly by.

Among my most treasured possessions were half a dozen flies, and two of these I attached to the cast with exquisite care. While so engaged, a shadow fell on the grass beside me and, looking up, I beheld a lank, shabby individual with a walrus mustache and an unhealthy face who, the night before, had helped with our luggage at the station.

"Water's too heavy for flies," said he, with an uptilting inflection. "This evening, yes; now, no—none whateffer. Better try with a worrum in the burrun."

He pointed at a busy little brook which tumbled down the steep hillside and joined the main stream at the garden end.

"C-couldn't I fish with a fly in the—the burrun?" I asked, for although I wanted to catch a fish very badly, for honor's sake I would fain take it on a fly.

"Indeed, no," he replied, slanting the tone of his voice skyward. "You cootn't. Neffer. And that isn't a fly rod whateffer."

"It is," I replied hotly. "Yes, it is."

But he only shook his head and repeated, "No," and took the rod from my hand and illustrated its awkwardness and handed it back with a wretched laugh.

If he had pitched me into the river I should have been happier.

"It is a fly rod and it cost two guineas," I said, and my lower lip trembled.

"Neffer," he repeated. "Five shillings would be too much."

Even a small boy is entitled to some dignity.

Picking up my basket, I turned without another word and made for the hotel. Perhaps my eyes were blinded with tears, for I was about to plunge into the dark hall when a great, rough, kindly voice arrested me with:

"Easy does it."

At the thick end of an immense salmon rod there strode out into the sunlight the noblest figure I had ever seen.

There is no real need to describe my colonel again—I have done so already—but the temptation is too great. Standing in my doorway, the sixteen-foot rod in hand, the deer-stalker hat, besprent with flies, crowning his shaggy head, the waders, like seven-league boots, braced up to his armpits, the creel across his shoulder, a gaff across his back, he looked what he was—a god. His eyes met mine with that kind of smile one good man keeps for another.

"An early start," he said. "Any luck, old fellar?"

I told him I hadn't started—not yet.

"Wise chap," said he. "Water's a bit heavy for trouting. It'll soon run down, though. Let's vet those flies of yours."

He took my rod and whipped it expertly.

"A nice piece—new, eh?"

"N-not quite," I stammered; "but I haven't used it yet, sir, in water."

That god read men's minds.

"I know—garden practice; capital; nothing like it."

Releasing my cast, he frowned critically over the flies—a Blue Dun and a March Brown.

"Think so?" he queried. "You don't think it's a shade late in the season for these fancies?" I said I thought perhaps it was. "Yes, I think you're right," said he. "I believe in this big water you'd do better with a livelier pattern. Teal and Red, Cock-y-bundy, Greenwell's Glory."

I said nothing, but nodded gravely at these brave names.

Once more he read my thoughts and saw through the wicker sides of my creel a great emptiness.

"I expect you've fished most in southern rivers. These Welsh trout have a fancy for a spot of color."

He rummaged in the pocket of his Norfolk jacket and produced a round tin which once had held saddle soap.

"Collar on to that," said he; "there's a proper pickle of flies and casts in that tin that, as a keen fisherman, you won't mind sorting it out. Still, they may come in useful."

"But, I say, you don't mean—" I began.

"Yes, go in; stick to it. All fishermen are members of the same club and I'm giving the trout a rest for a bit." His eyes ranged the hills and trees opposite. "I must be getting on with it before the sun's too high."

Waving his free hand, he strode away and presently was lost to view at a bend in the road.

I think my mother was a little piqued by my abstraction during breakfast. My eyes never, for an instant, deserted the round tin box which lay open beside my plate. Within it were a paradise and a hundred miracles all tangled together in the pleasantest disorder. My mother said something about a lovely walk over the hills, but I had other plans, which included a very glorious hour which should be spent untangling and wrapping up in neat squares of paper my new treasures.

"I suppose he knows best what he wants to do," he said."

So it came about that I was left alone and betook myself to a sheltered spot behind a rock where all the delicious disorder was remedied and I could take stock of what was mine.

I am sure there were at least six casts all set up with flies, and ever so many loose flies and one great stout, tapered cast, with a salmon fly upon it, that was so rich in splendor that I doubted if my benefactor could really have known that it was there.

I felt almost guilty at owning so much, and not until I had done full justice to everything did I fasten a new cast to my line and go a-fishing.

There is a lot said and written about beginners' luck, but none of it came my way. Indeed, I spent most of the morning extricating my line from the most fearsome tangles. I had no skill in throwing a cast with two droppers upon it and I found it was an art not to be learned in a minute. Then, from overeagerness, I was too snappy with my back cast, whereby, before many minutes had gone, I heard that warning crack behind me that betokens the loss of a tail fly. I must have spent half an hour searching the meadow for that lost fly and finding it not. Which is not strange, for I wonder has any fisherman ever found that lost fly. The reeds, the buttercups, and the little people with many legs who run in the wet grass conspire together to keep the secret of its hiding place. I gave up at last, and with a feeling of shame that was only proper, I invested a new fly on the point of my cast and set to work again, but more warily.

In that hard racing water a good strain was put upon my rod, and before the morning was out it was creaking at the joints in a way that kept my heart continually in my mouth. It is the duty of a rod to work with a single smooth action and by no means to divide its performance into three sections of activity. It is a hard task for any angler to persuade his line austerely if his rod behaves thus.

When, at last, my father strolled up the river bank, walking, to his shame, much nearer the water than a good fisherman should, my nerves were jumpy from apprehension.

"Come along. Food's ready. Done any good?" said he.

Again it was to his discredit that he put food before sport, but I told him I had had a wonderful morning, and he was glad.

"What do you want to do this morning, old man?" he asked.

"Fish," I said.

"But you can't always fish," he said.

I told him I could, and I was right and have proved it for thirty years and more.

"Well, well," he said, "please yourself, but isn't it dull not catching anything?"

And I said, as I've said a thousand times since, "As if it could be."

So that afternoon I went downstream instead of up, and found myself in difficult country where the river boiled between the narrows of two hills. Stunted oaks overhung the water and great boulders opposed its flow. Presently I came to a sort of natural flight of steps—a pool and a cascade three times repeated—and there, watching the maniac fury of the waters in awe and wonderment, I saw the most stirring sight in my young life. I saw a silver salmon leap superbly from the caldron below into the pool above. And I saw another and another salmon do likewise. And I wonder the eyes of me did not fall out of my head.

I cannot say how long I stayed watching that gallant pageant of leaping fish—in ecstasy there is no measurement of time—but at last it came upon me that all the salmon in the sea were careering past me and that if I were to realize my soul's desire I must hasten to the pool below before the last of them had gone by.

It was a mad adventure, for until I had discovered that stout cast, with the gaudy fly attached in the tin box, I had given no thought to such noble quarry. My recent possessions had put ideas into my head above my station and beyond my powers. Failure, however, means little to the young and, walking fast, yet gingerly, for fear of breaking my rod top against a tree, I followed the path downstream until I came to a great basin of water into which, through a narrow throat, the river thundered like a storm.

At the head of the pool was a plate of rock scored by the nails of fishermen's boots, and here I sat me down to wait while the salmon cast, removed from its wrapper, was allowed to soak and soften in a puddle left by the rain.

And while I waited a salmon rolled not ten yards from where I sat. head and tail, up and down he went, a great monster of a fish, sporting and deriding me.

With that performance so near at hand, I have often wondered how I was able to control my fingers well enough to tie a figure-eight knot between the line and the cast. But I did, and I'm proud to be able to record it. Your true-born angler does not go blindly to work until he has first satisfied his conscience. There is a pride, in knots, of which the laity knows nothing, and if, through neglect to tie them rightly, failure and loss should result, pride may not be restored nor conscience salved by the plea of eagerness. With my trembling fingers I bent the knot and, with a pummeling heart, launched the line into the broken water at the throat of the pool.

At first the mere tug of the water against that large fly was so thrilling to me that it was hard to believe that I had not hooked a whale. The trembling line swung round in a wide arc into a calm eddy below where I stood. Before casting afresh I shot a glance over my shoulder to assure myself that there was no limbo of a tree behind me to foul the fly. And this was a gallant cast, true and straight, with a couple of yards more length than its predecessor, and a wider radius. Instinctively I knew, as if the surface had been marked with an X where the salmon had risen, that my fly must pass right over the spot. As it swung by, my nerves were trained like piano wires. I think I knew something tremendous, impossible, terrifying, was going to happen. The sense, the certitude was so strong in me that I half opened my mouth to shout a warning to the monster, not to.

I must have felt very, very young in that moment. I, who that same day had been talked to as a man by a man among men. The years were stripped from me and I was what I was—ten years old and appalled. And then, with the suddenness of a rocket, it happened. The water was cut into a swath. I remember a silver loop bearing down-ward—a bright, shining, vanishing thing like the bobbin of my mother's sewing machine—and a tug. I shall never forget the viciousness of that tug. I had my fingers tight upon the line, so I got the full force of it. To counteract a tendency to go head-first into the spinning water below, I threw myself backward and sat down o the hard rock with a jar that shut my teeth on my tongue—like the jaws of a trap.

Luckily I had let the rod go out straight with the line, else it must have snapped in the first frenzy of the downstream rush. Little ass that I was, I tried to check the speeding line with my forefinger, with the result that it cut and burnt me to the bone. There wasn't above twenty yards of line in the reel, and the wretched contrivance was trying to be rid of the line even faster than the fish was wrenching it out. Heaven knows why it didn't snarl, for great loops and whorls were whirling, like Catherine wheels, under my wrist. An instant's glance revealed the terrifying fact that there was not more than half a dozen yards left on the reel and the fish showed no sign of abating his rush. With the realization of impending and inevitable catastrophe upon me, I launched a yell for help, which, rising above the roar of the waters, went echoing down the gorge.

And then, to add to my terrors, the salmon leaped—a winging leap like a silver arch appearing and instantly disappearing upon the broken surface. So mighty, so all-powerful he seemed in that sublime moment that I lost all sense of reason and raised the rod, with a sudden jerk, above my head.

I have often wondered, had the rod actually been the two-guinea rod my imagi-nation claimed for it, whether it could have withstood the strain thus violently and unreasonably imposed upon it. The wretched thing that I held so grimly never even put up a fight. It snapped at the ferrule of the lower join and plunged like a toboggan down the slanting line, to vanish into the black depths of the water.

My horror at this calamity was so profound that I was lost even to the con-sciousness that the last of my line had run out. A couple of vicious tugs advised me of this awful truth. Then, snap! The line parted at the reel, flickered out through the rings and was gone. I was left with nothing but the butt of a broken rod in my hand and an agony of mind that even now I cannot recall without emotion.

I am not ashamed to confess that I cried. I lay down on the rock, with my cheek in the puddle where I had soaked the cast, and plenished it with my tears. For what had the future left for me but a cut and burning finger, a badly bumped behind, the single joint of a broken rod and no faith in uncles? How long I lay there weeping I do not know. Ages, perhaps, or minutes, or seconds.

I was roused by a rough hand on my shoulder and a kindly voice demanding, "Hurt yourself, Ike Walton?"

Blinking away my tears, I pointed at my broken rod with a bleeding forefinger.

"Come! This is bad luck," said my colonel, his voice grave as a stone. "How did it happen?"

"I c-caught a s-salmon."

"You what?" said he.

"I d-did," I said.

He looked at me long and earnestly; then, taking my injured hand, he looked at that and nodded.

"The poor groundlings who can find no better use for a river than something to put a bridge over think all fishermen are liars," said he. "But we know better, eh? By the bumps and breaks and cuts I'd say you made a plucky fight against heavy odds. Let's hear all about it."

So, with his arm round my shoulders and his great shaggy head near to mine, I told him all about it.

At the end he gave me a mighty and comforting squeeze, and he said, "The loss of one's first big fish is the heaviest loss I know. One feels, whatever happens, one'll never—" He stopped and pointed dramatically. "There it goes—see! Down there at the tail of the pool!"

In the broken water where the pool emptied itself into the shallows beyond, I saw the top joints of my rod dancing on the surface.

"Come on!" he shouted, and gripping my hand, jerked me to my feet. "Scatter your legs! There's just a chance!"

Dragging me after him, we raced along by the river path to the end of the pool, where, on a narrow promontory of grass, his enormous salmon rod was lying.

"Now," he said, picking it up and making the line whistle to and fro in the air with sublime authority, "keep your eyes skinned on those shallows for another glimpse of it."

A second later I was shouting, "There! There!"

He must have seen the rod point at the same moment, for his line flowed out and the big fly hit the water with a plop not a couple of feet from the spot.

He let it ride on the current, playing it with a sensitive touch like the brushwork of an artist.

"Half a jiffy!" he exclaimed at last. "Wait! Yes, I think so. Cut down to that rock and see if I haven't fished up the line."

I needed no second invitation, and presently was yelling, "Yes—yes, you have!"

"Stretch yourself out then and collar hold of it."

With the most exquisite care he navigated the line to where I lay stretched upon the rock. Then:

"Right you are! Good lad! I'm coming down."

Considering his age, he leaped the rocks like a chamois.

"Now," he said, and took the wet line delicately between his forefinger and thumb. One end trailed limply downstream, but the other end seemed anchored in the big pool where I had had my unequal and disastrous contest.

Looking into his face, I saw a sudden light of excitement dancing in his eyes.

"Odd," he muttered, "but not impossible."

"What isn't?" I asked breathlessly.

"Well, it looks to me as if the joints of that rod of yours have gone downstream."

Gingerly he pulled up the line, and presently an end with a broken know appeared.

"The reel knot, eh?" I nodded gloomily. "Then we lose the rod," said he. That wasn't very heartening news. "On the other hand, it's just possible the fish is still on—sulking."

"Oo!" I exclaimed.

"Now, steady does it," he warned, "and give me my rod."

Taking a pair of clippers from his pocket, he cut his own line just above the cast.

"Can you tie a knot?" he asked.

"Yes," I nodded.

"Come on, then; bend your line onto mine. Quick as lightning."

Under his critical eye, I joined the two lines with a blood knot. "I guessed you were a fisherman," he said, nodded approvingly and clipped off the ends. "And now to know the best or the worst."

I shall never forget the music of that check reel or the suspense with which I watched as, with the butt of the rod bearing against the hollow of his thigh, he steadily wound up the wet slack line. Every instant I expected it to come drifting downstream, but it didn't. Presently it rose in a tight slant from the pool above.

"Snagged, I'm afraid," he said, and worked the rod with an easy straining motion to and fro. "Yes, I'm afraid—no, by Lord Bobs, he's on!"

I think it was only right and proper that I should have launched a yell of triumph as, with the spoken word, the point at which the line cut the water shifted magically from the left side of the pool to the right.

"And a fish too," said he.

In the fifteen minutes that followed, I must have experienced every known form of terror and delight.

"Youngster," said he, "you should be doing this, by rights, but I'm afraid the rod's a bit above your weight."

"Oh, go on and catch him," I pleaded.

"And so I will," he promised; "unship the gaff, young un, and stand by to use it, and if you break the cast we'll never speak to each other again, and that's a bet."

But I didn't break the cast. The noble, courageous, indomitable example of my river god had lent me skill and precision beyond my years. When at long last a weary, beaten, silver monster rolled within reach of my arm into a shallow eddy, the steel gaff shot out fair and true, and sank home.

And then I was lying on the grass, with my arms round a salmon that weighed twenty-two pounds on the scale and contained every sort of happiness known to a boy.

And best of all, my river god shook hands with me and called me "partner."

That evening the salmon was placed upon the blue ashet in the hall, bearing a little card with its weight and my name upon it.

And I am afraid I sat on a chair facing it, for ever so long, so that I could hear what the other anglers had to say as they passed by. I was sitting there when my colonel put his head out of his private sitting room and beckoned me to come in.

"A true fisherman lives in the future, not the past, old man," said he; "though for this once, it 'ud be a shame to reproach you."

I suppose I colored guiltily—at any rate, I hope so.

"We got the fish," said he, "but we lost the rod, and a future without a rod doesn't bear thinking of. Now"—and he pointed at a long wooden box on the floor, that overflowed with rods of different sorts and sizes—"rummage among those. Take your time and see if you can find anything to suit you."

"But do you mean—can I—"

"We're partners, aren't we? And p'r'aps as such you'd rather we went through our stock together."

"Oo, sir," I said.

"Here, quit that," he ordered gruffly. "By Lord Bobs, if a show like this afternoon's don't deserve a medal, what does? Now, here's a handy piece by Hardy—a light and useful tool—or if you fancy greenheart is in preference to split bamboo—"

I have the rod to this day, and I count it among my dearest treasures. And to this day I have a flick of the wrist that was his legacy. I have, too, some small skill in dressing flies, the elements of which were learned in his company by candle-light after the day's work was over. And I have countless memories of that month-long, month-short friendship—the closest and most perfect friendship, perhaps, of all my life.

He came to the station and saw me off. How I vividly remember his shaggy head at the window, with the whiskered cheeks and the gunpowder marks at the corners of his eyes! I didn't cry, although I wanted to awfully. We were partners and shook hands. I never saw him again, although on my birthdays I would have colored cards from him, with Irish, Scotch, Norwegian postmarks. Very brief they were: "Water very low." "Took a good fish last Thursday." "Been prawning, but don't like it."

Sometimes at Christmas I had gifts—a reel, a tapered line, a fly book. But I never saw him again.

Came at last no more cards or gifts, but in the *Fishing Gazette*, of which I was a religious reader, was an obituary telling how one of the last of the Mutiny veterans had joined the great majority. It seems he had been fishing half an hour before he died. He had taken his rod down and passed out. They had buried him at Totnes, overlooking the River Dart.

So he was no more—my river god—and what was left of him they had put into a box and buried it in the earth.

But that isn't true; nor is it true that I never saw him again. For I seldom go a-fishing but that I meet him on the river banks.

The banks of a river are frequented by a strange company and are full of mysterious and murmurous sounds—the cluck and laughter of water, the piping of birds, the hum of insects, and the whispering of wind in the willows. What should prevent a man in such a place having a word and speech with another who is not there? So much of a fishing lies in imagination, and mine needs little stretching to give my river god a living form.

"With this ripple," says he, "you should do well."

"And what's it to be," say I—"Blue Upright, Red Spinner? What's your fancy, sir?"

Spirits never grow old. He has begun to take an interest in dry-fly methods—that river god of mine, with his seven-league boots, his shaggy head, and the gaff across his back.

PART II

The
Warm Water
Mix

"They're in the River"

JOHN McPHEE

Among the spectators on the bridge, a cop appeared. He shouted, "Does one of you guys down there own a green Jeep?"

Ed Cervone shouted back, "Yes, Officer, I do."

"Well," the cop continued, with the slightest pause. "Your wife called. She wants you home. She thinks you're dead."

Laughter on the bridge—9:50 P.M.

It was not true that Marian Cervone was concerned about her husband. By her own account, the man is too unpredictable to worry about. She wasn't worried about Edmund, either. It was my wife, Yolanda Whitman, whose mind had been crossed by the ultimate possibility. This was a few years before the sudden bloom of cellular phones. I had no way to tell her why I was late, and deliberately breaking off that fish never crossed my mind.

Yolanda seems to remember the evening with total recall. For one thing, it was my turn to cook. "By nine o'clock, I was just plain mad," she has said for the record. "You were dithering too long. I was waiting for my dinner. You were taking your sweet time, failing in your responsibilities."

Yes.

"At some point after that, I shifted from mad to concern. You had fallen out of the boat. Gone through the rapids."

The rapids, not far from the bridge, cross a diabase ledge and are tumultuous in spring.

"It was pitch black. Cold. I imagined you with hypothermia in the river. So I called Marian. I told her I was worried because your absence was 'out of character.'"

Marian must have marveled that someone could seriously use a phrase like that about a husband. Marian said she would call back if she learned anything. After hanging up, she called the Lambertville police. She said her husband and son and a friend were out in a boat and had not returned "way beyond the time" she expected them. Would the police check the boat-launch parking lot and see if a green Jeep was there? The woman on the other end of the line said the police surely would.

A while later, the police called Marian, and Marian called Yolanda, who continues the narrative: "While I waited, a tear or two actually squeezed out. I had let myself wander into the impossible. Perhaps I was madder at Ed than at you—who knows? After Marian called back, I was again spitting mad. She said, 'They're still fishing.'"

Two hours, thirty minutes. At last the fish had come up enough in the river so that the people on the bridge caught glimpses of it as, now and again, it canted— silver flashing—and changed direction. We heard them go "Ooh!" We heard them shout, "Wow, what a huge fish!" When we, in the boat, finally got a glimpse of it, we thought it enormous, too. Toward the end, I kept pressing it, tightened the drag even more, a risky, foolish thing to do. I just hoped it would not make a sudden run. If it did so, at least I had turned off the anti-reverse button, and the reel could spin free.

The fish was close now. When it saw the boat, it dived. After it came up, and saw the boat again, it took off for the bottom of the river, slowly to rise once more. At some point in the last five minutes, Edmund tried for it with the boat net and missed. I finally worked it up to the side of the boat. It was still swimming, unspent. It did not roll over. It never gave up. On the second try, Edmund got it into the net, and the dart dropped out of its mouth. He brought into the boat a four-and-three-quarter-pound roe shad.

I still have the dart—secured with monofilament to a small piece of cedar shingle. It was only the second dart I had ever retired. On a bookshelf, I propped it up beside a dart of the same weight and colors, with which, on an upriver day the spring before, I had caught seventeen shad without changing or losing the lure. The chemically sharpened hook was a novelty I had succumbed to in a catalogue. That shipment of hooks was uneven, to say the least. Some of them were so weak they were bent out straight by the force of tugging shad. But not this one. Despite two hours and thirty-five minutes in the shad's mouth, the curve of the black steel looked as it had when I made the dart and festooned it with bucktail in a vise. At home, I studied the fish with a magnifying glass. It had not been hooked on the top of the head or in any other place on the outside. It was not foul-hooked. It was hooked in the roof of the mouth, very near the front, slightly off the midline, to the right. I saw a narrow hole there, and I put a toothpick in it, which did not come through to the outside. The connection of hook and shad had been something like a trailer hitch.

Mindful of the species' paper jaw and its legendary fragility, I would one day lay a shad on a dissecting table at the University of Massachusetts and show Willy Bemis just where my fish had been hooked.

"How would you describe that, Willy?"

"It's the ethmoid cartilage of the braincase. It's the part of the braincase that everyone would understand as, regionally, the nose. One solid cartilaginous structure forms the braincase during early development. This is the anterior tip of it. The brain is back in the center of the head. Most of the braincase is protected by bone, which would make it a very tough place for a hook to latch on to. But once you've got a hook past the bone and into that little piece of cartilage, it doesn't come out. If a hook goes through that, it's going to hook on to the fish in a very serious way. There's no way that fish is ever going to throw that hook."

The monofilament felt sandpapery. When I took it off the reel, it contracted instantly into coils from a hundred and fifty-five minutes of twisting. A thick mass of bunched contracted circles hopelessly intertwined, it looked like something an owl dropped.

I sent the reel to the Daiwa Corporation, in California, for an assessment. They wanted $54.40 to fix it, because the shad had bent the pinion gear, the shad had bent the drive gear, the shad had damaged the oscillating system and gone a long way toward wearing out the drag system. The reel required two new gears, a new pawl, a new worm shaft, and three new drag washers.

I still have some of the scales. They report the shad's age as three. For a female that young to be on the spawning run is more than uncommon. It's rare. The scales record strong growth in the river in the first summer, as the egg turned into a larva, and the larva into a juvenile. They record normal growth in the ocean in each of the following years. Then they show the shad coming back into the river—two years earlier than most females do.

Soon after that evening in Lambertville, I told this story to Richard St. Pierre, of the U.S. Fish and Wildlife Service. Headquartered in Harrisburg, on the Susquehanna River, he is a shad specialist, who has worked as a shad consultant on the Hudson River, the Columbia River, and the Yangtze. He said that it must have been a letdown for me to learn that the fish was not a striped bass or a sturgeon or a muskellunge "but just a shad."

It was not in any sense a letdown, I told him. I'm a shad fisherman. I was fishing for American shad.

The Black Bass as a Game Fish

JAMES A. HENSHALL

"He is a fish that lurks close all winter; but is very pleasant and jolly after mid-April, and in May, and in the hot months."—Izaak Walton

Those who have tasted the lotus of salmon or trout fishing, in that Utopian clime of far away—while reveling in its aesthetic atmosphere, and surrounded by a misty halo of spray from the waterfall, or enveloped by the filmy gauze and iridescent tomes, sung idylls, chanted paeans, and poured out libations in honor and praise of the silver-spangled salmon, or the ruby-studded trout, while it is left to the vulgar horde of black bass anglers to stand upon the mountain of their own doubt and presumption, and, with uplifted hands, in admiration and awe, gaze with dazed eyes from afar upon that forbidden land—that *terra incognita*—and then, having lived in vain, die and leave no sign.

It is, then, with a spirit of rank heresy in my heart; with smoked glass spectacles on my nose, to dim the glare and glamour of the transcendent shore; with the scales of justice across my shoulder—*M. salmoides* in one scoop and *M. dolomieu* in the other—I pass the barriers and confines of the enchanted land, and toss them into a stream that has been depopulated of even fingerlings, by the *dilettanti* of salmon and trout fishers; for I would not, even here, put black bass in a stream inhabited by salmon or brook trout.

While watching the plebeian interlopers sporting in an eddy, their bristling spines and emerald sides gleaming in the sunshine, I hear an awful voice from the adjacent rocks exclaiming: "Fools rush in where angels fear to tread!" Shade of Izaak Walton defend us! While appealing to Father Izaak for protection, I quote his words: "Of which, if thou be a severe, sour complexioned man, then I here disallow thee to be a competent judge."

Seriously, from Izaak Walton to the present day, the salmon and trout of Great Britain have been sung in song and story as game-fishes, and it is sufficient to say that they deserve all the praise bestowed upon them. And as our ideas of fish and fishing have derived mostly from English authors, it follows that many American writers and anglers have been obsessed by their teaching, even down to the present day, as in dry fly-fishing.

Now, while we have in America the same salmon as in Great Britain, and several species of trout equally as good or better than the brown trout, we also have many other game-fishes equally worthy, and among them the black bass.

I feel free to assert, that, were the black bass a native of Great Britain, it would rank fully as high in the estimation of British anglers as either the trout or the salmon. I am borne out in this by the opinions of British sportsmen whose statements have been received without question.

W. H. Herbert (Frank Forester) writing of the black bass, says:

"This is one of the finest of the American fresh-water fishes: it is surpassed by none in boldness of biting, in fierce and violent resistance when hooked, and by a very few only in excellence upon the board." (Fish and Fishing, 1850.)

Parker Gilmore ("Ubique") says:

"I fear it will be almost deemed heresy to place this fish (black bass) on a par with the trout; at least, some such idea I had when I first heard the two compared; but I am bold, and will go further. I consider he is the superior of the two, for he is equally good as an article of food, and much stronger, and untiring in his efforts to escape when hooked." (Prairie and Forest, 1874.)

In regard to the comparative gameness of the black bass and the brook trout the following opinions of American anglers are added. Seth Green, one of the fathers of fish-culture and a lifelong angler for trout, among other fishes, has this to say:

"This is among the finest sporting as well as food fish in America. Bites fiercely at fly or trolling spoon; makes a vigorous fight for life, liberty and happiness, showing a perfect willingness 'to fight it out on that line if it takes all summer,' and at last when subdued and brought to the table does honor to the cook who prepares it, and pleasure to the palate that enjoys it." ("Fish Hatching and Fish Catching," 1879.)

Robert B. Roosevelt, who, with Seth Green, was a Fish Commissioner of New York, and co-author of "Fish Hatching and Fish Catching," and a notable angler for salmon and trout, says of the black bass:

> "A fish that is inferior only to the salmon and trout, if even to the latter; that requires the best of tackle and skill in its inveiglement, and exhibits courage and game qualities of the highest order." (Superior Fishing, 1865.)

E. E. Millard, a veteran fly-fisher for trout for fifty hears, who has camped many summers on the famous Nipigon, and who is a true and faithful lover of the brook trout, has this to say in comparing the trout and the black bass as game-fishes:

> "When the acrobatic bass approaches with every spine bristling it signifies fight, and he dies battling face to the foe—not that the trout tamely submits at the first prick of the steel; far from it. He is a fighter, though not a scientific one, having no appreciation of the finer and more artistic points of the game. He looks the fighter, having the neck and shoulders of the pugilist, but is rather too beautiful, which, however, does not always follow, and there is lacking a little of the Irish in his composition, though when put to the crowning test, he hangs on with bulldog tenacity, lacking only the resourcefulness of the small-mouth bass, the generally recognized champion of finny warriors, and of whom I can well believe that, inch for inch and pound for pound, he is the gamest fish that swims." ("Days on the Nipigon," 1917.)

Now, while salmon fishing is, unquestionably, the highest branch of piscatorial sport; and while trout fishing in Canada, Maine, and the Lake Superior region justifies all the extravagant praise bestowed upon it, I am inclined to doubt the judgment and good taste of those anglers who snap their fingers in contempt of black bass fishing, while they will wade in a stream with brush and logs, catch a few trout weighing six or eight to the pound, and call it the only artistic angling in the world! While they are certainly welcome to their opinion, I think their zeal is worthy of a better cause.

The black bass is eminently an American fish, and is truly representative in his characteristics. He has the faculty of asserting himself and making himself completely at home wherever placed. He is plucky, game, brave, and unyielding to the last when hooked. He has the arrowy rush and vigor of the trout, the untiring strength and bold leap of the salmon, while he has a system of fighting tactics peculiarly his own.

Among anglers, the question is often raised as to what constitutes a game-fish, and what particular species are to be considered best among game-fishes. In coordinating the essential attributes of game-fishes, each inherent trait and quality must be duly and impartially considered. Their habits and habitat; their aptitude to rise to the artificial fly; their manner of resistance and struggle for freedom when hooked; their finesse and intelligence; and their excellence as food must all be taken into account and duly weighed.

The black bass is more advanced in the scheme of evolution, and exhibits traits of a higher organization than either the salmon or trout. It is worthy of note that the highest development of fishes is shown in those with spiny-rayed fins as in the black bass, striped bass, channel bass, etc., while those of a lower development have soft-rayed fins as in the salmon, trout, whitefish, pike, etc.

In the animal creation the highest intelligence is exemplified by the parental instinct or care of the young. This is shown in the highest degree among mammals, next among birds, in but few reptiles, and scarcely at all among fishes. In the two hundred, or more, families of fishes, those that evince any parental instinct or manifest any care of their young can be counted on the fingers of one hand. The black bass stands pre-eminent in this respect, and is a bright and shining example to all the finny tribe in its habit of watching and guarding its nest and caring for its young brood when hatched.

Most fishes in fresh and salt water abandon their eggs as soon as emitted and fertilized. The salmon and trouts deposit their eggs in the shallowest water and leave them to the tender mercies of predatory fish, birds, and reptiles during an incubation of two or three months.

The black bass will rise to the artificial fly as readily as the salmon or the brook trout, under the same conditions; and will take the live minnow, or other live bait, under any and all circumstances favorable to the taking of any other fish. I consider him, *inch for inch* and *pound for pound*, the gamest fish that swims. The royal salmon and the lordly trout must yield the palm to a black bass of *equal weight*.

That he will eventually become the leading game-fish of America is my oft-expressed opinion and firm believe. This result, I think, is inevitable; if for no other reasons, from a force of circumstances occasioned by climatic conditions and the operation of immutable natural laws, such as the gradual drying up and dwindling away of the small trout streams, and the consequent decrease in brook trout, both in quality and quantity; and by the introduction of predatory fish in waters where the trout still exists.

Another prominent cause of the decline and fall of the brook trout, is the erection of dams, saw-mills, and factories upon trout streams, which, though to be deplored, cannot be prevented; the march of empire and the progress of civilization can not be stayed by the honest, though powerless, protests of anglers.

But, while the ultimate fate of the brook trout is sealed beyond peradventure, in open, public waters, we have the satisfaction of knowing that in the black bass we have a fish equally worthy, both as to game and edible qualities, and which at the same time is able to withstand and defy many of the causes that will, in the end, effect the annihilation and extinction of the brook trout.

As to a comparison of game qualities as between the small-mouth bass and the large-mouth bass, I hold that, other things being equal, and where the two species inhabit the same waters, there is no difference in game qualities; for, while the small-mouth is probably more active in its movements, the large-mouth bass is more powerful; and no angler can tell from its manner of resistance whether he is fast to one or the other.

Both species of black bass rise equally well to the artificial fly; though, if there be any difference in this respect, I think the large-mouth bass has the advantage. In a letter Count Von dem Borne, of Germany (who was very successful in introducing and propagating the black bass in that country), wrote me that the large-mouth black bass rose better to the artificial fly than the small-mouth bass. My own experience rather favors this view, and it has likewise been brought to my notice by anglers in various parts of the country.

The current but erroneous opinion that the small-mouth bass exceeds the large-mouth bass in game qualities, has been very widespread, and has been much enhanced by the endorsement of several of our best ichthyologists, who unfortunately, however, are not, and do not pretend to be, anglers, but who imbibed this opinion second-hand from prejudiced anglers who ought to have known better. But as the black bass is becoming better known, and fly-fishing for the species is being more commonly practiced, this unfair and unmerited comparison is fast dying out.

Fish inhabiting swiftly-running streams are always more vigorous and gamy than those in still waters, and it is probable that where the large-mouth bass exists alone in very shallow and sluggish waters, of high temperature and thickly grown with algae, it will exhibit less combative qualities, consequent on the enervating influences of its environment; but where both species inhabit the same waters, and are subject to the same conditions, I am convinced that no angler can tell whether he has hooked a large-mouth or a small-mouth bass, from their resistance and mode of fighting, provided they are of equal weight, until he has the ocular evidence.

I use the expression "equal weight" advisedly, for most anglers must have remarked that the largest bass of either species are not necessarily the hardest fighters; on the contrary, a bass of two or two and a half pounds' weight will usually make a more gallant fight than one of twice the size, and this fact, I think, will account in a great measure for the popular idea that the small-mouth bass is the "gamest" species for this reason:

Where the two species co-exist in the same stream or lake, the large-mouth bass always grows to a larger size than the other species, and an angler having just landed a two-pound small-mouth bass after a long struggle, next hooks a large-mouth bass weighing four or five pounds, and is surprised, probably, that it "fights" no harder or perhaps not so hard as the smaller fish—in fact, seems "logy"; he, therefore, reiterates the cry that the small-mouth bass is the gamest fish.

But, now, if he next succeeds in hooking a large-mouth bass of the same size as the first one caught, he is certain that he is playing a small-mouth bass until it is landed, when to his astonishment it proves to be a large-mouth bass; he merely says, "he fought well for one of his kind," still basing his opinion of the fighting qualities of the two species upon the first two caught.

Perhaps his next catch may be a small-mouth bass of four pounds, and which, though twice the weight of the large-mouth bass just landed, does not offer any greater resistance, and he sets it down in his mind as a large-mouth bass. Imagine the angler's surprise, then, upon taking it into the landing net, to find it a small-mouth bass, and one which, from its large size and the angler's preconceived opinion of the species should have fought like a Trojan.

Now, one would think that the angler would be somewhat staggered in his former belief; but no, he is equal to the occasion, and in compliance with the popular idea, he merely suggests that "it was out of condition, somehow," or "was hooked so as to drown it in the struggle"; and so, as his largest fish will necessarily be big-mouth bass, and because they do not fight in proportion to their size, they are set down as lacking in game qualities—of course, leaving the largest small-mouth bass out of the calculation.

Gentle reader, this is not a case of special pleading, nor is the angler a creation of the imagination lugged in as an apologist for the large-mouth bass; he is a veritable creature of fish and blood, of earth earthy, and with the self-conceit, weaknesses and shortcomings characteristic of the genus *homo*. I have met him and heard his arguments and sage expressions scores of times, and if the reader will reflect a moment I am sure he will recognize him.

Many years ago I was at Gogebic Lake, Wisconsin, where, among a number of prominent anglers, were Dr. F., and Dr. T., both of New York City. Dr. F. had a very extensive angling experience in all parts of the country, and Dr. T. was well known as a participant in the fly- and bait-catching contests in the tournaments of the National Rod and Reel Association of that day.

Dr. T. was a firm believer in the superior game qualities of the small-mouth bass, and declared that he could invariably tell what species of black bass he had hooked, from its manner of "fighting." Dr. F. was confident he could not do so. The matter was finally put to a practical test, when Dr. T. was forced to acknowledge himself vanquished, and that he nor any other angler could make the distinction, for one fish was as "gamy" as the other. I might add that this result will be obtained wherever the two species exist in the same waters.

Mr. S. C. Clarke, a veteran angler of sixty years' experience, and whose opinion is titled to great weight, says:

> "I will say that, from an acquaintance with both species for more than forty years, from Minnesota to Florida, I have found little or no difference between them. I have taken them with fly, spoon, and bait, as many as fifty in a day (in early times), and up to six and a half pounds' weight."

A few years before his death, Fred Mather wrote as follows:

> "A bad name, given to the big-mouth bass when black bass first began to attract the attention of anglers, has stuck. It may interest a younger genera-tion of anglers to know that forty years ago these gamy fishes were hardly known to anglers, and as soon as they began to attract attention some per-sons, to show their exquisite discrimination, began to praise one to the detri-ment of the other. Dr. Henshall and I have had the courage to fight this, and to say that in game qualities there is little difference, and that what there is depends on the weight of the fish, two pounds being its fighting weight. Further than to say that the big-mouth is not so capricious about taking the fly as his brother—*i.e.*, will usually take it more freely—I have not room to go into this subject here. I have written all this before and intend to keep at it until justice is done to a noble game-fish."

Mr. Henry Talbott, an angler of wide experience, and who has written so entertain-ingly and instructively on black bass angling in the Potomac, says:

> "There are some anglers who consider there is but one black bass, the small-mouth, and that the other is useless for food, lacking in gamy quali-ties and only fished for by the misguided. In this they are mistaken, and it is a theory they will abandon and resent when their experience is wider.
>
> "It is possible that in the Florida lakes they may be tame sport, and there seems to be a general agreement that in some of the swamps of Ohio the big-mouth is an inferior fish, but there is yet to be found his superior where he has a fair chance.
>
> "Taking the two fish at their best, there is no man living can tell the dif-ference in their taking the fly, in their fight to the boat, or on the platter, by any other sign than that one has a more capacious smile than the other; and by the same token he is just a little the better jumper and will leave the water oftener after being hooked, and is as long in coming to the net as his cousin."

Owing to my admiration for the black bass as a game-fish, and my championship of its cause for many years, and my efforts to place it in the front rank of game-fishes, and my desire to have it placed in new waters, I am sometimes, thoughtlessly and unjustly, accused of being opposed to the brook trout, and of advising the stocking of trout streams with my "favorite" fish. Nothing can be further from the truth.

I am utterly opposed to the introduction of black bass into waters in which there is the remotest chance for the brook trout or rainbow trout to thrive. I yield to no one in love and admiration of the brook trout. I was perfectly familiar with it before I ever saw a black bass; but I am not so blinded by prejudice but that I can share that love with the black bass, which for several reasons is destined to become the favorite game-fish of America. "My offending hath this extent, no more."

Let us look this thing squarely in the face. I do not wish to disturb anyone's preference, but I do want to disabuse the minds of anglers of all prejudice in the matter. The brook trout must go. It has already gone from many streams, and is fast disappearing from others. It is sad to contemplate the extinction of the "angler's pride" in public waters, but the stern fact remains that in this utilitarian age its days are numbered and its fate irrevocably sealed. As the red man disappears before the tread of the white man, the "living arrow" of the mountain streams goes with him.

The trout is essentially a creature of the pine forests. Its natural home is in waters shaded by pine, balsam, spruce, and hemlock, where the cold mountain brooks retain their low temperature, and the air is redolent of balsamic fragrance; where the natural food of the trout is produced in the greatest abundance, and where its breeding grounds are undisturbed.

But the iron has entered its soul. As the buffalo disappears before the iron horse, the brook trout vanishes before the axe of the lumberman. As the giants of the forest are laid low, and the rank and file decimated and the wooden walls of the streams battered down, the hot, fiery sun leaps through the breaches, disclosing the most secret recesses of forest and stream to the bright glare of midday. The moisture of the earth is dissipated, the mosses and ferns become shriveled and dry, the wintergreen and partridge-berry, the ground pine and trailing arbutus struggle feebly for existence; the waters decrease in size and increase in temperature, the conditions of the food supply and of the breeding grounds of the brook trout are changed; it deteriorates in size and numbers and vitality, until finally, in accordance with the immutable laws of nature and the great principle of the "survival of the fittest" (not the fittest from the angler's point of view, but the fittest to survive the changes and mutations consequent on the march of civilization), it disappears altogether.

Much has been said about the "trout hog" in connection with the decrease of the trout. But while he deserves all the odium and contempt heaped upon him by the honest angler, the result would be the same were the trout allowed undisturbed and peaceable possession of the streams, so far as the fish-hook is concerned, while the axe of the lumberman continues to ring its death knell.

Let us, then, cherish and foster and protect the crimson-spotted favorite of our youthful days as long as possible in public waters, and introduce the rainbow trout, the Dolly Varden, the steelhead, the red-throat trout, or the English brown trout, when he has disappeared; and when all these succumb, then, and not till then, introduce the black bass. But let us give these cousins of the brook trout a fair trial first, and without prejudice. There are plenty of lakes, ponds, and large streams in the eastern states into which the black bass can be introduced without interfering with trout waters.

For many years to come brook trout will be artificially cultivated, and the supply thus kept up in preserved waters by wealthy angling clubs; but by the alteration of the natural conditions of their existence they will gradually decrease in size and quality, until finally they will either cease to be or degenerate to such a degree as to forfeit even this praiseworthy protection.

I must dissent from the statement sometimes made that the black bass is the bluefish of fresh waters. The black bass is voracious—so are all game-fishes—but not more so than the brook trout. The character of a fish's teeth determines the nature of its food and the manner of its feeding. The bluefish has the most formidable array of teeth of any fish of its size—compressed, lancet-shaped, covered with enamel, and exceedingly strong and sharp, in fact, miniature shark teeth— while the black bass has soft, small, brush-like teeth, incapable of wounding, and intended only for holding its prey, which is swallowed whole. The brook trout has longer, stronger and sharper teeth than the bass, and a large, long mouth, capable of swallowing a bigger fish than a black bass of equal weight. The mouth of the bass is very wide, for the purpose of taking in crawfish with their long and aggressive claws, and not, as supposed by some, for the swallowing of large fishes. The black bass gets the best of other game-fishes, not by devouring the fishes themselves, but by devouring their food. For this reason, more than any other, they should not be introduced into the same waters with brook trout. The pike or pickerel is the bluefish of fresh waters, and in dental capacity and destructive possibilities is not far behind it.

The brook trout, I think, is the most beautiful of all fishes, as a fresh-run salmon is the handsomest and most perfect in form. The salmon is a king, the brook trout a courtier, but the black bass, in his virescent cuirass and spiny crest, is a doughty warrior whose prowess none can gainsay.

I have fished for brook trout in the wilds of Canada, where a dozen would rise at every cast of the fly, and it would be a scramble as to which should get it—great lusty trout, from a half-pound to two pounds in weight—but the black fly made life a burden by day, and the mosquito by night. The glory and beauty of the madly rushing stream breaking wildly over the great black rocks, and the quiet, glassy pools below reflecting the green spires of spruce and fir, availed nothing to swollen eyelids and smarting brow.

I have cast from early morn till dewy eve, on a good salmon stream in New Brunswick, for three days in succession without a single rise. I have cast standing in a birch-bark canoe until both arms and legs were weary with the strain, and then rested by casting while sitting—but all in vain. The swift-flowing, crystal stream reflected back the fierce glare of the northern sun and flowed on in silence toward the sea. The fir-clad hills rose boldly on either side, and stood in silent, solemn grandeur—for neither note of bird or hum of bee disturbed the painful silence of the Canadian woods.

At such times would flash on memory's mirror many a fair scene of limpid lake or rushing river, shadowed by cool, umbrageous trees, and vocal with myriads of voices—where the black bass rose responsive to the swish of the rod and dropping of the fly. Or, should the bass be coy and shy, or loth to leave his lair beneath some root or shelving rock—the melody of the birds, the tinkle of a cow-bell, the chirp of a cricket, the scudding of a squirrel, filled up the void and made full compensation.

The true angler can find real pleasure in catching little sunfish, or silversides, if the stream and birds, and bees and butterflies do their part by him; while the killing of large or many fish, even salmon or trout, in silence and solitude, may fail to fully satisfy him.

I can find something beautiful or interesting in every fish that swims. I have an abiding affection for every one, from the lowly, naked bull-head, the humble scavenger of the waters, to the silver-spangled king who will not deign to soil his dainty lips with food during his sojourn in crystal streams, and I love the brook trout best of all. But, as an angler, I can find more true enjoyment, more blessed peace, in wading some rushing, rocky stream, flecked by the shadows of overhanging elm and sycamore, while tossing the silken gage to the knight in Lincoln-green, my ears conscious of the rippling laughter of the merry stream, the joyous matin of the woodland thrush, the purring undertone of the quivering leaves—my eyes catching glimpses of hill and meadow, wren and robin, bee and bittern, fern and flower, and my breath inhaling the sweet fragrance of upland clover and elder-blossom—I say I can find more true enjoyment in this—than paying court to the lordly salmon in his drear and silent demesne, or in wooing the lovely trout with anointed face, gloved hands, and head swathed in gauze. If this be treason, my brother, make the most of it. I am content. It is my honest conviction. After killing every species of game-fish east of the Rocky Mountains, from Canada to Florida, and some in foreign lands, I find the knightly bass and his tourney-field all sufficient.

THE CAPTURE OF THE BASS

My brother of the angle, go with me
This perfect morning in the leafy June,
To yonder pool below the rapid's foot.
Approach with caution; let your tread be soft;
Beware the bending bushes on the brink.
Disturb no branch, nor twig, nor leaf, my friend,
The finny tribe is wary.

Rest we here.
Behold the lovely scene! The rippling stream,
Now dancing, sparkling, in the morning sun;
The blue-eyed violet nodding at your feet;
The red-bird, all ablaze, with swelling throat,
The dreamy, droning hum of insect wings
Is mingled ever with the rustling leaves.
Sleek, well-fed cattle there contented stand,
On gravelly shoal beneath the spreading beech.
Across the narrow stream a sycamore,
A weather-beaten giant, old and gray,
With scarr'd arms stretching o'er the silent pool,
With gnarl'd and twisted roots bathed in the flood
For, lo, these hundred years.

Beneath those roots
With watchful eye—proud monarch of the pool—
A cunning bass doth lie, on balanced fin,
In waiting for his prey.

And now with rod,
With faithful reel, and taper'd line of silk,
With mist-like leader and two fairly flies—
Dark, bush hackles, both—I make a cast.
With lengthen'd line I quickly cast again,
And just beneath the tree the twin-like lures
As gently drop as falling autumn leaves;
And half-submerged, like things of life they seem,
Responsive to the rod and line.

But look!
Saw you that gleam beneath the flood? A flash—
A shadow—then a swirl upon the pool?
My hand, responsive to the sudden thrill,
Strikes in the steel—the wary bass is hooked!
And now with lightning speed he darts away
To reach his lair—his refuge 'neath the roots.
The singing reel proclaims him almost there—
I "give the butt"—the ever-faithful rod
In horse-shoe curve checks his headlong flight.
Right lustily he tugs and pulls, Egad!
But still the barb is fast.

The hissing line—
The rod now bending like a slender reed
Resists the tight'ning strain. He turns his course—
In curving reaches, back and forth, he darts,
Describing arcs and segments in the pool.
Ha! nobly done! as with a mighty rush
He cleaves the crystal stream, and at one bound,
Full half a fathom in the realm above
He nimbly takes an atmospheric flight—
His fins extended, stiff with bristling points—
His armor brightly flashing in the sun—
His wide-extended jaws he shakes in rage
To rid him of the hook.

And now I lower
The pliant rod in court'sy to the brave.
The line relieved, somewhat, of steady strain,
Outwits the wily bass—the hook holds fast!
Now back again he falls with angry splash
To seek the aid of snag, or root of tree;
For thus, my friend, he oft escapes, I trow,
By fouling line or hook—

He never sulks!
Not he; while life remains, or strength holds good,
His efforts never cease. Now up the stream—

Now down again—I have him well in hand.
Now reeling in, or erstwhile giving line;
He swims now fast or slow—now high or low.
The steady strain is still maintained, you see!
The good rod swaying like a wind-blown rush—
He surges thro' the flood.

Another leap!
Ye Gods! How like an angry beast he shakes
His brisling mane, and dives below again!
And did you mark, my friend, his shrewd intent,
As when he fell upon the slacken'd line?
If then he'd found it stretched and taut, I ween,
He would have made his safe and sure escape.
But haply then the tip was slightly lowered—
And so, with yielding line, the hook held fast.
Now truly, friend, he makes a gallant fight!
In air or water—all the same to him—
His spiny crest erect; he struggles still.
No sulking here! but like a mettl'd steed
He champs the bit, and ever speeds the best
With firm-held, tighten'd rein.

He's off again!
Now down the stream he flashes like a shaft
From long-bow swiftly sped—his last bold spurt—
The effort cost him dear—his worsted strength
Is ebbing fast. And now in lessening curves
He feebly swims, and labors with the tide.
And as I reel the line he slowly yields,
And now turns up his breast-plate, snowy white—
A vanquished, conquered knight.

And now my friend
The landing-net. With firm and cautious hand
Beneath the surface hold it. Take him in.
Now lift him out and gently lay him down.
How bright his tunic, bronze and glossy green!
A fitting rival to the velvet sward.

And see the ragged rent the hook hath made!
You marvel how it held him safe and fast!
'Twas by the equal and continual strain
Of supple rod and ever-faithful reel.
'Twas work well done.

Oh valiant, noble bass!
Fit dweller of the merry, brawling stream.
Thy once-loved pool beneath thy giant tree,
Thy fancied stronghold 'neath its tangled roots,
Shall know thee never more. Thy race is run!

Now in thy creel,
My doubting friend, we'll gently lay him down
Upon a bed of cool and graceful ferns,
Yet sparkling with the early morning dew—
A warrior in repose!

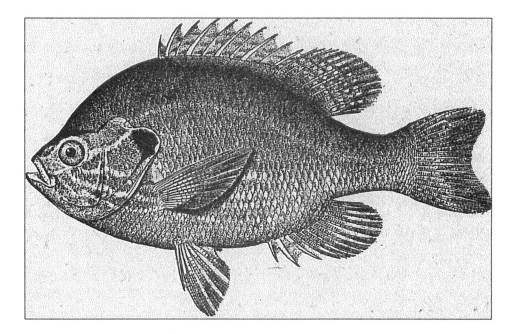

Red, White, and Bluegill

TED LEESON

Among angling aristocrats, Atlantic salmon have long been celebrated as "the fish of kings," no doubt because the two have so much in common: the aloof arrogance and inflated sense of self-worth, a fussiness about habitat, expensive tastes. And as far as I'm concerned, they deserve each other. Give me a panfish any day—a fish of the people, blue-collar rather than blue blood, a working-class fish, a fish for a great republic. I've never understood how the bald eagle, a scavenger and a thief, could have been chosen as our national symbol, whereas the honest, sweat-of-the-brow bluegill never even made the shortlist. I guess the Founding Fathers didn't fish much.

Panfish, of course, doesn't denote a particular species but a loosely defined assemblage with varying regional representatives—a little like Congress but harder working and better behaved. The core of the group comes from the Centrarchidae family—the sunfishes—itself a kind of melting pot whose chief ingredients include bluegills, pumpkinseeds, redears, red-breasts, green sunfish, warmouths, rock bass, and white and black crappies. A kind of odd-man-out, the yellow perch is not a sunfish but no less a panfish wherever it is found. I'm not aware of any single place that's home to all these species at once. They crop up in various mixes and proportions in different geographical areas, and membership in the category of panfish (or "bream" or "brim," depending on where you live) has always been a matter of shifting local interpretations, further complicated by a host of colloquial names: shell-cracker, stumpknocker, goggle-eye, sun perch, longear, speckled perch, white bass, and so on. In practice, the term ultimately falls into that set of expressions, like "I'll do it in a minute" or "I have strong feelings for you," that are universally understood but not necessarily taken to mean exactly the same thing by everyone.

Fishermen don't trouble themselves much about such discrepancies, instead focusing on the collective virtues of the fish. And foremost among their merits is a relentless availability. Like the other indispensables of American life—duct tape, canned chili, and WD-40—panfish can be obtained virtually everywhere. I've taken them in creeks and rivers, brackish water and fresh, 10,000-acre lakes and quarter-acre stock tanks, old quarry pits, prairie potholes, golf-course water hazards, abandoned strip mines, backyard ponds, irrigation ditches, and once, the ornamental fountain pool behind a fancy hotel. As a group, they are America's most widespread and abundant gamefish. And they are nothing if not game. I've caught them by accident and on purpose, on handlines, trotlines, poles cut from tree limbs, garage-sale spincast outfits, fly tackle that cost slightly less than my car, and every kind of gear in between. I've grabbed a few by hand and (in a mercifully brief period of angling dementia) jigged them up through 2 feet of ice. Equally ready for a few casual casts after work or the formalities of an organized expedition, panfish are a fish-of-all-trades, up for anything, anytime. They are a welcome counterweight to the forces of high-tech angling and a persistent reminder that fishing is finally about fish, not equipment.

Accommodating and enthusiastic, genial and cooperative, panfish are custom-cut for the neophyte. In the angling universe of my youth, they were the force of gravity that held everything together. The ones I could catch whetted my skills and honed my instincts. Those that proved better at being fish than I did at being a fisherman gave me a continuing sense of purpose. Without panfish, I might well have sunk into juvenile delinquency, or golf. The pinnacle of every summer was the day my father, a man who did not readily leave the house, squeezed our whole family into a station wagon and endured the eight-hour drive to a lake in northern Wisconsin. He herded us directly from the car into a rowboat where, except for a few moments stolen to dig more worms, we spent a week or two yarding in unimaginable numbers of perch and rock bass and bluegills. The little ones bit readily. And the bigger ones proved just discriminating enough to teach you something but still catchable enough that you could learn the lesson. At a time of life as yet uncorrupted by a lust for magazine-cover specimens, panfish fulfilled the greatest promise in all of angling—pure action.

We ate them too, by the stringerful, with butter and lemon and onions, fried, baked, broiled, and grilled, and best of all, without guilt. Even today, in a time when quality angling for high-profile species increasingly hinges on catch-and-release, you can still sit down to a plate of bluegills or crappies without the slightest twinge of conscience or the fear of a second-rate meal. They come by their name honestly, for a pan is the highest destiny of these sweet-eating fishes. Bony? Sure, a little. And a steamed crab is mostly shell. Who's that going to stop?

Once you've got panfish in your soul, they never really leave. Not many seasons ago, a friend and I extorted an invitation to a pay-to-play trophy trout lake in the high desert of eastern Washington. The morning's fishing, though not fast, produced some remarkable trout, among the biggest of my life. Noon found us prospecting the lower end of the lake. Approaching deeper water near an earthen dam, we suddenly doubled up—smaller fish, it was clear, but dogged and determined fighters. To our utter disbelief, they turned out to be a pair of identical yellow perch a full pound apiece, with deep blue-green backs and lemon-lime flanks that shaded into fat, cantaloupe bellies. With no real idea how they got there, but a pretty good one about how to get them out, we burned up half a box of trout flies and a whole afternoon happily catching perch in a $200-a-day lake where a 5-pound rainbow scarcely elicits a yawn. That evening when our host, proud of his fishery and eager for a report, asked how we'd done, we just told him, "Couldn't have been better."

And we meant it. In this age of scientific fisheries control, of measurements and projections that produce finely calibrated angling regulations, panfish may well be the last unmanaged gamefish in America, left to themselves, on their own as they've always been and doing just fine, thank you. It's ironic that a whole sector of the fishing industry now thrives on whisking anglers off for remote and pristine destinations to experience sport of unspoiled abundance, fishing "the way it used to be." Any 8-year-old kid with a cane pole, a bike, and panfish in his heart can lead you to just such a place.

And maybe that's what I like best about them: Panfish are the most democratic of gamefish. They do not care who fishes them and bite equally for everyone. They're unimpressed by the cost of your tackle, indifferent to the methods you use, unconcerned about the bait you favor, and sometimes, whether there's any bait at all. Panfish are angling's version of the single-shot .22—sturdy and dependable, workmanlike and unpretentious. If panfish formed a baseball team, they'd be the Cubs; if you could play them on a jukebox, they'd be Hank Williams tunes; if panfish were a beer, they'd be whatever's on sale.

Oh, and there's one last thing. Except for the more cosmopolitan perch, panfish are pure homegrown. Though, like much in American life, they've been exported around the world, panfish are indigenous only to North America, native to no other part of the globe. So picture this for a moment—a red-and-white bobber twitching above the slab of a sunset-colored bluegill. Now there's something worth printing on the back of a dollar bill.

Among the Northern Pines

LATHAN A. CRANDALL

We reached the lake in the evening, and started out bright and early the next morning to call upon some of the old inhabitants who wear fins and have a reputation for being scaly. A new and fascinating Dowagiac minnow caught the eye of a big bass before we had gone forty rods, and connections were promptly established. As he was being kindly but firmly persuaded to approach the boat he flung himself into the air, gave a twist and a wiggle and a shake and thus succeeded in appropriating that Dowagiac to his own uses. He has not been heard from since that brief interview, but it is safe to say that he is putting on airs as he dangles that rainbow-colored minnow before the eyes of his admiring relatives. We have sometimes doubted the truth of the old saw that it is unlucky to lose the first fish hooked, but all doubt on that point has been put to flight.

A day or two later five fine bass were caught one afternoon and hung over the side of the boat on a hastily improvised stringer. Rowing home the stringer parted through chafing on the side of the boat and the bass went their respective ways. Not content with this friendly slap, Dame Fortune—or inexcusable carelessness—permitted the string of the minnow pail, also hanging over the side of the boat, to break, involving the loss not only of the pail but of some four dozen A-1 minnows. When the Junior had captured a three-pound bass we concluded to tie him—the bass—up to a root that reached out over the water and to keep him until later. Just when he seemed to be thoroughly halter-broken he succeeded in untying the knot and we saw him no more. All this was bad enough, but to make a complete job of our discomfort the minnow-trap which was supposed to be busily at work luring bait for our use, suddenly and unaccountably disappeared. Then the outer pail of the new minnow-bucket was missing and the scaler could not be found. It rained and then rained some more. the bass absolutely refused to strike at a spoon-hook or pork rind or the new Dowagiac. Why did we ever leave our happy home?

It is always darkest just before dawn. The outer pail of the new minnow-bucket had been borrowed by a Methodist preacher who was camping nearby, and was returned the same afternoon. The minnow-trap had been rolled out into deep water by the under-tow, and within twenty-four hours of its disappearance was back in its accustomed place and hard at work. The scaler reappeared as suddenly and unaccountably as it had disappeared. A new stringer was easily manufactured and, with a plentiful supply of minnows, the bass needful to adorn the stringer were easily persuaded to come to hook. The weather-man repented of his unkindness and gave us days of glorious sunshine. The lake dimpled and laughed, the pines whispered all kinds of friendly messages, the red-squirrels scolded at us from the tree-tops where they were busy cutting off pine cones, and the chipmunks made friendly advances as we sat by the lakeside. The moon almost turned night into day and night loons called to us, "Ha! Ha! What's the matter with you? This is a beautiful world. Minnesota is the finest part of the world and this is the fairest spot in Minnesota. Cheer up!" And we did.

Now that we have gotten out of the dumps and life is worth living, let's go fishing. What shall it be? Or will you take anything that comes your way? There are bass and crappies and sunfish and great northern pike, not to mention rock-bass and perch. The natives aver that there are also enormous wall-eyed pike and we believe it, although they were always out when we called. Thanks be! there is not a pickerel in the lake. The great northern pike looks much like his kinsman, the pickerel, but differs in body-markings, gill-covers, general shape—being more stocky—and especially in palatableness. He is a vigorous fighter. Mr. Louis Rhead, in his book on "Fish and Fishing," says that neither the northern pike nor the pickerel has ever been known to rise above the surface of the water after being hooked. If that is correct, then something new under the sun has happened recently, for the writer, with eighty to a hundred feet of line out, had a nine-pounder throw himself entirely out of the water in his efforts to escape. The largest ever caught in this lake weighed thirty-six pounds, but numbers are taken that go over ten pounds each. They are nearly as gamey and quite as good eating as the muskallonge.

The crappies are more friendly. Early in our stay we located a "bed" which never failed to respond to a call. If there is any fish in these northern lakes that makes a more delicious dish than fried crappies, we want to be introduced to it. It is not all unusual to take them weighing a pound each, but this seems trifling when the Methodist preacher aforementioned tells us that he caught seventy-five in Lake Itasca in less than an hour which averaged two pounds each. Bass are here in abundance but were not responsive this summer. Those caught were ridiculously fat.

To cap the climax of attractions there is a trout stream only three miles away. Visit it? Rather. A friendly neighbor furnished horse and buggy and acted as guide. We had a few alleged angleworms, and even with these emaciated, scrawny apologies for bait we took enough trout to furnish a meal for each family represented by the anglers. The stream flows through a marsh and is fed by numerous springs. Where we first struck the brook one needed a magnifying glass to find it. How a six-inch trout manages to turn around in it passes understanding. It grows as it goes, however, and widens into quite a respectable stream during its journey of a mile.

For some years now the writer has been inflicting fish stories upon the unsuspecting public, and the impulse is within him to add more to those already told. He has a new supply growing out of the experiences of the summer, and it is hard to keep them bottled up. He would gladly particularize concerning the ten-inch trout that was waiting for him under the roots of a big tamarack just where the foam had formed a shady hiding-place, or mention specially some of the fights with the pike. But the cynical skepticism of assumed friends, the frivolous, not to say contemptuous comments made concerning the writer's previous contributions to piscatorial knowledge, have deeply wounded his sensitive spirit, and he cannot summon courage to challenge renewed unkindness.

Just why fish stories should be discredited so readily by those who do not fish it is difficult to understand. Why should a man who does not know the difference between a spoon-hook and an ostrich feather and who cannot tell a sunfish from a rainbow trout sit in judgment upon the solemn assertions of experienced anglers? This attitude of chronic unbelief concerning the testimony of honest men is unbecoming. We have heard many fish stories during the summer, all of them true. We have even heard varying accounts of the same incident and have believed them all. That comes from possessing a truthful spirit. A gentleman told us of seeing a string of five fine bass and some fifteen or twenty sunfish and perch caught by a cottager who came over from an adjoining lake. The next day another gentleman gave an account of the same catch and the number of bass had increased to twenty-five. On the third day, as vouched for by another gentleman, there were one hundred bass in that string and they averaged between four and six pounds. Now some suspicious individuals would scoff at the apparent discrepancies, but it is easy to reconcile the different statements. The first gentleman may have seen the catch early in the day and the other accounts may have been based upon later accumulations.

Among the most untiring fishermen met this summer were a father and son who chased the great northern pike with a zeal worthy of such a cause. One day the father informed me that they had caught a pike weighing fifteen pounds the day before. Soon after the son gave his version of the capture and said the pike weighed eighteen pounds. But why cavil? Are we to make no allowance for youthful imagination? Is a little matter of three pounds to be allowed to spoil a good fish story?

The writer ventures to record these experiences because they are not his own. Possibly he may be allowed to set down one other incident, inasmuch as it does not concern him personally: On the shore of the lake—the precise location was not given—once lived a farmer who owned a dog famed for exceptional intelligence. It occurred to the farmer that, as the dog loved the water and seemed interested in the fishing excursions which they took together, it might be possible to utilize the canine ability to practical ends. Fastening a trolling line to the dog's tail, he took him out upon the lake, threw him overboard and rowed rapidly to shore. Of course, the dog swam after the boat and had not gone far before he hooked on to a good-sized bass which he dragged after him to the land. The owner praised the dog and continued his training until the beast had become a proficient troller, entering into the sport with eagerness and zest. If the master failed to set him to work for a day or so the dog would bring the trolling line in his mouth and plead—as well as a dumb animal can—to be allowed to go fishing. If he caught a bass he would give two barks to announce the capture, and if a pike three barks, except in the case of an exceptionally large one, in which case he barked from the time the fish struck until he had landed it. If he had the misfortune to hook a rock-bass or a perch he would sneak down the shore to some unfrequented spot and there gnaw the intruder off the hook and then go back to work again. Would that we could record a long life for this most wonderful animal, but, alas! he came to an untimely end. When but four years of age, in the fullness of his powers, he begged to go fishing one lowering day. Soon after he had begun trolling up and down the shore the master heard his bark of victory and, as it was continued, knew that he had hooked a large fish. The barks soon took on a note of anxiety, gradually merging into fear. Rushing down to the shore the horrified farmer was just in time to see the dog being rapidly drawn backward despite his most heroic efforts. A moment later and a great pair of jaws opened and enveloped both dog and bark. When, now and then, on cloudy days, a sound comes across the water that somewhat resembles a bark, the residents say to each other, "There is the big pike that swallowed Perkins' dog." (The writer hastens to say that he did not see the dog nor the pike nor even the bark.)

By this time some reader may be interested to know where the lake is located about which we are writing. A journey of about two hundred miles almost due north from Minneapolis brings the traveler to Park Rapids, a live and growing town on the

Great Northern Railroad. One may not travel far in any direction from this town without coming across a lake. Three miles to the east is Long Lake, some nine miles in length with an average width of about three-fourths of a mile. It is a beautiful sheet of water, spring-fed, blue, with sandy beaches and broken, wooded shores. Here among the pines is the cottage where we spent a delightful outing.

Unless all signs fail, this section is soon to become the favorite playground of the Mississippi Valley. It has almost innumerable attractive lakes, the fragrant pines are everywhere, the air is pure and invigorating, the fishing is varied and first-class. Twenty-four miles from Park Rapids is Lake Itasca, whose fame has gone abroad, for it is here that the mighty Mississippi has its source. It lies within the state park, which includes thirty-six thousand acres of land, and here are found magnificent specimens of the great Norway pine, once so common over all this country. The superintendent of the park is given the privilege of conducting a summer resort on the shores of Lake Itasca, and the central lodge and adjoining cottages, all built of pine logs, are very attractive. An automobile trip on an ideal day gave an opportunity for visiting this interesting place. We wondered, as we approached the lodge, at seeing the boarders playing tennis and pitching quoits when ten rods away was the lake and fishing. But more intimate acquaintance with the lake dispelled the wonder. The shoreline is timbered and beautiful, but the water looks dead, and not a sand beach is to be seen. It is now all in the past except the memory. That will abide. The last afternoon of our stay we rowed across the lake and picked a gunny-sack full of hazel nuts, took a swim in the lake, and then built a fire on the shore over which we roasted the delicious sweetcorn, took our supper in the open, and rowed home as the shadows deepened and the crescent moon hung low in the western sky. We shall often recall the sunny days and peace-filled nights, the glory of the sunsets and the enticement of the beautiful lake. Possibly we shall feel, at times, the tingle generated by the big bass or the ten-inch trout. Certainly we shall live over again the picnics in the pine woods and the days spent in the boat voyaging in search of the wary bass.

Sacred Eels

JAMES PROSEK

We have not attained to the full solution of the exceedingly difficult eel problems,
but the steady progress of the last twenty years is full of promise for the future . . .
Altogether the whole story of the eel and its spawning has come to read almost like a romance,
wherein reality has far exceeded the dreams of fantasy.—Dr. Johannes Schmidt, 1912

My early encounters with eels were awkward, confused. My friends and I caught them by accident while fishing for trout or bass with worms. We never stopped to admire them; we were too shocked by their energy, frustrated by our inability to hold onto their slimy bodies, and just wanted our hooks back.

One December in Italy eight years ago, I stood at the edge of a lake next to my friend Larry Ashmead. A line of slender poles was sticking out of the water along the shore. A man nearby said the poles marked traps for catching eels, and I began to tell Larry what little I knew of the life history of freshwater eel.

Like those slender fish on the other side of the Atlantic, the eels in this lake were born in the middle of the Atlantic Ocean, somewhere east of the Bahamas, maybe several thousand feet deep. The discovery of the eels' spawning place was made in the early 1900s by the

Danish oceanographer Johannes Schmidt, who caught thousands of specimens of the larval stage of the eel in fine mesh nets in an amorphous region of the North Atlantic, several million square miles, called the Sargasso Sea. Observing these larvae, only a few millimeters long and a few days old, drifting in the surface of the ocean currents, Schmidt concluded that the adult eels had recently spawned, somewhere beneath his nets. News of the find, one of the most exciting in marine biology in the twentieth century, was published widely, in such magazines as *National Geographic*, in 1913, and the journal *Nature*. But it soon became clear that although Schmidt had solved a part of the "eel problem," he had merely stoked the fire. Although they knew at the surface where the eels spawned, no one had witnessed the adults spawning. It became then, perhaps, an even greater marine mystery.

Before the twentieth century, scientists both amateur and professional had concocted numerous explanations about how eels reproduced, many of them harebrained: that they were generated from horse hairs, or drops of dew, that they mated with snakes on the banks of rivers, or emerged from the carcasses of dead animals or the mud. It was not even known whether eels were asexual or had gender and reproductive organs until Sigmund Freud as a young medical student published the first paper on the location of the eel's gonads. As it turns out, the reproductive organs were virtually invisible until the fish began its journey in the sea. The larval stage of the eel—which looks nothing like the adult itself, but more like a leaf-shaped fish with fangs—was indeed known for centuries, named its own species, *Leptocephalus breverostris*. But until two Italian biologists in the late 1800s observed these fish metamorphosing into eels we didn't know the eel had a larval stage at all. Schmidt was determined to find out where these larvae, caught in the open ocean, came from. But even after Schmidt's discovery of the general vicinity of the Atlantic eels' spawning place, to this day, no one has witnessed an adult eel spawning in the sea, or seen an adult eel much beyond the river mouth on their way to the spawning grounds. His findings merely opened a larger can of eels.

"After the young are born in the ocean as little leaf-shaped fish," I said to my friend Larry, "they are spread randomly by ocean currents to the coasts of the Atlantic. After twenty years or so in freshwater, the adults return to the ocean to spawn and then die."

The eel is one of the few fishes that are catadromous—that is, it spends its adult life in freshwater but reproduces in salt. This life history is the opposite of that of the salmon, for instance, an anadromous fish, which spends its adult life in the sea but reproduces in freshwater. There are several other populations of catadromous eels around the world that spawn in other oceans but carry out very similar lives to the Atlantic eel.

Larry found all this hard to believe. Until his moment of doubt, I hadn't really stopped to consider what the eels went through to get to and from the small brooks and lakes where they spent their adult lives. The place where they would reproduce, and probably die, was thousands of miles away.

Some weeks later, Larry came across a 1941 story by Rachel Carson from *Under the Sea Wind*, called "Odyssey of the Eel." It is a tale written largely through the eyes of a female eel named Anguilla (the genus name for catadromous eels), inspired by Schmidt's discovery. The story begins by describing juvenile eels swimming to a small body of water called Bittern Pond, two hundred miles from the sea, "like pieces of slender glass rods shorter than a man's finger." And then, one dark rainy night in autumn, many years after she first entered freshwater, Anguilla leaves the pond, beginning her long journey back to the Sargasso.

Anguilla is drawn almost magnetically toward that place of warmth and darkness hundreds of feet below the surface of the ocean where she was born. Beyond that, the author imagines the rest, because once Anguilla leaves the mouth of the river, her life in the ocean is entirely a mystery: "No one can trace the path of the eels that left the salt marsh at the mouth of the bay on that November night when wind and tide brought them the feeling of warm ocean water—how they passed from the bay to the deep Atlantic basin that lies south of Bermuda and east of Florida half a thousand miles."

We don't know much more of the eel's life history today, nearly a century after Schmidt's discovery. What remains consistent about the eel is its ability to avoid our gaze. That ultimately was what attracted me to the eel.

It's not easy to get to like, or to know, the eel. It is dark and slippery, and not particularly beautiful at first glance. For me, the eel began as an idea. The idea was of the unseen journey, and the eel's intangible determination to reach a destination, a destiny that ends with death, and life. I'm still trying to figure out what to do with that idea, and whether trying to make sense of its ethereal qualities would somehow break the beauty of its incomprehensibility. In the course of my time spent with eels, I met other people who were as interested in eels as I was, people whose lives cross paths with the eel. Fishermen, scientists, slippery lovers of darkness themselves, who I began to call, in jest, "eelians."

Many eelians live lives like the eel, unseen, quiet, under the radar. For me, the unexpected paths that led to these people became wrapped in the original idea. One, Ray Turner, an eel fisherman of the Catskill Mountains in New York State, became a kind of prophet to me, who spoke in aphorisms that appeared alternately meaningless and prophetic, depending on the circumstances and delivery. "It's not the journey, it's the road," he once told me. Or, "Art is reality out of proportion." But the elusiveness of the eel was its beauty.

All around the world, the eel inspires fear, awe, and respect. Humans seem to have some visceral reaction to this minimalist fish, as they do the snake, a tempter of the innocent and virginal, an erotic symbol, a food source, a god. In some cultures the eel fills both the well of human spirituality and the stomach. The spawning areas and much of the life history of the world's catadromous eels is still a mystery, one that may be, as the indigenous people of New Zealand believe, best left unsolved. But it would be unfortunate if the opportunity to know the eel became lost. All around the world, catadromous eel populations are in serious decline. The causes are many and not always easily defined. If we do lose the eel, however, before we witness its spawning or know more about what fuels its determination to make the journey, or how it navigates in its migration, then, as the poet Wallace Stevens once wrote, "farewell to an idea."

I began my work on eels around 1998, and, as is the case when I dig into a topic, I mentioned my interest in eels with anyone who came within talking distance. I brought up eels in conversation with family, editors, artists, therapists, my barber, and one day with a friend named David Seidler, a screenwriter friend in Santa Monica. He asked me if I'd heard of the sacred eels in New Zealand. I had not, nor had I read anything about how important eels were to the culture and traditions of the Maori, the native Polynesians of New Zealand. There was, I would discover, a reason for this—Maori stories and traditions are passed on orally, and only between Maori.

As I found out on my first visit to New Zealand a few years before, a post-college trout-fishing trip with my friend Taylor, the Maori are genial, but don't go out of their way to share anything. Taylor and I saw Maori men in bars after their long days at work in the sawmills or slaughterhouses, but not much more than a grunt or nod passed between us. We trekked on Maori tribal land, hiked trails through old growth forests, fished crystal clear rivers with tall fern trees shading emerald pools, caught trout introduced by the British, and hung out with naturalized British people. But overall, the experience, though visually and physically fulfilling, felt superficial. I left New Zealand feeling empty, knowing that I was glimpsing only one small part of that country and little of its soul; in other words, its people. It was the first time in my travels that a pretty landscape was not enough for me.

As David told me more about the giant eels in New Zealand, I remembered then, while eating lunch on the bank of a remote river on that first trip with Taylor, that a slender dark shape, five feet long and big around as my arm, had come out of the shadows to eat a piece of the sandwich that I'd thrown in the water. I saw it so briefly that I wasn't sure I'd seen it at all. But as David spoke over the phone, it registered in my mind that the big dark fish had been perhaps the only native fish I'd seen on that trip, an eel.

David told me that it is a tradition of the Maori to keep ponds with sacred eels. The Maori feed the eels and protect them and in turn the eels protect the *iwi*, or tribe. The eels can be huge—six, seven feet—and feed right out of one's hands. The Maori say some of these eels are over 300 years old.

David, who grew up in America, knew the land of Kiwis from his years living there married to a Maori woman named Titihuiarangimoana, whom he met while working for a television company in Australia. His marriage gave him access to a world usually closed to pakeha, or white people. His introduction to the New Zealand wilds, or "bush" as it's called, was through fly-fishing for trout with a Maori man named DJ.

"I've seen some huge ones while trout fishing, mate," David said. "I was fishing in this mountain lake one day, wading through the shallows and went to step over this big log when . . . the log moved! It was a giant eel—big around as the fattest part of my leg. There was no stream running out of the lake, so I don't know how this eel would get to the sea to spawn, but they say that some small eels get up to high lakes when there's a typhoon, and they'll stay up there, sometimes over a hundred years, until the next big typhoon comes and washes them down the mountain."

David sent an e-mail to his friend DJ on the North Island in autumn of 2002, inquiring about eels on my behalf. DJ said he knew a thing or two about eels, but would try to find someone who might have more to say than he did on the importance of eels in Maori culture. Eventually, it was decided that the best person to lead me around New Zealand in search of eels was a twenty-three-year-old half-Maori woman named Stella August. Stella had just finished her graduate work at Waikato University in Hamilton. The subject of her thesis was the spring migration of glass eels on the Tukituki River, which flows toward to the eastern coast of the North Island, near her family's tribal land in Hawke Bay.

A few e-mail correspondences later, Stella agreed to set up an itinerary for me and to be my eel guide on a trip to New Zealand. Our trip was scheduled for February of 2004, summertime in the southern hemisphere.

In the meantime, in my research, I came across some Polynesian myths that involved eels, in the work of Joseph Campbell. Campbell explains in his book, *The Masks of God: Creative Mythology*, how the creation myth in India involving the snake made its way through Indonesia and was eventually inherited by the Polynesians, who replaced the snake, which was unknown in the islands, with the indigenous eel. "East of Indonesia, Melanesia, and Australia, throughout the island-studded triangle of Polynesia—which has Hawaii at its apex, New Zealand at one angle, and Easter Island at the other—the mythological image of the murdered divine being whose body became a food plant has been adjusted to the natural elements of an oceanic environment," Campbell wrote. "The voluptuous atmosphere of the lush Polynesian adventure will be different, indeed, from the grim holiness of the rabbinical Torah; nevertheless, we are certainly in the same old book—of which, so to say, all the earliest editions have been lost."

In several stories throughout the region, particularly in Samoa, a small eel is taken as a pet by a girl named Sina. Sina raises the eel in a coconut shell until it becomes too big, at which point she lets it go in a spring, but continues to feed it. One day when she's bathing in the spring the eel tries to pierce her vagina with its tail. The eel is killed and the head is buried, where a coconut tree grows. The nut of the coconut bears the mark of the eel's eyes and mouth. The story of the eel as a creature both loved but feared, and as a kind of detached phallus with a mind of its own, in consistent throughout the region.

Another Polynesian story, of which there are many variations, concerns a monster eel called Te Tuna, and the seduction of the god Maui's wife, Hine. Campbell likens Maui to a kind of Hercules of Polynesia. When Maui finds the giant eel Te Tuna in bed with his wife one night, he cuts off the eel's head with a hatchet. In the story, the head of the eel becomes all the saltwater eels of the world, and the tail becomes all the freshwater eels of the world.

It is not surprising, perhaps, that in the South Pacific region the word for eel, *tuna*, is a synonym for penis. There are many variations of stories of eels seducing women by a spring while they're washing clothes, or in their sleep, as well as stories of eels as monsters, but I found nothing specifically about the Maori and eels, or about sacred eels at all, until I stumbled onto the works of Elsdon Best.

Best was born in Tawa Flat, New Zealand, in 1856, the son of British immigrants. He is considered to be the foremost ethnographer of Maori society, which was diminishing rapidly even in the late nineteenth century. In his work, it is evident from the sheer proportion of pages devoted to the eel in his book, about two-thirds, that the eel was once the greatest inland food source for the Maori. He listed over two hundred local Maori names for the freshwater eel in his *Fishing Methods and Devices*. If the number of different words used to describe the nuances of an object in a language—like snow to the Eskimo—is evidence of its importance in a culture, then this fact alone, for me, confirmed the importance of eels in Maori life.

It was also in Best's work where I first read about the Maori monster called the *taniwha*, which most commonly takes the form of a giant eel.

In Maori Myth and Religion Part II, Best describes how Captain Cook, on his third voyage to New Zealand in 1777, gave us the first written record of what the natives there called *taniwha*: "We had another piece of intelligence from him, more correctly given, though not confirmed by our own observations, that there are snakes and lizards there of enormous size. He described the latter as being eight feet in length and big around as a man's body. He said they sometimes devour men."

Best, commenting on Cook's account, points out that the Maori man telling the story to Cook would certainly have known a lizard—though no eight-foot lizards exist in New Zealand—but would have never seen a snake. What the native described to Cook was the longfin eel of their freshwater rivers, *Anguilla dieffenbachii*, capable of growing to eight feet long and confirmed to live well over eighty pounds and a hundred years. Best also wrote that large eels were sometimes tamed and regularly fed. Offerings were sometimes made to these eels, and thought to be "sacred," they were respected like gods.

These Polynesian myths and traditions in the works of European writers, as they related to eels, were interesting to me, but at times dry. This was in part because the people who recorded them were not the authentic tellers of the tales. There was no Polynesian Homer to write them down. The soul of these stories was yet unwritten, was still in the minds of Maori elders in seaside and mountain villages in New Zealand. Because they were nature-based stories, they felt deflated and pale when told outside of any other context than the environment they came from. I slowly learned when I returned to New Zealand, the dangers that face the so-called pagan faiths. If the nature was endangered, the culture and ideas were as well.

Stella August was twenty-four years old when I visited New Zealand in 2004. Her mother is British, and her father was Maori. Stella's mother left home when Stella was nine, and she lived with her younger sister Wiki and their father on their tribal land on Kairakau Beach, a remote windswept coastline at Hawke Bay. Stella learned of her affinity for the sea and rivers through her father, and it was the sea that took him in a boating accident when a rogue wave overturned his skiff. He drowned, just off the beach near their home. Stella was sixteen at the time.

When her father died, Stella contacted her mother and asked if she would return to their tribal land to live with her and Wiki and help out on the farm. The mother had not set foot there since she'd left, years before. She agreed to return and has lived there ever since, tending to a herd of sheep and cows with her boyfriend Ray, and the help of cigarettes and cold Lion's Red beer to pass the time.

Drinking was just another part of living out there, a good hour and a half from the nearest supermarket.

Since Stella's father died, the elders of Ngati Kahagnunu had looked after her. Because of her love for the sea, she studied marine biology in college on a fellowship from her *iwi*, Ngati Kahanunu. When I met up with her, she had just handed in her master's thesis, was working part time in a coffee shop, and was organizing what she'd termed an "eel adventure" throughout New Zealand, for me.

Our scheduled meeting point was a Burger King on the second roundabout in Hamilton about a two-hour drive south of Auckland. She was wearing board shorts and a sweatshirt with surfer logos, and would not look directly into my eyes.

"You brought the sun," she said.

It had been raining for three weeks straight and New Zealand waterways had experienced some of the biggest floods in a lifetime. It was good weather, I supposed, for an eel.

We talked briefly about our itinerary there in the parking lot. Toward the end of our trip, I'd arranged for us to stay at a fishing lodge on the Mohaka River called Poronui Ranch. "That will be a good chance for us to sit down and make sure we both know where we're coming from," Stella said, with slight severity. "About what you're going to write."

I assured Stella that I would be sympathetic to the Maori culture. But she worried me when her tone turned defensive. She mentioned that the stories we would hear during our eel adventure were the "intellectual property" of her people. The Maori people had a right to be wary, even protective—the English colonists had lied to them, stole their language, customs, their spirituality (replacing it, with mixed results, with Christianity), and land. The latest assault in the eyes of some Maori, was the success of the film *Whale Rider*, about a young Maori girl learning the indigenous customs from her grandfather. Hollywood had made all kinds of money on this "intellectual property," and the Maori people hadn't received any measurable compensation. It was clear that Stella was conflicted about being my guide. She seemed happy that I'd shown interest in learning about her culture and sharing it with whoever cared to read, but also reticent about making known what was sacred and very personal, and being paid, though not much, to do so.

The movie *Whale Rider*, Stella agreed, was actually a very realistic portrayal of modern Maori life, especially in the instance of a young girl inheriting the culture from her reluctant grandfather, who traditionally would have passed that knowledge orally to a boy. But the boys in the modern Maori culture had no patience, they had attention problems, were fidgety, and more often then not got into trouble with drugs and alcohol. It was young women like Stella and her sister who were inheriting the faith and staging a cultural revival.

"I'm here," I said, repeating sentiments I'd shared in numerous e-mails over the previous months, "because of a genuine fascination for a very strange and fascinating fish."

She paused before answering. "Well, you and I are alike, then," she said. "But I didn't always like them. Eels. When my father brought them home, I wouldn't go near them. But my interest in fish is definitely because of my father." A lot of people were suspicious of me, Stella said, when she rang them up and told them she wanted to bring an American by to do research on eels in Maori culture. "The first thing they said was, 'Why does he want to know?' They've got a lifetime of experience, which traditionally is shared with those in their *hapu*, or sub-tribe, within the *iwi*. They're suspicious of science."

"I'm not a scientist," I protested.

She knew that, she said, but there was something she wanted me to understand about her culture. "I went to this big eel conference where the leading eel experts in New Zealand had gathered. Don Jellyman, a pakeha, probably the most famous, he's at NIWA"—the National Institute of Water and Atmosphere—"and was delivering a paper on his attempts to track eight large migrant eels from the river mouth to their spawning grounds with radio transmitters. He explained that all sign of the radio transmitters had been lost once the eels reached the edge of the trench off the east coast of the South Island. When Don sat down, Kelly Davis, who I hope will be available to see us, got up to represent the Maori. He addressed Don directly, saying, in front of everyone, 'Why do you need to know where they go? The juvenile eels come up the river in spring, the adults migrate out in the fall. My people have known this forever. What good will it do the fish to find the house where they breed?' Don was speechless."

I listened. And I learned not to assert too much, to ask too many questions, and to listen as best I could to what these individuals on our eel adventure had to share. Not an hour went by that Stella did not remind me that we would be meeting with the most knowledgeable people on eels in all New Zealand, that I was privileged to have time with them. As she advised, I had brought *koha*, or personal gifts, to give to them all: small art works I'd made, signed books.

Over lunch at her flat, Stella told me more about her love of eels, and about the time she spent with them. "Why do we have to try to understand everything that isn't understandable? Everyone wants to unlock everything. I'm conflicted because I'm Maori: I don't want to know where they go, and yet I've studied their movements in the rivers in a scientific way."

Our conversation returned to the idea of the *taniwha*, that important element of Maori stories. In the *Reed Dictionary of Modern Maori*, the translation of *taniwha* is "water monster, powerful person, ogre." It can make itself known at certain times to certain people, sometimes to warn them of danger. Stella pointed out that the most common form in which a *taniwha* shows itself is an eel. Usually a large eel.

"If you spear an eel that's a *taniwha*, or catch it in a net, it will cry like a baby or bark like a dog, or even change colors," Stella said. "If you killed a *taniwha*, you'd have a *matuku*, or curse, and start going crazy, like you're possessed."

In that case, she added, it meant you had broken *tapu*—something sacred, or off-limits.

Three weeks later, Stella and I were huddled in a tent, stranded in the bush with DJ. He had taken us up a small tributary of the Mata River he called Stony Creek, in the northeast corner of the North Island, so we might fish for trout and search for the big eels that often live in the headwaters of streams. The creek was in a remote piece of tribal land, thick with punga, the exotic looking New Zealand fern tree, the fronds of which hung over emerald plunge pools inhabited by large trout and eels. We'd been dropped off via helicopter four days before. In a driving rain, the river in the canyon rising, we waited for the weather to clear so we could be picked up at the appointed time. A day later, we were still in the tent, wet as water rats, hoping for a break in the rain so we could try to start a fire.

After four days in the bush, DJ was just starting to get comfortable enough with me to tell me what was really on his mind. He was, like all Maori I had come into contact with, a little reserved at first, even intimidating in his silence. His stature was imposing, tall and thin with dark skin, but strong, like a Native American cowboy. He had a long sage nose and a casual swagger and wore a silver pocket watch in a leather sack on his belt. The rain let up and, toward evening, the sky began to clear. Relieved that we'd probably fly out in the morning, we slipped from our tent, stretched our legs, and, after some effort, got a fire started. DJ pulled out his skillet to cook the two remaining steaks we'd brought. "I've seen some crazy things out here," he said, poking the fire, making a spot over the coals for the skillet to sit. "But it's more the things I've felt and haven't seen that stick with me."

DJ started to talk about the skillet and its history. He called it his family heirloom but with his Kiwi accent it sounded more like "hair-loom." His short "a" and "i" sounds were long and drawn out, pronounced like "ee"'s. I asked DJ if he had any stories of *taniwha*. I was eager to know more. But, as I was learning, he wouldn't be rushed.

"This was my dad's skillet," DJ said. "Most of the places I take people fishing and hunting in the bush are places I went hunting with my father as a boy. If I'm in an area I don't know I ask local people in the pub, the bros, or I have a yarn with the publican. I never take my white clients along, 'cause if I do, the bros won't talk. They won't even move their leeps, mate." DJ stoked the fire with a stick. A cool wind blew down the river valley.

One time, he said, he was up in the bush with friends on horseback, pig hunting. "We'd camped under this permanent shelter that heed been there foreever. We'd had a long day of hunting and we were cooking a big feed and all of a sudden the bush weent silent. You normally hear all these noises, the crickets and that, like now. Well, it all weent quiet, and then the horses started acting up, and then the dogs weent balleestic. We're told, you know, don't ever camp on the track, you're neever supposed to, but we deed, we were set up right on it." DJ flipped the steaks.

"I'm always trying to reason, and I thought, there's a logical reason why the horses are acting up. An expeerienced horseman could ride up in the dark and spook the horses. People do it all the time. It's possible. I waited for that horseman, but he neever came."

Stella asked if he had grabbed a gun.

"What good's a gun?" DJ asked. "I was in my sleeping bag with the top pulled over my heed. And then come this roar. I don't know how to describe eet, and I never heard eet since, and I'm not superstitious, but I have no way of explaining eet. Eet was like a jeet eengine, and loud, like deefening. I don't know what to call it, like a *taniwha* or what."

DJ split the steaks three ways and we sat on logs and ate. We made the fire bigger and were soon dry. To hear a personal *taniwha* story from DJ made me think. This wasn't a dry story told by a European ethnographer, it was an account told in the element from which it was derived. And the impact of the experience was as loud as the monster in his story. It was more impactful than a ghost story at a campfire, because you knew for sure by his tone and seriousness that DJ had experienced it, and had no logical reason to explain it. But in his spirit, in his Maori spirit, he believed it was a *taniwha*.

DJ knew I'd come to New Zealand to learn about eels in Maori culture. He'd been waiting for the right moment to tell me his version of things.

"The way I see eet," he said, salting his steak and taking a bite, "there are three players in a New Zealand river: the rainbow trout, the brown trout, and the eel. The eel is the cultural factor. The eel is the Maori factor. The trout is the British colonist. Everyone forgets about the eels because you don't see them. They're out at neeght mostly. You don't see the eel, but he's theere, and he's releentless in his eefforts to catch the trout. He's always stalking them. Ultimately he's the survivor. He can take the other two out eeny time. He might wait years to catch theem. 'Til they geet old and weak. The eel's got time. The eels been theere long before the British put theem in the rivers," DJ threw the gristle from his steak in the fire, "they'll be there eefter. We call that *morehu*, the survivor."

DJ's was a common sentiment among Maori in the early twenty-first century. The culture, buried underground for the better part of a hundred years, was re-emerging with a vengeance, and sometimes with some resentment for the descendents of the British colonists. The eel, I would come to find, was not only "sacred," but one of the most important creatures in Maori culture for a host of reasons—the lubricious creature seducing the wife of gods, a synonym of the penis, a protector, and the main traditional food source for the inland Maori. But most importantly, the eel was a symbol of what we were losing, the world over—that the loss of nature would equal a loss of culture, especially indigenous "pagan" culture, a loss of connection to the earth, and loss of soul.

This new world was not one I wanted to live in. And I began to rethink the assumptions I'd made about indigenous people from the things I'd read in the work of Campbell and Elsdon Best. I'd treated the stories about *taniwha* in the way that they were presented, as myth. But from the seriousness of tone in my conversations with Stella and DJ and others, I was finding out that what I had perceived as "mythology" was indeed very much a part of the spiritual reality of the Maori. And in many ways, the eelian thinking about nature, as an idea that couldn't be, and didn't need to be, pinned down, that would persevere, began to make a lot of sense.

As far as spirituality went, the idea at the source of, for instance, the Christian faith was much more portable and versatile than the core of the nature-based faith. The success of the Christian "myth" it occurred to me, sitting in that tent in the rain, listening to DJ's story, was its versatility, malleability, and portability. The Christian religion was based on the belief that the son of God, in human form, came to earth to take away our sins; this can be understood by any human anywhere in any environment in the world. The concepts of the Christian religion are promoted both in buildings built by people and in the open air. The difference with a nature-based faith like that of the Maori (and other indigenous peoples around the world) is that once you lose the Nature that the spiritual system is based on, you are also in danger of losing spirituality. If the eel is endangered is the Maori sense of spirituality also endangered? If a young Maori boy does not see a giant eel, is not awed by that six-foot writhing pile of muscle, can he have faith, truly, in a *taniwha*? What has happened to a large extent in the Maori culture is that the British immigrants began to destroy the foundation of the Maori faith. The Acclimitization Society (the established Department of Wildlife if you will) introduced trout to make the streams friendly for settlers from England, and they trapped the large eels, leaving them stranded on the bank, because they saw them as a threat to the introduced fish. Kelly Davis, an old Maori I spoke to later in the trip, said that he used to walk the banks of the river with his dad, kicking these large stranded eels back into the river. The British knew the quickest way to eradicate an indigenous culture, remove the creatures that are spiritually and gastronomically closest to them. The end of the eel for the Maori (and the whale and the kiwi) was the end of an idea. It is precisely what the Europeans did to the American plains Indians when they slaughtered hundreds of thousands of bison. Is there a connection between the loss of such natural wonders in New Zealand and the disillusioned youth of the Maori, especially the boys, who are turning to drugs and mischief instead of nature? When their energies and aggressions are not spent running around fishing and hunting do they turn to hostility? Toward their spouses, toward the government, toward everything? What becomes clearer and clearer to our 21st century society, with all our wisdom and reason, is that, although it is harder to imagine myth as a spiritual reality, we do need some form of spirituality. I found when I was in New Zealand, that when I let my "reason" fade, and imagined a giant eel living in a deep pool, one that warned off children from a dangerous current, or protected the surroundings of a place, or heard stories of areas of forest that were sacred, where there is a spiritual silence, where "no birds sing," I felt whole, I felt motivated, and I felt human.

Colors that Attract Bass

OZARK RIPLEY

How long ago man became acquainted with the fact that certain fish were attracted by colors it would be difficult to state to a certainty. Doubtless even the occupants of land in primeval days must have noticed it. If we were better posted on the subject anglers could tell more about the origin of certain lures, and upon which now for solution we have to resort to conjecture. Long discourses from time to time have been published about it, and yet have led to nothing tangible. But we do believe that the bass were not fished for with artificial lures until a short while before the Civil War, and then to no great extent. The early anglers had color fads and the present generation is just as devoted to them.

At one time a man who made for commerce artificial lures declared that blue was the most attractive color for game fish, especially bass and pike. His proofs were as far stretched as his logic. Nothing, however, did he mention about shades. His lures were of the spoon or spinner type. Later he must have suffered considerable alteration in his belief. His present all-potent lure relies on black and white for attractiveness and the model of his marvel has been changed very much.

The color subject for years has effected much study on the part of anglers, and the experts now agree that no one color is more dependable than another. Still, only recently a noted angler wrote a long article on the attractiveness of red, backing it up by his long experience. But his findings are somewhat ambiguous, as he started on the subject as applied to bass and confined his principal argument to pike.

As we consider colors, seemingly the ones who are most decided in their opinions toward one or the other are bait and fly casters who feature spinners to enhance the potency of their lure. It leaves this part unsolved—whether the fish they caught rose for the flash of their spinner or the colored fly trailing behind it. Perhaps by right we might call them color faddists, because each is positive that his statement of color effectiveness is irrefutably correct. Among them are many who are equally devoted to white as red or blue. And then comes along the other chap who fishes constantly and he is firm in his conviction that bass are better attracted by a contrast of colors than by any other presentation. There is some dependence to be placed on this, because so many anglers agree along the same channels most popular artificial baits follow color contrasts strongly. And one must remember that the selling of artificial baits successfully is guided a good deal by anglers' opinions.

Not long ago I met one of the largest manufacturers of wooden casting baits. He is what might be called a ubiquitous everlasting fisherman. He fishes North during the summer months, and winter finds him steadfast at the sport of bait casting for bass in Florida. Unlike most men commercially interested in baits, he says none is the best, and he would gladly give his advice on any fishing subject but colors. He has his favorites, plays them assiduously, and then acknowledges that they don't work out the same for all other anglers. He attributes all the criticisms ever aimed at his head to having the temerity in his younger days to state that on certain days one color surpassed the other as a killer.

The angling public accepted his statement broadly; not as he meant it, for waters he knew about and not others.

There is this much to colors while fishing with artificial lures for bass: If a man has a fixed belief in a color he will depend upon it, and give it greater opportunities to perform by shooting it into the places where striking fish ought to be.

How far anglers have ventured in colors is discernible from the supply of lures. The color variations are wonderful, the contrasts many and, then on top of this, the close-to-nature coloration is now among the most conspicuous.

We have all sorts of casting baits supposed to resemble some kind of live minnow or water denizen. The shape is there and the blending of pigments brings out effects often never seen in Nature. And yet some of these wooden lures, replicas of large minnows, are just so attractive in one conception of the creator as the other. When they depart from minnow resemblance in color, it matters not to bass. There are no minnows with red heads and white body, blue heads and white body, red heads and gold or silver body that live in lakes or streams. Still they will lure as many bass to their doom, as man in his wildest fancy, considering the available supply of this popular fish, expects. They are instances of color contrasts not by any means to be overlooked, anglers having such success with them.

A bass whether at play—if that is the time of the striking humor—or when hungry, perhaps is keyed up like a ball player to catch a ball, a hunter or some one playing a game that requires rapid concentration of their mind and sight on an object. Let it be the ball player, visualizing the ball to come at any moment in flight can be deceived into reaching out for and catching another of different color if it suddenly appears apparently from nowhere in his line of vision. This is not offered as the true explanation why colors attract fish but rather in the way of a suggestion and why bass strike lures.

A Dive for a Big Fellow

EDWARD C. KEMPER

It is not possible to write concerning one's own most tragic fishing moment without the frequent use of the personal pronoun. With this apology allow me to begin at the beginning: I am sure that I was a born fisherman. Mind you, I do not say "angler," the refined product, but "fisherman," a human being descended from an ancestor common to Ike Walton, Will Dilg, Sam Spicer, Van Campen Heilner, and some others we all know more or less; or ascended by the process of evolution from some ancestral persecutor of the finny tribe common to the fish hawk, the kingfisher and some others of like stripe whom we have all admired and envied on occasions.

By the time I had reached the glorious age of seventeen I was equipped with a nine-foot jointed rod, reel, linen line, and Cincinnati bass hooks. These deadly weapons were supplemented on all occasions by lots of creek minnows, which thrived well but not numerously in the big spring branch on my grandfather's plantation in the Shenandoah Valley, in Virginia, where I was raised. The south branch of the Shenandoah River is formed by the confluence of three smaller streams, known as North, Middle and South rivers. It was in the last-named stream, which works its arduous way along the foothills of the Blue Ridge Mountains, that most of my fishing was done, for there the conditions were ideal. The water was clear and cold. There were many riffles and swift chutes, and between them deep pools or stretches of quiet water.

My brother Bill and I fished together. Most of the time we waded, floating the live minnows down with the current to the ledges and pockets ahead of us. At other times, when the days were hot, we fished from the bank, in deeper water, and if the bass neglected us, we fell back on the basket of fried chicken always provided. Unfortunately we could not go fishing as often as we wished. We were permitted to go but every other day—the off days being spent in catching creek minnows for the following day's sport.

By some chance there came a day when Bill went elsewhere than bass fishing, so I went alone, loaded with a fine bucket of creek minnows, a fried chicken and the customary hopes for a big day. In this last I was not I was not disappointed. It proved to be the biggest and the saddest in what are now many days of angling experiences. To that time the biggest bass we had caught was a four-pounder, landed by Bill, and used by him as an irrefutable argument that he was a better fisherman than I. To catch one bigger was my burning ambition.

Upon reaching the river bank I decided to try out some favorite places by using brook trout methods—stalking the quarry, one might say. Imagine a big sycamore tree standing out from the banks into a wide mountain stream, its far-flung roots washed by a steady current of clear water slipping along five feet deep over a bottom of solid rock. By crawling out on the bank-fastened roots I was able to gain a place beside the trunk of the old sycamore and to cast a juicy minnow under its spreading branches toward the center of the stream.

For a moment nothing happened. The minnow worked downstream with the current some twenty feet out from the base of the old sycamore, and I was about to draw him in for another cast. It was never made. The line tightened and moved upstream quickly and steadily. There was going to be plenty of action. The boy at the end of the rod clung tensely to his perch and bided his time, hoping for the conventional pause and second run with its obvious import. But the bass had other intentions. He continued his steady course upstream until the line grew thinner and thinner on the spool, and there was nothing for me to do but strike.

Holding the reel handle and tightening the line until I could feel the pull of the fish, I yanked the hook and held on. And then the biggest, blackest, most formidable looking small-mouth I have ever seen (then or since) came to the top of the river. He didn't jump—he just looked around, rolled over, and started for the other side of the river. Had he come into the shore and gone under the roots of the big tree the tragedy would have happened sooner than it did. What to do was a problem. To land such a bass from that perch was impossible. To follow him, and try to land him on the other side of the river was a possible course; to tire him out, kill him on the rod, and lead him around the roots of the tree and back to the bank was another. It was the one I selected. Much now depended on the line and the rod. Both held in spite of a terrific strain, and the bass concluded to come back a bit and go upstream again. He did, not only once but several times.

By luck he was held out of the tree roots, and into the current, which had some advantages for him, and more for me. Finally he began to tire, to come to the top, and I could see him plainly in the dark, clear water. His red eyes glistened and his great fins worked back and forth. My heart beat like a trip-hammer, and I was frightened. I had hooked a bass so big and so strong that I didn't know what to do next, nor what the end was going to be. Then there came a change in the battle. The red-eyed warrior was visibly tiring and his efforts were becoming weaker. Slowly I worked back on the big roots, on which I had crawled out, holding the fish out from the tree, and now apparently exhausted on the top of the water.

At last I reached the bank below the tree. It was rocky, but not so steep, and I was soon at the water's edge, the great bass almost within my grasp. I thought he was done for, that he was beaten, that I had him. I bent and reached for his lower jaw, and at that cursed moment the gut on the hook, frayed to a shred, snapped in two and the big bass was free. He floated for an instant and then convulsively started for the bottom. Like a flash I threw the rod aside and sprang at him, into the water, with both hands gripping at him and on him, desperately striving to hold him against my chest but for a second, to sink some grip into his big body that would not slip. He was too quick. In a trice he was gone, and there I stood empty handed, up to my arms in cold water, exhausted for lack of breath. It was a bitter defeat administered by a worthy foe.

What did I do then? I went ashore blazing with anger. I didn't feel the wet clothes. I swore that I would some day catch that bass and be revenged. But I never did.

Only a year ago, after fifteen years' absence, I went back and fished from the roots of that sycamore tree for perhaps the hundredth time since the great victory of the biggest small-mouth I ever saw. All I got of him was experience, and a strange idea which formulated itself in later years, that any boy of seventeen who would so instantly spring into the water after escaping quarry must be a born fisherman, like an osprey or a kingfisher.

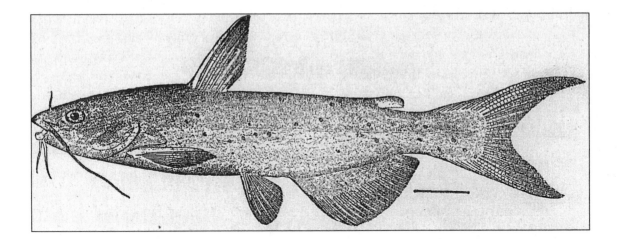

A Wise Ol' Cat

GEORGE V. TRIPLETT

I doubt whether any one of us can recall a more genuinely tragic moment than when his first little two-inch shiner wriggled off the hook and dropped back into the bosom of the old horse-pond. But that was in our chrysaloid stage before we had acquired the philosophic spirit in this greatest of all games of chance. Later we discovered that all angling has in it the blessed element of chance. If it were otherwise—quoting Dr. Van Dyke—it would "rob life of one of its principal charms and make fishing too easy to be interesting." Nevertheless, I have always somehow wished . . .

It was a long time ago and the retrospect brings up many things a bit alien to our modern sporting annals. For instance, in those days jugging was a gentleman's sport. This is not a "gone-are-the-days" lamentation—old anglers will know what I mean. Jugging was a form of fishing popular with our forefathers, like the netting of quails and the baiting of bears. It was a river sport and required plenty of room and patience and muscle. Almost any serene summer afternoon, when the old Ohio was drowsing along as clear and unruffled as the surface of a mirror, the juggers could be seen pulling their boats up towards the bend above town. To their jugs or buoys they would attach short lengths of strong cord, with big hooks, baited with liver or chunks of fat pork. The jugs would be cast overboard, about one hundred feet or more apart, the boats leisurely following them down the channel. Now and then a jug would disappear or go zigzagging across the river, and then there would be an exciting chase and the possible capture of a big channel cat that might tip the beam at fifty or a hundred, or even two hundred pounds.

One day when I was watching one of these strenuous exhibitions I got an idea. Why not go after one of those big fellows with rod and reel? That was before the big-game sea-anglers had begun to win buttons by conquering giant tunas and tarpons, but I must have had the budding faith of the Order, for that little idea grew and grew until it reached maturity. I became too obsessed by it to wait for a peaceful afternoon, and so an early midsummer morning found me pulling my boat up towards a long, low-water ledge of rocks that jutted out into the river almost to midchannel.

I doubt whether I have ever been able to make much improvement in my outfit— an old-time, one-piece, hand-made cane casting rod, light, strong, resilient and balanced to a hair, a valorous old smooth-running reel and a coil of sea-grass line, boiled to the fraction of a second in linseed oil and polished until it was almost transparent. That was the outfit with which I went forth to conquer a 200-pound channel cat.

I landed at the outer point of the ledge where the channel ran close in and deep. Baiting my hook with a generous slab of pork, I cast out. The big cork drifted down with the current for about a hundred feet and I awaited results. It was a long wait and the July sun was mounting higher and growing hotter. With another rig I skittered about for smaller fishes. Then suddenly the big cork disappeared and the reel began to buzz. When the cork bobbed up some fifty feet further away and started to perform queer antics I began to have expectations. Later on they assumed much acuter form. At last I had hooked a big channel cat. I had never caught anything heftier than a bass on that fine sea-grass line, but I had the broad Ohio all around me and the day was still young. It is true my hopes hung by a slender thread, but it was oiled sea-grass and my faith was that of all old-timers. With such a line they would have gone forth cheerfully to battle with a whale.

I have written elsewhere of the strength, tenacity and resourcefulness of a channel cat. This one was too busy ploughing the sandy bottom of the river or doubling and diving out in the deep water for me to learn whether he was just an ordinary rampageous cat or one of those dynamic veterans that I had seen tow a two-gallon jug at torpedo-boat speed. But at last I saw him. I had worked him around the inner side of the point and as he swung close in I could take his full measure. There is a term in the sportsman's lexicon called buck ague. If I did not contract a fully developed case of it just then I certainly had violent premonitory symptoms. But I held on to the rod and the sea-grass line held on to the fish.

Again and again he rushed off to deep water and as often I succeeded in bringing him in. I could see him plainly in these closer rushes and while doubtless he has grown some in my memory since that eventful morning, he seemed to be just about as big as I was, and I realized, then and there, that there was either the making of an angler or a champion channel cat out on the end of that lonesome ledge. I have never seen a big channel cat that knew when to quit. When they lie quiescent and appear to have given up, you had better corral your wits. You'll need them. It was so in this case. Off again, on again, gone again . . .

But of course that sort of thing could not go on all day. In fact probably it didn't last as long as I now think it did.

Finally I managed to coax my fish into a shallow cove where I could give him the *coup de grâce*. That is a very good way to put it now. I am willing to extend to this particular cat such assurance of my most distinguished consideration, though I wasn't thinking in such polite terms then. I had waded out into the water up to my knees and the time seemed to have come for eventualities. The big cat evidently had reached the same conclusion. When I started to maneuver him into a narrow gravelly pocket, once more he broke for deep water. As he rounded a little saw-toothed sliver of Carboniferous sandstone that had lurked out there in the swift currents for a hundred or a thousand years—waiting for that super-moment—the reel suddenly ceased its humming, the sea-grass line sagged in the guides and I saw a short quivering length of it go trailing out towards the channel and then disappear forever!

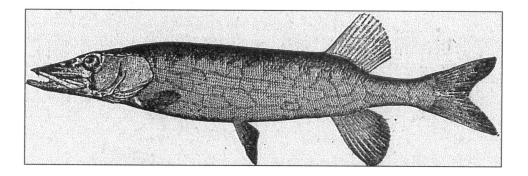

The Leopard of the Lake

LEONARD HULIT

The cooling days of early autumn had arrived, and Matt had been industriously plying his vocation of gathering frogs, and found they were not nearly so plentiful as earlier in the season, and he also realized that the gathering of the crops would soon begin with the farmers, and he usually had considerable work among them, taking corn and potatoes as pay. While he would greatly prefer gathering frogs or trapping, still corn and potatoes were essentials, and he would not shirk the duty when the time arrived. Already he had spoken to two farmers, offering his services, so there was plenty of work in line for him.

Aunt Mary, with her accustomed prudence, had been stocking their larder for the coming winter with such commodities as could be safely laid in, and a full barrel of flour as yet unopened stood in the corner of the kitchen, a thing which the little cottage had never before known. Thanks also to Matt's industry and good fortune, her purse was yet far from empty.

It was at the close of a blustery day. Considerable rain had fallen and there were fitful gusts of wind which swept the vines clambering about the little porch, now this way, now that, while there was a decided chill in the air.

"Where have you been gallivantin' now?" said the aunt as the lad came into the house, wet and with considerable mud clinging to his shoes, which roused her ire, and she said with her wonted sharpness, "I s'pose the scraper outside is a orniment an' not for muddy shoes."

Matt glanced down at his feet, then stepped outside and was soon industriously removing the offending mud; then he removed his shoes and dropped them in the shed with a clatter, and once more entering the kitchen sat down by the stove, his cap, as usual, draped to one side. He seemed buried in thought. His aunt, accustomed to these moods, said no more, knowing well that when the time seemed auspicious to him he would unbosom to her his conclusions.

For a long time he sat gazing out of the window. After a while he said: "Mr. Woodhull's goin' to send me some steeltraps when he's back in New York. I took a trip along the brooks an' bogs, and there's lots o' mus'rats this year, an' I seen some mink tracks, too. Fur'll be comin' on good time huskin's done. A dozen traps won't cost heavy. One good mink's skin'll about pay for 'em."

"You're a-goin' to be in the schoolhouse this winter," returned the aunt firmly, "an' you won't have time to tend to traps much. I want you to learn to read an' write good. You'll be called a reg'lar brook loafer next."

"Them as wants to let 'em," replied Matt stoutly. "Mr. Adams says dollars what comes honest is all right, an' I d'know but what mus'rat money's good as any, as long as it buys what we want; 'sides, them an' minks is pests. The's nights an' Sat'days to look after traps."

"It's your bein' along the brook an' in the woods all the time that I think most of, with your mind only on such things," responded his aunt. Matt made no immediate rejoinder, but got up and looked earnestly down the road, and then said: "I mos' forgot to say I met Mr. Stilwell to-day an' made a bargain with him for four loads of wood. I give him four days huskin' an' help him cart the wood when we want it."

Aunt Mary remained silent for a full minute, then asked: "How did you happen to think of the wood?"

"Well, I had sense to know we wanted it an' I knowed he had huskin' to do an' so when I was loafin' 'long the brook thinkin' o' nothin' in the rain I seen him in his meadow lookin' at where the mus'rats had been diggin' big holes all over, an' I made the wood bargain; 'sides, he is to give me ten cents apiece for all the mus'rats I trap on his land."

Aunt Mary looked the rebuke she felt and was framing her reply when a knock came on the door. "It's Mr. Adams," said Matt. "I seen him comin'."

That gentleman, clad in rubber clothing, took a seat, after receiving a warm welcome from the aunt. His many generous acts had won for him a warm place in her heart, and she was glad of his presence.

"Mr. Woodhull is going back to the city in a few days," began their visitor, after some commonplaces, "and I will soon leave on a business trip; so I just ran down from the store to see how you feel about trying for pickerel to-morrow if it does not rain too hard. The water is cooling down some, and if the weather is cloudy all the better."

Matt sat regarding his friend intently for fully a minute before making reply, then asked in his quaint way, "Is pickerel pike, Mr. Adams?"

"Well," he replied, "a pickerel is a pike, but a pike is not a pickerel," and he toyed with his watch charm, enjoying to the fullest the puzzled look on the boy's face. Matt slid down deeper in his chair, his hands clasping both knees, while his toe played abstractedly with the hearth of the stove. At length he said, "Unhook me, please, Mr. Adams, I've balked."

Aunt Mary and Mr. Adams both laughed at the drollery of the remark, and the gentleman then said: "The pike family is really a large one and embraces many important species, one of which is the pickerel, which can easily be told by its greenish color and chainlike markings along its side. It is found east of the Mississippi River in almost all streams, and is a good, game fish, frequently reaching the weight of from eight to ten pounds, while its cousin of northern lakes and rivers, a swift and hard-fighting fish called the muskellunge, often reaches the weight of from thirty-five to forty pounds."

Aunt Mary was deeply interested in the recital, and Matt, when Mr. Adams quit speaking, said, "What'd you say the name was?" Mr. Adams repeated the name, giving each syllable slowly, the boy repeating it under his breath, as could be told by the working of his lips. He made no further comment than "Twice as big as my carp, gosh!"

The following day proved dark and heavy. Clouds were scurrying across the sky as the three started for the old factory pond about five miles to the westward. It was a famous place for pickerel, as the pond had not been drawn down for many years, and large fish were reported to be had among the great patches of lily pads at the head of the stream.

Matt, as usual, sat in the rear of the wagon with his feet swinging, his discerning eye taking in every object within range. Minnows were in a pail near the lad, and had been taken from the creek before starting, as it was not certain that they could be found where they were to fish. Mr. Adams had remarked casually that he intended trying out some "plugs" he had with him, which elicited no reply from the lad. He merely cast an inquisitive look, remembering the "Lima bean" episode.

As soon as a boat had been secured the boy had gone down below the dam, where he was busily at work with a linen thread and small hook, and soon returned with several "sunnies," which he carelessly tossed into the boat with the remark: "Their bellies, with the fins left on, is prime for pike." As Mr. Woodhull rowed leisurely toward the head of the pond, Mr. Adams opened a tin box containing artificial frogs, as well as sundry plugs, spinners, and other paraphernalia entirely unknown to Matt. For a few minutes he gazed in mute wonder at the display and then asked bluntly, "What's them things?"

Mr. Adams explained the various articles and how they were used, none of which seemed to appeal to the boy's ideas of utility until a rather large "phantom minnow," with its green back and vari-colored sides was brought out. He examined it with a critical eye, turning it around and back, inspected the little spinners at the ends as well as the burrs of hooks on the sides, then said: "She looks as if the's some sense in tryin' her if you keep her goin' plenty an' jerk her about." Regarding the plugs he said nothing, and was soon busy arranging his line and hooks to his liking.

Both sides of the pond were lined with great patches of lily pads or "spatter-dock," as it was called, and it was well up to the head of the stream and between two patches of the lily pads that they made their first trial. The lad and Mr. Woodhull used minnows, placing their baits well up to the edge of the sheltering pads, while Mr. Adams, adjusting one of the incongruous-looking plugs, and with the help of the reel he was using, cast well over; then rapidly retrieving his line the lure could be seen darting from side to side as it approached the boat. Matt watched it eagerly, but made no comment. Several times Mr. Adams cast without result, and was changing to another type when Matt grabbed his pole with the quiet remark, "There she goes," and true enough his float was moving rapidly toward the pads with long dives, until it finally disappeared entirely. Then he struck and hooked his fish, and after much cutting around the boat Mr. Woodhull slipped the net under a fine three-pound fish.

There was just a trace of triumph in the lad's voice when he said, "I guess minnies is 'bout the thing when you want fish." Mr. Adams had put on his line one of those nondescript affairs with blunt nose and brilliantly painted sides, when it caught the lad's eye, and giving it a quizzical look he simply said, "That's worse than t'other one."

Standing up in the boat, Mr. Adams made a long cast over the stern and the plug landed with a splash close up to the pads, when there was another splash, followed by a great swirl, and the lure was sent whirling several feet over the water. Matt gasped and Mr. Adams chuckled. "That's on'y pike swearin'," said the boy as soon as he command words. "He's mad at seein' the thing an' tried to knock it out o' the pond."

It was such whimsical conceits that endeared the lad to his older companions, and it was an asset of which he was unaware.

Try as he would, Mr. Adams could get no more rises to his lure, while Mr. Woodhull and Matt each took a fish. "Seems 'ough it's a poor day for pluggin', Mr. Adams," said Matt with a giggle; "better fish with somethin' they want."

Mr. Adams made no reply, but seating himself he put on the phantom minnow and cast over to where he had had the first rise. As he began taking in line there came a splash and whirl in the water and his line began running out swiftly, while his rod bent and swayed under the impulses of a heavy fish. Matt became excited as the line cut swiftly through the water, and was worried, fearing the fish would get among the roots of the plants and tear loose, but there was a hand at the rod that had managed many such fish, and while giving full play to the quarry in open water, still he managed to steer it clear of all obstructions and gradually the pliant rod brought the unwilling captive nearer the boat in ever-narrowing circles.

Matt was standing ready with the landing net, his own rod neglected in his excitement. "Keep back the net," said Mr. Adams, as the fish made a rush by the side of the boat. "Never try to get a fish until it is led head first to the net, because when the slightest thing touches its tail it is sure to spring forward and is very liable to unhook." Following the instructions given, the net was placed directly in front of the fish on its next circle and was deftly lifted into the boat, much to the satisfaction of Mr. Adams and the joy of the lad, who fairly shouted, "Gee, what a whopper pike!" It was fully five pounds in weight and beautifully marked.

"This is the true pickerel," observed Mr. Adams, "and is clearly characterized by the chain-like links on the body, usually thirteen in number, on the center line from the gill opening to the tail. In colonial days it was known as the 'Federation Pike,' and still retains that title in some localities. It is always a bully among its fellows, depending more on hiding behind some cover, from which it darts out and seizes its prey, than on general pursuit. If we could have seen this fellow before he sampled my minnow we would have found him with body well behind the large roots of the lily pads and with head just protruding, watching every moving object, and when the splash came on the water and the bait began moving away his curiosity was aroused and he struck."

"He was a plum fool," said the irrepressible boy. "The's no sense as I can see in grabbin' what they don't know is good. The's no taste nor smell to that thing."

"Well," asked Mr. Woodhull, "don't you sometimes like to examine things you don't quite understand?"

"I suppose I do," was the answer, "but I don't bite 'em."

In all, ten fish were taken on that memorable afternoon, and all of good size. Matt had cleaned one of the sunnies and, using the belly with fins on, by skittering near the lily pads had hooked and landed one about the same size as the first he took.

"Seems 'ough they'll take a'most anything that's movin'," he commented.

"Yes," returned Mr. Adams, "there is nothing safe from their maws that is small enough for them to master. There are stories going about that are hard to believe true of the many things that have been found in their stomachs. Sure it is, however, that young ducks are not exempt, as well as many other objects. They have, as you can see, murderous teeth that, once set fast, are hard to release. They are a truly game fish, and are, in their way, as much so as either the trout or black bass, neither of which are in these streams."

As they rowed to the dam to make their start homeward Mr. Adams insisted on putting the large fish on Matt's string, saying as he did so: "Someone may give you a good price for it; anyway, you will have a beautiful specimen of the 'Leopard of the Lake.'"

A Big Fish, S-o-o-o-o Long

W. N. HULL

"Let's go blackfishing," said Will Potter, as we sat upon the broad veranda one beautiful morning after breakfast. "The tide is right to-day." And a party of four was soon made up, consisting of Will, Mabel, Fannie and the writer.

The first thing necessary was to provide bait. The best bait for blackfish is the fiddler. So we went back to the salt meadows to catch a quart or more of fiddlers. They look something like huge spiders, but have a shell like the crab, and good-sized pinching claws like the lobster. They live in holes and run along sidewise through the salt grass and sedge into the open places where water stands from the outgoing tide. You grab one as he runs, but had better see that he does not immediately grab you; he will pinch pretty hard if he gets a good hold.

Having collected a quart or so of these fiddlers in tin buckets, we gathered up the bamboo poles and started for the boat. As I passed the shed I felt a prompting to take with me a crab-net or dip-net. This impulse was so strong that I stopped to argue the matter.

"Take a crab-net, take a crab-net," said the prompter.

"Why should I take a crab-net? We are going fishing," I answered.

"Take a crab-net, take a crab-net," again urged the prompter.

"That's all foolishness," was the stubborn reply, and away I went with the party without the crab-net. How I regretted afterward that I had not obeyed the prompter!

A row of three miles brought us to good blackfish ground. It was close to the rocks that just showed above water when the tide was out, and off from which was deep water. Will was at the bow, Mable and Fannie in the middle, and I at the stern.

Blackfish bite best on the incoming tide. They suck along the rocks, feeding on what the tide has left there. What sport we had! Some one pulled in a fish every few minutes. They were big beauties, too—three, four pounds each. Presently Will gave a suppressed exclamation and when we turned we saw him standing up, grasping his pole tightly, and all excitement. He had hooked a big fish and was fighting to get him in.

Here is a royal battle—the struggle between a man and a fish! The man is strong, but hooks, lines and poles are weak, and blackfish are gamy. The man stands pale with excitement that almost destroys his judgment; the fish struggles desperately for liberty. The man lets the fish run, but keeps the line tight, trembling with fear lest line or hook break or the hook tear out of the flesh; the fish has no judgment, but with brute strength, dexterity and seeming cunning fights for escape. The man, if he is cool, calculates upon tiring out the fish, pulling upon him when his struggles cease or weaken; the fish, feeling this pressure, again exerts himself and darts away into the deep water, and if he catches the man off his guard in the tight line, he will give a sudden twist and a blow that will snap almost any line used to snare him.

The man says not a word, nor dare any of his companions advise him; it is his defeat or victory. Minutes are piling into half an hour, and yet the battle goes on. But the fish is weakening. Once he is pulled so near that we see his glistening side as he turns in the sunlight. The man gains confidence. This is a fish worth battling for. But away he goes again, and the line plays out. A word of encouragement from the girls, and again the captive is worked toward the boat.

Now he comes into everybody's view. An exclamation of delight bursts from the whole crowd: "What a fine fellow!" Now he comes so near that if I had obeyed the prompter and brought the crab-net I could have slipped it under him and made his capture certain. Up and up into the air he comes, a six-pounder, sure, almost into the boat, when the hook tears out and the fish falls back into the water and darts away, while the man drops upon the seat with a look of chagrin and disappointment upon his face hard to picture in words; but the Yankee ejaculation he utters is wonderfully expressive—"Gosh!"

Will could not be induced to cast his line again. He joked with Mabel and Fannie, baited their hooks, and tried to laugh off his disappointment, but nothing could bring him round to his own jolly self again except a return to land, a good dinner and a chance to tell the story of the big fish, s-o-o-o long, which he did not catch.

The 'Lunge

STEWART EDWARD WHITE

Dick and I traveled in a fifteen-foot wooden canoe, with grub, duffel, tent, and Deuce, the black-and-white setter dog. As a consequence we were pretty well down toward the water-line, for we had not realized that a wooden canoe would carry so little weight for its length in comparison with a birchbark. A good heavy sea we could ride—with proper management and a little baling; but sloppy waves kept us busy.

Deuce did not like it at all. He was a dog old in the wisdom of experience. It had taken him just twenty minutes to learn all about canoes. After a single tentative trial he jumped lightly to the very centre of his place, with the lithe caution of a cat. Then if the water happened to be smooth, he would sit gravely on his haunches, or would rest his chin on the gun-wale to contemplate the passing landscape. But in rough weather he crouched directly over the keel, his nose between his paws, and tried not to dodge when the cold water dashed in on him. Deuce was a true woodsman in that respect. Discomfort he always bore with equanimity, and he must often have been very cold and very cramped.

For just over a week we had been traveling in open water, and the elements had not been kind to us at all. We had crept up under rock-cliff points; had weathered the rips of white water to shelter on the other side; had struggled across open spaces where each wave was singly a problem to fail in whose solution meant instant swamping; had baled, and schemed, and figured, and carried, and sworn, and tried again, and succeeded with about two cupfuls to spare, until we as well as Deuce had grown a little tired of it. For the lust of travel was on us.

The lust of travel is a very real disease. It usually takes you when you have made up your mind that there is no hurry. Its predisposing cause is a chart or map, and its main symptom is the feverish delight with which you check off the landmarks of your journey. A fair wind of some force is absolutely fatal. With that at your back you cannot stop. Good fishing, fine scenery, interesting bays, reputed game, even camps where friends might be visited—all pass swiftly astern. Hardly do you pause for lunch at noon. The mad joy of putting country behind you eats all other interests. You recover only when you have come to your journey's end a week too early, and must then search out new voyages to fill in the time.

All this morning we had been bucking a strong north wind. Fortunately, the shelter of a string of islands had given us smooth water enough, but the heavy gusts sometimes stopped us as effectively as though we had butted solid land. Now about noon we came to the last island, and looked out on a five-mile stretch of tumbling seas. We landed the canoe and mounted a high rock.

"Can't make it like this," said I. "I'll take the outfit over and land it, and come back for you and the dog. Let's see that chart."

We hid behind the rock and spread out the map.

"Four miles," measured Dick. "It's going to be a terror."

We looked at each other vaguely, suddenly tired.

"We can't camp here—at this time of day," objected Dick, to our unspoken thoughts.

And then the map gave him an inspiration. "Here's a little river," ruminated Dick, "that goes to a little lake, and then there's another little river that flows from the lake and comes out about ten miles above here."

"It's a good thirty miles," I objected.

"What of it?" asked Dick, calmly.

So the fever-lust of travel broke. We turned to the right behind the last island, searched out the reed-grown opening to the stream, and paddled serenely and philosophically against the current. Deuce sat up and yawned with a mighty satisfaction.

We had been bending our heads to the demon of wind; our ears had been filled with his shoutings, our eyes blinded with tears, our breath caught away from us, our muscles strung to the fiercest endeavor. Suddenly we found ourselves between the ranks of tall forest trees, bathed in a warm sunlight, gliding like a feather from one grassy bend to another of the laziest little stream that ever hesitated as to which way the grasses of its bed should float. As for the wind, it was lost somewhere away up high, where we could hear it muttering to itself about something.

The woods leaned over the fringe of bushes cool and green and silent. Occasionally through tiny openings we caught instant impressions of straight column trunks and transparent shadows. Miniature grass marshes jutted out from the bends of the little river. We idled along as with a homely rustic companion through the aloofness of patrician multitudes.

Every bend offered us charming surprises. Sometimes a muskrat swam hastily in a pointed furrow of ripple; vanishing wings, barely sensed in the flash, left us staring; stealthy withdrawals of creatures, whose presence we realized only in the fact of those withdrawals, snared our eager interest; porcupines rattled and rustled importantly and regally from the water's edge to the woods; herons, ravens, an occasional duck, croaked away at our approach; thrice we surprised eagles, once a tassel-eared Canada lynx. Or, if all else lacked, we still experienced the little thrill of pleased novelty over the disclosure of a group of silvery birches on a knoll; a magnificent white pine towering over the beech and maple forest; the unexpected aisle of a long, straight stretch of the little river.

Deuce approved thoroughly. He stretched himself and yawned and shook off the water, and glanced at me open-mouthed with doggy good-nature, and set himself to acquiring a conscientious olfactory knowledge of both banks of the river. I do not doubt he knew a great deal more about it than we did. Porcupines aroused his special enthusiasm. Incidentally, two days later he returned to camp after an expedition of his own, bristling as to the face with that animal's barbed weapons. Thenceforward his interest waned.

We ascended the charming little river two or three miles. At a sharp bend to the east a huge sheet of rock sloped from a round grass knoll sparsely planted with birches directly down into a pool. Two or three tree trunks jammed directly opposite had formed a sort of half dam under which the water lay dark. A tiny grass meadow forty feet in diameter narrowed the stream to half its width.

We landed. Dick seated himself on the shelving rock. I put my fish-rod together. Deuce disappeared.

Deuce always disappeared whenever we landed. With nose down, hind quarters well tucked under him, ears flying, he quartered the forest at high speed, investigating every nook and cranny of it for the radius of a quarter of a mile. When he had quite satisfied himself that we were safe for the moment, he would return to the fire, where he would lie, six inches of pink tongue vibrating with breathlessness, beautiful in the consciousness of virtue. Dick generally sat on a rock and thought. I generally fished.

After a time Deuce returned. I gave up flies, spoons, phantom minnows, artificial frogs, and crayfish. As Dick continued to sit on the rock and think, we both joined him. The sun was very warm and grateful, and I am sure we both acquired an added respect for Dick's judgment.

Just when it happened neither of us was afterwards able to decide. Perhaps Deuce knew. But suddenly, as often a figure appears in a cinematograph, the diminutive meadow thirty feet away contained two deer. They stood knee-deep in the grass, wagging their little tails in impatience of the flies.

"Look a' there!" stammered Dick aloud.

Deuce sat up on his haunches.

I started for my camera.

The deer did not seem to be in the slightest degree alarmed. They pointed four big ears in our direction, ate a few leisurely mouthfuls of grass, sauntered to the stream for a drink of water, wagged their little tails some more, and quietly faded into the cool shadows of the forest.

An hour later we ran out into reeds, and so to the lake. It was a pretty lake, forest-girt. Across the distance we made out a moving object which shortly resolved itself into a birch canoe. The canoe proved to contain an Indian, an Indian boy of about ten years, a black dog, and a bundle. When within a few rods of each other we ceased paddling, and drifted by with the momentum. The Indian was a fine-looking man of about forty, his hair bound with a red fillet, his feet encased in silk-worked moccasins, but otherwise dressed in white men's garments. He smoked a short pipe, and contemplated us gravely.

"Bo' jou', bo' jou'," we called in the usual double-barreled North Country salutation.

"Bo' jou', bo' jou," he replied.

"Kée-gons?" we inquired as to the fishing in the lake.

"Áh-hah," he assented.

We drifted by each other without further speech. When the decent distance of etiquette separated us we resumed our paddles.

I produced a young cable terminated by a tremendous spoon and a solid brass snell as thick as a telegraph wire. We had laid in this formidable implement in hopes of a big muscallunge. It had been trailed for days at a time. We had become used to its vibration, which actually seemed to communicate itself to every fiber of the light canoe. Every once in a while we would stop with a jerk that would nearly snap our heads off. Then we would know we had hooked the American continent. We had become used to that also. It generally happened when we attempted a little burst of speed. So when the canoe brought up so violently that all our tinware rolled on Deuce, Dick was merely disgusted.

"There she goes again," he grumbled. "You've hooked Canada."

Canada held quiescent for about three seconds. Then it started due south.

"Suffering serpents!" shrieked Dick.

"Paddle, you sulphurated idiot!" yelled I.

It was most interesting. All I had to do was to hang on and try to stay in the boat. Dick paddled and fumed and splashed water and got more excited. Canada dragged us bodily backward.

Then Canada changed his mind and started in our direction. I was plenty busy taking in slack, so I did not notice Dick. Dick was absolutely demented. His mind automatically reacted in the direction of paddling. He paddled, blindly, frantically. Canada came surging in, his mouth open, his wicked eyes flaming, a tremendous indistinct body lashing foam. Dick glanced once over his shoulder, and let out a frantic howl.

"You've got the sea-serpent!" he shrieked.

I turned to fumble for the pistol. We were headed directly for a log stranded on shore, and about ten feet from it.

"Dick!" I yelled in warning.

He thrust his paddle out forward just in time. The stout maple bent and cracked. The canoe hit with a bump that threw us forward. I returned to the young cable. It came in limp and slack.

We looked at each other sadly.

"No use," sighed Dick at last. "They've never invented the words, and we'd be upset if we kicked the dog."

I had the end of the line in my hands.

"Look here!" I cried. That thick brass wire had been as cleanly bitten through as though it had been cut with clippers. "He must have caught sight of you," said I.

Dick lifted up his voice in lamentation. "You had four feet of him out of water," he wailed, "and there was a lot more."

"If you had kept cool," said I, severely, "we shouldn't have lost him. You don't want to get rattled in an emergency. There's no sense in it."

"What were you going to do with that?" asked Dick, pointing to where I had laid the pistol.

"I was going to shoot him in the head," I replied with dignity. "It's the best way to land them."

Dick laughed disagreeably. I looked down. At my side lay our largest iron spoon.

We skirted the left-hand side of the lake in silence. Far out from shore the water was ruffled where the wind swept down, but with us it was as still and calm as the forest trees that looked over into it. After a time we turned short to the left through a very narrow passage between two marshy shores, and so, after a sharp bend of but a few hundred feet, came into the other river.

This was a wide stream, smoothly hurrying, without rapids or tumult. The forest had drawn to either side to let us pass. Here were the wilder reaches after the intimacies of the little river. Across stretches of marsh we could see an occasional great blue heron standing mid-leg deep. Long strings of ducks struggled quacking from invisible pools. The faint marsh odor saluted our nostrils from the point where the lily-pads flashed broadly, ruffling in the wind. We dropped out the smaller spoon and masterfully landed a five-pound pickerel. Even Deuce brightened. He cared nothing for raw fish, but he knew their possibilities. Towards evening we entered the hilly country, and so at the last turned to the left into a sand cove where grew maples and birches in beautiful park order under a hill. There we pitched camp, and, as the flies lacked, built a friendship-fire about which to foregather when the day was done.

Dick still vocally regretted the muscallunge as the largest fish since Jonah, so I told him of my big bear.

One day, late in the summer, I was engaged in packing some supplies along an old fur trail north of Lake Superior. I had accomplished one back-load, and with empty straps was returning to the cache for another. The trail at one point emerged into and crossed an open park some hundreds of feet in diameter, in which the grass grew to the height of the knee. When I was about halfway across, a black bear arose to his hind legs not ten feet from me, and remarked *Woof!* in a loud tone of voice. Now, if a man were to say *woof!* to you unexpectedly, even in the formality of an Italian garden or the accustomedness of a city street, you would be somewhat startled. So I went to camp. There I told them about the bear. I tried to be conservative in my description, because I did not wish to be accused of exaggeration. My impression of the animal was that he and a spruce tree that grew near enough for ready comparison were approximately of the same stature. We returned to the grass park. After some difficulty we found a clear footprint. It was a little larger than that made by a good-sized coon.

"So, you see," I admonished, didactically, "that 'lunge probably was not quite so large as you thought."

"It may have been a Chinese bear," said Dick, dreamily—"a Chinese lady bear of high degree."

I gave him up.

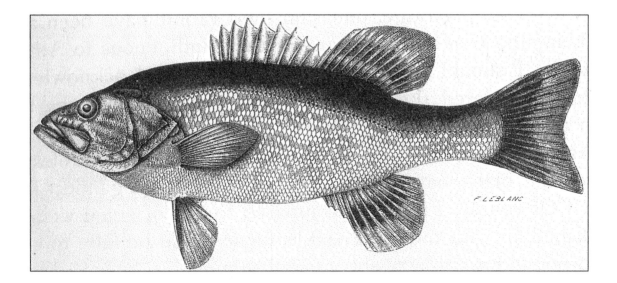

Slasher and the Shad

HART STILWELL

On the opening day of the Texas bass season eleven years ago, come May 1, I stayed home. Wandering around in the yard—probably daydreaming about the boys who were out snagging them—I stepped on a rake, and the handle came up and hit me so hard I have listed slightly to port ever since.

I took it as an omen, and from that day to this I have respectfully dedicated May 1 to a bronze-backed, big-mouthed fish. When I grow so old that I can no longer go forward under my own steam, then I'll have some loyal grandson bring me a tub of water with a bass in it, and I'll sit there in my armchair and angle for him. For I'm convinced that it's bad luck for me to stay away from the water on that opening day—bad luck and bad judgment too.

Still I never expect to catch a big one on that fateful occasion. I never have a ghost of a chance at that seven or eight-pounder that gets the prizes. And I'm not the only one. Maybe it's different in your part of the country, but down where I live we take it for granted that some rank dub who doesn't know the difference between a dry fly and a five-eighths-ounce plug will come waddling in with the biggest bass on the opening day—then go waddling out with the prizes with a smug look on his face.

After you see a thing like that happen year after year, you eventually reconcile yourself to it, like floods and high prices and the common cold. That is, I do. But not Judge and Doc.

As the years creep up on those venerable worthies in a manner that might discourage men of a weaker fiber, they derive from some unknown source a brand-new and youthful enthusiasm as the bass season rolls around each year. You will find them out there waiting for the crack of dawn, each vowing that he will bring in a bass the likes of which no mortal eye has ever gazed upon before.

And I guess that incident of the Slasher and the Shad was the high spot in their long career of setting aside the first day of May in honor of a sulky, savage, unpredictable fish.

Now, Doc and Judge have widely divergent views on the subject of catching bass, just as they have on about everything else where a difference of opinion is possible. And there's ample opportunity during two months of dry fishing to whip these views up to a climax for the opening day. So even though I don't ever get a bass worth mentioning, I do have the opportunity of hearing a vast amount of worldly wisdom upon the subject, and of seeing a minute fraction of that wisdom put into action by its proponents.

"Now, that," said Doc as we rounded a bend in Lake Olmito and hove into view of the little finger of land just above the bend where a dam had once been built, "is the home of the Slasher—right in next to that old elm stump you see there."

"Fiddlesticks," Judge suddenly exploded as he made a particularly hard cast, trying to reach some lily pads, and brought up short with a backlash.

"You don't believe it?"

"I don't know what you're talking about. I've got worries here of my own," and the Judge started milking the reel, while I eased off on the paddle. Doc cast steadily, doing a nice smooth job of it in that lumbering way of his. Yes, he'd fool a man who might think a big, fat fellow like Doc couldn't really handle tackle.

"We call this fish 'Slasher'," Doc explained, "because he's got a nasty habit of just slashing at a bait, then veering off and smacking it with his tail—or maybe bumping it. He intrigues me, the rascal."

"How do you know he's there?" Judge asked, and I felt it coming.

"Why, he lives there. I've had a dozen strikes from that fellow, and he's never felt a hook but once. That time I think I stuck him in the side as he passed."

"Fiddlesticks," Judge said again, and this time he wasn't talking about the backlash.

"Now, of course I haven't the slightest interest in winning prizes or other tokens that might be testimonial to ability that is well-established and recognized . . ."

"I got it out," Judge cut in, speaking of the backlash again. "Let's go on up the creek and get into some big ones." To Judge, Lake Olmito is and will always be a creek. It is, in reality, an old bed of the Rio Grande River, lined with beautiful ash, elm, ebony, and huisache trees, filled with clear water that harbors some of the finest fighting bass in our part of the country.

We had reached the spot where the Slasher was supposed to live, and Doc and Judge were both putting their lures in there, sliding them back into the water with that froggy plunk that marks the difference between a skilled bass fisherman and a dub. I eased off on the paddle, for I knew Doc would want to work the spot for several minutes, even if Judge didn't.

"There's no Slasher in that hole," Judge finally said. "No slasher, no cutter, no whizer—no, not even a perch. Let's move on."

"The old green-pasture hunting instinct working on him," Doc told me. And to Judge, "Do you come bass fishing so that you can race up and down here forever hunting something new?"

"I come to catch bass," Judge replied, "and when I see there are no bass in a spot, I like to move on to some other place. How long does it take you to search an empty barrel?"

"The Slasher hasn't stirred out of that hole in five years," Doc persisted. "Once I sneaked out here at night and tied a plug to that stump with a rubber band, the line leading to my rod down the lake there on the bank. I was determined to catch him. Next morning, I eased out in the boat and picked up the rod. I shoved the skiff out there to the middle, and then started working the lure back and forth . . ."

"Any man who would tie a plug to a tree with a rubber band ought not to be running around loose trying to tell sick people what's wrong with them. Let's move on."

At that instant the water boiled at Doc's plug and he leaned into the rod, but he leaned too soon. The fish missed. It was easy to see from the way he tore up the surface that he was a mighty bass.

"The Slasher," Doc sang out. "I told you he was there."

Both men got hot and started flinging plugs into that hole, while I gently eased the skiff back and held it in casting position. They kept tossing plugs in near the stump and working them out—Judge fast, as was his nature, and Doc gently and lovingly, as though each cast was his last for the season.

After perhaps five minutes of this Judge began to fret again. He is no man to cast at one spot by the hour, even though he knows there's a big fish in it. He insisted we move on up to the lake, and Doc insisted we work the hole a while.

"You take the boat and let me out," Judge finally said. "I refuse to cast in that one place all day."

Doc didn't answer for an instant. Then he said, "You take the skiff. I think I'll get out here and land that bass. He's in a striking mood, and I feel that all it takes is persistence."

Persistence. That was Doc's strong suit in life, and Persistence vs. Surprise was the basic conflict in their bass theories, Judge holding that the way to catch bass is to surprise them, while Doc argued that you simply had to wear down a fish's resistance.

"A bass is a strange creature," Doc explained as I paddled the boat toward the finger of land to let him out. "He's moody, and his mood will change at times with each cast of the plug. There is a definite cycle through which the fisherman must coax his fish."

"Cycles, persistence, pills—nuts," Judge exploded. "I've listened to that story now for twenty years, and never caught a bass by using it."

"At first the mood of your fish may be serene—calm and serene," Doc went on, with a sly smile at me, for Judge was anything but serene then. He was impatient to get going. Then perhaps after the fourth or fifth cast the mood changes to one of mild curiosity . . ."

"My mood is one of wild curiosity," Judge cut in. "I'm curious to find a place where I can catch some fish."

"Then with a few more casts of the plug, if these casts are delivered with the proper technique, his mood may change to annoyance." I had paddled the skiff up to the finger of land, and Doc was sitting there in the bow making a great show of getting his tackle in order, while explaining his bass theory. "Now we're getting places. That's the beginning—the first step toward victory. But don't get too anxious. The mood may suddenly shift back to serenity, and we have to start over at the beginning—start coaxing mildly . . ."

"I have passed through all the moods twice already," Judge said, "And now I'm rapidly getting back to anger."

"That's it," Doc said. "Anger. The test of a fisherman is to induce in his bass a mood of anger—burning, reckless anger. Then victory depends simply on a man's skill in handling his tackle.

We shoved off. "When I have to fiddle around studying the moods of a fish by the hour, then I'll take up needlepoint," Judge called as Doc clambered up the bank and we moved away. "You take a fling at them," he went on to me, moving to the stern of the skiff and taking the paddle. "Sometimes I marvel at the crackpot theories he can work out. Then again I marvel at myself for wasting my time listening to them. Now, it stands to reason that if you toss a plug out where a bass is and he sees it and doesn't strike—why, he isn't going to strike on the next cast, or the third cast, or the thirteenth or three-hundredth cast."

"But I have caught bass on the tenth or twentieth cast," I insisted.

"Then he just moved in. A bass strikes when he is surprised by the sudden appearance of something that resembles food. This tommyrot about getting one riled up so he'll hit a plug just for meanness simply amuses me. Who knows whether a bass is mad or hungry—or just simpleminded—or all three?"

That turned out to be a fairly dry fishing trip for Judge and me. I pointed out to him on several occasions that his Surprise Theory wasn't surprising anything much.

"They're not in a feeding mood," he explained.

The longer we fished, the faster Judge paddled, until we were gliding along at such a clip that I couldn't get the right action on my floating plunker. I'd cast, give it a quick plunk or two, and then we'd be dragging it along like a toy boat behind us. Finally I gave up and took the paddle, turning the fishing over to Judge.

He kept urging me to go faster, pointing to little spots up the lake where he was certain he would find a big one. And when we'd get there, he'd immediately see a better place, still farther away.

All he surprised, though, was a couple of little fellows just over the fingerling stage that nobody would care to mention in counting up the day's catch.

I took a whirl at fishing again and switched from a surface plunker to a small spoon and pork rind. I love to take my bass on a plunker, but it's a neat trick to turn when the surface of the water is as glassy as it was that morning.

I had better luck with the spoon, picking up a couple of fair-size bass.

Judge took another whirl at it and caught several bass just around legal size, which is about the size bass we usually take on the opening day. We put them all back. We don't carry a measuring stick, for we never take a bass out of the water unless he'll go three pounds, and the three pounds is judged by guess. At times the guessing gets mighty heated, and we have been known to bring in a bass weighing as little as two pounds. But when a man hasn't tasted broiled fish for several weeks he gets a warped idea of what it takes to tip the scales at three pounds.

As we rounded the bend we saw that Doc was standing in the same spot, casting gently away. When we neared him he made a motion for us to keep away. "I think I've got him almost in a mood for action," he called in a low voice. "He's reached the annoyance stage twice already, but slipped back into serenity again each time. I'm getting his feathers ruffled up now though."

"Let's move on," he called.

"Just a moment," Doc urged. "I'll get him now."

We waited several more minutes. There was another little flurry of arguing. Then Judge, always a man of action, stepped into the picture.

"Here I come," he said, and flung that big old floating plug of his at the stump, entirely ignoring Doc's warning for him to stay out of that hole. Doc figured he had staked a claim there, I guess, and it seemed there was some justice in his viewpoint.

Judge smacked that plunker up against the old stump, and started working it back rapidly, over water that had a slight riffle on it where the breeze got a clean sweep coming around the big bend.

There was a mighty swirl at the surface, and with a shout Judge jerked his surface lure so hard it left the water and jumped about halfway back to the boat. He'd seen the strike coming, and Judge can never wait for one when he sees it coming. The fish never touched his plug.

But as it boiled there at the surface, looking around angrily for that plug, Doc gently slid his bait into the water. The Slasher took hold.

Never will I forget the glow of happiness that spread over Doc's broad features as he leaned into that rod and brought forth a mighty leap from the Slasher in response.

And Doc gave us a fine example of fishing. He whipped that big bass down, even though there were several agonizing seconds when the Slasher went deep and got fast in the moss below.

"He'll go eight pounds," I guessed as I held him up and admired him after Doc had climbed back in the boat.

"Won't go much over seven," Judge said critically, and I gave him a dirty look. He examined the bass carefully, gazing down into its huge, open mouth in which a man could have stuck both his fists.

"Say, look at this," Judge said suddenly, reaching down into the bass's mouth.

"What is it?" Doc asked with concern.

"The tail of something sticking out." Judge reached down in the fish's mouth and pulled out a shad that the bass had evidently swallowed only a short time ago. The shad was fairly long and wide, but thin, a good, handy meal for a hungry bass of the Slasher's size.

"Now, can you imagine a bass striking right after stuffing himself full on a thing like that—so full he couldn't even swallow it?" Judge asked.

"You see? It's just as I said!" Doc cut in triumphantly. "Purely a matter of moods. I worked through the three cycles . . ."

"Fiddlesticks on your cycles," Judge cut in. "It was the surprise of that new kind of bait that got him."

Lost in admiration of the fish, I forgot my arguing friends. That was a noble bass, all right. The Slasher tipped the scales at seven pounds, eight-and-one-half ounces. But he didn't win anything. A dub who'd been using a surf rod and a lure weighted down with several sinkers ranged in a row above it, came waddling in with a bass that weighed seven pounds, ten ounces.

The Slasher had lost by an ounce and a half. And then Doc suddenly remembered that shad—the shad which Judge had so obligingly pulled out of the bass and tossed away. It weighed probably four or five ounces, so Judge had thrown away Doc's prize. The fireworks started. There was Doc, furious at the loss of his prize, vs. Judge, who argued—after his first shock—that no ethical angler would take a prize that way.

I haven't heard the last of it yet. And I probably never will.

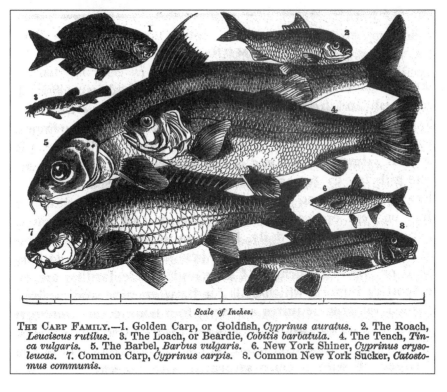

THE CARP FAMILY.—1. Golden Carp, or Goldfish, *Cyprinus auratus.* 2. The Roach, *Leuciscus rutilus.* 3. The Loach, or Beardie, *Cobitis barbatula.* 4. The Tench, *Tinca vulgaris.* 5. The Barbel, *Barbus vulgaris.* 6. New York Shiner, *Cyprinus crysoleucas.* 7. Common Carp, *Cyprinus carpis.* 8. Common New York Sucker, *Catostomus communis.*

Carp Fishing

FRANK FORESTER

This, I confess, I regard as very miserable sport; for though the fish is shy and wary, the difficulty in taking him arises only from his timidity and unwillingness to bite, and he is as lazy when hooked as he is slow to bite.

His proper haunts are deep, stagnant, slow-flowing streams, or ponds with muddy bottoms; and he lies under weeds, and among the stems and flat leaves of water-lilies, flags, and marsh-grasses.

Not indigenous to this country, he has been naturalized in the waters of the Hudson, where he is, for the present, protected by severe legislative enactments.

He will doubtless, ere long, become very plentiful; and as he is a rich fish when cooked *secundum artem*, and by many esteemed a great delicacy, he is likely enough to become a favorite with the angler.

Hofland thus describes the method of baiting the ground and fishing for Carp in England, and his directions are the best I have seen; they may be followed with implicit confidence:

"In rivers, the Carp prefer those parts where the current is not too strong, and where the bottom is marly, or muddy; and in lakes or ponds are to be found near beds of water-lilies, and other aquatic plants. Old Carp are very crafty and wary, and will not easily be taken by the angler; but young ones, when a pond is well stocked, may be easily taken in great quantities.

"Notwithstanding these instances of familiarity, it is by no means easy to make a large Carp familiar with your bait: to do this, the greatest nicety and caution must be observed; but if the young angler, who has been often foiled in his attempts, will patiently and implicitly follow my instructions, he will become a match for this cunning fish.

"Use a strong rod with running-tackle, and have a bottom of three yards of fineish gut, and a hook No. 9 or 10; use a very light quill-float, that will carry two small shot, and bait with a well-scoured red worm.

"Now plumb the depth with the greatest nicety, and let your bait just touch, or all but touch, the bottom; but you are not yet prepared; for a forked stick must be fixed into the bank, on which you must let your rod rest, so that the float will fall over the exact spot you have plumbed. Now throw in a sufficient quantity of ground-bait, of bread and bran worked into a paste, and made into little balls; or, in want of these, throw in the garbage of chickens or ducks; and all this is to be done on the evening of the day before you intend to fish.

"The next morning, if in summer, be at the pond-side where you have baited and plumbed your depth, by four o'clock at least, and, taking your rod and line, which is already fixed to the exact depth, bait with a small, bright, red, worm; then approach the water cautiously, keeping out of sight as much as possible, and drop your bait exactly over the spot you plumbed over night; then rest part of your rod on the forked stick, and the bottom of it on the ground.

"You must now retire a few paces, keeping entirely out of sight, but still near enough to observe your float; when you perceive a bite, give a little time; indeed, it is better to wait till you see the float begin to move off, before you strike, which you may then do smartly; and, as the Carp is a leather-mouthed fish, if you manage him well, there is no fear of losing him, unless the pond is very weedy. Be careful to have your line free, that, if a large fish, he may run out some of your line before you attempt to turn him; as he is a very strong fish, and your tackle rather light, you must give him careful play before you land him.

"The extreme shyness of the large Carp makes all this somewhat tedious process necessary to insure success; but I can safely assert, that I scarcely ever took this trouble in vain. Various baits are recommended for Carp,—such as green peas parboiled, pastes of all descriptions, gentles, caterpillars, &c.; but I have found the red worm the best, and next to this, the gentle, and plain bread-paste. Those who prefer a sweet paste may dip the bread in honey. Paste and gentle will answer better in autumn than spring. April and May are, in my opinion, the best months for Carp fishing; and very early in the morning, or late in the evening, is the best time for pursuing your sport."

The above mode of baiting bottom-grounds, and of fishing with the worm, in all its particulars, may be pursued with perfect success in all ponds and slow-running streams, for all the many species of the Carp family, which are, for the most part, the least carnivorous of fishes, and consequently the most difficult to allure, as the Bream, Roach, Dace, Chub, and Shiner, as they are provincially termed, though by no means identical with the European fishes of the same names. The Suckers (*Catastomi*), a sub-genus of the same family, will hardly take any bait whatsoever.

While fishing, as above described, both small river Perch and Eels of all sizes are likely to be hooked, as the baited bottom-ground allures all those species which seek their food at the bottom to its vicinity.

Bow-fin Fishing in the South Slang

ROWLAND E. ROBINSON

Sam Lovel and Antoine Bisette were taking after-dinner ease in a comfortable smoke at their summer camp near the mouth of Little Otter, and their talk was mostly of fishing.

"Ah'll tol' you what, Sam," said Antoine, reaching out lazily from his recumbent position, to the nearest stone, and knocking the ashes from his pipe, "Ah'll b'lieved dey ant no funs for feeshin' lak he was raght all raound here, me." Then getting to a sitting posture he tucked his legs crosswise after the not-latest fashion of a tailor, and began whittling a fresh charge from a plug of black tobacco. "'Cause you see, de feesh was so variety of it," he continued, looking askance at Sam to note whether this newly-acquired word was comprehended. "Dar was peek-erel an' pikes an' shad Ah ant ketch 'cause he come honly on de seine, an' basses, two kan' of it, Ah guess, tree, prob'ly, an' de sheephead you'll ant see yet an' de heel, he mek mah mouth tase good when Ah'll tink of it, an' de bull-paout mos' as mooch an' de mud-turkey more as bose of it. Dey was all good feesh, for mek mans felt plump when he ketch or heat it.

"Den dey was bow-fins an' leeng mek you lot o' fun for ketch, but, bah gosh! you ant want heat it an' say he good 'less you want tol' lie; no sah!

"Den dey was parches an' punkin' seed an' lot o' leetly feller dat was mek fer give de boy some funs, an' come in pooty good for mans when he can' ketch de beeg feller an' de bes' feller, an' he ant so bad for heat as no feesh 't all or bow-fins or clam.

"Bah gosh! Ah'll lak for see boy ketch all he can't carry of it an' feel so bigger as mans wid sturgeon, sem Ah'll was be feel when Ah was leetly boy in Canada an' carry home for show mah mudder all de ponkin seed Ah'll got.

"Ah'll weesh Ah'll can feel so beeg one tam more, but Ah'll can't 'f Ah ketch whale. Ah'll grow so modesty wid mah grow hol', an' Ah'll can't brag some more."

"It raly is tu bad 'baout you, Antwine," Sam remarked; "you'd orter git red o' your bashfulness."

"Ah'll can't help it, Sam. Dat was what Ah'll got for leeve wid Yankee so longs."

"But Ah'll tol' you, Sam, it mek me laft for hear dem feller up to Danvit brag when he come home wid string of traout baout half so longer as you finger of it, an' tol' all haow he ketch it an' when he ketch it, sem lak some mans tol' haow fas' hees hol' plug trot dat can't go so fas' as you roll barrel pot-ashins.

"What dem fellers tink dat go feeshin' for traout minny in brooks dey can step over, 'f dey feesh in waters lak dis, was so wide you can't holler crost it, an' ketch one feesh, dey mos' can't lift him?"

"Wal, I don't go altogether agin, nor with, what you're sayin', Antoine. The' is heaps o' fun in wrastlin with an' ol' lunker of a pickerel or pike, an' a bass is the beater o' the hull caboodle, fer he's julluk an' ol' sollaker of a traout, full o' fight an' tricks. But I hain't goin' tu go agin the fishing 'at I was brung up on, an' it makes me feel most as good as it did the fust time, when I go traoutin' along a lunsome brook with nobody anigh me but the birds a stoppin' their jinglin' tu watch me whilst I snatch aout the traouts, handsomer, 'f they be little, 'an any o' these mud-loafers.

"An' the smell o' the spruce an' balsam, sweeter 'n any these mashes affords 'cepten' them pond lilies, an' the wind a sythin' 'mongst 'em an' the brook allus a singin' an' invitin' you furder, to where it starts from, or to where it goes.

"An' if you're dry, you can flop yourself an' git a drink anywheres, 'at won't make ye stomerk sick, like this stuff. By the gret horn spoon! I wish't I hed a quart o' Stunny Brook this minute. I wish't the brook was beddin' right in my insides."

"Ah don't b'lieved water was very heal'ty for drink. It was bes' for feesh in, an' for whoman wash his close, Ah guess, an' bile patack. Ah tink some tam haow tire feesh mus' git for drink water, water all de tam. Prob'ly dat what mek him bit, fer git pull off of it. Bah gosh! Ah'll glad Ah'll ant feesh, but can git once a gret many while, leetly drops whiskee."

"Better stick tu what the fish du, Antwine, an' not hanker arter nothin' else. They don't."

"Ah'll don't b'lieve dat, Sam. Sometam, when Ah'll ketched hol' buster feesh, an' pull up mah leetly jaug fer treat mahsef, Ah'll seen heem ope hees maouth an' look so wishin' as if he'll askin' for jes' one jaw-fulls."

"Did ye ever try if one on 'em would take a snort?"

"No, sah!" Antoine answered, emphatically. "Ah'll ant goin' treat feller can't say 'Salut,' 'sides of dat, Ah'll ant never got more as Ah'll want mahsef—not quat so moch now," he added with a sigh, and then applied himself to lighting his pipe with a coal raked from the smoldering fire.

The fumes of the kindling tobacco seemed to inspire an idea. "Say, Sam, le's go up to Saou' Slang an' ketch some bow-fins, hein? Ah'll ketch some fraug an' we go have it some funs jes' for funs!" He rose quickly and made a motion as if to lead the way to the landing.

"Wal, I don't care," Sam assented, arising more deliberately, "Any fishin's better'n none," and he followed the Canadian toward the Creek.

When they reached the level ground of the shore, Antoine was alert for frogs, and was presently in pursuit of one that made flying leaps in the direction of the water. Locating the fugitive in a cluster of rushes, he made a clutch at him and secured him writhing in the midst of a handful of marsh herbage. Live bait not being required for the purposed fishing, Antoine ended the struggles of the captive by a rap on the head, and so caught and killed others till, when they neared the boats, he had a dozen dangling by their hind legs from his left hand. Here another broke cover and made for the safer shelter of the creek.

Antoine, dropping his bunch of dead frogs, made after this lively one. Running at full speed with hands uplifted to pounce upon his prey at its first brief halt, he was close to the water-line, vaguely defined among the growth of weeds, when his foot caught on a hidden stick of driftwood, and he fell headlong, ploughing half his length through weeds, water and mud. As he struggled upright from the ooze and floundered to firmer footing, all the expletives which he had gathered from two languages poured from his lips faster than the water and black mud of the marsh dripped from his garments. He rained imprecations on all the frogs that ever lived, and particularly on the one that caused his mishap, and grieved that those he had captured were not alive, that he might wreak vengeance on them; on the whole expanse of Little Otter's marshes, and on bow-fins, and on himself for being such a "sacre damn hol' foolish for go hunt dat cussed leetly jompey-jomp frawg for ketch some ant good for dev' bow-fins."

He had so far relieved himself, when he reached dry land, that Sam ventured to ask out of his laughter, "Did ye ketch the frawg, Antwine?"

"Ketch it? no!" sputtered the Canadian; "'less Ah'll ketch in mah mout. Ah'll ant ex-amine for see. Mebby Ah'll swaller. Bah gosh! 'f Ah tink he in mah stomach, Ah'll took vomitic for punish it."

He did not mind the wetting, for the shallow water was as warm as the weather, and he would not have minded it in a colder temperature if it had been in a better cause. So when he had cleared his clothes of mud, by scraping and ablution, and his burdened spirit by vigorous use of French and English, he was restored to good humor and enthusiasm in the prospective sport.

He took the oars, and, while Sam steered with a paddle, sent the scow surging upstream, noisily parting the quiet waters with her broad bow, and setting all the rushes of the marsh on either hand, and behind, aquiver with her wake. The water fowl, whose summer home was in the marshes, set up a clamor of strange cries as the boat's passage alarmed them or aroused their curiosity, but kept ever out of sight.

"Ah'll ant never see noting for belong to dat nowse," said Antoine, listening with uplifted oars. "Ah do' know 'f he was be bird or beas' or watry snaike. Ah guess he don't mud turkey, ant it? Ah'll hear folks said snaike mek nowse, but Ah'll ant mos' b'lieved it, 'less dis was snaike hollerin. He saound mos' hugly 'nough for it."

"Folks that lives here says it's birds; coots or fool-ducks some calls 'em, an' ma'sh chickens, an' they sca'cely ever see 'em till the last o' summer or int' the fall. But there's a reg'lar duck an' her hull fam'ly," said Sam, pointing forward with his paddle, and Antoine turning his head, saw a wood duck with her callow brood, a pretty fleet sailing in line along the rush border of the channel, faster than the scow, but with silent, arrowy wake. But their progress was not swift enough for the anxious mother, and she took wing, her ducklings following her low flight, running on the surface with a prodigious splashing and flutter of pinionless wings till they disappeared around the next bend.

When the scow rounded it, a broad landscape was disclosed, stretching to the mountains that lifted their blue peaks against the paler blue of the sky. Grandest of them all, the leonine front of Camel's Hump towered above its neighbors, and further southward the voyagers saw with a twinge of home-yearning their own as ill-named peak of Tater Hill, far beyond the strange homesteads and green fields of the lowland country.

Entering the narrow channel of the South Slang, the scow moved now more slowly. Her bow disturbed now and then some large fish that, making a gulp that sounded like plunging an inverted tumbler into the water, moved sluggishly off, marking its way with a slow under-water wake.

"Dat was bow-fins," Antoine explained. "He was here waitin' for us, an' when he mek dat nowse Ah spec he was smack hees mout' for dis frawg. Ah wish he'll gat dat feller Ah'll ant ketch, bah gosh!"

Not far up stream they found a stake which marked a favorite fishing-ground, and making the boat fast to it made ready for fishing. Their rods were not made of lancewood, greenheart, nor split bamboo, in fact were not made at all, but had grown at their own will from chance sown seeds of iron-wood, and were not rods, but only stout and rather crooked poles. The lines were such as carpenters used for chalking, with hooks as stout, and sinkers that might have served for plummets. Antoine skinned the hind legs of a frog, placed the tempting bait on his hook, and made a splashing cast that would have scared a wary fish out of the Slang. Sam followed his example, and both began the patient waiting which gives the angler time for the contemplation which so distinguishes his pastime.

A throng of swallows wheeled in swift circles around them or skimmed the quiet water, scarcely ruffling it where swallow and mirrored double briefly met. High above them a fish-hawk swung with moveless wing, in his lofty course. A king-fisher clattered along the channel's curves; a bittern gulped up his lugubrious strain in a marshy nook; a flicker cackled and drummed on a distant tree, and from further meadows came the jangle of bobolinks, and the clear, long drawn notes of meadow larks.

The marsh was alive with sunfish and perch, snapping eagerly at the swarming insects, but for a long half-hour nothing was allured by the angler's baits; nothing came to their line but the steel blue dragon flies that alighted one above another along the cotton cord, their slender bodies at right angles with it, as if it was a magnetized wire and they insects of steel. Sam amused himself with trying to duck them, but whether the line sank swift or slow not one glittering body or gauzy wing suffered wetting.

As he raised his pole slowly, after one of these futile attempts, it was as slowly but very strongly drawn down, till its tip touched the water, by a heavy, downright pull. Sam struck, and his line began to cut the water in a wide, deep sweep, singing as it went, and making the tough iron-wood writhe and tremble as the fish moved steadily toward the weeds.

"You'll gat it, Sam!" Antoine shouted. "Ah'll know it sem Ah'll see it was bowfins. Hang hol' of it! Kept it off de ma'sh 'less he ketch all de weed grow for ten rod!"

Sam held on stoutly and the fish gained no headway but what the spring of the pole gave him, while it bent till it almost cracked as he bored to right and left among the bottom weeds. At last he began to show signs of weakening, and Sam began towing him toward the boat, along with a great raft of up-torn weeds. But just as his uncouth form became discernible among the moving mass of vegetation, the strain proved too great for a weak spot in the line. It parted midway between hook and tip, and with dismay Sam saw the severed part trailed out of sight.

"Oh, bah gosh!" Antoine groaned, "dat was too bad for los' you fus' bowfins, too bad! too bad! But he an't wort' notings only funs an' you had some wid heem, 'f he'll did had de mos' an' laft at you naow. Fix off you line an' try 'gin, dey was more of it."

Sam unwound from his pole line enough to make up for the lost portion, tested every foot of it with pulls across his knee, bent on another hook, and was presently fishing again. It was soon Antoine's fortune to strike a big fish, which he handled with the skill born of experience, and with little ceremony brought to boat the wide-mouthed, small-eyed fellow, before half the fight was out of him.

"He'll ant han'some but he'll strong, as de dev' say, when he'll sew hees tore traouser wid lawg chain," Antoine remarked, as he unhooked his prize.

Indeed, this survival of the first form of fishes is no beauty, but he is a vigorous fighter, as tenacious of life as a turtle, and, when he can be found without his usual environment of weeds, might afford good sport with light rod and tackle. The fish seemed to have fallen into the mood of biting now, and the two anglers took several in rapid succession without further mishap to their stout tackle. As Sam unhooked an eight-pounder, as they guessed his weight, he noticed another line hanging from his broad jaws, and upon examination found it be the lost portion of his own, readily identified by the sinker and the hook which was fast in the fish's maw.

"By the gret horn spoon!" Sam remarked, "That feller's ekal to Bifmouthed Sile Baily 'at swallered his fork when he was eatin' in a hurry, an' then tucked his knife in tu keep it comp'ny."

"He want all de line you gat, Sam. He tryin' for stop de en' of dis bowfins feeshin' prob'ly."

When their bait was spent they had had enough of the sport, and, casting loose from the stake, took their way toward camp, while the shadows of the western shore slanted far across the deepened green of the marsh and the darkening water.

"What be we goin' tu du wi' these 'ere fish naow we've got 'em?" Sam asked, regarding the catch, as the scow slid up the shelving shore. "If we've got tu heave 'em away, seems tu me it's kinder useless fishin'."

"Wal, Sam, Ah do' know. We'll had de funs an' dat was what bowfins be mek for, prob'ly. Sartin he ant be made for han'some, or for heat. Ant you do not'ing honly for heat sometings? What you shoot skonk for, hein? You ant heat it, you ant peel hees skin for sol' it?"

"Skunks eat pa'tridges an' suck the 'aigs."

"Bowfins heat better feesh as he was," Antoine answered as laconically. "But if you feel so bad for t'row it, Ah'll streeng all dat bowfins and hitch heem in de water for some hol' bowfins heatin' mans come 'long for give it. Dey leeve week, prob'ly all summer so, till some mans come for give it. Der was hole feller leeve up de creek salt all he can't heat naow, for winter, sem lak codfeesh. An' some mans feed hawg of it."

So the fish were tethered to the edge of the marsh to await the coming of some appreciative native, and the anglers, wending their way to camp, rekindled the fire and soon had a fine pike-perch of the morning's fishing in the pan.

The shadows of night crept around them, darkening all their surroundings but the radiant circle of the camp fire, and still as they smoked the last pipe, Antoine discoursed of the pleasures of bowfin angling.

"Wal, arter all," Sam said, as he knocked the ashes from his pipe, "I'd ruther be a ketchin' them leetle traouts, Antwine." And who would not?

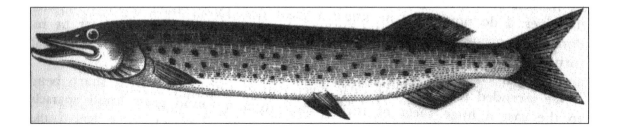

The Mascalonge (*Esox nobilior*)

JAMES A. HENSHALL

The specific name *nobilior*, long current for the mascalonge, and the one based on its earliest accurate description, was conferred by Rev. Zadoc Thompson in 1849 in "Notes on Certain Vermont Fishes," in the Proceedings of the Boston Society of Natural History, Vol. III, published July 18, 1849, and later he described it fully in the "History of Vermont," 1853, Part I. It is an excellent and appropriate name, and one that has become familiar to anglers. I have retained it, inasmuch as it was discarded, I think, for a very insufficient reason.

The specific name *masquinongy*, which has recently been given to this species in the books, is supposed to have been given to the mascalonge by Dr. Mitchill in 1824. His description, however, cannot now be found. It is alluded to by De Kay in his "Fishes of New York," in 1842, who gives its reference as "Mirror, 1824, page 297"; but I have searched for it in vain, as have others. De Kay merely says: "According to Mitchill, who describes a specimen 47.0 long and weighing thirty pounds, the fin rays are as follows: 'D. 21; P. 14; V. 11; A. 17; C. 26.' But this radial formula is just as applicable to Richardson's *E. lucius:* 'D. 20; P. 16; A. 18,' also given by De Kay. The size and weight of the alleged specimen of Mitchill would seem to indicate the mascalonge, but the great northern pickerel, *Esox lucius*, occasionally reaches a like size and weight. I once caught one weighing twenty-five pounds in northern Wisconsin, and saw several a little heavier, one of fully twenty-eight pounds.

Dr. Kirtland, in 1838, had, previous to De Kay, applied Mitchill's name *masquinongy* to a specimen from Lake Erie, and it is upon this evidence, principally, that this name has been adopted as the specific title of the mascalonge.

But afterward Dr. Kirtland used Thompson's name *nobilis* (meaning *nobilior*) and Le Sueur's name *estor* for the mascalonge. He also subsequently described the mascalonge from Lake Erie as *atromaculatus*, and one from the Mahoning River, Ohio, as *ohiensis*. From this it would appear that Dr. Kirtland, although a good naturalist in his day, was not at all clear in his estimation of the mascalonge.

There has been considerable controversy concerning the common or vernacular name of the mascalonge. Some claim it is from the French, and derived from the words "masque" and "allonge," which virtually mean "long face," and which is certainly nearer to the common pronunciation of mascalonge or muscalunge. Others claim it is an Indian name from the Ojibwa language, as "mash," meaning "strong," and "kinoje," meaning "pike." "Mash is also said to mean "spotted" and "deformed." From mash and kinoje come "maskinonge," as it appears as in the statutes of Canada. The name has been spelled in numerous ways, as evidenced in the Century Dictionary, which gives the following variations: maskalonge, mascalonge, maskalunge, maskallonge, masquallonge, masq'allonge, mascallonge, muscalonge, muskalonge, muskalinge, muskellunge, moskalonge, moscononge, maskinonge, maskanonge, maskenonge, maskenozha, maskinoje, and maskenonge, to which might be added muscalinga, mascalinga, etc. There is no authority or precedent for the name "muskellunge" as used by some writers and anglers, as neither the original French or Indian words have the letter "u" in either the first or last syllable. Moreover, the term "lunge" is in some sections applied to the lake trout. I am aware, of course, that the name has obtained considerable currency, but in much the same way that the black-bass is called "trout" in the South, and the pike-perch is denominated "salmon" in certain localities.

Rev. Zadoc Thompson, who was the first to call attention to the scaling of the cheeks as a diagnostic character, gives the vernacular name "masquallonge," and attributes it to French derivation, to which opinion I am inclined. As the most prominent writers on fish and fishing give it as "mascalonge," that name should be universally adopted, no matter what its origin, or whether derived from the French Canadians or the Chippeway Indians; that question is more interesting to philologists than to anglers. As an instance of inconsistency, or of the irony of fate, the books give the scientific name of the subgenus as *mascalongus*, from the French, and the specific name as *masquinongy*, from the Ojibwa.

The mascalonge is common in the St. Lawrence basin and the Great Lakes, more abundant in the lakes of northern Wisconsin, less common in the upper Mississippi River, Chautauqua Lake, New York, and Conneaut Lake, Pennsylvania, and rare in the upper Ohio River and tributaries. It has a long body, somewhat compressed, its depth being about one-fifth of its length; the head is large, about a fourth of the length of the body, and flattened, with the lower jaw projecting. It has a terrible array of teeth of assorted sizes. On the edge of each side of the lower jaw are several long, bayonet-shaped teeth, from one-half to an inch apart; in the front part of the tip of the projecting lower jaw are a few short but sharp teeth, recurved; in the front part of the upper jaw are three clusters of long, fanglike teeth, standing out amidst the smaller, cardlike teeth; on the edge of the forward half o the upper lip is a row of small, but very sharp, recurved teeth; back of these on the roof of the mouth (vomer and palatines), and extending back from the fangs in front to the throat, are three rows of cardlike teeth, recurved and very sharp.

The coloration and markings vary so much that several varieties have been needlessly established, as the variations are found in every locality, and do not seem to depend on habitat or environment. The usual color is dark gray, greenish or brownish, always darker on the back, lighter on the sides, and belly white or whitish. The fins usually have dusky or slate-colored spots or blotches; the lower fins and caudal fin are often reddish. The markings of the body vary a great deal. In the young the upper half of the body is covered with small, round black spots, which usually disappear or change their shape as they grow old. In mature fish the spots are more diffuse, sometimes enlarging to an inch or more in diameter, or by coalescing form vertical broad bands, while in others there are no distinct dark markings. And while all of these various markings are found in fish from the same locality there is no apparent structural difference.

I have examined and compared specimens from the St. Lawrence and Indian rivers, New York, Lake Erie, the Wisconsin lakes, Lake Pepin, Chautauqua and Conneaut lakes, Scioto and Mahoning rivers, in Ohio, and have seen preserved heads of large ones from Ohio, Kentucky, and Tennessee, and found that they all agree so well in the number of branchiostegals, squamation of cheeks and opercles, in dentition, fins, and in measurements, that they must all be considered as one and the same species. At the Chicago Columbian Exposition there were some twenty very large specimens of mounted skins from Canadian waters, in the exhibit of the Ottawa Museum, which showed well the variation in markings. Some still showed the dark spots on a gray ground; others were more or less distinctly barred with broad or narrow bands; others showed both bars and diffuse spots; and still others were of a uniform slate or grayish coloration, without markings of any kind. In the museum of the Cuvier Club, in Cincinnati, there are quite a number of mounted skins of mascalonge from the Wisconsin lakes, mostly large ones, that also show all of the various markings, as well as those of a uniform coloration.

About 1890 I donated to the Cincinnati Society of Natural History a specimen from Lake Erie; and in 1892 I donated to the United States National Museum two specimens from Lake Erie, and one from a tributary of the Muskingum River, in Ohio. All of these Ohio fish were from eighteen inches to two feet long, and all showed similar markings, being profusely covered with round black spots from an eighth to a quarter of an inch in diameter. Where the spots become diffused, and the bands are inclined to spread and coalesce, they are always more distinct toward the tail. In a mascalonge of less than a foot in length the spots are very black, very round, and quite small, not exceeding a sixth or an eighth of an inch in diameter.

Various appellations have been bestowed on the mascalonge to denote its rapacity, as the shark, wolf, or tiger of the waters, all of which are well merited by that fierce marauder. It subsists entirely on fish, frogs, snakes, and even the young of aquatic mammals and water fowl. Nothing in the shape of food comes amiss to him. He is solitary in his habits, lying concealed among water plants and rushes at the edges of the streams or channels and along the shores, or beside shelving rocks or banks in clear lakes, from whence he darts open-mouthed upon the luckless fish that approaches his lair. The number of fishes swallowed by a mascalonge during a single summer is almost incredible; and they are not minnows and small fry alone, such as are devoured by other predaceous fishes, but such as are old and large enough to reproduce their kind. It is fortunate that the mascalonge is comparatively a rare fish. As it is now being artificially propagated in some states, great care and judgment should be exercised as to the waters planted, so as not to jeopardize other and better game-fishes.

It spawns early in the spring and in very shallow water, where most of the eggs are devoured by frogs, turtles, fishes, and water fowl—a wise provision of nature when it is considered that the female deposits from one hundred thousand to three hundred thousand eggs. The eggs are quite small, about ten or twelve to an inch, and hatch in about two weeks. The mascalonge is the most valuable food-fish of its family, and is pronounced by some as being really excellent; but I consider it much inferior to the whitefish, lake-trout, pike-perch, black-bass, or brook-trout. While possessing no especial flavor, its flesh is firm and flaky, more so than that of the pike or pickerel, and it commands a ready sale in the markets.

It grows occasionally to an enormous size. I have taken it up to forty pounds, good weight. The late Judge Potter, of Toledo, Ohio, an angler of the old school, informed me that he had seen, in early days, many that weighed from fifty to seventy-five pounds. Mr. L. H. McCormick, formerly of Oberlin College, Ohio, saw one taken in a pound net that weighed seventy-two pounds. The late Dr. Elisha Sterling, formerly of Cleveland, Ohio, a contemporary of Judge Potter and the late Dr. Garlick, the father of artificial fish-culture in America, told me of one he once speared in Lake Erie that weighed eighty pounds, and said that those of fifty to sixty pounds were common in the forties.

The mascalonge is the best game-fish of its family. When of large size, from twenty to thirty pounds, it exhibits a bull-like ferocity when hooked, making furious dashes for liberty, and if not stopped in time will eventually take to the weeds. It exhibits great powers of endurance, but little finesse or cunning in its efforts to escape. It depends on main strength alone, swimming swiftly in straight lines, as might be inferred from its shape. Its long body does not admit of the quick doublings of the black-bass or brook-trout. If kept on the surface with a taut line it sometimes leaps into the air; but if allowed its own sweet will it bores toward the bottom, or endeavors to reach the refuge of weeds or rushes. One of less weight than twelve pounds, when hooked, can scarcely be distinguished from the pike or pickerel in its manner of resistance, and exhibits but little more gameness.

A black-bass rod of eight or nine ounces is sufficient for the largest mascalonge one is likely to encounter in these days. I caught one on the St. Lawrence, many years ago, that weighed thirty-two pounds, on an eight-ounce Henshall rod, and gaffed it in twenty minutes. Others have done the same even with a lighter rod. But it must be remembered that the weight of the fish, added to his fierce lunges, is very trying to a light rod, and I should not recommend one of less weight than eight ounces, which will answer for all emergencies in skilled hands. A good multiplying reel, a braided silk or linen line, size E or F, and Sproat or O'Shaughnessy hooks Nos. 3-0 to 5-0 on gimp snells, with brass box-swivel for connecting snell and line, constitute the rest of the tackle.

The best season for mascalonge fishing is in May or June, and in September and October, the latter months preferable. The most favorable hours are in the early morning and late afternoon. The middle of the day may be fished with a better prospect of success on cloudy, lowering days, with a brisk wind.

The best bait is a large minnow, either alive or dead, though a frog answers very well; and in the absence of either, a trolling-spoon, No. 4, with a single hook, may be utilized for casting. Rowing along in water from five to ten feet deep, the bait should be cast as far as possible to the edge of weed patches, reeling it again very slowly, or if the bait is alive it may be allowed to swim outside of the water-plants for a short time. By moving along continuously, and making frequent casts, this method is much more successful than still-fishing. When the wind is just right, or when the current is strong enough and the wind not contrary, it is a good plan to allow the boat to drift while casting.

As soon as a fish is struck and hooked the boat should be moved to deeper and open water at once, in order to give free play to the fish and lessen the probability of its taking to the weeds. In open water the angler has a better chance successfully to play and land his quarry, which should be kept on the surface as much as possible. He can be aided very much in his efforts by the careful and judicious management of the boat by a skilful oarsman.

When the mascalonge shows signs of weakness and can be drawn alongside, it should be gaffed at once. Not by striking at it with quick and violent motions, which serve only to frighten the fish and endanger the angler's tackle, but the gaff should be kept below the fish until it can be drawn over it, and then by raising it slowly and cautiously, until near enough, when by a quick upward and drawing motion, the point of the hook should be driven into the throat or breast of the fish, and by the same motion the fish should be lifted into the boat. It should then be killed by a smart stroke on the head, as a wound from its sharp teeth is no trifling matter. In the absence of a gaff-hook the fish should be more thoroughly exhausted before bringing it alongside the boat, when it should be struck a stunning blow on the head before being taken in.

The bait or spoon may be trolled along the edges of the channel, just outside of the weed patches, from a moving boat, with a line of thirty to fifty yards. In trolling, the revolving spoon, glistening and shining, is the attractive lure, and any addition of a minnow, or strip of fish or pork rind, or other bait, as is often resorted to by some, is entirely unnecessary. It adds nothing to the chances of hooking a fish, and should never be practiced by the consistent angler. He may use pork-rind if he wishes, but let it be used alone, on its own merits. A spoon is bad enough in any case, but it only makes it more reprehensible and repulsive, to the angler at least, to handicap it with bait of any kind; even the bunch of feathers that usually adorns the spoon should be discarded, as it is of no practical use.

Most mascalonge are taken, I am sorry to say, by trolling with a hand-line of heavy braided linen, size B or C, and a spoon of very large size, as large as No. 8, which seems to be the favorite size with hand-trollers. In this method of fishing the mascalonge hooks himself when he strikes the spoon. It is then drawn in, hand over hand, as the sailors say, with might and muscle. And as might be supposed, those who practice this method are loudest in their praise of the mascalonge as the "king of all gamefishes." A quick pull, a strong pull, and a pull all together, with the hauling aboard as soon as possible of the struggling fish, amidst much splashing and floundering, seems to be their estimation of gameness in a fish.

The foregoing remarks apply to fishing on lakes and quiet, weedy streams of the Northern states. In the clear and swifter waters of the upper Ohio, and its tributaries, the mascalonge lies in the deep pools during summer and fall, where it is taken by still-fishing. A large sucker, weighing from half a pound to a pound, is the favorite bait, with suitable rod and reel. The fish is given plenty of time to gorge the bait before striking, and this is quite important with so large a bait. Many large mascalonge, there called "pike," have been taken in this manner in those waters, events to be long remembered and talked about, while the head is carefully preserved for the admiration and envy of future generations of anglers.

Once when returning from a fishing trip to northern Wisconsin when mascalonge were much more in evidence than at the present day, I was carrying the head of a forty-pounder that just filled an ordinary tin bucket. At Appleton, while waiting for the train to Green Bay, the big head was the centre of an admiring group of anglers. Then came the natural and inevitable query, "Where did you catch it?" In order to avoid a long recital, which only could have done justice to the subject, and expecting the train at any moment, I replied, "An Indian speared it on Lake St. Germain." They looked at me as if I had seven heads; then one said: "Well! well! It requires an awful lot of moral courage to make such an admission." But I killed it, all the same, on a nine-ounce rod, and my Indian canoeman gaffed it.

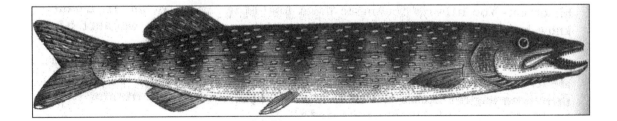

A Pickerel Yarn

FRED MATHER

Two Pritchard brothers, Tom and Harry, came from England and started to make and repair fishing tackle in Fulton street, New York, so long ago that the nearest date I can fix for it is the one so dear to our childhood: "Once upon a time." They are not recorded in the Chinese "Book of the Lily," which was written at the beginning of all things, and so must have come to New York after that period; but it was very long ago. The little shop upstairs was kept busy by anglers who knew of their skill, and also by some of the large fishing tackle houses, which found it more convenient than to send small jobs by express to their factories; and so the brothers found plenty of work to their hands while they lived.

The little shop was a place where one might drop in at any time and feel sure of meeting some of the old-time anglers of the city, and the talk would run on the nearby trout streams, rods, ferrules, flies, the prospect of a run of weakfish, the tides, the last big catch of sheepshead at the wreck of the Black Warrior, and such other things as are discussed where anglers most do congregate. There is no such place in New York City now, and never will be again until an angler's club is formed. I meet anglers occasionally in the different fishing tackle emporiums, but they are there on business and not for social talk, as was the case at Pritchards'. We needed such a place then and we need a club now.

Of Tom Pritchard I knew little; he was the eldest, wore gray muttonchop whiskers and attended to business; therefore, as Dame Juliana Berners says, "I write the less of him."

When I first knew Harry, some thirty years ago, he must have been a boy of about fifty years old, as convivial as opportunity offered and always ready to tell a story, the impediment in his speech increasing as he neared the climax, when his jaws would work but refuse to deliver a sound to all his yarns. As he put it: "I can s-s-s-sing and I can w-w-whistle, but I'm a s-s-sinner if I can t-t-talk," Frank Endicott once made Harry this proposition: "If you can't talk, don't try; you're too old to learn new tricks. When you've got a fishing yard to spin, just sing the introduction and descriptive part, and when you get to the last of it—where we are all willing to strain our credulity to believe you—just 'whistle o'er the lave o' it,' as the Scotch song goes. This will be a great relief to you, and will leave much veracity to your credit with all of us."

Harry was the man who was fishing for black bass on Greenwood Lake when a drunken "guide" tried to bail out of the perforated bait car which hung overboard, as has been related, but he had amplified the story with detail and climax until we enjoyed it as something of which we had never heard. But this is a digression.

"N-now Hi'll tell you a t-t-true s-s-story, an' Hi don't c-care hif you b-b-believe hit or not. You hallways puts m-me down for l-l-lyin', hanyway, an' Hi d-d-do' know has hits hany use to t-t-tell you hanythink m-m-more, you dwouldn't b-b-believe me, hanyway."

"Go on, Harry," said I, "the trouble with you is your excessive modesty. You evidently never expected me to believe that you killed a forty-foot shark on a sixteen-ounce rod while fishing for small fish in the waters of India, but your glowing account of your four hours' fight with the monster, after it had dragged you from the boat, and how you reeled in and gave line while treading water, bore the stamp of authenticity. Then, too, your reeling the great fish in and getting on its back, drowning it by pulling off your boots and jamming them into two of the gill openings, suffocating the fish with hands and feet in the other gill slits while you awaited death when the shark sank, is in memory as distinct as when you told it. I do not doubt the slightest detail, and have often rejoiced at your opportune rescue by the native fishermen, and your restoration to your regiment in Her Majesty's service. Please don't think that we entertain doubts of the truthfulness of your stories, even if such doubts sometimes cross your own mind."

"T-t-that's good. You think Hi don't hallways b-b-b-believe my hown s-s-stories. P'r'aps Hi don't b-believe 'em hev'ry time; hall Hi ask is for you to b-b-b-believe 'em."

"Let me explain," said I, "the funny man of the press has done much to injure the veracity of the angler. He has gone so far as to brand a palpable lie as a 'fish story,' thereby throwing discredit upon our guild. In his ignorance that a whale is not a fish he, in his skepticism, goes back many centuries, but now, Harry, let me go beyond the latter-day reporter, who has exhausted his wit upon the appetite of the goat, the disturbing influence of the mother-in-law, and the wholly fictitious accounts of the wealth of the plumber and the ice-man, into the question of the truthfulness of the fisherman. Is he less given to exaggeration than his brother who handles the gun? Is he more unworthy of belief than men who engage in other forms of sport or of business? I'll answer my own questions by saying that he is not, and in proof of this will point to the fact that I have even believed some of your stories."

"I move the previous question," said Mr. Endicott, "all this talk that Mather has shot off is irrelevant and not at all to the point. If Harry has a story to tell it should take precedence of all. Go on, Harry, and tell your story. I'll agree to believe a third of it and Mr. Scott and Fred will believe the other two-thirds. In that way the whole story will be believed without injuring our capacity for believing any stories that others present may inflict on us. Let her go!"

"Well, this here ain't much of a s-s-story, an' I don't care w-w-whether you b-b-believe or not, cause, it's as true as I sit 'ere on this stool, an' that's no lie. Y' see Hi was afishin' for p-p-pickerel up hon Greenwood Lake, hall by my lonesome, han I was a ketchin' s-s-small ones right fast han a keepin' c-c-count by sayin' that m-m-makes nine han' this un's t-t-ten, in that kind o' way ha 'avin' fun—"

"Hold on, Harry," said Endicott, "we want more detail. How big were these small pickerel, and what bait were you using?"

"Hi was b-b-baitin' with live minners, or k-k-killies has they calls 'em hin the salt-water. Hi hain't got h-h-hany of 'em left to prove they was my b-b-bait, but Hi'll task you to t-t-take my word for 'em. The p-p-pickerel was a-r-r-r-runnin' hextra small that d-d-day, han' the first si-s-singular thing that struck me was their r-r-regular size, han' I m-m-measured 'em. Hi'm a s-s-sinner hif they wasn't hall just heleven an' a harf h-h-hinches long to a fraction; and I sez to mys-s-self, sez Hi, this here's hall one s-s-school, hall hout o' one littler, but they're b-b-big henuff to take 'ome, so Hi fishes on."

"How many did you get on this remarkable day?" asked Mr. Scott.

"Hi'm a c-c-comin' to that hif you'll gi' me a c-c-chance. Y'see, Hi was hout for three days' f-f-fishin', an' Hi wanted to keep my f-f-fish halive till I left for 'ome; so Hi 'ad a fish car halongside, han' the p-p-pickerel were dropped into that as fast as Hi p-p-pulled 'em in. They was a-bitin' f-f-fast, an' about s-s-sundown Hi thought the car must be p-p-putty full, for Hi had counted f-f-forty-three, an' Hi'd quit. One m-m-more took hold, han' has 'e was a-kickin' hon the bottom of the boat Hi takes a look in the c-c-car, han' what do you think Hi s-s-see?"

"Well, Harry," said Endicott, "as I have followed the story, I should say that you must have seen forty-three pickerel in a mass and nothing more, because you have not mentioned taking in snapping turtles and other monsters. What else could you have seen? There's nothing remarkable in your yarn so far, that you should preface it, as you did, with the remark that we might not believe it. As far as I am concerned, I am willing to believe not only the third, to which I agreed, but the whole story as well. What did you see?"

"N-n-n-nothing!"

"But," said Mr. Scott, "you put the fish in the car; where were they?"

"Hin the b-b-boat. There was a slat hoff the b-b-bottom of that c-c-car, han' Hi'd been a-c-catchin' the same p-p-pickerel hall day, han' e' ——"

Harry's vocal cords gave out. We gravely shook hands, remarked upon the state of the weather and left him trying to finish the story.

A Big Muskellunge

W. N. HULL

The summer days began to drag. The brick walls of the city glimmered in the hot sunshine. Offices were like bake-ovens.

"Let's escape to the country," said Bob, fanning himself vigorously and mopping the perspiration from his jolly fat face.

"I know what's on your mind, Bob; you want another dog-fish."

"Let's go this time for muskellunge."

It was scarcely necessary for him to make the suggestion; I was ready to do anything to escape the terrible heat.

Next evening found us on board one of the boats of the Goodrich Line, steaming slowly out of the Chicago River and cutting a passage through the black veil of night which hung like a pall over the lake.

After a more refreshing sleep upon the cool waters of the lake than the summer had so far granted us, we landed next morning at Grand Haven. We transferred to a smaller steamer, and in two hours more we found ourselves fanned by the cool air of the upper lakes, and we turned into the Muskegon River and ran up to the city of Muskegon.

How delightful it is on a hot summer day to sit forward upon the upper deck of a lake steamer and be fanned by the rushing air as the boat speeds along!

We hire an electric launch to take us over to the other side of the bay, and there engage a man with a rowboat to row us up the bay while we take turns trolling for the muskellunge.

Our line is at least three hundred feet long and a good strong one. On the end is a monster spoon-hook, gaily ornamented with gaudy feathers. We want a large fish or none.

Bob now has the line on the stern seat, Charley is at the oars, and I am the gentleman at the bow. The gaff-hook lies near me, and I may have one stroke of skillful work to do. We are about fifty feet from the shore. Bob plays out two hundred feet of line, and Charley is rowing so slowly that there is scarcely a move of the water. The wind has risen slightly and raises a ripple upon the lake. This is favorable for a good catch.

An hour passes, and we have not had a strike. Charley says the fish are here, and we must be patient and keep a sharp lookout. We talk in low voices, and the fish are not frightened by anything uncommon among them this beautiful summer morning.

We started in at nine o'clock, and it is now ten. The movement and work are lazy and monotonous, and day-dreaming is creeping over the rower and the gentleman in the bow.

But Bob is alert. He has the business end of the expedition. He is an old fisherman and a true lover of the sport. He draws upon the line, causing the spoon to revolve more swiftly, and again lets it out, giving the spoon a slower movement.

Memory goes wool-gathering and roams across the continent. Again I am at Pacific Cottage on the Atlantic shore and the delightful days pass all too quickly; but my dreams are almost broken and we are almost upset by Bob, who springs to his feet shouting, "A strike! A strike!"

Sure enough, the line is playing out fast, and the "whale," as Charley calls him, is taking—we were about to say a bee-line, but probably it would be more correct to call it a fish-line—for his haunts in deep water. Bob holds him with a firm and skillful hand.

"He's well hooked," says Charley. "There's plenty of sport ahead for you city chaps. Ten to one you don't land him."

"I take you," says Bob, but does not take his eye off the line, nor his hands from the push and pull.

Now the fish changes his mind and shoots for the shore, but finding himself in shallow water, he turns again. In the shallow water we have caught glimpses that lead us to believe he is a rare fish.

"How much will he weigh, Charley?" I ask.

"With his own scales?" says Charley interrogatively, with a cunning look.

"Any way," I answer, and feel I have silenced Charley with my witty gun, but his reply takes a more practical turn:

"Don't count your chickens before they are hatched, nor weigh your fish till he is caught," and he slowly turns the boat as he sees the fish make a break up the lake.

"The line is all out, and he is actually pulling us along." It does seem so, and naturally we wonder if the line will stand the strain.

"Turn again, Charley; he's running down the lake," and Bob reaches rapidly hand over hand upon the slacking line.

The muskellunge is called the "wolf of the waters" and is the hardest fighter ever hooked. Bob's fish thrashes the waters like a mad bull. He jumps and he turns. He strikes with his tail, and whirls with a sudden wrench upon the line that tests its strength and his own jaws. But every effort and every swift run weakens him. He cares less and less for escape, and come s nearer the boat.

I have the gaff-hook ready.

"Pull him a little nearer, Bob," I shout.

"I can't do it," says Bob, "let him go again."

But he does not turn very far. Again Bob pulls him toward the boat, in and out, in and out for at least an hour and a half.

In the meantime Charley is telling how, away up in the mountain streams, two men in a canoe, with pole and reel, have great sport catching these big fellows that have crept up, like the salmon of the Pacific, as far as possible, to spawn.

"Strike him! Yank him in!" shouts Bob.

I am standing in the boat, keeping it as steady as I can, as I watch my chance. A wrong blow may break the hook or line and the fish will be lost.

"Next time, sure," I reply.

Now he comes so near that his whole body is seen, and he seems to be pausing to take breath. I take a careful blow with the gaff-hook and a sudden pull toward the boat. The fish comes in.

"Jump on him! Where's the hatchet?" shouts Bob. "He's the wolf of the waters, and will fight to the bitter end."

The hatchet lies at Charley's feet. He seizes it and with one blow with the sharp edge he splits the captive's head almost open, and the fish is surely ours; he quivers a little, and gives up his life.

"How much will he weigh now, Charley?"

"Thirty pounds," says Charley.

Later the scales reveal the fact that Charley was excited eight pounds, for the fish actually weighs but twenty-two pounds.

Bob's face is flushed with excitement. He chuckles and laughs, still keeping his eye upon the fish and stroking him occasionally all the way down to dinner.

"Isn't he a beauty?"

"Looks much like a pickerel."

"He is broader and more chunky."

"Tell you how we'll have him cooked. We'll have him stuffed, covered with slices of salt pork, and baked."

"If we had him down at the office we could bake him without an oven."

"Now, don't say office here; it sickens me to think of it."

But when we did return to the office, of all the stories Bob told to the calling friends, this is the one that he lingered longest over and made the most of. He always affirms that this was one of the best sporting events of his life.

The Shanty

JERRY GIBBS

The ice was dead gray. It stretched as far as you could see looking north up the big, ragged lake. Snow that had once brightened the surface had melted into hills of slush or two-inch-deep sheets of water that the wind riffled passing through. Beneath the water the ice showed bleakly. It was still safe, still over a foot thick, far from the blackness that would herald its final rottenness.

At the access parking lot stood remnants of a once-bustling ice-fishing village, shanties that had been hastily pulled during the thaws to prevent them being locked in when the weather turned again. The few ice houses still on the lake were owned by hard-core regulars who would fish them daily or nightly keeping watch on the weather.

It was the worst time of year in the North Country. Roads crumbled or turned to mud. Shrinking snow revealed mounds of preserved winter litter. Trees stood exhausted and bare. The crows had returned, though, and their sharp rasping knifed across the woodland valleys. You could say it was spring, the way it is spring in the North.

The two men and the big black Labrador retriever were 50 yards out heading south on the ice toward a long point guarding the entrance to a bay. The dog ran ahead, quartering, returning to check. Its owner, Bud Tuttle, pulled the sled that carried most of their equipment. The dog was very happy.

"Ought to harness your energy, foolish dog," Tuttle told the Lab. "This sled is getting waterlogged and heavy."

"Let me haul it for awhile," the other man said. He was a little shorter, but broader than Bud. His name was Earl Waite. The two were old friends who had not seen one another for some time.

"Nah," Bud told him. "I only let friends haul coming back–when I'm beat from digging holes."

"Right," Earl laughed.

Far off the point were several ice fishermen. Some had set out tip-ups but most worked short jigging rods or sticks for yellow perch.

"Don't know why they keep fishing out that far," Bud Tuttle said. "Those schools of yellows are moving in here by now. Those fish want deeper water they can find it off the point. Then it shallows fast soon as you get to the bay mouth. Course there's a better chance at a passing trout or salmon outside, but I pick up trout right at the drop, too."

Around the point, not far from it, stood a fragile shanty of wood framing and black roofing paper. "Look at that shack," Bud continued. "That's old René Tatro's. He's in there most all the time day or night. Anybody catches fish through a hole in the ice, it's him."

They sloshed a little way on without talking, then Earl said, "I haven't had a good perch feed in so long, almost forgot how they taste."

"Should get them," Bud said.

Earl took the auger and started the first hole. Bud set a jig rod and a Styrofoam cup of live maggot bait near the drilling, then dragged the sled through the slush-water angling toward the point. The dog splashed ahead like a spring colt. The first hole done, Earl walked over and the two men grabbed the auger together, alternating grips along the handle to cut the second hole fast. Then Earl returned to the first hole. He freed the hookless attractor spoon and ice flies secured to the jig rod guides and baited the fly hooks. He sent the silver spoon followed by the flies on droppers above it down the hole, found bottom and cranked up a few turns.

"Work from the bottom up, you never know where you'll hit them," Bud called over. "I'll be in a little deeper water here."

"You using the same rig?"

"I put on one of those Rapala jigs—you know, the things that swim around in little circles. Never can tell when a stray trout or pike might eat. I got the flies on above it."

It was quiet across the lake, then came the floating strains of a song sung in a dry, cracking voice.

"Who's singing?" Earl called over.

"That'll be old René in his shack," Bud laughed. "All the time he spends in there, guess he gets lonely. Keeps a bottle a rum for company. If he gets really tuned we'll have some music."

The first holes produced nothing and the two moved just off the point, drilling at new spots, Earl farther out, Bud closer in. Strains of a song in Quebec French came across to them from the shanty.

"He hasn't got started," Bud said. "You'll see. He switches back to English sometimes."

The dog appeared around the corner of the musical shanty, snuffling its edges.

"Ace, get over here," Bud yelled. The dog came up panting, nuzzled Tuttle's leg. "Good boy." He rubbed the dog's ears. "You leave the old man's shack alone, hear." Then he straightened. "Old Tatro's got a smelt system in there. Got a whole long trench he keeps open; a bunch of fishing lines spaced along it on a rack. Lines come off little wood spools, go through open brackets. Fish hits, he just plucks the line off, hand-over-hands it in unless it's a big one. They use the same thing up to the St. Lawrence fishing Tommy cod. Slick as owl dung in the rain. He won't get smelt now, though. Perch are just fine with him, too."

"Sounds like a production line," Earl said.

"He catches 'em, old geezer. I worry one day he'll slip through that trench after enough a that rum."

Earl counted off line in two-foot pulls. "It's deep," he said to himself. He cranked up until he figured he was at 15 feet. Overhead, streaks of thin clouds backed by a high, gray dome gave the sky the look of cool, polished tombstone. Far to the north the lake was empty. It seemed a very lonely place and Earl was glad he had company.

After a time, his second hole producing nothing, Earl started in. Bud had done no better. With Ace leading they headed around the point to the bay side closer to the old man's shanty. The black and gray shack sagged toward the left. "He builds it up new every year," Bud said. "It's not the strongest thing."

They drilled new holes inside the drop edge where the bottom rose from 40 to 18 feet. They drilled closer together, more for company than any insight into fish location.

René's shanty had been quiet for some time. Suddenly the old man's disembodied voice boomed across the ice. He sang in English this time, high in his nose in grand country fashion. First something about Texas ladies, then he segued into "90 miles an hour down a dead-end road . . . You gotta be bad to have a good time . . ." It was all delightfully incongruous for the time and place. Then Earl felt a peck and he struck with the jig rod.

He used the tip of the rod and his non-rod hand in a kind of alternating cat's cradle to pick up line and bring the fish in. He dropped the monofilament on the ice, the perch following.

"Nice," he said, "nice perch."

The fish was fat, gleaming brassy-gold, its black vertical bars vivid. It splayed its sharp-pointed gill covers, arched its spiny dorsal. Earl brought it to the bucket on the sled.

Hearing excitement Ace trotted back from one of his circuits, coming up just as a fish hit Bud's rig. "Just a couple feet off bottom," he said happily.

"That's where mine hit."

The dog danced, lunged for Bud's fish. "Ace, back!" Tuttle ordered. The dog backed reluctantly, wanting the fish. "You'll get fin-pricked," Bud grumbled affectionately, "not to mention slobbering dinner."

They took two more fish each but it was not fast and they spread out, drilling new holes, looking for the main school. They tried shallower, drilling a hole line, then moved out on the drop again and here they hit the school.

The fish were so tightly concentrated that holes a couple of yards apart meant the difference between an occasional fish or rapid action. They ended with four holes drilled in a cluster, alternating between them as one cooled and another became productive.

In his shack old René started in again singing ". . . we got winners we got losers, we got bikers we got truckers . . . an' the girls next door dress up like movie stars . . . I love this bar, I love this bar. . . ."

"He's getting there," Bud laughed.

"So are we," Earl said sticking another fish.

"Let's string out these holes and connect them," Bud said. "Make a trench like old René 's so we can keep moving right on top of the fish."

They augered new holes, connected the old ones. Then Bud grabbed the long steel ice spud from his sled and widened the slot. The opening was a long, rough rectangle.

Ace stayed with them now, feinting at each new fish, whining happily. Over in his shack René had launched into a sad-sweet ballad in Quebec French. Two crows circled overhead eyeballing for scrap bait. Just then Bud struck but this time his little jigging rod bowed over, line tearing from the reel with a soft zipping sound. "No perch!" he yelled.

Quickly Earl reeled in, ran over. The fish finished its first run and Bud was getting line back now, reeling smoothly. Then the fish went again. It was a shorter run but deeper, and when the fish was turned it came only a little way before going a third time, this run toward the point and just beneath the ice. Bud thrust his rod half down into the trench. "He's awfully close to the top. He'll cut me off on the ice edge if I let him."

Ace danced close, tail wagging, excited as the men.

"I got him coming," Bud said. He reeled faster now, gaining line. Then they saw the fish.

"Trout! Nice rainbow," Earl said. He raced for the sled. "You got a net?"

"Ah, no," Bud said worriedly. The fish was at the surface. It thrashed, showering Bud on his knees, reaching for it. Then it ran again forcing him to punch the rod into the trench.

"I have heavy line," Bud said. "If I can get him to hold on top a second I can scoop him with one hand, just swing him over."

The fish came. It lay on the surface, Bud holding it with raised rod, reaching under its belly with his other hand, scooping it, the fish arcing brightly through the air to the ice, gleaming, bold magenta stripe on its side. It arched its body, hard muscles lifting it from the ice. Earl grabbed it but instantly it slipped away. The fish spun on the ice, flopped, and Ace was on it but not fast enough. The rainbow's last effort took it from between the dog's feet back into the trench, the Lab after it, hitting the frigid water, diving.

"Ace!" Bud bellowed. He pounded with his boot heel on the ice. Earl jabbed his own jig rod under, searching. Bud ran to the sled, came back with the ice sieve, dropped to his belly. His arm up to the shoulder in the water, Bud swung the sieve in wide circles under water searching frantically for the dog.

"Ace, Ace!" he called. "Oh the damned, stupid . . ." He rolled over on the ice, his hand gone angry red. "I can't hold onto this scoop."

"Here give it to me." Earl grabbed the sieve. He was down now scooping at the other end of the wide trench.

A scream sliced the air. They saw René's shanty rock once before one black paper wall exploded, flimsy framing splintering, spewing the old man in green suspenders and baggy wool trousers. His white hair flared in ragged streamers, his eyes rolled madly, and from his sunken cavern-dark mouth came a wavering, tortured wail. René Tatro hit the ice running. He slipped to all fours, regained his feet, staggering for shore, not seeing the anglers, not seeing anything now but the safety of shore.

"La bête . . . sauvage!" he screamed, "the beast, the beast!"

He reached the shore, crashed into the woods. The two anglers were running now, heading for the destroyed shanty, reaching it, staring in. Inside was a shambles. Tackle was strewn everywhere. A half-filled can of corn had scattered kernels like confetti. Bits of lunch joined the yellow niblets. An empty rum bottle lay on its side. And in the middle of it all was Ace, tail beating as he wolfed down everything edible.

"Ace you fool!" Bud told the dog. "Come here." The dog even gave up eating to come. Bud grabbed the Lab around the shoulders and Ace shook his hindquarters showering both men.

"Can't believe this," Earl said.

"Oh yeah, it's real. Look at that setup. Ace must have boiled right up the middle of René's ice trench looking like the devil himself."

They both began laughing. They sat in the debris and could not stop laughing.

"That poor geezer. If he didn't think it was old Ned he likely thought it was the lake monster we're supposed to have," Bud said wiping tears from his eyes.

"Oh, I remember that—like the one in Loch Ness," Earl said.

"Ace you are a monster all right. Nothing's hurt with the fishing setup anyway," Bud pointed. "But the shack's sure finished."

"I'm shutting down this stove," Earl said. Ace squirmed to get back at the food.

"No more, you. You've done enough for the day," Bud told the dog. "I'm gonna call poor René. He won't believe me. Maybe I shouldn't tell him the truth. I bet he goes on the wagon for a while. Got to fix his shack for him. I wonder if I can ever get him back on the ice again."

"We better get out of here before we freeze," Earl said. "I'm starting to feel it."

"Same here. I think my arm's frozen," Bud said.

They staggered to the sled, started back fast toward the access, looking at one another, beginning to laugh again so hard that walking became difficult. The dog ran in front pleased with it all.

Finally Earl said, "You know, along with everything we have enough fish for supper."

"Good thing," Bud told him. "Nobody'll believe the rest."

Overhead along the shoreline two crows headed north into the silence of spring.

Fishing in the Ohio

JOHN JAMES AUDUBON

It is with mingled feelings of pleasure and regret that recall to my mind the many pleasant days I have spent on the shores of the Ohio. The visions of former years crowd on my view, as I picture to myself the fertile soil and genial atmosphere of our great western garden, Kentucky, and view the placid waters of the fair stream that flows along its western boundary. Methinks I am now on the banks of the noble river. Twenty years of my life have returned to me; my sinews are strong, and the "bowstring of my spirit is not slack"; bright visions of the future float before me, as I sit on a grassy bank, gazing on the glittering waters. Around me are dense forests of lofty trees and thickly tangled undergrowth, amid which are heard the songs of feathered choristers, and from whose boughs hang clusters of glowing fruits and beautiful flowers. Reader, I am very happy. But now the dream has vanished, and here I am in the British Athens, penning an episode for my *Ornithological Biography*, and having before me sundry well-thumbed and weather-beaten folios, from which I expect to be able to extract some interesting particulars respecting the methods employed in those days in catching Cat-fish.

But, before entering on my subject, I will present you with a brief description of the place of my residence on the banks of the Ohio. When I first landed at Henderson in Kentucky, my family, like the village, was quite small. The latter consisted of six or eight houses; the former of my wife, myself, and a young child. Few as the houses were, we fortunately found one empty. It was a log-*cabin*, not a log-*house*; but as better could not be had, we were pleased. Well, then, we were located. The country around was thinly peopled, and all purchasable provisions rather scarce; but our neighbors were friendly, and we had brought with us flour and bacon-hams. Our pleasures were those of young people not long married, and full of life and merriment; a single smile from our infant was, I assure you, more valued by us than all the treasures of a modern Croesus would have been. The woods were amply stocked with game, the river with fish; and now and then the hoarded sweets of the industrious bees were brought from some hollow tree to our little table. Our child's cradle was our richest piece of furniture, our guns and fishing-lines our most serviceable implements, for although we began to cultivate a garden, the rankness of the soil kept the seeds we planted far beneath the tall weeds that sprung up the first year. I had then a partner, a "man of business," and there was also with me a Kentucky youth, who much preferred the sports of the forest and river to either day-book or ledger. He was naturally, as I may say, a good woodsman, hunter, and angler, and, like me, thought chiefly of procuring supplies of fish and fowl. To the task accordingly we directed all our energies.

Quantity as well as quality was an object with us, and although we well know that three species of Cat-fish existed in the Ohio, and that all were sufficiently good, we were not sure as to the best method of securing them. We determined, however, to work on a large scale, and immediately commenced making a famous "trot-line." Now, reader, as you may probably know nothing about this engine, I shall describe it to you.

A trot-line is one of considerable length and thickness, both qualities, however, varying according to the extent of water, and the size of the fish you expect to catch. As the Ohio, at Henderson, is rather more than half a mile in breadth, and as its fishes weigh from one to an hundred pounds, we manufactured a line which measured about two hundred yards in length, as thick as the little finger of some fair one yet in her teens, and as white as the damsel's finger well could be, for it was wholly of Kentucky cotton, just, let me tell you, because that substance stands the water better than either hemp or flax. The main line finished, we made a hundred smaller ones, about five feet in length, to each of which we fastened a capital hook of Kirby and Co.'s manufacture. Now for the bait!

It was the month of May. Nature had brought abroad myriads of living beings: they covered the earth, glided through the water, and swarmed in the air. The Cat-fish is a voracious creature, not at all nice in feeding, but one who, like the vulture, contents himself with carrion when nothing better can be had. A few experiments proved to us that, of the dainties with which we tried to allure them to our hooks, they gave a decided preference, at that season, to *live toads*. These animals were very abundant about Henderson. They ramble or feed, whether by instinct or reason, during early or late twilight more than at any other time, especially after a shower, and are unable to bear the heat of the sun's rays for several hours before and after noon. We have a good number of these crawling things in America, particularly in the western and southern parts of the Union, and are very well supplied with frogs, snakes, lizards, and even crocodiles, which we call alligators; but there is enough of food for them all, and we generally suffer them to creep about, to leap or to flounder as they please, or in accordance with the habits which have been given them by the great Conductor of all.

During the month of May, and indeed until autumn, we found an abundant supply of toads. Many "fine ladies," no doubt, would have swooned, or at least screamed and gone into hysterics, had they seen one of our baskets filled with these animals, all alive and plump. Fortunately we had no tragedy queen or sentimental spinster at Henderson. Our Kentucky ladies mind their own affairs, and seldom meddle with those of others farther than to do all they can for their comfort. The toads, collected one by one, and brought home in baskets, were deposited in a barrel for use. And now that night is over, and as is the first trial we are going to give our trot-line, just watch our movements from that high bank beside the stream. There sit down under the large cotton-wood tree. You are in no danger of catching cold at this season.

My assistant follows me with a gaff hook, while I carry the paddle of our canoe; a boy bears on his back a hundred toads as good as ever hopped. Our line—oh, I forgot to inform you that we had set it last night, but without the small ones you now see on my arm. Fastening one end to yon sycamore, we paddled our canoe, with the rest nicely coiled in the stern, and soon reached its extremity, when I threw over the side the heavy stone fastened to it as a sinker. All this was done that it might be thoroughly soaked, and without kinks or snarls in the morning. Now, you observe, we launch our light bark, the toads in the basket are placed next to my feet in the bow; I have the small lines across my knees all ready looped at the end. Nat, with the paddle, and assisted by the current, keeps the stern of our boat directly down stream; and David fixes, by the skin of the back and hind parts, the living bait to the hook. I hold the main line all the while, and now, having fixed one linelet to it, over goes the latter. Can you see the poor toad kicking and flouncing in the water? "No"—well, I do. You observe at length that all the lines, one after another, have been fixed, baited, and dropped. We now return swiftly to the shore.

"What a delightful thing is fishing!" have I more than once heard some knowing angler exclaim, who, "with the patience of Job," stands or slowly moves along some rivulet twenty feet wide, and three or four feet deep, with a sham fly to allure a trout, which, when at length caught, weighs half a pound. Reader, I never had such patience. Although I have waited ten years, and yet seen only three-fourths of the

Birds of America engraved, although some of the drawings of that work were patiently made so long ago as 1805, and although I have to wait with patience two years more before I see the end of it, I never could hold a line or a rod for many minutes, unless I had—not a "nibble," but a hearty bite, and could throw the fish at once over my head on the ground. No, no—if I fish for trout, I must soon give up, or catch, as I have done in Pennsylvania's Lehigh, or the streams of Maine, fifty or more in a couple of hours. But the trot-line is in the river, and there *it* may patiently wait, until I visit it toward night. Now I take up my gun and note-book, and, accompanied by my dog, intend to ramble through the woods until breakfast. Who knows but I may shoot a turkey or a deer? It is barely four o'clock; and see what delightful mornings we have at this season in Kentucky!

Evening has returned. The heavens have already opened their twinkling eyes, although the orb of day has yet scarcely withdrawn itself from our view. How calm is the air! The nocturnal insects and quadrupeds are abroad; the bear is moving through the dark cane-brake, the land crows are flying towards their roosts, their aquatic brethren towards the interior of the forests, the squirrel is barking his adieu, and the Barred Owl glides silently and swiftly from his retreat, to seize upon the gay and noisy animal. The boat is pushed off from the shore; the mainline is in my hands; now it shakes; surely some fish have been hooked. Hand over hand I proceed to the first hook. Nothing there! But now I feel several jerks stronger and more frequent than before. Several hooks I pass; but see, what a fine Cat-fish is twisting around and round the little line to which he is fast! Nat, look to your gaff—hook him close to the tail. Keep it up, my dear fellow!—there now, we have him. More are on, and we proceed. When we have reached the end many goodly fishes are lying in the bottom of our skiff. New bait has been put on, and, as we return, I congratulate myself and my companions on the success of our efforts; for their lies fish enough for ourselves and our neighbors.

A trot-line at this period was perfectly safe at Henderson, should I have allowed it to remain for weeks at a time. The navigation was mostly performed by flat-bottomed boats, which during calm nights floated in the middle current of the river, so that the people on board could not observe the fish that had been hooked. Not a single steamer had as yet ever gone down the Ohio; now and then, it is true, a barge or a keel-boat was propelled by poles and oars; but the nature of the river is such at that place, that these boats when ascending were obliged to keep near the Indian shore until above the landing of the village (below which I always fixed my lines), when they pulled across the stream.

Several species or varieties of Cat-fish are found in the Ohio, namely the Blue, the White, and the Mud Cats, which differ considerably in their form and color, as well as in their habits. The Mud Cat is the best, although it seldom attains so great a size as the rest. The Blue Cat is the coarsest, but when not exceeding from four to six pounds, it affords tolerable eating. The White Cat is preferable to the last, but not so common; and the Yellow Mud Cat is the best and rarest. Of the blue kind some have been caught that weighed a hundred pounds. Such fishes, however, are looked upon as monsters.

The form in all the varieties inclines to the conical, the head being disproportionately large, while the body tapers away to the root of the tail. The eyes, which are small, are placed far apart, and situated as it were on the top of the forehead, but laterally. Their mouth is wide, and armed with numerous small and very sharp teeth, while it is defended by single-sided spines, which when the fish is in the agonies of death, stand out at right angles, and are so firmly fixed as sometimes to break before you can loosen them. The Cat-fish has also feelers of proportionate length, apparently intended to guide its motions over the bottom, whilst its eyes are watching the objects passing above.

Trot-lines cannot be used with much success unless during the middle stages of the water. When very low, it is too clear, and the fish, although extremely voracious, will rarely risk its life for a toad. When the waters are rising rapidly, your trot-lines are likely to be carried away by one of the numerous trees that float in the stream. A "happy medium" is therefore best.

When the waters are rising fast and have become muddy, a single line is used for catching Cat-fish. It is fastened to the elastic branch of some willow several feet above the water, and must be twenty or thirty feet in length. The entrails of a Wild Turkey, or a piece of fresh venison, furnish good bait; and if, when you visit your line the next morning after you have set it, the water has not risen too much, the swinging of the willow indicates that a fish has been hooked, and you have only to haul the prize ashore.

One evening I saw that the river was rising at a great rate, although it was still within its banks. I knew that the White Perch were running, that is, ascending the river from the sea, and anxious to have a tasting of that fine fish, I baited a line with a crayfish, and fastened it to the bough of a tree. Next morning as I pulled in the line, it felt as if fast at the bottom, yet on drawing it slowly I found that it came. Presently I felt a strong pull, the line slipped through my fingers, and next instant a large Cat-fish leaped out of the water. I played it for a while, until it became exhausted, when I drew it ashore. It had swallowed the hook, and I cut off the line close to its head. Then passing a stick through one of the gills, I and a servant tugged the fish home. On cutting it open, we, to our surprise, found in its stomach a fine White Perch, dead, but not in the least injured. The Perch had been lightly hooked, and the Cat-fish, after swallowing it, had been hooked in the stomach, so that, although the instrument was small, the torture caused by it no doubt tended to disable the Cat-fish. The perch we ate, and the cat, which was fine, we divided into four parts, and distributed among our neighbors. My most worthy friend and relative, Nicholas Berthoud, Esq., who formerly resided at Shippingport in Kentucky, but now in New York, a better fisher than whom I never knew, once placed a trot-line in "the basin" below "Tarascon's Mills," at the foot of the Rapids of the Ohio, I cannot recollect the bait which was used; but on taking up the line we obtained a remarkably fine Cat-fish, in which was found the greater part of a suckling pig!

PART III

A Touch
of Salt

Down to the Sea!

CHARLES KINGSLEY

Toward evening it grew suddenly dark, and Tom looked up and saw a blanket of black clouds lying right across the valley above his head, resting on the crags right and left. He felt not quite frightened, but very still; for everything was still. There was not a whisper of wind, nor a chirp of a bird to be heard; and next a few great drops of rain fell plop into the water, and one hit Tom on the nose, and made him pop his head down quickly enough.

And then the thunder roared, and the lightning flashed, and leapt across Vendale and back again, from cloud to cloud, and cliff to cliff, till the very rocks in the stream seemed to shake: and Tom looked up at it through the water, and thought it the finest thing he ever saw in his life.

But out of the water he dared not put his head; for the rain came down by bucketsful, and the hail hammered like shot on the stream, and churned it into foam; and soon the stream rose, and rushed down, higher and higher, and fouler and fouler, full of beetles, and sticks; and straws, and worms, and addle-eggs, and wood-lice, and leeches, and odds and ends, and omnium-gatherums, and this, that, and the other, enough to fill nine museums.

Tom could hardly stand against the stream, and hid behind a rock. But the trout did not; for out they rushed from among the stones, and began gobbling the beetles and leeches in the most greedy and quarrelsome way, and swimming about with great worms hanging out of their mouths, tugging and kicking to get them away from each other.

And now, by the flashes of the lightning, Tom saw a new sight—all the bottom of the stream alive with great eels, turning and twisting along, all down stream and away. They had been hiding for weeks past in the cracks of the rocks, and in burrows in the mud; and Tom had hardly ever seen them, except now and then at night: but now they were all out, and went hurrying past him so fiercely and wildly that he was quite frightened. And as they hurried past he could hear them say to each other, "We must run, we must run. What a jolly thunderstorm! Down to the sea, down to the sea!"

And then the otter came by with all her brood, twining and sweeping along as fast as the eels themselves; and she spied Tom as she came by, and said "Now is your time, eft, if you want to see the world. Come along, children, never mind those nasty eels: we shall breakfast on salmon to-morrow. Down to the sea, down to the sea!"

Then came a flash brighter than all the rest, and by the light of it—in the thousandth part of a second they were gone again—but he had seen them, he was certain of it—three beautiful little white girls, with their arms twined round each other's necks, floating down the torrent, as they sang, "Down to the sea, down to the sea!"

"Oh stay! Wait for me!" cried Tom; but they were gone: yet he could hear their voices clear and sweet through the roar of thunder and water and wind, singing as they died away, "Down to the sea!"

"Down to the sea?" said Tom; "everything is going to the sea, and I will go too. Good-bye, trout." But the trout were so busy gobbling worms that they never turned to answer him; so that Tom was spared the pain of bidding them farewell.

And now, down the rushing stream, guided by the bright flashes of the storm; past tall birch-fringed rocks, which shone out one moment as clear as day, and the next were dark as night; past dark hovers under swirling banks, from which great trout rushed out on Tom, thinking him to be good to eat, and turned back sulkily, for the fairies sent them home again with a tremendous scolding, for daring to meddle with a water-baby; on through narrow strids and roaring cataracts, where Tom was deafened and blinded for a moment by the rushing waters; along deep reaches, where the white water-lilies tossed and flapped beneath the wind and hail; past sleeping villages; under dark bridge-arches, and away and away to the sea. And Tom could not stop, and did not care to stop; he would see the great world below, and the salmon, and the breakers, and the wide wide sea.

And when the daylight came, Tom found himself out in the salmon river.

And what sort of a river was it? Was it like an Irish stream, winding through the brown bogs, where the wild ducks squatter up from among the white water-lilies, and the curlews flit to and fro, crying "Tullie-wheep, mind your sheep;" and Dennis tells you strange stories of the Peishtamore, the great bogy-snake which lies in the black peat pools, among the old pine-stems, and puts his head out at night to snap at the cattle as they come down to drink?—But you must not believe all that Dennis tells you, mind; for if you ask him:

"Is there a salmon here, do you think, Dennis?"

"Is it salmon, thin, your honor manes? Salmon? Cartloads it is of thim, thin, an' ridgmens, shouldthering ache out of water, av' ye'd but the luck to see thim."

Then you fish the pool all over, and never get a rise.

"But there can't be a salmon here, Dennis! And, if you'll but think, if one had come up last tide, he'd be gone to the higher pools by now."

"Shure thin, and your honor's the thrue fisherman, and understands it all like a book. Why, ye spake as if ye'd known the wather a thousand years! As I said, how could there be a fish here at all, just now?"

"But you said just now they were shouldering each other out of water?"

And then Dennis will look up at you with his handsome, sly, soft, sleepy, good-natured, untrustable, Irish gray eye, and answer with the prettiest smile:

"Shure, and didn't I think your honor would like a pleasant answer?"

Or was it like a Welsh salmon river, which is remarkable chiefly (at least, till this last year) for containing no salmon, as they have been all poached out by the enlightened peasantry, to prevent the *Cythral Sassenach* from coming bothering into Wales?

Or was it such a salmon stream as I trust you will see among the Hampshire water-meadows before your hairs are gray, under the wise new fishing-laws?—when Winchester apprentices shall covenant, as they did three hundred years ago, not to be made to eat salmon more than three days a week; and fresh-run fish shall be as plentiful under Salisbury spire as they are in Holly-hole at Christchurch; in the good time coming, when folks shall see that, of all Heaven's gifts of food, the one to be protected most carefully is that worthy gentleman salmon, who is generous enough to go down to the sea weighing five ounces, and to come back next year weighing five pounds, without having cost the soil or the state one farthing?

Or was it like a Scotch stream, such as Arthur Clough drew in his "Bothie"?—
"Where over a ledge of granite
Into a granite basin the amber torrent descended . . .
Beautiful there for the color derived from green rocks under;
Beautiful most of all, where beads of foam uprising
Mingle their clouds of white with the delicate hue of the stillness . . .
Cliff over cliff for its sides, with rowan and pendant birch boughs . . ."

Ah, my little man, when you are a big man, and fish such a stream as that, you will hardly care, I think, whether she be roaring down in full spate, like coffee covered with scald cream, while the fish are swirling at your fly as an oar-blade swirls in a boat-race, or flashing up the cataract like silver arrows, out of the fiercest of the foam; or whether the fall be dwindled to a single thread, and the shingle below be as white and dusty as a turnpike road, while the salmon huddle together in one dark cloud in the clear amber pool, sleeping away their time till the rain creeps back again off the sea. You will not care much, if you have eyes and brains; for you will lay down your rod contentedly, and drink in at your eyes the beauty of that glorious place; and listen to the water-ouzel piping on the stones, and watch the yellow roes come down to drink and look up at you with their great soft trustful eyes, as much as to say, "You could not have the heart to shoot at us?" And then, if you have sense, you will turn and talk to the great giant of a gilly who lies basking on the stone beside you. He will tell you no fibs, my little man; for he is a Scotchman.

No. It was none of these, the salmon stream at Harthover. It was such a stream as you see in dear old Bewick; Bewick, who was born and bred upon them. A full hundred yards broad it was, sliding on from broad pool to broad shallow, and broad shallow to broad pool, over great fields of shingle, under oak and ash coverts, past low cliffs of sandstone, past green meadows, and fair parks, and a great house of gray stone, and brown moors above, and here and there against the sky the smoking chimney of a colliery. You must look at Bewick to see just what it was like, for he has drawn it a hundred times with the care and the love of a true north countryman.

But Tom thought nothing about what the river was like. All his fancy was, to get down to the wide wide sea.

And after a while he came to a place where the river spread out into broad still shallow reaches, so wide that little Tom, as he put his head out of the water, could hardly see across.

And there he stopped. He got a little frightened. "This must be the sea," he thought. "What a wide place it is! If I go on into it I shall surely lose my way, or some strange thing will bite me. I will stop here and look out for the otter, or the eels, or some one to tell me where I shall go."

So he went back a little way, and crept into a crack of the rock, just where the river opened out into the wide shallows, and watched for some one to tell him his way: but the otter and the eels were gone on miles and miles down the stream.

There he waited, and slept too, for he was quite tired with his night's journey; and, when he woke, the stream was clearing to a beautiful amber hue, though it was still very high. And after a while he saw a sight which made him jump up; for he knew in a moment it was one of the things which he had come to look for.

Such a fish! ten times as big as the biggest trout, and a hundred times as big as Tom, sculling up the stream past him, as easily as Tom had sculled down.

Such a fish! shining silver from head to tail, and here and there a crimson dot; with a grand hooked nose and grand curling lip, and a grand bright eye, looking round him as proudly as a king, and surveying the water right and left as if all belonged to him. Surely he must be the salmon, the king of all the fish.

Tom was so frightened that he longed to creep into a hole; but he need not have been; for salmon are all true gentlemen, and, like true gentlemen, they look noble and proud enough, and yet, like true gentlemen, they never harm or quarrel with any one, but go about their own business, and leave rude fellows to themselves.

The salmon looked at him full in the face, and then went on without minding him, with a swish or two of his tail which made the stream boil again. And in a few minutes came another, and then four or five, and so on; and all passed Tom, rushing and plunging up the cataract with strong strokes of their silver tails, now and then leaping clean out of water and up over a rock, shining gloriously for a moment in the bright sun; while Tom was so delighted that he could have watched them all day long.

And at last one came up bigger than all the rest; but he came slowly, and stopped, and looked back, and seemed very anxious and busy. And Tom saw that he was helping another salmon, an especially handsome one, who had not a single spot upon it, but was clothed in pure silver from nose to tail.

"My dear," said the great fish to his companion, "you really look dreadfully tired, and you must not over-exert yourself at first. Do rest yourself behind this rock"; and he shoved her gently with his nose, to the rock where Tom sat.

You must know that this was the salmon's wife. For salmon, like other true gentlemen, always choose their lady, and love her, and are true to her, and take care of her and work for her, and fight for her, as every true gentleman ought; and are not like vulgar chub and roach and pike, who have no high feelings, and take no care of their wives.

Then he saw Tom, and looked at him very fiercely one moment, as if he was going to bite him.

"What do you want here?" he said, very fiercely.

"Oh, don't hurt me!" cried Tom. "I only want to look at you; you are so handsome."

"Ah!" said the salmon, very stately but very civilly. "I really beg your pardon; I see what you are, my little dear. I have met one or two creatures like you before, and found them very agreeable and well-behaved. Indeed, one of them showed me a great kindness lately, which I hope to be able to repay. I hope we shall not be in your way here. As soon as this lady is rested, we shall proceed on our journey."

What a well-bred old salmon he was!

"So you have seen things like me before?" asked Tom.

"Several times, my dear. Indeed, it was only last night that one at the river's mouth came and warned me and my wife of some new stake-nets which had got into the stream, I cannot tell how, since last winter, and showed us the way round them, in the most charmingly obliging way."

"So there are babies in the sea?" cried Tom, and clapped his little hands. "Then I shall have some one to play with there? How delightful!"

"Were there no babies up this stream?" asked the lady salmon.

"No! and I grew so lonely. I thought I saw three last night; but they were gone in an instant, down to the sea. So I went too; for I had nothing to play with but caddises and dragon-flies and trout."

"Ugh!" cried the lady, "what low company!"

"My dear, if he has been in low company, he has certainly not learnt their low manners," said the salmon.

"No, indeed, poor little dear: but how sad for him to live among such people as caddises, who have actually six legs, the nasty things; and dragon-flies, too! why they are not even good to eat; for I tried them once, and they are all hard and empty; and, as for trout, every one knows what they are." Whereon she curled up her lip, and looked dreadfully scornful, while her husband curled up his too, till he looked as proud as Alcibiades.

"Why do you dislike the trout so?" asked Tom.

"My dear, we do not even mention them, if we can help it; for I am sorry to say they are relations of ours who do us no credit. A great many years ago they were just like us: but they were so lazy, and cowardly, and greedy, that instead of going down to the sea every year to see the world and grow strong and fat, they chose to stay and poke about in the little streams and eat worms and grubs; and they are very properly punished for it; for they have grown ugly and brown and spotted and small; and are actually so degraded in their tastes, that they will eat our children."

"And then they pretend to scrape acquaintance with us again," said the lady. "Why, I have actually known one of them propose to a lady salmon, the little impudent little creature."

"I should hope," said the gentleman, "that there are very few ladies of our race who would degrade themselves by listening to such a creature for an instant. If I saw such a thing happen, I should consider it my duty to put them both to death upon the spot." So the old salmon said, like an old blue-blooded hidalgo of Spain; and what is more, he would have done it too. For you must know, no enemies are so bitter against each other as those who are of the same race; and a salmon looks on a trout, as some great folks look on some little folks, as something just too much like himself to be tolerated.

On Sea and Shore

LATHAN A. CRANDALL

Mr. W. D. Howells made a most pathetic confession some years ago in an article contributed to a well-known journal when he said concerning vacations, "Whatever choice you make, you are pretty sure to regret it." Either Mr. Howells was "out of tune with the universe" or he never tried Edgartown.

Lest some of our readers should assume some selfish motive as prompting this bold proclamation of Edgartown as an attractive spot in which to spend the summer days, let it be said that the writer does not stand in with any hotel proprietor or real estate dealer in this village by the sea—or elsewhere.

Just how Martha's Vineyard came by its name is not certain. One tradition has it that when, in 1605, Bartholomew Gosnold sailed from England for "Northern Virginia" and chanced upon No Man's Land, he gave it the name of Martha's Vineyard and that, for some unknown reason, this name was transferred to the neighboring island.

Still another tradition alleges that the first settler on the island had a loved daughter to whom he gave a tract of land where vines grew luxuriantly; and so not only her tract, but the whole island came to be known as Martha's Vineyard. Neither theory costs anything; they are probably about equally true—you can take your choice.

At the extreme eastern end of Martha's Vineyard is the quaint, restful village of Edgartown. Turn your face towards the sun-rise and you look across a narrow bay to

Chappaquiddick Island, lying like a giant earthwork to protect the village from the assaults of the ocean. Wouldn't you like to ramble about a bit? We'll start in at this ravine south of the town, for it was here that the first settler made his home. Considering that he built his log cabin in 1630, only ten years after the landing of the Pilgrims, it is not strange that nothing remains to mark the place of his abode but this grass-grown depression in the hill-side.

Going south along the main street we come to the old Mayhew house, built in 1698, and looking as if it proposed to stand for a few centuries longer. Tradition has it that during the Revolutionary War a cannon-ball passed through its walls, going in at the rear and coming out at the front. We stop just long enough to make an unsuccessful hunt for the hole, and then on to the Collins place. What is there especially interesting about this fairly modern house? Just this: that it was our home through many summer days, and we can never think of it or of its hospitable mistress without a thrill of delight. Out there in the front yard gleam the white grave-stones which mark the resting places of members of the family who died a hundred and fifty years ago. From the wide porch at the back of the house you look out over the bay to Chappaquiddick, and may even catch glimpses of the sea, looking either to the north or to the south.

We've rested long enough, and will resume our journey up the street to the Fisher house. Some day we will make a long stop here, for it is a pre-Revolutionary mansion and full of relics of the olden days. Here are quaint old deeds, some of them in the Indian language, and no end of curios gathered by members of the family during a prolonged stay in Spain.

If you've leisure, let's visit the piers. Time was when all was bustle here, but it is depressingly quiet now. Forty vessels in a single year sailed from this port in search of whales. An old record bearing the date of November 11, 1652, tells us that "Thos. Daggett and Wm. Weeks are appointed whale cutters for this year; voted the day above written." In those days whales were frequently cast upon the beach by severe storms, and whale cutters were appointed to insure a fair division of the spoil. Now the whaling industry is a thing of the past. One of the pathetic sights of the village is an old whaling vessel tied to the pier and slowly rotting away. It is many a year since the last of these vessels sailed from port, but if we are fortunate enough to meet one of the retired captains and can induce him to tell us something of his experiences, we shall come quite near enough to the hardships and privations of those heroic days. Do you see that man going along Water Street? He sailed a whaling vessel for forty years, and one of his voyages lasted six years lacking ten days.

You can take your choice between visiting the old burial ground on "Tower Hill" or going out for a sail. Take the sail? I thought so. Of course, there are brown old head-stones with quaint epitaphs up there on the hill, but who is that in possession of his senses would pass up the chance to go sailing in a Cape Cod catboat on such a day as this?

Here we on board the "Quickstep," one of the smartest boats on the coast, with a captain who knows the sea as a native New Yorker knows Broadway. While we are dropping down the bay before the light wind, you may like to hear of the gale when this same boat and captain were blown out to sea. The storm came up suddenly and the wind blew directly off shore. The captain was fishing just off the Muskeget shoals and tried hard to beat in, but in vain. When the gale had blown itself out, wrecks were strewn all along the coast, and the Edgartown people had given up the captain for lost; but on the fourth day he came sailing into harbor. Single-handed and alone he had fought the storm and had won the fight.

Isn't this a great day? and isn't this the ideal way of getting over the water? Better let the captain take the tiller, for we're coming to the bar and the channel is crooked. Now we're over and you can see Nantucket off there to the south. Where you see the rough water is Muskeget shoals, and the captain says that at certain tides the strongest vessel would be wrenched to pieces by the fierce currents and counter-currents. Did you ever see sky more blue or feel air more full of tonic? Don't worry! We shall curtsy a little, but the water is not rough enough to make trouble for the most sensitive landsman. Going around Chappaquiddick, Captain? Good! That is just about a twenty-mile sail.

Have I ever been out here when it was rough? Haven't I told you about the trip after mackerel when we had on board a load of theology? No? well, we shall have plenty of time for the story before we sight the light-house.

It was a nasty sort of a morning, but as friends had come over from Cottage City the night before for the express purpose of having a day with the mackerel we concluded to try it notwithstanding the weather. Dr. G. had brought along his boy of twelve, and as we sailed down the quiet water of the bay that boy was simply bubbling over with happiness. The lad besought his father to make an arrangement with the captain whereby he should spend at least a month on this boat the following summer. The captain seemed willing, and as we crossed the bar the boy was exulting in the assurance of long days of perfect bliss only one year ahead. The wind was blowing fresh from the north-west and as soon as we were out from under the shelter of the land the boat began to curvet and jump and roll and quick-step just as any respectable boat is bound do to under such circumstances.

In less time than it takes to write this down the joy of life had departed for that lad and he was carefully laid away. The lone layman of the party was a close second, and, losing all interest in mackerel, he stretched himself out on deck. The Professor followed suit, and Dr. G., after a heroic struggle, proceeded to part company not only with one breakfast, but, seemingly, with a dozen or more. The captain, who was an interested spectator of the process, murmured to the writer, "Holy mackerel! What an eater that man must be." All day we rolled and pitched, with three of the party groaning to be put on shore. We caught only a few mackerel, but we had a great deal of exercise.

How do we catch mackerel? As you are asking how we do it, and not how it is done by the heartless, unimaginative, commercialized Philistines who chase the schools in steam vessels, I'll tell you. The night before, the captain gets the fodder ready. I mean the fodder for the mackerel, not for the fishermen. It is about as nauseous a mess as one can imagine. Salted menhaden and the refuse from scallops are ground up together, forming a mass of about the consistency of thick molasses. There is the grinder now, just inside the cabin! Looks like a big coffee-mill.

We usually start early in the morning, sometimes before daylight, in order to take advantage of a favorable tide. When we are out to sea a sharp lookout is kept for that peculiar ripple on the surface of the water which denotes the presence of a school of mackerel. When we have sailed to the spot we "come-to" and drift with the tide, while dipperful after dipperful of the "chum"—as the sticky and malodorous mess is called—is thrown out upon the water. The mackerel will throng about the boat to feed upon this dainty, and then the fishing begins. Empty barrels on deck, a line—some fifteen feet long—in each hand, with hooks that are set into pieces of lead forming a "squid," and the sport begins. It is usual to bait with a piece of mackerel belly, pure white; but very often the greedy fish will bite at the shining lead. You do not stop to unhook the fish, but simply slap them over into the barrel behind you, and then out with the hook again. Sport? Yes, of a sort. Gets a little monotonous after a while. The captain fishes for the Boston market, so we have no twinges of conscience about catching as many as possible.

Do we catch anything besides mackerel? If you'll put out that line and the captain will sail along the edge of one of these "rips" you are very likely to have a practical answer to your question. Nothing that time; but the captain is coming about and we'll see what happens on the other tack. This is the poetry of sea-fishing. Here we are bowling along with a full sheet and—hang on to him! No, you have not hooked on to a railroad train but a blue-fish. Look out! Don't slacken on your line or you'll lose him. Hurts your fingers? Of course it does. You should have put cots on them. Give him a swing! Keep him clear of the boat! There!

There's your answer. He's the bravest, pluckiest, gamiest fish on the coast. We sometimes spend a half day or so fishing for bottom-fish like scup, black-fish, or even flounders, for they bite freely and bring a fair price in the market; but if you're fishing for sport, there is just one fish in these waters which fills the bill completely, and that is the blue-fish. Sometimes you fish for hours without getting a strike, and then all at once you run into a school of them. When this happens you have your work cut out for you. I remember a day at Block Island when the Doctor and I had sailed almost entirely around the island with our lines trailing unmolested behind the boat. Just as we were approaching the starting place the captain said, "Look at the bluebills jumping, over towards shore!" The bluebill is a small fish some four or five inches long, and favorite food for the bluefish. We tacked and sailed across the school, back and forth, again and again, and when the fray was over we had sixty blue-fish lying in the bottom of the boat that averaged over five pounds in weight.

There's the light-house; we'll soon be in. See that hotel on the hill? I've just time to tell you of something that happened there on a summer morning a few years ago. I met Dr. _____ on the Providence boat and he asked where we were stopping and if we had any fishing. When I told him of the "Quickstep" and Captain Frank and the mackerel, he said, "I'll be over Monday morning. I'm tired of Assemblies and Chautauquas and hotel piazzas." Monday found him with us, and arrangements were made to start at five o'clock Tuesday morning. The hour came, but Dr. ____ did not. The captain worried about the tide and the bar, and I volunteered to see what had become of our tardy friend. Pounding on the hotel door I finally managed to rout out the night watchman, who readily went in quest of the Doctor. Upon his return he reported that the would-be fisherman had been asleep, but was now dressing and would be down very soon. The minutes passed, the tide was ebbing, and no Doctor. Finally I suggested to the watchman that he make another trip to see if he could not accelerate the Doctor's motions. Reappearing after a little, the watchman said, "What do you think? That miserable old cuss had gone sound asleep again." "What a fall was there, my countrymen!" The D. D., the LL. D., the eloquent preacher, the famous lecturer, the renowned defender of the "faith once delivered to the saints," the man whose name is a household word among those affiliated with one of our largest Protestant bodies catalogued as a "miserable old cuss!"

Here we are, at the pier. Confess now, that for unadulterated pleasure a sail such as we've just had beats motoring, whether on land or water, out of sight. Independent of the wind in a motor boat? Yes, but not of the sputtering and chugging and smell. Remember what Tennyson says in Locksley Hall? I don't know that I can quote it accurately, but the idea is that a day in a cat-boat is better than a thousand years in a naphtha launch.

Tale of a Bonefish

C. BLACKBURN MILLER

John Adams lived in Toronto, Canada. Homer's habitat was a grass-grown flat in the shallows off the Florida keys, by road some 1,800 miles away. And though Kipling wrote: "East is East and West is West, and never the twain shall meet," his adjuration didn't apply to North and South, for John Adams and Homer did meet.

Adams first learned of Homer from the author, in answer to a letter to *Outdoor Life* asking for information on fishing in the keys. Whereupon he climbed into his car and rolled south those 1,800 miles. At Pirates Cove Fishing Camp on Sugar Loaf Key, Adams finally applied the brakes, to establish headquarters beneath the coconut palms that grow beside a sea of cerulean blue and emerald green.

It was on the dock the next morning that he met Earl McQuaid, veteran guide and bonefisherman. McQuaid was idly contemplating the efforts of a huge jewfish to scrape the barnacles from his hide against one of the dock supports, when Adams strolled up. For a time they both contemplated the antics of the goggle-eyed leviathan plainly outlined in the clear water.

Then: "Ever fish for bonefish?" asked McQuaid, apropos of nothing at all.

"No," replied Adams, still contemplating the jewfish.

"You've missed a lot, then."

"I probably have," Adams admitted. He shifted his gaze to the slight, energetic figure confronting him.

"Well, if that's the case, I don't suppose you've ever heard of Homer?"

Adams nodded. "Yes, I have."

The guide's face lighted with slightly suppressed enthusiasm. But then it took on a puzzled expression. "How come you've heard of Homer, when you've never fished for bonefish?"

Adams didn't elucidate. "Well," he said offhandedly, "perhaps it's a different Homer."

"Yes, I suppose it must be." And McQuaid stepped aboard his cruiser, which lay tied up to the pier. The conversation as far as he was concerned was ended.

But not for Adams. "I've come 1,800 miles to catch a bonefish," he said idly, looking away to where Bill the pelican sat composedly on the water.

"You've what?" McQuaid spun around on his heel.

"Just that. Eighteen hundred miles."

"Well then, you probably want to see Homer."

"I probably do."

Then Adams sat himself down on the stringpiece of the dock, to hear more about Homer from McQuaid's lips. It appeared that Homer was a bonefish of startling dimensions. Living in a state of single blessedness, he scorned the association of the school fish, and reserved for his solitary domain a long, narrow strip of flat that separated two deep channels. When the flooding tide crept up over the sanded bars, Homer would emerge from the deep water, and his shadow could be seen slowly cruising over the flat. His graceful, silvery body itself was harder to distinguish, as it was practically colorless in the brilliant sunlight.

McQuaid said he had guided many anglers to Homer's retreat, but to no avail. For one thing, the bonefish's voraciousness was tempered by extreme caution. Even the distant splash of a diving fish hawk would be sufficient to send the wary fish scuttling back into the safety of deep water. His speed on the get-away was something at which to marvel. One instant he would be visible at a distance of twenty feet—then, save for a swirl of sand, there would be nothing to tell of his departure: he was just gone.

And even when Homer's caution failed him, he was still tough. A few of McQuaid's clients had through infinite strategy succeeded in hooking the fish, but they brought home no evidence of those encounters but broken tackle and burned thumbs.

When McQuaid's story was done, Adams walked back to the camp dining room, his enthusiasm increasing by leaps and bounds. As he consumed his eggs, he listened indifferently to a fat man with a bald head, who sat at an adjoining table telling his wife of the delights of catching pot-bellied groupers on the reefs.

Adams consumed the rest of that day in going over his tackle and arranging for plenty of bait. Then he tossed through a restless night, during which a gigantic bone-fish sought with devilish insistence to get under the blankets and bite his toes. He arose in the morning hollow-eyed but jubilant, for the sun shone clear and there was a steady wind from the south that promised to continue all day.

After loading tackle, lunch, bait, and landing nets into an eighteen-foot skiff, McQuaid spun the engine wheel, and they headed up the channel, Adams sitting in the bow. In a while the channel began to wind in among low flats, where hummocks of sparse sea grass protruded above the tide. A small mangrove-grown key appeared, beside which the water deepened. Attaching a piece of stripped bait to his hook, Adams tossed it over and allowed his line to run out some sixty yards before he checked it. McQuaid decreased the speed of the boat, and sat intently watching the shadowed water.

They had passed the key when Adams felt a smashing strike. He raised his tip sharply in response, and a large barracuda shot into the air. The sun gleamed on the silvery gray back, making the black splotches on the sides darker by contrast. For a moment the long, sinuous body of the fish hung in the air as if suspended by invisible wires; then, amid a rainbow of spray, it dropped back into the channel. The line went slack, and for a moment the angler thought the hook had pulled out. "Look out, he's coming aboard!" shouted McQuaid. "Here he comes. Duck!"

As if in response the big fish leaped clear of the water, heading directly toward the boat. His keen, doglike teeth were distinctly visible as he sailed through the air not five feet from Adams's head. For a moment it had looked as if he would land squarely in the boat, but his frenzied leap carried him well past the bow, and with a curious half twist of his lean, powerful body he disappeared beneath the surface.

There followed a series of savage rushes, runs that carried the fish beneath and around the boat, demanding much dexterity on the part of the angler to keep his line free from the propeller. But at last the barracuda gave signs of weakening, and McQuaid made ready his persuader, a stout club of weathered mangrove wood. Adams worked the fish alongside, and it appeared to be reasonably quiescent, but McQuaid was not deceived. Grasping the wire leader, he raised the barracuda's head above the surface with what appeared to be loving care, then brought his club down with a resounding smack squarely between the fish's eyes. There was a convulsive shiver along the barracuda's sparse frame, and he was slid into the boat.

"We'd better be getting over to see Homer now," said McQuaid, opening the throttle.

The channel turned abruptly toward the south, skirting a skeleton key, and then zigzagged between the flats. McQuaid pointed out Homer's lair, half a mile ahead—a long, magenta-colored reef, formed like a hockey stick and bordering the channel.

Then he shut off the engine and manned an oar. "Can't afford to scare him," he said. "We'll have trouble enough without that."

Adams removed his trolling rig, ran his line through an egg-shaped sinker, and tied on a stout hook with a twelve-inch gut snell. (Gut is preferable, for the gleam of a wire leader in shallow water will sometimes alarm bonefish.) To the hook, finally Adams fastened a hermit crab by means of a rubber band.

McQuaid poled steadily along. Save for a small ray and a diminutive shark, there was no visible sign of life on the shoal.

"He hasn't come in yet," said McQuaid. "We'll pick out a likely spot, heave the hook over, and wait. Tide's on the make, and Homer will come with it."

"How do you know?"

"He always does."

Poling close in, they stopped at length in the shadow of a mangrove key and threw out a small anchor; then from beneath the seat in the bow McQuaid drew forth an ingot of lead. Upon this he cracked the shells of a number of hermit crabs, striking them with a padded hammer to prevent vibrations. Next he cut up several conchs and two large crawfish for chum. Then, baiting his own hook with a shrimp, he cast well out on the flat. Adams cast likewise, and the two settled down to watchful waiting.

For an hour there was no sign of activity. McQuaid threw bits of conch overboard for the tide to distribute, that they might lure Homer from hiding. But another twenty minutes passed before a dark shadow glided up from the deep blue water, a shadow that drifted over the shoal flat like a summer cloud across the sky. It stopped, and the surface was broached by a broad-flanged tail.

"That's him," whispered McQuaid. "That's Homer, all right. I can tell by the way he works."

Adams felt a sudden glow of feverish excitement. He was looking at last upon the mighty bonefish of which he had heard so much.

"Hold steady. He's feeding over to your bait."

And now the tail had disappeared, and in its stead a slender dorsal fin arose from the suggestion of an olive-green back. A scant three feet separated Homer from the bait.

"He's a-goin' to take it," McQuaid whispered.

But on soaring wing from the south came a large pelican, his white neck feathers reflecting the sun. At the edge of the channel, some fifty yards from where Homer was, the bird's observant eyes espied a small fish. In mid-flight he uptilted, described a half somersault in the air, and landed with a splash that could be heard half a mile away. Where Homer had been, there was only a slight swirl of sand to tell of his departure. Discouragement settled down upon Adams with all the suffocating tenacity of a damp blanket.

"He'll be back," consoled McQuaid.

"I don't know about that. He was badly frightened."

"You wait and see," said the guide. Complacently he reached for a sandwich from the lunch basket.

Another hour went by, and the little skiff was now floating with several inches of water beneath its keel. "Look over there!" the guide said suddenly.

Adams looked quickly over his shoulder and once more perceived the drifting shadow, some eighty feet away.

"He's a-goin up by us. Can you cast in front of him?"

Nervously Adams reeled in his bait, inspected it briefly, and drew back his rod for the cast. The tip swept forward, the bait and line sailed out about twenty feet—and stopped in mid-air, checked by that most mysterious of phenomena, a backlash. The angler plucked at the angry snarl with hasty fingers. At length the tangle was dissipated and Adams again reeled in to cast. The famous bonefish, however, had passed on.

"Cast over there anyway. He'll most likely be moseying around."

Obediently Adams cast, and the bait fell with a slight splash far out on the shoal. On the farther side of the flat Homer's tail again showed, as he nosed down into the marl after some shellfish that he had discovered. The tail soon disappeared; once more the dorsal fin was in evidence and the bonefish resumed his quest for food. He swam about in an erratic manner, then headed toward Adams's bait.

Once more the Canadian felt a wild hope surge within him. Once more the rod trembled in his grasp.

"Watch out! He's a-comin'."

McQuaid's advice was superfluous, for Adams was crouched upon the edge of his seat like a bird dog in leash. Even so, it happened so swiftly that he was taken unawares. The bonefish saw the bait lying on a strip of white sand, dashed on it, took it in full stride, and was away like a flash of light, tearing off yards of line in his mad rush for deep water.

Instinctively Adams clamped his thumb on the spinning reel drum, and the outer skin was quickly scorched from this member. The angler then remembered his leather drag and applied it; but he dared not put too much pressure on it, lest the six-thread line burn through. Homer whistled on his way.

From the center of the flat grew a thin mangrove sapling. Though only a few feet high, it represented a formidable obstacle if Homer should decide to take advantage of it; and that is exactly what he did. When he was several yards beyond the sapling, he suddenly changed his course so as to bring the line against the coral-incrusted trunk. Adams met this move by standing up in the boat and raising his rod tip, as high as he could reach. The bight of the line passed over the top of the little tree, and Adams breathed easier.

Still, McQuaid wasn't too reassuring. "Turn him back, if you can, before he reaches deep water. There's a shark out there, and he'll get him."

Gaspingly Adams signified that he would do his utmost, and increased the strain. The bonefish, now several hundred yards away, bowed to the superior force. He started down the reef, his speed undiminished; but Adams felt that he had scored a point in thus turning the fish, and his spirits rose again.

At this moment the zipping line cut across the back of a passing ray. That astonished creature leaped from the water in a mad spurt of fright, soared through the air for six feet, and dropped back into the water to disappear in a cloud of white mud.

Homer, with the hook firmly embedded in his jaw, now changed his tactics; he made for the boat. Adams reeled in frantically in an endeavor to retrieve the slack line, and McQuaid aided by waving his hat, causing Homer to veer.

The fish consumed the next twenty minutes in rushes, threatening repeatedly to carry out all the line. At last there came a time when Adams could stem these rushes with a minimum of effort, and he caught a glimpse of a silvery side as the fish gave to the strain.

But the bonefish was obstinate. He began circling the boat, keeping a good seventy feet between himself and the bent rod, and by presenting his flat side to the angler offered a maximum of resistance with but little effort on his part. Adams's wrist felt the strain, and ached wearily. But just when he thought he would have to change hands to ease the pain, Homer decided to call it a day and surrender.

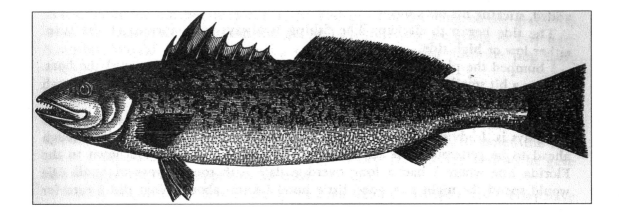

The Angler and the Weakfish

CHARLES BRADFORD

"The boats are in the breezy bay,
Fast by some point that juts its bar.

***

Or by some river mouth that pours
Its affluent current by the shores,
The fisher casts his baited line
To tempt the weakfish of the brine."
ISAAC McLELLAN

The doctor has come to my camp on the tiny island in the Great South Bay almost against his will—I forced the outing upon him by constant praising of the wild spot—and I feel that I must first make him comfortable and then show him the fishing. He is not at all himself. The long sail from the mainland, he says, has destroyed his usual good nature, but I tell him that it is hunger that makes him surly. "Living unnaturally, as you do in the city, Doctor, has destroyed your sense of appetite, and it has been so long a time since you were really hungry that you've forgotten what hunger is; you can't recognize it when, by a few hours of natural life, it returns to you, and you very naturally call your ailment by another name and attribute its origin to a false cause. I'll open some Little Necks for you, and while you eat them I'll broil you a sea bass." And I handed the old man a cup of sherry.

"Oh, I'll have none of your hungry yarn, nor any of your other yarns. I guess I know a little more about myself than you do," and the doctor looked real angry. "I couldn't eat in town, where I have every luxury; I couldn't sleep there, where I have a decent bed and decent roof over my head; and from what I see of this place I guess I'll starve outright or die of exposure here. I was a fool to listen to you. Why, this is the very worst sort of thing a man in my state of health should do—come out to a rough-and-tumble place like this. I wish I had gone back with the captain; that old numbskull, too, should have known better. Where are the decent things you said you had out here—the soft, clean beds, the fine stove, and all the other things?"

"Oh, don't fret so, Doctor. Everything will come in its order," I say to him. "Drink some sherry—it'll calm you. Here's your clams; now for a nice sea bass."

The shanty is not so bad as my visitor paints it. It has given me firm shelter for years, and some of the happiest days of my life have been spent within sight of its homely portal. Its island lies abreast of Bellmore, six miles distant on the mainland. The little house faces the ocean, whose breakers can be seen and heard rolling in on the wild beach a quarter of a mile to the south.

"Who owns this old place and what's it all about?" asks the doctor, the eating of the little clams and the sight of a fine sea bass giving battle at the end of my line reviving his spirits.

"I don't know the owner, Doctor. I took possession one summer's day some years ago—made for the open door during a terrific thunderstorm that overtook me in a small sailboat out there in the channel—and have never been disturbed, though spending several weeks here twice a year ever since."

The doctor is beginning to act agreeably. He offers to clean the sea bass while I catch another, but I hand him the rod and I set about cleaning the fish and building the drift-chip fire.

I could arrange for the doctor to take a nice weakfish, but decide it is better to first have the supper over and the beds made before we become really interested in the angle. So I let the dear old fellow take a two-pound bass, and then entice him from the play by putting the broiled fish on his knee.

The fish is cooked whole—head, tail, fins, and all—and I centre it in a great white platter, with thin slices of red pickled beet and a border of willow-green eel-grass.

"Well, you've proven three of your statements, at least," says the old man, pitching into the juicy flakes of the bass with the first natural hunger that has crossed his stomach in years, as he himself confesses; "I am hungry, as you said I'd be; fish are caught easily at the very door of the camp, and you really do cook and serve decently."

"And is not everything here really more pleasant than I described it?" I ask. "To-morrow at this time, my friend, you will admit as much."

The doctor is persuaded to eat the other bass and some thin strips of bacon, two huge potatoes roasted in the hot ashes, and a quantity of steamed soft clams raked out of a hotbed of seaweed.

"Now, Doctor, light your cigar and adjust your rod, and while you ply it upon the weakfish I'll clear away the supper mess and lay you a night couch where your sleep will prove 'sweeter and sounder, lighter and more luxurious than princes catch on beds of eiderdown and velvet'—here's your bait."

The day is nearing its end. The red sun is just dropping behind the fringe of dark-green upland, and already the flashes of Fire Island light pierce the gray shadows that gather in the east. The green herons are flying toward the island to roost, and the night herons are coming out to feed. The gulls gather on the loamy flats and exposed sandbars, and their restrained screams mingle with the cluck of the clapper rail, the whistle of the curlew, and the loud but mellow call of the golden plover and yellow shank, as they wing over the surf and meadow land.

The doctor, a few minutes before so surly with the world and himself, is now as calm and sweet-tempered as the tiny marsh wren that swings on the frail grassy stem at his feet, pouring out her evening hymn.

My companion stands on the sod banks and casts his crab bait into the tide, the green water now rushing in from the ocean, on whose plain the bounding whitecaps are made beautiful by the background of dark sky and the sunlit western heavens toward which they roll. Soon the tide will creep over the sod and flood the very island, but we shall not suffer any inconvenience. The little house rests high upon sturdy hardwood posts, and I have gathered up the outdoor cooking utensils, staked the boat safely, cut the salt hay for our beds, and gathered the chip-wood for the breakfast fire.

"You must cast out farther in the channel, Doctor," I call to my old friend, "or fish at the mouth of the little creek to your right. The sea bass, fluke, and blackfish frequent the spot you are attending, but the weakfish do not come in so close."

A cunning smile and a peculiar nod of the old angler's head tells me my advice will be heeded, but not upon the instant; he has something at his bait—a large fluke it proves to be—and he is playing the fish skillfully, for his tackle is delicate and his footing none too secure. The fish tugs heavily and, to the old man's astonishment, actually leaps out of the water and skims over the surface like a huge flat stone that is thrown to perform this service ere its weight will make it sink from sight. The fluke and the man battle for twenty minutes, but the angler gains the victory, and I tell him we shall have broiled flatfish if not planked weakfish for our morning meal.

Now the doctor removes his ounce dipsy and flails in the milder water at the creek mouth, and the crab meat, unhampered by any weight save that of itself and the hook, swirls with the current just as it might flow along at its own free will. It barely hides itself beneath the surface ere it is snapped by the game the doctor seeks, and the old man's rod again bends to the play, more violently now and with quicker movements than when the fluke tested its resiliency. We use the landing-net to secure this weakfish, because the locality does not permit of its being guided over the sod bank to the angler's footing, as the fluke was conquered. Here the bank is as yet a full foot out of water, while the spot where the great flatfish was landed allowed of the game being floated quite to the doctor's ankles.

My friend is now at the height of good nature, brought about by honest excitement, and as I take his rod and lead him toward the shanty, now without apparent foundation beyond the water that has flooded the whole meadow land, and appearing for all the world like a diminutive ark on stilts, I fancy I feel a slight quivering in his arm—the tremble of invigoration, not collapse.

"We'll go out in the boat and catch one more," says the doctor; "I'll handle the boat and let you take the fish."

"No, not to-night," I reply; "to-morrow, yes; and we'll make a glorious day of it, old friend; but no more tonight. You are tired, and that's all you can reasonably ask."

"But I'm not as tired to-night as I have been every night in town for the past half year."

"Ah, Doctor, your town tiredness is a different condition. There, 'mid the noise, the smoke, the frantic crowd, and all the unnatural disturbances of so-called civilization, you become fatigued, not really tired. Fatigue is killing; an honest tired feeling is health-giving. Fatigue is born of abuse; tiredness of exhilaration."

We go into the little house, now aglow with a bright, sweet-smelling wood fire, and the doctor's happy frame of mind goes on soaring higher and higher with every revealment. He sees the clean beds, made of rough pine wood and built against the wall one above the other like the berths of a steamship; the little shelves and cupboards in all the glory of their charges—tin tobacco boxes filled with every sort of spice and cooking condiment, and the hundred other homely but inviting articles stored here and there. Four square holes, one at each quarter of the dwelling, let in cool sea air on hot summer days, and stout wooden blinds protect these openings during storms.

The doctor and I talk a long time as we sit about the cozy fire, more than once filling the room with tobacco smoke so that we are obliged to open the door and fan the place with our coats.

I tell the old man all I know about the fishing and the natural history of the great lagoon, and he is a willing audience.

"The baymen, Doctor, say the Great South Bay is ninety miles long, six miles wide, and two feet deep. This is their deduction, and it is about correct, though, of course, in some places it is narrower than six miles and deeper, much, than two feet. There are channels twenty feet deep and open spots fully sixty feet in depth."

"Is flood tide the best for weakfish?" asks the doctor.

"Sometimes and in some places," I answer, remembering the reply of the bayman when I asked the same question years ago. "Most of my best fishing has been done just as the tide turns to run out and until it is about half out, though I have caught some nice fish on the incoming tide, as you took your four-pound fish this evening."

And so we chat until the doctor is made miserable by repeated efforts to keep awake; then we seek the berths, the old man being snugly housed in the lower one, and I blanketed to my chin in the one above him. Here we pass the night in sweet repose, lulled betimes by the booming of the surf, the splashing of the high tide, the leaping of heavy fish, the murmur of the mild wind, and the cry of the night bird.

"I may, peradventure, give you some instructions that may be of use even in your own rivers; and shall bring you acquainted with more flies than Father Walton has taken notice of in his *Compleat Angler*."

CHARLES COTTON.

Sea-Fishing in Simon's Bay

SIR GEORGE ASTON

Simon's Bay is a queer little place, dominated on one side by a mountain topped with gorgeous heaths and wild flowers and on the other side by immense docks, usually empty. Between them is old Admiralty House, with its lovely garden, and Simon's Town itself, straggling along the road between the mountain and the shore, and peopled chiefly by a colored parasitic population depending directly, as we all do indirectly, upon the British Navy for means of existence. For the sea-fisherman the bay has infinite possibilities, provided that he takes expert advice about time, tide and locality. You can fish with rod or hand-line from the huge breakwater; there your bait often seems to be anchored to the bottom. Something tells you that there is life in the thing at the other end of your line, and you long for a capstan or winch to put on an extra strain. It is a gigantic cuttlefish. Using your whole strength, you may detach his hold of the bottom only to se him let go the bait as it breaks the surface. There is but little sport to be had off the breakwater, but there are lessons to be learned. You may catch an "elf," a sporting little fish, excellent eating, but take care that the eating is all done on your side. Once I landed a little beauty, of about half a pound, and treated him as I would a small trout: I put my thumb in his mouth to force it open and extract the hook. Instead of opening wider, the little jaws closed like a vice, overlapping, and the tip of my thumb itself, which was left outside, bleeding profusely. A painful proceeding, avoided by experienced fishers in those waters.

For the best sport with the sea fishes of Simon's Bay you must use a boat, and for work beyond the shelter of the breakwater the bigger the boat the better. There is grand fishing with a hand-line for Cape salmon near the Lighthouse, well out in the bay, but it is sometimes a trying experience. During the summer weather it always seems to be blowing hard, and I never yet met a fisher keen enough to count seasickness of no account compared with his sport. The skipper of a certain Brixham trawler has a tale to tell of a certain friend in whose honor he provided a specially solid "plum duff," after riding for hours on a long glassy swell, and was promptly implored to return at once to harbor. As that friend was the writer of these notes, it may be assumed that a calm day was selected to try for Cape salmon by the Lighthouse. We dropped anchor in deep water near a ridge of rocks, fixing our position by cross-bearings known only to the initiated, and in about an hour and a quarter caught a heavier weight of fish than I have ever seen "landed" in the time, about 400 lb. The method sounds simple enough. We used big hooks, with huge chunks of mackerel as bait and no leads to weight our lines, two of which were held by expert Malay fishermen, who at first caught at least three fish to our one. We soon found out the reason. The weight of the great length of line we had to use, and the pull of the tide, made it very difficult to feel when a fish had taken the bait; you had to strike at what felt like only a touch. Then, again, knowing that we were after twenty-pounders, we treated them with respect and "played" them, thereby losing much skin from our fingers, wasting much time, and sometimes losing our fish. The long, nervous fingers of the Malays helped them to feel the least little tug, and instantly they hauled up, hand over hand, got their fish to the surface and into the boat, without leaving them time to diagnose the situation. Well, if catching fish is the only object of the fisherman, no matter how they are caught, I think that about twenty fish weight 400 lb. in an hour and a quarter should satisfy anyone.

But, from the sportsman's point of view, Simon's Bay has better to offer when the "snook" is about. Let me introduce him. On your way through the street of the little town you will notice him first with your nose. You will then see him hanging up, split open and smoked, by the sides of many doorways of houses and shops; and when properly cured and cooked, "Cape snook" is by no means to be despised. You may have a talk with some expert who warns you to beware of being bitten when you are extricating your hook from the mouth of a snook. You will see a Malay fisherman, directly he gets one into the boat, clasp it firmly under his left arm to hold its head steady; then a tremendous blow on the top of the fish's head with a boat's stretcher, belaying-pin, or what-not, to stop the snapping of its jaws, and then the hook can be safely removed. While waiting for our boat, we were told a gruesome story of an old fisherman who had neglected these precautions, was bitten in the hand by the poisonous teeth of a snook, and "before they could get him home to Kalk Bay he was a corpse!"

So much for snook in general. Now for the snook that gave me one of my most exciting experiences in forty years of fishing, in sea water and in fresh. This time I had only one companion, an Oxford undergraduate who had come out on a short visit to South Africa, and our boat was a very small one, a little twelve-foot skiff belonging to the flagship of the Cape squadron. The snook were good enough at that time to come close inshore, so we could keep well under the shelter of the breakwater, and there was no need to venture out into the nasty lop in the open bay. Before leaving England I had provided myself with a sea rod with a whole-cane butt and a green-heart top, quite a short rod, as a long one would be unwieldy to handle in a boat. It was impossible to get ashore to land a fish, as one does with a salmon, and a snook plays like a salmon, only very much more so. He turns mad directly he is hooked and makes wild runs incessantly, every bit of his great length wriggling and tugging furiously to get free. With so short a rod it is not easy to master such a fish, so I had also provided myself with an immense Nottingham reel, holding about two hundred yards of line. The first snook we can deal with briefly. He tore line off the reel as soon as he was hooked, but all went well, and we got him alongside and gaffed him in about five minutes. He weighed between nine and ten pounds. Now for the great experience.

The second snook I hooked made a mighty run, the reel screeching on hot bearings as he went. Before his run was at an end the reel came off the rod, banged down on one of the thwarts of the boat and bounded overboard, sinking, spinning as it went, to the bottom of the sea. There I was, helpless, holding up my rod, with a mad fish at one end of the line and a big reel at the other end, both making off at speed. They say that a drowning man remembers all the events of his life during his last few minutes. I have always wondered how they know that he does, but in my own great emergency I wished that I could remember whether I had fixed the end of my line firmly to the drum in the middle of the big reel. Anyhow, it was too late to do so now, and the only chance was to retrieve the reel from the bottom, meanwhile "hand-lining" the fish as best I could. It was impossible, of course, to control his mad rushes in any way. My "crew" rose to the occasion splendidly, got hold of the line in the direction of the reel, and hauled in, hand over hand, while I kept the recovered line clear of everything in the boat, so that the fish had run it out if he wanted to, which he did, frequently. By hauling up full speed hand over hand, my companion recovered the reel, still spinning, with plenty of line on the drum, after several ineffective attempts, as the reel sank spinning again whenever he slacked the line for a second to grab it. Landing that reel was as exciting a sport as landing any fish, but at last it was in the boat. The next step was to wind up on the reel the eighty yards or so of slack line in the boat, taking care to get no kinks in it, when the fish was taking out line in one direction and the reel in the other.

At last the line was on the reel and the reel on the butt of the rod; the fish chose that moment to make a rush across under the bows of the boat, followed by another rush back again across the stern, a maneuver which a few minutes before would have defeated us by making a bight of line round the part with which we were hauling the reel up from the bottom. The rest of the struggle followed the normal course, and the snook was in the boat about twenty minutes—seeming like twenty hours—from the time when he was hooked. He weighed twelve pounds.

So ended the most exciting experience I ever had when sea fishing, either in Simon's Bay or elsewhere.

Sharks on the Shell Bars

VEREEN BELL

We went for reds. But we hadn't been trolling more than fifteen minutes when we saw two triangular dorsal fins easing through the water near a shell bar a hundred yards away. That's when we forgot about the red fish . . .

We've done considerable coast fishing together, the six of us—Fondron and Emmett and I, and our wives—and we've learned some things. The main thing we've learned is that you can fish and be comfortable too. Some people think it's acceptable sport to spend six hours under a blistering Florida-coast sun in a small boat rank with old fish bait and ankle-deep in dirty brine. And, I might as well admit it, I'm one of them—if I can't do any better.

But we knew how to do better. From one of Panacea's mullet fishermen we rented a seine boat. Price, one dollar for the day. This boat is about twenty-four feet long, with plenty of width, a dry bottom, a six-foot seine deck at the stern end, and infinite seaworthiness. Room for portable ice boxes full of mullet and beer, vacuum jugs, gasoline cans, tackle boxes, a dozen rods, and reels of all sizes. Room for six people to fish without slapping one another in the face with bait slabs. Room to get up and move around and prevent *rigor mortis* from setting in. And finally, room for three motors—yes, three—on the capacious stern board.

After daylight the cars wound through the palmetto flatland bordering the broad, black Ochlockonee River mouth, and stopped beside an unoccupied fisherman's shack surrounded by tin cans. Floating serenely forty feet from shore was our yacht. Emmett shouldered his motor and waded out to it. When he had gunned the boat to the beach we loaded up.

Then we mounted the motors. My motor, a 9-horsepower one, went in the middle of the stern board. Emmett and Fondron had 4's, which they mounted on either side of mine. We shoved out a bit, then pulled the three starting cords simultaneously, and the three motors burst into life on the first pull. These modern motors don't have to be cajoled; they *go*. We nudged the levers open and the throbbing hum of the motors rose in harmony. Probably the people of the countryside muttered something about a distant squadron of naval planes from Pensacola and went back to sleep.

An incoming tide flooded upriver from the bay, and the wind that came with it chopped the black water, but the boat rode steady, and the battery of motors thrust it rapidly into the teeth of the tide. Fondron and the feminine element rigged redfish spoons while Emmett and I manned the outboards, steering with the larger motor. We knifed between the piles of the new Ochlockonee Bay bridge without slowing, and presently the water began taking on a greenish tinge. We were in the bay.

When we reached the shell bars we killed two of the motors and uptilted them, using one of the 4's for trolling. The three girls let out spoons astern. The water was shallow, only four or five feet deep. Startled mullet darted away over the shoals. Ahead, an occasional smear of white splash seemed to indicate striking reds.

About that time Flonnie, my wife, yelled, then tugged her line and said, "Shucks. Just raked bottom, I guess."

Life moved in the bay. Yonder in the shallows near the shore, white spray fanned upward where porpoises were giving the mullet hell. Once, not far astern, a tarpon rolled, showing his flag and for a few moments we held our breath, waiting for him to lam into one of the cruising spoons. But he either didn't see them, or didn't want them. Later, a hundred yards gulfward, a big whip ray leaped eight feet clear, flinging spray. For a monster of such personal ugliness, a whip ray takes the air with incredible grace. He leaps to rid himself of remoras, the little striped hitch hikers that cling to big fish by means of handy suction disks on their heads.

Suddenly Fondron, who had his 260 pounds up front to watch for shell banks, shouted, "Look!"

We looked—and saw two good-size sharks cruising around in a horseshoe formed by oyster bars. That's when we forgot about the reds.

We took off the spoons, and eased into the horseshoe's shallows. I had 15-thread line on my reel, about 150 yards of it, with a test pull of 456 pounds, while both of the fins we saw indicated sharks of 300 pounds plus. Emmett's line was bigger, being about a 24 thread. Fondron's had been on his reel so long he'd forgotten what it was. We quickly fastened big hooks onto eight-foot piano-wire leaders, baited up with half mullets, yelled "Duck!" to the excited girls, and let fling toward the spot we'd last seen the sharks. My mullet-head cast was about fifty feet.

Then we waited. Nothing happened. Maybe we had scared the sharks away. But that didn't seem likely. Sharks aren't likely to frighten easily . . .

Somebody hissed. Down to the right, a fin showed. Back of us, forty yards or more, were two other fins. The place was infested.

One of the fish turned our way, cruising lazily along the bar in water not three feet deep, with his tail waving leisurely back and forth. Emmett reeled in hurriedly, wound up, and hurled the big bait sixty feet through the air. The mullet plunked about four yards to the left of the shark. The dorsal fin swerved—toward the bait!

"He's going for it!" I whispered.

"Take it, boy, take it!" Emmett urged hoarsely.

The fin submerged. Our throats got tight, waiting. Three pieces of mullet out, and a hungry shark not ten feet from the farthest! You could hear the girls almost moaning with excitement, and my own pulse was tom-tomming. It was like sitting on a time bomb, wondering if this was the appointed moment for the explosion, or the next.

Still nothing happened. We knew the shark had by now passed Emmett's offering. Mine was close. Then Fondron grunted. His line was inching out. He braced himself and yanked the hook hard. And that set off the explosion!

"*Got him!*" Fondron yelled.

We knew that. We could see the line, taut as a fiddle string, razoring through the brine. We could hear the reel singing out. Emmett and I, on the raised stern deck, saw something else. The shark was angling sharply astern, and going like hell. We had a split second to realize that we both would have to try to jump that cleaving line. I had a momentary glimpse of myself clumping around on my knees, selling pencils. At the second the line would have attempted to cut our legs from under us, it went limp . . .

Broken line!

Fondron made a futile tug, then took a deep, shuddering breath and began coloring the clear air with a purple haze. I afterward noticed that the paint was blistered on his side of the boat. The girls didn't mind his language much—within another four months they were speaking to him again as if nothing had happened.

As for Emmett and me, we tried hard to sympathize with him, but we were so relieved not to be swept overboard or amputated at mid-thigh that I'm afraid we didn't sound sincere.

We cast baits out again.

Emmett said, "Fon, how you expect to catch a shark with an old piece of grocery string?"

I don't know what Fondron muttered, but it cooked the piece of mullet in his hand. He wound up and cast the bait, still smoking slightly, halfway to the shell bar.

"You own a whole hardware store full of fishing tackle," I put in, "and come off with line that—"

A shock ran up my line and jolted against my backbone. The reel hummed. Forgetting I was using a reel with no leather guard, I jammed my thumb against the wildly whirring spindle and lost about a square inch of skin. Finally I found the star drag.

"Crank up!" I yelled to Emmett.

He jumped to the motors. My line was melting fast. I was afraid I'd have none left by the time Emmett got a motor in the water and going. Then my rod tip ducked, something snapped, and I exhaled wearily and began winding in. The shark had rolled on my leader, kinked it, and broken it.

I sat down and called for a bottle of beer, while the others told me how I could have held him.

The crabs began finding our mullet. Every two or three minutes we'd have to reel in and shake a couple of them off. Virginia and Flonnie, who would sell their birthrights for a mess of deviled crabs, stood it as long as humanly possible.

"Let's get some of those crabs," they said. "We could catch dozens."

They rigged up a couple of fresh-water casting reels, baiting with mullet, and went to fishing. They caught several crabs immediately. Getting no further action from sharks, and seeing none rambling around, we watched the crabbing.

Abruptly Virginia's line went taut, and the little rod almost leaped out of her hand. She had several hundred pounds of shark on a freshwater casting outfit!

"What'll I do?" she cried above the throb and bump of the racing reel.

Not one of us could tell her anything to do, except hang on and yell, and she was already doing that. It ended soon—though not soon enough for Virginia—with a snapped line.

Not three minutes later my line tightened.

"This time you'll stick!" I vowed, and set the hook. Instantly the line began ripping out, whining hotly against the rod guides. "Crank up!"

The line evaporated off the drum, dancing and leaping. I heard one of the motors hiss, then break into a welcome hum. We had to get out of the horseshoe before the shark, already out of it, could cut back and take my line across the shell bar.

"Give it the gun!" Fondron yelled.

Then the reel drum ceased whirring. The terrific tug faded. And I knew I had an empty line. The shark was gone. When I reeled the 100 yards of line in, nothing was broken. Everything except the bait was there. And something else was there—the twenty yards of line that had been snapped off Fondron's rig earlier was tangled around my leader. Problem: was it the same shark? And did I hang him with my own hook, or did my tackle get tangled with the broken line that trailed from the shark's mouth? Or did I merely drag the loose line in as I recovered my own? Your guess is as good as mine. It only goes to prove that you can't tell what will happen when you're fooling with sharks.

Emmett hung one next, and lost him. Then we saw another shark lazing along the bars, looking for trouble. He took Emmett's bait. And he got his trouble. Emmett leaned on his rod with a back yank that would have sunk the hook into a coconut. The shark raced for the open end of the horseshoe.

Fondron spun the motor. It broke into life. Virginia, up front, manfully hoisted the anchor—she was the only one who could get to it. We slid out of the shell bars just before the shark would have taken the last of Emmett's line.

For fifteen minutes the shark ran wildly, with almost the abruptness of a tarpon—and with a lot more sheer horsepower. When he finally settled down to a steady pull we killed the motor.

Standing now on the bow, Emmett fought the shark, inching in a little line when he could, losing it back when the big fish wanted it. And all the time that mulelike shark towed a 24-foot seine boat with six people in it. He didn't knife it through the water. But he kept it following him. You could feel it moving, and behind there was a gentle wake. Sharks may not walk on their tails, or arch in the sunlight like some of our flashier game fish, but they don't have to apologize for brute pulling power.

Half an hour passed. I opened a bottle of cold beer and handed it to the sweating Emmett.

Fifteen minutes later Emmett gasped, "He's tiring!"

That was surprising. We had guessed it would take a least an hour and a half to bring him in.

Emmett fought all the line in except about ten yards. In the shimmering green water, a gray-white shape moved. Then a mighty thrash of the fish's tail showered spray over the boat, and he was running again.

A few minutes later, though, he was close once more. We had no gaff—we hadn't come for big fish. So Fondron got out the Colt Woodsman *.22* automatic pistol.

The shark broke water five yards away. And then we saw why he had become quickly exhausted. He was hooked, not in the mouth, but in the left pectoral fin. He had been forced to swim unnaturally, against a terrific side pull.

A bullet from the little gun galvanized him into furious action, and again the reel whined. But it didn't last long. Emmett pumped him up again. Presently he was alongside, his movements increasingly feeble.

The little gun spat. The shark convulsed considerably and, dying, rolled belly up. That upside-down position, the only one he hadn't tried, did the trick—it tore the hook out of the fin. The shark slid bottomward, headfirst, and we followed his descent until he gradually faded out of sight in the murky greenness—and became just another big one that got away.

We came back that afternoon with nothing to show for our trouble except a dozen crabs that could have been bought in town for twenty-five cents the lot. And they, it turned out, were dead and therefore no good. Not worth while, you say?

We planned to go back the next weekend.

But when we went looking for sharks, we never seemed to find them. So we went fishing for other things, with a crafty eye peeled for cruising dorsal fins, and we always took some bigger tackle along. No really heavy tackle. I had a reel that held about 140 yards of 18-thread line. I lost one shark because I had forgotten to wet the line beforehand, and it hung and broke.

When you hang a shark of 200 pounds on fairly light tackle like that, it's absolutely necessary to haul in the anchor and follow him a way. Otherwise he'll take out all your line, snap it, and keep helling it on away from there without any please-excuse-its. Once when I had a shark strike, there was some trouble with the anchor. My line was melting fast, so I tried tightening the drag a bit to slow him. I lost that shark too.

That night I removed the little wire spring that controlled the drag, making a no-drag reel of it, and put on a leather thumb guard. And that was the shape of my reel when I hung my next shark.

This time we went for sea trout. There were four of us now, so we used a smaller boat and two motors instead of three on the stern board. The day was hotter than the inside of a Bessemer converter. Fondron, in his bathing trunks, scoffed at the heat and made bold talk to the bubbling sun. "Shine on down, Josh, you might as well be shining on a lightwood knot."

Sea trouting on the coast is drift fishing. You drift over the shallow, grassy flats, then crank up and drift again. It was at the end of a drift, just on the edge of deep water, that we lost interest in the trout. Something took Fondron's trout bait and sprung his light casting rod into a bow. Just before the knifing line snapped, a big angry tail roiled the water ten feet behind the line, and we knew we had found sharks again. We wound in the trout line and rigged up the bigger outfits with eight-foot leaders. I put a mullet head on a 6/0 hook, and made my cast.

My bait waited about three minutes. Then a shark took it and said aloha. When I tried to set my hook my line went limp. The hook was too small. I put on one nearly twice as big, baited it with half a mullet, and cast.

Presently my line started leaping out again. I gave the rod a stiff back-yank—more, really, than was necessary, because a shark's mouth is meaty and it's usually easy to set the hook.

"Crank up!" I said. "I got him!"

Fondron leaped astern, gave the cord handle a hurried pull, and we were off. Meantime, though, the shark was racing seaward, whipping my line off as he went. The thumb guard, pressed hard against the whirring spindle, got so hot I could hardly keep my thumb on it. Before the first fifteen minutes of that fight were gone, I regretted my hasty action in removing the star drag.

It was forty-five minutes before the shark broke water, some sixty yards ahead of the boat. In that brief second he looked brown in the sun-drenched water. Finally, with arms aching and warm sweat rolling into my mouth, I inched him toward the boat. Again we had brought no gaff, so the little automatic .22 was used. At the impact of the first hollowpoint he made a mad run, and I had to pump him in again. Seven shots seemed to have no effect. About the tenth, he began to weaken, and went down. When I started pumping again, there was a leaden weight, and I knew he was dead.

We lashed him to the bow with the anchor line, and headed for shore. It was a long way in, even with both motors humming.

Hot? I sat up front with a cigarette and a bottle of beer, resting and sweating. Both the wives seemed half-stupefied by the heat.

Eventually the boat grounded on the beach at Ball Point. Fondron, with a sun-benumbed lack of expression on his face, murmured, "Thank the Lord!" He climbed out of the boat, but not on the land side. He stepped into the water and waded unsteadily out into the receding tide. Then he lay down with his face submerged and tried to cool his heat-soaked head.

"Shine on, Josh," his wife said, loud enough for Fondron, if not the sun, to hear. "You might as well be shining on a lightwood knot."

The Saga of the Yellowfin

MARK SOSIN

It wasn't my idea. The late Joe Brooks, a friend, master fly fisherman, and one of the first inductees into the IGFA Hall of Fame, spent time convincing me. "You can do it," he insisted. "You're young and strong with plenty of endurance." Joe felt that the time had come to catch a husky yellowfin tuna on fly and the place to do it was Bermuda. Without waiting for an answer, he simply said he would set up the trip.

Pete Perinchief, who never failed to let you know that he was On Her Majesty's Service and whose family had lived in Bermuda for three or four centuries, handled visiting fishermen. He was skeptical that anyone could catch a yellowfin on fly (which they call Allison tuna in Bermuda), so he brought his good friend Louis Mowbry with him to watch the attempt. Louis was the curator of the Bermuda aquarium and a man with impeccable credentials. My wife, Susan, and another friend of Pete's made up the party.

On July 3, 1969, we set sail for Challenger Bank aboard Captain Boyd Gibbons' Coral Sea. His brother, Terry, served as mate. The procedure is to anchor the boat in the shallower water of the bank and let out enough anchor line so the stem of the boat was near the dropoff to deeper water. The current would carry the chum over the edge and attract a variety of fish including the prized Allison tuna. Hog-mouthed fry was the chum of choice, a small silvery fish that flashed and radiated in the exceptionally clear water.

The tuna did not appear for a considerable amount of time, so everyone busied themselves catching a variety of other species. Suddenly, they were there, big, torpedo-shaped brutes moving swiftly through the slick as they feasted on the free food being drifted back to them.

Pete Perinchief changed his mind. Instead of letting me cast a fly to the tuna, he announced that all of us on board would catch one first on conventional tackle. To say I was disappointed was an understatement, but I remained silent. Pete, Louis, and their friend all caught a tuna, with only one man fishing at a time. It takes time to land an Allison on a 30-pound outfit. My concern was that the small school would leave our chum slick and my chance with the flyrod would be gone.

When the three men had caught their fish, Pete told me I had to catch one on regulation gear first. By the time I battled that tuna into submission, I wasn't so sure I could land one on fly. It was a tough fish and I was a bit winded when I finally brought that critter to boatside.

It's important to understand that state-of-the-art saltwater fly tackle in 1969 was not even close to what we use today. The rod was made from the traditional E-glass and would be considered a less desirable version of the modern 10-weight. Flylines were catalogued by letters in those days instead of numbers. The line was a GAAF which is about what a 10-weight is today. The late Myron Gregory had not yet sold his system of standardizing flylines with a numbering system. My reel was a Seamaster spooled with 275 yards of 30-pound test Dacron backing and the full flyline. The class tippet on the leader tested less than 12-pounds with a short, 30-pound test abrasion tippet that measured less than 12-inches.

A few tuna still fed aggressively in the slick when Pete suggested that now was the time to try one on fly. The flies I had tied for this undertaking were a combination of polar bear hair and Mylar, giving them that shiny appearance in the water that would hopefully attract a tuna. I'm a right-handed caster, yet they gave me the left side of the cockpit, so I had to release each cast on the backcast. The fly landed among the tuna and I started to strip it in short, sharp jerks. The tuna kept swimming around it, eating dead fry instead of the tempting polar bear and Mylar fly.

Frustration began to build. I was convinced that a tuna would grab the fly on the first cast and inhale it. It didn't happen. And, it didn't happen on the next dozen casts. I had come all this way to catch a tuna on fly and the ugly face of failure was staring right at me. My father cast and retrieved flies in chum slicks since the early 1940s and he caught fish. I did, too, under those circumstances, but then I never cast to a tuna before.

Finally, in pure desperation, I asked Terry Gibbons to toss a handful of fry right behind the boat. He did and I cast the fly in the middle of it. Instead of retrieving the fly, I let it drift with the chum. To this day, I can still see that tuna eat the fly going away from the boat and I vividly recall the flyline shooting off the deck the instant I set the hook. Until that moment, I had never read or heard of anybody else dead drifting a fly in a chum slick. Today, it is common practice.

The first run was devastating. That tuna kept going and going as the reel handle spun in reverse and backing disappeared at an alarming rate. The fish wasn't going to stop. We were anchored and no one was about to chase the fish with the boat. This was going to be a dead boat battle and I began to realize I was about to lose the tuna because the reel did not hold enough backing. You could see the gold of the reel spool between the remaining coils of Dacron. It was only seconds before it would end as abruptly as it started.

Not knowing what to do, I smacked the rod butt three or four times with my right hand. The fish stopped with a half-dozen turns of backing still on the reel. The tuna reversed direction and swam toward me. Now, I had to crank all the line back on the flyreel with a one-to-one retrieve.

Just when I thought things were under control, the tuna streaked for the horizon again. I could hear Pete Perinchief with his distinctive accent muttering his famed *Good God Miss Agnes* in the background. Once again, it appeared that I would be spooled, so I started hitting the rod butt again and it worked a second time. The fish stopped, turned around, and started swimming toward me.

As the fortunes of war changed and the result of the battle seemed to shift, the others on board began a discussion of how to handle this fish near the boat if I did in fact manage to land it. While I was in the throes of fighting that fish, my wife, an observer all day, heard them talk about grabbing the flyline, pulling the fish toward the boat, and gaffing it. She knew this was wrong and began to plead with them to talk to me first before they did anything. Fly fishing for big fish was new to them. Finally, she said, "You're going to break the fish off if you touch the leader, please don't do anything until you ask Mark."

They listened to her. I explained to Terry Gibbons that he had to free gaff the fish without touching line or leader. Equally important was how he gaffed the fish. "You want the fish swimming in a circle and moving away from the boat at the instant of gaffing," I explained. "Come up from behind the fish so the gaff does not pass in front of the line. That way, if you miss, the fish does not swim under the boat and break off and the leader does not break against the gaff."

Terry Gibbons gaffed that fish perfectly on his first attempt and threw it on the deck. I never physically touched the fish, allowing Pete and Louis to put it on ice and to weigh it back at the dock. The fish weighed 53 pounds 6 ounces on an officially certified scale and was the first tuna ever taken chumming. Obviously, it was a world record. For a long time, Pete Perinchief and Louis Mowbry erroneously concluded that the fish had to be sick for me to be able to land it. They later realized that the fish was perfectly healthy and that what they had witnessed pushed the frontiers of fly fishing that much further toward the horizon.

That catch is still considered by many to be a significant angling achievement.

Keeping Busy When Not on the Casting Deck

LEFTY KREH

It's more fun and certainly you'll catch more fish if you and your companion in a flats boat work as a team. While one stands on the platform, ready to throw at the next fish, his companion should be just as busy, maybe more so, than the person in the ready-to-fish position.

A major problem for the person on the bow is that the line remains free of tangles and obstructions. Wind blows the line around. It can slide unknowingly underfoot, or it can catch on a rod holder or a piece of gear in the boat, spoiling a cast. Because the fly fisherman is concentrating on seeing the fish and then making a good presentation, he is often unaware that disaster lurks nearby.

Sitting in the boat, the companion can observe what is happening to the line. He constantly makes sure all line is tangle-free. When the angler is false casting prior to throwing to a fish, his friend can alert him that his foot is on the line. If the caster or the boat changes position this can affect how the line is lying on the deck. His teammate constantly monitors the line to make sure it is okay to cast.

The companion can have ready additional flies and leader material. If the angler breaks off his fish either on a hook-up or during the fight, the companion has a leader tippet and fly ready. It is much quicker for him to repair the leader and attach the fly than the man standing on the bow.

Quite often one pattern isn't drawing strikes and a change in flies is needed. The friend can have several flies ready. He can quickly snip off one fly and tie on another. I make it a practice that anytime I miss on two hookups, I check the hook point for sharpness. If the man sitting behind the caster has a file ready, he can check the point and hone it in seconds.

If a fish is hooked and the companion sees that a knot is developing in the line, there is often time for him to remove the knot before the escaping fish pulls the line through the guides. I know of several times when my friend saved a fish by such quick action.

If a fish is hooked and there is some rough water, the friend can often step to the platform and help stabilize the fisherman as he fights his quarry.

Each time you reach a new fishing location line has to be pulled from the reel. This can be time consuming for the angler. But, if the companion will pull the line hand-over-hand from the reel, the chore can be accomplished in seconds. Sometimes the fly line has coils in it that can spoil the cast. *Again*, the companion can stretch the line to remove them.

Many fish are difficult to see on a flat. A snook hiding among the mangrove roots can be near impossible to spot. Despite its size, a permit can often be difficult to see—even for the guide on the poling platform. There are many indicators that help locate a fish on the flats. It can be a silvery flash in the water. A small shower of minnows indicates something chasing them. A subtle mud puff could tip off the anglers to a feeding bonefish. A tail that appears above the surface for only a moment can lead to a catch. A bird flying low over the flats will often briefly frighten a permit, bonefish, redfish, or tarpon. The guide and the angler are looking for all of these indicators. But, so can the companion. Many times it is the person that is not fishing that first locates a fish.

The guide usually stands on the poling platform, which is elevated above the deck. When the angler hooks a fish and brings it to the boat, the guide must stow the pole and climb off the platform to land the fish. All of this takes time and the boat either has to be staked out or anchored or is not under control during this time. Instead, the guide can maintain the boat if the companion will land the fish for his friend.

And, once the fish has been landed, the angler often wants a photograph of it. Many guides, especially outside the United States, know little or nothing about handling a camera or taking a good photo. This is where a friend can really help out.

Several years ago I realized something that took a long time to understand. I began to carry a fly swatter on flats boats. In Florida and the tropics there are biting flies that really hurt. These stinging bloodsuckers have caused many fish to escape, as the angler is distracted trying to kill the pests. Some of these flies are tough. I have knocked them unconscious with my hat, only to see them revive later and fly away. No so with a fly swatter. The companion can carry a fly swatter at the ready. Not long ago Mike O'Brien, a fishing buddy and I killed so many flies with my swatter that we actually wore it out. I piled a big number of their carcasses on the deck, laid the ruined swatter beside it and took a picture of what I called a "fly cemetery." The companion not only can keep these pesky critters from bothering either him or the fisherman, but it sure helps to pass the time when not fishing. And, I might add, there is a certain satisfaction in killing them.

I have seen many pairs of fly fishermen in a flats boat. One stands on the platform, ready to fish. The other person simply sits back and relaxes.

But the person who becomes a team player will get more fun out of the day, and both of them will probably catch more fish.

The Angler's Battle Royal: The Taking of the Tarpon

CHARLES F. W. MIELATZ

The man who has caught trout, black bass, or salmon, and has added to this the delight of shore fishing for tautog, bluefish, or striped bass, has many pleasant and exciting contests to remember; but if he should once get fast to a tarpon all his other fishing experiences—desperate as some of them may have seemed—will be eclipsed in a moment. The keen pleasure he took in recounting them will be gone. He will only remember that it was the tarpon which gave him the "battle royal."

To the trout fisherman wading down the brook, or drifting down the river with dainty tackle and beautiful flies; to the man who skirts the lily pads on quiet lake or broadening river with hellgrammite or phantom minnow; to him who haunts the rapid, and lures the royal salmon to attack some gaudy combination of color; to him who hies him to the shore to tempt the succulent tautog with crab, or chums for the voracious bluefish, or casts his bait into the swirl of dashing breakers to entice the striped bass—to each of these his first encounter with the Silver King will seem as though he had hooked one of those saucy little towboats which busy themselves towing leviathans about New York harbor.

Those true fishermen who have killed only small fish, especially those who have confined their labors to fresh water, will regard tarpon tackle as altogether too heavy for any kind of fishing. They will look at it, handle it, and then tell you that they believe in giving the fish a fair chance for his life—that they do not care for just the killing.

It would be interesting to have the opinion of that gentle angler, Izaak Walton, on the subject of tarpon fishing. But it would be more interesting to sit by and enjoy the tussle, to see the look of astonishment that would spread over his benign countenance when he beheld a piscatorial beauty two yards long break water at the end of his tackle. It would surely interrupt his train of contemplation. For he who hies him after tarpon has no use for shady nooks, wherein to sit him down with favorite author and enjoy himself till fortune smiles on him in an attack upon his lure. The tarpon fisherman must be up and doing.

Time and tide wait for no man, but the tarpon fisherman waits anxiously for the tide. The beginning of the flood is the best time, although the change to the ebb has also afforded good fishing. But the fact is that mullet, the staple article of food for the tarpon, are frequently possessed with a desire to come to inner waters in face of the ebb. This puts an end to fishing for the time being. For, when the mullet do appear, the tarpon are at once seized with a desire to kill all in sight. It is an interesting and even exciting spectacle to see a tarpon make preparations for a meal. It is not the kind of sport the fisherman is after, to be sure, but when the tarpon get started on a course of slaughter, it is not a bit of use to fish—better sit by and watch the performance. Tarpon do not make a first attack upon their food with their mouths. They have no teeth, except a roughening on the edges of the lips sharp enough to out the best line instantly, if it comes in contact with them. They secure their food by striking with their tails, and then turning about to pick up the fish stunned by the blow. When a school of tarpon comes up with a school of mullet, the big fish are so eager to get at their prey that the second rank will often leap clear over the advance line into the thick of the company of mullet, laying about them right and left with their tails, and lashing the water into foam flecked with the blood of the small fry. The mullet, on his side, has been equipped with means of escape, for he is able to make jumps that are remarkable for fish weighing, as he does, from two to three pounds. They spit through the air for fully twenty feet. A curious thing about this great jump is that the mullet make a series of three leaps before stopping. The moment the mullet perceive the second line of tarpon coming over the first they jump, with an indescribable result.

The most remarkable exhibition of this that it ever was my fortune to witness took place in Biscayne Bay, near Miami. The school of mullet was fully an acre in extent. They went into the air in a mass, followed closely by the tarpon. It was a wonderful sight, and meant a frightful mortality to the mullet, for the tarpon must have killed thousands of them.

Some tarpon enthusiasts fish three tides a day. I have known them to go out as late as ten o'clock at night, if it happened to be moonlight and the tide came right.

And curiously enough the fish did strike, though very few were killed. The exhibition given by the fish in the phosphorescent water made the experience well worth while.

There is one feature in tarpon fishing that the fisherman has reason to be grateful for. He does not have to sit about and wonder if there are any fish in the water. If weather and tidal conditions are right for fishing, there are always plenty of signs in evidence. The tarpon, like the porpoise, comes to the surface to blow. As the time for the change in the tide approaches, they may be seen in schools and pairs, showing their silvery sides on the crest of a wave for a moment, and then gracefully disappearing.

Some fishermen—the veterans, sometimes, but the new men always—are possessed with a wild desire to try to hook one when they see this preliminary performance. They may be seen frantically urging their boatman, first this way and then that, in the hope of cutting off a school in time to drag their bait before them, or to cast it among them. It is usually a vain effort, however, as the fish seldom begin to feed until the tide actually does turn. As a result of this unseemly haste, it is not unusual to see an impatient fisherman hooked to a jewfish (Warsaw), a follower of the tarpon, just at the time when the fish begin to feed and the propitious moment has arrived. I have seen the agony on his face while he tugged away at his jewfish, when the water all about was alive with tarpon, and a bait could not touch its surface before a fish would be there to take it. In fact, I have had experience myself, and know the feeling. Now it would seem that a jewfish, weighing from one hundred to three hundred pounds, might furnish fairly good sport in itself. But it is not tarpon, and there is nothing more to say.

Another thing you will observe about the true fisherman is that there are conditions under which his tackle counts for nothing. There are others under which he would rather do anything than give it up.

The tarpon fisherman, hooked to a jewfish at a critical time, no matter what his feelings may be in regard to the desire for tarpon, is bound to land that jewfish, and he does. It never once enters his mind that he could cut loose, re-rig, and go after the tarpon. On the other hand, a great deal of tarpon tackle, especially that for still-fishing, is so arranged that if a shark takes the bait he will cut loose the moment he closes his jaws. This will not worry the fisherman in the least. He simply puts on another snell, thanks his stars that he does not have to fight the shark, and goes on with his fishing.

But let me get back to the turn of the tide, and consider that the fisherman is not impatient: that he has made up his mind to do as his guide tolls him, which is, to reserve his ammunition until the proper time. The guide will row him out to the fishing grounds, where he will see the tarpon rolling about on the undulating surface as though they had not a care in the world. They will come up and blow within arm's length. This was to me perfectly exasperating before I learned the habits of the fish.

But see! there goes one swiftly, giving the surface of the water a sharp slap as he disappears. The tide has turned. Now, if you observe, you will see the fish are moving more quickly in all directions. Here and there one comes clear out of the water. They are feeding, and now is the time to try your luck. You look at your bait, a silvery leather fish, to see that it is properly fixed to the hook, and cast it, say, forty feet or so astern of the boat, and in a moment you have an embarrassment of riches. Two or three, aye even half a dozen, tarpon rush at your bait. You are so fascinated by their action that you forget to strike until too late. None will be hooked, but your bait does not come back to you; you try again. This time a fish gets the bait. You feel his tremendous blow, and set every muscle to hook him. Probably you do. But your leather fish, hooked through the eyes, has left these useful members on the hook, and shunted his body up the line. In a moment there is another strike, but as your unprotected line comes in contact with the tarpon's sharp, rough lips it parts, and away go hook and snell and fish. The program of the tarpon fisherman is many strikes, a few hooked, and fewer killed. This is his sport, and he keeps straight on with it. No sooner does your bait strike the water again than you feel a sharp rap. On the instant, you cannot quite make up your mind whether to strike or not. But the next moment a fish breaks water and goes down immediately over your bait. He has seen it, and it looked so much alive to him that he hit it with his tail, and then simply turned around to pick it up. You are prepared for what is coming, so you brace your-self for the shock.

You feel you have hooked the fish. He goes straight to the bottom, and though you are putting all the pressure you have on your thumb-brake, you cannot stop him. He goes fully seventy-five yards before he shows himself, and when you do get sight of him you see his back as he shoots out of the water in a tremendous leap, which takes nearly ten yards more of your line. He is going straight away from you, as you sit there pressing every ounce you have in you on the brake, in the hope of stopping him. He is a hundred and fifty yards away before you see him again. You try your best to hold him. The spool on your reel is much reduced by the outgo of line. Every bone and muscle in your arms and hands is aching from the pressure. Your guide in the mean time is backing water toward the fish with all his might. It is no use, however; you cannot do it. He comes out of the water again, as the last of your line goes off the reel with a shriek. At the same time, you feel a violent pull on the rod. As the new strain comes in an entirely different way, the rod is almost out of your hands before you adjust yourself to it. But you do hold it. There is a sharp report like a rifle shot a short distance away. You look in a dazed way after the fish. You see him jump wildly into the air a couple of times, turning over and over as he falls back into the water, and all is ended.

You feel as though you had had hours of struggle; the muscles in your arms and hands fairly ache; but it has really taken little more than a minute to accomplish all this. It does not profit you to wonder how it came about. It is the kind of thing that happens to the most skilful veterans, and they can explain it no better that can the novice. They will tell you that when the fish, breaking water, is headed away from you, especially when headed toward the open sea, you might as well make up your mind that he will get your line. The fish may be counted as a dead fish, for the friction on the line will cause him to keep up the struggle until his last spark of life goes out.

You simply put on another line or take another rod, and try it again. You trail your bait for some time without any sign of fish, and you are about making up your mind to the fact that fishing is over for that tide, when you suddenly feel the now familiar shock again. In an instant the fish is out of the water, and you see your bait go sailing through the air for a distance of twenty feet. You were caught napping, and you have missed your tarpon. This encourages you to try again. You still see fish breaking water here and there, but it is invariably at the other side of the pass. You chase first one school, then another, all in vain; till, finally, in compassion for your guide who has been rowing for hours, you decide to stop. But he objects, for he is a keen sportsman and does not want to go in without a fish. So you stick to it a while longer; but, at last, after missing another fish, and having a long interval of no signs, you conclude that fishing really is over for that tide, and the guide reluctantly heads the boat for shore.

Thinking of the number of times you have been taken off your guard, you determine to be vigilant as long as your bait is overboard, and you trail it across the pass for the last time. You keep a close watch as you are nearing the shore, and just as you are about to reel in finally, you feel a gentle pull on your line. Being ready, you strike. In fact, you would strike at anything just now. In another moment a mass of iridescent silver shoots into the air and falls back with a crash. Away goes the tarpon. He is hooked, and the battle is on. He does not run the line out fast, but moves around the boat with wonderful speed, and comes out of the water only a short distance away, shaking his head fiercely, and with a defiant expression in his almost human eyes. He dashes first in one direction, then in another, so rapidly that the guide is utterly unable to keep the stern of the boat pointed toward him. At one time he is off at right angles, and again he is right ahead of the boat, so that the line is running out over the bow. He keeps you turning and twisting in a way that is most tiring. The fish has been out of the water three or four times, giving a gymnastic performance of the first order, when down he goes to hunt for deep water. He gets there, too, in spite of all you can do to hold him. Now that he is down, he sulks. You pull and haul and lift with might and main, straining your tackle almost to the breaking point, but to no purpose. He will not budge. You have gradually worked the boat, so that it is just over the spot where the tarpon lies—a very bad place for it to be in. As you cannot move him you begin to think that the fish is off, and that your line has caught on something on the bottom. You finally conclude this is a fact. So you slack up to move the boat in another direction with a view to unhooking. This slacking of the line causes the fish to move. You put the strain on again at once, and he seems to give a little. Your tired muscles and aching fingers take on a new lease of life, and you go at him. You give him another lift. He comes up a little more. You are surely bringing him to the surface. You are putting in all the power you have. To encourage you and to be prepared for the unexpected—though he does not believe the battle to be half over—the guide makes ready with the gaff. After many pulls and much lifting, till your muscles are numb from the strain, you bring the big fish to the surface. The guide cautiously reaches out with the gaff. You are feeling highly elated, as you swing him slowly within reach, and are all ready to relax with a sigh of relief, when, in a flash, the fish, which has no intention of giving up, is away. In an unguarded moment you are the recipient of a crack on the fingers from the reel handle that makes you dizzy, and before you recover sufficiently even to think of putting pressure on the brake, the fish has not only gained a hundred yards of line, but has had a breathing spell. Well, you pull yourself together, grit your teeth, and go at him again.

Your guide is now backing toward the fish as rapidly as possible, to get in what line may be had that way before the fish moves again. Working the reel under this reduced pressure limbers you up a bit, and you begin to take notice again. But a hard fight is still before you. The tarpon recovers rapidly, and is now as fresh as ever. You reel in until you get a fairly good strain on him, doing it as gently as you possibly can, so as not to alarm him; and then you think it about time to stir him up a bit. So you give him a "yank."

He comes out of the water headed straight for the boat—and at the second jump it looks very much as though he were coming aboard. He strikes the water almost under the rod, however, and goes under the boat, out at the other end, and away. In the mean time, you have fully fifty yards of line to take in before you can get a strain on him again. This is no easy task, as your fingers tire more quickly now, and for the next half hour you will accomplish nothing beyond exasperating yourself. But then you begin to feel better. You are getting your second wind. Your fingers may be bleeding and your muscles tired, but you don't mind them. You stir up the fish as often as possible. You get in your line whenever you can, although he runs out lots of it at times. But you do not work as hard in getting it back. In fact, you are acquiring a great deal of knowledge about the sport of tarpon fishing.

At last he begins to weaken. His runs are shorter, his leaps do not lift him from the water—a final effort only brings his head above the surface. With the look of defiance still in his eye, he gives up the battle, and there is nothing more to do but to reel him within reach of the gaff. The guide puts a line through his gills, and you tow him to shore, where he is hauled out before you. What a thing of beauty he is, with his living silver sides, the deep green and gold of his back, and the wonderful iridescence of the underbody.

He measures six feet and ten inches in length, and the scales register one hundred and fifty pounds—just your own weight. As you look at the splendid fellow, a vague feeling of regret comes over you at the thought that such a thing of beauty should be dead. You would gladly give him back his life, for he has given your eye a feast of beauty in magnificent action, and he has called upon all your skill and endurance in The Battle Royal.

The Tarpon of Turner's River

A. W. DIMOCK

Marco is the name of a post office, but the place is called Collier's. Ask any child on the West Coast of Florida about Marco and he will shake his head, but mention Collier and the infant will brighten up and say: "Dat's Tap'n Bill!"

Island, bay, hotel, houses, boat-building plant, and even the atmosphere are, and always have been, Collier's. When Ponce de Leon was cavorting about the peninsula pestering the inhabitants with his inquiries about a spring, he stopped at Collier's. Everybody who goes down the coast stops there. The only way to avoid a long detour around the Cape Romano Shoals is to go through Collier's Bay to Coon Key, and one cannot pass through Collier's Bay without calling at the store.

Summer is the time to visit Collier. When the little mail boat lands me with my family at the dock Captain Bill meets me with:

"Well, how are you? The hotel isn't open, you know."

"Glad of it. That's why I am here. Where's that baggage truck?"

Then I wheel our baggage to the hotel, we select the choice rooms, and spread our belongings all over the place as if we owned the whole business. When the dinner bell rings we sit down with the family and occasional tramps like ourselves who stop in on their way down the coast. Instead of the colorless crowd of tourists who occupy the tables when the hotel is open, we meet itinerant preachers and teachers, lighthouse keepers and land seekers, scientists and Seminoles.

We take possession of the island, and wandering forth with big baskets return laden with a score of varieties of fruits from avocado, pears, bananas, and cocoanuts down through the alphabet to sapadilloes and tamarinds.

As evening approaches we sit on the sheltered piazza that overlooks the bay, and, if the tide favors, watch the porpoises at play, and, more rarely, witness the dizzy leaps of a dozen or a score of tarpon each minute.

From Collier's Bay to Coon Key the channel twists and turns among sand flats and oyster reefs, between wooded banks and around tiny keys without blaze or buoy, stake, or sign to point out the path. After years of observation and practice I can take a boat over the course, if the day is clear, without running on a bank more than once in three trips.

Yet a boy to the manner born has piloted me through the maze on a night so dark that I could scarcely see his face as I sat beside him. He chatted with me throughout the trip with his hand resting carelessly on the wheel which he idly swung to and fro without apparent thought or purpose. His every act was so casual that I had just figured out that we were hopelessly lost somewhere in the Ten Thousand Islands when he leaned past me to shut off the gasoline from the motor. A minute later the boat rubbed gently against some object that I couldn't see.

"Where are we?" I asked.

"At your own dock," was the amazing reply.

My captain carried us over the same course in the same mysterious manner and I was only sure we had passed Coon Key through the broader sweep of the wind and the gentle rise and fall of the boat on the slight swell from the Gulf. Going down the coast I got my bearings and felt rather than saw its familiar features. I was conscious of the nearness of Horse and Panther Keys, and off Gomez Point I had a mental picture of the old man for whom it was named as I last saw him at his home. He was then well along in his second century, and year by year his recollection of the first Napoleon, under whom he served, became clearer and of the details of their intimacy more distinct.

Sand-fly Pass, leading to Chokoloskee Bay, was our goal for the night, and nothing but a nose was needed to find it even in Cimmerian darkness. Its mouth was guarded by a pelican key, from which a rookery of the birds sent forth lines of stench as a Fresnal lens radiates light.

In the morning we entered Chokoloskee Bay, and crossing it anchored within the mouth of Allen's River, near the Storter store.

For nearly two miles Allen's River is a considerable stream. Beyond that distance it divides and spreads over flats until it is only navigable to a light draft skiff. Near the mouth of the river we caught and released a few tarpon of good size, but when a mile up the stream I struck a ten-pound fish I returned to the *Irene* and rigged up an eight-ounce fly rod. The fish rose best to a tiny strip of mullet, cast and skittered along the surface, or trolled. They preferred light flies to those of more brilliant coloring. Yet their tastes changed as often as the colors of a chameleon, and turned up their noses to-day at the lure that best pleased them yesterday.

The light fly rod is too flexible to fasten the hook in the hard mouth of the tarpon with any approach to certainty. In the beginning the fly fisherman will fail, nine times out of ten, to fasten the hook in the mouth of the striking tarpon. Then he will learn to thrust the butt of his rod away from the fish when it seizes the bait, and clutching the line or reel bring a strong, straight pull to bear on the hook in the mouth of the fish.

My first fish on the fly rod in Allen River weighed about four pounds, but it took longer to land than its predecessor of twenty times that weight. It led me into a narrow creek where an out-thrusting branch from the bank forced me to step out of the canoe in water waist deep. I followed the fish up the shallowing stream, walking on the bank when the bushes permitted and wading in the channel when trees came to the water's edge.

When the tarpon had had fun enough with me in shallow water it led me back to the deeper river. I nearly capsized the canoe as I got aboard while playing the fish, which cavorted up and down and across the stream, leaping several feet in the air every minute or two for a quarter of an hour before yielding.

In two days I had a score of strikes and landed half that number of tarpon after an average contest of an hour with each. The largest one was four feet long and weighed therefore about thirty-two pounds, but it was an exceptionally active fish and wore itself out in half an hour. By a series of frantic leaps, one of which took it over the bow of the canoe within reach of my hand.

During the two days' fishing there was seldom an interval of ten minutes between the landing of one tarpon and the strike of its successor. On the third day the tarpon were as abundant as ever and jumped all around the canoe, but not a strike could I get. If Solomon had ever fished for tarpon he would have added the way of a tarpon in the water to that of an eagle in the air, a serpent on a rock, and the other things that were beyond his comprehension.

We sailed to the south end of Chokoloskee Bay, where Turner's River connects it with the network of waterways through which tidal water flows in all directions around the big and little keys of the Ten Thousand Islands which extend from Cape Romano to Sable. Channels navigable to tarpon of the greatest draft connect Turner's River with the Gulf of Mexico, while from scores of tiny streams and shallow watercourses it collects the output of many tarpon nurseries.

I began business on Turner's River with an eight-ounce fly rod, and soon was fast to a ten-pound tarpon which thirty minutes later was captured and freed half a mile up the stream. Scarcely had a fresh lure been thrown out when there was a tug on my line and, as I believe, the largest tarpon that was ever caught on a fly rod shot a dozen feet in the air. Three times in quick succession it leaped violently, shaking its head to dislodge the hook.

Down the river the tarpon dashed till only a few feet of line was left on my little reel. The slight strain I could put on the line wouldn't have feazed a fish one tenth the size of the one to which I was fast. I needed more yards than I had feet of line to offer a chance of tiring this creature whose length exceeded mine by a foot. One more stroke of that propeller tail and my goose would be cooked.

I yelled to the captain to paddle for his life, regardless of the fact that he was already putting in licks that endangered it. Soon he was gaining faster than I could take in line and I shouted to him to slow up, changing the next instant to a cry to go ahead. When the trouble was over I asked the captain if I had screamed at him very often.

"Most all the time, but I didn't mind. I knew you was excited and didn't rightly know what you said," was his reply.

The line never again ran so low as in that first dash of the tarpon. Yet a hundred times the end of our hopes seemed near, but always the fish swam slower, or the captain paddled faster. The wild leaps of the creature were startling but welcome, for they tired the tarpon without carrying away line. We had followed the fish up, down, and across the river, and after an hour's struggle were well out in the bay, yet at all times we had kept within two hundred feet of our quarry.

Always we feared the tarpon's getting too far away. Sometimes the danger was of its coming too near, and more than once it sprang at us with wide-open jaws, falling short of the canoe by inches only, and once it sprang fairly against the captain, neatly capsizing the craft.

The sport of fishing is in inverse ratio to the size of the tackle compared with the activity, strength, and weight of the fish. Linus Yale, as skillful with trout as he was ingenious with locks, used to hitch his horse to a tree by a mountain brook near his New England home and forget for the day the anxieties of the inventor and the burdens of the manufacturer.

All trouble was left behind as he constructed a line from hairs in his horse's tail, attached a hook of his own forging, tinier than was ever made before, with an almost microscopic fly, and with a reedlike rod, made on the ground, captured the wariest trout in the brook. When with this flimsy tackle he landed a trout of large size he rejoiced more than when picking the Hobbs lock gave him world-wide fame.

As I followed my big fish the game increased in interest. It was more like chess than fishing. Strength availed little, for the utmost strain I could put on the line through the light rod was no restraint on the powerful tarpon. The creature must be made to tire itself out and do the chief work in its own capture and at the same time be kept within the narrow limits that the shortness of my line established.

When the reel was nearly empty the line was held lightly, while the captain paddled strongly. As we neared the quarry a quick twitch of the line usually sent the tarpon high in the air and off on another dash. As the reel buzzed the captain invited apoplexy by his efforts, while I encouraged him to increase them.

At times the fish seemed to be on to our game and refused to jump when called on. It even became immune to the splash of the paddle and made an ingenious move that threatened checkmate. The tarpon was beside us and the line short when it dived beneath the canoe and swam swiftly away on the other side. There is only one move to meet that attack, and it usually ends in a broken rod and a lost fish. I dropped the rod flat on the water, thrusting it beneath the surface elbow deep, while my finger kept a light pressure on the line. Happily the tip swung to the tarpon without breaking and the fish was played from a rod under water until the captain had turned the canoe around.

The strain of a single pound on a fly rod is more exhausting to the fisherman than ten or even twenty times that pull on a tarpon rod, and I was glad when the camera man said he had used his last plate and offered to change places with me. Usually when plates were out we got rid of the fish as soon as we could, but this was an unusual fish, destined to hold long the record for an eight-ounce rod capture, if once we could slide it over the side of the little canoe, The craft might be swamped the next minute, but the record would be safe.

The tarpon noticed the new hand at the bellows and went over his repertoire brilliantly. He traveled a mile up the river in search of a place to hide from the human gadfly that worried him and sulked under a bank for some minutes before allowing himself to be coaxed out. He pranced down the stream to the hay, with occasional leaps by the way, and the captain struggled mightily every foot of the course to keep within the limits of the line. In the bay a new terror possessed him and he dashed about as if crazy.

He saw his fate in the thing that he couldn't shake off, as the creature of the forest knows when the wolf is on his track, and he exhausted himself in his panic. Then he rolled over and lay quietly on his back with gasping gills in apparent surrender while the canoe was paddled beside him.

"I'm afraid we'll capsize if I take it aboard," said the captain.

"Get it in the canoe first and capsize afterwards all you want, only don't move till I measure it," replied the camera man.

After the tarpon had been found to measure six feet six inches, the captain got a grip on the corner of its mouth, and lifting its head over the side of the canoe was about to slide it inside when a powerful stroke of the fish's rail sent the head outboard and the captain was given his choice between swamping the canoe or releasing the fish. He let the tarpon go, for which I abused him at the time, but forgave him later when I saw that the hook was still fast in the creature's mouth. It was many minutes before the captain got another chance at the fish, but when he had renewed his hold and was ready to haul it aboard he sang out to me:

"I'll hang on to him this time if he lands me in—Halifax, so look out for the pieces of your canoe!"

But the tarpon slid into the canoe without a flutter, and slipping under the thwarts lay flat in the bottom. The trouble came later when, the rod having been laid aside, camera man and captain worked together to get the slippery thing out from under the thwarts and overboard. They would probably have swamped the canoe anyhow, but the tarpon made the thing sure and secured his revenge by a flap of his tail that landed him in the bay with his tormentors. It was a fitting end to the adventure, for, after the final scrimmage, canoe and canoe men sadly needed the scrubbing they got in the nearby shallow water to which they swam.

We hit the top of the tarpon season at Turner's River, on the West Coast of Florida, and for three days the fish stood in line, waiting their turn like metropolitans seeking good seats at the opera or holding their places in the bread line. No sooner had we turned loose an exhausted tarpon than a fresh one presented itself for the vacant chair. Twenty tarpon a day was our score, of fish that ran from ten to thirty pounds each. Most of them were taken on the fly rod, for which they were too large, as their weight was light for a heavy rod in such blasé hands as ours were becoming by that time.

Much of the action of a fly rod is wasted with a fish of the tarpon type weighing over five pounds, and much time lost from the camera standpoint, since it is hard to hold the fish near the canoe. A stiff, single-action, tournament style of fly rod fits the agile baby tarpon down to the ground, while a withy, double-action article couldn't follow for a minute the fish's changes of mind.

"These fish are too little for the big rod, too big for the little rod, and we have nothing between," I observed to the camera man just after landing on a tarpon rod a ten-pound fish in as many minutes.

"Let's go down the coast," was the reply. "There are big fish in the big rivers and babies in the creeks at the head of Harney."

I agreed to this as I threw out a freshly baited hook and trolled for another ten pounder. But it was a tarpon of ten stone or more that struck before twenty feet of line had run out, and as the creature shot up toward the sky I shouted:

"There's a seven-footer for you, the biggest tarp of the trip!"

It may have been the biggest, but I shall never know for sure. I threw myself back on the rod with a force that would have slung a little fish to the horizon and my guaranteed rod snapped like glass. I hung on to the broken rod and the tarpon played me for a few minutes, after which he sailed away with half of my line as a trophy.

Before running down the coast we went back to the Storter store in search of a substitute for the broken rod. The captain said he could make a better rod than the old one out of anything, from a wagon tongue to a flag pole. We bought a heavy hickory hoe handle which looked unbreakable, and furnished it with extra fittings which I had on hand. As we sailed down the coast I mended the broken rod and we entered on the new campaign with three heavy tarpon rods in commission.

We were cruising in the land of the crustacean. There were reefs of oysters along the coast. Oyster bars guarded the mouths of the rivers and great bunches of the bivalves clung like fruit to the branches of the trees. Beneath us was one vast clam bed, and dropping our anchor we drove poles in the mud down which we climbed and to which we clung with one hand while digging clams out of the mud with the other. We gathered a hundred or more, as many as the most sanguine of us believed we could eat. They ranged in size from that of the little neck of New York to giant quahaugs, of which single specimens weighed over five pounds.

Our anchorage that night was beside the little pelican key that separates the mouths of Broad and Rodger's rivers, and we roasted clams on the beach beside the latter. It was the toss of a copper which stream we should fish in the morning. Their sources and mouths were the same in each caw and a creek united their middles like the band of the Siamese twins. We chose Rodger's River because of its beauty, the great palms that adorned it, and the legends connected with its abandoned plantation, rotting house, and overgrown graves.

Big herons rose sluggishly from flooded banks before us and with hoarse cries flew up the river, dangling their preposterous legs. Fly-up-the-creeks flitted silently away, while lunatic snake birds, made crazy by worms in their brains, watched us from branches that overhung the stream, and when we were almost beneath them dropped into the water as awkwardly as if they had been shot.

We admired beautiful trees, great vines, fragrant flowers, and blossoming orchids as the tarpon bait was trolled from the trailing canoe, and from the mouth of the river to the cut-off no tarpon disturbed our meditations. Hurrying sharks showed huge fins above the surface, slowly rolling porpoises turned teen eyes upon us as they passed, otters lifted their little round heads, and a great manatee, frightened by a sudden glimpse of our outfit, left a long wake of swirls like those of an outgoing liner.

Crossing to Broad River by the crooked cut-off, we traveled a mile and a half to gain a third of that distance. Projecting roots held us back, overhanging branches brushed us harshly, while with bare faces we swept away scores of great spider habitations, suspended from bridges which their occupants had engineered across the stream. Yet I had little cause of complaint, since the only spiders that ran down my neck were the few that escaped the camera man, whose position in the bow of the leading craft gave him the first chance at the arachnids, or vice versa.

As there wasn't a tarpon in Rodger's River, we looked upon trolling down its companion stream as a mere formality, yet no sooner had I put out my line after turning down Broad River than the bait was seized by a splendid specimen of the silver king. The camera man missed the early leaps, for he had been slow in getting out his artillery, but after it had been brought into action he was kept busy. We were carried up into Broad River Bay, where the channels were so overhung with manatee grass that at every turn my line was loaded almost to the breaking point.

When the motor boat, maneuvering for position, got out of the middle of the channel, the propeller twisted a wad of the grass about the shaft and the motor stopped. Then Joe leaned over the stern of the boat, with head and arms under water as he tore at the clinging mass, while the camera man relieved his mind by energetic exhortation.

The tarpon led us through Broad River Bay to a series of deep channels which we had long known as the home of the manatee, several specimens of which we had captured there. The surrender of our quarry came after we had entered the broad, shallow, island-dotted bay that stretches from the heads of Broad, Rodger's, and Lossman's rivers across to the narrow strip of swamp prairie and forest that separates it from the Everglades.

After releasing the tarpon I fished no more till we were back in Broad River, when, again, on putting out my line, the bait was seized by a tarpon whose length we estimated at five feet since we never had a chance to measure it. The fish attended strictly to business, and after a few brilliant preliminary jumps, made straight for the cut-off, where, after turning a few corners and tying the line around some snags, it leaped joyously high in air, free of all bonds and in full possession of a valuable tarpon hook and a goodly section of costly line.

We traveled a mile down the river before throwing out another lure, and found ourselves in a tarpon town meeting. There were scores of them, leaping and cavorting, dashing hither and yon, and behaving as if at a big banquet, but it was a Barmecide feast, for not a food fish could be seen.

"Hang to 'em, if you can," called out the camera man as I baited my hook, "for I've had bad luck with the fish so far to-day."

"The next tarpon stays with me, or I go with him," was my reply, and the next minute one of the family was over my head, fiercely shaking his wide-open jaws to get rid of the hook. But the hook was fast and I hung to the line through the tarpon's first run, though the canoe was nearly capsized before the captain could head it for the flying fish. The thwarted creature, after three wild leaps, headed straight for the canoe, and diving under it brought the strain of his weight on the tip of the rod, which broke in two parts. I clung to the butt, and as the fish was of medium size soon brought it to the captain's hand, despite the broken tip.

We had now no rod nearer than the *Irene*, which was five miles distant, but the fish were in biting humor and the opportunity was not to be lost. There was a hand line in the motor boat, and I handed it to the captain, for my muscles were aching, and I thought to rest them with the paddle. The broken rod was left with the camera man, for both the hand line and the captain were strong, mix-ups with big tarpon certain, and a swim in the river the probable outcome.

One tarpon turned back so quickly, after towing us steadily for a quarter of a mile or so, that I couldn't change the course of the canoe till the fish had torn a dozen yards of line from the captain's hands and was that far behind us. The captain pulled fiercely, and the creature turned again and seemed to leap at me with wide-open jaws. Its weight fell on my arm and the side of the canoe, which would have capsized but for some quick balancing by my companion. Thereafter that afternoon the captain played the fish a bit less savagely, for which I was not sorry.

I had no dread of being swamped by a tarpon. It had happened before and would happen again, probably that very day, but I wanted it over, and expecting it every minute for hours got on my nerves.

It was late when the crisis came and we were near the mouth of the river, for each fish we struck had carried us down the stream with the ebbing tide. It was a tarpon of the largest size that turned away from an approaching hammerhead shark, and swimming beside the canoe shot high in the air directly above it.

I held my paddle without moving, waiting, waiting for the canoe to sink under me as it had done before. The captain rose to his feet as the tarpon turned in the air, and by a seeming act of volition threw himself clear of the craft.

"Glad I didn't wait for the spill," said the camera man as he turned the plate holder in his camera, "but I don't see how he missed you. What's become of the fish? Can't you get him to do it again?"

The tarpon had escaped. He had given the line a turn about the canoe, and of course it had broken.

The *Irene* was in sight of the mouth of the river as I tied a new hook on the broken line and told the captain I would troll until we reached the boat. But a tarpon lay in wait for me among the oyster reefs, and after he was fast, started back up the river. He was a hard fighter and so erratic in his dashes as he tacked up the stream that every few minutes I had to give him line to keep from capsizing.

"Can't you get that fish nearer the canoe?" shouted the camera man. "How can I photograph him when you're a mile apart?"

"I'll take him inside the canoe, if you want," I replied, though I had no notion of doing it.

I hauled on the line till the fish was twice his length from me and was trying to hold him there when the creature dived till the line ran straight down. Then it loosened, and like an arrow from a bow something shot up from the depths, dashing gallons of water in my face as it passed. I couldn't look up, but I wondered what would happen. Just as I concluded that this tarpon, like the last, had cleared the canoe in his fall, the craft gave a twist, a roll, and plunged me, shoulder first, beneath the surface!

It was a few yards' swim to an oyster reef, where the captain and I reembarked and were soon paddling for the *Irene*. It isn't worth while to change the few garments one wears when fishing for tarpon just because one has been overboard, so we sat on the deck as we were and ate clams on the half shell while Joe made clam stew for a second course and gave us our choice of stewed smoked turtle or clams for the next one.

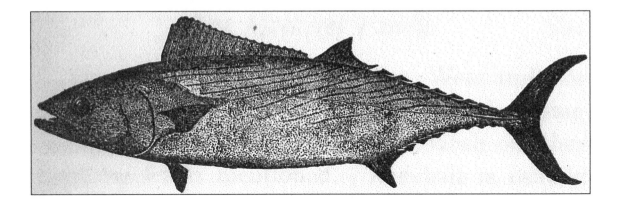

The King of the Mackerel

CHARLES F. HOLDER

Tuna angling is a purely a modern sport which I suggested ten or twelve years ago at the island of Santa Catalina, California, and, like many manly sports, it flashed into popularity and almost word-wide fame. The tuna is the horse-mackerel, the giant of the mackerel tribe, the doughty head of the family *Scombridae*; an ocean wanderer, a pelagic swashbuckler of the sea; now feeding upon bluefish, menhaden, or herring in the Atlantic, gorging itself with the great flying-fish or squid in the Pacific; everywhere a terror to the smaller denizens of the deep. For centuries it has been caught in great nets in the Mediterranean Sea, on whose shores it is considered a dainty; and from the mouth of the St. Lawrence to Cape Cod it is more or less common in summer and occasionally harpooned, its crescent-shaped tail being seen on many a longshore fish-house from Cape Breton to Swampscott, a talisman of good luck.

As to the time for tuna fishing, there is a difference of opinion. Some anglers are on the ground at daylight; others follow the schools at all times. I have had better luck, that is, more strikes, early in the morning on a rising tide, but the tuna is fickle game. At times it bites vigorously, then will cease without rhyme or reason, during which exasperating period schools of hundreds may be passed and crossed, the fish absolutely ignoring the various devices of the angler. The fishing-ground may be said to be from the point of Avalon Bay to Long Point, a distance of four miles, and from fifty feet to a mile offshore. The tuna is a strategist, and this shoreline, with its numerous open bays, the mouths of canyons, constitutes a series of traps, into which they can charge the flying-fishes; and when they are feeding, they can be caught on the edge of the kelp within twenty feet of the shore. The tuna does not travel in a single large school. That they arrive in a body is doubtless true, but when once on the ground they divide into small squadrons of from fifty to two hundred and are apparently preparing to spawn, playing on the surface, and on calm days, which are the rule in spring, they can be seen for a long distance, the spike dorsal out of the water, followed by the upper lobe of the sharp crescent tail. They are so tame that a boat can approach within fifteen or twenty feet of them before they sink, and it is an easy matter to follow and circle the school.

In fishing we are on the beach at daylight. To the east great bands of vermilion are piercing the sky, and the entire heavens are blazing with a rosy light, the advance guard of the sun that presently comes up over the Sierras on the mainland like a ball of fire. The boatman, who is just in with fresh flying-fishes, reports tunas all along shore, and a few moments later we are shoving off, seated in the stern of a wide-beamed yawl. She is rigged with a two-horse-power engine, but the boatman rows out into the bay, stopping to fasten on the leaders as we over-reel. This accomplished, he rows on while we unreel the entire line to soak it—an essential, as a dry line will burn off under the rush of a fish when the leather brake is applied. We are not out of the bay when a flying-fish is seen coming directly toward us, then another, and still another.

"Look out, sir!" cries the boatman.

Look out, indeed. Two fliers pass over the boat, my companion and I dodging them, catching one, and then, not ten feet from us, a torpedo seems to explode, and the still water flies into the air a mass of gleaming foam. Quickly another rod is taken, the living flier hooked on and cast. We are surely caught unprepared, yet zeee-ee-zee! a swirl of waters, a wail from the steel throat of the big reel, and the game is away. Gone? yes, gone, and if it must be acknowledged, two tuna men, who imagined they were cool under any circumstances, but have been robbed of bait and one hundred feet of line, and all in a moment, now sit dumfounded, then laugh at this phase of fisherman's luck. Manifestly the tunas could not wait for any lengthy preparation; they came in to meet us; we have met the enemy and we are theirs. The moral is, not to start from the beach until everything is in readiness and to be prepared for a strike the moment the bait is over, and all the time. A school of half a dozen tunas has entered the bay charging the flying-fishes, and is off up the coast, where we follow. Once around the point the tuna ground stretches away from point to point, four miles or more, of as beautiful water as the eye ever rested upon, with high rocky cliffs and blue-tinted mountains to the left, and everywhere as smooth as glass. Tunas are in a short time sighted, some leaping into the air, and as we move down the coast a heavy sea appears to be breaking on the Long Point rocks. But it is merely tunas feeding, each tuna as it rushes creating a whitecap; as hundreds are seen, the sight is a marvelous simulation of a storm on a sea of glass.

A flying-fish now comes soaring over the ocean a foot above it, and we know that just below is an eagle-eyed nemesis ready to pounce upon it like a tiger. We know that the tuna and its mate are swimming at an angle, canted, or, as the boatman says, with a "list," that its big, black, hypnotic eye may follow each move of the flier. The latter has soared nearly two hundred yards and begins to flag; its tail drops lower and lower, then touches the water to beat it furiously, at which there comes a rush of waters as the tuna attempts to seize its game. But the flying-fish in these few seconds of impact has stored a fresh supply of force, or inertia, and now soars away in a slightly different direction, a foot above the surface, the tuna still beneath it, uncertain whether to leap or to wait until the weary victim shall drop into its maw. It is here that we are treated to the lofty leaps of the tuna. If the latter is swimming deep in the chase, it occasionally dashes upward after the soaring fish, often missing it and rising ten or more feet into the air—a magnificent spectacle. Attaining its limit it turns gracefully and drops headlong into the sea. I have seen such a fish strike the flying-fish and send it whirling upward like a pinwheel. Again, the tuna will seize its prey in mid-air, as will a man-of-war bird.

While we have been digressing on came the flying-fish, crossing our bait by a lucky chance, or by the strategy of the boatman. We could almost feel the premonitory crash; every nerve was tingling with expectation; then twenty feet from the bait there was a rush, the tunas had sighted them, and for several feet they raced along, for there were two (generally the case), hurling the water, arrows aimed at the baits. They had been deflected from the flier, and while the water swirled astern, the cry of two reels rose on the morning air. Vainly the leather thumb-brakes were pushed upon the line; the latter slipped beneath it in feet and yards, then one reel became silent, the slack line telling the story of a flaw, or possibly too much thumb-power, or a rusty leader. Despite every effort the tuna tore the line from the reel, the boatman backing with all his strength, endeavoring to force sternway on the boat before the line was fully exhausted. Five hundred feet had slipped away and the boat was sliding through the water at a rapid rate when suddenly the line slackened, the game was gone. No, the line was doubling in, and springing to my feet I witnessed a splendid movement of the gamy fish, one which I have never seen repeated. The tuna had turned and was literally charging the boat, *el toro* of the sea, coming on like a gleam of light, its sharp dorsal cutting the water. I reeled with all my speed, knowing that if I was caught on the turn with an unknown amount of slack line, the end might come; but fifty feet had not been gained before the tuna was within fifteen feet of the boat, then seeing me it turned and was away like an arrow from a bow.

The big reel groaned as the crash came, but the brake was thrown off and my thumb played upon the leather pad with rare good luck, with just sufficient force to prevent overrunning. I gained enough line during this spectacular performance to stop the fish at three hundred feet, and held it by the thread of line while it towed the boat out to sea. A mile it took us, now plunging into the deep heart of the channel, to rise again with throbs which came on the tense line like heartbeats and found an echoing response. I gained ten feet to lose five, then would lose twenty to recover all, and more by vigorous "pumping," as the fish sulked and labored at the bottom of the sea. Suddenly I felt the line humming, vibrating like the cord of some musical instrument as the great fish rose, and as it reached the surface with a mighty swerve that gave the boatman active work to keep us astern to the game, it turned and again charged me. I rose, reeling rapidly as I watched the splendid trick; for trick it was, an attempt to take me unawares, running in on the line to break it if possible in the outrush. Again the fish turned hard by the boat and dashed away, this time inshore, towing us a mile or more, and within fifty feet of the rocks and their beard of kelp, where I succeeded in turning it, and now gained so rapidly that I had the fish within a short distance of the boat. The boatman was fingering his gaff, when, with a magnificent rush, the tuna tore from the reel three hundred feet of line, undoing the strenuous labor of nearly two hours. The fish appeared to be seized with a frenzy. It rushed around the boat at long range, plunged deep into the blue water as though searching the bottom for some obstacle upon which to rub the line, then rising with a strange bounding motion which was imparted to the rod, again charged the boat.

For three hours I fought this superb fish, during which it towed the boat from near Avalon to Long Point, then several miles in and out, repeatedly charging, never giving signs of weakening, always bearing away with its full force. At the end of three hours I again brought the fish to within fifty feet of the boat, when it again broke away and towed us four miles south, occasionally stopping to rush in, and once carried us out into rough water, towing the boat stern first against the heavy seaway so rapidly that I expected to see her fill; but by sheer good luck I turned the fish, and at the end of four hours brought it to gaff. Slowly it circled the boat and for the first time we saw that the fish was what we had suspected, of unusual size. As it slowly swam along, its big back of a deep blue, its white belly occasionally gleaming as I turned, its finarettes flashing gold, it presented a magnificent spectacle, a compensation for the hardest struggle I had ever made. Nearer it came, then it was turned at the quarter, the boatman's gaff slid beneath, and the big hook struck home. It was a clever gaff, but with a tremendous surge the tuna sounded, shivering the handle in the gaffer's hands, and was away taking the wreck with it. Fortunately I stopped the rush, and a few moments later again had the tuna alongside. This time a new gaff held it, the gamy creature, never conquered, never discouraged, lashing the water, hurling it over us, a last defiance. A nervous gaffer would have lost the fish at this stage, but the boatman held fast, and stepping on the gunwale pressed it down to the water's edge and cleverly slid the quivering, struggling tuna into the boat, where it pounded the planking with such vigorous blows that the small craft trembled from stem to stern. As its fine proportions were revealed, I realized that we had landed the largest tuna ever taken with a rod. Its actual weight was about one hundred and eight-seven pounds; its scale-record weight on shore after bleeding was one hundred and eighty-three pounds; its length was six feet four inches. This catch suggested the Tuna Club, and for two years this fish was the record catch of this organization. I have taken a number of tunas since, and have seen a large number caught, but have never known a fish that so thoroughly exemplified the word "game"; and in justice to this splendid fish, which is now in the possession of a Chicago angler, I must confess that a few moments more would have placed me *hors de combat*.

Among the exciting personal experiences incident to this sport which I recall was being capsized by a tuna nearly a mile offshore. I was trying the experiment of tuna fishing with a light jointed rod, seven and two-thirds feet long, weighing about fifteen ounces, which I used for yellowtail. I hooked my fish, and after a beautiful surface play of forty minutes brought it to gaff. Jim Gardner, the boatman, gaffed it cleverly and landed it, when the fish made a convulsive leap and fell upon the gunwale, capsizing the boat, which sank beneath us, rising bow up, covering the water with gaffs, oars, and other wreckage of the angler's art. My companion, Mr. Townsend of Philadelphia, could not swim, and was otherwise embarrassed by a heavy overcoat; and as the boat rolled over and evidently would not hold three, Gardner and I started to swim to the launch, which had been lying off, some distance away, and which was now coming up, while Mr. Townsend rested upon the bottom of the boat, assuring us that he was all right. As I neared the launch I heard the boatman's wife, who was aboard, scream that her husband was drowning, and turning, saw that Gardner had disappeared. Visions of certain big hammerhead sharks flashed through my mind; but as I stopped, endeavoring to look down into the blue depths, up he came, and I discovered that he still held my tuna by the gaff; in fact, he had never relinquished his grasp upon the handle, and was towing the fish, the latter, as it occasionally plunged downward, taking the plucky gaffer out of sight—a performance extraordinary in its nature, which was repeated three times. Each time Gardner, who was a professional swimmer previous to his boating career, dragged the tuna to the surface, and after an exciting and exhausting swim we were picked up, the launch and fisherman from shore reaching us about the same moment, Gardner securing a rope which is wife tossed him. I was burdened with a heavy corduroy hunting-suit and leggings, and found that I could not lift myself aboard, nor could the two men haul me in, so I was lashed to the rail, Gardner throwing his legs about the propeller. In this position we rested a moment, then by a supreme effort I was hauled in, and while the crew held me by the legs, I leaned over; and as Gardner lifted up the still struggling fish, I thrust my arm into its mouth and grasped it firmly by the gills; Gardner took a half hitch about its tail with a rope, and the men hauled upon my legs, and with a resounding cheer we dropped the leaping tuna into the cockpit—a laughable climax to a seemingly irrational and impossible fish story.

The Island

MARGOT PAGE

The Atlantic Ocean off Cape Cod is virtually boiling with fish, the brownish striped bass rolling slowly on their sides as they gulp the bait they have trapped on the surface. A layer of bluefish slash just underneath. A glint in the high summer sun, seagulls hover excitedly twenty feet above the water, one to a fish, dropping to the surface when they see a choice available morsel of baitfish.

Gleeful shouts pepper our twenty-one-foot craft as we stagger for balance in the pitch and rock of the waves. The fish move toward us and then away in predatory packs, marked by gulls and the agitated surface. In between frenzied moments of their activity, we wait at attention, scanning the surface of the water intently, heads swiveling. We're not looking at one another: all eyes are on the gulls and the water. We hold our fly lines at the ready.

Tom and I have brought Brooke along—now seven and a half, too smart for empty promises, too young for no reward—with the tantalizing promise of a boat ride to a tiny "desert island" off the Cape.

Our captain is Tony Biski, a burly, enthusiastic convert to fly fishing, about which he says, "Fly fishing is an art, something to do while you're fishing." Today he is taking us to the flats off Monomoy Point, the thin finger of sand pointing south from the Cape's elbow, home to seabirds, dunes, and many sea disasters of yore. But while we're coming off the high tide, we detour to The Rip where he's just received radio reports of blitzing fish.

My arm is firmly around Brooke's tubby, colorful life preserver. Her Barbie dangles from her hand as we skim over the high tide that covers the miles of undulating white sand we will later walk. Approaching the ocean side of Monomoy we can smell the distinctive oil slick produced by baitfish being shredded, and see gulls circling and diving—two sure indicators of large groups of working fish.

While Tony controls the boat, trying not to drift over the path of the fish, we swiftly lift our rods out of the keepers. Within a couple of casts, Tom hooks and lands two fish, and then—after a drawn-out fight into the backing—lands a twenty-pound striper. I, too, quickly hook a heavy fish and can feel him shaking his head against the line. Pulling him in, we see the flashes of blue—he is a large bluefish—just before he shakes himself one last time and bites off my tippet with his razored teeth.

We wait in a momentary calm, and Tony repositions the boat to where the gulls are working. The brown rolls start in waves towards us, a liquid earthquake, the gulls again fluttering above. Not used to a stripping basket, I have elected to leave my line free and as a result familiarize myself with every protuberance in Tony's boat. As I am having trouble casting any distance with the nine-weight rod into the wind, Tony suggests I use his eight-weight with a sinking line. Instantly my range improves and the deep ache in my shoulder disappears, but because of my excitement, I still cast badly and miss.

Seeing striped bass in such healthy profusion after the decline of the 1970s and 1980s is wild and exhilarating. They arc in chopping circles, swirls of beige backs breaking the surface as they twist and turn in deceptively lazy, vicious packs. Daytime fishing is, obviously, different from night fishing, because here you can see the fish moving up from the murky depths or prowling along the surface. You can see the take or kick yourself about what you're missing.

Of course, night fishing has its particular compensation: the sea's neon phosphorescence lights up the stripers as if they're electric.

And then there's always the indigo night.

***

By this time, Brooke's patience is beginning to fray. We have sold this expedition to her based on an island of sand and that is what she wants to see *right now*. Nearly an hour of this pitching and rolling is enough. She begins to complain. "You two are fishing maniacs," she cries with only marginal humor.

Fish are boiling towards us again and our attention is diverted from her crisis. We cast furiously into the watery chaos, hooking or missing as the case may be, forgetting about the small, unhappy member of our quartet. Soon, we hear the sound of pointed foot stamping, harrumphing, and covert groans. We are too preoccupied to respond.

Tom hooks a huge striper and our yells of delight set Brooke off in the opposite direction. Never one to hide her feelings, she shouts loudly, "I WANT TO GO TO THE ISLAND NOW!" But my attention shifts to Tom whose face is wreathed with joy as the giant bass runs down into the depths. He sets about bringing it in. Brooke will have no part of it. "NOOO MORE FISSSHHHHINNNGGG!"

To fend off impending disaster, Tom, at the same time he reels in his prize, launches into a long and complicated story involving a cockatiel at a pet store that has amazing adventures. As soon as she hears the magic words, "Once upon a time . . ." Brooke instantly settles into her rapt listening mode, but she is still suspicious enough of her good fortune to give no quarter. When Tom pauses to reel and pump the line and marvel at his luck for a few seconds, Brooke registers immediate vocal displeasure, and Tom resumes, seamlessly, the meandering thread of his story. When the fish is landed and released, the cockatiel's saga continues through my search for my fish ("No, Brooke, we can't leave until Mommy gets *her* fish," Tom explains.)

Mercifully, I finally hook and land a small striper, about twelve pounds, that takes me into the short backing. Tony, the captain, has been feeling the strain. He flicks a drop of sweat from his brow and grins happily. We take a couple of photographs, release the fish, and Tom gives me a kiss and formal congratulations on my first daytime striper. Brooke is moaning insistently. We zoom quickly back to the flats where the tide is receding.

"You've been spoiled, Margot, really spoiled," Tom teases with satisfaction. "You've seen it as good as it gets."

***

The high tide is on the wane, leaving crescent pillows of fawn-colored sand islands that turn white as they dry. On the horizon the emerald dunes that line Monomoy lend the seascape dimension and color under the reassuring blue dome of this enormous summer sky. Old fishing weirs spike in the distance, like startling, thin, tall fences sticking out of the ocean, grandfathered down in families through the area's salty legacy.

We jump out of the boat into knee-deep, clear ocean water. I strip to my bathing suit and anorak and wade over the firm flats, grateful to sink my feet into the fine, sugar sand. If you didn't know you were on the Massachusetts coast, you could be persuaded this was the Caribbean, so clear is the water, so smooth and white the sand.

In the distance, Tony stalks the flats like a muscular, nut-brown bear, his keen green eyes looking seaward always. Over on the other side of the island, Tom has flipped his stripping basket over his shoulder and is heading away; in one hand he carries his rod and with the other holds the hand of a little girl with a blonde braid who wears a shocking pink bathing suit and carries a bright blue pail, both colors visible at long distance. They range further, getting smaller and vaguer, one looking for shells and crabs, one looking for fish. Ocean treasures.

When we leave later that afternoon, Tony tells me he has named this little island for Brooke.

***

Several days later, Brooke is invited to play at the beach with friends. At this point in our vacation week, I am numbed from the medical problems of my father, a widowed stroke victim, who lives on the Cape year-round. We have come to visit him only to discover him in medical crisis. Though I have other things on my mind than fishing during this short reprieve from my unofficial nursing duty, I am drawn—hollow as I feel at the moment—to the water. We go again to the sea.

This day we hit low tide right on the nose. Tom and I are now enjoying the company of two Tonys, our captain again, Tony Biski, and our artist friend Tony Stetzko, who in 1981 held the world's record for a surf-caught striper (seventy-three pounds). The sheet of water on the flats we had skimmed over three days ago has now receded, leaving acres of white, rippled sand. Before Tony B. finishes anchoring the boat in the remaining tide, I plunge into the clean, warm ocean, readying my rod with one hand and adjusting a waist pack around my neck with the other. Shouted instructions drift on the wind behind me as the two Tonys rig up their tackle. Tom is out of the boat too, ranging wordlessly and rapidly out to the far flats through the knee-deep water. Tony S. strides out through the water calling eagerly to me, "You're too far, come in on this side of the slough, they're all in here." A pause, then a shout, "LOOK AT THEM . . . SEE THOSE HUGE SHADOWS, THERE THEY GO!"

Behind me there is a close splash, and I hear it and Tony doesn't. I whirl and see the boil and cast and instantly nail a large creature. Plunging, the beast runs out for a while, then eventually turns and bites the hook off.

We wait and shuffle along the slough, this being apparently a slow day on the flats, and Tony teaches me: *See the birds working over there, see the dark edge near the light band, that's where they're coming in, going after the bait, pushing them toward the beach. They like to rub their bellies on the sand, so they come in shallow. They're coming right in.* OH, LOOK AT THEM, OH HERE THEY COME, GET READY, GET READY, THEY'RE MONSTERS, OVER HERE, RIGHT IN FRONT OF . . . (cast, cast, cast, strip, strip, strip).

OH . . . *Oh . . . oh . . . there they go . . .* Tall and lean, Tony has long, dark Botticelli curls and a small, somewhat dashing scar on his cheek from a boating accident. A friend to all, he boyishly strides the Cape beaches like a great, excited heron.

We walk along the exposed tidal flats of this broad ocean floor, following the little rivers that flow through channels in the dead-low water. Stripers, blues, and maybe bonito are cruising along these miniature rivers, the Tonys explain to us, dining on nature's conveyer belt of sand eels and baitfish.

We come to the convergence of tidal flows where we catch a tidy number of stripers, fishing our striper patterns like nymphs, releasing them all after admiring their size or coloration. Someone brings me a live sand dollar to admire—I had only ever seen their bleached skeletons—and I place the brown-flanneled disk back in the ocean to, I hope, find a mate and make more sand dollars.

Then we amble back to our original starting position before the quickly incoming tide dissipates the still-feeding stripers off Brooke's Island's shores. While we walk back, Tony S. tells me how once he was so excited casting to a night blitz of fish that he dislocated his shoulder—which didn't deter him from completing the evening's fishing.

Now *that's* a fishing maniac.

***

By the time we reach the island, my intense need to catch fish has subsided. I have another mission.

After casting without success for a while, I wade back to the anchored boat by myself, grab a sandwich, soda, and a towel, and run back over the humped sand bar to where my carefully placed rod is about to get engulfed by wavelets. Safely repositioning it in a cradle of dark seaweed near the apex of the island, I spread my towel on the white sand of this crescent island and eat my lunch.

In the distance stand the optimistic, hazy figures of the men poised at the ready in the shimmering ocean. Around me, dunlins and yellowlegs twitter and scurry. As I relax, only the sound of the waves and the wind and the birds fill my ears.

Now it is time. I am overwhelmed trying to spread myself around to all those who need me—my father on the Cape, my husband and daughter, my work. Two households to run, an expanded team of nurses and home health aides' schedules to keep track of. How to keep my father safe and honor his wishes to stay at home when he needs twenty-four-hour care?

At this moment, I just want to run away. The nightmares of aides not showing up have made even my nights heavy. I can't get away from the image of my father's jaw clenched in pain, the helplessness of his frail body. The stuffiness of that old, hot, whaling captain's house.

I wait for the weariness, the confusion, the sadness to be washed out of me by the only salve I know.

The sand crystals coat my hand where it lies on the beach, the terns mew and cry, the sun warms my shoulders. There is a deep throb of a boat on the horizon and the sound of the waves' nurturing constancy as they throw themselves on the beach one after the other. Here, on this little island, miles from the mainland, there is no talking, no demands, no decisions I have to make. I am responsible, at this instant, only for myself. Not a human figure in sight except for the three sympathetic and somewhat protective men who have brought me here and are now gathered on the faraway boat to eat their lunch.

This is my oasis. Brooke's Island. The island of a young girl in a pink bathing suit with a bright blue pail, her blonde hair shining like a beacon.

Here, a bit of wonder returns to pierce my depression. Here, the breeze begins to blow and cleanse. The distant thrum of the boat engine, the calling of the plovers, the sandpipers, the steady fall of the waves, start to nibble at the mounting chaos of schedules, urinals, pain control, and emergency trips to the pharmacy for gauze, saline, rubber gloves, and medicine. I stand up and walk the receding perimeters of this white crescent island, now a mere patch curving out of the encroaching, resolute ocean. I mark off my territory, reclaiming myself from within my father's slow demise. No one is watching me, I am alone. My companions are back out on the flats, ever hopeful, ranging like a small pack of benign wolves.

He's suffered enough. Twenty-two years of paralysis.

***

The rivers of salt water are now slowly narrowing the spit of white sand. Little lapping rivers turn into wide ones, then become bays, and then merge with the ocean. Soon the foam will touch my toes and I will move further up the island.

I can't fill my mind enough with the seascape, the radiating light, the liquid sounds of the sea. But random thoughts intrude: images of the icy February ocean ahead. Worries from life back in Vermont. How in an hour we shall have to leave and I fear I won't be able to return to fish these flats for another year.

Eight long-necked cormorants skim low over the water's surface. They line the tidal islands, some with wings extended, frozen in mid-flap as they dry their feathers. Sandpipers hurry by me along the water's edge like race walkers in the park, beady dark eyes darting nervously. It's gratifying to note their healthy populations.

All of us have our own rivers, I remind myself, *with their own beginnings and endings. I am alone on mine, as is my father. I stand in awe of the wonder of circumstance and the mysteries of our lives.*

Tom splashes over with a bottle of mint iced tea and some sugar wafers. "They're *killing* them out in the rip! Wanta go or stay here?"

I elect to stay and he and the two Tonys speed out toward the Atlantic with lots of large hand-waves and big smiles.

I look around. Now I can be by myself on the planet, for this briefest of moments in time. Maybe I'll be lucky and they'll forget me and so I'll have to spend the night on the island.

This idea makes me excited and nervous.

I will bundle up in my windbreaker and towel. I have a Tootsie Pop, Snapple, and a pack of Kleenex in my waist pack, along with a juicy book, pen, and fat note-book. I will watch the glorious Cape Cod sun go down on my now-tiny island of twenty square feet. Then I will huddle and wait for the Perseid meteor shower, the silver dashes flashing so fast in the inky canopy you're not sure you even saw them.

With my rod and only one fly, I will catch a small bluefish, eat sushi, chew on some seaweed. Suck on the last of the lemon drops. Morning will come, a sunrise of indisputable hope and renewal. The striped bass will roil in, just for me, and I shall cast, catch, and release these great creatures from the ocean. Later in the day, the Coast Guard will pick me up on my deserted island, sunburned, thirsty, and I shall have been cleansed by the meteors, the salt winds, the cry of the terns. My fears of death and loss will have been swept away, and I will be ready to return to my father.

I am alone. Peace wraps me like an airy miracle. Slow and light.

∗∗∗

Some time later, the wavelets converge and move more rapidly up the white sand, devouring several inches a minute. I notice an insistent tone to the waves as they get closer. I pick up my gear and move it into the very middle of the exposed sand with a faint feeling of alarm. My crescent island is becoming a fingernail. I am under the assumption that this island stays dry but we are still two hours away from peak high tide. What if this is an abnormal tide? What if my whole island gets swallowed and my companions haven't returned?

I succumb to a brief moment of panic and then happen to glance over to a corner of the island where two seagulls are standing on a tiny crescent island of their own. At the same instant my eyes alight on them, their sliver of sand is being washed over by the first waves. The gulls, looking calmly out to sea, stand knee-deep in the rising tide and then confidently strut about their drowned island.

Again, I patrol my island as the tide comes up. I can measure its width in number of footsteps. And as I walk, I notice that I am not altogether alone. A strange speed-boat with one lone occupant has been making a couple of large circles around my island, watching me with craned neck, I now realize. I mildly speculate on what kind of weapon a graphite fly rod would make.

As I complete my tour with hands clasped behind my back, watching my feet making prints in the sand, Tom and the two Tonys suddenly appear, surfing in fast to the island on a big boat wake with anxious looks on their faces. It turns out they couldn't see me from afar, and when they finally spotted my vertical figure on the horizon, it looked as if I was engulfed by water, with that lone boat circling like a shark.

I also learn that my island does *not* remain dry at high tide.

We head for home. The guys are still talking with fevered interest about where the bass are, what and why they do what they do. Tony S. enthuses about plans to bring a mask and a raft the next time, so he "can swim down one of the rivers of eel grass *right next* to the bass." As we gather speed, I look behind me at Brooke's Island. A vessel in full sail moves majestically behind it as the slim patch of sand disappears in the waves.

We hit the rougher water, banging and slamming hard into the waves, the wind whipping strings of my hair into my mouth. Each hard satisfying crash pounds away the remnants of my depression. The pointed white nameless ghosts of a sailing regatta line the haze on the horizon. One has capsized.

Suddenly we are at the harbor mouth. Tony B. cuts the throttle.

The island is nearly underwater by now, but it is a comfort to remember that the tide will eventually turn.

Trailing the Sea-Bat

CHARLES F. HOLDER

The outer Florida reef, where the army of coral polyps has made its last stand against the Gulf Stream, was lying on the surface of what seemed a sea of molten steel. The wind was lead, and the blue expanse of the gulf had that strange oily appearance so often a characteristic of a dead calm in the tropics. In the west vermilion-tipped clouds—mountains of the air—rose high in the heavens, casting deep shadows over the green-topped creations of the wind, hurricane, or the prevailing tides. The keys appeared to be formed without rhyme or reason, but in reality nature could not have ordered better, as with their outlying banks and reefs they constitute a perfect harbor, a deep blue channel winding clear and distinct against the coral-covered lagoon, completely encircling Garden Key, the headquarters of hunters, sportsmen and anglers who find their way to the outer reef in search of adventure.

Some wit has described fishing in Florida in the summer as sitting in a Turkish bath holding a string, and I think the author of this mot found his inspiration on the reef on a warm day while trailing the sea-bat.

The heat was appalling, pouring down with such intensity that the shallows were too hot for comfort, and thick vaporous clouds waved upward from the bleaching coral sand, distorting every object along shore. For days the dead calm had continued; the long sleepy summer was at its height, and one had to pick his time for sport and diversion. There was an hour or two at sunrise for barracuda spearing, or for the beating jacks; a long siesta at midday, then a while toward evening perhaps when one could lure the dainty gray snapper or test conclusions with the big sharks which swam the blue channel at all times. Then came the night, often cool, to be spent on the water listening to the melody of negro rowers, the weird tales of Chief, a Seminole, who preferred the heat of the outer reef to the mosquitoes of the coast.

On such a night, when the only sound to break the stillness was the distant roar of the surf, there came out of the darkness, near at hand, a rushing, swishing noise; then a clap as of thunder, which seemed to go roaring and reverberating away over the reef, like the discharge of cannon. So startling was the sound, so peculiar, that the negroes stopped rowing, and one or two dropped their oars in consternation.

"Vampa fish, sah," said Paublo, the stroke oar, in a hushed tone, "an he mighty uncomfortable near, sah—jes over yander."

I thought so myself as the eight-oared barge now rocked in the sea made by the fish. In a few moments another jumped some distance away, and we could hear a splashing sound, which Paublo said was caused by the fins as the fish rushed through the water. The darkness was of that quality that could be felt, yet it was that described by Milton as "Dark with expressive bright" as the lagoon scintillated with phosphorescent light; every oar set the sea ablaze with silvery radiance, and ahead of the boat waves of fire seemed to go rippling away. Now another seething, hissing sound was heard, and a blaze of triangular light above some huge, dim fire body below, glided swiftly along; then a volcano seemed to rend the very sea, and out of a blaze of phosphorescent light that sent its radiations in every direction, rose a dim shape, cleaving the air to drop into another volcano, which opened to receive it with loud intonation.

"Sea Vampa, sure," Paublo whispered, as though he feared that the unknown would hear him. "Dey jes wheelin' an' wheelin', leapin', an' I reckon we'se in a bad place."

"Sea bat," grunted Chief, as the ladies expressed alarm. "They jump five, yes, eight feet high."

"How heavy are they?" I asked, thinking of possibilities.

"Three or four tons," replied Chief, sententiously.

This answer was unsatisfactory to some of the party, so we hauled close in shore near Long Key, where we listened to the explosions, as they seemed to be nothing else, caused by the crash of the return of the leaping fish. A school of sea vampires, sea bats, or devil fish, as men call them, had wandered into the lagoon. I knew them by reputation and hearsay, but never had seen one alive; and when I announced that I was going to take one on the following day, if they were still there, the negroes all protested, "One of dem vampas yander is twenty feet wide, 'deed he is. Five years ago a schooner seventy-ton burden, was layin' jes offen de pint yander; de capten had dun done gone ashore an' all de crew ceptin' de cook was a pickin' micramocs on de reef, jes ober yander wha yo' see de ole wrack a-layin', yes sah, jes yander under de cross. All at once dey hear de cook a-hailin' an' screamin' jes lak he crazy, an' lookin' up dere was de schooner, sails furled, anchor down, a-sailin' outen de channel. De cook he ran 'bout lak he crazy; he don' want to jump overboard cause he fraid of de sharks, so he jes yelled; an' de schooner sail on for half a mile, den stop, an' de men what had been follerin', clim board. What done it? why, de vampa fish. Yes, sah, he jes pick up de anchor an' tote it off."

Each man had some particular story to relate as to the dangerous character of the fish and its gigantic size and strength, intended to convince the listener that its capture was impossible. I found that some of these stories were true. A sea bat had towed a schooner up the channel, and while several attempts had been made to take one of these fish, it had never been accomplished in this locality. When I asked for a volunteer, after announcing my intention of trying this sport, the men were strangely silent. There was a superstition among them, that the fish had some demoniac power; that it could seize a man in its claspers and hold him beneath its cloak-like body and smother him. I finally secured the services of Chief and Paublo, and by daylight the following morning we were on the water, the men pulling across the channel to the long lagoon which formed the breakwater of the group to the east.

My boat was a light cedar affair, built in Boston, thoroughly seaworthy and prepared for the rough weather that is often experienced among the keys, by having under her forward and side decks rows of airtight cans, which more than once had proved to be of good service.

For weapons of offense I had the ordinary grains of the reef with which I had often taken large fishes. This harpoon consisted of a two-pronged spear attached to a steel cap which fitted closely upon a long, pliable yellow pine handle. The barbs of the points were movable; when they entered a fish they closed, but when the slightest strain came they opened and prevented the harpoon from tearing out. A stout line or rope was made fast to the grains and led up the pole, and three hundred feet of it coiled forward in a large half barrel. Besides this I had a sharp coral chisel to use as a lance in case of necessity. Thus equipped, we were ready for almost any game, at least of the sea.

The early mornings were usually ushered in by transformation scenes of splendid possibilities—staged in the heavens—and this was no exception. Long before the sun appeared, the east was a mass of crimson clouds; first deep, dark and ominous, gradually increasing in brilliancy, color and tint, until the sun burst forth in all his splendor.

We soon reached the spot where we had heard the thundering of the sea bat the preceding night, but the lagoon was apparently deserted. At Chief suggesting that the fish did not come so far up until full flood tide, we turned and rowed to the south, parallel to the great fringing reef against whose sunken coral rocks the surf broke sullenly. Long Key—a sandy spit since destroyed by a hurricane—Bush Key and the long fringing reef two or three miles in length, formed three sides of the lagoon, which at high water was from ten to twenty feet in depth and through a part of which ran a deep blue channel. Acres were covered with branch coral, while the rest of the bottom was either white sand, or had a scant growth of algae—the home of craw fish, crabs and various shell fish upon which I believed the big rays fed.

The men rowed slowly down the reef by an old ship blown in by a hurricane years before, now lying ghostly and still, with a corporal's guard of pelicans, frigate birds and gulls; down by Bird Key whose population of terns rose high in air with bewildering cries. I had begun to think that the morning was a poor time for vampire fishing when Chief stopped rowing and pointed to the east. I turned in time to see a black triangular object waved above the surface; it might have been the dorsal fin of a shark, yet no shark had so black a top-gallant sail, or, indeed, so large a one. Paublo was gazing at it; it was a rude awakening for him as I believe he had considered it a forlorn hope, and secretly prayed that we might not see the dreaded fish. I turned the boat in the direction of the fin and bade the men give way. The trim cutter shot through the still water like a gull. Where I had sighted the fish the lagoon began to dip into the deep channel of the Gulf Stream as it flows between Cuba and the Keys, and until nearly one hundred feet is reached every object on the bottom can be seen, so clear is the water.

We had almost reached the spot when not one, but five or six fins appeared, my exclamation causing the men to look around. I gave the tiller to Paublo, Chief taking the oars, and crept forward. As I picked up the grains I noted that I could see the bottom distinctly thirty-five feet below. We had happened upon a school of the monsters which were indulging in some game of the sea. There were, perhaps, ten or twelve in all, moving in a circle one hundred and fifty feet in diameter, and churning the water into a veritable maelstrom. Chief was slowly and noiselessly propelling the boat ahead, and we drifted about thirty feet from the circumference of the circle.

Surely these fleeting, glistening figures were the witches of the world of fishes, as no more diabolical creature could be imagined. They resembled enormous bats, and in following one another around the circle, raised the inner tip of the long wing-like fin high out of the water in a graceful curve, the other being deeply submerged. Imagine a fish shaped like a bat, the wings ending in graceful points, a vivid black on the upper surface and white beneath, a long whip-like tail, while from near the large and prominent eyes extended forward a pair of writhing, clasping finger-like tentacles three feet in length. Endow such a creature with marvelous activity and a constant desire to change its position and assume some extraordinary attitude, and possibly a faint conception of the actual appearance and personality of these strange creatures circling before me may be obtained.

As we slowly drifted nearer I could see them deep in the water, apparently going through a series of fantastic figures; now gliding down with flying motion of the wings; sweeping, gyrating upward with a twisting vertical motion marvelous in its perfect grace; now they flashed white, again black, so that one would have said they were rolling over and over, turning somersaults, were it possible for so large a fish to accomplish the feat. Since then I have been informed by one who had opportunity to watch them on many occasions, that this is what they were doing, and is really a common practice of the big rays. As I recall this strange performance, the huge creatures would suddenly turn over and shoot along upon their backs, thus displaying the pure white of the ventral surface, then again turning at the surface, move along with the remarkable, undulatory, bird-like motion. All this passed in rapid review, and fearing that they would become alarmed I gave the word, and Chief moved ahead.

I wished to select my game and make the throw as the fish turned, and to accomplish this I waited until several had passed. Finally we drifted directly in the path of the remarkable procession, the fishes paying no attention to the boat. One dived beneath her, another came careening up from below, standing directly on edge, as nearly as I could determine, and fairly exposed its broad back, not ten feet away ; and as it glistened in the sun I hurled the grains into it with all my strength. The pine handle seemed shot into the air as it rebounded, then we became witnesses to the extraordinary agility of this monster ray. It appeared to fly into the air, rising, an appalling mass of flesh, out of the seething waters, its side wings beating the heated air as it rose, then falling with a crash and the reverberating sound we had listened to the night before; fell as a square eighteen by ten feet and weighing tons might fall.

As the heavy waves from the impact struck the boat, I stumbled into the bottom, rolling out of the way of the jumping line that was now hissing from the barrel. The fish, after its first leap, had headed directly to the South, or out to sea, and the line was rising upward in coils. The Indian oarsmen rowed the boat ahead to lessen the strain when it should come, but so furious was the rush that I decided to check the fish before the rope was exhausted, and taking a piece of sail-cloth I grasped a coil and held on.

The boat was well under way, but the shock was terrific. Arms and muscles snapped, and for a moment the rope smoked through the cloth; then Chief dropped his oars and took it, and we were under way driving the fish by a single rein. I had used the boat to capture man-eater sharks, and as a precautionary measure to prevent the line from getting over the side, had a deep notch cut in the bow, in which it rested. With no little difficulty we succeeded in lifting it in place, the bow of the boat at the water's edge riding a heavy sea, which rushed ahead of us as an advance guard. In a short time the fish towed us into deep water, and then surged downward, keeping near the bottom, and we were forced as far astern as possible to keep the bow from going under. I noticed that Chief had taken out a big sheath knife, which he habitually carried in a leather scabbard, and held it in his teeth—a significant movement that was not lost on Paublo, whose terrified glance shot from the fast disappearing keys to the hissing line ahead and back again.

We were headed far out into the gulf, and for two miles the ray towed us at rapid pace. It was evident that if something was not done the line would have to be cut away or we would follow our wild steed indefinitely. I therefore directed the men to ship the oars and pull against it white I took a turn with the rope around the forward seat; but this powerful brake had no effect upon the fish. Then I determined to haul in and try to lance it. We were now a mile and a half, perhaps more, to the south of Bird Key in the open gulf and began to feel the long swell that ever rolled in from the west, while an ominous squall cloud as black as night, to the south dead ahead, did not add to the pleasures of the situation. The line was passed astern and we all "boused on," as Paublo expressed it ; now gaining a foot, again slipping back, hauling, straining every muscle, slowly but surely forcing the light boat upon the fish to the accompanying shouts of Paublo and Chief—"ah ho ah," "ah he ho," "all together now," "ah ho!" Then would come a rush; the line would smoke through our fingers for ten or twenty feet, and lying back until the flurry seemed to die away to haul again.

For some time we worked in this way, and I estimated that the fish was not more than twenty feet away, and had crawled out onto the little deck to peer down into the water, when the line rapidly rose, then turned so sharply to the left that I was nearly thrown overboard. The Seminole, who was in the stern, grasped an oar and aided in hauling the boat around; but she yawed and careened so that the water poured in; then the fish appeared at the surface forty feet away, its wing waving in the air like the black piratical flag it was, perhaps in derision, perhaps in defiance, then disappeared. The fish had turned the keeled boat in little more than its length and was now towing us directly back to the reef—a proceeding more than satisfactory as a storm was rapidly coming, and if caught we should have to cut away; so we sat with a turn of the line about the thwart on the alert for any move. Steam could hardly have towed us faster; we flew through the water throwing clouds of spray over the deck, racing with flocks of gulls that eyed us curiously, plunging among schools of Portuguese men of war and velellas, and in a short time without incident entered the lagoon, where I decided to bring matters to a finish and cut away rather than go to sea a second time.

Whether the great fish was accustomed to go to a certain feeding ground and now returned in its terror from mere force of habit, I do not know, but the fact remains that it was up the lagoon between Long Key and the outer fringing reef, into an almost perfect *cul de sac*, the water shallowing at every flap of its wonderful wings. I stood on the little deck and could see every movement of the strange fish, that in swimming over the white sandy bottom in water not over four feet in depth displayed its outline perfectly.

Chief had the oar, steering the boat after the fish, which, it was expected, would turn at any moment, while Paublo stood amidships holding the rope, which had a turn about the seat. The lagoon narrowed rapidly, and at high tide a small boat-channel was formed; at other times being too shallow and easily waded. Perchance the fish having passed this at flood tide, was again making for it, hoping to reach deep water, which was but a stone's throw away. The graceful, bird-like movement of its fins was a fascinating spectacle; a waving, undulatory motion which sent the ray along at a remarkable speed, and the slightest increase of which forced it over the white sand like the shadow of a dark cloud.

We were running parallel to the beach, and some men stopped and waved their hats as we shot by. Suddenly, without the slightest warning, the fish turned. I saw the pointed fin leap into the air until it stood upright, as the fish seemed to breast the water in the turn. I stepped back and shouted a warning to Chief. But it was too late. The bow of the boat was jerked, shivering and trembling, almost completely around, throwing Paublo over the rail into the lagoon, and was away almost before he recovered his feet and stood in water nearly up to his armpits looking at the retreating boat doubtless with amazement seasoned with relief, as he could easily wade to Long Key.

The fish headed for the outer reef, on which a heavy sea was breaking; drawing little or no water it could doubtless plunge over while the boat would either ground, or if it succeeded in making the reef, would doubtless be swamped in the surf. We took the line as Paublo dropped it, and surged upon it with all our strength, and were encouraged by finding that the fish was weakening. But we were rapidly approaching the reef; another haul and we were nearly on top of our quarry, whose long tail was under the boat, the mighty wings pulsating just ahead. A patch of coral now loomed up, and this fortunate obstacle turned the fish and in the whirl the fin seemed to rise almost over the boat, hurling the spray over us, and once more we were off up the lagoon headed for the *cul de sac*.

I gave Chief the rope, and taking the big square-edged lance sent in into the black mass. A cloud of blood followed, while the speed of the fish was increased so that the bow was well under water, flush with the deck. Again and again I lanced the fish, but the blade was a chisel-like affair, and did not penetrate more than five or six inches. There was a duplicate pair of grains in the boat, and this weapon was also hurled into the ray's back, but still it rushed on, seemingly as vigorous as ever. I fully expected to see it turn again, but it held its course, heading directly for the narrow tide channel between Long and Bush keys toward which Paublo was running along the beach of the former key. It was an exciting moment. The fish was alongside, yet we were going, as near as I could judge, at full speed.

Nearer we came, flying over the roots of mangroves, over patches of coral and sea-grass, into a narrow channel hardly four feet deep and not thirty feet wide, with a flat on each side partly bare. Not a tenth of a mile away the sea was beating on the reef, which meant liberty, if not life, to the fish. But fisherman's luck was ours. The tide was so low that it left but two feet in the upper head of the channel into which we ran. The fish discovered its error too late, but made a gamey attempt to rectify it, turning and lifting itself partly out of water, throwing oars, grains, and fishermen into the lagoon.

The turn cost the fish its life, as it ran high on to the narrow mud flat, where it beat the shallow water with its powerful wings, opened its cavernous mouth with great sucking gasps, every moment urging itself further out of its native element. Paublo, who had waded across the little channel in his exuberance, bounded on to the flat back of the monster and waved his hands aloft, while Chief ran in shore with the rope and presently had the fish securely fastened to a mangrove tree not fifty feet away.

We had earned our game and were well exhausted. Had it been high water, and could the ray have gone through the channel, which doubtless it often passed, it would have escaped.

Stretched upon the hot sands beneath the straggling mangroves, Paublo humming a low baccarole of his own invention, Chief silent, but with a long smile fixed upon his countenance, we could not believe but that the writhing black mass was a monstrous bird, one of the uncanny pterodactyls which geologists dream about; yet it was a noble quarry, "the struck eagle stretched upon the plain, no more through rolling clouds to soar again." The weight of the ray we could only conjecture, but it was doubtless several tons; and had this light and airy jumper sprang upon the boat it would have crushed it like paper.

When the tide was at the ebb the black vampire, as the men called it, was high and dry, and was paced off. It was eighteen feet from tip to tip, ten feet long from its mouth to the base of its tail, which was about seven feet in length. It is impossible to convey any adequate idea of the appearance of this devil-fish, sea vampire, this *Mania brevirostra* of science, which is so difficult to take that it more often runs away with boats than is captured, and of whose habits very little is known. Indeed, vampire fishing will never be a popular sport except among those who delight in an element of danger.

Mr. G. E. Northrop, of Chicago, captured a very large sea bat in the Gulf of Mexico in the summer of 1898, and in a letter to the writer described it as remarkable sport. The fish gave a hard fight, towing the heavy boat a long distance. Unfortunately the photographs of this fish turned out unsatisfactorily. In this connection, it is a singular fact that none of the popular works of the day appear to have a thoroughly correct figure of the fish, nor are photographs of it available so far as I know.

The big ray was almost jet black upon its upper surface, the back being rough; the under surface was white, with gray cloud effects here and there, giving it a marbled appearance. Popular fancy has given the fish a sting above the base of the tail, but this is a misnomer; it is without the serrated lance which marks many of the tribe which I took in these waters, one of which wounded a companion by striking its lances across his foot.

The mouth of the ray as we pried it open was of ominous dimensions, and afforded ample room for a man to lie very snugly coiled within. The teeth were very small, but the extraordinary feature of this fish—the one which has given rise to many tales, true and legendary—is its two tentacles or claspers, fleshy objects about four five inches wide and three feet long, which extend outward from each side of the mouth. Their office is undoubtedly to aid in securing food. When the fish is moving they are in constant motion, being whirled about like the tentacles of a squid, and that they are muscular and powerful has been demonstrated on many occasions. The natural movement of the claspers is inward, and when any object strikes between them it is instinctively held—a proceeding which explains the undoubted fact that these fishes can run away with large vessels.

At least five instances of this were heard of on the reef occurring from Tampa Bay to Garden Key, and the Hon. Wm. Elliott, formerly of Beaufort, S. C., a famous hunter of this game, reports two instances from that State. In every case the vessels, always at anchor, suddenly moved off in a mysterious manner and were towed greater or less distances. The ray had collided with the chain, and, true to its instincts, threw its two tentacular feelers or claspers around it and rushed ahead, thus lifting the anchor. That the claspers are very powerful is well shown by the experience of Mr. Elliott, who, in endeavoring to kill a large fish, which he had harpooned and run down, with a knife, felt his arm seized and held so securely that it became numb. He called to the men to hold the fish at all hazards; but it is obvious that if the animal which they had just hauled to the boat had made a rush and broken the harpoon or rope the sportsman would have been carried off in its embrace.

I never heard of an attack being made by the bat on the Florida reef; there it was supposed to catch crayfish, and employ the feelers to whip the food into its mouth.

That so enormous an animal can leap so easily and so high is remarkable, and I believe that this is a common pastime, as in later attempts to follow the fishes at night, I frequently heard the resounding crash that told of the return. The ray which I struck seemed to clear the water three feet, but Chief said that he had seen them jump five feet, while Mr. Elliott, already quoted, states that he has seen them bound ten feet into the air.

On the reef this fish was considered a dangerous animal, and never followed. Some years previous an attempt had been made to catch one which fouled a vessel's cable. The fish became impaled on the anchor, and when brought up broke away. It was then harpooned, but escaped after leaping partly on the boat, breaking the oars on one side, and seriously injuring the crew, who were crushed into the sinking craft. So the sea vampire, which was supposed to suffocate its victims with its cloak-like wings, was dreaded, and that anyone should consider it sport to follow such a creature and hunt it down was more than the ordinary reef negro could understand.

The people of upper Florida, Georgia, and the Carolinas, where the fish is also found, are equally afraid of it; yet, in 1845, to take one of these monsters was considered in these States the highest phase of sport, and the visitor to any of the hospitable plantations near Hilton Head would be sure to be invited to a sea vampire or devil-fish hunt. The sport was followed with great abandon, and one gentleman had a record of sixteen sea vampires taken with the harpoon in one season, the fish towing him from ten to twenty miles and fighting from one to five hours.

The waters of Port Royal Sound were the breeding grounds of the fish, and it is a singular fact that the wild excitement embodied in the sport was discovered in an attempt at retaliation on the part of the planters whose property had been destroyed by the rays. Those whose property abutted the Sound had water fences which marked the limits of their plantations seaward, and some had piers extending out into the water. The heavy posts, which would be in deep water at flood tide, were mysteriously hauled up, and I am informed by a gentleman from this section that the piles of wharves were occasionally similarly treated. For a long time the cause was unexplained, but finally a school of large rays was seen to sweep along and collide with the piles. The fish evidently threw their claspers about them and in the violent struggles which ensued wrenched them loose.

The sportsmen made the attack in eight oared barges propelled by negroes, and when the strike was made the barge rushed away toward the ocean, several other boats being caught as they passed until the fish was towing a procession of craft. This was the initial fish, which measured twenty feet across, and from that time on the exciting pastime became the sport above all others of the Sound region. The catches were marked by many sensational features. On one occasion Mr. T. R. S. Elliott was the harpooner, and when the fish was struck it cleared the water, striking the boat in the bow, sweeping away all the oars on one side, and sending her astern so violently that every man in the barge was thrown from his seat and one or two or two severely crushed. The man at the helm, James Cuthbert, was pitched headlong on to the deck, while Mr. Elliott took a flying leap into the air, landing upon the back of the struggling fish. He was fortunately hauled aboard before the ray got under way, and stood on the little deck, drenched, and raised a cheer as the boat moved off behind the wild steed.

The legend heard in the Pacific that this fish envelops its prey with its cloak-like wings may its traced to the ancient authors, among whom Oppian writes, "It is the broadest among fishes (*Eurotatos pantessin metichthusin*); and he further describes its habit of seizing mariners, sinking with them and smothering the victim beneath its wings. This belief is still held by the pearl divers off the South Coast. The truth is that while the fish makes a remarkable fight for its liberty, it is timid and never attacks; the fouling of anchors, the leaping upon boats being mere accidents attendant upon the movements of a large fish in agony and fear.

In following this spurt in Port Royal Sound the sharks were often a factor to be dealt with, attacking the wounded sea vampire in such numbers that while being towed by a fish Mr. Elliott took with a line as many as six hammerheads which were following the trail of blood; vicious monsters ranging up to nine feet in length.

In its peculiar somersaults the bat is not unique, as I have repeatedly observed the California banded sheepshead roll over and over; yet in so large a fish it is a remarkable act. Merely venturing an opinion I am inclined to think that this may be a feature of courtship, and nowhere have the strange gambols been so often observed as in Port Royal Sound. Here the fishes were repeatedly seen by Mr. Elliott, as I saw them once in the Gulf of Mexico, swimming in a circle, black and white flashing at intervals as they somersaulted; now swimming upon their backs; now vaulting into the air and while in this position falling upon the back. Sometimes the act would be performed in deep water, the flash of the white ventral side alone telling the story of the turn; again the water would boil at the surface, the horns appear and the huge fish would roll completely over until its tail lashed the air in its descent. So commonly was this trick performed that more than one of the fishes taken by Mr. Elliott was harpooned in the belly.

It is believed that specimens measuring nearly thirty feet across have been seen. Mitchell refers to one caught in the West Indies which required six oxen to drag it up the beach; but the average ray taken on American shores, which the sportsmen may expect to find in the summer months from Port Royal Sound to Garden Key and up the west coast of Florida, and in Lower California, will rarely exceed eighteen or twenty feet in width—large enough to afford some of the most exciting experiences in the annals of sport with the spear at sea.

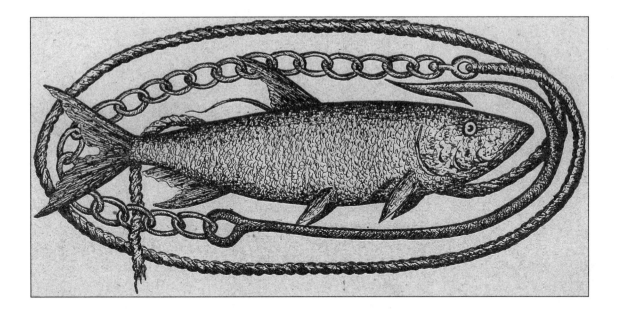

Byme-by-Tarpon

ZANE GREY

To capture the fish is not all of the fishing. Yet there are circumstances which make this philosophy hard to accept. I have in mind an incident of angling tribulation which rivals the most poignant instant of my boyhood, when a great trout flopped for one sharp moment on a mossy stone and then was gone like a golden flash into the depths of the pool.

Some years ago I followed Attalano, my guide, down the narrow Mexican street of Tampico to the bank of the broad Panuco. Under the rosy dawn the river quivered like a restless opal. The air, sweet with the song of blackbird and meadowlark, was full of cheer; the rising sun shone in splendor on the water and the long line of graceful palms lining the opposite bank, and the tropical forest beyond, with its luxuriant foliage festooned by gray moss. Here was a day to warm the heart of any fisherman; here was the beautiful river, celebrated in many a story; here was the famous guide, skilled with oar and gaff, rich in experience. What sport I would have; what treasure of keen sensation would I store; what flavor of life would I taste this day! Hope burns always in the heart of a fisherman.

Attalano was in harmony with the day and the scene. He had cheering figure, lithe and erect, with a springy stride, bespeaking the Montezuma blood said to flow in his Indian veins. Clad in a colored cotton shirt, blue jeans, and Spanish girdle, and treading the path with brown feet never deformed by shoes, he would have stopped an artist. Soon he bent his muscular shoulders to the oars, and the ripples circling from each stroke hardly disturbed the calm Panuco. Down the stream glided long Indian canoes, hewn from trees and laden with oranges and bananas. In the stern stood a dark native wielding an enormous paddle with ease. Wild-fowl dotted the glassy expanse; white cranes and pink flamingoes graced the reedy bars; red-breasted kingfishers flew over with friendly screech. The salt breeze kissed my cheek; the sun shone with the comfortable warmth Northerners welcome in spring; from over the white sand-dunes far below came the faint boom of the ever-restless Gulf.

We trolled up the river and down, across from one rush-lined lily-padded shore to the other, for miles and miles with never a strike. But I was content, for over me had been cast the dreamy, care-dispelling languor of the South.

When the first long, low sell of the changing tide rolled in, a stronger breeze raised little dimpling waves and chased along the water in dark, quick-moving frowns. All at once the tarpon began to show, to splash, to play, to roll. It was as though they had been awakened by the stir and murmur of the miniature breakers. Broad bars of silver flashed in the sunlight, green backs cleft the little billows, wide tails slapped lazily on the water. Every yard of river seemed to hold a rolling fish. This sport increased until the long stretch of water, which had been as calm as St. Regis Lake at twilight, resembled the quick current of a Canadian stream. It was a fascinating, wonderful sight. But it was also peculiarly exasperating, because when the fish roll in this sportive, lazy way they will not bite. For an hour I trolled through this whirlpool of flying spray and twisting tarpon, with many a salty drop on my face, hearing all around me the whipping crash of breaking water.

"Byme-by-tarpon," presently remarked Attalano, favoring me with the first specimen of his English.

The rolling of the tarpon diminished, and finally ceased as noon advanced.

No more did I cast longing eyes upon those huge bars of silver. They were buried treasure. The breeze quickened as the flowing tide gathered strength, and together they drove the waves higher. Attalano rowed across the river into the outlet of one of the lagoons. This narrow stream was unruffled by wind; its current was sluggish and its muddy waters were clarifying under the influence of the now fast-rising tide.

By a sunken log near shore we rested for lunch. I found the shade of the trees on the bank rather pleasant, and became interested in a blue heron, a russet-colored duck, and a brown-and-black snipe, all sitting on the sunken log. Near by stood a tall crane watching us solemnly, and above in the treetop a parrot vociferously proclaimed his knowledge of our presence. I was wondering if he objected to our invasion, at the same time taking a most welcome bite for lunch, when directly in front of me the water flew up as if propelled by some submarine power. Framed in a shower of spray

I saw an immense tarpon, with mouth agape and fins stuff, close in pursuit of frantically leaping little fish.

The fish that Attalano dropped his sandwich attested to the large size and close proximity of the tarpon. He uttered a grunt of satisfaction and pushed out the boat. A school of feeding tarpon closed the mouth of the lagoon. Thousands of mullet had been cut off from their river haunts and were now leaping, flying, darting in wild haste to elude the great white monsters. In the foamy swirls I saw streaks of blood.

"Byme-by-tarpon!" called Attalano, warningly.

Shrewd guide! I had forgotten that I held a rod. When the realization dawned on me that sooner or later I would feel the strike of one of these silver tigers a keen, tingling thrill of excitement quivered over me. The primitive man asserted himself; the instinctive lust to conquer and to kill seized me, and I leaned forward, tense and strained with suspended breath and swelling throat.

Suddenly the strike came, so tremendous in its energy that it almost pulled me from my seat; so quick, fierce, bewildering that I could think of nothing but to hold on. Then the water split with a hissing sound to let out a great tarpon, long as a door, seemingly as wide, who shot up and up into the air. He wagged his head and shook it like a struggling wolf. When he fell back with a heavy splash, a rainbow, exquisitely beautiful and delicate, stood out of the spray, glowed, paled, and faded.

Five times he sprang toward the blue sky, and as many he plunged down with a thunderous crash. The reel screamed. The line sang. The rod, which I had thought stiff as a tree, bent like a willow wand. The silver king came up far astern and sheered to the right in a long, wide curve, leaving behind a white wake. Then he sounded, while I watched the line with troubled eyes. But not long did he sulk. He began a series of magnificent tactics new in my experience. He stood on his tail, then on his head; he sailed like a bird; he shook himself so violently as to make a convulsive, shuffling sound; he dove, to come up covered with mud, marring his bright sides; he closed his huge gills with a slap and, most remarkable of all, he rose in the shape of a crescent, to straighten out with such marvelous power that he seemed to actually crack like a whip.

After this performance, which left me in a condition of mental aberration, he sounded again, to begin a persistent, dragging pull which was the most disheartening of all his maneuvers; for he took yard after yard of line until he was far away from me, out in the Panuco. We followed him, and for an hour crossed to and fro, up and down, humoring him, responding to his every caprice, as if he verily were a king. At last, with a strange inconsistency more human than fishlike, he returned to the scene of his fatal error, and here in the mouth of the smaller stream he leaped once more. But it was only a ghost of his former efforts—a slow, weary rise, showing he was tired. I could see it in the weakening wag of his head. He no longer made the line whistle.

I began to recover the long line. I pumped and reeled him closer. Reluctantly he came, not yet broken in spirit, though his strength had sped. He rolled at times with a shade of the old vigor, with a pathetic manifestation of the temper that became a hero. I could see the long, slender tip of his dorsal fin, then his broad tail and finally the gleam of his silver side. Closer he came and slowly circled around the boat, eying me with great, accusing eyes. I measured him with a fisherman's glance. What a great fish! Seven feet, I calculated, at the very least.

At this triumphant moment I made a horrible discovery. About six feet from the leader the strands of the line had frayed, leaving only one thread intact. My blood ran cold and the clammy sweat broke out on my brow. My empire was not won; my first tarpon was as if he had never been. But true to my fishing instincts, I held on morosely; tenderly I handled him; with brooding care I riveted my eye on the frail place in my line, and gently, ever so gently, I began to lead the silver king shoreward. Every smallest move of his tail meant disaster to me, so when he moved it I let go of the reel. Then I would have to coax him to swim back again.

The boat touched the bank. I stood up and carefully headed my fish toward the shore, and slid his head and shoulders out on the lily-pads. One moment he lay there, glowing like mother-of-pearl, a rare fish, fresh from the sea. Then, as Attalano warily reached for the leader, he gave a gasp, a flop that deluged us with muddy water, and a lunge that spelled freedom.

I watched him swim slowly away with my bright leader dragging beside him. Is it not the loss of things which makes life bitter? What we have gained is ours; what is lost is gone, whether fish, or use, or love, or name, or fame.

I tried to put on a cheerful aspect for my guide. But it was too soon. Attalano, wise old fellow, understood my case. A small, warm and living, flashed across his dark face as he spoke:

"Byme-by-tarpon."

Which defined his optimism and revived the failing spark within my breast. It was, too, in the nature of a prophecy.

Skelton's Party (selection)

THOMAS McGUANE

Skelton followed watching the drawn bow the rod had become, the line shearing water with precision.

"What a marvelously smooth drag this reel has! A hundred smackers seemed steep at the time; but when you're in the breach, as I am now, a drag like this is the last nickel bargain in America!"

Skelton was poling after the fish with precisely everything he had. And it was difficult on the packed bottom with the pole inclining to slip out from under him.

His feeling of hope for a successful first-day guiding was considerably modified by Rudleigh's largely undeserved hooking of the fish. And now the nobility of the fish's fight was further eroding Skelton's pleasure.

When they crossed the edge of the flat, the permit raced down the reef line in sharp powerful curves, dragging the line across the coral. "Gawd, gawd, gawd," Rudleigh said. "This cookie is stronger than I am!" Skelton poled harder and at one point overtook the fish as it desperately rubbed the hook on the coral bottom; seeing the boat, it flushed once more in terror, making a single long howl pour from the reel. A fish that was exactly noble, thought Skelton, who began to imagine the permit coming out of a deep-water wreck by the pull of moon and tide, riding the invisible crest of the incoming water, feeding and moving by force of blood; only to run afoul of an asshole from Connecticut.

The fight continued without much change for another hour, mainly outside the reef line in the green water over a sand bottom: a safe place to fight the fish. Rudleigh had soaked through his khaki safari clothes; and from time to time Mrs. Rudleigh advised him to "bear down." When Mrs. Rudleigh told him this, he would turn to look at her, his neck muscles standing out like cords and his eyes acquiring broad white perimeters. Skelton ached from pursuing the fish with the pole; he might have started the engine outside the reef line, but he feared Rudleigh getting his line in the propeller and he had found that a large fish was held away from the boat by the sound of a running engine.

As soon as the fish began to show signs of tiring, Skelton asked Mrs. Rudleigh to take a seat; then he brought the big net up on the deck beside him. He hoped he would be able to get Rudleigh to release this hugely undeserved fish, not only because it was undeserved but because the fish had fought so very bravely. No, he admitted to himself, Rudleigh would never let the fish go.

By now the fish should have been on its side. It began another long and accelerating run, the pale sheet of water traveling higher up the line, the fish swerving somewhat inshore again; and to his terror, Skelton found himself poling after the fish through the shallows, now and then leaning over to free the line from a sea fan. They glided among the little hammocks and mangrove keys of Saddlebunch in increasing vegetated congestion, in a narrowing tidal creek that closed around and over them with guano-covered mangroves and finally prevented the boat from following another foot. Nevertheless, line continued to pour off the reel.

"Captain, consider it absolutely necessary that I kill the fish. This one doubles the Honduran average."

Skelton did not reply, he watched the line slow its passage from the reel, winding out into the shadowy creek; then stop. He knew there was a good chance the desperate animal had reached a dead end.

"Stay here."

Skelton climbed out of the boat and, running the line through his fingers lightly, began to wade the tidal creek. The mosquitoes found him quickly and held in a pale globe around his head. He waded steadily, flushing herons out of the mangroves over his head. At one point, he passed a tiny side channel, blocking the exit of a heron that raised its stiff wings very slightly away from its body and glared at him. In the green shadows, the heron was a radiant, perfect white.

He stopped a moment to look at the bird. All he could hear was the slow musical passage of tide in the mangrove roots and the low pattern of bird sounds more liquid than the sea itself in these shallows. He moved away from the side channel, still following the line. Occasionally, he felt some small movement of life in it; but he was certain now the permit could go no farther. He had another thirty yards to go, if he had guessed right looking at Rudleigh's partially emptied spool.

Wading along, he felt he was descending into the permit's world; in knee-deep water, the small mangrove snappers, angelfish, and baby barracudas scattered before him, precise, contained creatures of perfect mobility. The brilliant blue sky was reduced to a narrow ragged band quite high overhead now and the light wavered more with the color of the sea and of estuarine shadow than that of vulgar sky. Skelton stopped and his eye followed the line back in the direction he had come. The Rudleighs were at its other end, infinitely far away.

Skelton was trying to keep his mind on the job he had set out to do. The problem was, he told himself, to go from Point A to Point B; but every breath of humid air, half sea, and the steady tidal drain through root and elliptical shadow in his ears and eyes diffused his attention. Each heron that leaped like an arrow out of his narrow slot, spiraling invisibly into the sky, separated him from the job. Shafts of light in the side channels illuminated columns of pristine, dancing insects.

Very close now. He released the line so that if his appearance at the dead end terrified the permit there would not be sufficient tension for the line to break. The sides of the mangrove slot began to yield. Skelton stopped.

An embowered, crystalline tidal pool: the fish lay exhausted in its still water, lolling slightly and unable to right itself. It cast a delicate circular shadow on the sand bottom. Skelton moved in and the permit made no effort to rescue itself; instead, it lay nearly on its side and watched Skelton approach with a steady, following eye that was, for Skelton, the last straw. Over its broad, virginal sides a lambent, moony light shimmered. The fish seemed like an oval section of sky—yet sentient and alert, intelligent as tide.

He took the permit firmly by the base of its tail and turned it gently upright in the water. He reached into its mouth and removed the hook from the cartilaginous operculum. He noticed that the suddenly loosened line was not retrieved: Rudleigh hadn't even the sense to keep tension on the line.

By holding one hand under the permit's pectoral fins and the other around the base of its tail, Skelton was able to move the fish back and forth in the water to revive it. When he first tentatively released it, it teetered over on its side, its wandering eye still fixed upon him. He righted the fish again and continued to move it gently back and forth in the water; and this time when he released the permit, it stayed upright, steadying itself in equipoise, mirror sides once again purely reflecting the bottom. Skelton watched a long while until some regularity returned to the movement of its gills.

Then he cautiously—for fear of startling the fish—backed once more into the green tidal slot and turned to head for the skiff. Rudleigh had lost his permit.

The line was lying limp on the bottom. Why didn't the fool at least retrieve it? With his irritation Skelton began to return to normal. He trudged along the creek, this time against the tide; and returned to the skiff.

The skiff was empty.

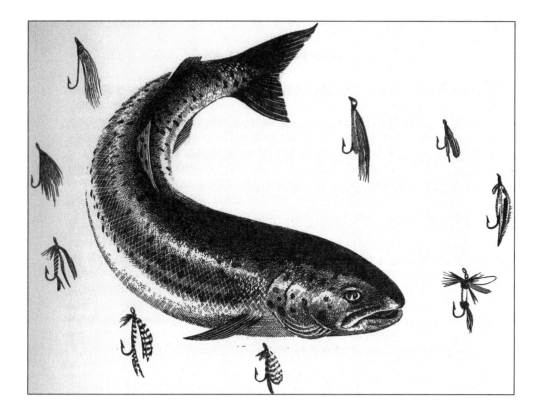

PART IV

Trout and the Lure
of Feathers

The Lakes at Inhluzane

TOM SUTCLIFFE

In those early years we had everything you could want for good stillwater fly fishing; trophy-sized browns and rainbows, even some double-figure trout, sections of lakes where the water dropped away off shelves and ledges and went down three or four meters, tall stands of reeds growing in glassy-green water, acres of waist-deep shallows crossed by old river beds, islands of weed like floating rafts and, in the weeds, the occasional pond-like openings that always held a fish or two.

Then there were countless clear inlet streams we fished as well. They ran in grass-lined, pebbled beds across bare veld, sometimes going underground, or flowing through a necklace of tiny pools roofed by hanging grass, widening as they got closer to the lake, but never getting much wider than you could easily step across. We surprised a lot of fish in these streams, mainly with big, bushy dry flies.

***

The aquatic life in the lakes was, to put it mildly, abundant. The shallow flats and the inlets and weed margins were alive with dragonfly nymphs, damsels, mayflies, snails, water boatmen, frogs, minnows and, of course, midges. The midge hatches some years were really good. Tall columns of insects would reach into the evening sky like the rising smoke of campfires, occasionally dense enough to just about blot out the setting sun (not really, but that's how we sometimes felt about them). Caddisflies danced erratically over the water along the bank pretty well every mild evening, and mayflies trickled off sporadically mainly in the shallow water around the weedbeds, never dense hatches but always a good filler. We had access to die richest aquatic soup you could dream about and we made the most of it.

We fished just about every way known to modem man--dry flies, emergers, nymphs, wet flies, deeply sunk attractors (we even occasionally trolled, which is one hell of a confession I know, but I can explain it). I suppose we fished nymphs most often, and then again, mostly on sunken weedbeds in waist-deep water—fairly large patterns, though later we got more technical and stand using smaller nymphs hung under tiny strike indicators. There were times that were just perfect for, say, fishing size 16 adult midges on the surface, times when a sunken dragon was exactly the right thing, times when you couldn't go wrong with a twitched DDD, and times, of course, when nothing short of a well-set stick of dynamite would make a trout take notice.

Also, we went through periods sort of obsessing over one or other specific technique. When we would concentrate for months on, say, snails, or emerging caddis pupae, or fishing midges, or imitating flies, ants, whatever, until eventually it slipped out of fashion, lost our exclusive focus and just took its place in our growing armory of strategies. We'd revisit them, sure, but only when conditions were right. The same held for flies. One or other pattern would come into fashion and we'd end up fishing it nearly exclusively for a couple of months, or until we just got tired of it. Then we would break down and go back to our normal philosophy of "fish the water the way that catches fish and stop fooling around trying to be smart."

We learned quite a bit during these academic spells, though. Most of our fads came to us straight out of the pages of the American Fly Fisherman and Fly Rod and Reel, from the early eighties on. Those two magazines were an inspiration.

But in the Inhluzane there was such a variety of water and such a variety of conditions that you could safely leave any special technique until you ran into exactly the right time to use it. And we got quite good at most techniques. Especially, we got good at casting in wind. You had to, to survive. In the end I felt I could east a fly through a keyhole in a gale from forty paces. Wisely I never put it to the test.

***

Float-tubes, when eventually they did come in, opened up even more opportunities. Suddenly we could fish silently just about anywhere we wanted (boats on lakes, on average, are just too noisy), or position ourselves for a perfect drift off structure we couldn't get to before, or even push deep into forests of reeds to locate hidden inner clearings big enough to get a fly into—and never before fished by man. That opened up some of the hottest trout spots I'd ever come across, but it was hard work, and 1 never really figured out how to land the fish I hooked. Over the years I got into some real hogs in these places, but I doubt I landed more than a couple. I settled for thinking it was just good fun hooking them in a place they'd least expected to bump into an angler, and left it at that.

Meanwhile, the Inhluzane's reputation for superb fly fishing grew, and before we knew it these was suddenly a lot more fly-fishing traffic, certainly more than we were used to. Happily, once we got over our resentment at actually having to share the place, there was never more traffic than actually mattered. The fly fishing up there remained a largely remote and authentic experience, likely still is. Generally, now that I think of it, the place at the time was not far short of what, if you happen to enjoy fly fishing, you could loosely call paradise.

***

There was one exceedingly remote, small lake on the farm North Star, a mile or so southeast of Hetherdon. A couple of acres of clear water in a sea of rolling grassland, its shallows squeezed up against the edge of a tall forest of wild chestnuts and yellowwoods on the southern slopes of a steep mountainside. We called it the Bush Dam, later just Bush, and it fished well, never any really big fish, but always good to visit. As the crow flies it was only a kilometer or two away, but it took us an hour to get there because the road was rough. In raw weather (which was often the case), it would have made a superb backdrop for one of those frontier-conquering Land Rover ads.

On its north shore a small stream came in cold from under the canopy of trees, and just beyond it there was a second feeder stream, even stronger, making a substantial through-flow of water. There were patches of piquant watercress in the streams and the cold spring water made a perfect mixer for the pale amber stuff, if you were that sort of connoisseur. Personally I didn't notice much difference, but I liked using the watercress in our salads. Mists rolled in any time and without notice and there were days when they got so dense you had to inch your way back to the truck along a fence, or shout for a response to get yourself orientated.

Many times the answering shout came from the exact opposite direction you thought it would.

The fish were, still are I'm sure, innocence itself. You could wade out and watch them feeding in clear water less than knee-deep. They were small, maybe a pound or two, very rarely three, smaller anyway than the fish we were used to at Inhluzane. I suspected the little pond might supplement itself with too much natural breeding for its own good, but the place was fine to us the way it was, because you could pretty well bet on getting fish any time you went there. Besides, we visited to experience the setting, as much as for the fishing. And because the fishing was easy, we could relax; just fish off the top of our heads a little (a pleasant change once in a while), and at the same time enjoy the bird life, the tall trees and the wildly-rugged scenery. But the road in was too dodgy for us to make a habit of going there.

I learned the fine art of using a motionless nymph on this lake. You watched a fish working a beat in knee-deep water, waited for a gap, laid out a nymph on a short line, let it settle to the bottom, then lifted the fly up when the trout swam into range. Deadly.

***

We put in enough time at Inhluzane to start believing we had become masters of stillwater trout. In truth, none of us ever was, though we got pretty serviceable at knowing exactly when to fish and when to home. Like, when light rain fell, or if a warm wind blew out of the west, we were on the water. If the wind got cold and came from the east, we wasted no time pulling our ferrules apart We had a neat rule of thumb about clouds, too. If they sat motionless over the mountaintops we knew we wouldn't catch much, But we had fishing, week in and week out, on any number of clear lakes, in countryside as pretty as any you could imagine, and we never fussed too much about any sudden change in the weather putting the fish down—we just rode it out. So we cut our stillwater teeth in grand style. We even invented a few flies along the way. One or two have stuck around, like the Zak, the DDD and the Rod-Eye Damsel. But we invented a hundred more that never got further than the edge of the Old Dam and, thinking back on some of them, more's the pity. As I said, you would expect, in time, there wasn't anything left that we didn't know about the trout in that lovely valley, or about fly fishing stillwaters generally.

Not so.

The fact is we learned something new every time we went there. I don't think we got near to actually mastering the fishing, though there were days when we thought we had. Rather, I suppose, we got pretty good at it when the fish were on, and knew more or less how to explain it when they weren't. I suspect that's about the outer limit of what's achievable in any type of fly fishing. About as close as you ever get to being called "an expert," and actually deserving the title. (Frankly, though, I've allways found the term a risky one in fly fishing.)

2000 Words of Heartfelt Advice

VERLYN KLINKENBORG

One spring morning many years ago, I woke up urgently needing to fish with a fly-rod. I'd never been fly fishing, and I hadn't fished at all since I was 12, a boy with a bait rod in a boat. All I remembered about fishing was that sunfish have spines and bullheads have barbels and that it's better to eat lunch as soon as you pull away from the dock, before the sandwiches start to smell like bait. That wasn't much to go on. I called my dad, a longtime fly fisherman. He gave me some good advice. "Start fishing," he said. But I lived in Manhattan. I had little money and no car. All I had was an appetite for an unfamiliar sport, an appetite aroused by the sudden dreamlike memory of sitting on shore when I was very young, watching my dad cast a wet fly in the White River near Meeker, Colorado.

As it happened, I learned to fly fish much as my dad had: I figured it out for myself. But there was a difference. He learned on the high mountain lakes and streams of Colorado. I built a fly rod—it was cheap and I wanted to build one anyway—and took it up to the roof of the building I lived in, which was narrow but nearly a hundred feet long. There in the swirling wind four stories above Third Avenue, I taught myself to cast, using a kiddie pool as my target. I practiced almost every evening for an entire summer. It would have been a ridiculous thing to do, if it hadn't been so effective.

The hardest part about being a beginner in any sport is knowing nothing. The problem isn't just what to learn, it's how to learn, a problem that's even worse in a sport like fly fishing, where a lot of emphasis is laid on tradition and on the supposedly scientific rigor of its best-known modern practitioners. In fact, fly fishing is often presented as a form of connoisseurship, which can be—and is often meant to be—very intimidating. But to some people, the apparent elitism of the sport is part of its attraction. So here's a rule of thumb. If you come across anglers, or angling writers, who make it sound as though the art of the dry fly gets passed down from firstborn to firstborn, ignore them. No one ever inherited a prose style or a casting stroke.

Fly fishing is basically a simple sport, no matter what you hear to the contrary. Casting is easy, not half as hard as learning to swing a golf club or rope a calf. Compared to spin-fishing and bait-casting gear, the equipment is mechanically simple. Fly fishing becomes elitist only if you want to own or lease private water, and in this country that's strictly a matter of cash, not breeding. The thing to remember is this: People spend enormous amounts of money for access to easy fishing. Really hard fishing is usually free. And no matter how far you progress in the sport or how exalted your ambitions become, there's no pleasure in angling as pure as the emotion you feel when you catch your first fish with a fly rod. That moment will echo down your sporting life, whether you find yourself casting for bluegills in a farm pond or for permit on Ascension Bay.

It's natural to want to sign up for fly-fishing school right away, and there are good reasons for doing so. The level of instruction and camaraderie at fishing schools can be very high, even though the enormous network of fly-fishing courses these days resembles a giant intake valve sucking beginners and their cash into the sport. I say, teach yourself instead. You'll be giving the tackle companies enough of your money anyway. Professional instruction can save you some time, but you learn nothing from the mistakes you don't make. Fly fishing isn't a product you consume while worrying about the shortness of time. It's a pursuit that gets interwoven with time itself. Teaching yourself, you learn about the techniques of fly fishing, of course, but, more importantly, you also get a chance to rediscover how you learn. That will be important on the stream. To paraphrase Heraclitus, you can never fish in the same river twice. Conditions are always different, minute by minute, cast by cast, and the ability to adjust to changing conditions—to instruct yourself quickly—is a good measure of an angler's success. If that sounds like mere philosophizing, wait till you find yourself at the onset of a Baetis hatch on the Bighorn River in early May.

Learning isn't just a matter of absorbing information. It's the act of winnowing information. I think the best, though not the fastest way to learn to fly fish is to read widely in the literature of the sport, which is a long-lasting pleasure in itself. Subscribe to the magazines; buy or borrow the books. (Watch the videos too.) Read everything and believe nothing until you've tried it out. Then keep what you can use and throw out the rest. Experience teaches you to read skeptically, and reading makes you a better judge of experience. Practicing on my rooftop long ago, I tried to copy the dissimilar casting styles of Joan Wulff, Lefty Kreh, and Charles Ritz. I also tried to ape every diagram in every fly-casting article I saw. Ultimately the dynamics of the cast itself—how a double haul felt when I did it right—taught me what I needed to know, but by trying out so many different casting styles I discovered that there is no single right way to cast. There is, instead, the broad range of what works.

Over the years, I've spent almost as much time watching anglers as I have fishing. It's a habit I picked up as a beginner, partly because I was lucky enough to be fishing with friends who were, and still are, vastly more skillful than I am. They never gave me advice, and I never asked for it, and yet their example meant every-thing to me. But in a way I've learned almost as much from watching men and women who were struggling with the sport. In their clumsiness, I could see my own, and I began to correct it little by little. I saw anglers for whom the loss of a fly or a tippet provoked a crisis, because it meant they had to tie an improved clinch knot or, worse, a blood knot. I saw anglers standing in water they should have been casting to, anglers casting to utterly barren stretches of river, anglers lashing the pool behind them with every backcast, anglers hopelessly entangled in the slack they had stripped from their reel, anglers whose rudeness had earned them the contempt of everyone around them.

And what I learned was that there's no substitute for practice or awareness or economy of motion or courtesy. Those are the fundamentals of fly fishing. These days, for instance, it's a fairly common habit to buy prefabricated leaders, knotted or knotless. When I began fly fishing I decided I wanted to tie my own leaders, fol-lowing the same logic that led me to build my first fly rod and tie my own flies. I bought Art Lee's *Fishing the Dry Fly on Rivers and Streams* and made up a couple of dozen leaders according to his formulas. (Tying leaders in the evening allowed me to pretend that I was fishing.) When I began, a blood knot was merely an aspiration, something I hoped one day to achieve. When I was done tying leaders several nights later, it was an instinct. Now I buy knotless leaders, but I still have a bombproof blood knot. The peculiar thing about learning to fly fish is this: every shortcut you take when you're a beginner ultimately diminishes your feel for the complexity, the sub-tlety of fly fishing. That's why, if at all possible, you should also learn to tie your own flies. The joy of catching a trout on a fly rod is compounded many times when you do it with a fly of your own making.

When I think back over my fly fishing education—thus far, that is—the single most instructive moment was an evening in June more than a decade ago. I had driven to the Catskills to interview a famous angler, and he invited me to go fishing with him. We drove along the Beaverkill, pausing here and there to look at the stream, and then we parked, geared up, and walked down to the river. I was tense with impatience, with nervousness. I wanted to wade right in and begin to pretend fishing, because, of course, what I really wanted to do was to watch this man fish. Instead, we sat down on a big rock near the high water mark. He didn't say much. He smoked a cigarette all the way down, and then he lit another one. He watched the water, and he tried to help me look where he was looking, although he couldn't actually make me see what he was seeing.

The current ran heavy along the far bank, and the river thinned out over a flat that ended on the near shore, so that most of that broad, beautiful river was in fact very shallow. Well upstream, at a picturesque distance, a couple of anglers were drifting dry flies along the edge of the deep current, a place that looked naturally inviting—to humans, at least. But that wasn't where this man was looking. His gaze ended at a line of rocks in water only a few inches deep, just a dozen yards upstream from us. I can't explain to you how long it seemed before I saw what he was looking at, but when I finally saw it I felt very stupid. It was the tail of a large brown trout, the tail an almost iridescent brown, glowing as it wriggled, half out of water. The fish was nymphing, nosing around in the sediment beneath the rocks. After offering me the chance, the man stood up, paid out line, made a single cast, and caught the fish, which he released.

It wasn't the cast, the catch, or the release that mattered to me, though they were elegant and unhurriedly efficient. It was the lesson about observation. Like most beginners, I had spent so much time thinking about gear and technique that I neglected the most important thing of all: the fact that my real subject was the river. I had watched the water every time I went fishing, watched it as I waded out to what I thought would be a good starting point, watched it as I made my backcast, as my fly drifted downstream. But I had never taken the time to sit down and absorb the river, to realize that what I should really be watching was the way the river differed from itself instant by instant. I had never realized that those differences—in light, in current, in sound—would show me trout, if only I could be patient enough to look for them. It was time to begin fishing in something besides my preconceptions.

That's a hard shift for most of us to make. It's easy enough to emphasize the rituals of fly fishing, its daily and seasonal rhythms, the languorous, almost supplicating beat of a long casting stroke. These are some of the things that make fly fishing a life-long sport, a sport of ever-deepening complexity. But those rituals and rhythms inevitably belong to the everyday world we inhabit, and they overlay, on the stream, a world we perceive only in flashes, when, for a moment, we're able to concentrate on the swiftness, the abruptness, the almost unimaginable profusion of what nature has laid before us. It is to lengthen those moments of concentration that one goes fly fishing, and a lifetime is barely long enough to learn what they contain.

About the Brown Trout

SAMUEL G. CAMP

Possibly you have heard some old trout fisherman—a man who has passed a good portion of his life in the woods and on the rivers and lakes of New England, fly-fishing for the red-spotted brook trout and hunting the white-tailed deer and the ruffled grouse—discourse concerning the game qualities and characteristics in general of the German or brown trout, *Salmo fario*, "made in Germany" and imported in 1882. If so, you have heard no good of the brown trout. You may have been more or less forcibly informed that the brown trout is a coarse fish; that he grows at the rate of one pound a year and fattens on the smaller red-spotted trout; that he lacks sporting blood and rises reluctantly to the artificial fly; that when hooked he furnishes a poor sort of fight compared with that of a speckled trout of equal size; that he is not as handsome a fish as the speckled trout; that, in fact, as a sporting proposition the brown trout is not to be considered.

Now the old trout fisherman is more or less correct in his conclusions; correct in so far, and only so far, as he assumes that the brown trout is not to be compared with the red-spotted brook trout, *Salvelinus fontinalis*; for no game fish, with the exception, possibly, of the salmon, which is very far beyond the dreams of most of us, will ever be so favorably esteemed as *fontinalis* has been, is now, and, thanks to the fish culturists, always will be.

In England, trout fishing means fishing for this same brown trout, and there they certainly consider it a true game fish. The reason why the brown trout has never come to his own in this country is because American anglers insist on comparing it with the "little salmon of the springs," to the inevitable detriment of *fario*.

Considered by itself, on its own merits, and leaving aside all odious comparison, the brown trout is a mighty good game fish. Its place, however, is not in the same stream with the speckled brook trout, for the very good reason that the growth of the brown trout, being almost a pound each year, as above stated, is much more rapid than that of *fontinalis*, and where the two co-exist, the brown trout preys upon his smaller speckled relative rapaciously, and to the latter's ultimate extinction.

Many of our former good trout waters have been rendered unfit for the red-spotted trout by logging operations, the introduction of foreign matter, and through various other causes. When the axemen have blazed their trail to the head waters of a trout stream, and cleared away the cool, green forest growth from its natal springs and tributary brooks, where the trout spawn and the fry grow to fingerlings, and the sun has had its way with the dismal "clearing," that stream is ruined for the native red-spotted trout; its temperature is raised beyond the point where the native trout will prosper and, in addition, with the removal of the overhanging foliage there is a consequent reduction of the insect food upon which *fontinalis* most thrives. It is in just such a stream that the brown trout, which does not demand water of a low temperature, and is naturally a tougher, hardier fish, will do well. A stream such as the above will yield good sport when planted with the brown trout. Do not conclude from this, however, that the brown trout is a coarse fish. It is not. The red-spotted brook trout, you must remember, is a charr, and the brown trout a salmon trout; and as salmon trout, *Salmo fario*, is no more a coarse fish than is any other similar member of the *Salmonidae*.

A certain trout stream that I have fished many times is inhabited by brown trout, running in weight up to five pounds, of course rarely, for although the books credit the brown trout with a capacity of attaining truly colossal proportions, we do not find them at all frequently; at least I have yet to raise one—I do not say catch.

It happened that one day I fished this stream in company with a friend who is much the sort of a trout fisherman that I have alluded to above—an expert, experienced, dyed-in-the-wool fly-fisherman, with an overweening admiration for the speckled brook trout and a small opinion of the brown trout.

We had fished down the stream until late in the afternoon with ordinary success, catching a fair number of native trout, but none of large size. There were now only two good pools left to fish, and the Old Angler was fishing ahead. The Old Angler started in on the Bridge Pool and I took the one upstream around a sharp bend. Leading down to the Bridge Pool is a pretty stiff riffle running on the left under overhanging cedars. The still water begins directly beneath the bridge, and a very little lower down there are two large submerged rocks. Between these two rocks there is generally a big brown trout; but the Old Angler did not know this. When I arrived it was all over. The Old Angler stood in mid-stream looking thoughtfully at a smashed fly-rod that dangled down into the water from his shaking hand. Also he was swearing softly, but with admirable taste and fluency. The Old Angler has since been heard to admit that possibly the brown trout has been maligned.

The fight of the brown trout is not as brilliant and erratic as that of the native, but it is, in its way, fully as effective. You will lose, in a day's fishing, just as many brown trout as native. As a general thing as much time must be taken to safely land a brown trout of, say, half a pound, as is needed for a red-spotted trout of equal weight. The red-spotted trout fights faster, but the brown trout puts a bulldog strain on the line and keeps it there; and he is never your fish until he is in the basket. Also, the brown trout, when hooked, will occasionally leap from the water and shake himself like a bass; a feat in which the native trout seldom or never indulges unless the fisherman is holding him too hard.

The brown trout rises to the artificial fly very freely, and any of the standard trout flies, hackles especially, when properly presented and seasonably used, will be successful. In habits the brown and red-spotted trout are very similar and consequently you should follow the same methods in fishing for either. There is a difference, however, in the manner in which they take the fly. A large red-spotted trout, when he has concluded that he wants a certain gaudy but palatable looking insect—perhaps a Royal Coachman—comes up leisurely, rolls over and sucks it in. But a brown trout will more often go at the fly like lightning, leaping clear of the water in his efforts, and if he misses he will do it again. He takes the fly viciously.

If there is a long rapid in the river, plentifully studded with rocks, you will find the brown trout lying in the fastest water, using the rocks as a shield from the current. Cast your flies for him directly into the foaming swirl below one of these rocks and very close to the rock itself. When hooked he immediately hurries down stream for a nice long distance, and you find yourself separated from your victim by many yards of roaring, white water. Then you may pursue two courses of action. You may, if you can, scramble down to your fish; or you may stand on a rock, with your rod bent double and yell. If you follow the latter course your fish whips himself off the hook in a little time; if you decide on the former you may make a killing or you may break a leg. In either event it is safe to say that, if you are without prejudice, you will acknowledge the brown trout a game fish.

The Trout and the Indian

GENERAL JOHN McNULTA

From my infancy I had heard tales of the Big Woods, but do not remember ever having then seen anyone who had been in them. A party was being made up to go there, and my father, when the time for starting came, on account of feeble health was prohibited from making the trip, as he had intended. I was in despair, as I was to be left behind, and all of the fond hopes that I had nourished were to be shattered—the big trout, the deer, the bears, the panthers, the wildcats and other varmints that I expected to kill, I would not see. And then, most of all the Indians, real wild Indians, but friendly, in whose wigwams I was going to rest, I would not see them. I was almost heartbroken. One of the party, however, with whom my father and I had been on a stream, volunteered out of pure sympathy to look after me.

Consent was then given that I might go, but the apprehensions under which I labored lest it be withdrawn, of which there was strong indication, are among the most painful reminiscences of my life.

We finally set off, three strong men and one small, freckled, scrawny boy. As one of the party facetiously remarked: "He is about the size of a pound of soap after a hard day's washing." And another said: "about two good mouthfuls for an ordinary bear," and my particular champion replied: "A small but very lively bait."

We got off on a steamer with a deck passage and Albany; fare one dollar for man, fifty cents for boy; canal boat from Albany to Utica. This was in 1847 or '48, and the New York

Central Railroad was, I think, being operated between Albany and Syracuse. We took the canal boat because it was cheaper than the railroad, and we also took a freight boat because it was cheaper than the packet boat—being one cent a mile, instead of two. It was slower, but time was of no value to us.

At Utica we hired a man with a team and wagon for the trip, but I do not remember the cost; it was approximately about what a sleeping-car porter would now expect as a tip for like time.

We went through Trenton over to Alder Creek and the big Black River Dam, where digging for a canal to Rome had just been started. Here we struck the primeval forest—no habitation beyond in that direction. A Mr. Williams had a sawmill at the dam, and there were a few small houses. We had traveled more than half the time in the woods after we left Trenton, often many miles at a time without seeing any sign of human life beyond the rough road over which we passed. A few miles before we reached Alder Creek, there was considerable clearing and a settlement of Welsh people, who were starting dairy farms.

From Alder Creek we diverged to the left and to the west, then northwest through the Steuben Hills, and again southwest on to Booneville, and there our team left us and went back to Utica. Here we met our guide, a Canadian-Frenchman voyageur named Marienne, who expressed in emphatic mixed English and Canadian-French his disapprobation of taking that puny, sickly petit garçon in the woods, who might get wet and die there.

After several days' delay we got started. There had been provided for me as a special guide and caretaker an Ojibway Indian of Herculean proportions, fully 6 feet 2 inches in his moccasins, and weighing, I judge, about two hundred pounds.

My long-desired wish to meet the Indians had been gratified, but the effect was not what I expected. I was afraid of the Indian, and it soon became evident that the Indian entertained grave apprehensions of some kind about me. I was constantly uppermost in his mind, whether for good or evil I could not determine, but feared the latter, and always felt great relief when he put away a big butcher knife that he carried in a leather sheath on a belt around his waist. I avoided being left alone with him, and as he did not know a dozen words of English and I did not know one word of Indian, our conversation was limited. My desire to know Indians had become fully satisfied, yet I thought if I could meet this particular Indian when he had no knife—in the city in the presence of a good-sized squad of policemen—it would be more satisfactory. I avoided being left alone with him and shied away from him on our journey. When we came to a stream I would slip out a few yards from camp and try my flies, and soon he left me to my ways.

At one of our camps I found an exceptionally good place for casting near the top of a rapid; the only place, however, to get room for a back cast was from a point of vantage on a tree fallen across the stream, upon which I crawled out. When in the act of making the first cast my feet slipped and down I went in the cold, swift water over head and ears, the current holding me up against the submerged limbs and body of the tree under which I was partly drawn with my head still under, but perfectly composed and with no apprehension, being a good swimmer and diver. With a good hold I was about to make a supreme effort to raise myself against the current, when I was pulled, almost jerked, straight up out of the water and found myself being held up in the air at arms' length by the Indian, about as he would hold up for inspection a muskrat that he had caught by the nape of the neck. He looked me in the face, made a grunt, and carried me to the bank. When he saw that I stood up and was all right, he gave two or three more grunts with a different inflection, while the expression of his countenance indicated satisfaction. Then it dawned upon me that the Indian thought I was in danger of being drowned, which I was disposed to resent as a reflection upon my resourcefulness as an angler, my skill as a diver and my all-around qualities as an amphibian.

An impulse came over me to make a run for camp and get away from him, but I could not run, as my boots were full of water. All men and boys wore boots then—calfskin boots, coming near to the knee. Boots indicated the line of demarcation between babyhood and boyhood. Then it occurred to me if I did start to run, the Indian could catch me before I reached camp. I pulled off my boots and rolled up my trousers ready for a run. Then I observed the Indian was without his butcher rod while he released the line from its entanglement. I did so because I was afraid to refuse, and reeled up while he released the hard-braided, heavily waxed linen line. When he came to the horsehair leader and single-hair snells and artificial flies on tiny hooks he was amazed and charmed. He had not only never seen but never heard of such an appliance. It was to him incredible that a fish could be caught without bait, on that imitation of an insect, and impossible to hold the fish on a single hair after he was hooked, or that that little hook would hold anything larger than a minnow. He made manifest his feelings in pantomime, and also indicated a desire to see the thing tried. This gave me some confidence in him, and I immediately began to gratify his desire.

A few casts brought up a good trout, fairly hooked and nicely held in the stiff current until successfully landed, the light rod showing all the curves from the straightness of an arrow to and beyond the perfect arch, the standard of a rod's capacity, to almost a perfect loop—the point of desperation, where nothing further in the way of line can be yielded, and where the only alternative is to hold or break. The little twig and single horsehair held in that swift current a vigorous two-pound trout—a true *Salvelinus fontinalis.*

The stoicism of the Indian melted away and was all gone; he was bubbling over with enthusiasm and continued to bubble until, without moving from that fallen tree, I had landed a full dozen, one a double of about a pound and a half each.

Radically opposite in race, in aspiration and traditions and physical endowments, two kindred spirits now communed together and understood every thrill and emotion that moved each. The man regarded the boy as he would a little weak bird fluttering between life and death, prematurely separated from the nest and brood. And the boy, terrorized by being alone in the wilderness with this gigantic savage, whose queer actions and dress filled him with distrust.

And then the desire of the Indian to witness a practical test of the angler's skill touched the boy's vanity. The interest and enjoyment of the Indian made a soul communion and coalescence, and all fears and distrusts were dissipated by confidence.

The two were children of one father, the one true and ever-living God, with like thoughts and aspirations. They became friends and remained so for life.

First of April

WILLIAM SENIOR

What struck me more than anything else, standing by the waterside in the somewhat dull morning of the 1st of April with which I am now concerned, was the extreme backwardness of the season. There was not the slightest spring of grass to be seen in the meadows, and you had to examine very closely to find the signs of budding in the trees. The hawthorns were beginning to shoot, no doubt, and the blackthorns, according to their custom, had flowered. But the clump of willows near which I stood arrested my attention, because I remembered that on the 1st of April of the previous year they were fairly toward development of leaf. Even now they had begun to sprout. But the willow shoots in a curious way, and the sprouting leaf at a little distance looks like something which has decayed, rather than like something which is about to burst into life. Flowers also were few and far between. I was treading on some ground ivy, which had fairly blossomed, and in the marshy places and near the river, a few celandines had opened their large yellow stars to catch what there was of sun. But, on the whole, it was a very wintry-looking 1st of April prospect, and of course, a moment's reflection would convince one, that this was only natural, for the series of floods had been long and vexatious, and, when the water had gone down, there had supervened nipping frosts and blighting east winds, which had put a strong check upon the forwardness which early in February was being remarked.

But looking about one to make notes of what there was or what there was not in meadow, wood, marsh, or hedgerow was not angling, and in the ten minutes, which I must confess had been spent in the above observations, might probably lose me that fish, of whose existence I was well aware. I knew of his being there during the first week of March. I saw him twice moving about between St. David's Day and Lady Day, and on the previous evening, just before the sun sent down, as I stood on the little wooden bridge spanning a turbulent torrent, which constituted a sort of extra by fall a short distance removed from the weir proper, I was delighted to find that my gentleman had not departed for foreign parts.

A very simple looking man, in that queer combination of nautical and farmyard costume so often to be seen by the riverside, sucked his short black pipe as he leaned upon the rail. He looked so innocent and confiding, and seemed so indifferent to anything connected with the water, gazing as he did at the moment with a far-off style at a distant hill crowned by clumps of trees, that I entered into conversation with him. Yes; he had no doubt there were some trout in the weir pool, and, indeed, he remembered that last year towards the fag end of the season a seven-pounder had been taken between the lasher and weir, and, now he came to think of it, he was also able to state that Tim Bridge, a 'stoopid sort o' feller,' working on the railway, had not more than two months ago been fined by the magistrates thirty shillings for taking a trout out of season from the very weir pool which was thundering in our ears. I was glad to hear that Mr. Bridges had suffered for his breach of the law, although, as the man had gone about from village to village showing his prize, and swiping at each exhibition, it was evident that he was unaware, until too late, of the crime he had wrought. It was a bad case, however, the fish being in miserable condition.

I ought, perhaps to remark that the weir pool at the spot of which I am writing was a very peculiar one. There was the small byfall to which I have referred; there was the weir proper; there was a broadish lasher, the whole between them making a very fair description of tumbling bay, flanked by strong individual streams. A little below, however, there were three small islands ranged at almost equal distances along the bed of the river, and as the bed had silted up between these islands, the stream from the byfall ran swiftly, close under the bank, which was hollowed out and steep. It was in one of the swift streams of this by-water, not far from where it roared under the little bridge, that the trout upon which I had fixed my affections was located.

"There's a pretty good trout feeding yonder," I said to the rustic, who still smoked upon the bridge, with the bowl of his pipe in an inverted position.

"No," he said, "I don't know much about fishing; but you may depend on't there's no trout here."

"Oh," I said, "I beg your pardon, you are mistaken. I have seen him there several times myself, and I mean to get him if I can to-morrow morning."

"Well, sir, I wish yer luck," he replied. "There'll be two or three gents a-fishing, I expect, off the warebeams in the morning. I see 'em going to the White Bull wi' their baskets and rods as I come along just now. You had better be early."

This, I told him, I intended to be, and the civility and intelligence of the man so impressed me that I offered him the choice of any cigar he might fancy from my case. On the morning of April the first I kept the resolution which I had informed my rustic companion I had made, and was at the waterside right early. It was very little after daylight, and, although the wind seemed to be backing a little towards the north, and, although it was a cold air, it was nothing like so piercing as it had been during the previous month.

I soon got to work, spinning over the spot where my trout had taken lodgings, but without success. I worked the stream thoroughly down to the end until breakfast time, toiling hard and executing every dodge with which I was acquainted. My marked trout would have none of me. Then I winced up my line, and disposing safely of the flight, strolled across within hail of two London anglers who had been similarly occupied for three hours over the weir pool. One of them said he had been broken away by a big trout; the other said he had repeated attacks made upon his bleak; but neither had anything to show for their operations. So I left them still trying, and cheering themselves with the interchange of an opinion that the sun would soon shine and infuse something of warmth into the chilly atmosphere.

For myself, I walked back to the White Bull, and resolved that if I could get no trout I would at least get breakfast. I was not a little surprised, though very much delighted, to find that when John, the waiter, with a look of triumph, whipped off the cover from the dish, there lay exposed to view a very shapely Thames trout that, in the full enjoyment of its physical proportions, would have weighed over three pounds. I asked no questions but attacked the meat, which did not, however, eat with the flavor which betokens the well-conditioned fish. Still, there it was upon the table, as the piece de resistance of the feast, and I did it ample justice.

"Where did you manage to get your trout, John?" I said, as the waiter came to see how I was getting on.

"Well, sir, I cannot exactly say where he came from, but I believe he was caught in the river here this morning."

"Oh, nonsense," I said; "impossible! I was out there at daylight myself, and there was not a soul about at that time, although the gentlemen who are stopping here came down to the weir soon after."

"Well, sir, to tell you the truth, I don't know; but I heard them say that the fish had been caught this morning."

Hereupon, when breakfast was over, I strolled round to the bar and into the smoking-parlor, where, as I expected, I found the landlord. I knew this gentleman of old, and scarcely hoped to receive any information from him; but I felt bound, as a matter of duty, to put him through the leading questions one asks on such an occasion.

"Well, I really don't know," he said. "The trout, of course, has been caught today. I shouldn't think of buying a fish out of season, but I never ask any questions. All I can tell you is that the trout was alive when he was brought here."

"What time did you get it?" I inquired.

"I can answer that question very exactly," he replied with a smile, "for the clock in the old church at Longtoncum-Burton was striking seven as I handed over two shillings and took in return the fish, which was still gasping, his gills opening slowly but unmistakably."

"May I ask from whom you bought it?" I then inquired.

"I bought it," he said, "from Bridges."

"What," I said, "do you mean Bridges, the same man that was fined thirty shillings for taking a trout out of season this side of Christmas?"

"Yes," he said, "that is the man, but he learned a lesson that time."

"Do you think Bridges caught the trout?"

"That I cannot say; as I told you, I never ask questions, because I know that if I did, in cases of that kind, I should generally hear lies in answer to them."

I did not quite understand the matter, nor did I feel satisfied about this Thames trout; and as I stood in front of the inn, looking up at the waxen buds which tipped all the branches of the great chestnut tree, and blowing up clouds of tobacco smoke to reach them if they could, I heard the voice of a man who was evidently in some stage of liquor—a voice thick and droning, and the words he spoke, run into each other as they were, at once attracted my attention, for those words were:

"And a blanked good trout it was, I can tell you."

I knew where the voice came from, and strolled round leisurely through the stable-yard, pas the kitchen, and so to the taproom, where I saw a laboring man stretched on a settle, with a small measure, apparently of gin, on the table, and an empty glass by its side. There were two other men sitting on each side of the fire smoking stolidly, and not paying, apparently, much attention to the gentleman on the settle. One of them spoke, remarking in a careless sort of tone:

"Well, that is two bob off the thirty, anyhow, Jim."

Here, then, was Mr. Bridges, who had sold the fish; and without beating about the bush, I said, pretending that we were old acquaintances:

"Hallo, Bridges, how are you? That was a good trout you got this morning."

"'Scuse me, sir," he said, "you've got the better on me, for I'm blest if I remember you. Howsomedever, that's neither here nor there; but I didn't catch the trout, you know."

"Who did, then?"

"A man we call Swankey hereabouts."

"A fisherman?"

"Not exactly to say a fisherman—a sort of poacher feller."

"When did he catch it?"

"I should say it was about three this morning he got that trout, but in the most queerest place you'd think on. What Swankey was partickerly pleased about was that one of them swells that is stopping here put him on to the fish last night. Then, d'ye see, Swankey, who never meant to'ed not been gone an hour afore he comes back wi' a bloomin' trout."

The reader will naturally observe at once that the person called Swankey was my innocent friend, to whose agreeable manners I had offered the generous tribute of a good cigar on the previous evening, and who had abused my confidence by slinking out in the raw, dark morning, and capturing the fish upon which I had set my desire for a good month past.

I am too much of a philosopher to fly into a rage over a trifle of this kind; but I must confess, as I took my rod and tackle, and strolled down once more to the river, I felt that Mr. Swankey had got, not only a Thames trout, but a thorough paced April fool in my humble self.

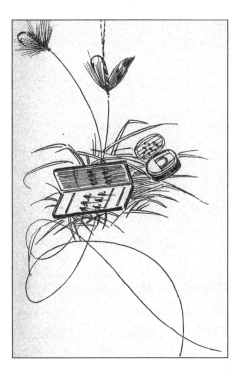

Practical Dry-Fly Fishing for Beginners

EMLYN GILL

"What is a dry fly?"

The question rather startled me for a moment, as I well knew that the man who asked it had been a thorough outdoor man all his life; had visited nearly all the haunts of big game in this country and in Canada; had shot at different times mountain sheep, mountain goat, moose, bear, antelope, elk, caribou, various kinds of deer, and other varieties of wild animals, and had as a rule carried at least one fishing rod with him on most of his trips, if not on all. Also I well knew that he had been successful in luring the finny fighters, as I had seen some of his records; and had also examined, mounted in his office, very fine, large specimens of bass, silver trout, ouananiche, muscalonge, and other game fishes.

A day or two before he asked me this question the July issue of *Field & Stream* had appeared containing an article that I had written on the dry-fly; this article did not attempt to go into the methods and technicalities of dry-fly fishing, but was simply intended to be a question put to American anglers, as to why this very fascinating branch of the sport was not practiced more generally in this country.

"The only mistake in your article," said this friend, "was that you did not even tell us what a dry-fly was. If you did not desire to go into technicalities, you should at least have described to us the fly mentioned."

And I apologize.

I had fully realized for several years that the vast majority of American fly fishermen had used only what are known as "wet flies," and that the knowledge of dry-fly fishing, as it has been practiced in England for many years, had been very limited in this country. But I must confess that I did not appreciate the fact that there was a very large body of anglers still in total ignorance of the meaning of the word "dry fly." English angling literature had been full of it for years; many books have been written upon the subject in England; in fact, books and sporting magazines have not only contained much about dry-fly fishing, but countless pages have been taken up with disputes about dry-fly methods between what are known as the "purists" and those who fish in other ways.

The dry-fly "purist," as he is known, casts his fly only when he sees a trout rising; he "stalks" the stream; if he sees a rise, he goes within casting distance of the spot, carefully places his fly so that it falls exactly where the trout had risen, or just above it, so that the fly will float down over the fish. If he does not get a rise, it is not incompatible with his code of ethics to try a fly of a different pattern; if he finally gives up in his attempt to catch this particular fish, he again "stalks" the stream, but does not make another cast until he again sees a rise. If no rises occur within his vision during the day, he does not fish.

This method of angling, sportsmanlike and commendable though it may be, and undoubtedly fascinating to its English devotees, is not, I believe, the kind of dry-fly fishing that would appeal to the majority of American anglers. Some of the strict "purists" call those who use other methods of dry-fly fishing "poachers," and it may be imagined that the disputes between the two schools are not always conducted in the most amiable manner. Whether or not we watch with amusement the more or less heated arguments among the various schools, over technical and what may appear to us minor details, yet we must give British anglers enormous credit for the deep, careful, scientific study that they have given for many years to the art of angling.

First, the expert English angler is an entomologist and knows upon what insects the trout feed, and as a rule finds out upon which insect they are feeding on that particular day and hour that he is on the stream; and from his fly box he selects a fly tied in exact imitation in size and color of the insect. Can that be said of the average American fly-fisherman?

He also endeavors to present the fly to the fish in the most natural manner possible. He knows that weak flying insects cannot swim against a current with the speed of a torpedo boat, and that they do not move about under the surface by fits, starts and jerks. He reasons that if a winged insect is on the surface of a running stream it can have but one motion; that is the motion imparted by the current. In other words, the fly simply *floats* on the surface of the water; and so his artificial lures are known as dry-flies or *floating flies*.

From this comes the whole theory of dry-fly fishing: To use a fly tied in exact imitation of a natural insect and so made that it will not easily sink; to allow it to float down over the trout, with no other motion than that imparted by the current. If any other movement is given to the fly the theory is that the trout will look upon it as entirely unnatural—something that it has learned to know that live flies will not do—and that therefore the lure will have no attraction whatever for the fish.

It is not probable that the average American angler would care to go on a stream and not cast a fly until he had seen a rise, even at the risk of the long-distance ignominy of being called a poacher by some of the English "purists." In the first place, he enjoys the practice of casting, whether the fish rise or not. Then again abundant experience has taught our American dry-fly fishermen that on some of our nearby streams they can often pass an entire day without seeing a trout rise at a natural insect. So the dry-fly fisherman of this country begins casting when he reaches the stream more or less "for general results," as the Englishman might think; but it may be said that the work of an American expert is not at all a bungling performance, and there is very little "hit-or-miss" about it. His methods may differ from those of the English "purist" in that instead of casting at the rise, he casts at what seems to him to be "likely spots"—that is, at those places where his experience has taught him that the trout hide, live and seek their food. There is nothing prettier to watch on a stream than the casting of a dry-fly expert. It is seldom except when watching him that I have seen flies light "like thistledown"; or that I have been deceived into thinking for a moment that an artificial fly was a natural insect as I saw it flutter down through the air to the surface of the water.

For the benefit of my friend the Camp Fire Club who asked me the question which appears at the beginning of this article, and for those anglers to whom the arts of dry-fly fishing still remain as a hidden book—in other words, for the very *beginner* in dry-fly fishing—I will try to explain as simply as possible the methods of dry-fly fishing as they are commonly practiced by some of our American anglers.

First, as to the equipment—rod, line, leader, flies and one or two other specialties used in dry-fly angling. I shall assume that the reader is thoroughly familiar with the rest of the equipment, such as clothing, waders, reel, creels, etc.

The rod for this form of angling should have plenty of what is commonly known as "back bone"; that is, it should not be weak or "whippy." It may be 9, 9½ or 10 feet long, though perhaps the 10 foot rod is the favorite. It is impossible to describe a rod by giving weight for length, for the very simple reason that one 9-foot rod of 6 ounces may have much less power, back bone and resiliency, than another rod of the same length weighing only 4½ ounces. What are known as 4 oz. or 5 oz. tournament rods, weighing 4½ oz. and 5½ or 5¾ oz., respectively, are in my opinion ideal rods for that purpose. Not, however, that tournament rods are at all necessary; I have several rods that are ideal for dry-fly fishing—one in particular, 9½ feet long, and weighing 5½ oz., full of back bone, snap and ginger, and easily capable of handling an English water-proofed "D" tapered line; and still it was not built for selecting a strong, powerful rod for dry-fly work. A heavier line is used than is commonly used in ordinary fly fishing for reasons that will be explained later; the rod also is called upon to do much more work, for in using the dry-fly, after each cast there must be several casts in the air or "false casts," for the purpose of drying the fly, before the insect again touches the water. Therefore your rod should be powerful, though not necessarily heavy; in fact, unless one likes to have a tired wrist at the end of the day, an unnecessarily heavy rod is anything but desirable.

As to the line, expert anglers will advise without qualification a waterproofed silk-line. While nothing can equal the best American-made split bamboo rods, the best English fly lines, while very expensive, are well worth the price and the trouble of getting them. They are waterproofed in a vacuum, so that the "dressing" may permeate every part of the line. Then they are rubbed down, and afterward dressed again. Just how many times this operation is repeated I do not know. But the completed product is a line of great beauty, smoothness and flexibility, and the angler who has not used one has a fresh pleasure before him in fly-casting. As to the size of the line, the same thing that was said of "weight for length" in rods may be said of lines, changing the expression to "weight for size." In a line it is the weight that counts; and lines of different makes designated by the letters "D," "E," or "F," vary both in size and in weight. It is probable, however, that the beginner in dry-fly fishing will be perfectly safe if he buys a good size "E," though I often use with much pleasure a "D" line. And by all means, whatever anyone else may tell you to the contrary, buy a tapered line, and have it tapered at both ends.

Next comes the leader. There are various opinions as to whether this necessary article should be tapered or not, and also as to the exact length that should be used. The beginner may study all these things out later, and be guided both by his own experience and that of others whom he will meet on the stream. It is safe to say that a large majority of dry-fly anglers both in England and America use a tapered leader, 9 feet long, and dry-fly leaders are commonly listed in this way in nearly all catalogues. It is true that a long, light leader is difficult to manage against a strong head wind, and in these weather conditions a leader of 6 feet might be better. The conventional dry-fly leader is tapered, and is rather coarse at the line end, tapering down to from fine drawn gut to the finest undrawn at the end where the fly is tied. Personally I prefer the fine undrawn gut for general fishing.

It has already been made plain that the flies are "tied dry"; that is, so that they will float. It is therefore necessary that the bodies of dry-flies shall be made of some material that will float readily, and that it will not become water-soaked easily. There are certain objections to the use of silk, as it changes color when wet and "dubbing," commonly used for the bodies of flies, becomes easily water-soaked and the fly consequently "soggy." So that now Mr. Halford, the English expert, recommends quill, horsehair and Rafia grass for dressing the bodies of floating flies. This, however, properly belongs to the fly-dressers' art, and not to beginners.

Most of our dry-flies come from England, though handled by the best American dealers, and all are tied as nearly as possible in exact imitation of live insects. It is customary to "paraffin" the flies from time to time to make them float better. For this purpose carry along with you on the stream a small bottle of paraffin oil, or one of the several preparations made specially for this purpose. It will also pay to buy a small "dry-fly oiler" made to carry this oil when you are on the streams. After tying the fly to the leader, put a small quantity of oil on the hackles and body of the fly. Carry a rag or old handkerchief with you, and with it "squeeze out" the superfluous oil.

The majority of dry-fly men also own a small tin of deer fat, though some consider its use unnecessary. With it they grease their line occasionally, or at least from 10 to 30 feet of it. The deer fat is best put on the line with the thumb and forefinger of one hand, and the line is then carefully rubbed down with a soft rag to remove the superfluous fat. The idea of the use of deer fat is to make the line float more readily. It is also claimed that it preserves the line.

While it has been made very plain that these words are written for the beginner only, yet I hope that the exact type of beginner that I have in mind will be equally well understood; he is not the tyro who has never as yet had the pleasure of using a fly-rod, or the man who has no knowledge of trout streams or the habits of trout. I assume that those who have asked me recently to write some dry-fly instructions of the simplest kind for the beginner are already good anglers. It is my hope that this article will be of some slight assistance to those who are fly fishermen, but who have not as yet tasted the pleasures of luring the trout with the dry-fly. It is not difficult to believe that the step from the expert wet-fly fisherman to the dry-fly expert is a comparatively short one, and easily accomplished by one willing to devote some thought to the subject, and some time to practicing on the streams. In this way it is probable that all our best American dry-fly anglers have become experts. They have first been expert wet-fly anglers; then their attention has been drawn to the dry-fly; they have received a few "points" from friends—enough to start with; they have practiced on the streams, perhaps somewhat crudely at first; they have read much of the very fine literature written in England upon the subject; they have been quick to understand the methods used by our English cousins; they have adapted and changed the English ideas to meet the conditions upon our streams, and in a comparatively short time they have become successively our pioneers and our experts in dry-fly angling.

It has already been noticed, possibly, what a part *naturalness* plays in dry-fly fishing; we have learned that the fly is in an exact imitation of the natural insect; it must be presented to the trout in an absolutely natural way, and when the fly is on the water, it must have a natural motion. It is not a case of hoping that by some lucky chance the trout may possibly take the feathered lure for "something good to eat," without knowing exactly the nature of the food presented. The trout must see that the fly is an insect upon which he has fed many times before; it must light on the water as he has seen thousands of other insects light; it must float down the stream in precisely the same manner that he has been accustomed all his life to see other insects float with the current. In other words, the very naturalness of the entire game must deceive the trout absolutely.

You must fish upstream, or up and across stream, and the beginner will make no mistake in following this advice blindly without being influenced by the arguments made pro and con by the wet-fly fisherman as to whether it is better to fish upstream or down. True it is not desirable that you cast directly ahead of you on the stream, so that you will "line the fish" as it lies with its head upstream. By "lining the fish" is meant casting the fly above the trout so that the leader comes down directly over its head and body, thus placing the fly, the head and tail of the fish and the angler all in a direct line. It is obvious that the fish may get a good view of the leader before it sees the fly, or that he may see the fly and leader simultaneously.

Before taking the beginner to the stream, even at the risk of repetition, it may be well to recapitulate and bring together the principal points of dry-fly fishing that we have already covered in a general way: 1. Use but one fly and that an imitation of a natural insect, and a fly that floats; 2. Cast this fly upstream, at or slightly above a spot where you know there is a trout, thorough having seen it rise, or a spot where your "fish sense" tells you that a trout may be; 3. Let the fly float down with no motion whatever except that naturally imparted by the current; 4. After the fly has floated down well below the place where you think the trout may lie, lift it very gently from the water and prepare for the next cast; 5. Make at least three or four casts in the air both to dry your fly, and to lengthen your line, and do not let the fly touch the water again until you see that the fly will strike the exact spot that you have picked out for it to land; 6. If you "bungle" your cast—this is, if the fly does not light at the spot that you intended—or if it does not light properly, with wing nicely "cocked" in the air, do not allow yourself to become excited and immediately jerk the fly from the water; let it float down as if you had made the finest cast possible, and then lift it out gently as before. By following this course you will lessen much the chances of frightening the trout, which may take the fly at the next cast as if nothing unusual had happened.

About making the casts in the air a word of explanation may be necessary, as this is something that is seldom practiced in wet-fly fishing. Strip the line from the reel with the left hand. Work the rod backward and forward as in regular casting, but hold the tip well up and allow the fly to move back and forth in the air without touching the water. But for several reasons do not swing your rod as if you were practicing with Indian clubs or beating a carpet, or as if you were taking any kind of daily exercise to strengthen your muscles. Let the wrist and spring of the rod do all the work. Let the tip of the rod describe only a small arc; that is, let it go only slightly beyond the perpendicular on the forward or on the back cast. Let the movement of the rod be gentle, and avoid all quick, sharp motions. In addition to being much better casting, the motion of the rod is not nearly so liable to alarm the trout. Before beginning to make these "false casts," your eye has picked out the exact spot on the water where you wish the fly to drop. When you see that you have enough line out, allow the fly to light very gently. Keep practicing until the fly falls as lightly as a small live insect would fall. Then let the fly float down with the current. As it comes down strip in the slack with the left hand, but do not strip so fast that you impart any unnatural motion whatever to the fly. When ready, lift the fly from the water as gently as possible, and then begin another series of "false casts."

Dry-flies are tied in two ways: First, with wings, which are generally upright; Second, they are tied "buzz," or with hackles and without wings. The winged fly should float on the water with its wings upright or "cocked." If the beginner cannot always make a fly light in this way, he need not be discouraged—the expert cannot do it either; often, very often, the fly will light on its side. Incidentally it may be interesting to know that the fly lights on the water with its wings "cocked" more often with the horizontal cast than with the overhead cast.

The Evolution of a Fly Fisher

JOAN SALVATO WULFF

I came into fishing as an innocent: my predatory skills, if I had any, were undeveloped. Loving woods and waters I caught calico bass and perch in the nearby Oldham Pond but, in trout streams, not knowing how to "read" water, nor the comfort, food, and safety needs of trout, I saw only the interesting patterns on the water's surface as if they were art.

If trout were rising I could be effective, but if they were not I became painfully aware of this lack of fishing instinct, especially in the company of anglers whom I think of as "natural born predators." In addition to understanding the hydraulics of the stream, to a man they had exceptional vision, as it related to water, seeing trout under the surface when I could not. A boyfriend, the late Johnny Dieckman, was the first of these and later in life Lee Wulff and Ed Van Put are the two who jump into my mind as always surprising me with their ability to catch fish.

With nothing to start with, I had to substitute my ability to fly cast to unlock the secrets of the stream, covering the water and learning inch by inch.

From this beginning, over the ensuing 70 years, I've been lucky enough to fish for most of the fresh and saltwater species that can be enticed to take a fly. Fishing, and especially fly fishing, has been the constant thread in my life. It's been a wonderful journey and, in the last several years, I have come to realize how differently I see the sport from when I began. It's an evolution I believe I share with others who have a passion for fly fishing.

The early stages of fishing are familiar to most anglers: the focus is on 1) the number. How many did you get? 2) The biggest fish. How big? Show me a photo. And then the most difficult: the wise old brown trout instead of the eternally innocent brookies; permit instead of bonefish. Feeling as if you've learned something.

These three stages play to our competitive nature; measuring ourselves against others whenever there is something to count. And they may stay with us forever in terms of particular species: most, biggest, most difficult. I, for instance, in the latter category, still feel the "need" to catch a 15-20 permit.

After Stage 3 the scope broadens; we enter the stages that are about more than catching fish.

It was Lee who raised my consciousness to Stage 4: giving something back to the resource; looking at the sport from the point of view of the fish. It's about preserving their gene pools as well as their habitat. Lee's wisdom, as early as 1939, that "a good game fish is too valuable to be caught only once" has been the concept that has let growing numbers of anglers enjoy the sport with, perhaps, the same number of fish.

The national conservation organizations are there to lead the way: the Federation of Fly Fishers, Trout Unlimited, the Atlantic Salmon Federation, the International Game Fish Association. I am a member of all of them and find that each group's efforts are distinct and necessary to keep our sport healthy.

In addition to making the sport more meaningful, there is another benefit to "belonging": gatherings of fishing experts willing to share their expertise at conclaves, symposiums, and club programs. It's a win/win situation for anglers of all levels. As involvement grows, your coterie of acquaintances expands and I can easily say that the best people I have ever met have been in this stage of my evolution.

If the first 3 stages are the "youth" of our fishing lives, "giving back" could be considered to be our "middle years," because there *is* more!

The golden years: Stage 5. *Just being there*. When people ask me to name my favorite place to fish, I can only say "wherever I am." And my answer to the question, "which is your favorite fish?" is "whatever I'm fishing for."

Evasive answers? Perhaps. It's just that, as my experience has broadened and I've learned the character of different waters and species of fish, I have come to love and admire them all. It's like partaking of good food. Think of how many different dishes you really love and appreciate each time you have them. Different, but equally wonderful. Remember, I'm talking about a lifetime.

In these years, *catching* fish has become less important; I can be fishless and still have had a good day. I can now fish "through" a companion and be as happy about their catch as they are because I know the challenges, and feelings of joy and satisfaction, that commemorate success.

These years are also a time when I can handicap myself if the fishing is too easy. Lee introduced the idea: "If you catch 3 fish on the same fly, change the fly. See what else they will take." "Reduce your tippet strength." "Use a smaller hook." Lee was an inspiration through the "pureness" of his approach. He always gave the advantage to the fish, through his simple tackle. He used no drag; just a click to keep the reel from overrunning, even with Atlantic salmon and tarpon. And with this tackle, he established a standard: one minute per pound to land the fish. The fish then had to swim away without the need to be revived. Lee's skills in playing fish were legendary.

I love this stage; the pressure is off! Challenge yourself! The competition is now with the fish—not other anglers.

I have one more stage to include in these golden years: #6. Replace yourself. This is about bringing young people into our sport. Unless we do this, our sport will be diminished; first in numbers of anglers and then, with fewer anglers working to preserve the habitat, in quality. Grandkids are the obvious and I am particularly blessed in this regard. I introduced Alex and Andrew to fly fishing when each became 5½ years old with two hands on the rod and a roll cast. They have both caught trout, and Alex has caught Atlantic salmon, on Royal Wulffs. Because I don't tie flies, I gave them fly tying lessons with a professional when they were 7. When I am long gone, they will be fly fishing together.

My cup runneth over.

Old age is approaching but I don't want to limit my enjoyment of the sport by defining it. In these past two years I have caught the largest tarpon of my life (approximately 125 lbs) and enjoyed sailfishing in Guatemala. This summer I was able to fish for steelhead on the Dean river in British Columbia, after hoping to for 40 plus years.

My most memorable fish are those I didn't land: a monster Atlantic salmon on Norway's Alta river, which played *me* for a few minutes, and another huge salmon on New Brunswick's Restigouche. The latter was on my last, "last cast."

It was nearly dark and, having covered the water from 20 feet on out, the cast was the longest I could make. The fish struck and dashed upriver, partly out of the water, which is how we knew he was a big one. Then he turned and raced downriver, into my backing. The guide thought the river was too high to follow the fish in the dark and headed back to shore, in spite of my protests. I found myself unhappily positioned 90 degrees from where the salmon was heading. The end was predictable: the fish never stopped—and nearly emptied my reel before the hook pulled out.

However, the reason I continue to think of this particular fish is not because I lost it, but because of the *wonder* of it all: how *magical* it was to reach out into that enormous river with a tiny artificial offering, when it was dark enough to keep me from seeing the fly land, and actually connect to a wild creature of such a size.

And magical it is. Starting as an innocent, this very ordinary woman has had an extraordinary life through the magic of fly fishing. And I plan to continue. So it's not over till it's over, and this very ordinary woman, having had an extraordinary life through the magic of sport fishing, plans to continue.

Pied Beauty

GERARD MANLEY HOPKINS

Glory be to God for dappled things—
For skies of couple-color as a brindle cow;
For rose-moles all in stipple upon trout that swim;
Fresh-firecoal chestnut-falls; finches' wings;
Landscape plotted and pieced—fold, fallow and
plough;
And all trades, their gear and tackle and trim.

All things counter, original, spare, strange;
Whatever is fickle, freckled (who knows how?)
With swift, slow; sweet, sour; adazzle, dim;
He fathers-forth whose beauty if past change:
Praise him.

A Bit of Luck

HARRY PLUNKET-GREENE

I had an experience with a trout on the Kennet, which I always associate, quite undeservedly, with "snatching." It was in 1922, and I was staying with Mr. Giveen, who had taken the Mill fishing from Col. Grove-Hills for the latter half of the season. He and I had often stood on the bridge at the top, where the water falls down from the lake of Ramsbury Manor, and hungrily objurgated the great fat three-pounders which laughed at us from beneath. These were rovers by profession, and never stayed long enough in one place to be fished for individually from below; and were up to every trick from above. They would lie with our noses on the ledge immediately underneath us, and dreamily watch the smoke from our pipes ascending to the blue; but the moment the top of a rod appeared over the edge, off they went. We tried concerted action many times, but as soon as ever one of the watchers disappeared from the bridge the pool was abandoned to two-year-olds. On this occasion I was passing by the sluice which forms a small side-carrier to the main fall and I put my head casually over the side, expecting nothing, and there right below me was a big golden trout tucked up under the boards, with his head down-stream and his tail up against the cracks where the water spurted through. He was doing no good there, so I felt it was my duty to get him.

It was an awful prospect. Immediately below him two planks ran across the sluice at intervals of about eight feet, and below them again in the fairway there was a veritable barricade of posts sticking up out of the stream in ragged profusion. There were three on the near side and two on the far side and a gaunt rubbing-post in the middle acting as a buoy, round which every sporting fish was in honor bound to double. Below these again there was another pole running right across the stream only four inches above the water, which swirled under it at a great pace. A more hopeless barbed-wire entanglement it would be hard to imagine to try and fish a fish out of, even if one hooked him. However, he was a beauty, and the fact that he was practically ungetable made it all the more exciting. I had up the ordinary tackle; by all the laws of caution I should have put up a ginger-quill with a No. 1 hook and a May-fly cast, but I reflected that if he got tangled up in the barriers a steel hawser would not hold him, and that if by some amazing fluke he ever came through, the fine tackle would be as good as anything else. Moreover, I should be able to swagger to the others about 4X casts and ooo hooks even more insupportably than before; so I stuck to what I had.

I stood well back where I could just see the tip of his nose and he could not see me, reeled in the line to within six inches of the cast, and gently dropped the fly on to him. It was at once carried out by the stream. I thought it was going to be hopeless, when to my intense delight the back eddy swirled it round at exactly the right moment and brought it over him again. It was then seized once more by the stream and carried off afresh. The process was repeated automatically without my having to do a thing, and there went my fly playing "last across with him," rushing up the backwater, tweaking his nose and dashing off downstream before he could say a word. I was so delighted and laughing so hard that I could not help crawling up to see the fun, and I put my head over to have a look. He was intently absorbed in the game and never saw me. He appeared to take no notice at first and treated it all with dignified unconcern, but as the impudent little beast dashed past him smothering him with insults he began to get impatient, and I saw his tail detach itself from the sluice-board and began to wag. Then he began to shake his head and bunch himself to attack. But nothing happened for a long time and I was just going to give it up, as my arm was getting tired from the unnatural position, when I had a wonderful bit of luck. There was a twig sticking out from the wall on the far side over the back eddy, and the gut caught over it, and, before I knew it, there was the fly bobbing up and down in the water, right in front of him. This was too much. His enemy was delivered into his hands.

He leaped at it, seized it, knew in a moment what had happened, and dashed off down-stream under the planks and through the posts and out into the pool at the bottom. There I had to leave him for a long time to settle himself, with my rod bent double under the first plank. Then the fun began. I cautiously passed it under this with one hand and retrieved it with the other and did the same with the second plank. All idea of keeping the line taut was perforce abandoned. I still had the six upright posts and the flat pole beyond to negotiate. If he once got tangled up in these it would be all over. He was near the top of the pool now, and I lay flat on the ground with the point of the rod out in the space between me and the centre post, terrified lest he should swim up on the near side of A post, catch sight of me, and dash down on the far side or pay a visit to X, Y or Z post. I clung to Mother Earth like a tiger-skin on a polished oak floor. Sure enough, up he came. He swam through the near channel and roamed about under my eyes (or the corner of one of them) for about a fortnight apparently, and then swam slowly back to the pool the same way he had come!

It was almost too good to be true! But the crux was still to be faced—there was still the flat pole to get under. It ran across the top of the pool, with a space of about four inches between it and the water. It was a bare two inches thick and it was quite rotten. I had to get the rod under it somehow (for I could never risk letting him out of the pool again), and I could only just reach it with my hand by holding on to the bank above with my toes and descending apoplectically towards the water. It cracked loudly the moment I touched it. I had to lean hard on the horrible thing with my right hand, pass the rod under with my left, scrabble it out again somehow with my right on the other side, change hands and work myself back up the bank. It groaned and shivered its timbers and fired off shots like a machine-gun—but the little iron-blue had squared it and it held. It was not all over even then, for if the fish had caught sight of me he would have dashed up through the uprights again; so I backed slowly out of sight into a withy-bed and stayed there till there was not a kick left in him. As a matter of fact, he had done it all for me by returning through the posts the same way he had come. The only credit I can take is for keeping out of sight and performing gymnastics with an almost superhuman skill for one of my size and weight. He weighed 2½ lbs.

Fishing with a Worm

BLISS PERRY

A defective logic is the born fisherman's portion. He is a pattern of inconsistency. He does the things which he ought not to do, and he leaves undone the things which other people think he ought to do. He observes the wind when he should be sowing, and he regards the clouds, with temptation tugging familiarly at his heartstrings, when he might be grasping the useful sickle. It is a wonder that there is so much health in him. A sorrowing political economist remarked to me in early boyhood, as a jolly red-bearded neighbor, followed by an abnormally fat dog, sauntered past us for his nooning: "That man is the best carpenter in town, but he will leave the most important job whenever he wants to go fishing." I stared at the sinful carpenter, who swung along leisurely in the May sunshine, keeping just ahead of his dog. To leave one's job in order to go fishing! How illogical!

Years bring the reconciling mind. The world grows big enough to include within its scheme both the instructive political economist and the truant mechanic. But that trick of truly logical behavior seems harder to the man than to the child. For example, I climbed up to my den under the eaves last night—a sour, black sea-fog lying all about, and the December sleet crackling against the window-panes—in order to varnish a certain fly-rod. Now rods ought to be put in order in September, when the fishing closes, or else in April, when it opens. To varnish a rod in December proves that one possesses either a dilatory or a childishly anticipatory mind. But before uncorking the varnish bottle, it occurred to me to examine a dog-eared, water-stained fly-book, to guard against the ravages of possible moths. This interlude proved fatal to the varnishing. A half hour went happily by in rearranging the flies. Then, with a fisherman's lack of sequence, as I picked out here and there a plain snell-hook from the gaudy feathered ones, I said to myself with a generous glow at the heart: "Fly-fishing has had enough sacred poets celebrating it already. Isn't there a good deal to be said, after all, for fishing with a worm?"

Could there be a more illogical proceeding? And here follows the treatise,—a Defense of Results, an Apology for Opportunism,—conceived in agreeable procrastination, devoted to the praise of the inconsequential angleworm, and dedicated to a childish memory of a whistling carpenter and his fat dog.

Let us face the worst at the very beginning. It shall be a shameless example of fishing under conditions that make the fly a mockery. Take the Taylor Brook, "between the roads," on the headwaters of the Lamoille. The place is a jungle. The swamp maples and cedars were felled a generation ago, and the tops were trimmed into the brook. The alders and moosewood are higher than your head; on every tiny knoll the fir balsams have gained a footing, and creep down, impenetrable, to the edge of the water. In the open spaces the Joe-Pye weed swarms. In two minutes after leaving the upper road you have scared a mink or a rabbit, and you have probably lost the brook. Listen! It is only a gurgle here, droning along, smooth and dark, under the tangle of cedar-tops and the shadow of the balsams. Follow the sound cautiously. There, beyond the Joe-Pye weed, and between the stump and the cedar-top, is a hand's breadth of black water. Fly-casting is impossible in this maze of dead and living branches. Shorten your line to two feet, or even less, bait your hook with a worm, and drop it gingerly into that gurgling crevice of water. Before it has sunk six inches, if there is not one of those black-backed, orange-bellied, Taylor Brook trout fighting with it, something is wrong with your worm or with you. For the trout are always there, sheltered by the brushwood that makes this half mile of fishing "not worth while." Below the lower road the Taylor Brook becomes uncertain water. For half a mile it yields only fingerlings, for no explainable reason; then there are two miles of clean fishing through the deep woods, where the branches are so high that you can cast a fly again if you like, and there are long pools, where now and then a heavy fish will rise; then comes a final half mile through the alders, where you must wade, knee to waist deep, before you come to the bridge and the river. Glorious fishing is sometimes to be had here,—especially if you work down the gorge at twilight, casting a white miller until it is too dark to see. But alas, there is a well-worn path along the brook, and often enough there are the very footprints of the "fellow ahead of you," signs as disheartening to the fisherman as ever were the footprints on the sand to Robinson Crusoe.

But "between the roads" it is "too much trouble to fish;" and there lies the salvation of the humble fisherman who disdains not to use the crawling worm, nor, for that matter, to crawl himself, if need be, in order to sneak under the boughs of some overhanging cedar that casts a perpetual shadow upon the sleepy brook. Lying here at full length, with no elbow-room to manage the rod, you must occasionally even unjoint your tip, and fish with that, using but a dozen inches of line, and not letting so much as your eyebrows show above the bank. Is it a becoming attitude for a middle-aged citizen of the world? That depends upon how the fish are biting. Holing a put looks rather ridiculous also, to the mere observer, but it requires, like brook-fishing with a tip only, a very delicate wrist, perfect tactile sense, and a fine disregard of appearances.

There are some fishermen who always fish as if they were being photographed. The Taylor Brook "between the roads" is not for them. To fish it at all is back-breaking, trouser-tearing work; to see it thoroughly fished is to learn new lessons in the art of angling. To watch R., for example, steadily filling his six-pound creel from that unlikely stream, is like watching Sargent paint a portrait. R. weighs two hundred and ten. Twenty years ago he was a famous amateur pitcher, and among his present avocations are violin playing, which is good for the wrist, taxidermy, which is good for the eye, and shooting woodcock, which before the days of the new Nature Study used to be thought good for the whole man. R. began as a fly-fisherman, but by dint of passing his summers near brooks where fly-fishing is impossible, he has become a stout-hearted apologist for the worm. His apparatus is most singular. It consists of a very long, cheap rod, stout enough to smash through bushes, and with the stiffest tip obtainable. The lower end of the butt, below the reel, fits into the socket of a huge extra butt of bamboo, which R. carries unconcernedly. To reach a distant hole, or to fish the lower end of a ripple, R. simply locks his reel, slips on the extra butt, and there is a fourteen-foot rod ready for action. He fishes with a line unbelievably short, and a Kendal hook far too big; and when a trout jumps for that hook, R. wastes no time in maneuvering for position. The unlucky fish is simply "derricked,"—to borrow a word from Theodore, most saturnine and profane of Moosehead guides.

"Shall I play him awhile?" shouted an excited sportsman to Theodore, after hooking his first big trout.

"——no!" growled Theodore in disgust. "Just derrick him right into the canoe!" A heroic method, surely; though it once cost me the best square-tail I ever hooked, for Theodore had forgotten the landing-net, and the gut broke in his fingers as he tried to swing the fish aboard. But with these lively quarter-pounders of the Taylor Brook, derricking is a safer procedure. Indeed, I have sat dejectedly on the far end of a log, after fishing the hole under it in vain, and seen the mighty R. wade downstream close behind me, adjust that comical extra butt, and jerk a couple of half-pound trout from under the very log on which I was sitting. His device on this occasion, as I well remember, was to pass his hook but once through the middle of a big worm, let the worm sink to the bottom, and crawl along it at his leisure. The trout could not resist.

Once, and once only, have I come near equaling R.'s record, and the way he beat me then is the justification for a whole philosophy of worm-fishing. We were on this very Taylor Brook, and at five in the afternoon both baskets were two thirds full. By count I had just one more fish than he. It was raining hard. "You fish down through the alders," said R. magnanimously. "I'll cut across and wait for you at the sawmill. I don't want to get any wetter, on account of my rheumatism."

This was rather barefaced kindness,—for whose rheumatism was ever the worse for another hour's fishing? But I weakly accepted it. I coveted three or four good trout to top off with,—that was all. So I tied on a couple of flies, and began to fish the alders, wading waist deep in the rapidly rising water, down the long green tunnel under the curving boughs. The brook fairly smoked with the rain, by this time, but when did one fail to get at least three or four trout out of this best half mile of the lower brook? Yet I had no luck I tried one fly after another, and then, as a forlorn hope,—though it sometimes has a magic of its own,—I combined a brown hackle for the tail fly with a twisting worm on the dropper. Not a rise! I thought of E. sitting patiently in the saw mill, and I fished more conscientiously than ever.

"Venture as warily, use the same skill,
Do your best, whether winning or losing it,
If you choose to play!—is my principle."

Even those lines, which by some subtle telepathy of the trout brook murmur themselves over and over to me in the waning hours of an unlucky day, brought now no consolation. There was simply not one fish to be had, to any fly in the book, out of that long, drenching, darkening tunnel. At last I climbed out of the brook, by the bridge. R. was sitting on the fence, his neck and ears carefully turtled under his coat collar, the smoke rising and the rain dripping from the inverted bowl of his pipe. He did not seem to be worrying about his rheumatism.

"What luck?" he asked.

"None at all," I answered morosely. "Sorry to keep you waiting."

"That's all right," remarked R. "What do you think I've been doing? I've been fishing out of the saw-mill window just to kill time. There was a patch of floating saw-dust there,—kind of unlikely place for trout, anyway,—but I thought I'd put on a worm and let him crawl around a little." He opened his creel as he spoke. "But I didn't look for a pair of 'em," he added. And there, on top of his smaller fish, were as pretty a pair of three-quarter-pound brook trout as were ever basketed.

"I'm afraid you got pretty wet," said R. kindly.

"I don't mind that," I replied. And I didn't. What I minded was the thought of an hour's vain wading in that roaring stream, whipping it with fly after fly, while R., the foreordained fisherman, was sitting comfortably in a sawmill, and derricking that pair of three-quarter-pounders in through the window! I had ventured more warily than he, and used, if not the same skill, at least the best skill at my command. My conscience was clear, but so was his; and he had had the drier skin and the greater magnanimity and the biggest fish besides. There is much to be said, in a world like ours, for taking the world as you find it and for fishing with a worm.

One's memories of such fishing, however agreeable they may be, are not to be identified with a defense of the practice. Yet, after all, the most effective defense of worm-fishing is the concrete recollection of some brook that could be fished best or only in that way, or the image of a particular trout that yielded to the temptation of an angleworm after you had flicked fly after fly over him in vain. Indeed, half the zest of brook fishing is in your campaign for "individuals,"—as the Salvation Army workers say,—not merely for a basketful of fish *qua* fish, but for a series of individual trout which your instinct tells you ought to lurk under that log or be hovering in that ripple. How to get him, by some sportsmanlike process, is the question. If he will rise to some fly in your book, few fishermen will deny that the fly is the more pleasurable weapon. Dainty, luring, beautiful toy, light as thistle-down, falling where you will it to fall, holding when the leader tightens and sings like the string of a violin, the artificial fly represents the poetry of angling. Given the gleam of early morning on some wide water, a heavy trout breaking the surface as he curves and plunges, with the fly holding well, with the right sort of rod in your fingers, and the right man in the other end of the canoe, and you perceive how easy is that Emersonian trick of making the pomp of emperors ridiculous.

But angling's honest prose, as represented by the lowly worm, has also its exalted moments. "The last fish I caught was with a worm," says the honest Walton, and so say I. It was the last evening of last August. The dusk was settling deep upon a tiny meadow, scarcely ten rods from end to end. The rank bog grass, already drenched with dew, bent over the narrow, deep little brook so closely that it could not be fished except with a double-shotted, baited hook, dropped delicately between the heads of the long grasses. Underneath this canopy the trout were feeding, taking the hook with a straight downward tug, as they made for the hidden bank. It was already twilight when I began, and before I reached the black belt of woods that separated the meadow from the lake, the swift darkness of the North Country made it impossible to see the hook. A short half hour's fishing only, and behold nearly twenty good trout derricked into a basket until then sadly empty. Your rigorous fly-fisherman would have passed that grass-hidden brook in disdain, but it proved a treasure for the humble. Here, indeed, there was no question of individually-minded fish, but simply a neglected brook, full of trout which could be reached with the baited hook only. In more open brook-fishing it is always a fascinating problem to decide how to fish a favorite pool or ripple, for much depends upon the hour of the day, the light, the height of water, the precise period of the spring or summer. But after one has decided upon the best theoretical procedure, how often the stupid trout prefers some other plan! And when you have missed a fish that you counted upon landing, what solid satisfaction is still possible for you, if you are philosopher enough to sit down then and there, eat your lunch, smoke a meditative pipe, and devise a new campaign against that particular fish! To get another rise from him after lunch is a triumph of diplomacy, to land him is nothing short of statesmanship. For sometimes he will jump furiously at a fly, for very devilishness, without ever meaning to take it, and then, wearying suddenly of his gymnastics, he will snatch sulkily at a grasshopper, beetle, or worm. Trout feed upon an extraordinary variety of crawling things, as all fishermen know who practice the useful habit of opening the first two or three fish they catch, to see what food is that day the favorite. But here, as elsewhere in this world, the best things lie nearest, and there is no bait so killing, week in and week out, as your plain garden or golf-green angleworm.

Walton's list of possible worms is impressive, and his directions for placing them upon the hook have the placid completeness that belonged to his character. Yet in such matters a little nonconformity may be encouraged. No two men or boys dig bait in quite the same way, though all share, no doubt, the singular elation which gilds that grimy occupation with the spirit of romance. The mind is really occupied, not with the wriggling red creatures in the lumps of earth, but with the stout fish which each worm may capture, just as a saint might rejoice in the squalor of this world as a preparation for the glories of the world to come. Nor do any two experienced fishermen hold quite the same theory as to the best mode of baiting the hook. There are a hundred ways, each of them good. As to the best hook for worm-fishing, you will find dicta in every catalogue of fishing tackle, but size and shape and tempering are qualities that should vary with the brook, the season, and the fisherman. Should one use a three-foot leader, or none at all? Whose rods are best for bait-fishing, granted that all of them should be stiff enough in the tip to lift a good fish by dead strain from a tangle of brush or logs? Such questions, like those pertaining to the boots or coat which one should wear, the style of bait-box one should carry, or the brand of tobacco best suited for smoking in the wind, are topics for unending discussion among the serious minded around the camp-fire. Much edification is in them, and yet they are but prudential maxims after all. They are mere moralities of the Franklin or Chesterfield variety, counsels of worldly wisdom, but they leave the soul untouched.

A man may have them at his finger's ends and be no better fisherman at bottom; or he may, like R., ignore most of the admitted rules and come home with a full basket. It is a sufficient defense of fishing with a worm to pronounce the truism that no man is a complete angler until he has mastered all the modes of angling. Lovely streams, lonely and enticing, but impossible to fish with a fly, await the fisherman who is not too proud to use, with a man's skill, the same unpretentious tackle which he began with as a boy.

But ah, to fish with a worm, and then not catch your fish! To fail with a fly is no disgrace: your art may have been impeccable, your patience faultless to the end. But the philosophy of worm-fishing is that of Results, of having something tangible in your basket when the day's work is done. It is a plea for Compromise, for cutting the coat according to the cloth, for taking the world as it actually is. The fly-fisherman is a natural Foe of Compromise. He throws to the trout a certain kind of lure; and they will take it, so; if not, adieu. He knows no middle path.

"This high man, aiming at a million,
Misses a unit."

The raptures and the tragedies of consistency are his. He is a scorner of the ground. All honor to him! When he comes back at nightfall and says happily, "I have never cast a line more perfectly than I have to-day," it is almost indecent to peek into his creel. It is like rating Colonel Newcome by his bank account.

But the worm-fisherman is no such proud and isolated soul. He is a "low man" rather than a high one; he honestly cares what his friends will think when they look into his basket to see what he has to show for his day's sport. He watches the Foe of Compromise men go stumbling forward and superbly falling, while he, with less inflexible courage, manages to keep his feet. He wants to score, and not merely to give a pretty exhibition of base-running. At the Harvard-Yale football game of 1903 the Harvard team showed superior strength in rushing the ball; they carried it almost to the Yale goal line repeatedly, but they could not, for some reason, take it over. In the instant of absolute need, the Yale line held, and when the Yale team had to score in order to win, they scored. As the crowd streamed out of the Stadium, a veteran Harvard alumnus said: "This news will cause great sorrow in one home I know of, until they learn by to-morrow's papers that the Harvard team acquitted itself creditably." Exactly. Given one team bent upon acquitting itself creditably, and another team determined to win, which will be victorious? The stay-at-homes on the Yale campus that day were not curious to know whether their team was acquitting itself creditably, but whether it was winning the game. Every other question than that was to those young Philistines merely a fine-spun irrelevance. They took the Cash and let the Credit go.

There is much to be said, no doubt, for the Harvard veteran's point of view. The proper kind of credit may be a better asset for eleven boys than any championship; and to fish a bit of water consistently and skillfully, with your best flies and in your best manner, is perhaps achievement enough. So says the Foe of Compromise, at least. But the Yale spirit will be prying into the basket in search of fish; it prefers concrete results. If all men are by nature either Platonists or Aristotelians, fly-fishermen or worm-fishermen, how difficult it is for us to do one another justice! Differing in mind, in aim and method, how shall we say infallibly that this man or that is wrong? To fail with Plato for companion may be better than to succeed with Aristotle. But one thing is perfectly clear: there is no warrant for Compromise but in Success. Use a worm if you will, but you must have fish to show for it, if you would escape the finger of scorn. If you find yourself camping by an unknown brook, and are deputed to catch the necessary trout for breakfast, it is wiser to choose the surest bait. The crackle of the fish in the frying-pan will atone for any theoretical defect in your method. But to choose the surest bait, and then to bring back no fish, is unforgivable. Forsake Plato if you must,—but you may do so only at the price of justifying yourself in the terms of Aristotelian arithmetic. The college president who abandoned his college in order to run a cotton mill was free to make his own choice of a calling; but he was never pardoned for bankrupting the mill. If one is bound to be a low man rather than an impractical idealist, he should at least make sure of his vulgar success.

Is all this but a disguised defense of pot-hunting? No. There is no possible defense of pot-hunting, whether it be upon a trout brook or in the stock market. Against fish or men, one should play the game fairly. Yet for that matter some of the most skillful fly-fishermen I have known were pot-hunters at heart, and some of the most prosaic-looking merchants were idealists compared to whom Shelley was but a dreaming boy. All depends upon the spirit with which one makes his venture. I recall a boy of five who gravely watched his father tramp off after rabbits,—gun on shoulder and beagle in leash. Thereupon he shouldered a wooden sword, and dragging his reluctant black kitten by a string, sallied forth upon the dusty Vermont road "to get a lion for breakfast." That is the true sporting temper! Let there be but a fine idealism in the quest, and the particular object is unessential. "A true fisherman's happiness," says Mr. Cleveland, "is not dependent upon his luck." It depends upon his heart.

No doubt all amateur fishing is but "play,"—as the psychologists soberly term it: not a necessary, but a freely assumed activity, born of surplusage of vitality. Nobody, not even a carpenter wearied of his job, has to go fishing unless he wants to. He may indeed find himself breakfast-less in camp, and obliged to betake himself to the brook,—but then he need not have gone into the woods at all. Yet if he does decide to fish, let him

"Venture as warily, use the same skill,
Do his best, . . ."

whatever variety of tackle he may choose. He can be a whole-souled sportsman with the poorest equipment, or a mean "trout-hog" with the most elaborate.

Only, in the name of gentle Izaak himself, let him be a complete angler; and let the man be a passionate amateur of all the arts of life, despising none of them, and using all of them for his soul's good and for the joy of his fellows. If he be, so to speak, but a worm-fisherman,—a follower of humble occupations, and pledged to unromantic duties,—let him still thrill with the pleasures of the true sportsman. To make the most of dull hours, to make the best of dull people, to like a poor jest better than none, to wear the threadbare coat like a gentleman, to be outvoted with a smile, to hitch your wagon to the old horse if no star is handy,—this is the wholesome philosophy taught by fishing with a worm. The fun of it depends upon the heart. There may be as much zest in saving as in spending, in working for small wages as for great, in avoiding the snapshots of publicity as in being invariably first "among those present." But a man should be honest. If he catches most of his fish with a worm, secures the larger portion of his success by commonplace industry, let him glory in it, for this, too, is part of the great game. Yet he ought not in that case to pose as a fly-fisherman only,—to carry himself as one aware of the immortalizing camera,—to pretend that life is easy, if one but knows how to drop a fly into the right ripple. For life is not easy, after all is said. It is a long brook to fish, and it needs a stout heart and a wise patience. All the flies there are in the book, and all the bait that can be carried in the box, are likely to be needed ere the day is over. But, like the Psalmist's "river of God," this brook is "full of water," and there is plenty of good fishing to be had in it if one is neither afraid nor ashamed of fishing sometimes with a worm.

Nuptial Dress and Etiquette

O. W. SMITH

Any angler who has fished for the eastern brook trout along toward the fag end of the season, when the ripened leaves of the sumac begin to whisper of frosts to come, knows full well what I mean by "nuptial dress." Is there in Nature a creature more beautiful that *Salvelinus fontinalis* when on courting bent? Then, if ever, he deserves the appellation, "flower of fishes"? What angler has not heard the phrase, "glow of the trout"? No one who has taken the fish late in the season will quarrel with that word "glow"; for actually the body is possessed of an irradiate brilliancy impossible of description. Then, too, the *texture* of the skin is somehow different from other fishes, a condition to be expressed only by the word "velvety." To me fishing for brook trout is comparable only to picking violets in the springtime; and I have much the same feeling when I behold a basket of carefully packed and preserved speckled trout that I have when I see a generous bowl of native violets on the drawing-room table. No, I am not going to attempt the impossible and describe a trout garbed in nuptial robes; I leave that task for the poet and painter.

We who have angled much for the speckled beauties have learned through experience to seek them as the Open Season wanes well up towards the headwaters of streams; indeed, even little, unimportant confluents, possessed of scarce six inches of water save in seldom pools, will turn out pound fish and even better. To those unacquainted with the habits of this lover of the rills, the size of the fish sometimes taken from the little creeks will be a matter of surprise. Only last season, along toward the last days of August, I was fishing in a certain famous trout stream with but meager results; then one day I made my way to a distant hay-marsh where I knew a little spring creek found its source. One could not much wonder that the map-makers had missed the stream altogether; for rods at a time it made its way beneath the ground, and when its waters did smile up at the glaring sky it was through an opening only a few inches wide. Yet from the creek I took six fish, each the exact replica of the first, in size and beauty equaling anything taken from the larger stream. Perhaps had I remained longer I might have doubled or even tripled the catch; but six were all I could use and to take more would have been to have laid myself open to a certain charge which I hope I never justly deserved. Perhaps those fish were simply seeking colder water, but their brilliant coloring seemed to indicate that the reproductive instinct was strong upon them.

Late in the fall I have found large fish away up where there was not sufficient water to cover their back fins, and have lain for hours watching their interesting courtship. Even a stream apparently possessed of only a few fish will turn out an unbelievable number during the spawning season. It is this habit of the trout, ever seeking waters higher up as the season wanes, that leads the experienced fly-fisherman to visit the pool above when he misses large fish in a pool before-time inhabited. But the fishing of the little streams deserves a chapter by itself, and those interested in fishing will find the matter more fully treated in chapter ten.

Perhaps nowhere will we find a better description of a trout courtship than in "The Trouts of America," by Mr. William C. Harris, than whom no ichthyological writer is more competent to write. He says: "Arrived at the spawning grounds in October or later on, the female shapes with industrious care a little nest in the gravel, fanning it clean with her tail and removing the larger pebbles in her mouth; the male, all the while, moving slowly and gracefully above, below, and around his mate, as if to let her see and admire the gorgeous bridal robe of olive velvet and gold with which nature had adorned him. After displaying for a few moments with natural vanity the beauty of his nuptial array, approaches her, rubs his body against her side; and soon after she enters the nest, emits a few eggs, which the male fertilizes by ejecting milt upon them. This process continues until the reproductive act is ended. Scarcely five percent of the ova of the female is productive, owing to several causes, the main one being the destruction of the eggs by the hordes of minnows and other spawn eating animals; the trout, both male and female, leaving the ova unprotected immediately after spawning."

Numbers of trout are taken during the spawning season, for then the opportunities for the poacher are almost unlimited. The fish are in shallow water and almost unprotected and can easily be speared and shot. Indeed one who understands the fish's ways can even take them in his hands, though only the knowing can do so. Again and again I have visited trout streams during the spawning season only to find the banks of open pools well ornamented with empty rifle and shotgun shells. Of course it would be very easy to net the fish, and no doubt numbers are so taken. One reason why many streams remain practically unprotected is because in the Middle West, October and November are the open months for hunting and the game wardens are busy elsewhere; but I am persuaded that some time could be advantageously spent by the wardens guarding the trout streams. The illegal fisherman is bad enough at any time, but when he becomes a fish-murderer he deserves no sympathy or consideration. Why, in mercy's name, continue to plant fry if we are not going to protect the adult fish when they most need protection?

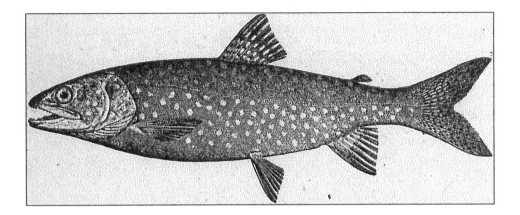

The Value of Observation

GEORGE M. L. LABRANCHE

Several years ago I was looking on at a tennis match between the champion of America and one of the best men England ever sent to this country, and as I watched their play I could not help but marvel at the accuracy with which the players placed their shots. Their drives were wonderful for direction and speed. On nearly every return the ball barely cleared the net and was seldom more than a few inches above the top as it passed over. A friend who knew many of the experts told me how they attained to their remarkable precision. It was the custom of many of them, he said, when preparing for the big matches, to practice for accuracy by driving the ball against a wall. He said this was particularly true of the American champion, and that it was not unusual for him to use up a dozen or more balls in a day's practice. The wall had painted across its face a line of contrasting color at a height from the ground equivalent to that of the top of a regulation tennis net, and upon the line were painted a number of disks about ten inches in diameter. Standing at a distance from the wall equivalent to the distance of the base-line of a regulation tennis-court from the net, the player would return the ball on its rebound from the wall, striving each time to so place it that it would strike just above the line. The accomplishment of a satisfactory score after a succession of drives would convince the player that he had good control of his stroke, and he would then turn his attention to the disks, against each of which he would drive twenty or more shots, taking them in turn and keeping a record of hits in each case. The accuracy developed by such practice was truly remarkable, and I hesitate to mention the number of times in succession one expert made clean hits—it seemed an incredible number.

I have seen golfers practicing the weak places in their game for hours with as much zeal and earnestness as if they were playing a match, and a polo player of my acquaintance practices his strikes upon a field at his home, riding his ponies as daringly and recklessly as though a championship depended upon his efforts. The devotees of these and similar active sports are keenly alive to the necessity of constant practice, that spirit of competition which is so much a part of them making any endeavor that will aid toward high efficiency or improve game or form, seem worth while. And in all sports, particularly those in which the competition is individual, whenever and wherever opportunity presents itself there will be found hundreds of enthusiasts following every ply of the expert, keenly studying his method, observing his form, and absorbing and storing the knowledge so gained for their own practice later on court or field. So, too, even though competition has no place in fly fishing, and should have none, the angler ought to strive always to "play a good game." He should practice the tactics of his art with the same zeal as do the followers of competitive sports if he hopes ever to become an expert fly fisherman in the highest sense of that misused term.

The casual angler who looks upon fishing as merely incidental to his periods of recreation, during which his chief concern is the recuperation of tired brain and unstrung nerves, may feel that he is making a business of his pleasure by devoting much time to the study of his angling. In a measure this is true, and it would be asking much, indeed, of him who thinks of fly fishing only as a pastime. But to him who realizes that it is a sport—a sport that is also an art—there is no incident, complex or simple, that is unworthy of his attention and consideration. No sport affords a greater field for observation and study than fly fishing, and it is the close attention paid to the minor happenings upon the stream that marks the finished angler. The careless angler frequently overlooks incidents, or looks upon them as merely trivial, from which he might learn much if he would but realize their meaning at the time.

Of greatest importance to the dry fly angler is that mastery of the rod and line that enables him to place his fly lightly and accurately upon the water. I venture to assert that one who has had the advantage of expert instruction in handling a rod, and is thereby qualified to deliver a fly properly, will raise more trout upon his first attempt at fishing a stream than another who, through he knows thoroughly the haunts and habits of the fish, casts indifferently. The contrast between the instructed novice and the uninstructed veteran would be particularly noticeable were they to cast together over the same water in which fish were rising freely. Whether or not the novice would take more fish than the veteran is another question. Lacking experience, the novice would probably hook few fish and land fewer. But he would be starting right, and the necessity of overcoming later on that bad form likely to be acquired by all who begin without competent knowledge of the veteran who would come to him in time.

The beginner should watch the expert and should study particularly the action of the rod. He should note that the power which impels the line forward stars from the butt, travels the entire length of the rod, is applied by a slight forward push rather than by a long sweep, and ends in a distinct snap. He will soon learn that the wrist must do the real work, and no better scheme for teaching this has ever been devised than the time-honored one of holding a fly book or a stone between the casting arm and the body. The proper action of the rod will be best learned if he fasten that part of the butt below the reel to the forearm with a piece of string, a strap of leather, or a stout rubber band, the effect of which device will be to stop the rod in an almost perpendicular position when the line is retrieved. The pull of the line as it straightens out behind him will be distinctly felt, will give him a good idea of the power and action of his rod, and sever as a signal for the forward cast. He should practice casting as often as his spare time will allow—over water when possible, but over grass if necessary. He should not wait until the stream is reached and actual fishing problems begin to press upon his notice for solution. His mind will then be occupied with many other things; hence, the knack of handling the rod should have been already acquired.

After the beginner is satisfied that he can properly place and deliver his fly he should turn his attention to study of the fish and the currents of the stream. If he has been a wet fly angler his experience will stand him in good stead, as it will qualify him to locate the likely haunts of the fish. Long and varied though his experience may have been, however, the use of the dry fly will open avenues of observation and knowledge that were hidden from him while he practiced the old method. My own experience is responsible for this rather broad statement, but not until after I had become an ardent advocate of the dry fly, and had abandoned the wet fly for good and all, did I realize the truth of it. In the beginning I was ever on the alert for rising fish, and, instead of boldly assailing promising water, wasted much time, on many occasions, scrutinizing the water for some indication that a fish was feeding. In this way I frequently discovered non-feeding fish lying in places where I had not expected to find them. Such fish were then the more easily approached because I was able to assume a position myself that would not disclose my presence. Just as frequently, too, I have seen fine fish cruising about, and have taken many that might have been driven away by the slightest movement on my part. In many cases I have been compelled to remain absolutely motionless for ten or fifteen minutes before a fish would come to rest long enough to make worth while an attempt to get a fly to it. nearly every time, too, that a fish has been hooked I have seen it actually take the fly—an action always instructive, because fish vary greatly in their manner of taking, and interesting, because in it lies one of the real charms of fly fishing.

The continued use of a floating fly upon water where the angler sees no indication of feeding fish, but where experience tells him that they may lie, seems to develop in him a remarkable keenness of vision. This is a direct result, perhaps, o the attention he gives to his fly. My own experience is that while I am watching my fly float down-stream some stone of irregular formation, peculiar color, or difference in size fro others about it, lying upon the bottom, arrests my eye, with the effect of making the water appear shallower or clearer than it really is. My fly appears to be the center of a small area upon the surface of the water through which everything is seen as clearly as though through water-glass, the shadow of the fly itself upon the bottom often being plainly discernible. Anglers who fish the dry fly learn to identify the living shadow that appears suddenly under the fly as a trout ready to take it on its next drift down-stream, and to recognize a fish as it sidles out from the bank or swings uncertainly toward the fly just as it passes the boulder that shelters him. In either way an interesting opportunity is afforded, particularly for exercising a very necessary attribute—self-control.

It may be that many happenings I now see upon the stream passed unnoticed when I used the wet fly because of some lack of concentration and observation. If this be so, I have the newer method to thank for the development of those faculties. I have learned not to overlook a single minor happening. Perhaps my keenness to ascribe some meaning to the slightest incident has resulted in the building of many fine structures of theory and dogma upon poor foundations. This may be true, but I am certain that their weaknesses have always become apparent to me in time; and, on the other hand, I am just as certain that I have been greatly benefited by my habit of close attention to the little things that happen on the stream. For instance, I cherished the belief for many years that one advantage of up-stream fishing lay in the fact that when the fly was taken the hook was driven into the fish's mouth instead of being pulled away, as in down-stream fishing. I thought this to be one of the strongest arguments in favor of up-stream fishing, and, theoretically, it is. But I know now that many fish that take a floating do so when they are headed down-stream. While there are still many reasons why up-stream fishing is the better method, this particular argument no longer has weight with me.

As I remember it, the strongest admonition of my early schooling on the stream was never to remain long in one place. I was taught to believe that if a rise was not effected on the first few casts subsequent effort on that water was wasted—that the trout would take the fly at once or not at all. I clung to this belief for years, until one day I saw a fine fish lying in shallow water and took him after casting a dozen or more times. Since then I have taken fish after upwards of fifty casts, and I rarely abandon an attempt for one that I can see if I feel certain that it has not discovered me. Even when I have not actually seen a fish, but have known or believed one to be lying near by, the practice has proven effective. Thus I have had the satisfaction of accomplishing a thing once believed to be impossible; but I have gained more than that: I have learned to be persevering and, what is still more important, deliberate. The man who hurries through a trout stream defeats himself. Not only does he take few fish but he has no time for observation, and his experience is likely to be of little value to him.

The beginner must learn to look with eyes that see. Occurrences of apparently little importance at the moment may, after consideration, assume proportions of great value. The taking of an insect, for instance, may mean nothing more than a rising trout; but the position occupied by this fish may indicate the position taken by others in similar water. The flash of a trout, changing his position preparatory to investigating the angler's fly, will frequently disclose the spot occupied by him before he changed his position; and, later on, when the fish are not in the keenest mood for feeding, a fly presented there accurately may bring a rise. The quick dart up-stream of a small trout from the tail of a pool is a pretty fair indication that a large fish occupies the deeper water above; it indicates just as certainly, however, that the angler has little chance of taking him, the excitement of the smaller fish having probably been communicated to his big relative.

The backwater formed by a swift current on the upstream side of a boulder is a favorite lurking-place of brown trout. I was fishing such places one day, and found the trout occupying them in rather a taking mood. In approaching a boulder which looked particularly inviting, and while preparing to deliver my fly, I was amazed to see the tail and half the body of a fine trout out of the water at the side of the rock. For a moment I could not believe that I had seen a fish-the movement was so deliberate and I came to the conclusion that it was fancy or that a water-snake, gliding across the stream, had shown itself. Almost immediately, however, I saw the flash of a trout as he left the backwater and dashed pell-mell into the swift water at the side of the boulder. Down-stream he came until he was eight or ten feet below the rock, when, turning sharply and rising to the surface, he took from it some insect that I could not see. Up-stream again he went, and shortly resumed his position in the dead water, showing half his body as he stemmed the current at the side of the rock. Once more this performance was repeated, and I knew I had stumbled upon an interesting experience. Hastily measuring the distance, hoping to get my fly to him before some natural insect might excite him to give another exhibition of gymnastic feeding, I dropped it about three feet above him, and, contrary to my usual method of retrieving it as it floated past the up-stream side of the boulder, I permitted it to come down riding the top of the wave, when the same flash came as the trout dashed after it. The fish could be plainly seen almost directly under the fly. As it reached the rapidly flattening water below the rock, he turned and took it viciously, immediately darting upstream again. He was soundly hooked, however, and I netted a fine fish lacking one ounce of being a pound and a half. My experience heretofore had been that if a fly were placed a yard or so above this point and allowed to float down to the rock a feeding fish would rush forward-often as much as two feet-and take it, immediately turning or backing into his position again. I had assumed from this observation when the fly passed the rock or backwater without a rise it should be retrieved and another try made. This fish satisfied me, however, that when really feeding, or when inclined to feed, trout may be lured comparatively long distances by inviting-looking morsels. Either he did not decide to take the fly until just as it was passing him or else he liked the exercise of the chase. In any event, he was not peculiar in his habit, because four more fish were taken in the same manner the same day.

In most cases when the fly is cast above a boulder lying in swift water (which I consider, under certain conditions, one of the best places to look for brown trout) it will be taken as it approaches the rock, the trout darting out and retiring immediately to avoid being caught in the swifter water on either side of his stronghold. But if it is not taken, and is permitted to float down with the current, it may bring a response.

It was a somewhat similar observation which prompted the practice and, I must say, rather dubious development of what some of my friends are pleased to call the "fluttering" or "bounce" cast. This cast is supposed to represent the action of the fluttering insect, the fly merely alighting upon the water, rising, alighting again, repeating the movement three or four times at most; finally coming to rest and being allowed to float down-stream. It rarely comes off, but when it does it is deadly; and, for the good of the sport, I am glad but when it does it is deadly; and, for the good of the sport, I am glad that it is difficult, though sorry, too, for the pleasure of accomplishing it successfully is really greater than that of taking fish with it. The cast is made with a very short line-never over twenty-five feet-and the fly alone touches the water. The action of the fly is very similar to that produced by the method known as "dapping," but instead of being merely dangled from the rod, as is the case when "dapping," the fly is actually cast. It should be permitted to float as far as it will after its fluttering or skipping has ceased. The beginner practicing the cast will do well to cast at right angles to the current, and he should choose rather fast water for his experimenting. The speed of the water will cause the fly to jump, and the action it should have will be the more readily simulated than if the first attempts are made on slow water.

I had made a flying trip to the Brodhead, and, with that strange fatality which seems so often to attend the unfortunate angler rushing off for a weekend in the early season, found the stream abnormally high and horrible weather prevailing. After many attempts to get into the stream, with results equally disastrous to my clothing and temper, I abandoned all idea of wading and walked and crawled along the bank, casting my fly wherever I could but rarely finding good water that could be reached, and rising but a few small fish. As there was a gale blowing in my face directly down-stream, it was practically impossible to place a fly where I wished with any delicacy, and I decided to abandon the sport after trying a pool just above me that I knew contained big fish. My first cast on this water, made during a lull, fell lightly, but brought no response, and after a further half dozen fruitless attempts I began to think of the fine log fire at the house. I made one more cast, however, this time in the teeth of the wind. Using but twenty-five feet of line and a short leader, I was able to straighten both in the air. The wind kept all suspended for an instant, the fly, accompanied by a small part of the leader, finally falling upon the water, where I remained but a fraction of a second, the wind whisking it off and laying it down a foot away. This happened five or six times as the fly came down-stream, and during the time it was traveling a distance of not over eight or ten feet five trout, each apparently over a pound in weight, rose to it, but missed because it was plucked away by the wind just in time to save them. I did not get one of them, and, as it was practically impossible to continue casting under the prevailing conditions, I left the stream. It was brought home solidly to me that day, however, that it was the *action* of the fly alone that moved the fish—and my day was not badly spent. I cannot say as much of the many other days since then that I have spent in what I feel were rather foolish attempts to imitate the effect produced by the wind on that day.

The study of the positions taken by big fish when they are feeding, and those which they occupy when they are not, I san important part in the education of the fly fisher. Each time the angler takes a good fish or sees one feeding, if he will note in his diary its position, the condition of the water, temperature, atmosphere, time of day, and the insect being taken, he will soon have an accumulation of data from which he may learn how to plan a campaign against particular fish at other times. Extremely interesting in itself, the study of insects is of great value to the angler in his attempts at imitation, and the information gleaned from autopsy might not be acquired in any other manner.

It may be said to be an axiom of the fly fisher that where a small trout is seen feeding rarely need a large one be looked for. But the actions of a small fish in sight may sometimes indicate the presence of a larger one unseen. The taking of a fine trout on a certain stream in Sullivan County, on August 27, 1906, after one of those long periods of drought so common in recent years, convinced me of this. I had been waiting for even a slight fall of rain, and, quite a heavy shower having come up the evening before, I started for this stream. Upon my arrival there I was surprised to learn that not a drop of rain had fallen in weeks, and that the shower which had been heavy twenty miles away had not reached the vicinity. While driving from the station to the house at which I was to stop. Along a road that paralleled the stream, the many glimpses I had of the latter filled me with misgivings. At one point the stream and road are very near each other, and, stopping my driver, I got out looking at a famous pool below a dam which had long outlived its usefulness. It was a sizzling-hot day, and at that time—eleven o'clock—the sun was almost directly overhead; yet in the crystal-clear water of this pool, with not a particle of shade to cover him, lay a native trout fourteen inches in length which afterward proved to weigh one pound three ounces. Too fine a fish, I thought, as I clambered back into the carriage, to be occupying such a place in broad daylight, and I promised myself to try for him later in the afternoon. Returning about six o'clock, I found him in the same position, and during the full twenty minutes I watched him, while he appeared to be nervously alert, he never moved. Notwithstanding the fact that everything was against me, and knowing that the chances were more than even tat the fish would see me, my rod, or my line, I made plans for approaching him; yet, busy as I was, I could not rid my mind of this ever-recurring thought: with all the known aversion of his kind to heat, and their love of dark nooks, why was this fish out on such a day? Why did he not find a place under the cool shade of the dam? With the instinct strong within him to protect him by hiding, the impulse must have been much stronger that forced him to take so conspicuous a stand—a mark to the animals which prey upon his kind. As there were absolutely no insects upon the water, and scarcely enough current to bring food of other sort to him, he could not have been feeding. The only reason, then, to account for his being there—the thought struck me forcibly enough—was his fear of a bigger fish. The logical conclusion was that if a fish of his inches (no mean adversary) exposed himself the one that bullied him must be quite solid. I tested this fellow's appetite with a small, pinkish-bodied fly of my own invention, and, standing about forty feet below and considerably to the left, dropped it three or four feet above him; but, although it was certain he could see the fly, he made no attempt to go forward and take it. As it neared him, however, he rushed excitedly to the right and then to the left, taking the fly as it came directly over him, and, before I could realize what had happened, came down-stream toward me at a great rate. As he was securely hooked, I kept him coming, and netted him quietly at the lip of the pool.

That this fish did not take the fly the instant it fell meant to me that he was afraid to go forward into the deeper water which harbored his larger fellow; and his action as the fly appeared over him meant that, while he wanted it badly enough, he would not risk an altercation with the other, which might also have seen it. When he did finally decide that the coast was clear, he took it quickly and rushed down toward the shallower water where he might be secure against sudden attack.

If some of the theories developed in those few moments appear fanciful, it must be remembered that my mind was occupied with the thought that the pool contained a larger fish, and the conclusions based upon the subsequent actions of this smaller one only tended to strengthen this belief. Fanciful or not, I was rewarded a few minutes later by the sight of a monster tail breaking the surface just under the water that trickled over the apron of the dam. Having prepared a gossamer leader, preferring to risk a smash to not getting a rise, I dropped a small Silver Sedge—which I used because it could be more plainly kept in sight—almost immediately in the swirl and was at once fast in a lusty fish. After many abortive attempts to lead him into the diminutive net I had with me, I flung the thing, in disgust, into the woods. I finally beached the fish and lifted him out in my hand. He was a fine brown trout, eighteen and three quarter inches in length, and weighed, the next morning, two pounds nine ounces.

While I was engaged with this fish another rose in practically the same spot under the apron of the dam. Hurriedly replacing the bedraggled fly with a new one, I waited for the trout to show himself, which he did presently, and again I was fast—this time in one of the best fish I have ever seen in these waters. It seemed an interminable length of time, though probably not over ten minutes, that I was engaged with this one, and it was impossible to move him; he kept alternately boring in toward the dam and sulking. In one of the latter fits I urged him toward me somewhat too strongly, and he was off. Immediately I was afforded a sight of what I had lost as he leaped clear of the water in an evident endeavor to dislodge the thing that had fastened to his jaw. The smash made as he struck the water still resounds in my ear, and when I say that this fish would have bone close to five pounds I but exercise the right to that license accorded all anglers to attempt to describe the size of the big ones that get away. Having one good fish in my creel, however, I really had some basis for my calculation—at any rate, he was one of the best fish I have ever risen. Examining my leader, I found it had not broken, but the telltale curl at the end proved that, in the fast-gathering gloom, I had been careless in knotting on the fly.

The Demon of the Foam

H. PRESCOTT BEACH

It is a wild, swirling river that opens when you leave the placid Lake St. John; dark and rest-less, full of rifts and eddies. The path of this torrent is far from smooth, blocked as it is by jagged ledges and polished, water-worn boulders that push back and fret the eager stream. Round and round the hollowed basins scooped out of living rock by the struggles of the waters pent up like caged beasts, the currents whirl like giant mills. The wheels of these mills are never idle. Years as numberless as the creases cut by the tide in the hard, black stone have passed since first the flood felt the rough barriers thrown across its way, driving its drops back into this weary bondage, where to-day they are still slaving, grinding the blackness into bub-bles that rise and drift and shine. An outstretched arm of the reef gathers in these gleaming jewels as they come and piles them in a mass, an island of floating foam. These islands are the gleaming spots that flash upon you when first the birch-bark feels the throbbing, the heaving of the river and leaps forward like a living thing. Strange, startling is the effect of these creamy mounds that lie here and there upon the sullen swirls like ivory set in ebony. They are too like old ivory, stained and discolored, for with them are gathered in all the chips and saw-dust and dead boughs and stumps that have come down from the woods.

Queer moths and millers hover all day around the yellow islands. They dance and flit untiringly over the drift, seeking their tiny prey—miniature sea terns skirting little shores.

Brown, drab, buff and black flecked with scarlet, twinkle in the sunshine and skim over the surface in airy play. Now and again there is a ripple on the water, a crease, a wrinkle, a dimple in the foam; sometimes it is a heavy splash and one or more of the dancers disappears. As the sun gets higher the dance grows livelier; thousands of wings are beating time in the warmth and glow, and as the revels swell the revelers one by one drop and are lost. What is this little flurry, this stir upon the froth that brings such sudden end to these innocent moths? Only is a dark form visible for an instant; a waving toss of a glistening tail, a plunge and the thing is gone. This is a very dance of death! And this specter, this destroyer—half seen and half imagined—swift, cunning and relentless, who and what is it? It is the Demon of the Foam. It is the Ouananiche.

Through the mists of early morning that hang over the rapids is gliding a bark canoe. Three men are in the craft; one gray-haired and old who peers through the fog, and two are keeping the course with strong strokes of their paddles. These are bold spirits who hold their way amid this rush of water—who do not jump when the bark grazes an ugly rock—or quivering, slides over a hidden ledge to dash her mouth into a caldron below. They only smile when she careens against a floating timber and drinks—yes, stoops and drinks—a bucket-full of green water, though he of the gray hair clutches the thwart more tightly and leans lower to the far side. Too many times have these weather-painted Chippewas felt their way down this same path of whirlpools to feel uneasy when the bright fringe of a wave curls over the edge and the swash sprinkles their skins. They were boys upon this same stream, swimming its maddest freshets and knowing its every turn and trick. The one at the bow is On-ik-mah (the kingfisher) and the stout fellow at the stern is Mon-ah-quic (the paddle-lover) both trusty and two of Patterson's best guides. The elder man amidships—still young in his love for ways in the woods, the streams and the open sky; too full of wonder; too wrapped in watching this unquiet scene to feel afraid—is my old self, and we are shooting Le Grande Décharge.

Into calm and still water at last we slip; calm and still only as compared with yon wild mill-race above, for does it not boil and seethe all around us who drift along the foam? It is here I put together my well-tried split-bamboo and, with feverish fingers, thread the eyelets with the filmy gray silk. The slender thing shakes like an aspen in my hands as I feel for my fly-book, hardly able in my panic of anticipations to unfasten the leathern strap. Then a moment of indecision. My eye runs over the gorgeous bits of feather and is led from blue to crimson, from crimson to green, from green to gold, from gold to black and from black to white, each seeming more alluring—more beautiful—than the last. Then I forsake them all and, turning to the last leaf, my finger plays among a few flies of quiet tones. Here are the Hackles, brown, red and gray; here is the Dun Midge and the Montreal; and here, half-hidden by less worthy wings, is nestled the tempter of them all—the Silver Doctor.

"A famous medicine-man thou art, too, old friend," I murmur as I bend it fluttering to the leader, "and many a seemingly incurable case they power has overcome. Would that the human leech of to-day had so little of show and pretense as though in thy modest cloak, and but a half of thy unfailing skill. Here stretch thy wings again!"

The guides, with paddles stayed, leaned forward to watch as the invisible line followed the speck of gray that shot out toward the nearest patch of foam. Among a band of brown millers it alighted gayest of all the dancers, and fell as with tired pinions, helpless to the water, there to struggle for life. its small tumult does not disturb the others, who skip on as aimlessly and as lightly as before, but down below, in the shadow of that reef of bubbles, fierce eyes are watching—eyes that see every speck that floats and even the reflections of things in the air. Instantly and without warning, there comes a tumbling leap of foam, and from the island rises a sharp fin that plunges in again. It has tried for the Doctor and it missed him. Another cast and the M. D. flickers away over beyond the outside of the eddy. Barely does he strike, when—splash! again the rise and the silvery moth has gone. The pliant rod curls to a round letter O when I draw back and find that the hook has gone home. The Demon has caught this latest dancer and has carried him down to his cave. Now the water swirls again, broken by an angry leap, and the Demon thrashes out into the mid-tide. It feels the goad now and knows this victim has a sting. Gladly, Ouananiche of the Foam, wouldst cast forth this bitter morsel, but it clings; it grapples thy cruel jaw with a strength that never yields to thine!

Back, back to its old haunt it returns, diving deep into the green gulf, striving hard to drag loose the unfeeling line, shaking its strong head in madness, rushing fast and hard. Turn from the tangled float of logs beyond, good fish! What! You will not? Oh, how that stout reed bends and writhes when I give this mighty fish the butt! It is a struggle, and for an instant I feared; then felt the pull lessen and the furious fellow lunged past the canoe in full flight up-stream. Nothing can check him for thirty yards or more, when he flashes to the top and vaults high into air; then his strength ebbing, he turns with the tide and, fighting out toward the centre, hangs sullen and lies still. A sharp shaking sends him on—this time weak but still game— and taking advantage of the eddies, he whirls off around a low boulder. Was he free? No! The line had followed over the top, not twisted around the rock where it would surely have parted, and the Demon is not yet free. No charm for him now in the swarm of gay flies; he settles deeper in the basin and digs for the bottom. Persistently I urge him upward—rebelling, sulking, but slowly giving way. His dark mottled back gleams for a moment beside the bark when I raise him and Kingfisher, with a ready net, lifts him into the boat.

I take a long breath of triumph. This is a good fish—a four-pound catch—and I rise in the bark and point out another pool below where a heavy plunge has just sent the spray flying. Thither we go and, letting the canoe drift against a big snag, I send the Doctor flying out over the foam. For a time he pirouettes and prances all in vain. Nothing heeds his antics and yet beyond, every moment or two, a rise tells the death of some real living harlequin. Kingfisher yawns and I glare at him. What does the man want? Does he think I am a magician that I should land four-pound fish every other minute? He avoids my glance and says something in Chippewa to the other. They look off at the clouds and smile. I demand to know what he said and do not believe it when he calmly replies, "That day was got warm 'fore noon." There is no time to scold, for—whiz! My reel calls me back to fishing. A demon has hooked himself during the discussion and now he is carrying my good line down stream at a furious rate. No giving this chap the butt! We follow in the birch-bark, keeping clear of the thick brush and dead debris that is jammed among the rocks, and corner him in a narrow hole. Here he gives battle for the first and last time; here he smashes my favorite tip, and here at the end I bring him to net—savage to the very finish—a giant Ouananiche of seven pounds.

Kingfisher unbent himself so far as to smile a dignified approval on the great flapping fish; then relapsed into his ordinary grave image condition.

Once more we found a temporary harbor in a rocky cove behind a high point of hemlocks half a mile below the Grande Décharge. Here the flecks or spots of foam were small, not more than a yard across, and slowly floated around with the eddy. In some places one could see as many as four Ouananiche feeding beneath and around one mass of bubbles, their sharp dorsal fins cutting the surface in every direction. Surely, this was a promising lair.

"Too much feesh; no bite any!" was Kingfisher's comment, but it was not until I had exhausted my stock of flies and had sent flitting over the pool, Scarlet Ibises, Coachmen, Parmachene Belles and Seth Greens without even a passing nibble, that I had faith in his diagnosis. Why it was so I could not discover. Here were the fish, and big ones too; they were feeding, too, as was testified by their long leaps and flashing springs after the live moths. At last I hit upon an expedient. I had often heard of trolling for the Ouananiche but had never believed it possible to accomplish any good results in that way. In my breast-pocket was a tin case filled with miscellaneous traps and among them a brass pickerel-spoon which I had made after a peculiar design of my own. It had slain its scores of pickerel and many bass and, as results showed, was ready to conquer new foes.

I bent it on a stout braided line and, biting over the line a split buckshot just above the spoon, insured its sinking to a depth of six inches or so, even when the canoe moved at a rapid rate. The guides sent us spinning across the pool and behind gleamed the new bait which I have named the "Golden Death." Scarcely had we gone a dozen paddle-strokes when a smashing tug made me brace myself for a struggle. It was a monster; but with a tearing plunge he freed himself and was gone in a shower of spray. Another snatched as he let go and that one, too, managed to shake out the grapple of hooks at the first jump. The third—a smaller fish—took the whole thing fairly and, badly struck, bolted for the shore. Of course, with a heavy linen line I "snubbed" him easily and, though he finned it furiously, dragged him in after a few minutes of resistance.

Barely did that big of whirling brass touch the water again ere a mighty fellow attacked and captured it, throwing himself a full yard out of water when he felt the barb. Wildly he dove and tugged below; eagerly he worked the line out toward the river; swiftly he headed for his deep hole below and, oh! How he withstood my remorseless twitches and heavy pulls, reaching out with every ounce of muscle (and he was all muscle) for his old den. Despite my every effort he gained his stronghold— down oh! so far—and there he lay unmoving. No device could start or stir him from his hiding place now; see-sawing the line, jerking it, sagging back till I feared it would part, were of no avail. Then suddenly, of his own accord, he tore up to the very edge of the canoe, skating past our very eyes with slack enough to free himself ten times over if he had not been frightfully hooked. Three or four times he dashed into the air, turning complete somersaults, then made six or more short, mad rushes like a bull, once charging the canoe and scraping its side as he went under the bottom. When at last he came, breathless and beaten, to the net he bit and snapped at the meshes as if he would tear all to bits. In the bottom of the birch-bark he lay, angrily clashing his jaws till he died. Though not so large as my second fish, he was more powerful. Five more of these beautiful captives we took with the spoon in this placid cove under the overhanging hemlocks, and then, no more appearing, we gave up a little before noon and put ashore for lunch.

There on a bank of soft moss, with those great trees leaning over me and the broad, curling, petulant river before me, I lay and smoked after our simple meal. On broad, green leaves lay the noble, handsome fish. Bravely had they fought and bravely died, and it was with almost a reverent touch, when we headed home for the Island House now two miles away, that I laid them in the basket. It was my first day of many, many happy ones among the grandest fish in all the Canadas—the king of the whirlpools, the Ouananiche, Demon of the Foam.

Salmon-Fishing

A. G. WILKINSON

Although the salmon is the acknowledged king of fishes, and the taking of it the most royal of sports, yet comparatively few indulge in the pastime. There are certainly many, and those too among the foremost men of our country, who concede fully the benefits to be derived, not only from open-air life and exercise, but from having some pursuit or specialty outside of business and profession,—call it hobby, if you will,—which, while it gives rest to certain faculties of the mind, equally exercises and strengthens others. They realize truly that life is better than fame, and sound lungs and good digestion than a fat purse; but the difficulties in the way of taking salmon turn most of these in a different direction for their recreation.

The three principal hindrances to salmon-fishing in this country are: the great trouble in obtaining either a lease of a stream or a permit for the best part of the season; the great distances to be traveled, and consequent loss of valuable time; and the large expense as compared with other sorts of outdoor amusements.

The region where salmon can at the present day be taken, in sufficient numbers to reward one for the attendant trouble and expense, is a circumscribed one. Beginning at Quebec, and following down the river St. Lawrence, the salmon-streams are very numerous upon the northern shore, and extend far away to the Labrador coast. Among them are the well-known Laval, Godbout, Trinity, St. Margaret, Moisic, St. John's, Magpie, Mingan, Great and Little Romaine Rivers.

The range of mountains on the north shore runs within a few miles of the St. Lawrence, and hence the rivers upon that side are very short and rapid, giving but few good pools, and are, as a general thing, very difficult to fish. Only a few good streams are found on the south shore, among which are the Rimouski, Grande Metis, and Matane. Passing down the Gulf of St. Lawrence, we come to the Basin of Gaspé, into which flow three admirable streams; and farther on, upon the north shore of the Bay of Chaleurs, and at its western end, are some of the best, including the famous Restigouche, fished yearly by Englishmen who cross the Atlantic for that express purpose; also the Cascapedia, made more noted through Mr. Dawson's charming letters from there, where, at a good ripe age, he took his first salmon. The Nipisiguit on the south shore of the Bay of Chaleurs and the Miramichi on the eastern coast of New Brunswick are the last salmon-streams of any account until we come to Nova Scotia, where there are a few upon its south-east coast below Halifax.

In Cape Breton there is a single good river, the Margarie. Here and there small streams are found in other parts of New Brunswick and in the Island of Anticosti, but practically salmon-angling is confined to the rivers of Canada East and those of the northern part of New Brunswick, which includes the Miramichi.

But few of the rivers we have mentioned debouch near a steamer landing, and all others are difficult of access. To reach these latter the angler must manage in some way to get transportation for many miles over a rough country, where it is difficult to find horses, wagons, or roads; or he must charter a small sailing-vessel and run along a most dangerous coast, carrying with him both canoes and men. The Restigouche and Matapediac are reached with comparative ease from Dalhousie, a landing-place of the Gulf Port steamers. This line of steamers also touches at Gaspé Basin, leaving passengers just at the mouths of the three streams flowing into it. These are the York, St. John, and Dartmouth, called by the natives the South-west, Douglastown, and North-west. These rivers are among the best stocked in Canada. The scenery about them is most varied, and in this respect unlike most other parts of Canada, where one tires of the monotony of mere grandeur and longs for the picturesque. They flow chiefly through deep gorges, or canyons, and between mountains, which occasionally rise to the height of a thousand or fifteen hundred feet. Beautiful lakes, filled to repletion with brook-trout, are found on the high land between the rivers, which for quite a distance flow within a few miles of one another. These streams are very rapid, and in early spring are almost torrents, and yet they have very few falls around which a "carry" must be made. Comfortable houses have been erected at some trouble and expense every ten or twelve miles on those parts of the York and St. John which abound in good pools.

The Canadian Government exercises complete control of the principal salmon-streams, both in their tidal and fluvial parts. Leases are commonly given for several years, but occasionally a schedule of vacant rivers is published, giving "upset" or minimum prices at $500 in gold. The very fact that such advertisement is made indicates of itself that the rivers are not, for some reason, very desirable. The best rivers are leased for eight or ten years, and upon the likelihood of a vacancy, numerous applicants bring influences to bear to secure the chance at once.

It is understood that as a general thing leases of the better class of streams are not to be given to the "States" people, as they call us of the United States. Our political anglers often remark that it is more difficult to lease a good salmon-stream than to secure an election to Congress. A thousand dollars has been paid for the use of the fluvial part only of a first-class stream for a single season, this including, of course, all the fittings and canoes, etc. Add to the cost of a "permit" the traveling and camping expenses, and the price of good salmon tackle, which is always of the most expensive sort, and you swell the sum-total of a summer trip to quite an amount.

While the Canadians are so tenacious of their leases, and naturally desirous of keeping the best streams for themselves, yet they are most generous and kind to their "States" friends. Often, one is not only accorded a permit to fish, but receives an invitation to make, for the time being, all the accessories and fittings of the stream his own, including houses, canoes, and cooking-utensils. My invitation, some years ago, from that genial sportsman, Mr. Reynolds, of Ottawa, was to make the York River my own, paying simply for my men and provisions. His guests kill every year many salmon to his one, and he enjoys their success far better than his own. An Indian would wish him, in the happy hunting-grounds, the exclusive right of the best stream. We can only express our heartfelt wish that for a score of years to come he may continue yearly to take his 47-pound salmon in his favorite stream.

To the cost of stream and tackle must be added the great uncertainty of getting fish. One may secure the best stream, purchase the best tackle, and travel a thousand miles to no purpose, for *Salmo salar* is a very uncertain fish, and the worst sort of a conundrum. Sometimes he comes early and sometimes late; sometimes he goes leisurely up the rivers, lingering accommodatingly at the pools, and seemingly in good mood for sporting with flies; and sometimes, when kept back by the ice of a late spring, he goes for the headwaters at once, only stopping when compelled by fatigue, and then having no time to waste upon flies. Last year, with scores of salmon, by actual count, in the different pools, often not more than one in a pool could be tempted to rise to our flies. All these combined causes make the number of salmon-anglers small.

A stream being secured, the selection of tackle is an easy matter. A water-proofed American-made silk line of about three hundred feet, tapering gradually at each end, so that it may, when worn, be changed end for end, is the one generally used in this country. A simple reel with click is the best, and it may be of hard rubber or metal, as preferred. If of metal, it is usually nickel or silver plated. In olden times, the Scotch salmon-angler strapped around his waist a roughly made wooden reel of large size, called a pirn. It was entirely unconnected with the rod, along which the line was carried by rings, beginning quite a distance above the hand. In the old Scotch works upon angling, we read of the gaffer singing out to his laird, "Pirn in! pirn in! you'll be drowned and coot" (drowned and cut), by which he meant, "Reel in, or your line will bag and be cut off by getting around the sharp edges of the rocks."

The Scotch poaching angler suspends by straps under his outer garments a capacious bag of coarse linen for concealing his salmon, while quite innocently he carries in his hand a string of trout. Mr. Scrope once caught a poacher with a salmon in his bag, and demanded how it got there. The reply was, "How the beast got there I dinna ken. He must ha' louped intil ma pocket as I war wading."

The leader, of nine to twelve feet nearest the hook, is of the best selected silk-worm gut, which should stand a test of four or five pounds strain. This gut is made by taking the silk-worm just before it begins to spin its cocoon, and soaking it in vinegar some hours. The secreting glands of the worm are at that time filled with the mass of glutinous matter from which the silk of the cocoon is to be spun. One end of the worm, after it is thus soaked, is pinned to a board, and the other stretched out some eight or ten inches and secured. When this is hardened, it becomes the beautiful white, round gut of commerce, which, when stained water-color, and dropped lightly in the pool, will not be noticed by the fish.

In the matter of rods, the conservative man still clings to a well-made wooden one of greenheart or other approved wood, of which the taper and strength are so accurately proportioned that the addition of but a few ounces at the end of the line carries the main bend or arch nearer the butt end. Those who are not so conservative, and who are fond of lessening in every practicable way the somewhat tedious labor of casting the fly, choose a rod of split bamboo, which weighs about two pounds. My own weighs but twenty-seven ounces, although nearly sixteen feet long. No one will risk himself upon a stream without extra rod, reels, and lines, and if he takes a greenheart and split bamboo, he has two as good rods as are made. One who has long used a heavy wooden rod has at first a feeling of insecurity and a distrust of the slender bamboo, which can, if necessary, be wielded by a single strong arm. It is said an old Scotchman, handling one of these rods for the first time, exclaimed: "Do ye ca' that a tule to kie a saumont wi'? I wad na gie it to my bairnies to kie a gilsie wi'." It should be explained that a grilse is a young salmon just returned from a first trip to the sea. After its second trip, it returns a salmon proper, with all the characteristic markings. It often happens that a grilse (called by the Scotch "gilsie," or salmon-peel) is larger than a salmon one or two years older, the varieties differ so in size. The young of the salmon are first called parrs, and have peculiar spots and dark bars, or "finger-marks," as they are called. At eighteen months, they are some six inches long, and the following spring silver scales grow over the bars and spots, when they are called smolt, retaining that name until they go to sea. For a long time the parr was held to be a species of trout, and entirely distinct from salmon. Mr. Scrope, the author of "Days and Nights of Salmon-Fishing," a work now extremely rare, held long and animated discussions with James Hogg, the "Ettrick-Shepherd," upon this subject, which was settled practically by a Mr. Shaw, of Drumlanrig, who tagged a parr and identified it again as a full grown salmon in 1836.

The manufacture of a fine rod of split bamboo is a work requiring great skill and judgment, not unlike that required to make the far-famed Cremona violin. The rods are made usually from Calcutta bamboo, as it has a larger proportion of enamel with tough fiber and long growth between joints. In the Japanese bamboo, the fibers follow the joints too closely, and so must be cut into in straightening the pieces. Our American cane is lighter, and the enamel is very hard and elastic, but the inner woody fiber is soft as well as brittle. Sometimes several invoices of Calcutta cane will not contain one suitable piece for rod-making. The canes mildew on the passage, and this injures the fibers. Sometimes they are injured in being straightened over a fire, and often a single worm-hole ruins the entire piece. Just as our forest trees have the thickest and roughest bark on the north side, so the bamboo has thicker and harder enamel upon whichever side was exposed to storms. In making fine rods not only the best cane is selected, but the best side of this selected cane is preferred.

The split bamboo rod is an instance in which nature is successfully improved. The cane in its natural growth has great strength as a hollow cylinder, but it lacks the required elasticity. The outer surface or enamel is the hardest of vegetable growth, and is made up largely of silica. The rod-maker, by using all of the enamel possible, and by his peculiar construction avoiding all the central open space, secures great strength with lightness, and nearly the elasticity of steel itself.

In making a rod, some ten or twelve feet of the butt of the cane is sawed off and split into thin pieces or strands. These pieces are then beveled on each side, so that when fitted together they form a solid rod of about half the diameter or less of the original hollow cane. This beveling is done with a saw, or a plane if preferred, but more expeditiously by having two rotary saws or cutters set at an angle of sixty degrees to each other, in case the rod is to be of six strands. The strip is fed to the cutters by means of a pattern which, as the small end of the strip approaches, raises it into the apex of the angle formed by the cutters. This preserves a uniform bevel, and still narrows each strand toward its tip end so as to produce the regular decrease in size of the rod as it approaches the extreme end. These strips can also, if desired, be filed to a bevel by placing them in triangular grooves of varying depths in a block of lignum-vitae. The pieces are then filed down to the level of the block, which is held in a vise during the operation.

The six or twelve strips as required, being worked out, and each part carefully tested throughout its entire length by a gauge, are ready for gluing together, a process requiring great care and skill. The parts should be so selected and joined that the knots of the cane "break joints." The parts being tied together in position at two or three points, the ends are opened out and hot glue well rubbed in among the pieces for a short distance with a stiff brush. A stout cord is then wound around the strands from the end glued toward the other portions, which are opened and glued in turn, say eight or ten inches at a time. A short length only is glued at one time so that slight crooks in the pieces can be straightened, and this is done by bending the rod and sliding the pieces past each other. During the gluing all inequalities and want of symmetry must be corrected or not at all, and so the calipers are constantly applied to every side at short intervals, and any excess of thickness corrected by pressing the parts together in a vise. Figure 1 shows a section of a length of bamboo cane from which the strips indicated by spaces marked off are to be sawed. Figure 2 is an end view of the six strands properly beveled and glued together. This length or joint of the rod is made up of six sectors of a circle whose diameter is greater than that of the rod, and hence it is necessarily what in common parlance might be called six-cornered. Figure 3 is an end view, natural size, of a six-stranded salmon-rod tip at its larger end; and Figure 4 is a longitudinal view of a piece of a Leonard trout-rod tip of

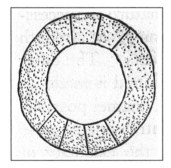

Figure 1

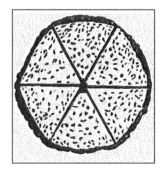

Figure 2

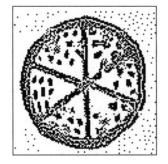

Figure 3

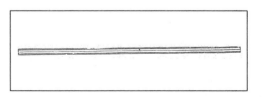

Figure 4

twelve strands now lying before me. This figure gives the size as accurately as the calipers can determine it, and shows what vast amount of skill, patience, and untiring industry is required in the art we have been describing.

The ferrules are water-tight and expose no wood in either the socket or the tendon part. Bamboo is so filled with capillary tubes that water would be carried through the lengths and unglue them, if it could once reach the ends where the joints of the rod are coupled together; hence the necessity of careful protection at this place. The entire rod when finished is covered with the best copal coach varnish. By taking care to renew the varnish from time to time, no water need ever get to the seams.

In spite of the prejudice against what has been called a gentleman's parlor rod, they have steadily gained in favor. Twenty-five years ago, a London firm made split-bamboo rods, putting the enamel inside. Naturally enough, with the soft part of the cane exposed to wear and weather, and nearly all the enamel sacrificed, they did not find favor in the eyes of thoughtful or scientific anglers. At least, Mr. Phillippi, living at Easton, Pa., conceived the idea, in 1866, of putting the enamel upon the outside, where it would do the most good. Next, Mr. Green and Mr. Murphy put their heads together, and made rods of this sort of four strands, and finally the old well-known firm of A. Clerk & Co., New York, introduced into the market the Leonard rod of six and twelve strands, and have since been supplying Europeans with all they get of this article.

I have taken not a little pains to get, as far as possible, a correct history of this somewhat remarkable invention. My own rod of this kind has been used in both rain and shine for several seasons, and is now in perfect order. In careful tests, I have never yet seen a rod of its weight, or of its length and any weight, that could throw a fly quite as far; and, light as it is, it brought last year to gaff in twenty minutes a thirty-five pound fish, which my friend Curtis gaffed for me, off the high rock at the "Big Salmon Hole" of the York. Any rod with which one has killed many and large fish is, naturally, held to be perfection upon the stream; but the rod we have been describing is beautiful as an *objet de vertu*, and in the library becomes a source of joy to every admirer of skilled workmanship, though he be not familiar with its use.

The angler must keep just strain enough on the rod to prevent the hook from dropping out of the mouth of the fish,—which in this case measured forty-eight inches in length,—while his friend, after having skillfully hooked him with a prodigiously long gaff, is drawing him forward so as to use both hands in lifting him upon the rock. As some of our skillful surgeons perform even the delicate operation for a cataract equally well with either hand, so must the successful salmon-angler have become ambidextrous. In casting he must be able, of course, to use either hand forward at will, and when one arm has become lamed by holding the rod, as it rests against the waist in playing a fish, and takes nearly all the strain while the other manipulates the reel, he must be able to change the position of the reel upon the rod, and work it with his left hand while his right manages the rod. This left-handed arrangement will have the reel on top in its proper position, and the right hand taking all the strain.

The scientific angler, as soon as the fish is hooked, turns his rod over and brings his line uppermost, so that it hugs and strains the rod equally at every inch of its length, leaving to the rings their proper function of simply guiding the line.

Having, through Mr. Curtis's kindness, received an invitation from Mr. Reynolds, as already mentioned, to fish his river, the York, accompanied by any friend whom I might select, I provided myself with a Norris greenheart and a Leonard bamboo in the way of rods, and with an assortment of proper flies.

It is, however, in the selection of friends to accompany us that we find the greatest difficulty connected with a projected excursion for salmon. One may have plenty of friends who would make camp-life delightful, and whose presence at the festive board "would make a feast of a red herring"; but they cannot be ordered for a trip, like tackle. Your choice must, as a matter of course, be very much restricted. You will never trust yourself in camp with your best friend unless you have seen him under fire; that is to say, unless you know how he will stand the thousand and one annoyances incident to long journeys with poor conveyances and still poorer hotels; with black flies, sand-flies, mosquitoes, fleas, and worse. The best companion of the library, the drawing-room, and the watering-place, although possessed of the most kindly attributes, oftentimes becomes absolutely unendurable when quartered for a day or two on the banks of a Canadian river, with limited cuisine, unlimited numbers of insects, and poor luck at angling. Never go with one who is painfully precise, and who wishes to have everything his own way and at once. Such a man might as well stay away from Gaspé, where the natives always have their own way, and never, under any circumstances, hurry. Never go with one who is over-excitable or enthusiastic, for it isn't just the thing to have a man standing on his head in a birch-bark canoe every time he gets "a rise," or the canoe takes a little water running down rapids. The experienced angler chooses a friend who is deliberate, and takes all ills philosophically, and, if possible, one with that fortunate disposition which permits him to keep both his head and his temper under all circumstances. Other things being equal, he selects an admirer and follower of Brillat-Savarin, for he has ever remarked that one who fully enjoys and appreciates the best of dinners is just the one to endure with equanimity the worst, if no better is attainable.

To be eighteen miles from the main camp when fish are rising as fast as they can be killed, and to have but three pieces of pilot-bread for the angler and his two men, and to be forced to go without supper and breakfast, or else give up the sport and return, will bring the bad out of any man if it is in him.

Your companionable angler need not always take things quite as coolly as did a well-known editor who, once upon a time, while engaged in pulling in a blue-fish, after sawing his fingers with a hundred or more feet of line, was seized with hunger and fatigue, and, taking a hitch about a cleat, satisfied his inner man with sardines and crackers. To the surprise of all his companions, after finishing his lunch and resting his fingers, he pulled in the fish, which had swallowed the hook so far down that it had to be cut out. Of course, the first few feet of the line which he used was wired so that it could not be bitten off.

Here is a sketch from life of a jolly English gentleman, who gets thoroughly disgusted every time he loses a fish. He then, without saying a word, quits the business, puts his back against a smooth tree, and takes a short nap, leaving others to thrash the pools. It is worthy of note that one need never fear meeting snobs, swells, or disagreeable people fishing for salmon. The air of a first-class stream seems fatal to all such.

The last of June, 1874, found Mr. Lazell and the writer tired out with close attention to duties, and with barely frame-work enough left "to veneer a decent man upon," rendezvousing at the office of Fred. Curtis, Esq., in Boston, prepatory to setting out for Gaspé Basin, Canada East. An idler cannot appreciate fully the enjoyment we felt in anticipation of several weeks entire freedom from business of any sort. To get so far from civilization that no irascible inventor can find you and argue his case until your head seems ready to burst; no client can bore you for hours without giving a single important fact in his case; and where you will hear of no impecunious creditor's paper going to protest,—is woth a large amount of preliminary toil.

After having, as Lazell asserted, taken an outfit sufficient for a whaling voyage, we devoted still a day to getting little odds and ends which Curtis's experience had taught him to provide—things which seemed superfluous, and in fact almost absurd, and yet worth their weight in gold when one is thirty miles from a settlement. Lazell finally, getting a little out of patience, sarcastically insisted upon our taking a crutch, in case any one should lose a leg. Six weeks later, when my unfortunate friend, after cooling off too suddenly from a twelve-mile walk on a hot day, found himself unable to use one leg, and hence was deprived of his turn at the distant best pool, we turned back the laugh by suggesting the crutch which we had failed to bring. The only desirable thing we did forget was a box of Bermuda onions. These could not be procured in Canada, and were ordered thither from Boston by telegraph. They only reached us ten days after our arrival upon the stream; and if a tippler longs for his drams as we did for the onions, after a diet of fish and salt meats, we pity him.

To one about to make a trip to Canada East, we would say: Start in all cases from New York, even though you live in Boston. Take express trains direct from New York to Montreal without change, and then the Grand Trunk Railway or night steamer to Quebec. We started twice from Boston, going once by Portland and the Grand Trunk, and once by the Passumpsic Railroad. One can on these routes endure waiting from six or seven P.M. until ten P.M., and then, after two hours' additional travel, waiting from midnight until three A.M. at Newport, Richmond, or Island Pond; and at Richmond being crammed in a small room packed with French-Canadian laborers who never heard of a bath—I say one *can*, but he doesn't wish a second experience of the same sort. The Frenchman's remark, that all roads are good which lead to victory, didn't console us when we arrived in Quebec on time.

A day in the quiet, quaint old city of Quebec is not without pleasure and profit. One goes away feeling that, after all, heavy taxes with progress and improvement are not such objectionable things. The quiet of Quebec is broken but once each day—upon the departure of the steamer for Montreal.

In Quebec, salmon-anglers get their supplies usually from Waters of John Street, Upper City, who from long experience needs only to be told the size of your party, the time of your stay, and approximately, the limit as to expense. When you go aboard your steamer, everything will be found there admirably packed, with not an article, wanting,—not even extra corks for stopping opened and partially used bottles,—and the genial old countryman himself, with bill of lading in hand, awaiting your coming to wish you good-bye and alore of sport and salmon.

Tuesday, the last day of June, 1874, at two o'clock P.M. we set sail in the "Secret," formerly the fastest of the Southern blockade runners.

We were due in Gaspé Basin at four A.M. Thursday, but were delayed by storm, and did not arrive off the Cliffs until one P.M. for quite a distance before reaching Gaspé Head, which is at the immediate entrance of the Bay, we sailed past long lines of small boats anchored at intervals of a few hundred feet. Into these boats we could see with a glass the cod-fish pulled at rapid rates.

The last few miles of sea-coast is a rugged, nearly perpendicular cliff, in some places over eight hundred feet in height, and resembling somewhat the Dover Cliffs, but more remarkable in appearance. As we turned Gaspé Head, the sun shone out warm and bright, the water became more quiet, and our lady passengers were able to get on deck, and to enjoy themselves for the first time since leaving Quebec.

So well had our kind friend Reynolds arranged matters, that all our men, with horses for taking us with our luggage up the stream, were awaiting us at the wharf.

We delayed a little to receive the honest welcomes of a score or more of the inhabitants, who, having learned that friends of Mr. Curtis had arrived, lost no time in paying their respects. Our friend Curtis has a way of going around the world, dispensing favors right and left, and but few prominent persons in Gaspé had not at some time received the much coveted permit for a day's fishing, accompanied with flies and leaders, or something else equally desired. We were now to reap the rewards of his thoughtfulness about little matters.

One can be made uncomfortable by a thousand little annoyances, and he will be, if in any way he gets the ill-will of the people near his stream. If he acquires a reputation for bargaining and paying small prices for services rendered, he had better at once give up his stream and seek another as far from it as possible. Accompanied with the honest hand-shake of some of the hardy fishermen was their assurance that they should as usual expect all our worn-out flies and frayed leaders upon our return from the river, and also any spare fish we thought not worth sending home. Their universal "so long" in place of good-bye amused us not a little, but why they use it or whence it is derived we could not conjecture.

Half a mile from the landing we stopped upon high ground near the residence of Mr. Holt (then our efficient Consul at Gaspé), to enjoy our surroundings.

At our feet was the Bay, by common consent scarcely less beautiful than the Bay of Naples, which it resembles when seen from a certain point. In the hazy distance was the indistinct line of the Gaspé Cliffs, and our steamer rapidly making her way to the Gulf. The sun lighted up most beautifully the intense green of the forests, which were broken here and there by neat white cottages and their surrounding patches of still brighter green. Although the very last of June, the foliage was not yet burned by the summer's sun, and the grass was but just greening.

Six miles from the settlement the road became a mere path, and we took to our saddles, which the thoughtful George had stowed in our two-horse wagon. Two miles farther and we were at the first pool of the river called the High Bank Pool. We determined at once to try it and throw our virgin fly for salmon. Setting up our rods, we scrambled down the steep gravel bank with the enthusiasm of school-boys. Insects of various sorts were there long before us, and soon we were compelled to send Coffin up the bank for our veils. The veils used are of the thinnest silk *barége*, in form of a bolster-case open at both ends, which are gathered upon rubber cords. One cord goes around the hat-crown and the other around the neck under the collar. These veils perfectly protect the face from insects, but do not allow smoking, and interfere slightly with the vision; I therefore discarded them, and now use a brown linen hood with cape buttoning under the chin. The pests were so persistent that we were glad to put on linen mitts, which tie around the elbow and leave only the finger-tips exposed. Finally, the little brutes drove us to anointing our finger-tips with tar and sweet-oil, a bottle of which usually hangs by a cord from a button of the angler's coat. A philosophical friend once insisted that it only required the exercise of strong will to endure the pests, and that protection was effeminate. The second day, he looked much the worse for wear, his handsome face disfigured with swellings, and his eyes almost closed from the poison of the bites.

We now worked away in comparative comfort until I saw Lazell, who was a few hundred feet distant, suddenly dash off his hat and commence slapping his head with both hands as if determined to beat out his brains. I concluded that he must have had a rise, and that, contrary to his custom, he had become excited. Going to him, I found that the black flies, baffled at all other points, had found the ventilating eyelet-hole upon each side of his hat-crown, and had poured in through them in hordes upon the top of his unprotected head. Getting no rise, I climbed up the bank to await my more persevering friend. (It may be noted, in passing, that we learned a few days later that we had not cast within several hundred feet of that part of this pool where salmon usually lie.) Soon my friend's head appeared over the bank with apparently a good stout stick thrust completely through it, hat and all, as if some stray Micmac had shot him with a roughly made arrow. The solution of this was that Lazell had plugged up the holes in his hat with a broken rod, and thus cut off the flies from their favorite foraging grounds.

It is a fact not generally known that the farther north you go, the larger and more venomous are the mosquitoes, according to the late lamented Captain Hall, of Arctic fame, one knows little of the annoyance of these insects who has not been in Greenland during the summer months. After a summer upon the Gaspé streams, a person of even large inquisitiveness doesn't long for any more information upon that branch of natural history. They are so troublesome there that, to fish comfortably, it is necessary to protect the face and neck, and cover the finger-tips with a mixture of tar, sweet-oil, and pennyroyal. Gaspé insects seem fond of newcomers, and our blood afforded them a favorite tipple. Seriously, however, we were not much inconvenienced, as we took every known precaution against them, and not only had our rooms thoroughly smoked with smudges, but kept large smoldering fires around the houses the greater part of the time. When ladies fish, a smudge is kept burning upon a flat stone in the canoe.

We reached our comfortable quarters at House No. 1 at nine P.M. while it was still light. We found that our house was clapboarded, and contained two comfortable rooms; one with berths like a steamer's, which were furnished with hair mattresses and mosquito-bars; the other served as sitting and dining room. A large log house adjoined and was furnished with a good cooking stove, while a tent was already pitched to serve as quarters for our men—five in number. Stoves and furniture are permanent fixtures of the houses at the different stations, as are the heavier cooking-utensils, so that in moving up the stream one has merely to carry crockery, provisions, blankets, and mosquito-bars,—which latter are of strong thin jute canvas. Above the first house, the men make your beds of piles of little twigs of the fragrant fir-balsam, whose beauties have been recorded by every writer upon angling. Near each house is a snow-house, dug into the hill-side and thickly covered with fir-boughs and planks. The snow is packed in them in winter by the men who go up for that purpose and to hunt the caribou that frequent the hills adjoining the river. The snow lasts through the season, and is more convenient than ice. If one drinks champagne, he has but to open a basket upon his arrival and imbed the bottles in the snow, and he has at any moment a *frappe* equal to Delmonico's best. The fish as soon as killed are packed in the snow, as are the butter, milk, and eggs when brought up every two or three days by the courier, who remains at the Basin ready to start for you at any moment that letters or telegrams arrive. Our courier delighted in surprises for us such as baskets of native strawberries and cream for our dessert. Ten cents at Gaspé buys quite a large basket of this exquisitely flavored wild berry.

I have been thus minute in describing our surroundings, because I believe more comfortable and complete arrangements are found on no other stream. It is all very well to camp out under an open, "lean-to" or tent, and exceedingly healthful and enjoyable, but we rather enjoyed this comfortable way of living. Standing for six hours or more daily, while throwing a fly or killing a fish, is hard work for one of sedentary habits, and gives enough exercise and oxygen to make one wish for good living and quarters; and with this open-air life one may indulge his appetite with impunity if he can get the food, for his digestion and assimilation are at their best.

The difference between the temperature at midday and midnight in the mountainous regions along the Gaspé salmon-streams is notable. One day last season, the air at nine A.M. was 74°, at two P.M. 84°, and at half-past seven P.M. 51°. We were anxious to get approximately the temperature of the water of these northern streams to compare with the water of streams farther south, which had been stocked with young salmon by Professor Baird, United States Fish Commissioner, and so made the best observations possible with a couple of ordinary thermometers. At the bottom of one pool in the York, near the mouth of the Mississippi Creek, which is a roaring little branch of the York coming down from the snow of the neighboring mountains, the water at midday was but 40° Fahrenheit, while the air was 78°. In other pools on this river we found the temperature at noon to be 44° at the bottom and 44° at the surface, with the air at 60°. This was well up among the mountains, thirty-five miles above the mouth of the river. Lower down the stream, 48° bottom, 48° surface; and sometimes after a very warm day, 47° to 48° at eight o'clock P.M. Ten or fifteen miles distant, upon the Dartmouth, which flows through a less mountainous country and has longer and more quiet pools and less shaded banks, we found the pools varying from 55° to 59° when the air was 60° to 70°.

Upon the first morning of our arrival, we *did not* get up at three A.M., when the day was just dawning, and order up our men to get breakfast. We had been in northern latitudes before, and took the precaution to hang our rubber overcoats over the windows to darken them, thus keeping out the early morning light and securing a long night's sleep. Our first day opened with a drizzling rain which forbade fishing. After coming a thousand miles, and with but six days' "permit" upon our stream, a rainy day seemed like a misfortune.

About ten o'clock, the sun came out, and I went to the pool directly in front of the house, to practice casting with both hands as well as get used to standing in a cranky canoe. Soon a fish rose and hooked himself, only making it known by spinning off a few feet of line as he dropped back to position at bottom of pool. A fish will thus hook himself nine times in ten of the fly comes slowly over him with a taut or at least straight line behind it. More fish are lost by too quick striking them than by other bad management. The steel-like tip of the rod upon the slightest pull at the fly springs forcibly back and fixes the hook at once. I had resolutely determined never to strike, and have never done so. I may have lost a fish by it, but am sure more would have been lost by striking. Of course, a strong, quick pull is given after the fish is hooked and has started the reel in order to imbed the hook more firmly. Soon my reel was furiously whirling. I had read about the "music of the reel" and all that sort of thing *ad nauseam*, as I had often expressed it, but somehow, after hearing a salmon in his first fierce run upon that reel with a stiff click, the wonder was that people had not written more about it.

One cannot afford entirely to ignore book teaching. Having read and re-read every standard author on salmon-angling, my rod-tip was at once, and without thought, lowered when this lively little fellow made his first leap in the air, and showed the beautiful silver of his sides. It was done just as the fingers strike the proper key upon a musical instrument, when the player's mind is too far away perhaps to name the tune he has unconsciously run into. Of course, if you do not lower your rod-tip the fish, falling upon a taut line, will break himself loose. This fish showed no disposition to leave the pool for the rapids below, but went first to one side, and then to the other, sweeping around by the farther shore, and jumping clean from the water each time he turned. It was impossible to keep below him, so rapidly did he change place. In spite of all the strain which be safely put upon him, he would now and then get a hundred feet below the rod and rest there in comparative ease, with the force of the current balancing my strain upon him in an opposite direction. When you can keep abreast of your fish, or a little below him, the current, weight of line, and your strain of two or three pounds all in the same direction will soon tire him out.

Most anglers greatly miscalculate the force exerted by the rod, and will speak of using many pounds' strain. An actual test with a spring balance upon various rods showed that rarely is a strain of three pounds put upon the fish, and, in fact, few rods can raise a pound weight at the end of a line.

As my fish became tired and slowly passed the gaffer, he tried to gaff and missed. This goaded the fish to more desperate running and plunging in the direction of a projecting tree-trunk lying upon the water. If he could have reached it, he would have run under and then jumped back over it, leaving the line fast while he broke himself free. Soon his runs were shorter and his jumps less frequent, and finally, from very weakness, he would turn upon his side. I swung him gently toward the gaffer, who in his eagerness had waded nearly waist-deep into the pool. In an instant the fish was struggling at the end of the cruel gaff, making hard work for the brawny arms, and in a moment more he was laid upon the shore, where old William Patterson gave him the *coup de grâce* with a stout short stick carried for that purpose in every canoe. Just at the moment of gaffing many fish are lost; for if more strain is exerted than usual, the hook breaks out of the well-worn hole in the jaw, and if the strain is relaxed a moment before the gaff is in, the line lets the hook drop out of the enlarged opening.

My trip and trouble had not been in vain, as my first salmon had been hooked and played to gaff without the slightest assistance. Before putting him in the snow, I lighted my pipe and sat quietly to admire and talk to him. It seemed wonderful that the little thread of silk-worm gut could have conquered so brave a fish.

Finding but few fish in the lower pools, we broke camp on Monday, and set out for House No. 2, at what is called the Big Salmon Hole. The men assured us that it would be impossible to pole the canoes with ourselves and provisions over the shoal rapids, and that in several places they would have to unload and make a "carry." In order, then, to favor our men, Mr. Lazell and I set out to walk the distance, with the cook to show the way and carry our tackle. We could risk the wetting of our extra clothing and provisions, but not care to have our rods floated down the stream, in case of an overturn. Of itself, a twelve-mile walk is not objectionable, but when one must climb over a dozen fallen trees at every hundred yards, it becomes monotonous. Six miles from camp we to the North Fork, a roaring brook of perhaps eighteen inches in depth. Lazell, with his wading-boots, stalked triumphantly across, while the cook and I went down a quarter of a mile to cross upon a tree which, some years ago, had fallen and formed a natural bridge. There was no path along this wind-swept gorge, and trees were piled upon trees, making many windfalls to be gotten over. At the end of a long half hour we came back to where Lazell was awaiting us. Could we have met the man who said there was a "pleasure in the pathless woods," he would have fared badly. The truth was that the dead-wood of the bridge had broken under our weight, and we were wetter than if we had waded the branch. Often upon this trip we touched, with our rod-cases or gaff, the partridges which unconcernedly flew up and lighted on the lower branches of the trees. We reached the pool, and killed a fish before the canoes arrived. The next morning, Annette, Lazell's gaffer, came tumbling down from a tree where he had been sent to point out where the salmon were lying, and ran to the house yelling as if crazy, "Mr. Lazell has got his first fish, and he's a whopper!" Sure enough he had on a fish, and it commenced sulking at once. He had lighted his pipe and taken his seat just where one of Mr. Reynolds's friends, in 1873, took his breakfast while holding his sulking fish with one hand. Having gone to the pool with my light bamboo, to which he was unaccustomed, he was unprepared for heavy fighting, as he felt insecure and had a dread of breaking it.

Now and then, by rapping on the metal butt of the rod with a stone, the vibrations of the line would start the fish into making a short run and lazy jump. The men all put the fish at thirty-five pounds, and more than a pound or two out of the way. Soon the fish began quietly working for the deepest part of the pool, and in spite of all the strain my friend was willing to put on him, finally got there under the edge of a sharp ledge. The salmon commenced sawing upon the line whenever a strain was brought to bear, and this necessitated giving line at once. After working for one hour and forty minutes, the leader parted.

Without a word, Lazell took his own greenheart rod, and in a few minutes was busily casting at the very upper end of the pool, above where he had hooked the first fish. As good fortune would have it, he soon hooked a large one which came down the pool and tried the same game, but he managed to stop him and slowly swing him away from the center of the pool each time. Quite soon the fish ran and jumped enough to weaken himself, and was brought up to the gaffer. This was my friend's first salmon, and it weighed thirty-three pounds.

The skill of our men in gaffing struck us as remarkable, for during the season they missed for us but a single fish. Not the same romance attaches to them as to Indians, and they do not present that statuesque appearance while gaffing, but they are a thousand times more reliable, and always know better where the fish lie, and how quickest to aid you to circumvent and kill them. The Gaspé men can give even the best of anglers a valuable hint occasionally which it is quite safe to follow, as it often saves a fish. They come from that good old stock, Scotch-English, and are as true as steel. Money and jewelry were safer in our camps than at home in the way of our servants. They never touch a drop of liquor, and work faithfully from morning till night. Even after long and tedious hours of poling up rapid streams, under a hot sun, they are ready to anticipate your slightest wish. All the men ask for, beside fish, is pork, hard bread, sugar, and black tea. Without the latter they are good for nothing. They make the tea in the tea-kettle itself, and drink several large tincupfuls at a sitting. Following this by a five minutes' pull at a pipeful of navy plug tobacco, they are ready for work.

In favorable seasons, the Big Salmon Hole of the York is good for two or three fish daily; and as Lazell was unable to walk by reason of cooling too rapidly after our twelve-mile walk, it seemed best to leave to him the exclusive use of this and the other pools near House No. 2. On Wednesday, therefore, I set out for the Narrows, near which are the last and best pools of the river, leaving two men to come with the canoe and luggage, and taking one with me. We arrived before noon, and, after lunch, carefully inspected the pools. By crawling quietly to the edge of low cliffs, or climbing trees, we could count the fish by scores, lying quietly behind small stones or just at the edge of the current, with heads upstream. At first, one unaccustomed to it only sees large numbers of dark, smooth stones, as he expresses it; but soon a little wavy motion of the lower end of the object is seen, and you find that they are all salmon, only the dark backs being visible as you look down upon them. They rest in these pools for several days, to gain strength for leaping the falls just above. Often one hundred and fifty have been counted in the lower or long pool at the Narrows, and frequently not more than a single one will take the fly.

The matter of taking a fly seems to be one of sheer sport. It is a well established fact that salmon eat nothing during the several months they remain in the rivers. Before entering the Gaspé streams they gorge themselves with capelin, a small fish resembling our smelt. Quite often fish which we killed at the lowest pools had undigested parts of capelin in their stomachs. As their digestion is known to be very rapid, this indicates a high rate of speed against a swift current up fierce rapids and over falls. A bit of dried leaf seems to amuse them as much as an artificial fly. Dropping a leaf quietly off a tree into a pool, we could see a salmon rise and take it, and after getting to the bottom open his mouth and let it float up to the surface again, when other fish would take it, one after the other, apparently enjoying the sport like kittens at play. So distinctly could we see the salmon that we easily traced the scars of the nets, which are found on large numbers. Many we take have an eye entirely blinded from the wound made by the twine. At one time, just under the upper falls, I was for some fifteen minutes so near a salmon that I could have touched him with the end of my rod. The water was shallow and clear, and gave a good opportunity of closely watching the king of fishes as he majestically sailed around, probably wondering whether he would succeed in his leap over the falls. Dozens of his fellows were coming up at intervals to look at the falls, but not one could be tempted to take the slightest notice of any fly in our books, although we were out of their sight and threw our flies within a few inches of their noses.

We had with us rods, reels, gaffs, and, unfortunately, a new and untested package of leaders. The run of the first fish hooked parted a leader. A second leader shared the same fate; and a third was taken by a salmon who determined to leave the pool and go down the rapids below. Testing our leaders with the spring balance, we broke them at a pound or pound and a half strain, although they had previously received a thorough soaking. We were in a bad predicament; salmon everywhere; pools full of them, and seeming eager to rise, and no suitable leaders with which to take them. We made the best of it, and with what patience we could, awaited the canoe with our large fly-books containing new gut. From this we afterward tied leaders which stood a strain of five pounds, and were soon engaged in trying to overcome a strong, lively fish.

Presently our head man sung out, "You must lose your fish or get a drenching." A small dark cloud came over the near mountain, traveled rapidly down the gorge, and before one of the men could bring a rubber coat from the house, a few hundred yards distant, the rain was pouring upon us. The rapidity with which heavy showers follow down the gorges and course of the streams at Gaspé is somewhat startling to a new-comer. Of course, the fish must at all hazards be killed; and, of course, this particular fish was not in half the hurry to come in out of the water that we were, but tried our patience in many ways, sometimes taking us in the canoe where we couldn't wade, and sometimes through quite deep water where we did not wish to take the canoe and disturb the pool. It was thirty-five minutes before faithful old William had him quiet at the bottom of the canoe. He, as well as all our men, preferred to get us into a canoe before gaffing, when practicable, for they then felt much more sure of the fish. The Gaspé-built canoes are very long, and if the angler passes one of the men and steps to the extreme end, he can with perfect ease swing the fish to the gaffer at the other end, always taking great care not to reel in his line beyond its junction with the leader. If he does this and the gaffer misses, or the tired fish gets up life enough for a short spurt, then the knot sticks in the tip ring, and good-bye to fish and tip. It is with some reluctance that we differ with so good an authority as Norris, in his "American Anglers' Book," but we prefer canoe gaffing. We were all thoroughly soaked with rain, and I was additionally uncomfortable from having gone over the tops of my rubber wading stockings in water, which at two P.M. was only 42° Fahrenheit. As there were but three hours more of this the last day of our permit, we could not afford to lose a moment. As soon as the sun came out, I hooked a second fish, and worked away busily until in the three pools I had killed five, when I stopped, wearied as well as satisfied with salmon-fishing, resisting our man's most urgent entreaties to "kill another, and make it a half dozen." I have never made a large score or killed a very large fish, but this work of three hours and a half was quite satisfactory, and is here given:

1	Fish	of	22	lbs.,	Fairy	Fly.	
1	"	"	22	"	"	"	
1	"	"	24	"	Jock	Scott	Fly.
1	"	"	21½	"	Silver	Doctor	Fly.
1	"	"	23	"	Silver	Gray	Fly.
—			—				
5			112½. Average, 22½ lbs.				

The healthful excitement as well as open air exercise enabled without ill effects to endure this three and a half hours' wetting.

At half-past four A.M. next day, the canoe went down with the fish, and I walked to Middle House, where I found Lazell in good spirits over one thirty-three pound fish and other smaller ones. Hastily packing, we set out in our canoes for House No. 1, where we took in additional fish and luggage. Running down the rapids between sharp rocks, both out of the water and under its surface, where all your safety depends upon the accuracy of your men's knowledge, their nerve, and the strength of rather slender spruce setting-poles, is quite exciting to a novice. At the word "check her" from old William at the stern, young James throws his entire weight suddenly upon his pole in the bow. Several times the pole broke, and necessitated quick work in dropping the pieces and grasping a second one, which is always kept within reach in running rapids. Upon breaking a second one, in all likelihood we would have got an extremely unlucky dipping.

We reached Gaspé the same day, having made thirty-five miles since half-past four A.M., and were in time to have our fish packed in snow and forwarded by the afternoon steamer for Quebec. For transportation, the fish are first "drawn" through the gills, then filled with snow and packed two in a box. The snow is then rammed solid around them until it resembles in consistency a cake of ice, and the box is placed inside of 2 much larger ones. The space between the two boxes is now filled with sawdust. At Quebec, the boxes are examined and refilled, if necessary, before forwarding by rail. Our fish left Gaspé Thursday, were in Boston in good condition the Tuesday following, and were served at the Somerset Club just a week after they were killed. With ice in place of snow, the packing is usually a failure.

Finding a letter at Gaspé inviting us to fish the Dartmouth, we went over to that river on July 10th, taking horses to a place called by the habitants Lancy Cozzens, which we presumed to be a corruption of *L'anse aux cousins*. From this point we proceeded by an invention of our own. One of the three canoes had a small sail, and holding another canoe by our hands upon each side of it, we voyaged very independently until we tried to tack under a very stiff breeze—a performance which didn't take place exactly to suit us. Reaching the narrower part of the stream, we took our setting-poles in orthodox fashion, and soon reached camp, where we found a commodious wall-tent ready pitched, and all needed cooking-utensils, as well as a salmon for supper, left in the house by some departing friends.

The sea-trout had just commenced running up the river, and gave us most serious annoyance. The sea-trout is anadromous, and follows up the salmon some weeks later. An old trout-angler believes you not quite sane, and much less serious and truthful, when you positively assure him that oftentimes before you can reach a salmon you must play to gaff a half dozen or more sea-trout, varying in weight from one to five pounds. That a five-pound trout can be an annoyance, and a serious one at that, isn't readily comprehended. You can't hurry a large trout, but must play and tire him out. Occasionally your man from a tree-top will tell you just where a fine salmon is lying, and, perhaps, that he started for the fly and missed it at your last cast. The next cast, a sea-trout, which is quicker than a salmon, snatches your fly the moment it strikes the water, and in the next few minutes flounders all over the pool, putting an effectual stop to salmon-fishing. Now is the time for self-control—for quietly lighting a cigar and strolling back to camp. Sometimes an irascible angler seizes the trout the moment he is off the hook and hurls him vindictively against the cliff.

This same abused sea-trout, however, when broiled before the tire in an open wire broiler, with a bit of salt pork clamped upon him, or rolled in buttered and wetted papers, and roasted under the embers, is preferable to salmon, and is more often eaten by the Gaspé anglers. The sea-trout and the common brook-trout, *Salmo fontinalis*, are taken side by side in the same pools; and so great is the apparent dissimilarity, that it seems impossible that they are one and the same species, the sea-trout merely being changed by his trip to sea, as some naturalists assert. The spots on the brook-trout are much more clearly defined, and have the light color upon their edges, while the markings of the sea-trout seem not to be distinct spots so much as irregular markings akin to those of the mackerel. This is as it appears to us who are not naturalists.

It is notable that although the three Gaspé rivers flow into the same bay, and for long distances within a few miles of each other, yet the fish are so different as to be readily distinguished one from another by the natives. The fish run up earliest in the York, and those taken even in the lowest pools are of larger size than those of the other streams. Of course, those that are strong enough to get to the upper pools early in the season before the river has run down are extremely large. The last runs of fish in the York are perhaps a trifle smaller than the general average of the St. John, where the early and late runs are of more nearly the same average size. So the fish of the Tay, in Scotland, are a month earlier than those of the Tweed, and presumably in this case because the snow gets out of the former much the sooner. The fish of the St. John are slightly shorter and fuller than those of the York, resembling more nearly the *Salmo quinnat* of California. A few seasons since, the St. John was so jammed with the logs of a broken-up lumber raft that the fish were blocked out of it, and that year its peculiar fish were taken in the York. The next year, the St. John was clear, and its fish went back to it. A few seasons later grilse and young salmon were taken in the York which slightly resembled the St. John fish. The parent fish returned to their own stream. Their offspring, which were hatched in the York, remained in that river.

On the Dartmouth, the extreme northern of the three rivers, the so-called nightingales are singing continually, commencing at three A.M., at the first gray of the morning. These birds are probably a kind of sparrow, and by no means true nightingales; but so sad and sweet were their plaintive notes, that by a sort of fascination we would lie awake to listen, at the expense of some hours of needed sleep. During two seasons upon the other two rivers, only a few miles distant, not one was heard. After some practice in imitating them, we thought the following musical notation gave a very good idea of the song, which varied slightly with different birds, and at different times with the same bird. Between each double bar is a single song. Numbers 1 and 2 are different songs of one bird, and Numbers 3 and 4 are songs of another bird.

The terms of lease of a Canada salmon-stream require the lesser to maintain a guardian upon the river at his own expense. A comfortable log-house of a single room is usually built just below first pools, and the guardian occupies it during the few months of angling and spawning season. This expense is quite light, sometimes only a hundred dollars in gold. In addition, the Government appoints and pays overseers, who are assigned to special districts and are expected rigidly to enforce the law regulating the net fishing in the tidal part of the rivers, and particularly to see that the nets taken up over Sunday. The Gaspé rivers flow through so wild and inaccessible a country that it is impossible for poachers to reach the pools and carry away fish in large quantities except in canoes, which must pass the guardian's house.

If the Government would offer a bounty for every sheldrake killed, it would greatly aid in keeping the streams better stocked. In the stomach of a young sheldrake will be found sometimes six or more parr, as the young of salmon are called. When we consider the numbers of broods raised each year on a stream, and that both young and old are gormandizing parr all day long, we see that thousands upon thousands of fish are yearly lost in this way alone: These little parr, by the way, often bite at the fly, which is so large for them that they can only grasp some of its feathers, and hang on so well that you throw them several yards as you withdraw to make a fresh cast. The finger-marks or bars identify them at a glance.

One evening, while on the Dartmouth, we were surprised by a visit from the guardian and the overseer, who came to dine and spend the night with us. They bragged a little of a big fish the overseer had captured in an unaccountably short time. Upon examining the tackle, we found that the line practically ended at the reel, where it joined a worthless cord, and that even this apology for a line had not been wetted. The rod was a shaky affair that couldn't possibly kill a lively five-pound trout. The hook was covered thickly with rust. In their canoe we found a fish of over thirty pounds. One eye was covered with an opaque substance which had grown over it on the line of an old net scar. The other eye had across it a recent cut, which had totally destroyed its sight. The fish was then totally blind, and in all likelihood had broken out of a net a few nights before. These cunning jokers had made a sharp and well-defined cut in the jaw where fish are usually hooked, and they had gaffed him as he lay unable to see the approach of the canoe. We were glad that they had thus saved the fish from a lingering death, sooner or later, by starvation; but raising a blind fish to a fly, and killing him with a rickety bait rod and worthless line, was too much for our credulity. We never informed them that we had seen through their little fish-story, and presume that they had many a laugh at having made "States" men believe that blind salmon could be taken with a fly.

Wednesday, July 15th, found the usually quiet and sleepy little settlement of Gaspé in great commotion. Some people were out on the house-tops with spy-glasses, and others rushing down to the wharf, where a goodly number had already collected. Going to the upper rooms of the Gaspé Hotel, to which we had just come from the Dartmouth, we saw a beautiful yacht coming rapidly up the Basin under full sail. Soon she was abreast the wharf, giving all a view of her exquisite proportions, and, passing slowly up where the York merges itself in the waters of the Bay, grace-fully swung into position and dropped anchor. She was the "Palmer," well known in both this country and Europe for victory over the "Cambria," and famous as well for being the winner of numerous other races. Soon we received a call from her owner, Mr. Rutherfurd Stuyvesant, who was to have the York the rest of the season. A little later we met the rest of his party, and were invited to pass the evening on board the yacht. The ladies braved a ten days' voyage from New York, and part of it in rough weather, off what sailors call the " nastiest of coasts," and were to brave the mosqui-toes and black flies as well,—hoping to rival the Countess Dufferin, who had a few weeks before thrown a fly, hooked and played to gaff a large fish upon the St. John.

We returned home by the "Secret," leisurely stopping at various points, as our fancy dictated. While at a certain place, the steamer touched with the mail, and was to remain two hours. Could the mail be opened at once, and we receive our letters, we might wish to hurry on by that very steamer. We therefore brought all our bear upon the obdurate postmaster, to induce him to open the small pouch with mail for his office, and give us our letters at once while the steamer was still at the landing. His constant reply was: "It cawnt be done. Government business cawnt be hurried. The mail is too lawge, too lawge."

When the steamer arrived, he was the first to board her. He chatted consequen-tially with the officers for more than an hour. They were all on our side, and tried apparently to shake him off. Finally, with the little pouch (which he wouldn't entrust to his clerk on our side) under his arm, he slowly and with the firm, determined tread of a militia captain on training-day, moved off toward the post-office. Fifteen minutes would have sufficed to distribute the mail; but not until the steamer's last whistle blew did he put the letters into the boxes. He reckoned without his host, however; for a friend was quietly watching, and in an instant took our letters and started for the steamer at full run, yelling at the top of his voice. Good old Captain Davison just then remembered that he had forgotten something, and took time enough with the steamer's agent to enable us to glance hastily over our letters, and ascertain that we could go by that steamer.

In 1874, Mr. Curtis exchanged his old river, the St. John, for the Dartmouth, in order that the former might be set aside for the Governor General. Earl Dufferin having been called to England in the summer of 1875, it fell to Mr. Curtis's lot to have the use of both streams, and I accompanied him for a few weeks' recreation.

To reach our stream from Gaspé, we were obliged to take ourselves and all our luggage across the swollen York by repeated trips in a small dug-out, at a place some six miles from its mouth. After crossing, our provisions and luggage were taken in large boxes mounted upon stout timber sled-runners, this being the only conveyance that would stand a nine-mile trip over a slightly widened forest trail. We took saddle-horses, but yet found the trip most tedious by reason of the "windfalls" which had to be cut away by our canoe-men, who carried axes for the purpose, and by the swamp mud through which we frequently had to wade our horses.

The fishing of 1875 was comparatively a failure, less than twenty being killed by three of us during a week on the St. John. A friend of mine, Douglass, one day hooked an ugly fish, which played him all known pranks, and seemed, in addition, to extemporize a few for the occasion. The fish leaped out of water enough to make it exciting, but not enough to tire himself out. He tried pulling constantly backward and forward in quick, short jerks, which is the worst thing a fish ever does. This makes the coolest angler nervous and anxious, for unless line is upon the instant given, the hook is pulled out, or the gut broken. The fish came down in view of the house, when, comparing the pluck and strategy of the fish with the skill of our friend, we counted the fish a trifle ahead. Of course, when near either bank, the men took care to keep on the shore side of the fish, so that when he suddenly rushed for deep water he would not pass under the canoe and break loose. In spite, however, of all precautions, the fish made a dash to run under, and one of the men gave a quick, powerful push on his setting-pole, which unfortunately rested upon a flat, slippery rock. The next instant our view was cut off by an immense pair of caribou hide boots, which seemed suspended in mid-air. The fish was just at the canoe, and the greenheart was taking the last possible ounce of strain. The line could not run out fast enough to relieve the rod, and we awaited its snapping. Equal to the emergency, Douglass, remembering an old trick of Curtis's, threw the rod behind him, and with reel end in the water and the tip ring resting on the edge of the canoe, the line ran safely and swiftly out. Douglass then tired and killed his fish, which weighed fifteen pounds— about the average of the St. John fish.

The non-angling reader by this time surmises that the only way to bring a salmon to the gaff is to tire him, by keeping a constant steady strain upon him, with the shortest practicable line. The greatest dexterity and skill of the angler and his men are required to keep the canoe always in such a relation to the fish as to make this possible. Half your score depends upon the quickness of the men, who must, if you are on shore, be so near you with the canoe that if the fish starts down a rapid, they can take you in upon the instant, and follow him. How patiently would our faithful fellows sit on the crossbar of the canoe, and only now and then, when the flies and mosquitoes were unusually troublesome, break silence with "I don't care if I do take a little o' yer *fly-ile*."

To give the general reader an idea of the way in which anglers make up their scores for distribution among their friends, we give an old one, which still stands among the best made in America:

F. Curtis's Score of Salmon-Fishing, York River, Lower Canada, for one evening and the following day, 1871.

TWO HOURS, THURSDAY EVENING, JULY 6.

1 Fish, 18 pounds weight . . . fly, Jock Scott.
1 Fish, 22 pounds weight . . . fly, Robin.
1 Fish, 25 pounds weight . . . fly, Robin.
1 Fish, 26 pounds weight . . . fly, Silver Doctor.
1 Fish, 34 pounds weight . . . fly, Curtis.
1 Fish, 32 pounds weight . . . fly, Curtis.
1 Fish, 26 pounds weight . . . fly, Curtis.
1 Fish, 31 pounds weight . . . fly, Robin.
1 Fish, 17 pounds weight . . . fly, Robin.
1 Fish, 22 pounds weight . . . fly, Robin.
1 Fish, 24 pounds weight . . . fly, Silver Doctor.
1 Fish, 23 pounds weight . . . fly, Robin.
1 Fish, 26 pounds weight . . . fly, Robin.

Total weight for both days, 326 pounds. Thursday's average, 22¾ pounds. Friday's average, 26⅙ pounds each, and gross weight 235 pounds. Whole average, 25 1/13 pounds.

Sunday is the only day in camp when all are sure to be at home for an early dinner and in condition to enjoy and appreciate a good one. On week-days, the cook, who never leaves camp, does not serve dinner until half-past seven, so as to give all time to return from the pools, which are often a few miles distant. If one gets a sulking fish late in the afternoon, he may be detained until long after the dinner-hour, and it is by no means a very rare occurrence to have a fish gaffed by the light of a birch-bark torch.

Canada fishing-laws forbid throwing a fly Saturday evening after six o'clock, but of course must allow killing a fish previously hooked. On Sunday, all are somewhat rested, and appetites are always keener after the day's rest which follows excessively hard work out-of-doors.

On Sunday, July 4th, 1875, Mr. Reynolds sent word that with three friends he would come over and take dinner with us on our glorious Fourth. As his name is a synonym for hospitality, we were quite anxious to show no shortcomings ourselves in that direction. Our six men and the cook were assisted by Curtis himself, who undertook the unheard-of thing of making a loaf of cake on a salmon-stream. How he succeeded is best told by his own letter to his sister, who had given him the cake recipe:

"I used every available dish in camp—spilled the flour all over my clothes and the floor, and then rubbed it well in with butter, of which latter I melted one mess too much and the other too little. Took a vote, and found a majority of one for stirring it with the sun. Think, after all, I stirred it the wrong way; and certainly put in too much egg-shell to make it settle well for all the plums, currants, citron, etc., nearly settled through the bottom of the small wash-bowl in which I baked it, while some large lumps of sugar failed to get crushed at all. The cake was, however, quite passable. To be sure, I forgot to butter the dish, and had to dig the cake out in small pieces and glue them together; but that was a mere trifle, and my success was greater than could be reasonably expected from so *doughty* a matter. The cow which I had driven up from the settlement and put in our old and now unused snow-house, *so as to keep her*, came to grief by breaking her leg on her way down the steep rocky river-bank to get water."

Our admirable courier came up from the Basin early in the morning with a clean pocket-handkerchief full of lettuce leaves, the size of a silver dollar, which he had procured from the minister's wife, who had raised under a cold frame the only lettuce in the settlement. Coffin complained bitterly of the imposition of the lobster-dealer, who, learning that his purchase was for "States" men, charged him ten cents each for lobsters of about five pounds weight, while he sold them commonly to the packer opposite Gaspé for fifty cents a hundred, large and small as they run. So plentiful are lobsters around Gaspé Basin that a few moments suffice to get a basketful hooked up with a peculiar sort of gaff made expressly for the purpose.

A heavy shower overtook our friend, between the two rivers. They had, in honor of the special occasion of a Fourth of July dinner with their American friends, dressed themselves in gorgeous apparel of white flannel. What with the rain which had soaked them and beautifully distributed the usual face dressing of tar and sweet oil over large geographical surfaces, the stains of tree-drippings and the wadings through the marsh at the end of the lake, they presented a sorry appearance. Nothing could induce them to remain and dine in such plight, and so after a little rest and a modest lunch of crackers they left us. Our bill of fare, which in accordance with camp custom we had had written on bark, was quite elaborate.

Thursday, we received from our friend Reynolds a kind invitation to occupy the York River for a week. Curtis and I accepted, Douglass going off by steamer to take a fortnight upon the Matapediac. We packed luggage in long rubber army-bags, and slung them across the back of an apology for a horse sent up from Gaspé, and went directly over the mountains to House No. 1, where we found canoes and extra men awaiting us, and then pushed directly for the Narrows.

In lifting one of our canoes over a slight fall, we swung her around and half filled her with water, soaking our blankets, boxes of bread and crackers, as well as sweetening the men's tea with brown sugar *en masse*.

Just below the Narrows canoes cannot be used, but the fishing must be done while standing and wading in from one to two and a half feet of water. Rubber wading-stockings are worn, with very large canvas shoes over them, the soles studded with soft metal nails to prevent slipping upon the rocks. In a moment of excitement, while following a fish, one frequently gets in over the tops of his stockings, and the subsequent carrying of a few gallons of water in these, for-the-time rubber-bottles is neither comfortable nor easy. Curtis improves upon the stockings by a pair of boots and trowsers, such as are used by the Baptist clergy, and which permit wading above the waist. Another of his improvements is a vertically adjustable piano-stool arrangement in his canoe, which, while voyaging, lets one down near the bottom to keep the center of gravity low and prevent capsizing, and which when casting can be turned up for a high seat. This, of course, is only to be used as last indicated when one is lame or very much inclined to laziness.

At the pools, some distance below the Narrows, are found numbers of fallen trees, projecting nearly at right angles to the low riverbanks. These trees are the occasion, to nearly all anglers, of the loss of a few fish. Poling rapidly under them, while intent upon a running fish, they find their elevated rod within a few inches of the obstruction. On the instant, the rod is thrown forward, and this gives slack line to the fish and enables him to free himself. A second and too late thought tells him, what every one of course knows, that a line from a given point before him on the water to the top of his rod, when held upright, is precisely the same as from the same given point to the top of his rod when it is dropped horizontally in the same vertical plane. Nine times out of ten an inexperienced angler forgets this, and does not quickly throw his rod to the center of the river, and thus preserve his rod and keep a uniform strain upon his fish.

The old log-house at the Narrows is replete with pleasant reminiscences. On the pine doors, cupboards, and window-casings are scores and sketches illustrating amusing incidents of life upon a salmon-stream. Sadly we note the names of one or two who, alas! can never gladden us again with their presence.

Higgs's well-known copy of Bagster's first edition of "Izaak Walton" is bound in wood from the door of Cotton's fishing-house, *"taken off by Mr. Higgs, near the lock, where he was sure Old Izaak must have touched it."* Following out somewhere this conceit, we made our sketches and notes upon the soft bark of some of the old birches that overlooked our quarters.

Empty Baskets Change the Tune

ALEXANDER MACKIE

The good March Brown in April, May,
Your labor sweet will better pay,
But when the pink wild roses blow
Or heather blooms, 'tis time to show
The blue-nosed worm.

"The thing's amiss," some critics sneer;
"'Tis dirty work and torture sheer,"
Yet empty baskets change their tune,
And they discard, in leafy June,
The fly, for worm.

Two Old Trout of the Pools,
and the Little Dry-Fly that
Finally Accomplished Their Ruin

EMLYN GILL

The author's early experiences with the floating fly were neither fruitful nor encouraging; but he fully realizes that this lack of success was entirely his own fault, and was due both to a lack of knowledge of dry-fly methods and to an insufficiently aroused interest in them. One day several years ago he saw in a tackle shop some flies different from any in his fly-books, and having been told that they were the English floating flies, laid in a small stock of them, while the tackle-dealer briefly explained how they were used. Afterward these flies were taken on several trips, but were unthought of and unused. One day he met an angler who had used the dry-fly method of fishing and who seemed to be enthusiastic about it. The author made up his mind that he would try the floating fly at the very next opportunity that presented itself. But it must be remembered that he had been a confirmed wet fly fisherman for more than thirty years, and while he had advanced in the wet fly art so far as to use only a single small fly, and leaders fully as fine as those made for dry-fly angling, yet when he reached a stream it was natural for him to think of the lures that had been his companions since boyhood and not to attempt to branch out into new fields.

But one May day, four or five years ago, when on a week's end fishing trip, he was driven to a point verging upon exasperation by a large trout which persisted in rising leisurely from a hole beside an old stump in a pool that had been a favorite of the author's for several years. When its first rise was seen the angler placed over it one of his most attractive wet flies with a feeling of confidence that the trout could not resist it. But resist it he did, not only on the first cast, but on succeeding casts. Then the pool was rested, and another favorite fly was tried with the same result. The trout was still rising occasionally, but paid no attention to the artificial lure; once it arose just as the imitation touched the water and within a few inches of it, apparently entirely unconcerned about the wiles of the angler attempting to lure it to destruction. Again the pool was rested and the trout soon attacked with another pattern. It happened that this was not the first day that the same tactics had been tried both by the writer and his friends, and this particular trout had gained a well-deserved reputation. To make the matter worse, the author, in a fit of vainglorious boasting, had made arrangements at the inn that morning to have this fish cooked for his dinner that very evening.

Finally, having reached a point bordering upon total discouragement, the angler sat down to take a rest and to think things over. In a few minutes there was a "plop," and another big swirl by the stump. The trout was still doing business at the same old stand, but the angler had apparently closed up shop and ceased to take interesting the affairs going on about him.

But in a moment he sat erect, with the appearance of a man who had solved a great and weighty problem. An idea had suddenly flashed through his mind! A tiny japanned vest-pocket eyed-fly box lay open before him, and he was gazing intently at its long neglected contents. There were within this box little whirling duns, Wickham's fancies, Jenny spinners, black gnats and coachmen—all beautifully tied English floating flies. He selected a whirling dun, which has ever since been one of his favorite lures. It was carefully knotted to the filmy leader, and a moment after the next rise of the fish it was floating in the centre of the swirl with wings erect. Then something took place that had not happened before in this spot that season, so far as records showed; the old trout had sucked in the little dun, apparently without the slightest suspicion that it was not a natural insect, and the hook was firmly imbedded in its mouth.

This should have been a lesson to me, but I must confess that it was not. True, I often thought of this episode and admitted that the dry-fly on that occasion had saved the day; furthermore, I listened more attentively when anglers spoke of the floating lure; but the microbe of enthusiasm had not as yet reached its mark.

The following spring I went to the same stream and fully intended to give the dry-fly a thorough try-out. But when the opening day of the season dawned, the morning after my arrival, the habits of a lifetime had full possession of me, and the dry-flies were forgotten. This was in the middle of April. After returning from this trip, there came a feeling of regret that I had not spent at least a part of the time fishing with the floating lure, and so I hurried back to the stream early in May, fully intending that this trip should be devoted exclusively to practice with the dry-fly. The results were neither good nor bad; the fishing seemed to be poor that week, and I used the wet fly and dry-fly alternately, fortune favoring one about as much as the other. I performed one surprising feat, however, with the floating fly that I have always attributed to amazing good luck rather than to particularly good management. It was well known to local and visiting anglers that a large trout occupied an almost impregnable position in the upper part of a long pool above a dam, and it had been considered impossible to reach it with any known lure, without giving it previous warning of danger. It could not be cast for from below, and rocks and bushes made it impossible to assail it from either side; while above, a barrier of rocks was made higher by an old pine tree that had fallen across the stream. Many anglers had schemed to take this trout, but none had succeeded in making even a good attempt at doing so. To make a long story short, I cast a fly from above the fallen pine tree and over it, without even seeing the water in which the fish lay. The floating fly was so cast that it must have drifted down over the trout; in an instant I either heard, or imagined that I heard the "plop" of a rising fish, and we were at once engaged in a struggle, neither of us in sight of the other. How it was possible from that position to "play" this trout to a standstill without getting hopelessly tangled I did not know; but in a short time it showed signs of weakening, and I laid my rod on the top of the barrier formed by the rocks and the pine tree, clambered over as fast as I could, picked up the rod again, and the fish was soon in the net.

By this time I had begun to be somewhat accustomed to the use of the dry-fly, but still lacked the confidence in myself necessary to handle it to the best advantage. The following winter I most fortunately came across Mr. Halford's early books and read them greedily. The naturalness of dry-fly methods as described by him was absolutely convincing, and I became enthusiastic over what I then began to consider the most artistic and beautiful of all methods of angling. Afterward I had the great good fortune to meet some of our dry-fly experts, and now feel competent to go upon the streams alone and at least *learn* new things about this delightful art.

The incidents related have been written so much with the idea of entertaining the reader, as with the hope that they will point a moral to the beginner with dry-fly, with the result that he will start in at once to *master* dry-fly fishing instead drifting along aimlessly until a chance happening compels him to realize the desirability of becoming a skillful dry-fly angler.

At first, if an angler has been a wet fly fisherman all his life, the dry-fly and the methods of its use may seem somewhat strange to him when he takes them up; in other words, he is apt to lack that confidence in himself and the dry-fly that he has when casting the wet fly, to the handling of which he has become thoroughly accustomed. Many are wont to imagine, at first, that there is something more difficult about dry-fly angling than fishing with the sunken lure. This, I think, is not so when one has acquired the knack of it. It may be possible for a bungling fisherman to meet with success in some wilderness waters, or at times in streams nearer civilization when they are high and discolored. But to be a finished wet fly angler one must possess as much skill as the dry-fly fisherman. Nothing but experience can teach a man where the trout lie in the streams; if one starts right, and is shown how, it is comparatively easy to cast a fly skillfully. There are no insurmountable obstacles in the way of becoming a successful dry-fly angler that do not confront the user of the sunken fly.

But *give the dry-fly a chance*; one without previous practice cannot go upon a stream for one day, and meeting with no success rightfully condemn the dry-fly, as has been done the past year by several friends and acquaintances of the author. How many times have not one but many anglers spent an entire week fishing with wet flies on some well-known trout stream, without taking altogether more than a few small fish? My advice to the beginner with the dry-fly is to go ahead and *make* a success of it, without being discouraged by real or fancied obstacles. The first rise to the imitation insect, as it floats down the stream in plain sight of the angler, will give the beginner a thrill he has seldom had when he has felt the tug of a trout taking the sunken fly. The dry-fly game is *worth while*, and no one should hesitate to make any efforts necessary to overcome what may appear to him to be difficulties in the way of becoming an accomplished dry-fly fisherman.

The author is intensely interested in seeing the use of the dry-fly spread in America for several reasons, of which the principal one is, perhaps, that it will give a greatly added pleasure to our anglers. It is a delicate and artistic method of taking trout, and I have found almost without exception that dry-fly experts have such a great love of the game, that a heavy creel at the end of the day is not the principal consideratum. In these days of depleted streams it is most necessary that the doctrine should be spread broadcast that the one pleasure of trout fishing, apart from the joy of being close to nature, is the matching of one's wits against the cunning of the trout. He alone deserves the title of sportsman who returns carefully to the water all trout that he does not need for food; as soon as the fish is taken into the net, all the sport to be had with that particular fish is over, and when killed and put into the creel it has become simply *meat*.

I apprehend that one of the discouragements with which the dry-fly beginner is liable to meet for some time to come will be improper tackle, foisted upon him, unintentionally, perhaps, by dealers who themselves are not familiar with the flies and leaders used by dry-fly experts, and who think that they have made their best efforts to secure a supply of proper tackle. Some friends have complained that dry-flies used by them last season could not be made to float; while I have heard certain dealers recommend leaders almost strong enough for salmon fishing, and yet they did it without intent to deceive. Therefore, whenever he can do so, it will be advisable for the beginner to consult some expert dry-fly angler before purchasing tackle, especially flies and leaders. If the enthusiasm over this method of fishing becomes general among fly-fishermen, as it now bids fair to do, it will be only a short time before all our best tackle dealers have a full and proper equipment of dry-fly necessities.

The Big Trout of the Hog-Back

O. W. SMITH

How a fisherman loves his favorite streams! There is no love like a first love, after all. Many years ago—I don't care to remember how many—I first fished for trout in the Pine River, Waushara County, Wisconsin, and since then I have visited that stream every year with one exception—that year was lost. Now, when the birds are nesting, I long to worship at the shrine of the Red Gods. I smell the smoke of the camp-fire; I hear the entrancing murmur of the musical Pine and the splash of the leaping trout; I see the foam-flecked pool at the foot of the Dane's Meadow, and so well acquainted am I with it that I almost feel as though I could cast a fly blindfolded. When the Red Gods thus call in the springtime it is hard to remain at desk or counter. This getting acquainted with a stream is an advantage; for you learn every fall, current and hole, and can cast almost without looking. Then, too, some big fish—usually THE big fish—gets away and you dream all winter long that he is waiting for you at the foot of the rapid or beneath the great cedar log where he broke away—waiting just for you! Why he is waiting for you, why some other fellow may not have caught him, you can't explain, but you believe he is waiting for you—now, don't you? Of course there are certain advantages in fishing a new stream: you see new country and solve new problems, but there is nothing quite like fishing the old stream. It's the first love; it's getting back home again—that's what it is.

I first visited the West Branch of Wolf River up in Shawano County, Wisconsin, on the 21st day of May, '03, and twice during the year 1904 I made that long, weary journey; then I said I'd go no more, but when the 15th of April, 1905, rolled around and the bud began to swell, while the yellow-throats shouted, Wichety! witchey! wichety! from every willow copse I found myself longingly looking north-westward, while I listened for something—the music of Hemlock Falls. We experienced no trouble in making up a party. The man the Game Warden filled the place admirably; the Butcher was to have made a 4th but at the last moment business gripped him and we three were compelled to go on alone. To my mind three is not an ideal party—two one-sided like a jug handle. Neither do I like a large party; to my mind, even four are too many. Of course with four you can fish two and two, but when you have an odd number you have—well, an odd man. I think two the ideal party. A small tent, a few supplies, good fishing and a congenial companion—what more can mortal want here below?

Our first camp was on a little creek some 6 or 8 miles northwest of Cecil. I find by referring to my notes that we did not reach the creek until after sundown and the lateness of the hour compelled a hasty camp—therefore, an uncomfortable one. I, for one, was glad to get up. The night was very cold and as soon as it was light enough to get about I built a fire and soon three shivering figures were huddled about it. A heavy frost lay white and cold upon the ground and the little creek was frozen over, as I found when I went to get water for coffee. O! but that coffee was good!

"Say, Parson!" said the Merchant as he scraped up a handful of frost with which to cool his coffee, "you said we'd have nice warm weather, but if that's not frost, dum me if it ain't frozen dew!" "Blamed if I don't believe it's snow," grumbled the Game Warden in turn. "No, it's not snow," I replied, "for it was too cold to snow; if you don't believe me, just go down and look at the hole I chopped in the ice when I got the water." "You don't mean that the creek was frozen over?" exclaimed the Game Warden; "well, if that is so, it accounts for my cold feet." "Hope they didn't get cold clean through," remarked the Merchant, "for if they did we'll have frosts until July." "And you can sell some more of your all cotton woolsocks," retorted the Game Warden. "Yes, on time," returned the Merchant. O! but they were good men, those two fellows; the frost did not affect their spirits in the least but seemed to have a contrary effect.

We did not linger long after breakfast but were soon upon the road and bowling along between giant red pine (wrongly called Norway pine), whose smooth reddish trunks marked with pike-like reticulations towered from 80 to 120 ft. above us. If I were a poet I would sing the praises of the red pine as Longfellow did of the Hemlock—so immaculate, sturdy and independent, I know no tree possessing more character. Reaching Keshena, we tarried only long enough to replenish our larder;

then on, over sand beaten hard by much rain. From Keshena Falls, where we crossed the Wolf River, on we were continually crossing little trout streams—streams fragrant with precious memories—and I must have tired the boys with my stories of the large trout I caught in bygone years and the larger ones that got away. Just let me mention three of those clear, purling brooks: Oshkosh, Stockbridge, Chickininny. Now can't you hear them laugh as the red and gold trout leap and splash and play? If Shakespeare had known the music of Indian names he never would have caused a character to ask "What's in a name?"

Taking two trout fresh from the water—one from the West Branch and the other from the Chickininny—the observer would find it hard to believe that they were of the same species. The fish from the first-named stream is short and chunky, its back is a greenish black with prominent vermiculations, the belly is a bright orange red, while the red spots upon the side are prominent. The fish is a typical Eastern brook trout as described by Jordan and Everman. The fish from the latter stream is long and slim, of a silvery, washed out color, with no prominent markings; often the red spots are entirely absent. The West Branch fish is more active as becomes so clipper-built a body—leaping clear from the water time after time in its efforts to reach the fly and upon occasion taking it in mid-air. Indeed, the fish seems to delight in acrobatic feats and leaps just for the fun of the thing. Now the fish of the Chickininny are logy, lack gusto and enthusiasm, will come to the landing net almost without protest. When one remembers that the two streams are not more than 10 miles apart and both empty into the same stream the wonder grows. I have caught a few dark trout in the West Branch but I have never taken a light fish from the Chickininny and the Indians told me that they were not to be found in the stream. Commend me to the clipper-built fighter of the West Branch every time.

We reached our old camp-ground just above Hemlock Falls at 12:30 and after a hasty lunch set about building a permanent camp, for we were to remain until the last of the week. Hemlock browse was cut and laid "just so" to form our bed. A stone fire-place was built with crane all complete. Fire-wood enough to last the week was cut. A dining table was built and a tarpaulin which we carried for that purpose stretched above it. At 4 o'clock all was completed and we shouldered our rods and set out to get enough fish for supper; it did not take us long and we were back at the tent before dark with a pan of dressed fish just the right size for frying. Fish, potatoes, bread and butter and coffee made a meal to remember. I will not soon forget that night around the campfire. The little glade in which our tents were pitched up was surrounded upon all sides by tall hemlocks, which reached up and up until they seemed to touch the stars, forming a splendid background for the flashing firelight. It was pleasant to lie wrapped in my fur coat, listening to the Game Warden's yarns; for he has had interesting experiences and a few close shaves, and the Merchant could spin good yarns, for in his younger days he had been a log-driver and a noted one too; then when the conversation would flag I would tell of my adventures with the Sioux Indians, for once in my life I was a missionary among them. So that evening and others passed in pleasant conversation.

The next day I suggested to the Merchant that we visit the Hog-back—a locally famous spot some 3 miles down the river of which the Indians had often told me but which I had never visited. He was nothing loath, for anything in the way of a new experience is always welcome to him; so we set out, following a trail which Nolan, an aged Indian friend, told me led to the Hog-back. The Merchant led off, setting a stiffish pace, and I soon tumbled to his game; he was trying to wind me, but daily walks of 4 and 5 miles had rendered my leg muscles like iron and I was not worried; when I noticed the perspiration standing out on his neck I suggested that he walk a little faster and he let out another notch, though it required an effort to do so. When we reached the Hog-back he was steaming but game, and never squealed, though he has never led off since. The Hog-back is one of the strangest rock formations it has ever been my good fortune to behold. Let the Reader imagine a dam, with rounded top 10 ft. high and 5 rods long, carved out of solid granite with one end broken down, through which water rushes with great force and noise and he will have a mental picture of the Hog-back. The photograph was taken from the south bank, therefore the ledge is in the distance and appears smaller than it really is. Let the Reader remember that it is about a rod from the Merchant to the end of the ledge and about 4 rods from the end of the ledge to the further shore. The rock upon which the Merchant is standing bears witness to the fact that at one time the dam was complete. What an upheaval there must have been when Mother Earth built that great dam! What could have been the cause? How long ago was it built? Nolan, my Indian friend, told me that the river men had destroyed the beauty of the place and I can well believe it. What must it have been like before dynamite destroyed the south end? One glance at the picture is enough to convince a trout fisher that a large trout had its home in the hole just below the rock. A trout *did*, and in as few words as possible I will tell you the story of his capture.

I reached the Hog-back alone, the Merchant having stopped to fish a likely looking hole a few rods above, where the trail hits the river. Experience has taught me that the deepest hole is a little below the fall and that the proper way to reach it is if possible to cast from above the fall—not into the moil of water but upon the comparatively quiet water farther down. So, just above the rock on which the Merchant is standing in the picture, I paused and examined my tackle, finding everything O.K. I sent my fly, a Royal Coachman, out on the wings of the wind. It was a good place for a cast and it was a good cast. For an instant my line hung in the air—a graceful curve; then quickly changed to a double curve or letter S; then straightened out and the fly poised light as thistle down above the foam-pitted water, as though in doubt whether to descend or to fly on in mid-air forever, but, feeling the restraining line, it settled upon the water. at once without any preliminary skirmishing as is so often the case, a great pair of jaws opened and my fly disappeared—without any fuss or furor but calmly, dispassionately, inevitably as Fate. I had caught a glimpse of the great head and wide open jaws and waited with beating heart for the rush, but to my surprise it did not come. The seconds, hour long in duration, dragged by, and nothing was doing. There was something uncanny about the whole proceeding. When it was impossible to wait another second, I began to reel in slowly, and the fish—an inert dead-weight followed. I never experienced anything just like it and I began to think that I would land my quarry without a struggle. But when the fish reached the boiling water below the rock it awoke from its sleep, trance, bewilderment or whatever it was, and did things a-plenty. The way it dashed about that little rock-bound pool more than made up for its former inertness. I could only say in helpless impotence, as did the Dutchman the other day when his team ran away: "You son-vun-guns vent den." In my eagerness to do something I stepped out upon a wet rock, slipped and went into the water, which fortunately was only shoulder-deep but O! so cold! When I say that ice and snow yet remained in unexposed-places, the reader can imagine how cold that water was. Striking outside the swiftest current, I was able to keep my feet, but the trout spied my legs as it rushed by in one of its great circles and promptly dashed between them, over the Hog-back, up into the quiet water above; happily the line did not foul and my reel was soon madly shrieking as the rushing fish ate up the reserve line. As quickly as possible I passed the rod between my legs and faced about, pressing my burning thumb upon the madly flying spool, and when the reader remembers that my hands were beneath the water he will see that I was seriously handicapped. I shouted for the Merchant, but the hemlock and cedar threw back my shout with mocking laughter. Would no one come? Suddenly a shadow darkened the water and I looked shoreward, to see the grinning face of my Indian friend Nolan. Talk about angels! As though finding a man in ice-cold water was an ordinary thing, he asked imperturbably, "What do in there? Water blame cold yet." "Big fish going up there!" I chattered—"stop him!" a gleam of intelligence shot across his swarthy face, while the lust of battle lighted his eye and he sped away up the bank in a manner to belie his 70 odd summers, while I waded to the shore, my reel still spinning and the reserve line diminishing rapidly as the spool grew smaller. When Nolan got above the trout he promptly jumped into the water, which was waist-deep, and by dint of splashing turned the trout, and I breathed once more. At this juncture the Merchant appeared upon the bank, and, seeing the Indian in the water, shouted, "Here! you old fool! you'll catch your death of cold!" "Fool yourself," returned Nolan, "blame big trout on Parson's line—go and help land!" realizing that something extraordinary was taking place, the Merchant dropped his rod and came to my aid, but the battle was about over and the trout easily brought to net. Shivering, chattering, Nolan and I shook hands, while the Merchant built a fire. "Nolan," said I, "you take the trout, for without you it would have got away." "No, no," he replied, "you take um home to squaw and papoose." "Parson," said the Merchant, as we stood about the welcome fire, "you are the confoundedest fellow to get into scrapes when you go fishing that I ever knew. Do you remember the fight at Hemlock Falls?" as though I ever could forget! I experienced no ill effects from my wetting and have had many a hearty laugh over the battle at the Hog-back.

I might tell you of each day's adventures and I flatter myself that they would prove interesting, but space forbids. Thursday night, our last night on the stream, was warm and before morning we experienced a thunderstorm—the first of the season; it was impossible to sleep; the vivid lightning played among the hemlock tops, while heavy thunder boomed and crashed. As I lay awake watching the fiery serpents crawling about upon the canvas roof, I found myself repeating:

"You sulfurous and thought-executing fires—
Vaunt couriers to oak-cleaving thunderbolts!—
Singe my white head! And thou, all-shaking thunder, Strike flat the thick rotundity o'
the world!
Rumble thy—"

But just then a great hand was clapped over my mouth and I perforce kept silent.

The next morning we were early on the road; for we planned to spend one night on the Chickininny and have a try at the red-bellied trout. We reached the stream a little after noon, set up our tent and got everything ready for the night; then we went fishing. We fished the stream carefully, yet not a fish did we get. At 5 o'clock we were back at the tent—wet, hungry and disgusted, but after a hearty supper of bacon and eggs we felt better and held a consultation. As it was necessary that I reach home the next day, I suggested that we start out and drive all night; the other boys were nothing loath, so at 6 we started. At Keshena we refilled our lantern and made ready for the long journey. While our rig stood in front of the store there was a muttering of distant thunder in the west. "Do you hear that, boys?" said the store-keeper. "You'd better put out your team and stay with me, for we're going to have a wild night—black too—for there is no moon and you'll miss your way among the trails on the east end of the Reservation." But the lust of travel was upon us and we bade him a gay Goodby, jumped into our rig and drove out of town. It *was* a black night, and it *did* rain all night long, and we *did* have trouble keeping the road. At midnight we stopped on the shores of Mud Lake, to feed our horses and make coffee; we had trouble when we attempted to start a fire, but when the coffee was made how good it tasted. What a picture we must have made, standing about the little fire in the dense woods, while the rain pelted us unmercifully. Well, it was disagreeable, but one of the pleasantest things to look back upon; for the disagreeable is pleasant in perspective. We reached home the next day, tired and sleepy, but satisfied with our trip and I more than satisfied with the battle at the Hog-back.

The Finest Trout in the World

HARRY PLUNKET-GREENE

It might naturally be supposed that if one had the fishing of a trout-stream like the Bourne one would not leave an inch of it unexplored, but it was a fact that up to this time none of the rods had ever taken the trouble to investigate the top quarter-mile of the water. Savage and Sharkey had somehow got it into their heads that there was nothing worth troubling about above the "lagoon" immediately beyond the viaduct, and as they lived close to the top of the fishing, all the rest of us, myself included, had tacitly accepted this as a matter of fact. Nowadays the whole of this region is a vast watercress bed, and anyone looking out of the window of the train, when passing over the viaduct, would never realize that there was, or ever had been, a river there at all; but in those days there were two streams above, as well as below, the bridge, meeting a little way up and stretching as one, for a quarter of a mile to the end of the fishing.

We had all of us come on occasions as far as the hatch below this final stretch, but, in the belief that the water above was a blank, had always turned back when we got there.

On August 31st of this year, the last day of the season, I found myself at this hatch at about six o'clock in the evening. I had got four fish averaging 1½ lbs., but it had been a bad rising day, cold and windy. At six o'clock it suddenly turned warm and calm, and I was sitting on the hatch smoking a pipe before going home, when I thought that, just for fun, I would walk up to the end of the water. I expected nothing, and had half a mind to leave my rod behind and saunter up with my hands in my pockets. I got over the fence and rolled up on to the bank unconcernedly, and, as I did so, from one weed-patch after another there darted oft a series of two-pounders racing upstream like motor-boats. I dropped like a stone, but the damage was done. I just sat there cursing the day I was born and myself, not only for having lost the chance of a lifetime—for the iron-blues were beginning to come down back—but for having left this gold-mine undiscovered and untouched for two years—and to-day was the last day of the season! If there had been any handy way discovered of kicking oneself physically as well as mentally I should have been unrecognizable when I got home. Every fish was under the weeds long ago, and I might just as well pack up my traps and clear out.

There was an old broken-down footbridge about a hundred yards above me, and I thought that I would go up to it and explore the reach beyond, more with a view to the possibilities of next year than with any hope for present. I got down from the bank and circled round through the meadow. I got to it, and was just picking my way across its rotten planks when under my very feet I saw a small nose appear, followed by a diminutive head and the most enormous shoulder I ever remember to have seen in a chalk stream. I froze stiff where I stood, except that my knees were shaking like aspens, for there right underneath me was gradually emerging the fish of my life. I do not mean to say that I have not caught bigger fish before and since, but this was a ver-itable star in the dust-heap, a Cinderella stealing out of the kitchen that we all despised, and the romance of the thing put him (*pace* Cinderella) on a pedestal of fame from which I have never taken him down.

It was agonizing work, for he swam up in the most leisurely way at a rate of about an inch in every five seconds, while I was straddled across two wooden planks, either of which might have given way at any moment, and had to pretend that I was part of the landscape. He was immediately under me when he first showed up and I could easily have touched him with my foot. What fish will see and what they will not see will ever remain a mystery! It was then about half-past six (old time), the time of day when one's visibility is most clear, and yet he took not the smallest notice of me. He just strolled up the middle of the stream contentedly as though he were having a smoke after dinner. I can still feel my joints creaking as I sank slowly to my knees and got my line out. It fell just right and he took no more notice of it than of a water-rat, I tried again and again, lengthening the cast as he moved up, and at last he rose towards it, examined it carefully and, horror of horrors!, swam slowly after it down-stream through the bridge under my feet! It would have been laughable if it had not been so tragic. There was I pulling in the slack like a madman, and leaving it in wisps round my knees, scared lest he should see my hand move; and he passed me by without a word and disappeared into the bowels of the bridge.

I just knelt there and swore, trying to look over my shoulder to see if he had gone down below. There was no sign of him, and the situation was painful in the extreme, for my knees were working through the rotten woodwork, and if I tried to ease myself I should either bring the bridge down with a crash or anyway evict Cinderella for good and all.

I bore it as long as I could, and was just going to give it up and scramble out anyhow, when I saw that nose slide out again beneath me, and my old friend started off on his journey up-stream once more.

I began on him with a shorter line this time, and he took the fly at the very first cast like a lamb. If he was a lamb as he took it he was a lion when he had it. Instead of running up-stream, as I hoped and expected he would do, he gave one swish with his tail and bolted down through the bridge, bending the rod double and dragging the point right under. It was done with such lightning speed I had no time to remonstrate. I threw myself flat on my stomach and got the rod sideways over the bridge, and then the fight began. I was on one side of the bridge, and he was half-way to Southampton on the other. He got farther and farther downstream, going from one patch of weeds to the next, and digging and burrowing his nose into the middle of it, while I just hung on, helpless, waiting for the end. He quieted down after a bit, and finding that he could not rub the annoying thing out of his nose on the south side he determined to explore the north, and he began to swim up towards me. I must have been a ridiculous sight, spread-eagled on the rotting planks with splinters digging into my legs and ants and spiders crawling down my neck, vainly endeavoring to hold the rod over the side with one hand, to wind in the line with the other, and to watch him over my shoulder all at the same time. Fortunately, I must have been invisible from below, but the moment he got under the bridge he saw the rod and tore past me up-stream with the reel screaming. But now we were on even terms and there was a clear stretch of water ahead, and I was able to play him to a finish. I was really proud of that fight, for, in addition to the cramped style which I was compelled to adopt, it took place in a stream ten feet wide, half-choked with weeds, and I got him on a 000 Ironblue at the end of a 4x point. He weighed 3½ lbs. when I got him home, and I have always bitterly regretted that I did not get him set up, for, with the exception of an 1½-pounder in the hall of Longford Castle, caught in the Avon by one of the family on a "local lure" (the name of which neither fork nor spade would dig from me), he was the most beautiful river-trout in shape, color and proportion I ever saw.

Winter Angling

FRANK S. PINCKNEY

The best winter angling is to be had in that charming interval between the hallowed old holidays and that sloppy period which, of late years, heralds the slow approach of spring in these our latitudes.

The practice of angling at this season of the year for large trout, immense black bass and preternatural mascalonge, has grown of late to proportions which seem to warrant some special mention of so delightful, if unseasonable, a sport, as well as some description of the tackle and paraphernalia required for its enjoyment.

For the winter angler a first-class outfit is of prime importance. The poles should be of well-seasoned hickory or hard maple, from eight to ten inches in diameter, in sections about three feet in length. These need not to be divested of their rich covering of curved, bronzed and lichened bark, but should be fitted, fresh from the sheltered pile, with careful skill into an old-fashioned open fire-place, about which, in years agone, the angling forefathers of the angler of to-day told marvellous tales of deeds of "derring do" with "dipseys," bobs and poles; and about which now *his* children list with wonder, not unmingled with some tinge of incredulity, to his yet more wondrous recitals of brave contests and curious captures with dainty rods and delicate reels.

The winter angler's wading shoes may be made of any soft material that will protect his feet should they chance to slip from the old brass fender down upon the sombre painted brick hearth below, during some delicious drowse. Most anglers have lady friends—fair cousins and others, who make them nicely with substantially embroidered lily-pads and firm strong rosebuds and vigorous elastic daffadowndillys. These are a good protection—but the soles?

Two dollars and a half, without hob nails, and no deduction for small feet! Even winter angling has its drawbacks.

The winter angler's fishing coat should be warmly quilted to protect him from the cold, and may be of a color to suit his complexion if he has one. It should be given him by his wife or "ladye faire" as a sample of her skill in manipulating the needle and—the dressmaker.

As to the kind of lure required, much must depend upon taste of the individual angler, but it certainly ought to be hot and not have *too* much water in it.

For protection against black flies, midges and mosquitoes he may, if he likes, smear his face and hands with oils either of tar or of pennyroyal, or he may build a "smudge" on the table, but the most successful winter anglers I know use for this purpose a hollow tube of convenient length with a bowl at one end and a set of teeth, either real or artificial, at the other. The bowl may be filled with any harmless weed capable of *burning* slowly as, for example, tobacco. As a rule, one of these will answer the purpose, but if the flies are especially troublesome, or the angler should chance to be bald-headed, he may be forced to ask a brother angler to come to his assistance with a contrivance of a similar nature. Together they will probably be able to defy all attacks of the black flies or even the blues.

As to creels (or baskets) the merest mention will suffice. At the nearest newspaper office will be found one of suitable size and fair proportions. It is called a "waste basket" and is specially constructed to hold the abnormal catches made by winter anglers.

Possibly the highest charm of winter angling (or as some call it, "Fireside Fishing") is the grand wide ranging freedom of it. Three vast realms are at one's command. The realm of Memory, with its myriad streams of recollection filled with the fish and fancies of the Past. The realm of Anticipation bright with golden dreams of the coming open season, and lastly the realm of Pure Lying, wherein from the deep, dark pools of his own inner turpitude the angler at each cast hooks a speckled-sided Hallucination *(Salmo Hallucionidus)*, a large-mouthed Prevarication (*Micropterus Prevaricatrix*) or a silver-gleaming Falsehood (*Salmoides Falsus*), each more huge than the other, and all "beating the record" quite out of the field.[1]

---

[1]NOTE—The writer respectfully submits this nomenclature to revision by Dr. Henshall, an unquestioned authority.

What wonderful vistas, what remotely narrowing perspectives, stretch away into the vague distances of the first two of these grand realms! How far reachingly the life-lines of anglers uncoil in both directions from the reel of time—"playing" the hoarded treasures of memory at one end, and making tournament casts into the future with the other! Are not the time-worn rodcase and the well-thumbed fly-book and note-book on his table, side by side with the last daintily tapered product of his plane, rasp and scraper—his rod, just finished for the coming summer—which, perchance for him may never come?

Is he not at once reveling in the past and dreaming of the future?

There is no sport, when known in all its branches, that is so fully an all-the-year-round delight as is angling.

Many an idle hour of the long winter evenings may be pleasingly passed by the angler in "going over" his tackle, oiling his reels, airing his lines, and re-arranging his flies, freeing them from the moth and rust that do corrupt. He is but a slovenly worshipper at the shrine of the good Saint Izaak, who casts aside his panoply after the last bout of autumn and gives no thought to it again till spring makes her annual jail-delivery of imprisoned life. Constant care of the belongings of his art, be he fly or bait fisher, is characteristic of the faithful angler, and only simple justice to the tackle maker. There is nothing sadder or more dejected-looking than a crippled rod and a neglected "kit" full of snarled lines, rusty hooks, and moth-eaten flies.

In the matter of winter angling, the fly-fisherman has a decided advantage over him who uses bait alone. The art for him has more side issues. He may, if he can, learn to tie flies or contrive and construct new-fangled fly-hooks. The effort to learn will probably ruin his temper and break up his domestic relations if he has any, but it is not for me to say that "*le jeu ne vaut pas la chandelle*." If no domestic ties trend him toward caution as yet, and he dreads none in the future, he may even venture the attempt to make his own rods.

Let me say a word here of amateur tackle-making from the standpoint of personal experience. It is agreeable—it is even fascinating, but it does not *pay*; very few have the mechanical deftness, the patience, taste, and judgment combined to really excel in any of its branches. No young man with a career to make for himself by dint of constant toil or close application to a business or profession has any right to devote to these arts the time and attention they demand if even a fair degree of skill is to be attained. For the angler of "elegant leisure" this has no weight perhaps, but he too will, as a rule, find better tackle than he can make, readily at his command at a cost so inconsiderable as to quite justify me in saying that his amateur work will not *pay*—for, if he be young, out-of-door sports will far better serve to lay up in his still developing frame the treasures of health and vitality for future use. There are those, indeed, for whom it is a proper employment of time and who are endowed with the peculiar faculties required. To such it is a charming occupation, a delightful distraction, and a choice factor in the enjoyment of the winter angler by the fireside.

Every angler ought to keep a record or diary of his angling bouts. Most anglers do so, I think. Therein should be recorded not only the weight and size of daily catch, the number saved, and the number *thrown back*, (I look back with especial pride upon my record in this direction), but also some jottings of scenes, impressions, and incidents. Reading therefrom years after at the fireside he will detect a faint perfume of old forests in the winter air, and hear again in fancy the swirl of swift waters sweeping among mossy rocks.

I take up my own, quoting from it almost at random. Note, if you please, how, in untamed words, have expressed themselves the exhilaration of the stream—the tingling of healthy blood through ample veins—the joy in nature's aspects, and the delightful sense of unrestraint that comes only of fresh air, of wholesome exercise, of angling.

"*May 20th.*—. . . The streams hereabout lack two important elements which are the charm of my favorite—kill, to *wit*, picturesqueness and the possibility of large trout—large, I mean, for our mountain brooks where still found au naturel. I went over the other day to Bright's Run. I don't know exactly where it is, and I consider it (next to Bright's disease of the kidneys) the very worst thing Bright has developed. It is a stream such as might properly empty into the Dismal Swamp, and find itself quite at home there. It is totally devoid of romantic beauty—and nearly so of trout. I never worked so hard in my life for twenty-two little ones, that put me to the blush as I put them in the basket. I was perpetually in a row with the overhanging thickets and the underlying logs, and my thoughts were a monologue of exclamation points. I would not angle in Bright's turgid waters again for all the trout the most minute analysis might discover in them.

"Yesterday I had a much more agreeable day without a seven-mile ride on a pesky buck-board. I went quite alone, up the Buckhill as far as the Fall. This is a pleasant stream full of Nature—and sawdust—with here and there a speckled trout and here and there a black snake. (By special permission of Mr. Tennyson.) There really are now and then cool little nooks which make one envy the trout; and an occasional spring dripping with a fresh *rat-tat-tat* over rocks and moss and into one's whiskey in spite of all one can do. This sort of thing is what makes a trout-stream after all. You may catch a whale in a goose-pond but it isn't angling. To me much depends upon surroundings. I like to form a picturesque part of a picturesque whole. Even when there is no audience in the gallery.

"Given, a dark glen fringed with pines that sigh and pine high up aloft—a pool whose sweep is deep, around which rocks in tiers, mossy as tombstones centuries old, bow their heads in mourning—heads crowned with weeds, and grave-mounds of mother earth, and pallid flowers, pale plants and sapless vines that struggle through shadows of a day in coma, laid in the hearse of night, without a proper permit, and I am happy. I don't know just why, but if I meet an undertaker I mean to ask him. All these deep, dark hiding spots of nature seem but so many foils to the keen sense of life and thrills of vitality that fill me. My nervous system sparkles against such somber back-grounds.

"Then, too, the Fall was lovely. Next to Niagara, the Kauterskill and Adams', this Buckhill Fall is one of the most successful, in a small way, that I know of. It might be bigger and higher and have twenty-five cents worth more water coming over it out of a dam; but for a mere casual Fall gotten up inadvertently by nature, it is very good, in an amateurish sort of a way, you know!

"There is, I believe (hang it, there always is!) a romantic legend connected with—but stay!—you already guess it. Big Buck Indian—years ago—in love with mother-in-law—commits suicide—jumps over the ledge—ever since on moonlight water the color of blood (probably tannery just above the Fall), Buck Kill, now corrupted into Buckhill. In the march of civilization the last *impedimenta* to be left by the wayside are the beautiful superstitions of ignorance.

"I am now quite alone here. A young music composer, hitherto my companion, left yesterday, so I am handcuffed to solitary confinement.

"By the way, my composer was a voluntary exile from the domestic arena. He had but recently married—to formulate it by proportions—say about a ton of mother-in-law to about an ounce of wife, and when the contest waxed fiercer than became the endurance of a sensitive nature, he packed his bag and came a-fishing. He was a capital angler—a phenomenal musician and had an appetite and digestion like one or more of the valiant trenchermen of England's merrie days, so he solaced his grief with Sonatas and buckwheat cakes in the mornings and tears and gingerbread in the evenings. He was a born genius and as beautiful as a dream, so I advised him to go home, choke his m-in-l, kiss his wife and live happily all the days of his life. I think he has gone to try the plan.

"Speaking of buckwheat cakes, you can go out here most any time and catch a nice mess running about a half a pound and *game* all the way through. No! No! I'm thinking of the trout! I mean they are light as a feather, and taste to me just as did those I had half enough of when I was a lad with my good old Presbyterian grandmother, who would not 'set' the batter on Saturday night lest it should 'work' on the Sabbath.

"Just here I wish to record an event which has happened to me while yet each detail is fresh in my memory.

"The day had been showery, yet the fishing had been very poor, so I went at sunset to try my luck in the stream near the house, where are some fair pools and a semi-occasional trout.

"The darkness had begun to gather, indeed it was so dark that I knew only by the instinct of habit where my flies fell upon the water, for I could not fairly see them. I had just made a cast by a little rock which protruded somewhat above the surface into a small pool behind, and was slowly drawing my line toward me, when I perceived a frog seated upon the rock, watching the proceedings with some apparent anxiety. Hardly had I made out his frogship in the gloaming, when pop! he went into the water. 'Kerchung!' At this instant I felt a *strike* and returned the compliment sharply, so as to set my hook well in and make sure of my trout. He was very *game*, and I was obliged to play him with a five and a half ounce rod for some time, but finally landed him in good form, only to discover that instead of a trout I had taken froggy on a black hackle fly, setting the hook firmly into the thin membrane which connects the two hind legs and just where the tail *ought* to be. This left him the fullest freedom of action and gave him so good a chance to fight me that I never suspected him of being anything less than a half-pounder. He must have jumped from the rock directly on to the fly trailing behind it and been thus hooked by my 'strike.' MEM.—This story is gospel, but better not tell it where you enjoy an exceptional reputation for veracity.

"*July 10th*. . . . Nothing has happened! Nothing ever does happen here. Delightful existence, free from events! I remember hearing Homer Martin once say that it was the height of his artistic ambition to paint a picture without objects. The confounded objects, he said, always would get wrong and destroy his best effects. How far this was intended to be a humorous paradox and how far the suggestion of an artistic ideal, I know not, but I surely somewhere have seen a painting—from whose brush I cannot say—which quite nearly fulfilled this strange condition. It represented a horizon, where met a cloudless, moonless, starless summer sky and a waveless, almost motionless sea—these and an atmosphere. The effect was that one could perceive where the sea ceased and sky began. I wonder if it would not be thus with a life quite devoid of events—would one be able to distinguish such from Heaven?

"The charm of it is that it leaves both the physical and intellectual in one to develop freely. When a cow, grazing in a woodland pasture, comes at noonday to the brook to drink and then calmly and not without a certain ungainly majesty of movement, crosses the deep pool and climbs the steep bank on the other side, by no apparent motive urged save of her own sweet will, she always looks refreshed and filled in some sort with the stolid bovine expression of great contentment. Mark how different it all is when the same cow crosses the same brook driven by the barefooted urchin with a gad and shrill cries and a possible small dog in the background. How wearily and breathlessly she wades, and with what distressful pantings she climbs, and how unhappy and enduring and long-suffering she appears, as you watch her shuffle away down the cow-path homeward! It's the Must that hurts. It's the barefooted urchin Necessity with his infernal gad Ambition and his ugly little cur dog Want, always chasing and shouting after one, that makes it so tiresome to cross the stream.

"Then, too, as to the mind. Shall not one gain better intellectual growth when beyond the reach of the imperial ukase of daily custom which fixes the mind upon and chains the tongue to some leading event of the passing hour?

"In swift and endless succession come foul murders, robberies, revolutions, sickening disasters, nameless crimes, and all the long list of events, and are as so many manacles upon the mind.

"I hate Events. They bore me. *All except taking a pound trout.*

"Alas! what a rent these last words make in the balloon I have been inflating! Logic (another troublesome nuisance, evolved, probably, at Hunger's Point) forces me from the clouds to earth and insists that I shall accept a trite aphorism: 'Little events fill little minds; great events for big ones.'

"Then if I take refuge in the cowardly device of saying I don't want a big mind, what becomes of my theory of intellectual development as the outgrowth of an eventless life!

"I decline to follow out more in detail this or any other line of argument. One can't argue in the face of such an event as a thermometer in the nineties away up here in the mountains.

"This chance allusion to logic reminds me that I have recently heard from a dear old angling friend. He writes incidentally that since his return to his active professional duties he has made money enough to pay many times over the expenses of his recent two weeks' fishing bout with me. I have written him that he might find it well to start at once upon another trip. I have no doubt there exists a certain correlation of forces whereby a week's fishing, with its resultant increase of oxygenation, and rebuilding of gray tissue, accurately represents a certain amount of possible mental labor and thus, indirectly, a fixed sum of money.

"It is then alarming to think how abnormally rich a man might become if he fished all the time."

If I have quoted somewhat at length vaporings of others in my note book it has been only to suggest to others, whose angling experiences are and have been wider and more varied than my own, how readily they can organize a "preserve" for winter angling. Believe me, no event, no feeling, no passing observation of your surroundings can be too trivial to record, and each written line will, in years to come, suggest a page of pleasant memories when as "Nessmuk" says—

"The Winter streams are frozen

And the Nor'west winds are out."

Nothing Fishy About Trout

DAVE BARRY

There comes a time when a man must go into the wilderness and face one of Mankind's oldest, and most feared, enemies: trout.

For me, that time came recently in Idaho, where I go every summer. Many people think Idaho is nothing but potato farms, but nothing could be further from the truth: There are also beet farms.

No, seriously, Idaho is a beautiful state that offers—to quote Emerson—"nature out the bazooty." This includes many rivers and streams that allegedly teem with trout. I say "allegedly" because until recently I never saw an actual trout, teeming or otherwise. People were always pointing at the water and saying, "Look! Trout!" But I saw nothing. I wondered if these people were like that creepy little boy in the movie *The Sixth Sense* who had the supernatural ability to see trout.

Anyway, on this Idaho trip my friend Ron Ungerman—and "Ungerman" is NOT a funny name, so let's not draw undue attention to it—persuaded me to go trout fishing. We purchased fishing licenses and hired a guide named Susanne, who is German but promised us that she would not be too strict.

Susanne had me and Ron Ungerman (Ha ha!) put on rubber waders, which serve two important purposes: (1) they cause your legs to sweat; and (2) they make you look like Nerd

Boy from the Planet Dork. Then we hiked through roughly 83 miles of aromatic muck to a spot on the Wood River that literally throbbed with trout. I, of course, did not see them, but I did see a lot of blooping on the water surface, which Susanne assured us was caused by trout.

But there was a problem. To catch trout, you have to engage in "fly casting," a kind of fishing that is very challenging, and here I am using "challenging" in the sense of "idiotic." When I was a boy, I fished with a worm on a hook, and it always worked, and I will tell you why: Fish are not rocket scientists. They see a worm, and in their tiny brains they think, "Huh! This is something I have never seen before underwater! I had better eat it!"

But with "fly casting," you wade into the river and attempt to place a "fly"—a furry little hook thingy weighing slightly less than a hydrogen atom—on top of the water right where the trout are blooping. You do this by waving your fishing rod back and forth, using the following rhythm, as explained to us (I am not making this up) by Susanne: "CO-ca CO-la, CO-ca CO-la." On your third CO-la, you point your arm forward, and the "fly," in a perfect imitation of nature, lands on your head. Or some-times it forms itself into a snarl that cannot be untangled without the aid of a chain saw AND a flamethrower.

At least that's what kept happening to me and my friend Ron Ungerman. (Yes! "Ungerman!") We stood there for hours, waving our rods and going "CO-ca CO-la," but most of the time we were not getting our flies anywhere near the blooping. The trout were laughing so hard at us that they considered evolving legs so they could crawl onto land and catch their breath.

But Susanne was a good teacher, and very patient, and finally, just when I thought I would never ever catch a trout, it happened: I got a citation for not having my fishing license with me. Really. I left the license back in the car. The Idaho Fish and Game official who cited me was very polite, and so was I, because he was wearing a sidearm. I considered asking him if I could borrow it to shoot a trout, but there's probably some rule against THAT, too.

As the day wore on, our efforts—"CO-ca CO-la; CO-ca CO-la"—took on an air of desperation, because it was becoming clear that Susanne, a true professional, was NOT going to let us leave until we caught a blooping fish. So you can imagine how blooping happy we were when Ron (Ungerman) finally managed to haul in a trout. It was not a large trout. It was the length of a standard Cheeto. But it WAS a trout, dammit, and it meant we could stop.

Later, Ron and I agreed that it had been a lot of fun and we would definitely never do it again. So, to any trout reading this column I say: You are safe from us. And to the Idaho Fish and Game Department, I say: You'll never take me alive.

In Praise of Trout—And Also Me

PAUL O'NEIL

Angling for the noble trout with an artificial fly is widely defined in literature as an exercise in contentment—a process hardly less stupefying, apparently, than an overdose of goof balls. Bait fishermen consider the practice effete, like tennis as it was played by young females in 1890. Bartenders, undertakers and other sentimental kibitzers assume it denotes high purpose, since fly fishermen—ah damned fool expression!—are alleged to be purists. Fishing experts, and particularly those who write for sporting publications, make fly fishing sound like lion hunting. Experts never have a moment's doubt as to what fly pattern to use, never cast over a trout weighing less than two pounds and never fail to bring the monster to net after 1) a thrilling battle, which went on long after night fell over the clear pool, or 2) a very short tussle, really, due to the fantastic skill with which the quarry was played.

During my twenty years of fishing with a fly, each and every one of these assumptions and, definitions has caused me vague hot recurring unease and guilt—the sort of fleeting pangs a second-story man with a hangover might experience at the sound of a Salvation Army band. It seems impossible that there could he a grain of truth in any of them, but the fisherman's hand-maiden, alas, is doubt and he is often impelled to ask, "Why am I not a better man?"

The maniac who engineered my worst August afternoon—this was five years ago, but I will remember it if and when I am ninety—typifies the sort of phenomenon which occasions such self-analysis. My first response to his appearance was simple astonishment. He held a wobbling glass rod high in air and, as he lurched slowly downstream, he jiggled and jerked from ankles to head and plucked at his monofilament line—thus activating the lure tied to its end—like Billy Sunday's own bullfiddle player. The man never stopped; he must have trained for his performance as Dempsey trained for Willard or Hackenschmidt trained for Gotch.

"How ya doing?" he cried as he sloshed up, still jerking spastically, to my side. "No good," said I. "Ought to use a minnow," said he, pointing with his chin to his own line. He then shut off his engine for a moment and opened his creel. "Five," said he.

He lied. There were only three. But each beautiful trout was fifteen inches long. I felt—I cannot deny it—like an orphan child at the wading pool.

It was a moment in which it was impossible not to wonder—even though one could pick no worse time for fishing a fly than an August afternoon—whether a real expert would have been standing there, as was I, with an empty creel and an emptier expression being patronized by an inartistic and greed-riddled bait-using cretin. It was also impossible not to wonder, once the first awful shock had passed, whether I would not have reacted more charitably if I had been truly dedicated, truly sporting and pure. I was privy, after all, to fresh air, sunlight, the sight and sound of running water, the loom of green and gentle Catskill heights and the chance to speak generously to a fellow sportsman—all of the ingredients of contentment, certainly, if man ever possessed them. It did no good. I waited steaming with avarice, until the interloper vanished from view and then attached a streamer fly which imitated the minnow he seemed to have used and did my fruitless best to ape his curious style. Ninety per cent of fly fishermen, in my opinion, would have fallen prey to the same lamentable instincts (and would doubtless have failed, as did I) provided they, too, evaded observation by their peers.

It would be incorrect to say that the fly fisherman never enjoys tranquility, never appreciates nature or is incapable of high purpose—even to the point of freeing the trout he has hooked for the masses to snaffle. All are possible as long as the trout are decent enough to rise to the angler's fly in the first place. These conclusions are based, I must confess, on personal speculation, as is my conviction that fly fishermen tend to be competitive, status conscious and crafty types skilled in the low arts of gamesmanship.

I was enormously encouraged in these views, however, by a recent visit—my first—to the gambling hells of Las Vegas. I was startled out of my wits by the boiler factory din—the crash of slot machines, the cries of crap shooters, the sound of music in which I was enveloped at an hour when most people are eating breakfast. But, for all that, the unlikely scene was instantly familiar. Everyone in the big casino—from the old ladies yanking away after jackpots to the high rollers at the dice table—

betrayed that complete obliviousness of all other humans and wore that look of mingled cupidity and resignation I had seen on scores of dry-fly pools.

My own case may very well be worse than the average. I not only bear the scars of a thousand old frustrations and anticipate a thousand more but must admit, after a score of years flailing away at streams, that intolerance and prejudice have encroached on my mind as mildew does on last year's cantaloupe. I would rather catch an eight-inch trout than an eight-pound bass. I am incapable, in fact, of understanding why one wants to fish for bass in the first place—or for perch, or for muskellunge, or for pike. Ted Williams seems, at least from afar, to be an absolutely splendid fellow. What impels him to pursue the tarpon—a piscatorial slob with a cheap suit of theatrical armor and a mouth like a vacuum cleaner? Trout, *si*! , Salmon, *si*! you can make fishmeal of the rest for all of me.

I am against roads. I am against detergents. I am against insecticides. I am against logging. I am against flood control. I am not against golf, since I cannot but suspect it keeps armies of the unworthy from discovering trout, but I pity them for playing it when they could be putting a fly on the water.

I have been brought to this condition not only by the beautiful, the disconcerting, the succulent trout, but by the Catskill stream in which I have wooed it—come heat, cold, high water, low water, mud, bulldozers, the New York City Board of Water Supply and locals bent on dumping used tires and old tin cans—for lo these two decades. Esopus Creek is a famous Catskill trout stream; not so famous as its sisters, the Beaverkill and the Neversink, but famous enough, thanks in good part to the fact that fishing writers, like many other kinds of writers, tend to live in New York and to find life there far more significant than life in Colorado, Minnesota or Oregon.

The Esopus rises as a trickle of cold, clear water on the shady slopes of Slide Mountain, the Catskills' highest (4,204 feet) elevation, and ends up, after enduring many lesser indignities, in the faucets, sinks and fire hydrants of the Bronx, Manhattan, Brooklyn, Staten Island and Queens. My addiction to it, nurtured perhaps by some inner masochism, stems from this contrast between promise and fulfillment.

It is a lovely little river. It runs north, then east, then southeast in a twenty-five-mile circle around a cluster of green, ledge-scarred little mountains—Panther, Wittenberg, Terrace, Garfield, Romer, Cross, Pleasant and Cornell—before its broadening valley angles off, still into the east, to blend after another twenty-five miles with the great valley of the Hudson. Its fall is gradual and it presents, mile after mile, that orderly succession of gentle riffles, noisy, boulder-strewn rapids and long, slow pools in which both trout and fisherman are most likely to prosper. It gathers size and authority from two main tributaries as well as dozens of little hollows, cloves and kills; and these brooks—Woodland Valley Creek and Stony Clove Creek—are pleasant trout streams in their own.

The Esopus is an old American landmark. Henry Hudson paused just off the gates of its valley—as he sailed up the Hudson River—in 1609, and there were Dutch and eventually British settlements there from 1614 onward despite bloody raids by the Sopus, a collection of river Indians from whom it got its name. The centuries have left their imprint. State Highway 28 parallels it along the route of an ancient wilderness path and the roadside is littered, between stretches of farmland, with houses, motels, gas stations, stores and little summer resorts. Hamlets with dusty memories—Phoenicia, Boiceville, Shandaken, Allaben, Big Indian—toe up to the highway for the motorist's dollar. But the towns are quiet, comfortably weatherworn and resigned. The summer boarding houses doze amid weedy lawns. Tree-edged meadows often intrude between road and wandering river. The soft mountains, which rise abruptly and overlook all, are clothed in unbroken wilderness.

One can drive from New York City to Phoenicia in just two and a half hours, but deer drink in the mist-hung stream at dawn and the fisherman can wade all through a weekday morning in midsummer and never see another soul. At humid dusk, with the last shine of light on the water, he can fancy that he and the angler silhouetted just upstream are alone on the continent. The Esopus nevertheless can drive him out of his mind. It is victimized so steadily by both man and nature that its wounds, illnesses and distortions of personality, its slow recoveries and its sudden relapses gradually become the major preoccupation of his existence; and he finds himself—even on those rare occasions when the creek is clear, its temperature normal and its water level perfect—cringing in sure anticipation of horrors to come.

The Esopus is tortured by weather. The unprecedented series of hurricanes which belabored the last Coast between 1938 and 1955 almost wrecked its whole system. Tropical deluges accompanied these great storms and roaring, mud-colored floods rolled great boulders down the streambeds, toppled trees, ate out of banks, scoured away insect life and killed thousands and thousands of trout. The scars are still evident along all the creeks. Winter clogs them annually with ice; the snow melt of early spring makes them frigid torrents, and the still of July and August leaves them appallingly low and warm.

Man, meanwhile, labors cheerfully to further the damage. Trout streams are treated with reverence in England and men devote their lives to the art of managing them. But in the U.S. streams are fair game for any lunatic with a bulldozer. Roads are more important. So is a fallacious theory of flood control by which wandering, rock-blocked sections of brooks and rivers—the very sort of water that trout need for their survival—are straightened and flattened into sluices which speed up flow and cause worse damage farther on.

The fisherman can do little in response but fulminate. The creek's torturers are all men of goodwill and are equipped, each and every one, with valid and logical reasons for the depredations—just as were the early tanners who razed the valley's original hemlock forests in the half century after the War of 1812. Only the bark of these great trees was used; the bare hills were left littered, as by endless acres of great bones, with their rotting trunks. New forests of beech, maple, oak and other leafy trees have mercifully replaced them in the last century, but the beds of the streams are given scant chance to recover from the steam shovels and bulldozers of road builders and flood control engineers.

But if the Esopus is endlessly put upon and lamentably accident prone, it has one even more exasperating quality. It is loaded with trout and, though it often makes the fisherman's life a living hell and often seems on the verge of disintegration, he simply cannot—or at any rate *I* simply cannot—walk away and leave it to its own fiendish devices.

The New York City Board of Water Supply dammed its lower valley in 1912 and formed the Ashokan Reservoir, a wide twelve-mile lake into which the stream now empties. In so doing, it inadvertently provided Esopus trout with their own little ocean: a deep, feed-rich haven from which huge rainbows and browns launch themselves, the first in the spring and the latter in the fall, on salmonlike spawning runs to the farthest kills and hollows and to which they return, their genetic duties accomplished, to shelter during the rest of the year. Despite its difficulties, thus, the river stocks itself naturally with wild trout and these progenitors of the big brood fish valiantly defy man's best efforts to eradicate them.

They are benefited, in the process, by the Shndaken Tunnel, an eighteen-mile aqueduct which runs north beneath the hills to tap another Catskill reservoir and which feeds extra water into the Esopus and thence, eventually, into New York's hydrants and dishwashers. This enormous conduit, known locally as the "portal," makes the river unique.

In drought season, when every other Catskill stream—including the upper Esopus and its tributaries—is dreadfully low and warm, the lower river is kept high and cool by the flow from the tunnel mouth. It is kept so high for long periods that, in fact, it can hardly be fished at all; the water department, naturally, is more interested in shooting 500 million gallons a day toward the Bronx than in an angler stranded at streamside by raging rapids. The portal water does ease off in August, it is true, often bringing the fisherman negotiable riffles and slow, gliding pool surfaces. But it brings in late-season silt as well, so that the tantalizing stretches of water, rendered more turbid day by day, are usually the color of bad coffee by the end of the month.

In moments of understandable despond I sometimes think desperately of other trout water—crystalline, virginal, shadowed—and particularly of a little lake hidden high on the northwest's Mount Rainier which I once found by dint of secret directions an old friend cunningly extracted from a knowledgeable ranger. I was the fourth human to fish it. It was rimmed by fir, reflected the great, white dome of the peak like a mirror and, more delightful yet, attracted swarms of flies and bugs from a green marsh which bordered one area of its shoreline. The dry-fly fisherman wants his trout near the surface and I could not see but, in the absolute stillness, could hear the fish splashing away at their insect banquet. They were lovely creatures—a species of cut-throat known as Montana black-spotted trout—with scarlet fins and bellies tinted softly with old rose. But they were also, alas, without discrimination; they took any fly I offered.

There was no trail to the lake. I scared myself half to death working up through vertical cliffs to find it and suffered more grievous fright on the way down; for I was privileged, during the latter process, to look past my shoes at treetops two thousand feet below. But the fishing in itself was simply too easy and, even in memory, does not compete with the Esopus—which not only justifies greed and other less admirable human qualities by its own displays of temper, but makes any minor vic-tory a Roman triumph and provides a steady atmosphere of awful suspense. I could easily drive to the Schoharie, the Beaverkill or the upper Delaware from the rambling and rickety summer house I inhabit in Woodland Valley, but in the last two decades, no matter how disappointing the local fishing, I have never gambled a day on trying them. I have invested so many hours of frustration in the Esopus and its tributaries that the prospect of losing even one unlikely dividend because of absence is more than I can quite bring myself to contemplate.

Water constitutes only one part of the puzzle a fisherman is eternally trying to solve. The other part, of course, is the fish he is trying to extract from it. A trout is not, to put it mildly, gifted with intellect; one would be impelled to say, after the most cur-sory inspection of his mental apparatus, that he is downright stupid. A great many non-addicts, as a result, find the angler a hilarious spectacle. There he stands, draped in more equipment than a telephone lineman, trying to outwit an organism with a brain no bigger than a breadcrumb, and getting licked in the process. But the fisherman is engaged—or he should be—in a far more complex sort of reasoning. He is trying to understand the trout's environment and to predict the trout's response to it. The trout, if stupid, has his own low cunning—or is equipped, at any rate, with a subtle set of instincts—and he responds to what is happening around him with amazing accuracy. In thus interacting with the stream in which he lives, he creates the illusion of enor-mous wisdom and instills a sense of gloom and mental inadequacy in his pursuer.

He is both wary and greedy, and the pull of these two aspects of his nature makes him subject to starling alteration of behavior. When the water is full of feed, as during a big hatch of mayflies, nature seems to bet that the benefits of a full stomach far out-weigh any danger which may be encountered in achieving it, and the trout will roll and splash recklessly within a yard of a fisherman's waders.

But when he is feeding heavily, he also becomes fantastically selective. He will stuff himself on insects, sometimes so small that they can barely be seen with the naked eye, until he bulges like an Indiana hog, and he will go right on choking them down as long as the supply holds out. Since nature does not want him to waste energy capriciously, however, he will ignore the biggest and most delicious bugs and flies of other species while he is concentrating on the predominant insect of the moment. He will ignore even the tidbits on which he is feeding, if they do not wash almost directly into his mouth, and will hardly move an inch, right or left, while doing so.

When such a big drift of feed ceases, however—and it is a phenomenon which can tail off in a matter of seconds—the trout's *modus operandi* changes completely. As far as the fisherman is concerned he simply seems to vanish, since his natural sense of alarm reasserts itself and he either takes cover behind rocks or in the depths of pools or beneath the distorted light of riffles, or flashes away to such shelter at the first tiny change in the pattern of light or shadow on the water above him. Having retreated, however, he drops his fastidious airs and gulps anything edible which comes his way.

Each of these manifestations of the trout's personality confronts the angler with dilemma. But each presents him, simultaneously, with glorious opportunity. When a trout is feeding selectively, he will refuse any artificial fly which does not duplicate the size, the color and, in an impressionistic sense, the shape of the type upon which he is dining. Give him that, though, and he will grab it with suicidal joy—and so, on the next cast, will the trout who was feeding only a few feet from him. All sorts of little things will disturb him when he is skulking behind a rock; but if he is convinced that he is not being gulled, he will often sip in any old fly the angler puts over him. The practice of fly fishing is based on these twin revelations, and the hopes, the dreams and built-in despondency of the fly fisherman revolve around them.

There are hundred of fly patterns, large and small—dry flies, which float on top of the water, and wet flies and imitations of nymphs, which are induced to wash along under the surface. If a fisherman were able to choose just the right imitation and present it at the right place at the right moment in the right way, he could hook a trout on every cast. He cannot do it. He could not do it with the aid of a computer. But once in a while he can feel himself on the verge of it. If he labors to understand the entomology of streams, keeps notes, memorizes miles of water, always casts with care, fishes continuously and is lucky, he will enjoy occasional brief but dazzling moments of absolute triumph—moments in which he can believe he is the reincarnation of Attila the Hun and the possessor of a mind as penetrating as that of Sherlock Holmes himself. If he enjoys this sort of self-image—and, personally, I find the role of Attila rather attractive—he will be addicted to the fly forever.

He prays for a big hatch of aquatic inserts. In the Northeast this usually means a hatch of mayfly, a little creature obviously invented for the fisherman's special benefit. The mayfly spends most of his life as a nymph—an ugly little underwater bug which lives, depending variously on his type, on almost every variety of river bottom. During this phase he does his poor best to keep the trout from eating him. He is finally moved, however, to splendid self-sacrifice. He rises to the surface and changes, in a few seconds, into a dun—a delicate and beautiful little fly with four upright wings, two or three tiny tails and a slender body. The dun bobs on the current like a little sailboat, flutters and, if he is still undevoured, flies slowly upward and away.

In so doing, the mayfly performs several wonderfully unselfish functions. There is no point in fishing a dry fly—or a wet fly either—if no trout can see it; when fish are feeding on the bottom, an angler can beat the water into a froth without attracting their attention. As the nymphs rise, however, the trout rise with them, eating them en route like peanuts. At the surface the fish begin sucking in the floating duns—and are thus positioned to suck in a dry fly which imitates them.

The mayfly is kind enough to engage in these rites on a schedule the fisherman can often anticipate. *Epeorus pleuralis* (often known as Iron Fraudator), the blue-gray mayfly which is first of the species to appear in the spring, may be expected on is first (of the species to appear in the spring, may be expected on the water at one o'clock, E.S.T., during the last week in April and the first days of May. The fisherman who is equipped with a dry Quill Gordon, size 12 or 14, can expect to slay trout with ease and precision for fully forty-five minutes.

The Esopus watershed is inhospitable in late April; the hills are rust brown under bare trees, wet snow falls with the rain, and the streams are often too high, too cold or discolored. I find it beautiful. A fly fisherman should think of insects rather than fish, for it is they—since the trout merely respond to their presence—which are the real key to a full creel. The knowledge that Iron Fraudator is absolutely bound to hatch during the week, and at an hour which allows a long, leisurely breakfast, is as bracing as possession of a chart indicating buried treasure.

But the season's exasperations begin in April too. Early mayflies are enormously obliging, but they do not appear simultaneously on the whole river and the fisherman can slop along from pool to pool, maddened by the certainty that duns are appearing somewhere along the stream, and yet never find them—or rising trout—at all. Subspecies of the wonderful insect appear, one after another, through May, June and early July, changing in color from iron blue—through subtle shades and blendings of gray, olive and brown—to creamy yellow forms. Famous old dry fly patterns imitate all the important types; the Hendrickson, the Red Quill, the Grey Fox, the March Brown, the Light Cahill were all invented to match specific mayflies and to take fish when they are hatching. But as the season progresses, the fisherman often finds several different sorts on the water at the same time and can be moved to borderline neurosis while attempting to discover which one predominant insect the trout are actually rating at the moment he casts a fly over them.

There are works of practical entomology (*Matching the Hatch* by Ernest G. Schwiebert, Jr., *Streamside Guide to Naturals and Their Imitations* by Arthur B. Flick) which provide him with thorough background; but he is often balked, nevertheless, as he stands in midstream glaring wildly around him, for clues as to what is going on in the water. Some forms of mayfly—and the artificial flies which imitate them—are remarkably alike. The Hendrickson and Red Quill, in fact, are exactly the same save for the winding on the shank of the hook. But the trout will take one and refuse the other. They not only refuse the fly, they insult the fisherman. A trout will rise within a quarter inch of a fly which is too big or admits light improperly or is slightly off shade and will contemptuously splash water on it. He will jump clear of the surface and land on the other side of it. There are times when he seems to spit on it. But he will not touch it. And he will refuse a fly which matches the emerging duns in every respect if he has decided, for reasons known only to himself, to keep feeding just below the surface on the supply of rising nymphs.

Nature, it must be admitted, has provided the baffled angler with certain helpful signs and portents. A trout usually rises gently if he is feeding on the surface, but tends to splash and roll if he is feeding on nymphs or spent insects floating just beneath it. There are experts who maintain they can identify sixteen different kinds of rises (amongst them the sip, the slash, the double-whorl, the suck, the pyramid, the bulge and hump, and the spotted ring) and instantly announce just how the fish is feeding by noting the way he disturbs the water. But if a man can see dozens of rising trout and cannot make them pay the slightest heed to his artful casting, he has a tendency to quit thinking. Usually he takes refuge in trial and error and begins changing flies at random—a process which involves juggling his rod, a knife, a fly box and a bottle of dope in which he dunks each successive lure to make it float, and doing it all while up to his hips in a turbulent creek.

If he enters into this rigmarole at dusk, he must eventually ask himself an awful question: if he cuts the fly off the end of his leader, will there be light enough to allow his replacing it with another pattern? He can see dim, aluminum-colored flashes where fish are rising in the dark pool. He takes the course of courage and boldness. He cuts. He instantly regrets it. Swarms of no-seeums sift down and bite him like clouds of red-hot pepper. He cannot swat. He is standing motionless, holding a No. 16 Light Cahill toward the dim sky with one hand and trying to poke the invisible end of his synthetic gut leader through its invisible eye with the other. He grunts and sweats. He may even make small moaning sounds. But eventually he admits the cruel truth. He is disarmed. He turns, disconsolately, to wade ashore. At this moment he is subject to a final indignity and, if he is truly unlucky, he will be claimed by it. He slips in the darkness, lurches wildly, tumbles arse over tea kettle. The vehemence, the utter foulness of the profanity which can be induced by this common, even comic little accident is shocking, and the witness who laughs does so at his peril.

But the angler needs more than a knowledge of entomology—although this is a first requirement—to attack trout successfully on streams as cranky as those of the Catskills. He must do more than cast well, too. The fly must be presented correctly, but casting is simply a means to an end and is a far simpler process than is generally believed. After a few months of practice, any fool ought to be able to put a fly within a couple of inches of his target; he should be able to avoid getting hung up in trees and have mastered the trick of dropping loose line on the water to compensate for the drag of current. This is not to say there are no difficult casts. If an angler sees a big fish rising under an overhanging branch and has to reach out to the limit of his rod's power to deliver his fly, there is a very good chance he will manage any number of embarrassing mistakes. But on most water the long, difficult cast is seldom necessary. It is my opinion that motivation is more important than technique and that the successful fisherman catches trout when others do not because he possesses sneaky and atavistic instincts which heighten his perception and his ability to concentrate, and make him respond to all sorts of unkind little signals from his subconscious mind.

Something of this sort occurs in my own case, I believe, out of simple hunger. A great many fishermen are uninterested, or at least profess to be uninterested, in small trout. But in most streams—and certainly in the Esopus, save for the preseason and postseason spawning runs—there are very few fish of any other kind.

I am an eight-inch trout fisherman. I must admit I enjoy being an eight-inch trout fisherman. I sometimes keep seven-inch trout. A nine- or ten-inch trout looks like an absolute leviathan to me. I admire their beauty. I like the bulge a collection of them makes in my wet canvas creel. I am grateful to them for the fact that they are as selective, if not always as wary, as big trout and that the intellectual problems and gratification involved in luring them at the fly has little to do with their size or weight. But essentially, I like the way they taste and, when I wade into the stream, I am after something special to eat.

This does not mean that I am insensitive to the social delights of landing a big fish. A few big brown trout do skulk in deep holes or beneath boulder-studded white water during the summer and a few more seem to begin their autumnal spawning run as early as August. These monsters—anything longer than sixteen inches or heavier than two pounds is a monster in the Esopus—may rise to the surface for a few minutes during really big spring fly hatches, but mostly they stay deep and invisible, think dour thoughts and eat such minnows and small trout as incautiously invade their lairs. The chances of hooking one of them on a fly are remote in the extreme despite the experts and their interminable creeds about casting. But if the angler wants to be considered absolutely compleat and even perhaps occult—and a fly fisherman would not be a fly fisherman if he did not welcome such rumors—he simply has to produce a monster at least once.

Between May and September real, live, exciting news in Phoenicia concerns only one topic: trout. John McGrath and Joe Holzer who preside over its two grocery stores are fishermen. The Folkerts brothers, Herman and Dick, who run its social center—a combined tackle and golf shop, soda fountain, newspaper stand, bus stop and sporting goods store—are consummate anglers. So is Fred Muehleck, whose racks of ancient Payne, Leonard and Hardy rods are wondrous to behold. So also is Phil Halzell, his Woodland Valley neighbor and stream-side companion of thirty years' standing. Half the inhabitants, in fact, are fishermen and the other half cannot avoid listening to them. Let someone—anyone—catch a monster by whatever means (a construction stiff once lifted a big brown out of Woodland Valley Creek with a clamshell power shovel) and the news flashes up and down the valley roads with the speed of light.

Three summers ago, after going year on year without even seeing a monster, I caught two of them in one three-week period—a two-pounder of 17 inches and a three-pounder which measured 20½ inches. I am willing to admit that I took each of them into town, lugged them through the crowd of people waiting for the Pine Hill-Kingston line bus and thence into Folkerts' tackle shop to be measured, weighed and admired by hangers-on from the soda fountain. While nobody has since spoken of me as a veritable artist with a fly rod, I have reason to believe that I am no longer considered a mere dilettante from New York. I have, in fact, heard several generous remarks about my prey, and one man, whom I did not discourage, seemed to be under the impression that I was able to track down monsters at will.

Honesty compels me to say that I hooked both of them by accident. In each case, a stray current sucked my over fly down deep beside a sunken boulder and presented it to the fish, whose presence I did not remotely suspect, in a completely natural way—an effect no one could have achieved otherwise in a month of trying. Both leviathans, I am sorry to relate, acted like Bowery drunks after I put the iron to them. A three-pound trout, of course, will put a splendid arc in a four-ounce rod, but neither of my fish seemed to have any concept of the thrilling fight which was expected of them. The bigger one ran out of steam after half stranding himself in a shallow riffle while I was trying to lead him into a quiet pool for the big battle. I simply fell on him, wrestled him two out of three falls and carried him ashore. And though both were wrapped in cheesecloth and lovingly poached in a court bouillon, neither of them, alas, tasted very good.

Smaller trout—if they are fat, wild and freshly caught—are something else again. The prospect makes my entire endocrinological system thump, palpitate and clank like a houseful of old-fashioned steam radiators on the first day of winter. It has been my privilege to sample the haute cuisine of Paris, New York, San Francisco and New Orleans, but neither Maxim's nor Le Pavillon have offered me anything to match the tender and delicate taste of these lovely fish, They should, to my mind, be rolled in corn meal, sizzled for four or five minutes in bacon fat (better, for reasons I do not understand, than butter) and served with a fresh green vegetable or salad, a baked potato, or macaroni with a bland cheese sauce. The exterior of the trout, properly done, is crisp and gold; the interior, white, moist and of a flavor, subtle but poignant, as to pierce the very soul. If the air of the dining room is faintly perfumed by fireplace wood smoke, the hilt will taste better: and if one drinks a clear, icy martini while they are cooking and a half bottle of well-chilled Moselle while they are being consumed, he will find himself, when all are gone, sitting mindlessly, happily motionless while his inner being relives and resavors the sensations which have been visited upon it and congratulates itself upon a turn of fortune too splendid to be quite believed.

My memories of such orgies and my unbridled appetite for more of them have a great deal to do, I am convinced, with what successes I may manage in my contest with the Esopus. There are days when some curious perceptiveness—simulated, I can only assume, by messages from my digestive tract—allows me to strike at the split second a trout takes my sunken, drifting nymph, although I can neither see nor feel the fish before it is magically hooked. I am incapable of remembering telephone numbers or even, at times, the names of people I have known for years, but I can visualize miles of stream in infinite detail. The Esopus has its obvious and easily remembered water: the Greeny Deep, Twin Rooks, the Spanish Farm, the Pool-in-Front-of-Bill-McGrath's-House and a succession of noisy cascades known, simply, as Down at Elmer's Diner. But I know hundreds of minor riffles, rock-divided eddies and patches of slack water; I know how they change at various river levels; I remember how fish behave in them and I remember when shadow, if any, falls on them, morning and evening.

The Catskill fisherman needs such information just as the prospector needs an understanding of rock formations—not that the knowledge is likely to produce riches in either case, but because it keeps hope alive. He needs a very good, very expensive fly rod for the same reason, even though in nine hundred ninety-nine out of a thousand situations one can fish just as well with a cheap glass rod.

A fine rod is made of a particularly hard and resilient cane from North Vietnam's Tonkin region. Its delicate sections are machined to tolerances of a thousandth of an inch to produce a specific and particular bending mode or "action." It is simple, exquisitely balanced and beautiful to see—at once an efficient tool and a work of art. The very process of removing a good rod (in my case an eight-foot Orvis) from its aluminum case, of jointing it up and carefully attaching an English reel (no others click so satisfyingly when spun) does something to the spirits comparable, I imagine, to climbing into the cockpit of a Spad or polishing up a set of safecracker's drills. When the fisherman's hand closes on its smooth, cork grip he is armed as Arthur with Excalibur and anticipates triumph almost automatically as he wades into a stream.

Once in a while, furthermore, even on streams as exasperating as the Esopus or its feeders, he will win an enormous victory. I cannot help but feel that my own performance during the hurricane of 1955 was absolutely brilliant. On considering it in retrospect, in fact, I am able to discover in myself qualities so admirable that I would be inclined to discount them were it not for the penetrating, even pitiless, honesty with which I have reviewed the episode. I will go so far as to say that I rose as a phoenix from the ashes of defeat and that I hoped and was rewarded while all others were cast down by despair.

The hurricane and its accompanying deluge made a horrible mess of our Catskill streams; they poured down their valleys under opaque curtains of rain in roaring, muddy floods. It made a mess of my house, too. The roof leaked, and when I put pans under the drips, I was impelled to endure something very like a xylophone concert. Forced into the open by this ungodly racket, I took my rod, drove five miles to the end of the Woodland Valley road and began walking upstream under the trees. I was as wet, in five minutes, as if I had fallen into a swimming pool; but I pressed sternly on and, after two miles, came upon the splendid and gleaming phenomenon I had hoped but not actually expected to find.

Under normal conditions Woodland Valley Creek betrays itself at this high point of its valley only in little skeins and trickles of water among shadowed, mossy rocks. But now it was ten feet wide and, since there were no clay banks to discolor the water, it ran clear as crystal. The native brook trout of the Northeast had been extinct in ninety-five per cent of the Esopus system for a long time—very probably since the tanners cut the hemlocks more than a century ago. But brookies, which had somehow endured year after year in the shadowed trickles of water here, were feeding voraciously in the swollen creek. They were absolutely beautiful fish with a sheen of electric blue, white piped fins, mottled backs and crimson spotted sides. I hooked them for two hours, released all but five of the handsomest, since even a hungry man could hardly deny they had earned the right to freedom, and splashed back down through the rain feeling as though I had discovered the Mother Lode.

Despite such bagman's satisfactions, however, I must confess that my pursuit of artistry, restraint and purity of purpose has progressed very slowly, if at all. But I strive. I have a model: an erect, wispy and grave old gentleman whom I encountered at midday on the Esopus above the portal five years ago and have admired, wistfully, ever since.

The sun was bright. The stream was low and clear. It was not a time to fish at all, for any movement sent trout flashing to cover in the still, brilliantly lighted pools and I was carrying a rod only as insurance against some unlikely opportunity. As I strolled along inspecting a stretch of water I had not seen for a long time, I became conscious of the old gentleman only when I saw him bend, perhaps seventy yards below me, and then straighten, net in hand. But in that instant, even at that distance, I saw that the net contained the dark, curved form of a very big trout—a monster, or, at the very least, a monster junior grade.

When he came slowly upstream, minutes later, I began to understand what a feat he had managed under those absolutely impossible conditions. He did not show me the fish or even allude to it. He had wrapped it in newspaper and had contrived to get most of the resulting package into his creel. If I had not had that glimpse of it in his net, I might not have known he had a fish at all.

He must have been eighty; I doubt if he weighed much more than a hundred pounds and he walked slowly and with care. But I could only assume that he had come to the river with his sheets of old newspaper because he expected to stalk that one particular fish and that he had fully expected to land it. He nodded at me, glanced at my rod and, after reaching into a pocket, produced a roll of leader so fine that it was almost invisible. It must have tested less than a pound. He snapped off two feet of it simply by breaking the fragile stuff between his fingers. "Use this as a tip," he directed. Then he pulled out a plastic box, removed a tiny, curiously bedraggled black fly and handed it to me as well. "Try this," he said. "I tie them during the winter."

This was the fly and this was the weight of leader with which, quite obviously, he had subdued his thick, heavy trout. He had been forced, on such water, to take a long, long, almost impossible cast to avoid frightening his quarry. In teasing up such a fish, indeed, he had very probably had to drop the fly again and again, and each time as lightly as thistledown. And having hooked the monster, he had played it coldly and delicately at the end of that gossamer tip, knowing one slightest false move would lose him the game.

He fixed me with a stern eye until I had tied on his contributions and then, apparently satisfied that he had prepared me, too, for higher things, nodded and turned away toward the road. I knew better—that he had only prepared me for a few fruitless casts on such a day. But I got down on my hands and knees, for all this, to approach a pool formed by the confluence of a little side stream called the West Kill and then, sitting up slowly to avoid alarming its inhabitants, I looked carefully for evidence of opportunity.

The pool was deep, blue and still, but there were gnats dancing over the faint currents at its head and I felt that I saw an occasional tiny disturbance on its surface. I lighted a cigarette, and then made a long cast and promised myself that I would let my fly lie on the quiet water until I had finished smoking. But impatience and lack of faith were soon my undoing. I yanked the line off the water in dissatisfaction after three puffs and cast a foot to the right of its first position. As the line was still in the air, the biggest brown trout I have ever seen broke water like a runaway torpedo and fell back with a shattering splash. "Good Lord!" I cited in astonishment and cupidity—I talk to myself considerably when fishing—and, moved to mindless activity, made still another frantic cast. And this time I saw that my little fly was gone and realized what I had done. The big fish had sucked it in at the split second I had retrieved my line and I had broken off the hairlike leader without the slightest sense of having done so. The monster had jumped because my hook was imbedded in its lip. Had I concentrated, had I waited one second longer . . .

Ah, well. I will, given a bit of luck, be eighty years old myself one day and I like to think a certain improvement in both skill and moral tone will have become evident at that point and that the Esopus—or what is left of it—will yield to the superior man. And, if one matures late, one can always look forward to ninety.

PART V

Some Adventures
on Water

The Miramachi it ain't, so all right, it's 116th St.

JOHN BRYAN

The stretch of the Hudson River that flows past New York City is polluted. Its fish are contaminated with poly-chlorinated biphenyls (PCBs) and its banks are littered with filth. Its few human visitors do not frequent the Miramichi, nor are they familiar with the Gaspé. But the Hudson is a five-minute walk from my apartment on 112th Street in Manhattan, and I have learned to throw flies into its thickness.

On an evening I usually take a dozen or so stripers and snappers or baby bluefish, but occasionally the river whisks me beyond that, directly to Valhalla. As it did one Saturday in late September.

With only three hours before dark, I braved the traffic of the West Side Highway, strung my rod and began to make preliminary casts into the river. My 116th Street beat is a rocky stretch of bank that extends two blocks to a concrete sewer outlet on the left and eight blocks to the right to the bay south of 125th Street. The bank is strewn with man-size rocks, placed there as both highway support and river curb, and the water drops gradually to 30 feet, where stripers and bait-fish cruise. At low tide, the slimy rocks are laden with assorted debris.

I have the 116th Street beat memorized. The boulder with the blue paint. The flat sitting rock where I rest occasionally. The hole with the cable growing from it. The concrete sewage outlet below, and the three sewage pipes above. The tiny "driftwood beach" that I sometimes comb. And the standing rocks that I jump to and from.

I have some of the river's hazards conquered (I hate to say "licked"). Backcasting between traffic. Double-hauling past flotsam. Cleaning my line on every 10th cast.

And I know the river's rhythms. High tide at my beat is 2½ hours later than at the Battery. Change of current takes three hours. Sewage flows often—but not always. Dusk and dawn are the best times, regardless of the tides—unless dead low is combined with a full sewage flow. Then I wouldn't even stick a poacher's line in the river.

That September evening my first casts were downstream, parallel-to-the-bank 50-footers. I was darting a bright weighted streamer—a No. 2 hook with a lot of lead, tinsel and white hair—on a 12-foot leader with a four-pound tip on a sinking line. I retrieved the fly along the rocks as fast as I could yank it.

After five minutes of no fish, I opened my duffel and inflated my raft. Eight minutes of foot-pumping was all it took. A $20 Macy's job, it was similar to the one I used during my school years in North Carolina for floating streams and farm ponds. This one, though, was for the Hudson, for the out-of-casting-distance schools of snappers and stripers that are common to the river. No oars, just a sculling paddle, but with it you can go faster than with oars if you paddle right.

The vinyl raft was large and firm, each of its three compartments permeated with the smell of the Hudson. I was now ready for a quick takeoff if far-off stripers were sighted. Until then I would fish the shoreline boulders.

The river was in good condition. The incoming tide, still an hour from high, was clean and relatively free of debris. I say relatively because there is always garbage floating along the banks of the Hudson in Manhattan. Some days it is so bad that it's impossible to retrieve an ungarnished fly. When the tide is dead low and the sewage outlets are active, the water is filled with floating and half-floating objects of every description. The visibility is down to zero and the smell is not pleasant. But that day no sewage was issuing from the outlets and the flotsam was minimal.

On my first upstream cast I got an immediate strike, and I was into a small bass. A 12-incher, silvery with purple-black stripes. I released it and proceeded to catch five more, all small, all in front of the same upriver boulder.

Small stripers are everywhere along the Hudson rocks in the summer (they begin to leave as cold weather arrives). It's easiest to find them with a spinning rod. Just cast along the rocks before and after high tide, retrieving with the current.

Busily releasing small stripers, I scarcely noticed the arrival of the two visitors. When I turned and saw them, they were sitting in my raft in the grass, clutching matching pints of no-name moonshine.

"How ya doin'?" I delicately inquired. "You gonna float around in this thing?" one of them asked.

"Yeah, do this thing hold you up?" said the other.

"Well, for one person it's all right, if you're careful. It can tip over, though, if you don't know what you're doing." I was lying.

"I think we'll take a ride in it," one of them said. "Where's your other oar?"

Tricky situations weren't uncommon on my Upper West Side beat, but this was the first time my raft had been in jeopardy. Both men were bigger than I am, and although they were obviously more than a little drunk, I knew I couldn't stop them if they wanted to take a ride on the raft.

"I'll tell you, right now's not really the best time for a float on the river," I said. "See that log? See how fast it's moving? The currents are really dangerous now. In about an hour the tide will slow down and I'd be glad for you to borrow the raft then. My name's John, and I come down here to fish the river a lot. I've never seen you guys though. What are your names?"

"John, you're my main man. I'm Thomas, and this is my main man Maxwell. You be here in an hour?" I nodded. "Then we'll see you later. We'll float that damn thing all over this damn river."

Thomas and Maxwell wandered off through the screeching traffic. I had lied again. I had no intention of being there when they returned. In a few seconds I was floating upstream with the incoming Hudson tide.

Sculling strongly, I was quickly out toward midriver. I laid down the paddle and cast the streamer toward the edge of one of the many Hudson currents. The river is often like that, like a hundred streams all flowing side by side at different speeds. While rafting, I can adjust my relative speed by entering the various subcurrents, and it is at the junctures of these currents where the fish most often feed. On a calm day you can see snappers working 50 patches across the river. Larger disturbances mean stripers, or sometimes even shad. Once I caught several large shad on my Hudson streamers.

Out away from its shoreline the river is pleasant. With some imagination you can even sense its origins. The Hudson begins 300 miles to the north in the Adirondacks near Mt. Marcy in a fishless two-acre lake called Tear of the Clouds. Spilling gently down, it gradually becomes the wild and rapid upper Hudson, home of native brookies and implanted browns and rainbows that feed on Adirondack mayflies. Stifled at the base of the mountains, the river becomes sluggish, held in check by locks and dams. The trout become carp, and the mayflies houseflies. Pristine tributaries become paper-mill runoffs. Near Troy the sewage takes over. And below the Troy Dam the river first tastes salt and begins to take on the character it has on my beat. The tides extend 154 miles up to Troy and back down past Albany, Kingston,

Poughkeepsie, West Point, Croton, Haverstraw Bay, Spuyten Duyvil, the George Washington Bridge, 116th Street. The carp become stripers, the stripers that I was looking for.

Once a school of stripers is located, it pays to move gradually with the current. The baitfish are drifting, and the stripers follow. When I'm bank-fishing and have found a school, I walk slowly along the rocks as I catch and release fish, finally arriving either at the big concrete sewer outlet downriver or the steep gravel bank upriver. Then I return to my starting point to pick up another school.

I sculled the raft, hoping to find a current that would let me drift with some fish. Nearby the surface erupted with six frenzied splashes. Then a smaller splash—my streamer. One strip and a fish was on, pulling hard, taking line, as the raft swung around. The fish was a good one, larger than the 12-inchers I had caught earlier, but not so large that I couldn't slow its runs. Back and forth, the raft rotated with the fish's lunges, zigzagging with the river's flow. I retrieved line gradually, enjoying the bent rod and the tight line. The fish came to the surface 30 feet away and shook its head; a striper. Again it surfaced, and then plunged toward the bottom. But the fish tired, and I soon put my thumb into the jaw of my best Hudson striper. My scale said 3½.

I debated for an instant whether I should keep the bass, for photographs or something. (Hudson River fish shouldn't be eaten because of the high levels of PCBs.) Or to show Steve, my Sheepshead Bay friend who scorns the Hudson, who won't fish my 116th Street retreat with me. But I decided not to bother, and I put the hefty fish back into the river.

Two false casts and the fly was out again. I stripped and felt a tug. Another pleasing battle and another weighed striper. Longer than the first, but thinner and not as heavy.

The next 24 casts produced stripers. I counted. My record had been 39 straight on a rainy Friday in 1975, but they had been 15- and 16-inchers. These were all at the magic three-pound mark. And they were tiring me. An hour and a half of bent graphite had begun to fatigue my forearm. Striper after striper. Schooling 40 feet away from me, moving together with the tide. I wished I had tagging equipment. Each year I resolve that I will tag my next year's fish, but I still hadn't gotten around to it. Beautiful 20-inch fish. But no whoppers. Tugs and pleasure-boaters passing, waving as I landed and released my catch.

More splashing and I flexed the rod for a cast while simultaneously seeing a dozen teenagers on the rocks, each heaving stones in my direction and shouting words I could not understand but which did not sound like pleasantries. My sculling paddle got me out of range without injury, but the stripers were soon behind me, and the record 39 was no longer endangered.

The tide had begun to change and I floated almost motionless amidst the back eddies of the reversing Hudson. Prime time for big stripers. When the high tide comes and lingers for 30 minutes and then begins its retreat, bottom dwellers and baitfish are aroused, and hungry cows supposedly feed.

Small snapper schools pitty-patted gently across the river, but I was looking for splashes, not dimples. I searched the eddies with the streamer, but the next few minutes produced nothing. The teenagers soon tired of their sport, and I moved back to fish near the shoreline. My "main men" weren't there, and I moved north of the 116th Street launching area. I wearily rolled short casts into the rocks as sunset approached, but the fish were apparently somewhere else, and the brief strips produced a half-hour void.

The sun finally dropped into the Jersey bluffs, and I beached the raft near the concrete sewer outlet. I sat dangling my legs from the concrete, slow-pulling the worn-out streamer as I finished the day. Then, a final strike! The fish ran downriver. On my feet, feeling the line through my gloved right hand. Then mono, then Dacron backing. There was no stopping it. The rod was not jerking, just a constant double bend. Line burning across my forefinger.

I held the rod high with both hands at the reel, the buckskinned right hand letting line flow from it. I put pressure, too much pressure, on the line and the fish, but it wouldn't slow. The backing began to vanish and I watched as the reel spool gradually came into view. With only a few feet left, I struck the fish hard, holding the line tightly, bending the rod behind my shoulder. I heard and saw a huge boil 100 yards away where the fish rolled. For a few seconds it stopped, and then with renewed strength moved again. Before I knew it the backing was at its end. The rod strained, the line held for a moment, then parted at its last knot.

The line, the backing, the leader, the fly and the cow bass were gone. As was the day.

After a minute of squeezing a deflating raft, I gathered myself and recrossed the zooming traffic. I walked through Riverside Park, nervously watching for Thomas or Maxwell or the teenagers.

Tired, I leaned forward as I negotiated the 116th Street hill up to Broadway. I watched three street kids playing tag—Shorty, Jolly and Black Lagoon. Black Lagoon was "it." Further up the hill I passed a giant man with a black eye and a bandage around his head. At the top of the hill was Broadway, and it was there that the breeze off the Hudson lost its force. And it was there that I reentered the city of New York, five minutes away from a productive—if somewhat odoriferous—fishing paradise. As usual, I remembered to take a last deep breath of the Hudson before crossing the street to climb the five flights of stairs to my apartment.

An Exploring Expedition

W. C. PRIME

There is a lake over the mountains, some forty miles from the Rookery, which I had long desired to see; but I could never persuade a friend to go with me on an exploring expedition. A recent extension of the railway had made it somewhat more accessible, if I was to give credit to the information given me by a baggage-master, who assured me that the railroad crossed an old wood-road which led in three or four miles to the lake.

There is, I think, a love of novelty in all anglers. We prefer to fish new waters when we can, and it is sometimes pleasanter to explore, even without success, than to take fish in familiar places. New and fine scenery is always worth finding. But I could not beat these ideas practically into the brain of either Steenburger or Doctor Johnston, and I resolved therefore on a solitary expedition to the lake.

I had not then, what I now possess, and strongly recommend to roving anglers, a patent India-rubber raft, made in two cylinders, with a light frame to sit on. This boat or raft, packing in a small compass when not "blown up," weighs less than fifty pounds, and can be carried on a man's shoulders to any lake or pond. I have frequently used it on water never before fished, and to reach which it was necessary to climb hills so steep and so covered with alternate rock and under-brush that two men would have found it quite impossible to carry up safely any boat, however light. An axe and an auger wherewith to build a raft were therefore essentials to my equipment, and these, with some hard bread and sandwiches, and one heavy and one light fly-rod, made up the sum total of my luggage.

Taking the forenoon accommodation train up the road, I went forward to find my old informant, the baggage-master, or, if not him, some other one who could supplement my scanty knowledge of the locality I was seeking.

Luckily there was a man who said he knew all about it, and, after riding forty miles or so, the conductor stopped his train at a road-crossing in the woods, I tumbled out, and civilization at once departed from me, drawn by the power of steam.

It had been a sudden idea, and the realization was somewhat discouraging. Alone in the woods, with sundry traps in the way of luggage, and with no other guide than the words of the confident individual I had met on the cars, who said that the lake lay at the foot of a hill to which he pointed across the forest, I set out, and after a half-mile tramp came on the traces of a clearing, and, soon descending into a hollow, found a saw-mill. Two men who were running it were evidently astonished at the appearance of a traveler, but they very good-naturedly offered advice, to wit, that, if one wanted trout-fishing, he could find it then and there in the mill-dam, but that, if he went to the lake he would find no trout, for nobody ever could take trout there except through the ice in the winter.

"What size do they take them then?"

"Oh, sometimes five or six pounds."

This was the same story I had heard at a distance, and it confirmed my hopes. I chatted a while with the sawyers, and tried the contents of their pond. A few casts brought up some small trout, and at length a very decent fish, perhaps a pound in weight, rose to the scarlet ibis. Landing him, and leaving him with the others for the use of the men, who had never before seen fly-fishing, and were astonished at the process, I pushed on in the afternoon toward the unknown lake or pond. The road became less a road and more a path as it ascended hill after hill, winding and pleasant, but always tending upward. At last it opened on a large clearing where stood a ruined log-house, deserted long ago, and a tolerably decent barn, in which there was a small quantity of dry hay. This was an unexpected luxury, for I had calculated on a night in camp. I took possession of the only tenantable end of the log-house, deposited my packages, and resolved to make this my headquarters, since it was evident the lake was distant not over a mile at most. Then taking a light rod I plunged into the forest, and in less than half an hour emerged on the banks of the lake. It lacked an hour of sunset, and there was but little time for the examination of the shores. Boat there was none. The unbroken forest surrounded the sheet of water. There was no time this evening to construct a raft, and if I was to have trout for supper, it must be by casting from the shore, and so I went to work at once.

In visiting a new lake like this, the chances are always against the fisherman. He knows nothing of the special haunts of the trout, and can form no opinion of the shape of the bottom of the pond—an idea of which is generally necessary to guide one in looking for this fish. The safest rule is therefore to seek for the main inlet, and, if the water is here found shoal, to wade out far enough to get a cast over deeper water. Beginning on this rule, I had a long hunt for the inlet, and it was after sunset before I found it. It happened fortunately that there was an accumulation here of old driftwood, well packed together, which supported me, and I had a good clear back cast. For ten or fifteen minutes it was all vain work. Nothing broke the surface which had life. The gloom began to settle on the lake. It grew cold withal, and the wind was sharp. I frankly confess that by this time I wanted fish because I was hungry. If supper were to be confined to three or four pieces of hard bread, it was not to be regarded with any earnest longings and joyous anticipations. If, on the other hand, I could look to the rich salmon-colored meat of a trout as waiting me in the old log-house, it was something worth thinking about.

And as I thought about it, he rose with a heavy rush, and slashed the tail-fly with his own broad tail and went down again. Cast after cast, and he would not rise again. So I fell back at last on the old white moth, and, taking off all the other flies, cast this alone, in the twilight which was now almost darkness. He came up at it at the first cast, and took it, head on, following the fly from behind. It is not often on still water that a trout takes a fly with his mouth before striking it with his tail; but they sometimes do it on a white fly in the evening, and from this fact it seems likely that they regard it as an animal moving in the water and not as a fly at all.

He took it and turned down; then, as he felt the hook, swayed off with a long, steady surge, and circled half around me. Supper was tolerably certain now, and my appetite at once rose. In less than five minutes I had him, a good, solid three-pounder, in the landing-net, and at once struck a bee-line for the log-house in the clearing.

The cabin was nothing to boast of as a shelter.

The roof was tight over the end opposite the chimney, but the windows were destitute of glass, and the breeze, which had sprung up freshly before I left the lake, was talking loudly to itself inside of the place as I approached it. There was plenty of wood around the old hut, and in ten minutes I had the chimney blazing at a terrible rate. Fire-light is as much a polisher in-doors as moonlight outside. It smoothes down all the roughness of an interior. It reddened the walls of the cabin and covered them with dancing images. I had nothing in the way of eatables except the trout, hard bread, and some salt. The salt was the great article. It was on the faith of that salt that I had ventured on the expedition. With a few pinches of salt and a good rod or gun, one may live luxuriously for a while, if he have luck. Without the salt—only imagine it. You may not think much of it as a thing to possess, but just reverse the picture and imagine fish and game in abundance without it, and you may thereby find in some measure what it is worth.

I recall oftentimes a scene at Wady Haifa where the palms of Ethiopia bear golden fruit, but where salt is worth more than golden dates. There I have bought bushels of luxurious fruit for a single handful of the condensed brine from the far-off sea.

One half of the trout was turning before the blaze, hung on the small end of a birch sapling; the other half was reserved for breakfast, for it was by no means certain that any other food was to be found. A pile of hay from the barn made a soft bed in the sheltered end of the room. While the fire burned I mused, and before the musings had assumed form the trout was cooked, and then my supper was ready and eaten, the bed looked more and more inviting, and by nine or ten o'clock I was sound asleep in the corner.

Morning found me sleeping. The sun and air were streaming in at the window-frames innocent of sash or glass. But while the question of breakfast was under discussion, a voice came in by the same avenues with the sunshine and wind, singing a cheery song, and I saw the tall form of one of the sawyers of the mill swinging along toward the wood in the direction of the lake. He pulled up at a hail and turned to the cabin.

"Glad to see you lively this morning," he said in a hearty voice. "I thought I'd come over and bring you suthin' to eat; expected to find you in camp, down along the pond." Then, entering the cabin and seeing the half of the last night's trout hanging before the fire—"Well, you seem to ha' taken care of yourself. You don't say you got that feller last night with one of them little poles o' yourn?"

We made a substantial meal together at once, and the best thanks that could be given my friend were visible in the justice done to his corn-bread and hard eggs. He had come three miles across the country on this hospitable errand, and was delighted when I proposed to him to spend the day on the lake, and promised to go home with him in the evening.

The first work was the building of a raft. To the uninitiated it is often a puzzle how rafts are constructed by fishermen in the forests, and possibly there are not many sportsmen who have regarded an axe and an auger as parts of an outfit. The two things are essential to a forest expedition, and in going to fish an unknown sheet of water one might almost as well leave his rod behind him as these tools. There are ways of getting on without the auger, but a raft lashed together with withes is a dangerous craft. I have had such a one part with me in mid-lake, while I swam ashore with my rod in my hand, losing even the fish I had taken. In the present case I had both tools. The construction of the raft was very simple. Two pine-trees supplied six logs, each about a foot in diameter, which were rolled into the water and floated side by side, a few inches apart. Across these, smaller timbers were laid, the axe shaping them down flat where wooden pegs were driven in auger-holes through them into the heavy logs. It was but little over an hour's work to complete it, for the timber was at hand in good size and quantity. Then we covered the raft with balsam boughs, to stand or sit or lie down on, and a couple of long poles finished the furniture of the vessel, which we pushed out at the inlet of the lake. The day was so much more beautiful than the previous one that the lake appeared like a new place, and the trout were rising on the surface here and there in a way which indicated that the warm sunshine had brought out some small flies, invisible to the eye at a distance, but satisfactory as indicating that the fish were on the feed. It was nearly ten o'clock when I began casting. But nothing rose to my flies till I had changed them twice or oftener, and had on at length three small gnats, a dun, a yellow, and a black, and then came the first strike at the yellow, a half-pound fish soon killed. Another at the yellow again, a somewhat larger fish, gave me some slight work, and a third took the yellow once more, and thereupon I changed: the dropper yellow, the tail-fly yellow, and intermediate a small scarlet ibis. The first cast made with this new bank, as some men call the arrangement, cost me the scarlet fly. A large fish took the dropper, and at the same instant another struck the ibis. They headed in opposite directions, and the very stroke of the two parted the slender thread. I landed but one of that cast, and only once after that had two at the same time, and then saved them both.

The sport continued good till about one o'clock, and then ceased. The breeze rippled the water, the flies were increasing in number in the warm sunshine, but feeding time was over and the fish went down. I have seen the same thing often on other waters.

The object of the expedition was accomplished. There were trout in the lake—they would rise to the fly. Over a dozen beautiful large fish, and nearly another dozen which ran below a half pound each, were fair evidence of the contents of this water. Six of the smaller fish had been taken with bait by my friend, the sawyer. He had cut a birch rod, and with hook and line which I supplied, and the fin of a trout for bait, which he kept constantly moving near the bottom of the lake, he had captured a half-dozen fair-sized fish.

So we left the raft to drift toward the leeward side of the lake, and started for the log-house in the clearing; and thence, carrying heavy weight, we trudged over the hills to the home of my friend of the mill.

It is one of the most pleasant incidents, not uncommon either, in the life of a roving angler, to find the hospitality of a warm American country home. There is no other country in the world where such incidents can happen, for nowhere else are there outlying farms and homes in the forest, in which one can meet with that measure of refinement and cultivation which marks American farmers' families.

Books, magazines, and newspapers find their way into the remotest settlements, and it is a pleasing fact that newness or freshness in the literature is not an essential to its enjoyment. Life glides on so evenly that there is no thirst for novelty, no excitement which requires peculiar stimulus. It is the custom of many anglers whom I know to gather in the autumn all their old magazines and literature of various kinds, and send it to such distant homes in the forest, where it helps the winter through, and where the giver finds, and is sometimes glad to find it in the spring.

My sawyer friend brought me to such a house. The firelight was shining from the kitchen hearth through the open door as we approached, and an old woman, with a bright and sunny smile on her face, welcomed her son and his guest on the threshold. The two lived together here, in a snug frame house, low down in the valley, and only a half-mile from the open country where was a small village and a church. "If it were daylight, you could see the church," said the old lady, "but as it is, you can only see the lights in Alice Brand's farm-house."

And later in the evening, after we had dined, or supped, royally, and were sitting before the hearth talking of this, that, and the other thing, the old lady told me a story about Alice Brand's farm-house.

Forty years ago Stephen Brand was a farmer in the valley near the church, well to do in the world, and, as he hoped, with some treasure laid up where it could not corrupt. At all events, Stephen was a light in the church, and had been a judge, or something of the sort, in his county. For a long time the stout old man had served his country, and he was beginning to be weary.

He had one son; but Walter Brand, the child of his old age, was a wanderer, and his wife Alice, the daughter of the clergyman, lived in the old house with Stephen, and cared for him and superintended the domestic duties of the home-farm.

Alice had been a favorite in the village before her marriage, and most persons thought well of the match; but Walter was a restless boy, and although sole heir to his father's wealth, which was not small, and although he had a gentle wife at home that loved him truly and fondly, he yet preferred to rove, and seldom returned to the old place under the elms.

They had one child. He was a boy, and from his birth was so like the old man that you were startled and almost frightened at the strange resemblance. There was an old look on the child's face that grew tenfold older every year that he lived, and when he was seven, you might have taken his countenance for that of a man of seventy. He was hopelessly deformed. This sorrowful truth began to force itself on the mother's mind before he was two years old, and at length there could be no doubt of the fact. Like all deformed children of tender-hearted parents, he was far more dear to his mother on this very account, and she cherished him as a very gem lost out of heaven and found by them. And such he was. There was a depth of quiet beauty in his childish soul that passed all sounding. No one seemed to penetrate its mysteries except the old man, his grandfather, and he would sit for hours looking into the large black eyes of the boy, and apparently gazing into the very soul of his pet. They grew to each other. The old man for his sake came half way back to his childhood and met him—for the boy seemed to be half way to old age, even at six years old. Alice was happy in that growing love, and watched them with eyes full of tears at the thought that ere long the old man must go down to silence, and the boy live on alone.

Sometimes they would walk together, and sit down under a tree on the river bank and talk. No one knew what they talked of in such moments, but doubtless the grandfather had visions of the world he was entering, and communicated them to the boy. And so years traveled along, and they all grew older together, and when once in a while Walter came back, the house was happy. But a change came. The cheek of Stephen Brand grew paler and paler as he grew more feeble, and he felt that the hour was approaching when he must go away by the dark road; and the boy's life was so knitted to that of his grandfather, that he too seemed visibly to fail from day to day. It was a curious circumstance, and did not fail to attract the attention of the family and the neighborhood, and wise old women prophesied that the boy would not out-live the old man.

And now the two talked constantly and steadily from morning till night and late into the night. Sometimes they were seated by the fire in the old hearth, sometimes in the large chairs facing each other that stood in Stephen's room, and as the spring advanced they sat sometimes under the large elm that was near the well, and oftener still on the river bank by the spring. And their conversation was no secret, but was of the high and blessed promises for the future, of the light that shone all along that otherwise dark sad road they were traveling. Alice wept in secret every day, but never let them see her tears. She went cheerfully about her household work, and in the dull routine of a farmer's life sought to forget the bitterness of the coming separation.

It came at length. One pleasant morning in the summer, when the birds sang with unusual cheer, and sky and earth seemed to come close together in their affection, the inseparable two walked feebly out together, and down to the old seat on the river bank. Alice was alarmed about them, and followed them herself, but when she saw them seated safely she returned and worked sadly on until noon. But they did not return as usual, and she hastened down the pathway across the field, and sought them by the spring. But they were not there. A wild terror seized on her, and she sank trembling on the seat, beside the old man's hat which lay on it. A brief search revealed the sad story. The boy had sought something in the edge of the water, and in his feebleness had fallen. The old man had tried to rescue him, and perished with him. The two were found together, and together carried to the old farm-house, out of which the light had now forever gone.

"Ah," said the old lady, "I've heard the passing-bell many, many times in the valley, but I never heard it sound so strange as it did that afternoon when it came up the valley and I counted it. It was ever so long before I got to eighty-seven, and then I knew that Stephen Brand was gone, and I was just thinking how lonesome poor little Steve would be, when it struck again. Upon my word, sir, it almost knocked me off my chair; and when I counted fourteen, I just sat here trembling all over, and then I fell to crying like any child."

"Mrs. Brand still lives on the farm, I suppose?"

"Alice, you mean? Oh yes. The death of the two who had been so close to her was a heavy affliction, and she was pretty much broken down; but it brought a blessing that repaid her, for Walter came home at once, and somehow their old love sprang up again quite fresh, and he did not go away, and they settled down into a happy sort of life. They're living in the old house now. It's Alice's, for the old man left it to her and not to Walter. He'd be glad to see you, sir. It isn't often he hears from his old friends in the city. She's my cousin, Alice is. Sam, why don't you walk down to the farm and see Walter? It'll do him good, for he's getting old and growing stiff. Sam, you're not afraid of ghosts?"

"No, no, I thank you. But I'm too content with your hospitality to go away from it to-night," I said, in reply to Sam's proffer of an escort for the call. But I noticed that it was the allusion to ghosts that had started him out of his easy seat, and I looked for an explanation.

"It's not strange," said my hostess, "that superstitious people should have made a ghost story out of the curious life and death of the old man and his grandson. But for a man six feet high and well educated as Sam is, I call it absurd."

"Sam believes it?"

"Sam declares he saw them. The people used to say they two haunted the side of the brook. Sam goes fishing for trout sometimes of an evening down the hollow, and he declares he saw them one night, the tall old man and the little boy, moving along in the edge of the bushes and looking and pointing toward the old house. But as to its being ghosts he saw I never believed it, for I always thought the ghosts were Tim Stevens and his boy on their way to steal Alice Brand's chickens. She generally misses some about the time the ghosts are around."

A Furcoated Fish

B. F. WILDER

I declined with thanks when Mr. Dilg first asked me to write on this subject. You see, the word "Tragic" pertains to tragedy—a mournful or fatal event, and I have had no tragic moments, not while fishing, anyway. Moreover, though of an industrious, diligent nature, always anxious to be up and doing, lest I overtax myself I have to fight constantly against an impulse to work. But this struggle with my innate self has been, I regret to say, sometimes mistaken for laziness; and unquestionably Mr. Dilg fell into this error, for in a terse phrase he rebuked me for the sin of sloth. Smarting under the injustice, but convinced of the futility of argument, I sat down at my typewriter. This is the result:

As we left the dock the guide took two healthy minnows from the bait pail and placed one on the Madame's hook and one on mine, hooking them lightly through the lips. We committed their bodies to the deep, the guide got the boat under way, and the Madame and I began trolling for bass.

I had watched closely the operation of baiting, but had been unable to determine from the minnows' faces whether they had experienced pain, for their expression had not changed at all. While meditating on this subject I had a strike, and an instant later a bass broke beautifully. The Madame was wildly excited—it was her first fishing trip—and broke into a sort of anthem. "Don't lose him!" she chanted, with appropriate gestures. "Don't lose him.

Whatever you do, don't lose him!" Her chant was soothing, the fish was hooked hard, and a few minutes later we netted it.

Presently the Madame had a strike, and up shot a mighty bass with her hook fast in its jaw. I proffered advice and admonition, and even offered to take the rod if she felt herself unequal to the task before her, but my attentions were misinterpreted. The heretofore gentle Madame turned on me and announced that this was her first bass, that she proposed to catch it herself, and that any interference would be construed as an unfriendly act. Well, we hadn't been married very long, and I didn't volunteer more advice; though when the big fish lay gasping in the boat, I did venture to say that I would rather die than catch a bass by such unscientific methods. But this remark I would have willingly withdrawn a few minutes later, when by a series of unfortunate accidents I lost a fine pickerel.

Trolling became a flat failure. For an hour or more we worked up and down the lake. Then the guide suggested that we try bait-casting on a near-by reef. Now I was not a good bait-caster. Of course, I knew how the trick was done, for I had read a number of good works on the subject. But whenever I had attempted to put my acquired precepts into practice, it had been my misfortune to fall into the hands of boatmen of the baser sort, whose censorious comments made it impossible for me to devote my entire attention to the mastering of the art.

To this day I remember one man, impatient and profane, who bitterly reviled me even while I attempted to relieve him of my hooks. He said that my technique was faulty and demanded the attention of a surgeon—purged of lamentation and impure expletive, that is what his wicked speech summed up—and this, mark you, though the location of his wound made it impossible for him to see what I was doing for his comfort. This experience, coupled with some others, had made me diffident, and I accepted the guide's suggestion with reluctance.

Things worked well, at first. Neither the Madame nor I tried for distance, and as for accuracy, all we had to do was to keep our lines reasonably well apart. The guide, seated in the bow, watched our first casts closely. Then he heaved a deep sigh and devoted his attention to the pages of a newspaper.

Our take was meager. Yellow perch and a small blue-eyed fish, which the guide called ruck bass, were all that came to our hooks, and after black bass these left something to be desired. I thought that with a longer line I might attract the attention of some wandering small-mouth, so I attempted an underhand cast and put some power in it. But the minnow burst on the guide's jaw, which was where it shouldn't have been.

For a moment the guide rocked on his seat, as if about to dive overboard. Then, half rising, he demanded to know why I had done that. I apologized for the accident, explaining that if he had not raised his head at the critical instant the minnow would have cleared him, and advised him to think no more of it and continue his reading. During my explanation he watched me closely, appearing at times about to interrupt, but the logic must have appealed to him, for after a slight hesitation he said that he guessed he had finished his paper. He added that we had better go back to the hotel now for we were about out of bait. So we trolled again, quite close to shore.

Presently we saw a long, lithe creature, black in color, which the guide declared to be a mink, busy with a turtle at the water's edge, and we stayed our course to watch. Whenever the turtle would put forth its head or flippers, the mink would snap; but so long as the turtle remained within his shell, the mink was powerless to harm. The contest seemed to be a stand-off, for though the turtle could not regain the water, neither could the mink bite through the shell. When the mink saw us, it suspended operations upon the turtle and regarded us fearlessly, arching its back and darting its head in and out with a curious snaky motion.

I threw one of our few remaining minnows on the shore, and the mink left the turtle and ran toward the minnow. The beast was almost incredibly swift, and its snaky movements were accentuated by the obstacles in its path. It seemed to glide over these instead of climbing them. For a moment it sniffed here and there, seeming to use its nose instead of its eyes. Then it located the minnow and pounced on it. In an instant that minnow was inside the mink.

A brilliant thought came to me, and I reeled in my line and made a cast to shore. The mink picked up my bait and I struck and hooked the beast. Instantly it darted into a near-by brush pile, and for a few moments I "played" it there; then I pulled it out and into the water.

For excitement bass fishing is nothing to mink fishing; but I prefer it. A bass is limited, so to speak. It won't leave the water to run about on land, neither will it dart up the handle of a landing net to bite viciously at one's fingers, but the mink did both of these things. And after some minutes of spectacular battling it remained at the end of the leader, snapping its wicked looking teeth, seeming to regret that the length of the rod kept it out of the boat, apparently as fresh as when it began to fight.

"How are you going to take it off the hook?" I asked the guide.

"I'm not going to," responded that worthy, briefly. Clearly there was no profit in pursuing that course further. Willingly would I have cut the line, had I been sure the mink would escape, but there was an air about the beast which made me believe it would employ its liberty improperly. We seemed to have aroused its evil impulses, and if it should join our party—No, we couldn't risk it. Though the mink wasn't large, our boat was too small for four.

"Can't you think of something?" I asked, turning again to the guide.

"I didn't know you wanted me to," he answered. "Most folks like to play their catch as long as it'll fight. They say they like a good battle."

"So do I," I rejoined, with dignity, "but this struggle appears to lack a successful termination, the only thing that makes fighting pleasurable. Employ your native cunning. You should be more than a match for a mere mink!"

"I could hit him with an oar," the guide said, doubtfully.

"Certainly you could," I replied. "I am surprised that you have not already done so."

We were mistaken. Even though its movements were hampered by the line, that mink could swim like a seal; it was impossible to hit it. After some futile attempts we sat and listened to our captive's clicking teeth. It seemed to be whetting them. Uneasily I wondered how long the hook's snell would last.

Raising my eyes from contemplation of this spectacle, I became aware of a woman, far up the terraced hillside, watching us through field-glasses. And suddenly a thought came to me, a thought which, by comparison, made my previous uneasiness a mere nothing.

"Do people ever tame minks?" I asked.

"I've been worrying about that for the last five minutes," the guide answered nervously. "That mink was too darned tame! I've seen a lot of mink, and usually you don't see 'em at all. Just a sort of a black flash," he added illuminatively. "Gosh! I hope not. There's only one party lives anywhere near here, but if I'm mixed up with catching anything of hers, I'll never hear the last of it!"

"Is that her?" I asked ungrammatically, pointing to the female watching us.

"My soul and body, yes!" gasped the guide. "And she's a-coming," he continued wildly, as the woman broke into a loping run toward us. "We're in for it!"

His terror was contagious, and seated on thorns I watched her rapid approach. To think that I had made the long trip from New York only to be bawled out by a wild woman for catching a tame mink! Slipping and sliding on the steep places, loping on the levels, nearer and nearer she came, and I sat silent, dismally apprehensive. At length she stood panting on the lake's brink.

For a moment she could not speak. Then: "What you got down there?" she demanded hoarsely, one long, gaunt hand pointing at the mink, the other shading her snapping eyes from the noonday sun.

There was no immediate reply. No one seemed willing to take up the burden of conversation. The guide, with the air of one guilty of a crime involving moral turpitude, stared fixedly at his feet. The Madame's frightened glance turned wildly between the tall female and me. Though I dreaded the termagant's tongue, I rose to my feet, took off my hat and began:

"Madame," I said, "I would not like to say what I believe it to be." ("I'll bet you wouldn't!" whispered the guide hoarsely.) "It is evidently a savage beast," I continued, with a wicked look at the guide, "for it seized our bait and then attacked us.

We all have been placed in great bodily fear, and my wife has suffered extreme mental perturbation. If it is possible to establish the beast's ownership, it is my intention to bring suit for damages."

"Well, I can tell you what it is," replied the woman vehemently; "and if that lazy lummox you've got for a guide was any good, he'd have told you! It's—"

"If you can guarantee us protection," I interrupted, bent upon making all possible defense before the storm should break, "we will liberate that beast by cutting the line."

"If you do, I'll have the law on you!" shouted the woman, shaking her fist at me. "You've got a mink that's been catching my chickens—that's what you've got! And if you let him go, I—I—I don't know what I'll do to you!"

"W-w-what did you say?" I stammered feebly, unable to comprehend instantly the great change in our fortunes.

"You heard me!" answered the remarkable woman. "You wait right here till I come back. I'll get a meal sack. Then you reel the nasty mink up short. I'll hold the sack open, and we'll put him in and drown him. Wait right here."

As she departed, the Madame and I drew long breaths of relief and smiled happily at each other. The guide took off his hat and wiped his forehead. "Do you mind if I smoke my pipe, Marm?" he asked. "It seems as if it might kinder clear my mind," he added pathetically.

"Go ahead," the Madame answered cheerfully; and the guide, after filling his pipe with the worst tobacco money could buy, poisoned the atmosphere with great gouts of smoke.

For a time he smoked in silence; then he turned to me. "If I'd stopped to think," he said heavily, "I could have told that that there mink warn't no tame mink. But that woman kinder terrifies me—always did. I wouldn't a-missed it, though—now that it's over. Gosh, you're a wonderful liar!" And the glow of honest admiration upon his features indicated that his latter remark was intended as a compliment.

"I couldn't see any reason for your fear," I said loftily, choosing to ignore fulsome praise of a disreputable, but useful, accomplishment.

"That's all right. If you weren't scared, you hid your feelings well," he rejoined dryly. "Anyway, if it had been her mink, you'd have just gone back to the city. I'd have to leave home. Sssssssh! She's coming back."

She came, and she brought a sack with her. Aided and abetted by her, also admonished, directed and supervised, we drowned the mink. And as it perished, she engaged us in conversation, a conversation to which the Madame and I contributed little and the guide nothing at all. As we withdrew the mink's dripping corpse from the lake, I asked the guide where I could have the skin mounted. But he was not fated to reply, not while that tall, thin female was present, anyway.

"You take it to the fish undertaker in the village," she commanded. "Good-bye."

That's all. As you see, the story contains nothing tragic, but I warned you of this at its beginning, so don't blame me. The mink? Oh, it occupies the post of honor among our fishing trophies.

The Sportsman Tourist

JOHN A. LANT

A few years ago I found my domicile in famed Sleepy Hollow, near Tarrytown. The little brook that passed my door leaped into the Pocantico nearby the rock whereon the oldest inhabitant averred that Irving sat and fished. It was an ideal spot to lure a dreamer. The living waters of three brooks met and mingled. Well, indeed, might this spot be hallowed in the memory by the legend, which recalls the brook "with just murmur enough to lure one to repose," hard by the then old schoolhouse.

In an idle moment, I, too, sat upon that rock, with, by chance, rod and line. A quiet, cool, refreshing spot, indeed. A limpid pool below formed near an old wall, over which a wooden bridge was thrown. Swirling bubbles gathered, lingered, and then strung off as the ripples danced along. Overhanging branches nearly touched the water, and vines trailed along the banks. By no special direction my line floated down to this spot. In a lazy, listless way I drew the line back too quickly. I had unconsciously perpetrated a skilful play. A sturdy fish rose to seize the bait. I saw the white belly and sudden splash. My former experience gave me to understand that I had lost a beautiful trout. I was not long in solving the secret. By cautious lingerings I lured many trout. Knowledge came with experience, and day by day I took practice lessons at my door. With confidence and courage I ventured to adjacent streams and favorite pools, always with success, when the strictest caution was observed. I studied the habits of the trout and lured him with every variety of seasonable bait and color. I was loth to deceive the noble trout with artificial fly, preferring the natural variety, but occasionally added a bit of color, which may have appealed to a passion other than that of gluttony.

My earliest and best rods were improvised from that stately purple-crowned, jointless weed known as "Pride of the Meadow." In the spring they may be seen in great clusters, brown and bare, of ample length for fishing. I found them admirably light, but at times insufficient. It occurred to me they might be strengthened by inserting a slender one inside another, and then bind on a handle upon which to fasten the reel. A better rod could not be devised for trout. The "admirable apparatus" of the artist angler has many a scar in its polished surfaces, not dreamed of by my more natural substitute

The result of my first season's catch, and it was a short one, footed up four hundred and seven good trout, within twenty-six miles of the great metropolis, and my second, in a single month's opportunities, and a dry season at that, footed eighty-seven.

No trout was counted or taken which was less than seven inches. Numerous evidences of these catches can be seen in my fishing books of fins, skin and tails. The skin of a two-and-a-half-pounder in part, forms a cover decoration for this volume.

I record these investigations along brooks in the immediate vicinity of Tarrytown, twenty-six miles from New York, the Pocantico, the Saw Mill river, and the Bronx. The Sprain, near Yonkers, is a good trout stream, also the lower Saw Mill river. These are accessible by rail, boat or wheel. Several experts have satisfactory stories to tell that would astonish the yearning angler, whose dreams encompass the Adirondacks.

The past year I visited that region, the Catskills, and wandered far into the Green Mountains of Vermont, but at last yield the palm of success to my native brooks as above.

Memories of Mahseer

P. R. BAIRNSFATHER

"CANNY, now! Get him by the gills—that's the lad!"

Then a tremendous heave, a mighty tail outflung, a sickening glimpse of hooks hanging free, and the fish was gone.

"Idiot! what for did ye no take a better grip? I tell you, you'll never see the like o' yon fish again. Man, I would rather have lost my pension!"

In moments of excitement the Colonel always lapsed into broad Doric, and the object of his wrath, his last joined subaltern, stood there dripping mud and water, and with never a word to say. He, too, was suffering as keenly as the other from the despair that comes with such disappointments, and he realized that there was no excuse for having so bungled his share of the disaster. The mahseer that had gone before, needless to say a monster, had been played for hours till it was thought that there was not a kick left in it, and as its captor proudly steered it towards the bank, the subaltern had volunteered to land it, but the last kick had evidently been held in reserve. The boy did what he could to retrieve the position, and flung himself bodily on the top of the fish, and actually held it for a moment in his arms, striving to get firm hold of the slippery scales. But not all the sterling qualities that afterwards won him a well-earned V.C. availed him on this occasion, and so one more great fish went to join the lost legion, and one more fishing story was left minus the dry proof always exacted by them that scoff. Yet, even at the risk to which we fishermen are not insensible, I maintain that this must have been an exceptional mahseer, for it was the talk of the regiment at the time I joined. Moreover, the Colonel was not a man given to exaggeration, and, seeing the fish at close quarters, he stoutly declared that the 6 ft. 1 in. of subaltern were, with reasonable margin, none too much to cover it. The reader, therefore, bearing in mind that a mahseer is, roughly, proportioned much as a salmon, can form some sort of estimate of its probable weight. And at that we must leave it.

Yet surely the most amazing feature of this contest remains to be told, and that is the bait which the mahseer, after much reluctance to feed at all, had at last been induced to take. This was a swallow! Ordinary baits had failed signally; spoon, with minnows both natural and artificial, had been tried without success; and the old Colonel, with his henchman, sat, weary and despondent, on the bank. Suddenly they noticed what appeared to be a fish of unusual size repeatedly coming to the surface of the water just below a neighboring bridge. Some swallows were skimming the water at that spot, and whether the fish was actually attracted by them or not, the incident gave the Colonel the idea which proved an inspiration. The subaltern was told off to shoot a swallow, and it was on this, fitted to a stout triangle, that the lost mahseer had been hooked. That mighty mahseer are occasionally taken is illustrated by one that a friend of mine brought back, not long after the adventure described above, from Tangrot, on the Jhelum, in those days the Mecca of enthusiastic fish men, a fish that measured exactly the same number of inches as his wife—not, it must be confessed, a tall woman, but at any rate not less than five feet. Touching further records of lost giants, I could tell how I once saw a big fish break in a trice, by sheer weight and strength, a four-ply of copper wire between spoon and trace. The line had got caught round the reel-handle in trolling from a boat, and there was no possibility of freeing it before the end came. Not all the monsters have been lost, however, for Mr. Murray Aynsley killed a brace of 104 lb. and 101 lb., both in the Cauvery.

Size and weight are not everything to the true fisherman, who looks for other virtues in his favorites, including a readiness to take some orthodox lure, a spirit of battle when hooked, and a presentable appearance when finally brought to the gaff; and I think that the mahseer can hold its own with some of the best sporting fishes of other lands. Those who have no acquaintance with it may be inclined to underrate its good qualities when they learn that it is a carp, and, like its more homely cousin, a ground-feeder; for the ordinary pond carp undeniably suggests a sluggish quarry entailing hours of waiting beside a float and a hook baited with worm or paste, without in every case much of a struggle at the end. In the case of the carp, the environment of quiet waters may have produced the characteristics that fail to appeal to those who have known better days with salmon and trout, but the mahseer is a very different proposition for the angler to deal with. Living in some of the strongest streams possible for fish life, it too has the qualities of its environment—strength, speed, and dash equal to those of any fresh-run salmon—and its first characteristic rush is such as to inspire a prayer that all is well with the tackle. A carp it may be by race, but to the ordinary carp of our acquaintance the mahseer is as a lean wild boar of the jungle to the fat prize pig in its sty.

Indeed, the mahseer has been styled the Indian salmon, and from the angler's point of view the proud title, is well deserved. It is to be caught in the same kind of rivers and with much the same lures as the salmon, though it must be confessed that it prefers spoon to the fly. It plays in much the same fashion, and the salmon-fisherman's allowance of a minute to the pound would not be excessive with a big mahseer on the rod, while that first wild rush, the invariable opening of the proceedings, is all in the mahseer's favor. In it the fish may fly off at one fell swoop with a hundred yards of line, the leverage on which makes a ten-pounder feel like double the weight. What would Izaak Walton have said to such a fish, seeing that he used no reel, and, when fast to an extra-heavy trout, used to throw his rod into the river and follow as best he could. As a further analogy to the salmon, it should be noted that the mahseer, though it does not, like the other, go down to the sea, has its periods of migration up and down the big Indian rivers, and it was, thanks to his special knowledge of this habit, which he long kept to himself, that a friend of mine used to make sensational catches of mahseer such as turned his brother-fishermen green with envy, his record including over a ton within a month, while on his best day he caught 446 pounds' weight of fish.

There is another advantage which the premier fish of India has over the salmon, and that is that it is never out of season. Owing in all probability to a habit of spawning at various times of year, there are no sluggish autumn fish and no kelts. On the other hand, it is only fair to say that, though eatable soon after capture by sportsmen with a healthy appetite, the mahseer does not compare in this respect with a fresh salmon, though in appearance it suffers little by comparison. We must, however, substitute the larger head and tail, and in place of the beautiful silver of the salmon, suggestive of its stay in the sea, the mahseer's hue is a burnished gold, singularly in keeping with the clear water and fierce sun of its natural haunts.

As I sit over the fire and let my thoughts go back to the pleasant days spent with my old Ringal rod on one or other of the great northern rivers—Ganges, Jumna, Chenab, Beas, or Jhelum—how the memories crowd, and what a remembering of happier things! True, as recalled haphazard, my experiences seem to have been singularly free from sensational episodes, yet they are probably the more typical on that account. These reminiscences seem to centre chiefly round Sialkot, in the north Punjab, where my regiment arrived, one memorable day in 1890, for a three years' spell. I was glad enough to be moved there, for this was the very spot that I had heard of some years earlier from a retired brother officer who had himself enjoyed good sport in the neighboring waters. Here it was that Muchee Bawan might be reached, the very name of which, in the vernacular, signifies home of fish. The best of news awaited me on arrival at our station, for it seemed that the fishing had been utterly overlooked for years, so that those of us who fished had all the satisfaction of rediscovering this once famous ground. It further transpired that, although only thirty miles distant, the road was so troublesome as to be considered next to impossible; but every fisherman will appreciate our satisfaction on learning of this difficulty of approach. From our own bungalow we could plainly see the Pir Punjal mountains, an outlying range of the Himalaya, from which the Tawi River flowed to join the Chenab twelve miles from Sialkot, and Muchee Bawan, the desired, lay somewhere hidden in the misty valley below. Our patience was sorely tried while the cold weather and drill season ran their course, after which, in April, the thermometer steadily rose to punkah heat, and then came the longed-for time for leave. We had arranged to ride as far as possible, camp and baggage being sent forward on camels, which, of course, furnished the usual diversions, one flatly refusing to enter the ferry-boat, and another as obstinately declining to leave it. At long last, however, we pushed on to our journey's end, studiously neglecting a number of attractive pools that we might the sooner make our goal, nothing short of Muchee Bawan itself, unfished these ten years, but previous to that period recognized as incomparable. Our difficulties of transport were by no means light. There was no road, and the only way of getting to the spot was through a deep gorge. There was no footway, and the only mode of travel was by raft. Then where were the raftmen, we asked, only to be told that they were either dead or gone elsewhere. Here, indeed, was an Eastern problem, with, as we surmised, an Eastern solution, for baksheesh ultimately proved the means of producing as many raftmen as we needed, though not before the day was at an end. Daybreak next morning found us at the water's edge, all impatience to be gone; but the raftmen were hurrying matters forward in usual Eastern fashion—that is to say, by sitting round their shriveled goatskins and chattering. It was not, by the way, baksheesh that put new life into the proceedings this time, but anyhow the men quickly and cheerfully grasped what was required of them. The skins were softened in the water and blown up through one of the legs, a rickety old native bedstead lashed to each four skins with odd lengths of string, loin-cloth, or pugaree, and the rafts were ready in reasonable time. An odd procession it was that now started out on the deep, still water of the gorge, the sides of which gradually narrowed till the fairway seemed to end altogether. And the method of propulsion was also curiously simple. The water was too deep for poling, and there would have been no room for paddles, so that four swimmers were allotted to each raft. Naturally the progress was slow, since, with their hands resting on the edge of the raft, they could only use their legs, not in the strong froglike stroke familiar and the weather was normal. We had simply struck an off day on which not a fish could be tempted, and the occasion was at once sadly memorable for the most complete blank I ever scored, but also gloriously associated with what is, perhaps, the reddest-letter day in all my fishing diaries. It fell out in this way. We—that is to say, my good C.O. and myself—had fished three whole days with no result whatever. On the evening of the last day, still doggedly trying every pool we came to, we reached camp, and it was small blame to the C.O. that, having had enough of it, he fell a victim to the lure of tea. Just then, as luck would have it, I noticed some small gulls screaming excitedly over a pool that I knew well some way downstream. It had never been a good pool, and my hopes were not very high; but the birds seemed to mean small fry, and the small fry might mean big fish. Any-how, there were still two clear hours of daylight, and this was our last day, so I resisted the call of tea and set out for the pool. What a sight met my eyes! The water was simply alive with fish, their backs now and then appearing out of water as they dashed after the fry, for all the world like a school of miniature porpoises. So I got to work at once, and the result recalled that first memory of Muchee Bawan. As soon as the spoon touched the water, two or three mahseer would rush for it at once, the best fish generally winning. I was nervous of the result, for it was clearly a case of fishing against time, and I had with me only the light rod and gear. Fish after fish was landed without mishap, and not one of them disgraced its order by omitting that first grand rush and the good fight to follow. Mercifully, the tackle held, and only the coming of night put a stop to the orgy. At length it was no longer possible to see the spoon strike the water, and the sensation of playing the last fish of the day without any notion of the direction in which it was next going to dash provided a fitting climax to a crowded hour. Thirteen fish I had caught in the time, scaling in all just 51 lb. Here, then, was a great happening of the unexpected, the more interesting to me because it had falsified the dictum of our greatest authority on Indian fishing, who holds that any attempt to catch mahseer after sunset is the one thing hopeless. To this generalization my agreeable experience had at any rate furnished a notable exception.

It will not have escaped the reader's notice that the general size of the mahseer that we caught in Muchee Bawan was distinctly mediocre. It must, however, be remembered that the Tawi is only a small tributary stream incapable of raising really big fish, and the charm of the fishing lay in the preference we had for quantity rather than size, as well as for the opportunity of using lighter rods and tackle than are indispensable for mahseer of larger size. For these bigger fish we had to go to the Chenab itself, a much easier jaunt, since the river lay only twelve miles from the station on a good road, so that we could even canter out for an evening's fishing after the day's work and be back the same night. Here it was a matter of trolling from boats with a long line out, the boat being pulled upstream by a rope. On bad days, when the fish were not in the right humour, it was monotonous work, and, as we invariably sat facing the west, the persecuting glare of the sun on the water made us yet more impatient of our ill-luck. Yet there were the other days on which we came in for great reward, for fish weighing from 10 to 50 lb. were quite within the range of moderate expectation, while monsters of far greater weight were known to dwell in the river, and we were ever in hope of hooking one of these. Many we took out of the Chenab in our time, but never the monster. In the end, however, my regiment held the record with a fish of 52 lb., though we were handsomely beaten in actual best take for a single day, for the C.O. of another gallant regiment, able to grant himself leave when we could not get away, and never forgoing the privilege, landed one fine day the much-envied score of sixteen fish to his own rod. Great fish they were, too, the total weight of them being nothing less than 200 lb. No wonder we found some little difficulty in congratulating him!

Here, too, in the Chenab, the conditions under which we caught our fish were ever a mystery. Water, weather and season would be apparently identical on the days of great success and those other days with never a fish. Some days we would troll over the same stretch of water times and again without result. Then, all of a sudden, the fish would come at the bait as if possessed. This was the case on the day that gave me my first forty-pounder. My companion, already into one which proved almost as heavy, had landed in order the better to play his fish, and I, resisting the usual temptation of offering good advice, essayed to prove my pet theory, that mahseer have a certain moment at which they must feed, by taking a cast from the shore. The theory held good in practice, for, sure enough, next moment I had him, and then came a splendid fight. It was a strenuous dance he led me up and down the bank for thirty-five glorious if anxious minutes. Happily, the channel was clear, and there was little or no danger from rapid or snag, yet, with such a heavy fish in play, no minute was free from anxiety, and every mad rush seemed to mark the end. When at last the fish took to rolling over and over far out in the stream, it seemed impossible that the gut could bear the strain, and, as a matter of fact, my misgivings on the subject proved well-founded, for, as I afterwards discovered, the gut was actually severed and disaster had been averted only by its having jammed so tightly between the treble hooks as to hold the great fish in its final struggles. It was a good thing that I was spared this knowledge until the fish was safe on the bank, else I might not have had the courage to go through with it. Three more, all of them good fish, we got out of that reach, and the luck was such as to carry us through many another less successful day.

These were great times no doubt, yet I wonder whether, after all, the simpler incidents much earlier in my Indian days were not even happier! There was the far-off time, for instance, when, under the spell of my first introduction to mahseer, I would gallop out a good nine miles on a hot weather morning, starting at 3 A.M. so as to be on the water an hour or so before sunrise. The ignoble bait used on these occasions was nothing more than a pellet of dough, and the one pool had to be assiduously groundbaited for days before my visit. Not a fish would move after the sun was once on the water, so the sport had to be short and sharp, and it was fun of the best while it lasted, for I never once remember drawing blank. A few lumps of dough were thrown into the pool on arrival, just to attract and locate the fish, after which came the cast, a rush from all directions, and a fish on the rod, its size depending on which first got to the bait. The madness of the first rush was particularly noticeable here, probably owing to the eagerness of the fish to make good its prize in presence of so much competition. Half a dozen would be the usual morning's take, and I was able to get back in good time to provide fresh fish for the mess breakfast. True, these fish never exceeded a weight of from one to five pounds, but even that was satisfactory when contrasted with my previous experience of nothing but small trout at home. In the more sophisticated moods of after years, such sport would have seemed too trivial to be thought of, but in those early days it was very welcome.

It was about that period that there befell me one of those incidents which the fisherman never forgets. I was not actually on a fishing trip, but had been told by an old hand that at a certain spot on the marching road to Cashmere, whither I was bound after ibex, a small stream joined the Jhelum River, and that if I were to try a cast or two at the junction, I might reasonably look forward to hooking something enormous. The rod was therefore taken along and the expert's instructions obeyed to the letter. A frog was to be the lure on this occasion, and it was, indeed, about the only sort of bait appropriate to this season of dirty flood water, though I never again fell thus far. At any rate, the result warranted the experiment, for I had not been fishing more than ten minutes when the jerk came and the mahseer was off in its proverbial non-stop rush, fortunately upstream and in the slacker current above the tributary. I could form no estimate of its size, but I knew that I had never felt anything like it before. It was absolutely beyond control, though I could plainly see that if the fish once got out in the mainstream, it would be all over in a moment. Up and down the water it raced, backwards and forwards, with nearly all my line out, alarmingly close to the main current, yet mercifully turning just at the crucial spot, wholly of its own sweet will, for I had no control over its movements whatever. Ten minutes of this followed, and then the fish suddenly determined to go downstream. It showed no sign of tiring, and of course I was brought up all standing by the tributary stream, too deep to be crossed except by swimming. This was out of the question, as I could never have got across while holding on to the rod with such a fish at the other end. Then it was that my young attendant, whom I had so far overlooked, had an inspiration.

"Give me the rod, Sahib," he said. "I can easily take it over, while you run round by the bridge."

This suggested a happy solution of the difficulty, and, after warning the youngster to hold on like grim death, I raced for the bridge. The young fellow swam like a duck, and the mahseer behaved just as I could have wished. Feeling it once again at the end of the rod, when I took it from the native, I all but laughed aloud in the certainty of success. Alas! Whether its anger had been roused by the unavoidable jerking of the rod during the swim, or whether it simply judged the time had come to put an end to such fooling and get to business, the grim fact remains that, within a few moments of my recovering the rod, the fish dashed off downstream and out in the middle. No check was possible, and, as the mahseer lurched and struggled, borne down by the irresistible current, I got one unforgettable glimpse of its proportions. I rushed madly down the bank, helplessly watching the line disappear off the reel until it was all out. Then came one final pull, and the fish of my life was gone.

Here, then, though it ended in dismal failure, was the greatest moment in all my memories of mahseer. Yet, as has been said, it was but one of many happy fishing episodes, and it would be hard to say whether, if there is any comparison between the two, it really gave me more excitement than that remote triumph when, as a boy, I successfully guddled an enormous half-pound trout while the other boy, more mindful of home instructions, dutifully paused to remove his boots. I wonder!

The One That Got Away (selection)

HOWELL RAINES

No, I was oppressed by the sheer weight of something more personal—my own amateurishness in the face of this new kind of fly fishing. I had gotten cocky about my ability to catch trout and bass, including some large ones. But in saltwater environments, the heavy rods and lines, the persistent winds, the greater distances needed even in routine casts—all these factors converged to form a nexus of neuromuscular chaos. Whenever it was mentioned that I had written a book about fishing, I made a point of telling people that my skills were modest. Then I would pick up a rod and prove it.

But hell's hammers, I didn't want to think of myself as clumsy, either. Somehow the abundance of Christmas Island, where it is possible to catch plenty of easy fish, sharpened the contrast between those fish and the hard ones that Lefty or the other experts might catch. I'm talking about the ghostly torpedoes you sometimes glimpsed on the turbulent rim of the islands, where the easeful shallows brushed up against the fertile, brutal surge of the blue Pacific. I particularly liked these ocean flats, which were bands of shallow, protected water between the coral reef and the shore. It is an environment of great violence, beauty and motion: gulls, terns, pipers zipping by within inches of your head, angelfish and blacktip reef sharks at your feet, and always the big combers marching in to die in shuddering explosions against the coral ramparts of the barrier reef. Fishing those flats, with the cannonade of the waves always in your ears and the spirals of white spume leaping incessantly toward the sky, was a little like standing behind a fortified line during a battle, protected improbably from a world of violence that stretched to the horizon. In those spots, if you trained your eyes on the area where the clear water stranded off into the deeper green underbelly of the incoming waves, you'd see the most intimidating bonefish, the sovereign loners, a full yard long, which didn't need to slide into the knee-deep flats to nibble little stuff. In their passing, these fish put me in mind of what Isak Dinesen said about elephants. They moved along as if they had an appointment at the end of the world.

In the precincts of such fish, one day Tabaki spoke.

"Big bone. He's coming along the edge of the deep water."

Sure enough, moving steadily through the green murk was a gray shape five or six times the size of the fish we had been catching in droves in a long march across an amiable flat.

"You can't reach him from here. Let's move out. Don't splash."

We took an intersecting line to try to get ahead of the fish. It was coming steadily on an unveering course, out there in about four feet of water.

"Cast now, as far as you can," Tabaki said, in that voice guides use when they suddenly care whether a particular fish is caught. It is a voice very different from the one they use when they are saying, in effect, you paid your money, here's your shot, I do this every day.

He was watching the relationship between my false casts and the fish. On the fourth or fifth stroke, he said, "Let it go."

I did. To my surprise, the fly landed in the edge of the deep water. Maybe my best cast ever. Not dead-on, but plausible.

"Let it sink," Tabaki said. "He might see it."

I let it sink without hope, satisfied simply that the cast had not been a humiliation.

"Now, strip, strip," he said.

Dear hearts, I wish to tell you that this lordly fish swung toward the fly as inexorably as doom's pendulum, not hastening in the least until the last instant, when it closed on the fly in a rush and took it and was the biggest fish of our trip and one of the biggest ever taken at Christmas Island, where a seven- or eight-pound fish is a large one.

I wish to tell you that and I suppose I could, but it did not happen.

The cast was not quite good enough, or my luck was not the supremely obliterating luck you need to make up for a cast that is not quite good enough. A few times in a fishing life that kind of luck will come along, but it did not come to me on this day in the Republic of Kiribati.

Nor was my casting good enough for the other edge-cruising gorillas we spotted on the ocean flats where the big ones would from time to time come looming along under the combers. Just as well, Tabaki explained, since a bonefish that strong and that close to the reef will simply bore over the edge and cut you off on the coral and that would break your heart more cleanly than a bad cast. I would have been willing to take my chances on that kind of heartbreak.

PART VI

Anglers All—and
Matters Philosophic

The Man Who Lived Two Lives in One: Zane Grey

ROBERT H. BOYLE

There never has been anyone quite like Zane Grey. Famed as the author of *Riders of the Purple Sage* and fifty-seven other Westerns tinged with purple prose, Grey ranks as the greatest bestselling novelist of his time. For years the total sales of his books fell behind only the Holy Bible and McGuffey Readers. At his death in 1939 his novels had sold more than 15 million copies in the United States alone, and thirty years later they were still selling at the rate of 750,000 to a million books a year. Magazines paid Grey as much as $85,000 for the serial rights to a single work, and Hollywood transferred epic after epic to the silver screen. Gary Cooper, Cary Grant, Warner Baxter, Warner Oland, Richard Arlen, Richard Dix, Randolph Scott, Wallace Beery, Roscoe Karns, Harry Carey, William Powell, Jack Holt, Jack LaRue, Billie Dove, Lili Damita, Fay Wray, Jean Arthur and Buster Crabbe are among the stars who got their start in Zane Grey movies.

On film or in print Grey's Westerns enthralled the public. The books were stilted, awkward and stuffed with painful dialogue ("If you think I'm wonderful and if I think you're wonderful—it's all really very wonderful, isn't it?"), but they throbbed with the narrative drive of a true storyteller and the fervor of a moralist who made certain that virtue triumphed over evil on the range. "Never lay down your pen, Zane Grey," John Wanamaker, the white-haired merchant prince, once advised, putting a friendly hand on the novelist's shoulder. "I have given away thousands of your books and have sold hundreds of thousands. You are distinctively and genuinely American. You have borrowed none of the decadence of foreign writers . . . The good you are doing is incalculable."

Grey received acclaim and money (and some critical brickbats) for his writings, but in another field his distinction was almost beyond compare—he was one of the finest fishermen the world has ever known. In the words of Ed Zern, who edited the anthology *Zane Grey's Adventures in Fishing*, "It is reasonable to assume that no one will ever challenge his right to be known as the greatest fisherman American has ever produced." It has been said that the dream of many American males is to have $1 million and go fishing. "Well," writes Zern, "Zane Grey had $1 million, and he really went fishing."

Grey is the classic case of the compulsive angler. He was truly obsessed by fish. "Not many anglers, perhaps, care for the beauty of a fish," Grey wrote in *Tales of Fishes*, one of his eight books on angling, "but I do." He would rhapsodize on the beauty of a huge tuna that "blazed like the sword of Achilles" or marvel over the shimmering colors of a dolphin, only to feel a pang because the dolphin was dying and he was "the cause of the death of so beautiful a thing." The leaping of fish absolutely fascinated him, and even fish fins and fishtails had what he called, with a flourish, "a compelling power to thrill and excite me."

From black bass to blue marlin, Grey pursued fish the world over with unmatched avidity. He explored and established new fishing grounds and techniques in Florida, California, Nova Scotia, New Zealand and Australia. He took great delight in fishing where no one had ever fished before, and his sense of anticipation was so keen that even arranging tackle for a trip gave him exquisite pleasure. He was the first man to catch a fish weighing more than 1,000 pounds on rod and reel. In his day he held most world records: 582-pound broadbill swordfish; 171-pound Pacific sailfish; 758-pound bluefin tuna; 318-pound yellowfin tuna; 1,040-pound striped marlin; 1,036-pound tiger shark; 618-pound silver marlin; 111-pound yellowtail; and a 63-pound dolphin. The record for the yellowtail and the yellowfin tuna have not been beaten since the International Game Fish Association began keeping records in 1938. Grey was held in such high regard that the Pacific sailfish was named for him, *Istiophom greyi*. Hardy's in England manufactured a Zane Grey reel, while in the United States there was a Zane Grey bass bug, a Zane Grey steelhead fly and a Zane Grey teaser.

Grey had his bad days fishing—he once passed 88 days without a strike—but he remained enthusiastic. "The enchantment never palls," wrote. "Years on end I have been trying to tell why, but that has been futile. Fishing is like Jason's quest for the

Golden Fleece . . . something evermore is about to happen." When something did, Grey wrote about it exuberantly. If he made an unusual catch he would wire *The New York Times*. There were some critics who thought him guilty of exaggeration. A friend, Robert H. Davis, the editor of *Munsey's Magazine*, wrote Grey, "If you went out with a mosquito net to catch a mess of minnows your story would read like Roman gladiators seining the Tigris for whales." Davis added, "You say, 'the hard diving fight of a tuna liberates the brute instinct in a man.' Well, Zane, it also liberates the qualities of a liar!" Grey cheerfully reported these comments himself in *Tales of Fishes*. Such criticisms did not bother him. But he was vexed and angered when his sportsmanship was called into question, as it was on a couple of occasions.

Zane Grey's passion for fishing, which, by his own admission, grew stronger through the years, started in his childhood. "Ever since I was a little tad I have loved to chase things in the water," he wrote. He was born in Zanesville, Ohio, on January 31, 1872. His Christian name was actually Pearl, and the family name was spelled Gray. After college he dropped Pearl in favor of his middle name of Zane, and he changed spelling of Gray to Grey. He also shaved three years off his age, according to Norris F. Schneider, the foremost authority on Grey, and on his death obituaries reported he had been born in 1875.

Grey came from pioneer stock. His great grandfather, Colonel Ebenezer Zane, settled what is now Wheeling, West Virginia in 1770 and moved into Ohio after the Revolution. Zanesville is named for him. Grey's father, Dr. Lewis Gray, was a farmer and a preacher who eventually became a dentist with a practice in the Terrace section of Zanesville.

The oldest of five children, young Pearl was so mischievous that he was known as "the terror of the Terrace." On one occasion he destroyed a bed of imported tulips planted in front of the Zanesville Historical and Art Institute. The name Pearl, especially in conjunction with the name Gray, apparently bothered him considerably. The only time he ever liked it was during his adolescent years, when he strove to dramatize himself by dressing in pearl-gray suits.

He was six when he saw his first fish. "Looking down from my high perch into the clear pool directly under me, I saw something that transfixed me with a strange rapture. Against the sunlit amber depths of the little pool shone a wondrous fish creature that came to the surface and snapped at a bug. It flashed silver and rose." The experience stayed with him. In school and church Pearl Gray was a dreamer. "I dreamed, mostly of fields, hills and streams . . . As I grew older, and learned the joys of angling, I used to run away on Sunday afternoons. Many a time have I come home late, wet and weary after a thrilling time along the river or stream, to meet with severe punishment from my outraged father. But it never cured me. I always went fishing on Sunday. It seemed the luckiest day." Dr. Gray told Pearl the only good fishermen who had ever lived were Christ's disciples, but the boy paid no heed; and he became the admirer of a local bum named Muddy Mizer who was always fishing on the Muskingum River.

Besides fishing, Pearl's other love was baseball, a sport at which he and his brother Romer, called R.C., excelled. Pearl was a pitcher, and he and R.C. played semipro ball around Ohio. Dr. Gray wanted Pearl to become a dentist, and he had him start by polishing sets of false teeth on a lathe. His pitching arm stood him in good stead. When the family moved to Columbus, Pearl unofficially went into practice on his own, pulling teeth in Frazeysburg until the Ohio Dental Association compelled him to stop. He continued playing baseball, and after one game a scout from the University of Pennsylvania offered him a scholarship. His father allowed him to accept it on the condition that he major in dentistry.

At Penn, Grey was at first highly unpopular. Ignorant of student traditions, he accidentally entered the upper class section of a lecture hall one day and triggered a riot in which his clothes were torn off and the room wrecked. After another contretemps he was chased by sophomores into a stairwell, where he managed to hold them off by hurling potatoes. His name and his refusal to go along with the crowd, to smoke, to drink or to gamble, made him the butt of jokes, and he escaped by spending most of his time reading in the library and playing baseball. He proved to be so good a ballplayer that, as he wrote later, "The bitter loneliness of my college days seemed to change. Wilborn, captain of the track team, took me up; Danny Coogan, the great varsity catcher, made me a member of Sigma Nu; A1 Bull, the center on the famous football team that beat Yale and Princeton and Harvard, took me as a roommate."

Grey played left field for Penn. His one lapse came in a game against Harvard, when he accidentally stepped into a hole and a fly ball hit him on the head, allowing the winning run to score. Ordinarily his fielding was excellent. He once made a catch that helped Penn beat the Giants at the Polo Grounds. In his senior year he came to bat in the ninth inning against the University of Virginia with Penn trailing by a run. There were two out and a man on second. A verbose professor shouted, "Grey, the honor of the University of Pennsylvania rests with you!" Grey homered to win the game.

Grey was graduated with a diploma in dentistry in 1896. He opened an office in Manhattan on the West Side, and there he languished. He did not like the city, and he got away whenever possible. He played baseball for the Orange Athletic Club in New Jersey, and he became the youngest member of the Camp Fire Club. There a fellow member suggested that Grey write a story about his bass fishing on the Delaware. He did, and the story—his first effort—was published in *Recreation* in May 1902. The appearance of the article gave him direction, and he began writing an historical novel about his ancestor, Betty Zane, who carried gunpowder to her brother,

Colonel Zane, during the siege of Fort Henry in the Revolution. All winter Grey labored over the book in a dingy flat. Upon completing it he drew the cover and inside illustrations. No publisher would accept *Betty Zane,* and, after a wealthy patient offered to back it, Grey had it printed privately. Sales were nil, but in a visit to Zanesville in 1904, Grey grandly announced that he given up dentistry to devote himself "exclusively to literature."

In 1905 Grey married Lina Roth of New York, whom he had met a few years earlier while he was canoeing down the Delaware in one of his escapes from dentistry. She had faith in her husband and a bit of money to boot, and he gave up his practice to write while living in a house overlooking the Delaware in Lackawaxen, Pennsylvania. There he wrote, hunted, fished and savored "the happiness that dwells in wilderness alone." R.C., by now a professional ballplayer, chipped in with an occasional dollar, and Zane later repaid him by making him his official secretary and constant fishing companion.

Grey followed up *Betty Zane* by writing a couple of other books about the Ohio frontier, *The Spirit of the Border* and *The Last Trail,* which the A. L. Burt Company eventually published. They were flops. But Grey hung on, and in 1907 he went west with one Buffalo Jones, visiting the wilder parts of Utah and Arizona. Jones had a ranch on the rim of the Grand Canyon, where he was hybridizing black Galloway cattle with buffalo and calling the offspring cattalo. In his spare time he liked to lasso mountain lions. Grey loved it all, and, upon returning to the East, he wrote a book about Jones, *The Last of the Plainsmen,* which he took to Harper, a firm that had rebuffed him previously. Eagerly he awaited word and, hearing none, he visited the publishing house, where an editor coldly informed him, "I don't see anything in this to convince me that you can write either narrative or fiction." It was the bleakest moment in Grey's life. He was 36 years old, he had abandoned dentistry, his wife was pregnant with their first child and he had failed again. "When I staggered down the old stairway and out into Pearl Street I could not see," he later recalled. "I had to hold on to an iron post at the corner, and there I hung fighting such misery as I had never known. Something came to me there. They had all missed it. They did not know . . . and I went back to Lackawaxen to the smile and encouragement that never failed me."

He promptly wrote his first Western novel, *The Heritage of the Desert.* Harper yielded and published it in 1910—the year of the birth of his first son, Romer—and Grey thought he was at last on his way. Quickly he wrote *Riders of the Purple Sage,* but Harper rejected it as too "bulgy." Grey asked a vice-president of the firm to read the manuscript. He liked the novel, and so did his wife, who stayed up until three in the morning to finish it. The book was published, and Grey was permanently established. In fifteen years *Riders of the Purple Sage* sold two million copies. Grey also turned out half a dozen juveniles, many of them dealing with his baseball experiences. In *The Young Pitcher* he wrote of the potato episode at Penn and drew himself as Ken Ward, the hero. His brother, R.C., also called Reddy, was Reddy Ray, spark plug of the team. In *The Shortstop*, Grey named the hero after Chase Alloway, a professional player he had known in Ohio. (In the Western *The Lone Star Ranger* Grey named one of the villains Chess Alloway.)

Although comfortably off, Grey continued to write feverishly. He could not abide waste of time. As a writer and as an angler Grey was a finisher, and he followed both callings to the hilt. "It is so easy to start anything, a fishing jaunt or a career," he wrote, "but it is an entirely different matter to finish. The men who fail to finish in any walk of life, men who have had every opportunity . . . can be numbered by the millions." At top speed, Grey found he could write 100,000 words a month. He would pen himself up in his study, where he would sit in a Morris chair, writing in longhand on a lapboard, furiously chewing the top of a soft No. 1 pencil when a sentence failed him. He compiled notebooks of vivid phrases and expressions, and he often thumbed a worn copy of a book, *Materials and Methods of Fiction*, by Clayton Milton. Grey's son Romer said, "That was father's bible. It had a greater influence on his writing than any other work." Grey wrote only one draft of a book; he left the finishing of the manuscript to his wife. When not writing he fished. He knew a long stretch of the Delaware by memory. "I own nearly a thousand acres of land on it," he wrote. "I have fished it for ten years. I know every rapid, every eddy, almost, I might say, every stone from Callicoon to Port Jervis. This fifty-mile stretch of fast water I consider the finest bass ground I have ever fished." In July, when the river was low, he would scout the water for big bass by going upstream and drifting face down on a raft. "I see the bottom everywhere, except in rough water. I see the rocks, the shelves, the caverns. I see where the big bass live. And I remember." When the time came to fish, Grey became part of the landscape; he trod the slippery stones "as if I were a stalking Indian. I knew that a glimpse of me, or a faint jar vibrating under the water, or an unnatural ripple on its surface, would be fatal to my enterprise." Not every visiting angler exalted the fishing; some referred to Lackawaxen Creek as the Lackanothing or Lackarotten.

With money coming in, Grey and R.C. began fishing in Florida. They went after bonefish, snook and tarpon. Grey was among the first to go after sailfish, and he did so well that other fishermen flocked to the Gulf Stream. He was intrigued by wahoo, then seldom caught, reasoning that they could be taken because "all fish have to eat." He caught wahoo, and he helped put the Keys on the map. Wherever he went, he fished. On a trip to Mexico to gather material for a novel, his train chanced to pass by a jungle river, the Santa Rosa. Immediately Grey wondered, "Where did that river go? How many waterfalls and rapids hastened its journey to the Gulf? What teeming life inhabited its rich banks? How wild was the prospect! It haunted me!" In time he made the trip in a flat-bottom boat. On a trip to Yucatán, he happened to hear of "the wild and lonely Alacranes Reef where lighthouse keepers went insane from solitude, and where wonderful fishes inhabited the lagoons. That was enough for me. Forthwith I meant to go to Alacranes." Forthwith he did. There he met a little Englishman, Lord L., and "it was from him I got my type for Castleton, the Englishman, in *The Light of the Western Stars.* I have been told that never was there an Englishman on earth like the one I portrayed in my novel. But my critics never fished with Lord L."

Grey never lost any time. On a fishing trip he was up before everyone at four in the morning, transcribing the adventures of the previous day. If fishing was slack, he worked on a book until breakfast. He wrote much of *The Drift Fence* and *Robbers' Roost* at sea, and he piled up such a backlog of books that *Boulder Dam*, which he wrote while off on a trip in the 1930s, was not published by Harper until 1963.

In 1914 Grey started going west to Catalina each summer, where he tried sword-fishing. In his first year he spent over three weeks at sea, trolling a total of 1,500 miles. Grey saw nineteen swordfish but did not get one strike. Instead of becoming discouraged, he was pleased. "By this time," he wrote, "I had realized something of the difficult nature of the game, and I had begun to have an inkling of what sport it might be." On the twenty-fifth day Grey sighted a swordfish, which he hooked. But the fish broke away, and Grey was sick at heart. The following summer found him back in Catalina. "I was crazy on swordfish," he admitted. To get his arms, hands and back into fighting trim, he rowed a boat for weeks on end. His patience and training were rewarded—he set a record by catching four swordfish in one day.

Between gathering material for novels and advising on movies and fishing, Grey began to visit Southern California so frequently that he moved his family to Los Angeles in 1918. Two years later he bought the small estate in Altadena that now serves as the headquarters of Zane Grey, Inc. Once established on the West Coast, Grey took up steelhead fishing in Oregon, and on a trip down the Rogue River he ran into a prospector who offered to sell his shack and land. Grey bought the place at Winkle Bar as offhandedly as he would buy a dozen new rods. He also owned some land and a small hunting lodge in Arizona. He shuttled from one place to another, writing, fishing, hunting, and gathering material. "[The year] 1923 was typical of what I do in the way of work and play," he replied to an admirer who had asked what a typical year was like.

The pleasant paradox, however, is that my play turns out to be valuable work. January and February I spent at Long Key, Florida, where I wrote, read, fished and wandered along the beach. The spring I spent with my family in Altadena, California, where I wrote and studied, and played with my family. Tennis is my favorite game. During this season I motored with Mrs. Grey down to San Diego and across the mountains to El Centro and Yuma, through the wonderful desert land of Southern California. June found me at Avalon, Catalina Island, a place I have found as inspiring as Long Key, and infinitely different. Here I finished a novel, and then began my sword-fishing on the Pacific. My brother, R.C., and I roamed the sea searching for giant swordfish. Sometimes we ran a hundred miles in a day. The sea presents a marvelous contrast to the desert. It inspires, teaches, subdues, uplifts, appalls and remakes me. There I learned more of nature than on land. Birds and fishes, strange sea creatures, are always in evidence. In September I took Mr. [Jesse] Lasky and his [Paramount] staff to Arizona to pick out locations for the motion picture, *The Vanishing American*. Upon the return I parted with the Lasky outfit at the foot of Navajo Mountains . . . I, with my guide Wetherill, with selected cowboys and horses, tried for the third time to reach Wild Horse Mesa. In October I went to my hunting lodge in the Tonto Basin, where the magnificent forests of green pine and silver spruce and golden aspen soothed my eyes after the long weeks on sea and desert. Here I hunted and rode the lonely leaf-covered trails, lay for hours on the Rim, listening to the bay of hounds, and spent many a pleasant evening round the camp-fire, listening to my men, the gaunt long-legged and lead-faced backwoodsmen of the Tonto Basin. November and December found me back again at Altadena, hard as nails, brown as an Indian, happy to be home with my family, keen for my study with its books and pictures, and for the long spell of writing calling me to its fulfillment.

Grey always had some new adventure going. A Norwegian named Sievert Nielsen, a sailor turned prospector, read Grey's novel *Desert Gold* and wrote to him under the misapprehension that the story of the treasure in the farfetched plot was true. Grey was so charmed with the letter that he invited Nielsen to see him. They became friends and hiked across Death Valley for the thrill of it.

Grey's success at landing big fish prompted a correspondence with Captain Laurie Mitchell of Liverpool, Nova Scotia. Mitchell, who was to become one of Grey's fishing companions, was enthusiastic about giant bluefin tuna off Nova Scotia. He himself had landed only one—it happened to be a world-record 710 pounds—and had lost between fifty and sixty of the big fish. Other anglers had caught perhaps a total of ten. The fish were simply too tough for ordinary tackle. This was just the sort of challenge that appealed to Grey, who promptly began laying plans to fish in Nova

Scotia. He reasoned that his swordfish tackle would be adequate for the tuna, provided that the boat from which he was fishing was fast and maneuverable. He had two light skiffs built in Nova Scotia, and from Florida he ordered a special launch, twenty-five feet long and equipped with two engines capable of doing eighteen miles an hour. The launch was so designed that at full speed it could turn on its own length. Grey installed Catalina fighting chairs in each boat.

Within a couple of weeks Grey proved his strategy to be right. He hooked three tuna and landed two, one of which was a world-record 758 pounds and the largest fish of any species ever caught on rod and reel.

Before leaving Nova Scotia, Grey fulfilled a boyhood dream of buying "a beautiful white ship with sails like wings to sail into tropic seas." The three-masted schooner, which he called *Fisherman*, held the record for the run from Halifax to New York City. Grey scrupulously made certain she never had been used as a rumrunner; ever the teetotaler, he would not have a bootlegger's boat as a gift. He had *Fisherman* outfitted with all the tackle that "money could buy and ingenuity devise," and, with R.C. and Romer, he set sail for Galápagos, Cocos Island, the Gulf of Panama and the Pacific coast of Mexico. On this trip he caught a 135-pound Pacific sailfish, the first known to science, but otherwise fishing conditions were not good because of an abundance of sharks.

Broadbill swordfish remained Grey's great love. In 1926 at Catalina, he and his brother caught a total of 10, including Zane's world-record 582-pounder. In that same year R.C. caught five marlin, all weighing more than 300 pounds. No other angler had then caught more than one 300-pound fish, and the 354-pounder taken by R.C. was a world record. It was a great year for the brothers, and, as Grey wrote, "Not the least pleasure in our success was to run back to Avalon with the red flag flying at the masthead, to blow a clarion blast from the boat's whistle, and to see the pier filled with excited spectators. Sometimes thousands of visitors massed at the end of the pier to see the swordfish weighed and photographed. On these occasions R.C. and I would have to stand the battery of hundreds of cameras and shake hands until we broke away from the pier."

Not everyone cheered Grey. He and R.C. broke early with members of the Catalina Tuna Club over Grey's choice of tackle. Although a light-tackle man in freshwater, Grey used very heavy tackle for big game fish. He argued that fish that broke off light tackle either became prey to sharks or died.

Grey accepted the invitation of the New Zealand government to investigate the big-game fishing possibilities in that country. Captain Mitchell and R.C. went with him. They revolutionized local practices; instead of fishing with bait deep down, they took fish by trolling. Grey caught a world-record 450-pound striped marlin and a record 111-pound yellowtail, while Captain Mitchell set a record with a 976-pound black marlin. Grey's greatest pleasure, however, was finding copies of Westerns in even the remotest homes he visited. "This was surely the sweetest and most moving of all the experiences I had; and it faced me again with the appalling responsibility of a novelist who in these modern days of materialism dares to foster idealism and love of nature, chivalry in men and chastity in women."

Back home, Grey had difficulties in Arizona. In 1930 the state passed game laws and established seasons, and Grey, accustomed to hunting bears whenever the mood was on him, was angered. He felt that he was entitled to hunt year round, because he had put Arizona on the map. When a warden refused to issue him a resident license Grey was "grossly insulted," and he gave up his lodge in the Tonto Basin. "In twelve years my whole bag of game has been five bears, three bucks and a few turkeys," he said. "I have written fifteen novels with Arizona background. Personally it cost me $30,000 to get material for one book *To the Last Man*. My many trips all over the state have cost me $100,000. So in every way I have not been exactly an undesirable visitor." He was so indignant he said he would never return and, as a parting shot, he said that the game commission and the Forest Service had sold out to "the commercial interest." As a case in point, he cited the north rim of the Grand Canyon as nothing more than a "tin-can gasoline joint." Grey felt strongly about the Grand Canyon, so much so that he could not bring himself to write about it. It was simply too marvelous to describe.

Fishing in the Pacific lured him more and more. He revisited New Zealand and Tahiti, where he caught his record 1,040-pound striped marlin. The fish was mutilated by sharks; had it not been, it would have weighed 200 pounds more. When the Australian government asked him to explore big-game fishing there, Grey went to Australia and landed his record tiger shark off Sydney Heads. Always the unknown beckoned. He spent $40,000 for a steel-hulled schooner originally built for the Kaiser, and another $270,000 went into refurbishing the ship, which he named *Fisherman II*. His dream of dreams was to fish the waters of Christmas Island off Madagascar, where there were reports of sailfish twenty-two feet long. Equipped with six launches, *Fisherman II* embarked for Christmas Island on a round-the-world cruise. The ship was 195 feet long, but she had a narrow twenty-eight-foot beam and she rolled, even in a calm sea. Even Grey got sick. "We had so much trouble it was unbelievable," said his young son, Loren. "We got as far as Totoya in the Fijis. The captain was ill. The chief engineer had appendicitis. We were there for over a month or more with costly repairs. Father finally called the trip off because of a pressing business matter with his publisher." Eventually Grey gave up on the ship, and she ended her days as a cannery tender for a West Coast tuna fleet.

While steelhead fishing in Oregon in 1937 Grey suffered a stroke. Romer and a guide carried him to a car and got him home, where he recuperated. Within a year he seemed recovered. He went to Australia to fish and then back to Altadena to write, before going on to Oregon for steelhead. There he insisted that Loren and three friends fish "not only all day, but every day in the week," said Loren, who became a professor of education at San Fernando Valley State College. "We finally had a big fight with him and said we wanted to go home. If he wouldn't let us go home, would he at least let us go into town on weekends and live it up a little bit? He finally gave in, so we'd fish just five days a week."

Determined to make a complete recovery, Grey worked out with a rod in a fighting chair set on the porch of the west wing of his house. Every day Grey would battle imaginary fish, pumping the rod perhaps 200 times before calling it quits. He was getting ready for the next expedition. It never came. On October 23, 1939 Zane Grey died. His workouts in the fighting chair apparently had been too much for him. He once wrote, in his younger days, "There is only one thing wrong with a fishing day—its staggering brevity. If a man spent all his days fishing, life would seem to be a swift dream." For Zane Grey, compulsive angler, the swift dream was over.

Thaddeus Norris

FRED MATHER

When I bought a farm near Honeoye Falls, Monroe County, N. Y., in 1868, to begin raising trout, I also bought a book entitled "American Fish Culture," which was published in that year by Porter & Coates, Philadelphia, and the author was Thaddeus Norris. Just who he might be, or what he might know of the subject, I did not know, but it was the first publication of its kind that I had heard of, and I bought it. It has little value to the fishculturist to-day, but it gave all that was then known about breeding trout, salmon, oysters and other things, and yet I had much to learn. I do not think he said so in the book, but at that time he had gone into trout breeding at Bloomsbury, N. J., had tried it a year or two and sold out to Dr. J. H. Slack, who ran the place until he died, some five or six years later.

In September, 1873, I was called to Washington to consult with Professor Baird, the United States Fish Commissioner, and there I met Mr. Norris, and we struck up a friendship which lasted until he died. I was then forty and he was sixty-two. He was a lovable old man whom many people called "Uncle Thad," and I soon dropped into the habit of addressing him so. Business over, he said: "Freddy, I'm going down to Betterton to fish for perch, and I'd like to have you go with me. Will you do it?"

"Where's Betterton?"

"I think there is a previous question before the house. Let us finish one at a time. The question is: Will you go?"

"Yes."

"Well, now that we have settled that, the next thing is to take up your question. Betterton is in Kent County, Md., and is a paradise for the angler who is contented to fish for white perch. It is not on the map, has no post-office, and therefore we can rest assured that we can't be called home by the demands of either family or business. There is no village of Betterton, only a few scattered farmhouses, and unless I am greatly mistaken it is a place that would just suit such a quiet, easy-going fellow as I take you to be."

"No railroad whistles, umbrella menders, steamboat nor church bells to destroy a morning nap?"

"Nothing of the kind, my boy; the place is on the Eastern Shore. At the upper end of Chesapeake Pay is the confluence of the Susquehanna, Northeast, Elk and Sassafras rivers, all within sight, and a grand sight it is over the upper end of the bay, and Betterton is about a mile below the mouth of the Sassafras. So much for geography. Anything else?"

"Not a thing. You've asked me to go to Betterton with you and I am your guest. I haven't the slightest curiosity how we are to get there, whether we walk, row, sail or swim. I did not bring any fishing tackle, but can easily get what will be needed for white perch. I suppose none of them weigh over 100 lbs."

"No; there is a law which limits their size, but you'll find 'em tip to the limit. Come up and stop with me in Philadelphia to-night and give no thought to fishing tackle or other thing. We will talk fish until bed-time and possibly dream of them before morning."

That night one of the most lovable of men spread his heart wide open and captivated me. When I was a young man I was fond of the society of some older ones, and I say "some" advisedly, now that I have had my hair bleached and am posing as a blond, a condition which I insist is not due to "peroxide," or any other preparation, but has been brought about solely by Anno Domini which you can't buy in a drug store. I find that I like boys—that is, if they are the kind of boys which I like. There's just as much difference in boys as there is in dogs; some wouldn't have you like 'em under any circumstances, and as for old men, they are boys who have been boiled down and all their traits intensified. A disagreeable boy will grow into——— Pardon me, we were going fishing.

We took an Ericsson steamer somewhere above Chestnut street, Philadelphia, about 4 P.M., and went through the canal from Delaware City to Chesapeake City, down the Elk River and into the bay, reaching Betterton at the uncomfortable hour of 4 A.M. Neither of us grumbled—we made light of having to turn out at that time ; and now, while writing this sketch, nearly a quarter of a century later, and with an experience as much riper, it seems to that "Uncle Thad" and I had the one common trait of accepting whatever came to us without grumbling.

As old Nessmuk said, "Bismillah, it is well!" Others say, "Kismet, it is fate!" And in these sayings lies all the philosophy contained in that scriptural warning which says that it is "no use to kick against the pricks." Resignation to the inevitable has preserved my life where others have died. Norris had the same turn of thought, and as we walked up from the landing to the house where we were to stop, he said: "The only thing I prefer to getting out of bed at 4 o'clock in the morning is sitting up all night."

I remarked that I would prefer sitting up two nights; but we had not far to walk. Our host, Mr. Thomas Crew, was astir, as is the custom of farmers and dwellers in the country, and we entered his hospitable home, lay down and had our sleep out, because Crew said the tide would be about right four hours later. About 8 o'clock we had finished breakfast and were sailing away to the perch grounds, some two miles distant, with young Jim Crew as captain as well as crew. There were some other boats there, and more came later, making eleven in all, and about fifty anglers. As we anchored, Jim pulled out a half-bushel basket of peaches—and such peaches! I realized that we were right where peaches grow in both quantity and excellence. The tide ran from two to three miles an hour that day, the ebb being strongest. The average depth of the water was 30 ft. We used 9 ft. bass rods, with multiplying reels and a dipsy of 2 oz. "Dipsy," in the Philadelphia language, means a piece of wire to keep two hooks on short snells apart, and a sinker hangs at proper depth below. It is said to be a corruption of "deep sea," but I never heard it east of New York, and rarely there, although the thing is sometimes used about New York Harbor, and called a "spreader." We used shedder crabs and angleworms, the former being plenty and the latter scarce, owing to the lightness and dryness of the soil. Some of the anglers used clams and shrimp.

Our largest perch that day weighed 18 oz. The average was perhaps less than half that weight. Captain Jim did not fish, and we two filled three peach baskets with such good measure that they ran over. Perhaps we counted them, but I don't remember. From conversation with the men in other boats we estimated the catch of the entire party that day at 6,000 white perch, besides a few other fishes, and Jim said it was not a very good day for perch.

Filled to overflowing with humor, Uncle Thad was as charming a man as one could wish for on a month's trip. He was past middle age and not strong nor active, but bright as a button. His "American Angler's Book" was the first good American book on angling. It treated of native fishes and methods of fishing, while all other fishing books up to that time were rehashes of English publications. It was first published by E. H. Butler & Co., Philadelphia, in 1864, who printed two editions. Of the last, Porter & Coates bought 699 copies in 1865, with all the plates, and issued an edition with their imprint. This was a volume of 692 pages, and the only edition I have.

The latter firm printed editions in 1881, 1886 and 1891, each being of 250 copies. In the last three editions there is an excellent obituary notice, written by his friend, Mr. Joseph B. Townsend. My volume is well thumbed, for I still delight in the quaint stories in which he embodies information, especially in those charming pages which he calls "Dies Piscatoriae." If any man is entitled to be called "The American Walton" it is Thaddeus Norris. His book may not be read by scholars who regard Walton as an English classic to be studied by non-anglers as a choice bit of literature, but it can be read with pleasure by anyone who appreciates clean humor, even if he cares nothing about fishing. Some years ago it was proposed that I should edit "The American Angler's Book," but business forbade. I am indebted for many of the above facts and dates to Mr. J. B. Townsend, Jr., of Philadelphia.

The winter of 1875-76 I spent at Lexington, Va., quartered in the Military Institute, together with my assistant, Mr. Wm. F. Page, now a well-known fishculturist; and I ran down to Richmond and met Uncle Thad by appointment, and tried to get him to go to Lynchburg to fish for pike with my friend Captain Jack Yeatman, of that city, who was an excellent angler, and had a rod that I wanted Norris to see. It was a natural bamboo, carefully smoothed inside where the partitions had been, and the line was run through the inside of the cane. "This," said Captain Jack, "puts the strain on all points, instead of a few, where the rings are." This idea has been put on the market since, but I have a notion that it is very hard on lines. Time did not permit Mr. Norris to go there. He arranged with me to go to Philadelphia in the spring and try to build an aquarium for the Centennial Exposition. I went, tried, and failed for want of financial support.

That summer it was my custom to visit Uncle Thad in his home on Logan square every Tuesday evening, and we would go up into his workshop where the justly celebrated "Norris split-bamboo rods" were made, and often talk until "the wee sma' hours ayont the twal." If we talked of fishing, it was not of perch catching at Betterton, but of grander sport. We had both fished, but not in unison, with Dan Fitzhugh of grayling memory, and our thoughts turned to that royal and generous angler. We would repeat some of Dan's stories; Uncle Thad would slap his knee and laugh until the tears came, and say "Dan was a glo-o-rious fel-low!" and then we gave a few moments of meditation to Dan.

In his "American Fishes," 1888, Professor C. Brown Goode says, writing of the white perch: "In a single paragraph Mr. Norris, who, making no profession of scientific skill, has been one of our best observers of fishes, has given almost the only reliable information which has ever been collected regarding this species."

It so happened that the Philadelphia Academy of Sciences met at the corner of Logan square and Race street every Tuesday night, and we would often get a tip from Professor Cope if the talk was to be about a lot of prehistoric fishes, mammals and birds, in a densely scientific manner in which we had no interest whatever, or whether the discourse was to be upon the fishes of to-day. In the latter case we often spent a profitable hour on many evenings.

I recall one of these fish was on the table and was to be the subject of the lecture. It was a salt water fish which is not caught by anglers and is never in the markets. It was about 1 ft. long, heavy-bodied and triangular, the back being the apex; it had a greenish color, a body like jelly, and was covered with a thick skin on which were many tuberculous or spiny plates.

"What kind of a fish is that, Fred?"

"Well, Uncle Thad, that is a lumpsucker or lumpfish. Notice its build. It is so weak behind that it can't swim much, but see its ventral fins—how they are modified into a sucking disk on its breast, whereby it can hold fast on a rock and let the tide bring food to its mouth."

"Don't you wish that you were that kind of a sucker? What did you say its name was?"

"Lumpsuckers or lumpfish on our coast. In England it is called sea-owl, cock-paddle, and it doesn't seem to mind what they call it—at least it never resents these names. That's all I know about the fish."

"Then you don't know what these musty old scientifs call this queer-looking beast?"

"Oh, yes; they call it *Cyclopterus lumpus*. I didn't know you were after that."

"Lumpus, lumpus; and they call the tomcod *Microgadus tomcodus*, and one species of catfish *Ameiurus catus*. Now, honestly, my boy, don't you think we can make as good Latin as that? Well, well, it is lumpy, sure enough. But lumpus! Let's go back to the workshop and digest the scientific information we have obtained here to-night. If we get more at one sitting we may not be able to assimilate it, and may not be able to retain what we have learned."

There were banjos in those days. They are rare now. They have put frets on them and made them merely guitars with a calf-skin head, on which can be played operatic music, but not real banjo music, which in these degenerate days is called "rag time." . . .

Uncle Thad's banjo had a serious fracture in the cranium. Mine was in a trunk in storage, but he had to have it got out in order to properly recite the mishaps of "Johnny Booker," "Uncle Gabriel," and other epics. Our national instrument had no frets upon it, nor additional strings to play difficult marches and operas; in fact, it was a banjo, and not a hybrid guitar and mandolin . . .

One night after the old man had finished "Dandy Jim," I said: "Uncle Thad, once I attended a dance down in Texas and was greatly interested in the orchestra, which consisted of only two pieces—a fiddle and a boot; both were good in their way, and if the dancers missed the fiddle when conversation was loudest, the boot heel gave them the correct time. I have noticed that in your enthusiasm you have emphasized certain crescendo passages with your heel, which might offend any musical ear which was trying to sleep on the floor below."

"I think you are right in this matter," he said. "Where the orchestra consists of a banjo and a boot, the latter should subordinate its tones or be abolished entirely. Perhaps the banjo should be hung up until next Tuesday night and I'll tell you how Fish Commissioner Reeder, of this State, had his nose sunburned. Do you know H. J. Reeder?"

"Very well. Met him when his father was Governor of Kansas, and since that time he has been a fish commissioner and I have met him frequently and have had much correspondence with him. We've all had our noses burned, blistered and peeled in the sun. Was Reeder's nose an exception in any way?"

"No," said the veteran angler; "it was as susceptible to the influence of the sun as a Maryland peach, and that's the point. I made some verses on it to an original meter. I'll read 'em:

"'The shades of night were falling fast.'"

"Yes, that is original, and grand! How on earth did you ever come to think in that direction?"

"Never mind about the applause until the curtain if about to descend, and please do not interrupt again until this lyric is finished.

"The shades of night were falling fast,
As o'er the Bel.-Del. Road there passed
A sun-burned nose, with face attached,
That had been to the South dispatched
For catfish!

"'Neath forehead high and yaller hair
Was a Grecian nose and complexion fair,
A bright blue eye and curled up lash,
And lie ever kept shouting through his mustache:
Oh, catfish!

"'Oh, don't go out,' quoth Howard; 'stop!
It's awful hot where the white-caps hop;
You'll burn your nose on the upper side,'
But the ghastly fisherman still replied:
'More catfish!'

"The boat at length came up to land,
With a sun-burned nose, a line-cut hand,
And a barrel of fish bought for a price;
Says the nose-burned man, 'they're remarkably nice,
Fresh catfish!'

"Now, young man, be warned by me,
If ever again you go to sea,
Bear this painful burn in mind
And leave your tender nose behind,
For catfish!"

Tears big as goose eggs came to my eyes as I grasped the poet's hand and asked his pardon if the ceiling below should fall out account of my tears; I'm so easily affected. When he handed me the paper I pocketed the poem in order to give it to an appreciative world, which his modesty forbade him to do.

The workshop of Uncle Thad—I love to call him so—differed from that of the rod-maker of to-day. The latter has his ferrules drawn by an expert, who perhaps draws tubes for microscopes and telescopes; and they fit throughout the whole length, and never throw apart. In Uncle Thad's day—and he was abreast of the time in rod-making, if not ahead of it—he made his ferrules by hand and brazed them, afterward smoothing them with flat files, grinding them together with emery powder and oil, and then burnished them in a lathe.

I handled many of his rods, and wanted one. I feared to tell him so, because the notion might occur to him to give me one; so I had a friend buy a rod for me, and I used it several years, its value increasing each season, until it was stolen from me in a car while returning from a fishing trip.

If I had used that rod until it was "superannuated" it would be in an honored place on my wall in company with a pair of buffalo horns from the only buffalo I ever killed, a pair of snowshoes worn in Wisconsin in 1856, a banjo made by my own hands, and a sword which I wore in the early '60's, which was "Held by the Enemy," as the title of a play goes, for over a quarter of a century.

In the day on which things happen they are merely incidents which are not forgotten, but laid aside as trifles. Half a century later, or even half of that, they assume an importance which is surprising. An instance of this is my reminiscence of perch fishing at Betterton. There was nothing of importance to record; but the lapse of time serves to figure Uncle Thad Norris in a strong light, and to bring up the man so that I can attempt to sketch him in a manner that will interest people who never knew him . . .

Thaddeus Norris was born near Warrenton, Fauquier county, Va., in 1811, and moved to Philadelphia about 1835, where he resided until his death, which occurred on April 11, 1877. A widow, two sons and two daughters survived him.

An incident occurred which illustrates his dry humor. We were looking at some fish in the tanks at the Centennial Exposition, when a noisy sort of fellow introduced himself to Mr. Norris as "a brother of the angle," and after a long recital of his exploits, said: "Yes, Mr. Norris, I'm the boss fisherman of western Pennsylvania, and I catch more fish than anyone I ever met."

"I am always pleased to meet a thorough angler," said Uncle Thad, very seriously. "I suppose you fish with the fly?"

"Always, Mr. Norris; always."

"Always rig the line properly with a float and sinker?"

"Oh, yes, always use the float and sinker."

"That's right; I see that you are really an expert angler, and I am glad to know you."

Mr. Norris never smiled, nor did his eye change when it met mine, and the man suspected nothing. After the man departed Uncle Thad said: "I often meet such men, and I sized him up for a man who knew nothing of fly-fishing and would need a float and sinker if he tried to cast a fly."

Genial Uncle Thad! When I read of his death the words came upon me "like the falling of a great oak in the stillness of the woods."

The Angler

WASHINGTON IRVING

It is said that many an unlucky urchin is induced to run away from his family, and betake himself to a seafaring life, from reading the history of Robinson Crusoe; and I suspect that, in like manner, many of those worthy gentlemen who are given to haunt the sides of pastoral streams with angle rods in hand, may trace the origin of their passion to the seductive pages of honest Izaak Walton. I recollect studying his *Compleat Angler* several years since, in company with a knot of friends in America, and moreover that we were all completely bitten with the angling mania. It was early in the year; but as soon as the weather was auspicious, and the spring began to melt into the verge of summer, we took rod in hand and sallied into the country, as stark mad as was ever Don Quixote from reading books of chivalry.

One of our party had equaled the Don in the fullness of his equipments: being attired *cap-à-pie* for the enterprise. He wore a broad-skirted fustian coat, perplexed with half a hundred pockets; a pair of stout shoes, and leathern gaiters; a basket slung on one side for fish; a patent rod, a landing net, and a score of other inconveniences, only to be found in the true angler's armory. Thus harnessed for the field, he was as great a matter of stare and wonderment among the country folk, who had never seen a regular angler, as was the steel-clad hero of La Mancha among the goatherds of the Sierra Morena.

Our first essay was along a mountain brook, among the highlands of the Hudson; a most unfortunate place for the execution of those piscatory tactics which had been invented along the velvet margins of quiet English rivulets. It was one of those wild streams that lavish, among our romantic solitudes, unheeded beauties, enough to fill the sketch-book of a hunter of the picturesque. Sometimes it would leap down rocky shelves, making small cascades, over which the trees threw their broad balancing sprays, and long nameless weeds hung in fringes from the impending banks, dripping with diamond drops. Sometimes it would brawl and fret along a ravine in the matted shade of a forest, filling it with murmurs; and, after this termagant career, would steal forth into open day with the most placid demure face imaginable; as I have seen some pestilent shrew of a housewife, after filling her home with uproar and ill-humor, come dimpling out of doors, swimming and curtseying, and smiling upon all the world.

How smoothly would this vagrant brook glide, at such times, through some bosom of green meadow-land among the mountains: where the quiet was only interrupted by the occasional tinkling of a bell from the lazy cattle among the clover, or the sound of a woodcutter's axe from the neighboring forest.

For my part, I was always a bungler at all kinds of sport that required either patience or adroitness, and had not angled above half an hour before I had completely "satisfied the sentiment," and convinced myself of the truth of Izaak Walton's opinion, that angling is something like poetry—a man must be born to it. I hooked myself instead of the fish; tangled my line in every tree; lost my bait; broke my rod; until I gave up the attempt in despair, and passed the day under the trees, reading old Izaak; satisfied that it was his fascinating vein of honest simplicity and rural feeling that had bewitched me, and not the passion for angling. My companions, however, were more persevering in their delusion. I have them at this moment before my eyes, stealing along the border of the brook, where it lay open to the day, or was merely fringed by shrubs and bushes. I see the bittern rising with hollow scream as they break in upon his rarely-invaded haunt; the kingfisher watching them suspiciously from his dry tree that overhangs the deep black mill-pond, in the gorge of the hills; the tortoise letting himself slip sideways from off the stone or log on which he is sunning himself; and the panic-struck frog plumping in headlong as they approach, and spreading an alarm throughout the watery world around.

I recollect also, that, after toiling and watching and creeping about for the greater part of a day, with scarcely any success, in spite of all our admirable apparatus, a lubberly country urchin came down from the hills with a rod made from a branch of a tree, a few yards of twine, and, as Heaven shall help me! I believe, a crooked pin for a hook, baited with a vile earthworm—and in half an hour caught more fish than we had nibbles throughout the day!

But, above all, I recollect, the "good, honest, wholesome, hungry" repast, which we made under a beech-tree, just by a spring of pure sweet water that stole out of the side of a hill; and how, when it was over, one of the party read old Izaak Walton's scene with the milkmaid, while I lay on the grass and built castles in a bright pile of clouds, until I fell asleep. All this may appear like mere egotism; yet I cannot refrain from uttering these recollections, which are passing like a strain of music over my mind, and have been called up by an agreeable scene which I witnessed not long since.

In a morning's stroll along the banks of the Alun, a beautiful little stream which flows down from the Welsh hills and throws itself into the Dee, my attention was attracted to a group seated on the margin. On approaching, I found it to consist of a veteran angler and two rustic disciples. The former was an old fellow with a wooden leg, with clothes very much but very carefully patched, betokening poverty, honestly come by, and decently maintained. His face bore the marks of former storms, but present fair weather; its furrows had been worn into a habitual smile; his iron-gray locks hung about his ears, and he had altogether the good-humored air of a constitutional philosopher who was disposed to take the world as it went. One of his companions was a ragged wight, with the skulking look of an arrant poacher, and I'll warrant could find his way to any gentleman's fish-pond in the neighborhood in the darkest night. The other was a tall, awkward, country lad, with a lounging gait, and apparently somewhat of a rustic beau. The old man was busy in examining the maw of a trout which he had just killed, to discover by its contents what insects were seasonable for bait; and was lecturing on the subject to his companions, who appeared to listen with infinite deference. I have a kind feeling towards all "brothers of the angle," ever since I read Izaak Walton. They are men, he affirms, of a "mild, sweet, and peaceable spirit;" and my esteem for them has been increased since I met with an old *Tretyse of Fishing with the Angle*, in which are set forth many of the maxims of their inoffensive fraternity. "Take good hede," sayeth this honest little tretyse, "that in going about your disportes ye open no man's gates but that ye shet them again. Also ye shall not use this forsayd crafti disport for no covetousness to the encreasing and sparing of your money only, but principally for your solace, and to cause the helth of your body and specyally of your soule."

I thought that I could perceive in the veteran angler before me an exemplification of what I had read; and there was a cheerful contentedness in his looks that quite drew me towards him. I could not but remark the gallant manner in which he stumped from one part of the brook to another; waving his rod in the air, to keep the line from dragging on the ground, or catching among the bushes; and the adroitness with which he would throw his fly to any particular place; sometimes skimming it lightly along a little rapid; sometimes casting it into one of those dark holes made by a twisted root or overhanging bank, in which the large trout are apt to lurk. In the meanwhile he was giving instructions to his two disciples; showing them the manner in which they should handle their rods, fix their flies, and play them along the surface of the stream. The scene brought to my mind the instructions of the sage

Piscator to his scholar. The country around was of that pastoral kind which Walton is fond of describing. It was a part of the great plain of Cheshire, close by the beautiful vale of Gessford, and just where the inferior Welsh hills begin to swell up from among fresh-smelling meadows. The day, too, like that recorded in his work, was mild and sunshiny, with now and then a soft-dropping shower, that sowed the whole earth with diamonds.

I soon fell into conversation with the old angler, and was so much entertained that, under pretext of receiving instructions in his art, I kept company with him almost the whole day; wandering along the banks of the stream, and listening to his talk. He was very communicative, having all the easy garrulity of cheerful old age; and I fancy was a little flattered by having an opportunity of displaying his piscatory lore; for who does not like now and then to play the sage?

He had been much of a rambler in his day, and had passed some years of his youth in America, particularly in Savannah, where he had entered into trade, and had been ruined by the indiscretion of a partner. He had afterwards experienced many ups and downs in life, until he got into the navy, where his leg was carried away by a cannon ball, at the battle of Camperdown. This was the only stroke of real good fortune he had ever experienced, for it got him a pension, which, together with some small paternal property, brought him in a revenue of nearly forty pounds. On this he retired to his native village, where he lived quietly and independently; and devoted the remainder of his life to the "noble art of angling."

I found that he had read Izaak Walton attentively, and he seemed to have imbibed all his simple frankness and prevalent good-humor. Though he had been sorely buffeted about the world, he was satisfied that the world, in itself, was good and beautiful. Though he had been as roughly used in different countries as a poor sheep that is fleeced by every hedge and thicket, yet he spoke of every nation with candor and kindness, appearing to look only on the good side of things: and, above all, he was almost the only man I had ever met with who had been an unfortunate adventurer in America, and had honesty and magnanimity enough to take the fault to his own door, and not to curse the country. The lad that was receiving his instructions, I learnt, was the son and heir apparent of a fat old widow who kept the village inn, and of course a youth of some expectation, and much courted by the idle gentlemanlike personages of the place. In taking him under his care, therefore, the old man had probably an eye to a privileged corner in the tap-room, and an occasional cup of cheerful ale free of expense.

There is certainly something in angling, if we could forget, which anglers are apt to do, the cruelties and tortures inflicted on worms and insects, that tends to produce a gentleness of spirit, and a pure serenity of mind. As the English are methodical even in their recreations, and are the most scientific of sportsmen, it has been reduced among them to perfect rule and system. Indeed it is an amusement peculiarly adapted to the mild and highly-cultivated scenery of England, where every roughness has been softened away from the landscape. It is delightful to saunter along those limpid streams which wander, like veins of silver, through the bosom of this beautiful country; leading one through a diversity of small home scenery; sometimes winding through ornamented grounds; sometimes brimming along through rich pasturage, where the fresh green is mingled with sweet-smelling flowers; sometimes venturing in sight of villages and hamlets, and then running capriciously away into shady retirements. The sweetness and serenity of nature, and the quiet watchfulness of the sport, gradually bring on pleasant fits of musing; which are now and then agreeably interrupted by the song of a bird, the distant whistle of the peasant, or perhaps the vagary of some fish, leaping out of the still water, and skimming transiently about its glassy surface. "When I would beget content," says Izaak Walton, "and increase confidence in the power and wisdom and providence of Almighty God, I will walk the meadows by some gliding stream, and there contemplate the lilies that take no care, and those very many other little living creatures that are not only created, but fed (man knows not how) by the goodness of the God of nature, and therefore trust in him."

I cannot forbear to give another quotation from one of those ancient champions of angling, which breathes the same innocent and happy spirit:

> Let me live harmlessly, and near the brink
> Of Trent or Avon have a dwelling-place,
> Where I may see my quill, or cork, down sink,
> With eager bite of pike, or bleak, or dace;
> And on the world and my Creator think:
> Whilst some men strive ill-gotten goods t' embrace;
> And others spend their time in base excess
> Of wine, or worse, in war, or wantonness.
> Let them that will, these pastimes still pursue,
> And on such pleasing fancies feed their fill;
> So I the fields and meadows green may view,
> And daily by fresh rivers walk at will,
> Among the daisies and the violets blue,
> Red hyacinth and yellow daffodil.

On parting with the old angler I inquired after his place of abode, and happening to be in the neighborhood of the village a few evenings afterwards, I had the curiosity to seek him out. I found him living in a small cottage, containing only one room, but a perfect curiosity in its method and arrangement. It was on the skirts of the village, on a green bank, a little back from the road, with a small garden in front, stocked with kitchen herbs, and adorned with a few flowers. The whole front of the cottage was overrun with a honeysuckle. On the top was a ship for a weather-cock. The interior was fitted up in a truly nautical style, his ideas of comfort and convenience having been acquired on the berth-deck of a man-of-war. A hammock was slung from the ceiling, which, in the daytime, was lashed up so as to take but little room. From the centre of the chamber hung a model of a ship, of his own workmanship. Two or three chairs, a table, and a large sea-chest, formed the principal movables. About the wall were stuck up naval ballads, such as "Admiral Hosier's Ghost," "All in the Downs," and "Tom Bowline," intermingled with pictures of sea-fights, among which the battle of Camperdown held a distinguished place. The mantel-piece was decorated with sea-shells; over which hung a quadrant, flanked by two wood-cuts of most bitter-looking naval commanders. His implements for angling were carefully disposed on nails and hooks about the room. On a shelf was arranged his library, containing a work on angling, much worn, a Bible covered with canvas, an odd volume or two of voyages, a nautical almanac, and a book of songs.

His family consisted of a large black cat with one eye, and a parrot which he had caught and tamed, and educated himself, in the course of one of his voyages; and which uttered a variety of sea phrases with the hoarse brattling tone of a veteran boatswain. The establishment reminded me of that of the renowned Robinson Crusoe; it was kept in neat order, every thing being "stowed away" with the regularity of a ship of war; and he informed me that he "scoured the deck every morning, and swept it between meals."

I found him seated on a bench before the door, smoking his pipe in the soft evening sunshine. His cat was purring soberly on the threshold, and his parrot describing some strange evolutions in an iron ring that swung in the centre of his cage. He had been angling all day, and gave me a history of his sport with as much minuteness as a general would talk over a campaign; being particularly animated in relating the manner in which he had taken a large trout, which had completely tasked all his skill and wariness, and which he had sent as a trophy to mine hostess of the inn.

How comforting it is to see a cheerful and contented old age; and to behold a poor fellow, like this, after being tempest-tost through life, safely moored in a snug and quiet harbor in the evening of his days! His happiness, however, sprung from within himself, and was independent of external circumstances; for he had that inexhaustible good-nature, which is the most precious gift of Heaven; spreading itself like oil over the troubled sea of thought, and keeping the mind smooth and equable in the roughest weather.

On inquiring further about him, I learned that he was a universal favorite in the village, and the oracle of the taproom; where he delighted the rustics with his songs, and, like Sinbad, astonished them with his stories of strange lands, and shipwrecks, and sea-fights. He was much noticed too by gentlemen sportsmen of the neighborhood; had taught several of them the art of angling; and was a privileged visitor to their kitchens. The whole tenor of his life was quiet and inoffensive, being principally passed about the neighboring streams, when the weather and season were favorable; and at other times he employed himself at home, preparing his fishing tackle for the next campaign, or manufacturing rods, nets, and flies, for his patrons and pupils among the gentry.

He was a regular attendant at church on Sundays, though he generally fell asleep during the sermon. He had made it his particular request that when he died he should be buried in a green spot, which he could see from his seat in church, and which he had marked out ever since he was a boy, and had thought of when far from home on the raging sea, in danger of being food for the fishes—it was the spot where his father and mother had been buried.

I have done, for I fear that my reader is growing weary; but I could not refrain from drawing the picture of this worthy "brother of the angle"; who has made me more than ever in love with the theory, though I fear I shall never be adroit in the practice of his art; and I will conclude this rambling sketch in the words of honest Izaak Walton, by craving the blessing of St. Peter's master upon my reader, "and upon all that are true lovers of virtue; and dare trust in his providence; and be quiet; and go a angling."

What and Who Is an Angler?

THADDEUS NORRIS

It is not my intention to offer any remarks on the antiquity of angling, or say much in its defense. Dame Juliana Berners, Izaak Walton, and more recent authors, have discoursed learnedly on its origin, and defended it wisely and valiantly from the aspersions and ridicule of those who cannot appreciate its quiet toys, and who know not the solace and peace it brings to the harassed mind, or how it begets and fosters contentment and a love of nature.

I ask any caviller to read Dr. Bethune's Bibliographical Preface to his edition Walton; and then Father Izaak's address to the readers of his discourse, "but especially to THE HONEST ANGLER," and accompany him in spirit, as Bethune by the quiet Lea, or Cotton by the bright rippling Dove; and if he be not convinced of the blessed influences of the "gentle art," or if his heart is not warmed, or no recollections of his boyish days come back to him, I give him up without a harsh word, but with a feeling of regret, that a life-time should be spent without attaining so much of quiet happiness that might have been so easily possessed, and quoting a few sad words from Whittier's Maud Muller, only say "it might have been."

Many anglers, such as Sir Humphrey Davy and Sir Joshua Reynolds, besides some of my own acquaintance, have sought its cheering influences in advanced life. I know of one whose early manhood and maturer years were spent on the boisterous deep, and who, though now past eighty, is still an ardent, but quiet angler; and when no better spot can be found, he will even fish through the ice in winter for roach. No doubt his days have been lengthened out, and the burden of life lightened, by his love of angling.

But how sweetly memories of the past come to one who has appreciated and enjoyed it from his boyhood, whose almost first penny, after he wore jacket and trousers, bought his first fish hook; whose first fishing line was twisted by mother or sister; whose float was the cork of a physic vial, and whose sinkers were cut from the sheet lead of an old tea chest! Thus rigged, with what glad anticipations of sport, many a boy has started on some bright Saturday morning, his gourd, or old cow's horn of red worms in one pocket, and a jackknife in the other, to cut his alder pole with, and wandered "free and far" by still pool and swift waters, dinnerless—except perhaps a slight meal at a cherry tree, or a handful of berries that grew along his path—and come home at night weary and footsore, but exulting in his string of chubs, minnows, and sunnies, the largest as broad as his three fingers! He almost falls asleep under his Saturday night scrubbing, but in the morning, does ample justice to his "catch," which is turned out of the pan, crisp and brown, and matted together like a pancake.

In *my* school days, a boy might have been envied, but not loved for proficiency in his studies; but he was most courted, who knew the best fishing holes; who had plenty of powder and shot; the best squirrel dog, and the use of his father's long flint-lock gun. And I confess, as I write these lines with my spectacles on, that I have still a strong drawing toward this type of a boy, whether I meet him in my lonely rambles, or whether he dwells only in my memory.

Sometimes the recollection of our boyish sports comes back to us after manhood, and one who has been "addicted" to fishing relapses into his old "ailment"; then angling becomes a pleasant kind of disease, and one's friends are apt to become inoculated with the virus, for it is contagious. Or men are informally introduced to each other on the stream, by a good-humored salutation, or an inquiry of "*What luck?*" or a display of the catch, or the offer of a cigar, or the flask, or a new fly; and with such introduction have become fast friends, from that affinity which draws all true anglers together.

But let me ask what is an angler, and who is a true angler? One who fishes with nets is not, neither is he who spears, snares, or dastardly uses the crazy bait to get fish, or who catches them on set lines; nor is he who is boisterous, noisy, or quarrelsome; nor are those who profess to practice the higher branches of the art, and affect contempt for their more humble brethren, who have not attained to their proficiency, imbued with the feeling that should possess the true angler.

Nor is he who brings his ice chest from town, and fishes all day with worm or fly, that he may return to the city and boastingly distribute his soaked and tasteless trout among his friends and brag of the numbers he has basketed, from finger-lings upwards.

Anglers may be divided into almost as many genera and species as the fish they catch, and engage in the sport from as many impulses. Let me give, "en passant," a sketch of a few of the many I have met with.

There is the Fussy Angler, a great bore; of course you will shun him. The Snob Angler, who speaks confidently and knowingly on a slight capital of skill or experi-ence. The Greedy, Pushing Angler, who rushes ahead and half fishes the water, leaving those who follow in doubt as to whether he has fished a pool or rift carefully, or slurred it over in his haste to reach some well-known place down the stream before his companions. The company of these, the quiet, careful angler will avoid.

We also meet sometimes with the Spick-and-Span Angler, who has a highly var-nished rod, and a superabundance of useless tackle; his outfit is of the most elabo-rate kind as regards its finish. He is a dapper "well got up" angler in all his appointments, and fishes much indoors over his claret and poteen, when he has a good listener. He frequently displays bad taste in his tackle, intended for fly-fishing, by having a thirty-dollar multiplying reel, filled with one of Conroy's very best relaid sea-grass lines, strong enough to hold a dolphin. If you meet him on the teeming waters of northern New York, the evening's display of his catch depends much on the rough skill of his guide.

The Rough-and-Ready Angler, the opposite of the aforenamed, disdains all "tomfoolery," and carries his tackle in an old shot bag, and his flies in a tangled mass.

We have also the Literary Angler, who reads Walton and admires him hugely; he has been inoculated with the sentiment only; the five-mile walk up the creek, where it has not been fished much, is very fatiguing to him; he "did not know he must wade the stream," and does not until he slips in, and then he has some trouble at night to get his boots off. He is provided with a stout bass rod, good strong leaders of salmon gut, and a stock of Conroy's "journal flies," and wonders if he had not better put on a shot just above his stretcher fly.

The Pretentious Angler, to use a favorite expression of the lamented Dickey Riker, once Recorder of the city of New York, is one "that prevails to a great extent in this community." This gentleman has many of the qualities attributed by Fisher, of the "Angler's Souvenir," to Sir Humphrey Davy. If he has attained the higher branches of the art, he affects to despise all sport which he considers less scientific; if a salmon fisher, he calls trout "vermin"; if he is a trout fly-fisher, he professes con-tempt for bait fishing. We have talked with true anglers who were even disposed to censure the eminent Divine, who has so ably, and with such labor of love, edited our American edition of Walton, for affectation, in saying of the red worm, "our hands have long since been washed of the dirty things." The servant should not be above his master, and certainly "Iz. Wa.," whose disciple the Doctor professed to be, considered it no indignity to use them, nor was he disgusted with his "horn of gentles." But the Doctor was certainly right in deprecating the use of ground bait in reference to trout, when the angler can with a little faith and less greed soon learn the use of the fly.

The *Shad-roe Fisherman.*—The habitat of this genus (and they are rarely found elsewhere) is Philadelphia. There are many persons of the aforesaid city, who fish only when this bait can be had, and an idea seems to possess them that fish will bite at no other. This fraternity could have been found some years back, singly or in pairs, or little coteries of three or four, on any sunshiny day from Easter to Whitsuntide, heaving their heavy dipsies and horsehair snoods from the ends of the piers, or from canal boats laid up in ordinary—the old floating bridge at Gray's Ferry was a favorite resort for them. Sometimes the party was convivial, and provided with a junk bottle of what they believed to be *old rye*.

Before the gas works had destroyed the fishing in the Schuylkill, I frequently observed a solitary individual of this species, wending his way to the river on Sunday mornings, with a long reed pole on his shoulder, and in his hand a tin kettle of shad roe; and his "prog," consisting of hard-boiled eggs and crackers and cheese, tied up in a cotton bandana handkerchief. Toward nightfall "he might have been seen" (as James the novelist says of the horseman), trudging homeward with a string of pan rock and white perch, or "catties" and eels, his trousers and coat sleeves well plastered with his unctuous bait, suggesting the idea of what, in vulgar parlance, might be called "a very nasty man."

But let us not turn up our scientific noses at this humble brother; nor let the home missionary or tract distributor rate him too severely, if he should meet with him in his Sunday walks; for who can tell what a quiet day of consolation it has been to him; he has found relief from the toils and cares of the week, and perhaps from the ceaseless tongue of his shrewish "old woman." If his sport has been good, he follows it up the next day, and keeps "blue Monday."

We have seen some very respectable gentlemen in our day engaged in fishing with shad roe at Fairmount Dam. The bar even had its representative, in one of our first criminal court lawyers. He did not "dress the character" with as much discrimination as when he lectured on Shakespeare, for he always wore his blue coat with gilt buttons: he did not appear to be a successful angler. "Per contra" to this was a wealthy retired merchant, who used to astonish us with his knack of keeping this difficult bait on his hooks, and his skill in hooking little white perch. Many a troller has seen him sitting bolt upright in the bow of his boat on a cool morning in May, with his overcoat buttoned up to his chin, his jolly spouse in the stern, and his servant amidship, baiting the hooks and taking off the lady's fish. The son also was an adept as well as the sire. Woe to the perch fisher, with his bait of little silvery eels, if these occupied the lower part of the swim, for the fish were all arrested by the stray ova that floated off from the "gobs" of shad roe.

As we love contrasts, let us here make a slight allusion to that sensible "old English gentleman," the Admiral, who surveyed the northwest coast of America to see, if in the contingency of the Yankees adhering to their claim of "fifty-four forty," the country about Vancouver's Island was worth contending for. He was an ardent angler, and it is reported, that on leaving his ship he provided stores for a week, which comprised of course not a few drinkables; as well as salmon rods and other tackle, and started in his boats to explore the rivers and tributaries, which, so goes the story, were so crammed in many places with salmon, that they could be captured with a boat hook; and still with all the variety of salmon flies and the piscatory skill of the admiral and his officers, not a fish could be induced to rise at the fly. He returned to his ship disheartened and disgusted, averring that the country was not worth contending for; that the Yankees might have it and be——; but it would be indecorous to record the admiral's mild expletive.

The True Angler is thoroughly imbued with the spirit of gentle old Izaak. He has no affectation, and when a fly cast is not to be had, can find amusement in catching sunfish or roach, and does not despise the sport of any humbler brother of the angle. With him, fishing is a recreation, and a "calmer of unquiet thoughts." He never quarrels with his luck, knowing that satiety dulls one's appreciation of sport as much as want of success, but is ever content when he has done his best, and looks hopefully forward to a more propitious day. Whether from boat or rocky shore, or along the sedgy bank of the creek, or the stony margin of the mountain brook, he deems it an achievement to take fish when they are difficult to catch, and his satisfaction is in proportion. If he is lazy, or a superannuated angler, he can even endure a few days' trolling on an inland lake, and smokes his cigar, chats with the boatman, and takes an occasional "nip," as he is rowed along the wooded shore and amongst the beautiful islands.

A true angler is generally a modest man; unobtrusively communicative when he can impart a new idea; and is ever ready to let a pretentious tyro have his say, and good-naturedly (as if merely suggesting how it should be done) repairs his tackle, or gets him out of a scrape. He is moderately provided with all tackle and "fixins" necessary to the fishing he is in pursuit of. Is quietly self-reliant and equal to almost any emergency, from splicing his rod or tying his own flies, to trudging ten miles across a rough country with his luggage on his back. His enjoyment consists not only in the taking of fish: he draws much pleasure from the soothing influence and delightful accompaniments of the art.

With happy memories of the past summer, he joins together the three pieces of his fly rod at home, when the scenes of the last season's sport are wrapped in snow and ice, and renews the glad feelings of long summer days. With what interest he notes the swelling of the buds on the maples, or the advent of the bluebird and robin, and looks forward to the day when he is to try another cast! and, when it comes at last, with what pleasing anticipations he packs up his "traps," and leaves his business cares and the noisy city behind, and after a few hours' or few days' travel in the cars, and a few miles in a rough wagon, or a vigorous tramp over rugged hills or along the road that leads up the banks of the river, he arrives at his quarters! He is now in the region of fresh butter and mealy potatoes—there are always good potatoes in a mountainous trout country. How pleasingly rough everything looks after leaving the prim city! How pure and wholesome the air! How beautiful the clumps of sugar maples and the veteran hemlocks jutting out over the stream; the laurel; the ivy; the moss-covered rocks; the lengthening shadows of evening! How musical the old familiar tinkling of the cow-bell and the cry of the whippoorwill! How sweetly he is lulled to sleep as he hears

> The waters leap and gush
> O'er channelled rock and broken bush!

Next morning, after a hearty breakfast of mashed potatoes, ham and eggs, and butter from the cream of the cow that browses in the woods, he is off, three miles up the creek, a cigar or his pipe in his mouth, his creel at his side, and his rod over his shoulder, chatting with his chum as he goes; free, joyous, happy; at peace with his Maker, with himself, and all mankind; he should be grateful for this much, even if he catches no fish. How exhilarating the music of the stream! how invigorating its waters, causing a consciousness of manly vigor, as he wades sturdily with the strong current and casts his flies before him! When his zeal abates, and a few of the speckled lie in the bottom of his creel, he is not less interested in the wild flowers on the bank, or the scathed old hemlock on the cliff above, with its hawk's nest, the lady of the house likely inside, and the male proprietor perched high above on its dead top and he breaks forth lustily—the scene suggesting the song—

> The bee's on its wing, and the hawk on its nest,
> And the river runs merrily by.

When noon comes on, and the trout rise lazily or merely rip, he halts "sub tegmine fagi," or under the shadow of the dark sugar maple to build a fire and toast trout for his dinner, and wiles away three hours or so. He dines sumptuously, straightens and dries his leader and the gut of his dropper, and repairs all breakage. He smokes leisurely, or even takes a nap on the greensward or velvety moss, and resumes his sport when the sun has declined enough to shade at least one side of the stream, and pleasantly anticipates the late evening on the still waters far down the creek. God be with you, gentle angler, if actuated with the reeling of our old master! whether you are a top fisher or a bottom fisher; whether your bait be gentles, brandling, grub, or red worm; crab, shrimp, or minnow; caddis, grasshopper, or the feathery counterfeit of the ephemera. May your thoughts be always peaceful, and your heart filled with gratitude to Him who made the country and the rivers; and "may the east wind never blow when you go a-fishing!"

The Fisherman's Song

THOMAS D'URFEY

Of all the world's enjoyments,
That ever valued were;
There's none of our employments
With fishing can compare:
Some preach, some write,
Some swear, some fight,
All, golden lucre courting.
But fishing still bears off the bell,
For profit or for sporting.
Then who a jolly fisherman, a fisherman will be
His throat must wet,
Just like his net,
To keep out cold at sea.

The country squire loves running
A pack of well-mouthed hounds:

Another fancies gunning
For wild ducks in his grounds:
This hunts, that fowls,
This hawks, Dicks bowls,
No greater pleasure wishing,
But Tom that tells what sport excels,
Gives all the praise to fishing.
Then who a jolly fisherman, . . .

A good Westphalia gammon
is counted dainty fare;
But what is't to a salmon
just taken from the Ware?
Wheat ears and quails,
Cocks, snipes, and rails,
Are prized, while season's lasting,
But all must stoop to crayfish soup,
Or I've no skill in tasting.
Then who a jolly fisherman, . . .

Keen hunters always take to
Their prey with too much pains;
Nay, often break a neck too,
A penance for no brains:
They run, they leap,
Now high, now deep,
Whilst he, that fishing chooses,
With ease may do't, nay, more to boot,
May entertain the muses.
Then who a jolly fisherman, . . .

And though some envious wranglers,
To jeer us will make bold;
And laugh at patient anglers,
Who stand so long i' th' cold:
They wait on Miss,
We wait on this,
And think it easy labor;
And if you'd know, fish profits too,

Consult our Holland neighbor.
Then who a jolly fisherman, a fisherman will be
His throat must wet,
Just like his net,
To keep out cold at sea.

The Devout Angler

COLLIN D. B. ELLIS

The years will bring their anodyne
But I may never quite forget
The fish that I had counted mine
And lost before they reached the net.

Last night I put my rod away
Remorseful and disconsolate,
Yet I had suffered yesterday
No more than I deserved from Fate.

And as I scored another trout
Upon my list of fish uncaught,
I should have offered thanks, no doubt,
For salutary lessons taught.

Alas! Philosophy avails
As little as it used to do.

More comfort is there still in tales
That may, or may not, be true.

Is it not possible to pray
That I may see those fish once more?—
I hear a voice that seems to say,
"They are not lost but gone before."

When in my pilgrimage I reach
The river that we all must cross,
And land upon that further beach
Where earthly gains are counted loss,

May I not earthly loss repair?
Well, if those fish should rise again,
There shall be no more parting there—
Celestial gut will stand the strain.

And issuing from the portal, one
Who was himself a fisherman
Will drop his keys and, shouting, run
To help me land leviathan.

Observations on the Practice of Angling

AMERICAN ANGLER'S GUIDE

For Angling may be said to be like the Mathematics, that it can never be fully learned, at least not so fully but that there will be still more experimenting left for the trial of other men.—Walton

Angling generally, in this country, is not necessarily so scientific as in many parts of Europe. Our streams being larger, more numerous, and less fished, except in a few instances near our large cities, heavier tackle in some cases may be used, and less skill required. In angling for trout in the country streams, where immense quantities are found, the less skilful angler, with coarse tackle, will often succeed in filling his basket in a very short time. But as railroads increase, and access becomes more easy to the different fishing grounds, the fish will become more shy, greater skill will be required, and finer tackle indispensable, to complete success. Hence where a worm for trout, a piece of bread for perch, or a strip of pork for pickerel, have been used, natural or artificial flies, and small fish, attached to the finest possible kind of materials, will be needed. Therefore the true Angler should make himself thoroughly acquainted with the most approved modes of Angling, and the best materials for his proper equipment.

The *Artificial Fly*, so much used in England, finds but little favor in this country, not because it is not as good a bait, but because more skill is required in using it; consequently many of our Anglers only fish in the spring months, when the water is thick and turbid, and the worm can be used, while the more experienced sportsman from foreign parts,[1] will astonish the native by his dexterity in throwing the fly and killing an almost incredible number of fish, where the unbeliever regarded tile fly as a useless article of tackle. There are some that attain to greater proficiency in fly-fishing than others, as is the case with almost any kind of sport. But the skill necessary to success in this branch of our subject, is not so great as the novice imagines: certainly it is the more genteel, as well as the most pleasant mode, as those who have successfully tried it can testify. It is therefore to be hoped it will be more generally adopted by

All who seek the lake or brook,

With rod and line, and float and hook.

Great improvements have been made within a few years in the manufacture of artificial baits. Every variety of fish and insect has been most successfully imitated, defying almost the scrutiny of the Angler, and certainly the object of his sport. These improvements every brother of the angle should adopt, and thereby remove the objection of the few who oppose the art on Bacon and Byronic grounds.[2]

As the enjoyment of angling naturally makes the sportsman a keen observer, he should pay particular attention to the winds, those

"Unseen currents of the air,"

as Bryant has it. Walton says: "You are to take notice, that of the winds, the south wind is said to be the best. One observes that

'—When the wind is in the south,

It blows the bait in the fish's mouth.'

Next to that, the west wind is believed to be the best; and having told you that the east wind is the worst, I need not tell which wind is the worst in the third degree: and yet (as Solomon observes) 'that he that considers the wind shall never sow,' so that he that busies his head too much about them, if the weather be not made extreme cold by an east wind, shall be a little superstitious; for as it is observed by some that there is no good horse of a bad color, so I have observed that if it be a cloudy day, and not extreme cold, let the wind set in whatever quarter it will, and do its worst, I heed it not, and yet take this for a rule, that I would willingly fish standing on the lee shore; and you are to take notice that the fish lies or swims nearer the

---

[1]Parties are often made up in England for fishing in the Canadas and the United States.
[2]Byron and Bacon both objected to angling on account of the necessity which then existed of using various live animals on the hook as baits.

bottom, and in deeper water than in summer; and also nearer the bottom in a cold day, and then gets nearest the lee side of the water."

Sir Humphrey Davy says: "For fly-fishing,

A day with not too bright a beam,

A warm but not a scorching sun."

Also, "never fish with your back to the sun, as your shadow is thrown on the water, and the fish are frightened at your movements." These are important instructions to the Angler, and the high source from whence they come should be considered by him as law. It would be well to notice here, also, that after protracted rains or severe storms, the Angler should fish at the bottom if he expect sport, and that it is useless to angle after a long drought in summer, or in the autumn or spring, when the high east, or cold north winds blow.

In fresh water angling the best time is early in the morning, or at the close of the day. The proper time for salt water angling depends upon the tide. The best time is at the last of the ebb or the first of the flood, whether at morning, at mid-day, or at night.

In all kinds of angling it is necessary to be very cautious, but particularly in taking the wily trout. Many novices in the art wander up and down streams, and wade creeks, with little or no success, from the want of this—a proper requisite of every good Angler. The more skilful also, sometimes fail from the same fault.

A story is told, which serves tell to show the necessity of caution. An Angler, who had risen with the sun, and fished till near noon-day without success, was outdone by a knowing one, who, with proper precaution, passed his rod and line between the legs of the Angler (which like his line were pretty well stretched) into a hole underneath the hank. He soon had a bite, and succeeded in taking a two-pound trout, almost before the astonished tyro was aware of his presence.

Some are of the opinion that trout, and similar fish, can hear[3] the tread on the ground. It is certain that it will start at the least noise, when nothing can be seen. Salter, in his "Angler's Guide," says: "Keep as far from the water as you can, and go quietly and slily to work, for fish have so many enemies that they are suspicious of everything they see, feel, or hear; even the shaking of the bank of a river (under which they frequently lie) will alarm them, and spoil the Angler's sport, etc.; and also, when two or three Anglers are fishing near each other; therefore avoid agitating the water by trampling on the bank unnecessarily; drop your baited hook in the water gently, and you will kill more fish than three Anglers who act differently."

---

[3]Smith, in his "History of the Fishes of Massachusetts," says that the acoustic apparatus is boxed up in the solid bones of the skull, so that sound propagated through the water gives a vibratory motion or tremor to the whole body, and which, agitating the auditory nerve, produces hearing.

Blaine also says: "*Avoid every thing that may attract the attention of the fish*: stand so far from the water's edge as you can, and never let your shadow fall on the water. If possible, take advantage of a bush, tree, etc., completely to conceal the person. When an Angler fishes near home, an artificial screen of rushes, twigs, etc., may be employed for that purpose. In dropping or dipping with the natural fly, the greatest caution is necessary to keep completely out of view of the fish; not only the shadow of the screen, but that of the rod also, should be kept from falling on the water."

The dress of the Angler is of great importance in trout angling. If it be true, as before stated, that this timid inhabitant of the brook is disturbed by the least motion, certainly the best means should be taken to render any motion imperceptible. There are two colors of dress for angling, desirable on different occasions. If your sport be in the summer, and lie mid the brilliant green foliage of the trees, bushes, and meadows, your dress should undoubtedly be green throughout. On the contrary, should you be pleased to enjoy yourself in autumn, when nature has changed the scene, and draped herself in sober brown, the most proper uniform is a drab from top to toe. A disciple of Walton, who angles on Long Island, and takes more trout than any ten sportsmen who visit that delightful resort, is represented as standing still as a ghost, his rod extended in his hand, without any apparent motion, equipped in drab pantaloons, drab vest, drab coat, and drab hat; and so quiet is he in his movements, that he will take a mess of trout, when a person but a few yards distant would hardly be aware he moved a muscle. How different from many who profess to understand the art, and who go whipping and splashing the water for miles around.

As health is of great importance, the lover of this sport should adopt the physician's prescription, and "keep the head cool and the feet warm." To this end he should provide himself with a pair of water-proof boots, to be ready should he wish to wade the stream, or cross a marsh. He should pay strict attention to all laws regarding angling, and all rules laid down for bridge, boat, or brook fishing, and on no account transgress the laws of the different States with respect to spawning time, and the size of the fish to be taken.

It is much to be regretted, that there are many who call themselves Anglers, who set all laws at defiance, by taking many kinds of fish out of season; such conduct is unworthy a sportsman, and should meet with rebuke from every member of the angling community.

Finally, let the disciple of the rod

"Use all gently,"

and when he has made up his mind to pass a few days, or even hours, in this delightful amusement, let him be fully prepared with *everything necessary, and everything in order.*

Note to *Don Juan*, Canto XIII

LORD BYRON

And angling, too, that solitary vice,
Whatever Izaak Walton sings or says;
The quaint, old, cruel coxcomb, in his gullet
Should have a hook, and a small trout to pull it.

It would have taught him humanity at least. This sentimental savage, whom it is a mode to quote (among the novelists) to show their sympathy for innocent sports and old songs, teaches how to sew up frogs, and break their legs by way of experiment, in addition to the art of angling, the cruelest, the coldest, and the stupidest of pretended sports. They may talk about the beauties of Nature, but the angler merely thinks about his dish of fish; he has no leisure to take his eyes from off the streams, and a single *bite* is worth to him more than all the scenery around. Besides, some fish bite best on a rainy day. The whale, the shark, and the tunny fishery have somewhat of noble and perilous in them; even net fishing, trawling, etc., are more humane and useful. But angling!—No angler can be a good man.

Fishin' Jimmy

ANNIE TRUMBULL SLOSSON

I was on the margin of Pond Brook, just back of Uncle Eben's, that I first saw Fishin' Jimmy. It was early June, and we were again at Franconia, that peaceful little village among the northern hills.

The boys, as usual, were tempting the trout with false fly or real worm, and I was roaming along the bank, seeking spring flowers, and hunting early butterflies and moths. Suddenly there was a little plash in the water at the spot where Ralph was fishing, the slender tip of his rod bent, I heard a voice cry out, "Strike him, sonny, strike him!" and an old man came quickly but noiselessly through the bushes, just as Ralph's line flew up into space, with, alas! no shining, spotted trout upon the hook. The new comer was a spare, wiry man of middle height, with a slight stoop in his shoulders, a thin brown face, and scanty gray hair. He carried a fishing-rod, and had some small trout strung on a forked stick in one hand. A simple, homely figure, yet he stands out in memory just as I saw him then, no more to be forgotten than the granite hills, the rushing streams, the cascades of that north country I love so well.

We fell into talk at once, Ralph and Waldo rushing eagerly into questions about the fish, the bait, the best spots in the stream, advancing their own small theories, and asking advice from their new friend. For friend he seemed even in that first hour, as he began simply, but so wisely, to teach my boys the art he loved. They are older now, and are no mean anglers, I believe; but they look back gratefully to those brookside lessons, and acknowledge gladly their obligations to Fishin' Jimmy. But it is not of these practical teachings I would now speak; rather of the lessons of simple faith, of unwearied patience, of self-denial and cheerful endurance, which the old man himself seemed to have learned, strangely enough, from the very sport so often called cruel and murderous. Incomprehensible as it may seem, to his simple intellect the fisherman's art was a whole system of morality, a guide for every-day life, an education, a gospel. It was all any poor mortal man, woman, or child, needed in this world to make him or her happy, useful, good.

At first we scarcely realized this, and wondered greatly at certain things he said, and the tone in which he said them. I remember at that first meeting I asked him, rather carelessly, "Do you like fishing?" He did not reply at first; then he looked at me with those odd, limpid, green-gray eyes of his which always seemed to reflect the clear waters of mountain streams, and said very quietly: "You wouldn't ask me if I liked my mother—or my wife." And he always spoke of his pursuit as one speaks of something very dear, very sacred. Part of his story I learned from others, but most of it from himself, bit by bit, as we wandered together day by day in that lovely hill-country. As I tell it over again I seem to hear the rush of mountain streams, the "sound of a going in the tops of the trees," the sweet, pensive strain of white-throat sparrow, and the plash of leaping trout; to see the crystal-clear waters pouring over granite rock, the wonderful purple light upon the mountains, the flash and glint of darting fish, the tender green of early summer in the north country.

Fishin' Jimmy's real name was James Whitcher. He was born in the Franconia Valley of northern New Hampshire, and his whole life had been passed there. He had always fished; he could not remember when or how he learned the art. From the days when, a tiny, bare-legged urchin in ragged frock, he had dropped his piece of string with its bent pin at the end into the narrow, shallow brooklet behind his father's house, through early boyhood's season of roaming along Gale River, wading Black Brook, rowing a leaky boat on Streeter or Mink Pond, through youth, through manhood, on and on into old age, his life had apparently been one long day's fishing—an angler's holiday. Had it been only that? He had not cared for books, or school, and all efforts to tie him down to study were unavailing. But he knew well the books of running brooks. No dry botanical text-book or manual could have taught him all he now knew of plants and flowers and trees.

He did not call the yellow spatterdock *Nuphar advena*, but he knew its large leaves of rich green, where the black bass or pickerel sheltered themselves from the summer sun, and its yellow balls on stout stems, around which his line so often twined and twisted, or in which the hook caught, not to be jerked out till the long, green, juicy stalk itself, topped with globe of greenish gold, came up from its wet bed.

He knew the sedges along the bank with their nodding tassels and stiff lance-like leaves, the feathery grasses, the velvet moss upon the wet stones, the sea-green lichen on boulder or tree trunk. There, in that corner of Echo Lake, grew the thickest patch of pipewort, with its small, round, grayish-white, mushroom-shaped tops on long, slender stems. If he had styled it *Eriocaulon septangulare*, would it have shown a closer knowledge of its habits than did his careful avoidance of its vicinity, his keeping line and flies at a safe distance, as he muttered to himself, "Them pesky butt'ns agin!" He knew by sight the bur-reed of mountain ponds, with its round, prickly balls strung like big beads on the stiff, erect stalks; the little waterlobelia, with tiny purple blossoms, springing from the waters of lake and pond. He knew, too, all the strange, beautiful under-water growth: bladderwort in long, feathery garlands, pellucid waterweed, quillwort in stiff little bunches with sharp pointed leaves of olive-green,—all so seldom seen save by the angler whose hooks draw up from time to time the wet, lovely tangle. I remember the amusement with which a certain well-known botanist, who had journeyed to the mountains in search of a little plant, found many years ago near Echo Lake, but not since seen, heard me propose to consult Fishin' Jimmy on the subject. But I was wiser than he knew. Jimmy looked at the specimen brought as an aid to identification. It was dry and flattened, and as unlike a living, growing plant as are generally the specimens from a herbarium. But it showed the awl-shaped leaves, and threadlike stalk with its tiny round seed-vessels, like those of our common shepherd's-purse, and Jimmy knew it at once. "There's a dreffle lot o' that peppergrass out in deep water there, jest where I ketched the big pick'ril," he said quietly. "I seen it nigh a foot high, an' it's juicier and livin'er than them dead sticks in your book." At our request he accompanied the unbelieving botanist and myself to the spot; and there, looking down through the sunlit water, we saw great patches of that rare and long-lost plant of the *Cruciferae* known to science as *Subularia aquatica*. For forty years it had hidden itself away, growing and blossoming and casting abroad its tiny seeds in its watery home, unseen, or at least unnoticed, by living soul, save by the keen, soft, limpid eyes of Fishin' Jimmy. And he knew the trees and shrubs so well: the alder and birch from which as a boy he cut his simple, pliant pole; the shad-blow and iron-wood (he called them, respectively, sugarplum and hard-hack) which he used for the more ambitious rods of maturer years; the mooseberry, wayfaring-tree, hobble-bush, or triptoe,—it has all these names,—with stout, trailing branches, over which he stumbled as he hurried through the woods and underbrush in the darkening twilight.

He had never heard of entomology. Guénée, Hübner, and Fabricius were unknown names; but he could have told these worthies many new things. Did they know just at what hour the trout ceased leaping at dark fly or moth, and could see only in the dim light the ghostly white miller? Did they know the comparative merits, as a tempting bait, of grasshopper, cricket, spider, or wasp; and could they, with bits of wool, tinsel, and feather, copy the real dipterous, hymenopterous, or orthopterous insect? And the birds: he knew them as do few ornithologists, by sight, by sound, by little ways and tricks of their own, known only to themselves and him. The white-throat sparrow with its sweet, far-reaching chant; the hermit-thrush with its chime of bells in the calm summer twilight; the vesper-sparrow that ran before him as he crossed the meadow, or sang for hours, as he fished the stream, its unvarying, but scarcely monotonous little strain; the cedarbird, with its smooth brown coat of Quaker simplicity, and speech as brief and simple as Quaker *yea* or *nay*; the winter-wren sending out his strange, lovely, liquid warble from the high, rocky side of Cannon Mountain; the bluebird of the early spring, so welcome to the winter-weary dwellers in that land of ice and snow, as he

"From the bluer deeps

Lets fall a quick, prophetic strain,"

of summer, of streams freed and flowing again, of waking, darting, eager fish; the veery, the phoebe, the jay, the vireo,—all these were friends, familiar, tried and true to Fishin' Jimmy. The cluck and coo of the cuckoo, the bubbling song of bobolink in buff and black, the watery trill of the stream-loving swamp-sparrow, the whispered whistle of the stealthy, darkness-haunting whippoorwill, the gurgle and gargle of the cow-bunting,—he knew each and all, better than did Audubon, Nuttall, or Wilson. But he never dreamed that even the tiniest of his little favorites bore, in the scientific world, far away from that quiet mountain nest, such names as *Troglodytes hyemalis* or *Melospiza palustris*. He could tell you, too, of strange, shy creatures rarely seen except by the early-rising, late-fishing angler, in quiet, lonesome places: the otter, muskrat, and mink of ponds and lakes,—rival fishers, who bore off prey sometimes from under his very eyes,—field-mice in meadow and pasture, blind, burrowing moles, prickly hedge-hogs, brown hares, and social, curious squirrels.

Sometimes he saw deer, in the early morning or in the dusk of the evening, as they came to drink at the lake shore, and looked at him with big, soft eyes not unlike his own. Sometimes a shaggy bear trotted across his path and hid himself in the forest, or a sharp-eared fox ran barking through the bushes. He loved to tell of these things to us who cared to listen, and I still seem to hear his voice saying in hushed tones, after a story of woodland sight or sound: "Nobody don't see 'em but fishermen. Nobody don't hear 'em but fishermen."

But it was of another kind of knowledge he oftenest spoke, and of which I shall try to tell you, in his own words as nearly as possible.

First let me say that if there should seem to be the faintest tinge of irreverence in aught I write, I tell my story badly. There was no irreverence in Fishin' Jimmy. He possessed a deep and profound veneration for all things spiritual and heavenly; but it was the veneration of a little child, mingled as is that child's with perfect confidence and utter frankness. And he used the dialect of the country in which he lived.

"As I was tellin' ye," he said, "I allers loved fishin' an' knowed 'twas the best thing in the hull airth. I knowed it larnt ye more about creeters an' yarbs an' stuns an' water than books could tell ye. I knowed it made folks patienter an' commonsenser an' weather-wiser an' cuter gen'ally; gin 'em more fac'lty than all the school-larnin' in creation. I knowed it was more fillin' than vittles, more rousin' than whisky, more soothin' than lodlum. I knowed it cooled ye off when ye was bet, an' het ye when ye was cold. I knowed all that, o' course—any fool knows it. But—will ye b'l'eve it?—I was more'n twenty-one year old, a man growed, 'fore I foun' out why 'twas that away. Father an' mother was Christian folks, good out-an'-out Calv'nist Baptists from over East'n way. They fetched me up right, made me go to meetin' an' read a chapter every Sunday, an' say a hymn Sat'day night a'ter washin'; an' I useter say my prayers mos' nights. I wa'n't a bad boy as boys go. But nobody thought o' tellin' me the one thing, jest the one single thing, that'd ha' made all the diffunce. I knowed about God, an' how he made me an' made the airth, an' everythin', an' once I got thinkin' about that, an' I asked my father if God made the fishes. He said 'course he did, the sea an' all that in 'em is; but somehow that didn't seem to mean nothin' much to me, an' I lost my int'rist agin. An' I read the Scripter account o' Jonah an' the big fish, an' all that in job about pullin' out levi'thing with a hook an' stickin' fish spears in his head, an' some parts in them queer books nigh the end o' the ole Test'ment about fish-ponds an' fish-gates an' fish-pools, an' how the fishers shall l'ment—everything I could pick out about fishin' an' sech; but it didn't come home to me; 'twa'n't my kind o' fishin' an' I didn't seem ter sense it.

"But one day—it's more'n forty year ago now, but I rec'lect it same's 'twas yest'day, an' I shall rec'lect it forty thousand year from now if I'm 'round, an' I guess I shall be—I heerd—suthin'—diffunt. I was down in the village one Sunday; it wa'n't very good fishin'—the streams was too full; an' I thought I'd jest look into the meetin'-house 's I went by. 'Twas the ole union meetin'-house, down to the corner, ye know, an' they hadn't got no reg'lar s'pply, an' ye never knowed what sort ye'd hear, so 'twas kind o' excitin'.

"'Twas late, 'most 'leven o'clock, an' the sarm'n had begun. There was a strange man a-preachin', some one from over to the hotel. I never heerd his name, I never seed him from that day to this: but I knowed his face. Queer enough I'd seed him a-fishin'. I never knowed he was a min'ster; he didn't look like one. He went about like a real fisherman, with ole clo'es an' an ole hat with hooks stuck in it, an' big rubber boots, an' he fished, reely fished, I mean—ketched 'em. I guess 'twas that made me liss'n a leetle sharper'n us'al, for I never seed a fishin' min'ster afore. Elder Jacks'n, he said 'twas a sinf'l waste o' time, an' ole Parson Loomis, he'd an idee it was cruel an' onmarciful; so I thought I'd jest see what this man'd preach about, an' I settled down to liss'n to the sarm'n.

"But there wa'n't no sarm'n; not what I'd been raised to think was the on'y true kind. There wa'n't no heads, no fiistlys nor sec'ndlys, nor fin'ly bruthrins, but the first thing I knowed I was hearin' a story, an' 'twas a fishin' story. 'Twas about Some One—I hadn't the least idee then who 'twas, an' how much it all meant—Some One that was dreffle fond o' fishin' an' fishermen, Some One that sot everythin' by the water, an' useter go along by the lakes an' ponds, an' sail on 'em, an' talk with the men that was fishin'. An' how the fishermen all liked him, 'nd asked his 'dvice, an' done jest 's he telled 'em about the likeliest places to fish; an' how they allers ketched more for mindin' him; an' how when lie. was a-preachin' he wouldn't go into a big meetin'-house an' talk to rich folks all slicked up, but he'd jest go out in a fishin' boat, an' ask the men to shove out a mite, an' he'd talk to the folks on shore, the fishin' folks an' their wives an' the boys an' gals playin' on the shore. An' then, best o' everythin', he telled how when he was a-choosin' the men to go about with him an' help him an' larn his ways so's to come a'ter him, he fust o' all picked out the men he'd seen every day fishin', an' mebbe fished with hisself; for he knowed 'em an' knowed he could trust 'em.

"An' then he telled us about the day when this preacher come along by the lake—a dreffle sightly place, this min'ster said; he'd seed it hisself when he was trav'lin' in them countries—an' come acrost two men he knowed well; they was brothers, an' they was a-fishin'. An' he jest asked 'em in his pleasant-spoken, frien'ly way—there wa'n't never sech a drawin', takin', lovin' way with any one afore as this man had, the min'ster said—he jest asked 'em to come along with him; an' they lay down their poles an' their lines an' everythin', an' jined him. An' then he come along a spell further, an' he sees two boys out with their ole father, an' they was settin' in a boat an' fixin' up their tackle, an' he asked 'em if they'd jine him, too, an' they jest dropped all their things, an' left the ole man with the boat an' the fish an' the bait an' follered the preacher. I don't tell it very good. I've read it an' read it sence that; but I want to make ye see how it sounded to me, how I took it, as the min'ster telled it that summer day in Francony meetin'. Ye see I'd no idee who the story was about, the man put it so plain, in common kind o' talk, without any come-to-passes an' whuffers an' thuffers, an' I never conceited 'twas a Bible narr'tive.

"An' so fust thing I knowed I says to myself, 'That's the kind o' teacher I want. If I could come acrost a man like that, I'd jest foller him, too, through thick an' thin.' Well, I can't put the rest on it into talk very good; 'taint jest the kind o' thing to speak on 'fore folks, even sech good friends as you. I aint the sort to go back on my word,—fishermen aint, ye know, an' what I'd said to myself 'fore I knowed who I was bindin' myself to, I stuck to a'terwards when I knowed all about him. For 'taint for me to tell ye, who've got so much more larnin' than me, that there was a dreffle lot more to that story than the fishin' part. That lovin', givin' up, suff'rin', dyin' part, ye know it all yerself, an' I can't kinder say much on it, 'cept when I'm jest all by myself, or—'long o' him.

"That a'ternoon I took my ole Bible that I hadn't read much sence I growed up, an' I went out into the woods 'long the river, an' 'stid o' fishin' I jest sot down an' read that hull story. Now ye know it yerself by heart, an' ye've knowed it all yer born days, so ye can't begin to tell how new an' 'stonishin' 'twas to me, an' how findin' so much fishin' in it kinder helped me unnerstan' an' b'l'eve it every mite, an' take it right hum to me to foller an' live up to 's long 's I live an' breathe. Did j'ever think on it, reely? I tell ye, his r'liging 's a fishin' r'liging all through. His friends was fishin' folks; his pulpit was a fishin' boat, or the shore o' the lake; he loved the ponds an' streams; an' when his d'sciples went out fishin', if he didn't go hisself with 'em, he'd go a'ter 'em, walkin' on the water, to cheer 'em up an' comfort 'em.

"An' he was allers 'round the water; for the story 'll say, 'he come to the seashore,' or 'he begun to teach by the seaside,' or agin, 'he entered into a boat,' an' 'he was in the stern o' the boat, asleep.'

"An' he used fish in his mir'cles. He fed that crowd o' folks on fish when they was hungry, bought 'em from a little chap on the shore. I've oft'n thought how dreffle tickled that boy must 'a ben to have him take them fish. Mebbe they wa'n't nothin' but shiners, but the fust the little feller'd ever ketched; an' boys set a heap on their fust ketch. He was dreffle good to child'en, ye know. An' who'd he come to a'ter he'd died, an' ris again? Why, he come down to the shore 'fore daylight, an' looked off over the pond to where his ole frien's was a-fishin'. Ye see they'd gone out jest to quiet their minds an' keep up their sperrits; ther's nothin' like fishin' for that, ye know, an' they'd ben in a heap o' trubble. When they was settin' up the night afore, worryin' an' wond'rin' an' s'misin' what was goin' ter become on 'em without their master, Peter 'd got kinder desprit, an' he up an' says in his quick way, says he, 'Anyway, I'm goin' a-fishin'.' An' they all see the sense on it,—any fisherman would,—an' they says, says they, 'We'll go 'long too.' But they didn't ketch anythin'. I suppose they couldn't fix their minds on it, an' everythin' went wrong like. But when mornin' come creepin' up over the mountings, fust thin' they knowed they see him on the bank, an' he called out to 'em to know if they'd ketched anythin'. The water jest run down my cheeks when I heerd the min'ster tell that, an' it kinder makes my eyes wet every time I think on 't. For 't seems 's if it might 'a ben me in that boat, who heern that v'ice I loved so dreffle well speak up agin so nat'ral from the bank there. An' he eat some o' their fish! O' course he done it to sot their minds easy, to show 'em he wa'n't quite a sperrit yit, but jest their own ole frien' who'd ben out in the boat with 'em so many, many times. But seems to me, jest the fac' he done it kinder makes fish an' fishin' diffunt from any other thing in the hull airth. I tell ye them four books that gin his story is chock full o' things that go right to the heart o' fishermen,—nets, an' hooks, an' boats, an' the shores, an' the sea, an' the mountings, Peter's fishin'-coat, lilies, an' sparrers, an' grass o' the fields, an' all about the evenin' sky bein' red or low-erin', an' fair or foul weather.

"It's an out-doors, woodsy, country story, 'sides bein' the heav'nliest one that was ever telled. I read the hull Bible, as a duty ye know. I read the Epis'les, but somehow they don't come home to me. Paul was a great man, a dreffle smart scholar, but he was raised in the city, I guess, an' when I go from the gospils into Paul's writin's it's like goin' from the woods an' hills an' streams o' Francony into the streets of a big city like Concord or Manch'ster."

The old man did not say much of his after life and the fruits of this strange conversion, but his neighbors told us a great deal. They spoke of his unselfishness, his charity, his kindly deeds; told of his visiting the poor and unhappy, nursing the sick. They said the little children loved him, and every one in the village and for miles around trusted and leaned upon Fishin' Jimmy. He taught the boys to fish, sometimes the girls too; and while learning to cast and strike, to whip the stream, they drank in knowledge of higher things, and came to know and love Jimmy's "fishin' r'liging." I remember they told me of a little French Canadian girl, a poor, wretched waif, whose mother, an unknown tramp, had fallen dead in the road near the village. The child, an untamed little heathen, was found clinging to her mother's body in an agony of grief and rage, and fought like a tiger when they tried to take her away. A boy in the little group attracted to the spot, ran away, with a child's faith in his old friend, to summon Fishin' Jimmy. He came quickly, lifted the little savage tenderly, and carried her away.

No one witnessed the taming process, but in a few days the pair were seen together on the margin of Black Brook, each with a fish-pole. Her dark face was bright with interest and excitement as she took her first lesson in the art of angling. She jabbered and chattered in her odd patois, he answered in broadest New England dialect, but the two quite understood each other, and though Jimmy said afterward that it was "dreffle to hear her call the fish pois'n," they were soon great friends and comrades. For weeks he kept and cared for the child, and when she left him for a good home in Bethlehem, one would scarcely have recognized in the gentle, affectionate girl the wild creature of the past. Though often questioned as to the means used to effect this change, Jimmy's explanation seemed rather vague and unsatisfactory. "'Twas fishin' done it," he said; "on'y fishin'; it allers works. The Christian r'liging itself had to begin with fishin', ye know."

But one thing troubled Fishin' Jimmy. He wanted to be a "fisher of men." That was what the Great Teacher had promised he would make the fishermen who left their boats to follow him. What strange, literal meaning he attached to the terms, we could not tell. In vain we—especially the boys, whose young hearts had gone out in warm affection to the old man—tried to show him that he was, by his efforts to do good and make others better and happier, fulfilling the Lord's directions. He could not understand it so. "I allers try to think," he said, "that 'twas me in that boat when he come along. I make b'l'eve that it was out on Streeter Pond, an' I was settin' in the boat, fixin' my lan'in' net, when I see him on the shore. I think mebbe I'm that James—for that's my given name, ye know, though they allers call me Jimmy—an' then I hear him callin' me 'James, James.' I can hear him jest 's plain sometimes, when the wind's blowin' in the trees, an' I jest ache to up an' foller him. But says he, 'I'll make ye a fisher o' men,' an' he ain't done it. I'm waitin'; mebbe he'll larn me some day."

He was fond of all living creatures, merciful to all. But his love for our dog Dash became a passion, for Dash was an angler. Who that ever saw him sitting in the boat beside his master, watching with eager eye and whole body trembling with excitement the line as it was cast, the flies as they touched the surface—who can forget old Dash? His fierce excitement at rise of trout, the efforts at self-restraint, the disappointment if the prey escaped, the wild exultation if it was captured, how plainly—he who runs might read—were shown these emotions in eye, in ear, in tail, in whole quivering body! What wonder that it all went straight to the fisher's heart of Jimmy! "I never knowed afore they could be Christians," he said, looking, with tears in his soft, keen eyes, at the every-day scene, and with no faintest thought of irreverence. "I never knowed it, but I'd give a stiffikit o' membership in the orthodoxest church goin' to that dog there."

It is almost needless to say that as years went on Jimmy came to know many "fishin' min'sters"; for there are many of that school who know our mountain country, and seek it yearly. All these knew and loved the old man. And there were others who had wandered by that sea of Galilee, and fished in the waters of the Holy Land, and with them Fishin' Jimmy dearly loved to talk. But his wonder was never-ending that, in the scheme of evangelizing the world, more use was not made of the "fishin' side" of the story. "Hain't they ever tried it on them poor heathen?" he would ask earnestly of some clerical angler casting a fly upon the clear water of pond or brook. "I 'should think 'twould 'a' been the fust thing they'd done. Fishin' fust, an' r'liging's sure to foller. An' it's so easy; fur heath'n mostly r'sides on islands, don't they? So ther's plenty o' water, an' o' course ther's fishin'; an' oncet gin 'em poles an' git 'em to work, an' they're out o' mischief fur that day. They'd like it better'n cannib'ling, or cuttin' out idles, or scratchin' picters all over theirselves, an' bimeby—not too suddent, ye know, to scare 'em—ye could begin on that story, an' they couldn't stan' that, not a heath'n on 'em. Won't ye speak to the 'Merican Board about it, an' sen' out a few fishin' mishneries, with poles an' lines an' tackle gen'ally? I've tried it on dreffle bad folks, an' it allers done 'em good. But"—so almost all his simple talk ended—"I wish I could begin to be a fisher o' men. I'm gettin' on now, I'm nigh seventy, an' I ain't got much time, ye see."

One afternoon in July there came over Franconia Notch one of those strangely sudden tempests which sometimes visit that mountain country. It had been warm that day, unusually warm for that refreshingly cool spot; but suddenly the sky grew dark and darker, almost to blackness, there was roll of thunder and flash of lightning, and then poured down the rain—rain at first, but soon hail in large frozen bullets, which fiercely pelted any who ventured outdoors, rattled against the windows of the Profile House with sharp cracks like sounds of musketry, and lay upon the piazza in heaps like snow. And in the midst of the wild storm it was remembered that two boys, guests at the hotel, had gone up Mount Lafayette alone that day. They were young boys, unused to mountain climbing, and their friends were anxious. It was found that Dash had followed them; and just as some one was to be sent in search of them, a boy from the stables brought the information that Fishin' Jimmy had started up the mountain after them as the storm broke. "Said if he couldn't be a fisher o' men, mebbe he knowed nuff to ketch boys," went on our informant, seeing nothing more in the speech, full of pathetic meaning to us who knew him, than the idle talk of one whom many considered "lackin'." Jimmy was old now, and had of late grown very feeble, and we did not like to think of him out in that wild storm. And now suddenly the lost boys themselves appeared through the opening in the woods opposite the house, and ran in through the sleet, now falling more quietly. They were wet, but no worse apparently for their adventure, though full of contrition and distress at having lost sight of the dog. He had rushed off into the woods some hours before, after a rabbit or hedgehog, and had never returned. Nor had they seen Fishin' Jimmy.

As hours went by and the old man did not return, a search party was sent out, and guides familiar with the mountain paths went up Lafayette to seek for him. It was nearly night when they at last found him, and the grand old mountains had put on those robes of royal purple which they sometimes assume at eventide. At the foot of a mass of rock, which looked like amethyst or wine-red agate in that marvelous evening light, the old man was lying, and Dash was with him. From the few faint words Jimmy could then gasp out, the truth was gathered. He had missed the boys, leaving the path by which they had returned, and while stumbling along in search of them, feeble and weary, he had heard far below a sound of distress. Looking down over a steep, rocky ledge, he had seen his friend and fishing comrade, old Dash, in sore trouble. Poor Dash! He never dreamed of harming his old friend, for he had a kind heart. But he was a sad coward in some matters, and a very baby when frightened and away from master and friends. So I fear he may have assumed the role of wounded sufferer when in reality he was but scared and lonesome. He never owned this afterward, and you may be sure we never let him know, by word or look, the evil he had done. Jimmy saw him holding up one paw helplessly, and looking at him with wistful, imploring brown eyes, heard his pitiful whimpering cry for aid, and never doubted his great distress and peril. Was Dash not a fisherman? And fishermen, in Fishin' Jimmy's category, were always true and trusty. So the old man without a second's hesitation started down the steep, smooth decline to the rescue of his friend.

We do not know just how or where in that terrible descent he fell. To us who afterward saw the spot, and thought of the weak old man, chilled by the storm, exhausted by his exertions, and yet clambering down that precipitous cliff, made more slippery and treacherous by the sleet and hail still falling, it seemed impossible that he could have kept a foothold for an instant. Nor am I sure that he expected to save himself, and Dash too. But he tried. He was sadly hurt. I will not tell you of that.

Looking out from the hotel windows through the gathering darkness, we who loved him—it was not a small group—saw a sorrowful sight. Flickering lights thrown by the lanterns of the guides came through the woods. Across the road, slowly, carefully, came strong men, bearing on a rough hastily made litter of boughs the dear old man. All that could have been done for the most distinguished guest, for the dearest, best-beloved friend, was done for the gentle fisherman. We, his friends, and proud to style ourselves thus, were of different, widely separated lands, greatly varying creeds. Some were nearly as old as the dying man, some in the prime of manhood. There were youths and maidens and little children. But through the night we watched together. The old Roman bishop, whose calm, benign face we all know and love; the Churchman, ascetic in faith, but with the kindest, most indulgent heart when one finds it; the gentle old Quakeress with placid, unwrinkled brow and silvery hair; Presbyterian, Methodist, and Baptist,—we were all one that night. The old angler did not suffer-we were so glad of that! But he did not appear to know us, and his talk seemed strange. It rambled on quietly, softly, like one of his own mountain brooks, babbling of green fields, of sunny summer days, of his favorite sport, and ah! of other things. But he was not speaking to us. A sudden, awed hush and thrill came over us as, bending to catch the low words, we all at once understood what only the bishop put into words as he said, half to himself, in a sudden, quick, broken whisper, "God bless the man, he's talking to his Master!"

"Yes, sir, that's so," went on the quiet voice; "'twas on'y a dog sure 'nuff; 'twa'n't even a boy, as ye say, an' ye ast me to be a fisher o' men. But I hain't had no chance for that, somehow; mebbe I wa'n't fit for 't. I'm on'y jest a poor old fisherman, Fishin' Jimmy, ye know, sir. Ye useter call me James—no one else ever done it. On'y a dog?

But he wa'n't jest a common dog, sir; he was a fishin' dog. I never seed a man love fishin' more'n Dash." The dog was in the room, and heard his name. Stealing to the bedside, he put a cold nose into the cold hand of his old friend, and no one had the heart to take him away. The touch turned the current of the old man's talk for a moment, and he was fishing again with his dog friend. "See 'em break, Dashy! See 'em break! Lots on 'em to-day, ain't they? Keep still, there's a good dog, while I put on a diffunt fly. Don't ye see they're jumpin' at them gnats? Ain't the water jest 'live with 'em? Ain't it shinin' an' clear an'-" The voice faltered an instant, then went on: "Yes, sir, I'm comin'—I'm glad, dreffle glad to come. Don't mind 'bout my leavin' my fishin'; do ye think I care 'bout that? I'll jest lay down my pole ahin' the alders here, an' put my lan'in' net on the stuns, with my flies an' tackle—the boys 'll like 'em, ye know—an' I'll be right along.

"I mos' knowed ye was on'y a-tryin' me when ye said that 'bout how I hadn't been a fisher o' men, nor even boys, on'y a dog. 'Twas a—fishin' dog—ye know—an' ye was allers dreffle good to fishermen—dreffle good to—everybody; died—for 'em, didn't ye?—

"Please wait—on—the bank there, a minnit; I'm comin' 'crost. Water's pretty—cold this—spring—an' the stream's risin'—but—I—can—do it'—don't ye mind—'bout me, sir. I'll get acrost." Once more the voice ceased, and we thought we should not hear it again this side that stream.

But suddenly a strange light came over the thin face, the soft gray eyes opened wide, and he cried out, with the strong voice we had so often heard come ringing out to us across the mountain streams above the sound of their rushing: "Here I be, sir! It's Fishin' Jimmy, ye know, from Francony way; him ye useter call James when ye come 'long the shore o' the pond an' I was a-fishin'. I heern ye agin, jest now—an' I—straightway—f'sook—my—nets—an'—follerd—"

Had the voice ceased utterly? No, we could catch faint, low murmurs and the lips still moved. But the words were not for us; and we did not know when he reached the other bank.

A Painter, an Angler, and Some Others

WILLIAM SCROPE

Exploring one morning the upper parts of the river, with my trout rod in my hand, I came to a little meadow in a vale where the stream played in mazes beneath hanging coppices. In this sequestered spot, I espied a gentle angler—I may say particularly gentle. His mode of fishing appeared so novel, that I was induced to pry a little into it; so I ventured to approach him, and asked what sport he had been having.

"Oh, glorious, glorious—perfectly enchanting! All Paradise is around me!"

I took notice, however, that although he held his rod pretty much in the usual piscatorial position of altitude, his fly was by no means on the water, but lay very comfortably dry upon the furze on the bank side, and that, whatever his hand might pretend to be doing, his mind was not at that moment particularly bent upon a capture. Whilst he stood entranced, I took the liberty of lifting up the lid of his basket, in which I descried nothing but a pair of gloves—not a fish reposed in it. It was clean, new, and Cockney-like, and I ventured to give him a hint to this effect.

"Well now I declare, sir, that is very singular; because I certainly caught two trout, and put them into my creel. But I dare say you are a little absent, and did not notice them; I am somewhat absent myself occasionally."

He examined the basket, and found only gloves by themselves—gloves.

"Where can I have put them?"

"Indeed I can't guess, sir."

He then began to shuffle about and examine his waistcoat pockets and those of his pantaloons, nay, actually his fob.

"Perhaps, sir, you did not find quite room enough in your fob, and put them into your coat pocket for fear they should soil the basket."

"Bless me! so I did; and here they are, truly. I see now how it is; in a hurry, and whilst I was wrapt in admiration of the scenery, I put the gloves where the fish should have been, and *vice versa*—nothing could be more natural."

This he said with simplicity worthy of the golden age. But he declared that although he was not at that moment very intent on the sport, he did like the fishing exceedingly. "Because," said he, "it requires no parade of attendance, like other field sports; it leads to the most beautiful spots; and I take up my rod and my painting box at any hour I please, and saunter over the flowery meads, in a state of tranquil enjoyment, amidst all the most pleasing images of rural life."

I observed there was considerable excitement in fishing occasionally, as well as tranquility. "For instance, now," said I, "there is a sea trout in that run of water that will make your heart dance, if you should happen to hook him; I saw him put his head up at the cheek of the current, and he had a willful look, and is likely to make most pernicious runs when hooked; for these sort of fish are very active and strong. If you will give me leave, I will change your trout fly for a larger one, and instruct you how to proceed, as from the nature of your tackle I conclude you are not accustomed to fish of this description. There now—go a little higher up the stream; throw above him, and bring the fly gently round; and if he comes at it, do not strike him too hard, or you will break your slender tackle. If you get hold of him, we shall see how he is to be managed; he will put your tranquility to the test, I promise you."

He grasped the rod, and held it aloft; then, after a considerable pause, "He is exactly in the right spot," said he. "Precisely," I replied.

"What a rich red tone of color he has—how well it tells in the shadow! He will come in capitally."

"He is not red, I assure you, but clear as silver, and I wish he may come in capitally."

"Bless me! he looks red to me, and I must take him immediately; he is exactly the thing I wanted." So saying, to my amazement, he dropped the rod, and pulled out a sketch book, in which he began painting a red cow in water colors that was reposing under a hawthorn bush on the opposite bank, just beyond the stream where the fish was lying, and which had been the real object of his remarks. When he had done with the cow, however, I put the rod once more into his hands, and reminded him of the fish.

"Now throw a few yards above the spot where you see the water boiling around the large blue stone. Very well; advance a step every trine you throw. Capital! Now you are precisely at the fish. Strike him gently if he rises. Well done!—by Paul Potter you have him! Hold up the top of your rod, and keep an even steady pull upon him."

"How can I keep a steady pull upon such a wild animal? Why he springs out of the water, and whizzes about in it, like that fire-work called a serpent."

"Be steady—be steady, or he will whiz you about with a witness. Shorten your line; get into the water, and follow him."

"What a cruel speech! Why I never learned to swim. You are exceedingly inconsiderate indeed, sir."

"Swim! why the water on this channel is scarcely over your ankles, and I will help you if you should happen to stumble."

"Then we should both meet a watery grave together. I have often read of such calamities."

"In with you—in with you, I say, or he will be off. There, I told you so; he has broke your line; and, pray pardon me, but pretty work you have made of it with your tranquility."

"Well, as it seems to make you so uneasy, I will go a little way into the water, though I shall not enjoy it."

"Why, what is the use of wetting yourself, now, you have lost the fish?"

"True, true—I did not sufficiently consider that; so now I will go back, and see if I can improve my cow."

This was abundantly philosophical; but intelligible enough to me, who being very much addicted to painting myself, know how absorbing a passion it is.

The cow was a good cow—drawn in a clean and decisive manner, with a correct knowledge of the anatomy of the animal. I praised accordingly, and we began naturally enough to talk upon the principles of landscape painting; and as we both agreed pretty well as to those principles, so we both laid down the law with as much confidence as if we were the lineal descendants of Zeuxis or Apelles—a fashion, I must observe, most particularly prevalent at the present day. I fear it is not worth while to notice our remarks . . .

Then, having beguiled the attention of Mr. Tintern (for that was the stranger's name) from the summits in which he had been soaring, I found him quite ready to receive an impression of a more humble kind, and he attended me in my walk, nothing loth. I was very much gratified with his company; for, besides his talent and simplicity of character, there was such an appearance of benevolent feeling in much of his conversation, which I have not thought it necessary to mention, that no one could avoid being taken with him.

I commenced operation at the Carry-wheel, which is nearly at the head of the Pavilion-water, and had not made four casts before I hooked a fish. He was evidently diminutive; but, dwarf as he was, he thought a good deal of himself, and was prodigal of the little strength which nature had given him. I thought him conceited, and so hauled him on shore at once without any ceremony. He proved to be a river trout of four pounds—a silly-looking creature enough.

Well, I went forward and caught a few gilses and salmon in the upper Pavilion-water, not worth mentioning, except as the sport had the effect of rousing my new friend from his abstraction; indeed I met with nothing remarkable till I came to the Kingswell Lees. Now every one knows that the Kingswell Lees, in fisherman's phrase, fishes off land; so there I stood on *terra durra* amongst the rocks that dip down to the water's edge. Having executed one or two throws, there comes to me a voracious fish, and makes a startling dash at "Meg with the muckle mouth." Sharply did I strike the caitiff; whereat he rolled round disdainful, making a whirl in the water of prodigious circumference: it was not exactly Charybdis, or the Maelstrom, but rather more like the wave occasioned by the sudden turning of a man-of-war's boat. Being hooked, and having by this turn set his nose peremptorily down the stream, he flashed and whizzed away like a rocket. My situation partook of the nature of a surprise. Being on a rocky shore, and having a bad start, I lost ground at first considerably; but the reel sang out joyously, and yielded a liberal length of line, that saved me from the disgrace of being broke. I got on the best pace I was able, and was on good ground just as my line was nearly all run out. As the powerful animal darted through Meg's Hole, I was just able to step back and wind up a few yards of line; but he still went a killing pace, and when he came near Melrose Bridge he evinced a distressing preference for passing through the farther arch, in which case my line would have been cut by the pier. My heart sunk with apprehension, for he was near the opposite bank. Purdie, seeing this, with great presence of mind took up some stones from the channel, and threw them one by one between the fish and the said opposite bank. This naturally brought Master Salmo somewhat nearer; but still for a few moments we had a doubtful struggle for it. At length, by lowering the head of the rod, and thus not having so much of the ponderous weight of the fish to encounter, I towed him a little sideways; and so advancing towards me with propitious fin, he shot through the arch nearest me.

Deeply immersed, I dashed after him as best I might; and arriving on the other side of the bridge I floundered out upon dry land, and continued the chase. The salmon, "right orgillous and presumptive," still kept the strength of the stream, and abating nothing of his vigor, went swiftly down the Whirls; then through the Boat shiel, and over the shallows, till he came to the throat of the Elmwheel, down which he darted amain. Owing to the bad ground, the pace here became exceedingly distressing. I contrived, however, to keep company with my fish, still doubtful of the result, till I came to the bottom of the long cast in question, when he still showed fight, and sought the shallows below. Unhappily the alders prevented my following by land, and I was compelled to take water again, which slackened my speed. But the stream soon expanding, and the current diminishing, my fish likewise traveled more slowly; so I gave a few sobs and recovered my wind a little, gathered up my line, and tried to bring him to terms. But he derided my efforts, and dashed off for another burst, triumphant. Not far below lay the rapids of the Saughterford: he would soon gain them at the pace he was going, that was certain; see, he is there already! But I back out again on dry land, nothing loth, and have a fair race with him. Sore work it is. I am a pretty fair runner, as has often been testified; but his velocity is surprising. On, on—still he goes, ploughing up the water like a steamer. "Away with you, Charlie! Quick, quick, man—quick for your life! Loosen the boat at the Cauld Pool, where we shall soon be." And so indeed we were, when I jumped into the said craft, still having good hold of my fish.

The Tweed is here broad and deep, and the salmon at length had become somewhat exhausted; he still kept in the strength of the stream, however, with his nose seawards, and hung heavily. At last he comes near the surface of the water. See how he shakes his tail and digs downwards, seeking the deep profound—that he will never gain. His motions become more short and feeble; he is evidently doomed, and his race well-nigh finished. Drawn into the hare water, and not approving of the extended cleik, he makes another swift rush, and repeats this effort each time that he is towed to the shallows. At length he is cleiked in earnest, and hauled to shore: he proves one of the grey scull, newly run, and weighs somewhat about twenty pounds. The hook is not in his mouth, but in the outside of it; in which case a fish being able to respire freely, always shows extraordinary vigor, and generally sets his head down the stream.

During the whole period of my experience in fishing, though I have had some sharp encounters, yet I never knew any sport equal to this. I am out of breath even now whenever I think of it. I will trouble any surveyor to measure the distance from the Kingswell Lees, the starting spot, above Melrose Bridge, to the end of the Cauld Pool, the death place, by Melrose Church, and to tell me how much less it is than a mile and three-quarters—I say I will trouble him to do so; and let him be a lover of the angle, that he may rather increase than diminish the distance, as in good feeling and respect for the craft it behooves him to do. I will likewise thank my contemporaries and posterity to bear in mind that the distance about to be measured by this able surveyor was run at an eclipse pace, always allowing for some slight abatement in speed pending our immersion.

Whilst I was taking a rest on the greensward, the heated face of my excellent new friend appeared through the alders. He could not, however, be fairly said to be in at the death; the *coup de grace* having been already given about five minutes. He expressed the greatest astonishment at the swiftness and result of the race, and at the power of the fish, who had been able to distress two full-grown men so completely. He owned he was much excited, but thought fishing for salmon would be too turbulent an amusement for him; though perhaps he might have kept up with a good pony, had the ground been passable by such a beast. Poussin, Virgil, the Apennines, all were forgotten; and he began to enter warmly into the spirit of the present, and was curious to know by what particular tactics one can contrive to get the better of such a large furious monster, as he expressed it, with such apparently inadequate means, when a small sea trout broke him with all the ease imaginable. As I now reckoned upon his attention, I told him as follows—how to manage a large salmon, and how a large salmon may manage us:—

"When you get hold of a *monstrum horrendum ingens* of a fish, say of some five and forty pounds, you must anticipate a very long and severe battle. If, therefore, you have a disposable Gilly with you, despatch him instantly for some skilful fisherman, as well to assist you when you are exhausted with fatigue, as to bring your dinner and supper; not forgetting a dark lantern, that you may not be beaten by the shades of night—a circumstance by no means improbable. At the first onset you will probably be obliged to keel) your arms and rod aloft, in order to steer clear of the rocks. This action, with a heavy rod and large fish on your line, is very distressing, if continued even for a short time; and it will be necessary to repeat it often, if the channel is not very favorable; and in that case your muscles will ache insupportably, if they at all resemble those of other men. The easiest position, when it is safe to use it, is to place the butt of your rod against the stomach as a rest, and to bring the upper part of the arm and the elbow in close contact with the sides, putting on at the same time an air of determination.

"If your leviathan should be superlatively boisterous, no one knows what may happen. For instance, should you be in a boat, and he should shoot away down the river, you must follow rapidly; then, when he again turns upwards, what a clever fellow your fisherman must be, to stop a boat that has been going down a rapid stream at the rate of eight miles an hour, and bring it round all of a sudden in time to keep company with the fish, who has taken an upward direction! And what a clever fellow a piscator must be, if he can prevent twenty yards of his line, or more, from hanging loose in the stream! These sort of things will happen, and they are ticklish concerns. All I can do is to recommend caution and patience; and the better to encourage you in the exercise of these virtues, I will recount what happened to Duncan Grant in days of yore.

"First, you must understand that what is called 'preserving the river' was formerly unknown, and every one who chose to take a cast did so without let or hindrance.

"In pursuance of this custom, in the month of July, some thirty years ago, one Duncan Grant, a shoemaker by profession, who was more addicted to fishing than to his craft, went up the way from the village of Aberlour, in the north, to take a cast in some of the pools above Elchies Water. He had no great choice of tackle, as may be conceived; nothing, in fact, but what was useful, and scant supply of that.

"Duncan tried one or two pools without success, till he arrived at a very deep and rapid stream, facetiously termed '*the Mountebank*': here he paused, as if meditating whether he should throw his line or not. 'She is very big,' said he to himself, 'but I'll try her; if I grip him he'll be worth the handing.' He then fished it, a step and a throw, about half way down, when a heavy splash proclaimed that he had raised him, though he missed the fly. Going back a few paces, he came over him again, and hooked him. The first tug verified to Duncan his prognostication, that if he was there 'he would be worth the handing'; but his tackle had thirty plies of hair next the fly, and he held fast, nothing daunted. Give and take went on with dubious advantage, the fish occasionally sulking. The thing at length became serious; and, after a succession of the same tactics, Duncan found himself at the Boat of Aberlous, seven hours after he had hooked his fish, the said fish fast under a stone, and himself completely tired. He had some thoughts of breaking his tackle and giving the thing up; but he finally hit upon an expedient to rest himself, and at the same time to guard against the surprise and consequence of a sudden movement of the fish.

"He laid himself down comfortably on the banks, the butt end of his rod in front; and most ingeniously drew out part of his line, which he held in his teeth. 'If he tugs when I'm sleeping,' said he, 'I think I'll find him noo'; and no doubt it is probable that he would. Accordingly, after a comfortable nap of three or four hours, Duncan was awoke by a most unceremonious tug at his jaws. In a moment he was on his feet, his rod well up, and the fish swattering down the stream. He followed as best he could, and was beginning to think of the rock at Craigellachie, when he found to his great relief that he could 'get a pull on him.' He had now comparatively easy work; and exactly twelve hours after hooking him, he cleiked him at the head of Lord Fife's water: he weighed fifty-four pounds, Dutch, and had the tide lice upon him."

Thus Duncan Grant has instructed us how to manage a large salmon. Let us now see how a large salmon may manage us.

In the year 1815, Robert Kerse hooked a clean salmon of about forty pounds in the Makerstoun Water, the largest, he says, he ever encountered; sair work he had with him for some hours; till at last Rob, to use his own expression, was "clean dune out." He landed the fish, however, in the end, and laid him on the channel; astonished, and rejoicing at his prodigious size, he called out to a man on the opposite bank of the river, who had been watching him for some time.

"Hey, mon, sic a fish!"

He then went for a stone to fell him with; but as soon as his back was turned, the fish began to wamble towards the water, and Kerse turned, and jumped upon it; over they both tumbled, and they, line, hook, and all went into the Tweed. The fish was too much for Rob, having broke the line, which got twisted round his leg, and made his escape, to his great disappointment and loss, for at the price clean salmon were then selling, he could have got five pounds for it.

Thus you see how a large fish may manage us.

I must tell you that the above-mentioned Robert Kerse has long been a distinguished character on the Tweed. At a secluded spot, where the woods and rocks dip down to the margin of the river, and where its current is opposed by a rocky barrier through which it has worn its way in frightful gorges, the gaunt figure of Auld Rob of the Troughs has been seen any time these forty years. He is very tall and bony, and when working his boat with the canting pole amongst the rapids, or looking down aloft ready to strike, he cuts a most formidable Salvator Rosa-like appearance. Rob is now highly seasoned with the saltiness of time, being nearer eighty than seventy years old; drinks whiskey like water, his native element; and to this day runs after the hounds, when they come near, like a boy of fifteen. He is a genuine lover of all sports, and has begot numerous sons and daughters: of the former, four are game-keepers, and fishermen on Tweed, Tiviot, and Ettrick, to the Duke of Bubbleuch, Lord Lothian, and Lord Home. They are remarkable as claiming a regular descent from Saxon ancestors in the most remote times, and are an active, athletic, clean-limbed race of men, keen of eye, and swift of foot, of good pluck, and altogether amphibious, loving the heather and mountain flood better than the street and servants' hall. Stalwart men would they have been in a Border Foray had they lived in the time of Johnny Armstrong. Such and so great are the Kerses; but they will not go down to posterity like the Purdies, "carent quia Vate sacro"; neither could the old river god Rob himself contend with the otter so valiantly as Charlie Purdie. Whether it was that he had a sort of fellow-feeling for an animal that was amphibious like himself, and followed the same profession, or from what other cause I cannot say, but Rob did not particularly shine in a fair stand-up otter fight, as you shall hear.

In the latter end of September, 1839, Kerse had set a cairn net at the Clippers, "a little below Makerstoun House, but on the bank of the river opposite to it; and on going to the cairn to examine the net, he saw a young otter sitting on, and entangled in it; he threw more of the net over it, whilst drawing it to the land, and when he had caught hold of the tail, and was carrying it off, a large otter, which he described as "a she ane," five feet in length, jumped out of the water, ran up the bank after him to use his own words, "like a mad bear," and commenced a furious attack upon hint. Rob had nothing to defend himself with but his hat; and as he was holding the young one with one hand, he found he was likely to have the worst of it, and to be bitten by the one animal or the other. So he threw the whelp to the old one, saying, "Ay, ye she devil, ye may get her, twae to ane is odds." They both swam away; that is, the two otters, not Kerse.

On looking after them he saw two other young ones trying to make past the point of the cairn, which, owing to the strength of the current, they seemed unable to effect: Kerse thought he would try the thing again, so he laid hold of one of them and pulled it out also by the tail; scarce had he done this, and had begun to take to his heels, ere out again jumped the old one, and attacked him; but this time Rob had provided himself with a large stone, and hit the old beast on the back, when he again set off and carried the young one with him which was afterwards given to Lord John Scott. During the whole contest, says Rob, "the auld beast keepit squeeling, and makin' a noise something like a horse, when he gies a snore."

Fishing

REVEREND THOMAS BASTARD

Fishing, if I, a fisher, may protest
Of pleasures is the sweet'st, of sports the best,
Of exercises the most excellent,
Of Recreations the most innocent.
But now the sport is marred, and wot ye why?
Fishes decrease, and fishers multiply.

Crazy for Rivers (selection)

BILL BARICH

That autumn, I went a little crazy for rivers. The weather was unusually mild in northern California, where I live, and I had some time to spare and couldn't imagine a better way to spend it than in the high mountain country as the leaves began to fall. I fished the Merced and the Stanislaus, the Kings and the North Yuba, and I had some luck on them all and might have fished the Tuolumne, too, if nature hadn't dealt me a setback. It was a good period in my life, calm and reflective, even happy. The days flowed by unbroken, in perfect sunlight, and often I found myself thinking back over the years and thanking the heavens I'd come to be where I was, knee-deep in a trout stream with a fly rod in my hand.

Some people are born anglers, but I was not, even though my father had a passion for fishing. When I was a boy, I used to hear him complain about his distance from a decent lake as he dodged the traffic between our Long Island home and his office in Manhattan. He'd grown up in rural Michigan, the last of twelve children. His older brothers had taught him to love the outdoors, so he came by his longing honestly. His father—my grandfather, a stocky Slav always dressed for a wedding in a three-piece wool suit from Dubrovnik—was fond of the woods, as well, and saw no irony in decorating the tavern he owned with his cherished forest creatures (deer, moose, even hawks) stuffed and mounted.

For some reason, I'd met only a couple of my paternal uncles, so I enjoyed being told stories about them, especially about John, the eldest, who was a legendary hunter. He had shared a bed with my father for a while. That wasn't uncommon in large families in those days, and it might never have been mentioned at all, except that John talked and hunted in his sleep. In the middle of the night, he'd sit bolt upright in a trance, grab my father by the shoulders, shake him, and shout, "There's a bear in the room! Oh, no! He's going to attack us!" My father never saw the bear, of course, but it seemed real to him, and he would shiver and whimper until John stuck out an arm like a rifle, took deliberate aim, and fired a fatal shot.

"Blam! Got 'im!" he'd cry. "We're saved!" Then he would roll over and go back to sleep.

Though I couldn't have known it then, not when I was still a child myself, I understood later that my father told such stories because he missed the folks on the Upper Peninsula and felt nostalgic for his youth and its sporting pursuits. His success in business had separated him from much that he cared about and had affection for, so every summer he would saddle up his family for a two-week vacation at a fishing resort, ordinarily in Minnesota—my mother was from there—but once in darkest Maine, at Sebago Lake, where I was puzzled and a bit frightened by the taciturn, stiff-spined, pipe-smoking men in flannel shirts, who were already cutting firewood in July.

I got my first fishing lessons on those trips, but I was a lackluster student. I could swing a Louisville Slugger with aplomb and even hit the long ball, but I was terribly awkward with a spin rod. Whenever I snarled my line or tossed a Jitterbug into a tree, my father would become flustered, carrying on about the minutes he was losing as he untied the knots and retrieved the plugs from limbs. He had a temper back then and lacked the patience to be a sympathetic teacher. We hardly ever caught any fish, either, so my brother, David, and I, being enterprising lads, would amuse ourselves by liberating minnows from the minnow bucket, shooting at squirrels with a Whammo slingshot, and conducting stupid giggling fits whose sole purpose was to further annoy the old man.

The only rewarding fishing I ever had on vacation, in fact, was courtesy of Carl Peterson, my mother's father, who guided us kids around Paradise Lake in a rowboat, in 1956. Carl managed an apartment building in St. Paul and bought me my first official cowboy outfit—chaps, spurs, boots, the works. I liked him a lot, although not as much as I liked my Uncle Ned, a former star player in a semi-pro baseball league, who worked as a mailman and let me walk his route with him sometimes. Ned always had a powerful thirst, and if the weather happened to be humid, we would be forced to stop at a few saloons along the way, where my uncle would polish off a quick draft beer, often paid for by an admiring fan, while I thumped the pinball machine and developed bad habits at an early age.

Carl Peterson didn't fish much himself, but he had patience in his favor and knew that children in boats are most content when they have something to do. He let us fish for easy-to-catch crappies instead of the tricky bass or pike my father went after, and we hauled in so many of them so fast that we got our picture in the local paper holding up a stringer to show off our forty or fifty victims. It still astonishes me to see how proud I look, a sophisticated East Coast youth of thirteen with his hair styled in a fashionable "Hollywood" crew cut (flat on top and slicked back at the sides), secretly imagining his future as a rock-and-roll star, even as he poses with a bunch of dead crappies at Paradise Lake.

I really hated fishing by the time I turned sixteen. I rebelled against the entire concept of a family vacation and whined and protested until my parents agreed to let me stay home alone. (Not incidentally, that was the summer I lost my virginity to a lusty cheerleader in my very own upstairs bedroom, treating her to an ice-cream pop from a circling Good Humor truck immediately afterward because I had no idea what else to do.) I thought that sitting in a boat in the middle of nowhere was the dumbest activity known to mankind and swore I would never fish again—and I might have kept my promise, too, if my brother hadn't intervened by accident, thirteen years later.

I had taken Horace Greeley's advice by then and migrated west to seek my fortune, although not to *work* for it. I was living in San Francisco, in a spacious Haight-Ashbury Victorian that we renters failed to dust even once during our tenancy. My hair, suffice it to say, was not in a Hollywood crew cut anymore, and I'd mastered the fine art of slacking. As for David, he had what we referred to as a "straight" job (book salesman in Manhattan), but he'd managed to finagle a transfer to California so he could savor the hippie glories I'd described to him. On a whim, he brought some of my father's old tackle with him, and we passed a comical evening sorting through it, laughing as we dredged up the names of the long-forgotten lures—Hawaiian Wigglers in lurid purple skirts, an evil black Sonic, a wacky Crazy Crawler, and a single Lazy Ike, yellow with bright-red polka dots.

We stored the tackle in the basement, where it languished. It might have stayed there forever, or at least until our landlord evicted us, if I hadn't fallen for a new girlfriend and invited her on a romantic trip to the Sierra Nevada. Not that I'd ever been to the Sierra Nevada myself, but that hardly matters when you're wild about someone. I studied the maps and made the plans and knew in my heart that we would be all right wherever we landed, as long as the place had a bed. After packing the car and loading the cooler, I went downstairs at the last minute and grabbed one of the vintage spin rods and a reel, South Bend and Zebco respectively, although I wasn't truly conscious of why I might be doing it and moved about as a person does in a daze or a dream.

We wound up in a rustic cabin on Stuart Fork of the Trinity River, in the shadow of the Trinity Alps. The cabin resembled a packing crate inside and had an icebox instead of a fridge, but it fronted on the river and was blessed with an open-air porch, where we slept on a lumpy mattress and gazed up at the brilliant stars and moonlit peaks and felt that we must be the most fortunate couple on earth. We went hiking, played games of cribbage, and cooked steaks over the coals, and yet not once did it occur to me that I was reliving the family vacation. I was still very young then and blind to so many things, and I didn't realize how a past experience can touch us deeply, can shatter us or set us free, even though we've never reckoned with its power. But I know it now. The past is never wholly gone.

Those days in the mountains were glorious days. It was late in September, but the afternoons were still blazing hot, and we liked nothing better than a nap on the porch after lunch, with the sun falling all around us and the air rich with the scent of sun-warmed pines. One afternoon, I woke before my girlfriend and stood looking at the river, so low and clear I could count the pebbles of the streambed. Trout in there? I doubted it, but I rigged up the rod for fun, rolled up my jeans, and waded barefoot into the water. I could see the sun glinting off the spoon I'd bought at the resort's store and could hear some Steller's jays bickering in the tall trees, and I drifted so far away from Stuart Fork that when a fish hit my lure, it had the effect of yanking me out of the clouds and back into my body.

High up leaped a silvery little rainbow, as hooked in the moment as I was.

A River Runs Through It (selection)

NORMAN MACLEAN

We somehow couldn't get started that morning. After Paul and I had left home, Father put away his fishing tackle, probably thinking he was putting it away for good, so now he couldn't remember where. Mother had to find most of the things for him. She knew nothing about fishing or fishing tackle, but she knew how to find things, even when she did not know what they looked like.

Paul, who usually got everyone nervous by being impatient to be on the stream, kept telling Father, "Take it easy. It's turned cooler. We'll make a killing today. Take it easy." But my father, from whom my brother had inherited his impatience to have his flies on water, would look at me visibly loathing himself for being old and not able to collect himself.

My mother had to go from basement to attic and to most closets in between looking for a fishing basket while she made lunches for three men, each of whom wanted a different kind of sandwich. After she got us in the car, she checked each car door to see that none of her men would fall out. Then she dried her hands in her apron, although her hands were not wet, and said, "Thank goodness," as we drove away.

I was at the wheel, and I knew before we started just where we were going. It couldn't be far up the Blackfoot, because we were starting late, and it had to be a stretch of water of two or three deep holes for Paul and me and one good hole with no bank too steep for Father to crawl down. Also, since he couldn't wade, the good fishing water had to be on his side of the river. They argued while I drove, although they knew just as well as I did where we had to go, but each one in our family considered himself the leading authority on how to fish the Blackfoot River. When we came to the side road going to the river above the mouth of Belmont Creek, they spoke in unison for the first time. "Turn here," they said, and, as if I were following their directions, I turned to where I was going anyway.

The side road brought us down to a flat covered with ground boulders and cheat grass. No livestock grazed on it, and grasshoppers took off like birds and flew great distances, because on this flat it is a long way between feeding grounds, even for grasshoppers. The flat itself and its crop of boulders are the roughly ground remains of one of geology's great disasters The flat may well have been the end of the ice age lake, half as big as Lake Michigan, that in places was two thousand feet deep until the glacial dam broke and this hydraulic monster of the hilts charged out on to the plains of eastern Washington High on the mountains above where we stopped to fish are horizontal scars slashed by passing icebergs.

I had to be careful driving toward the river so I wouldn't high-center the car on a boulder and break the crankcase. The flat ended suddenly and the river was down a steep bank, blinking silver through the trees and then turning to blue by comparing itself to a red and green cliff. It was another world to see and feel, and another world of rocks. The boulders on the flat were shaped by the last ice age only eighteen or twenty thousand years ago, but the red and green precambrian rocks beside the blue water were almost from the basement of the world and time.

We stopped and peered down the bank. I asked my father, "Do you remember when we picked a lot of red and green rocks down there to build our fireplace? Some were red mudstones with ripples on them."

"Some had raindrops on them," he said. His imagination was always stirred by the thought that he was standing in ancient rain spattering on mud before it became rocks.

"Nearly a billion years ago," I said, knowing what he was thinking.

He paused. He had given up the belief that God had created all there was, including the Blackfoot River, on a six-day work schedule, but he didn't believe that the job so taxed God's powers that it took Him forever to complete.

"Nearly half a billion years ago," he said as his contribution to reconciling science and religion. He hurried on, not wishing to waste any part of old age in debate, except over fishing. "We carried those big rocks up the bank," he said, "but now I can't crawl down it. Two holes below, though, the river comes out in the open and there is almost no bank. I'll walk down there and fish, and you fish the first two holes. I'll wait in the sun. Don't hurry."

Paul said, "You'll get 'em," and all of a sudden Father was confident in himself again. Then he was gone.

We could catch glimpses of him walking along the bank of the river which had been the bottom of the great glacial lake. He held his rod straight in front of him and every now and then he lunged forward with it, perhaps reenacting some glacial race memory in which he speared a hairy ice age mastodon and ate him for breakfast.

Paul said, "Let's fish together today." I knew then that he was still taking care of me, because we almost always split up when we fished. "That's fine," I said. "I'll wade across and fish the other side," he said. I said, "Fine," again, and was doubly touched. On the other side you were backed against cliffs and trees, so it was mostly a roll-casting job, never my specialty. Besides, the river was powerful here with no good place to wade, and next to fishing Paul liked swimming rivers with his rod in his hand. It turned out he didn't have to swim here, but as he waded sometimes the wall of water rose to his upstream shoulder while it would be no higher than his hip behind him. He stumbled to shore from the weight of water in his clothes, and gave me a big wave.

I came down the bank to catch fish. Cool wind had blown in from Canada without causing any electric storms, so the fish should be off the bottom and feeding again. When a deer comes to water, his head shoots in and out of his shoulders to see what's ahead, and I was looking all around to see what fly to put on. But I didn't have to look further than my neck or my nose. Big clumsy flies bumped into my face, swarmed on my neck and wiggled in my underwear. Blundering and soft-bellied, they had been born before they had brains. They had spent a year under water on legs, had crawled out on a rock, had become flies and copulated with the ninth and tenth segments of their abdomens, and then had died as the first light wind blew them into the water where the fish circled excitedly. They were a fish's dream come true—stupid, succulent, and exhausted from copulation. Still, it would be hard to know what gigantic portion of human life is spent in this same ratio of years under water on legs to one premature, exhausted moment on wings.

I sat on a log and opened my fly box. I knew I had to get a fly that would match these flies exactly, because when a big hatch like this or the salmon fly is out, the fish won't touch anything else. As proof, Paul hadn't had a strike yet, so far as I could see.

I figured he wouldn't have the right fly, and I knew I had it. As I explained earlier, he carried all his flies in his hat-band. He thought that with four or five generals in different sizes he could imitate the action of nearly any aquatic or terrestrial insect in any stage from larval to winged. He was always kidding me because I carried so many flies. "My, my," he would say, peering into my fly box, "wouldn't it be wonderful if a guy knew how to use ten of all those flies." But I've already told you about the Bee, and I'm still sure that there are times when a general won't turn a fish over.

The fly that would work now had to be a big fly, it had to have a yellow, black-banded body, and it had to ride high in the water with extended wings, something like a butterfly that has had an accident and can't dry its wings by fluttering in the water.

It was so big and flashy it was the first fly I saw when I opened my box. It was called a Bunyan Bug, tied by a fly tyer in Missoula named Norman Means, who ties a line of big flashy flies all called Bunyan Bugs. They are tied on big hooks, No. 2's and No. 4's, have cork bodies with stiff horsehair tied crosswise so they ride high in the water like dragonflies on their backs. The cork bodies are painted different colors and then are shellacked. Probably the biggest and flashiest of the hundred flies my brother made fun of was the Bunyan Bug No. 2.

I took one look at it and felt perfect. My wife, my mother-in-law, and my sister-in-law, each in her somewhat obscure style, had recently redeclared their love for me. I, in my somewhat obscure style, had returned their love; I might never see my brother-in-law again. My mother had found my father's old tackle and once more he was fishing with us. My brother was taking tender care of me, and not catching any fish. I was about to make a killing.

It is hard to cast Bunyan Bugs into the wind because the cork and horsehair make them light for their bulk. But, though the wind shortens the cast, it acts at the same time to lower the fly slowly and almost vertically to the water with no telltale splash. My Stone Fly was still hanging over the water when what seemed like a speedboat went by it, knocked it high into the air, circled, opened the throttle wide on the returning straight away, and roared over the spot marked X where the Stone Fly had settled. Then the speedboat turned into a submarine, disappearing with all on board including my fly, and headed for deep water. I couldn't throw line into the rod fast enough to keep up with what was disappearing and I couldn't change its course. Not being as fast as what was under water, I literally forced it into the air. From where I was I suppose I couldn't see what happened, but my heart was at the end of the line and telegraphed back its impressions as it went by. My general impression was that marine life had turned into a rodeo. My particular information was that a large Rainbow had gone sun-fishing, turning over twice in the air, hitting my line each time and tearing loose from the fly which went sailing out into space. My distinct information was that it never looked around to see. My only close-at-hand information was that when the line was reeled in, there was nothing on the end of it but some cork and some hairs from a horse's tail.

The stone flies were just as thick as ever, fish still swirled in quiet water, and I was a little smarter. I don't care much about taking instructions, even from myself, but before I made the next cast I underlined the fact that big Rainbows sometimes come into quiet waters because aquatic insects hatch in or near quiet waters. "Be prepared," I said to myself, remembering an old war song. I also accepted my own advice to have some extra coils of line in my left hand to take some of the tension off the first run of the next big Rainbow swirling in quiet water.

So on this wonderful afternoon when all things came together it took me one cast, one fish, and some reluctantly accepted advice to attain perfection. I did not miss another.

From then on I let them run so far that sometimes they surged clear across the river and jumped right in front of Paul. When I was young, a teacher had forbidden me to say "more perfect" because she said if a thing is perfect it can't be more so. But by now I had seen enough of life to have regained my confidence in it. Twenty minutes ago I had felt perfect, but by now my brother was taking off his bat and changing flies every few casts. I knew he didn't carry any such special as a Bunyan Bug No.2 Yellow Stone Fly. I had five or six big Rainbows in my basket which began to hurt my shoulder so I left it behind on shore. Once in a while I looked back and smiled at the basket. I could hear it thumping on the rocks and falling on its side. However I may have violated grammar, I was feeling more perfect with every Rainbow.

Just after my basket gave an extra large thump there was an enormous splash in the water to the left of where I was casting. "My God," I thought before I could look, "there's nothing that big that swims in the Blackfoot," and, when I dared look, there was nothing but a large circle that got bigger and bigger. Finally the first wave went by my knees. "It must be a beaver," I thought I was waiting for him to surface when something splashed behind me. "My God," I said again, "I would have seen a beaver swim by me under water." While I was wrenching my neck backwards, the thing splashed right in front of me, too close for comfort but close enough so I could watch what was happening under water The silt was rising from the bottom like smoke from the spot where lightning had struck A fair-sized rock was sitting in the spot where the smoke was rising.

While I was relating my past to the present rock, there was another big splash in front of me, but this time I didn't bother to jump. Beaver, hell! Without looking, I knew it was my brother. It didn't happen often in this life, only when his fishing partner was catching fish and he couldn't. It was a sight, however rare, that he could not bear to watch. So he would spoil his partner's hole, even if it was his brother's. I looked up just in time to see a fair-sized boulder come out of the sky and I ducked too late to keep it from splashing all over me.

He had his hat off and he shook his fist at me. I knew he had fished around his hat band before he threw the rocks. I shook my fist back at him, and waded to shore, where my basket was still thumping. In all my life, I had got the rock treatment only a couple of times before. I was feeling more perfect than ever.

I didn't mind that he spoiled the hole before I had filled my basket, because there was another big hole between us and father. It was a beautiful stretch of water, against cliffs and in shadows. The hole I had just fished was mostly in sunlight—the weather had become cooler, but was still warm enough so that the hole ahead in shadows should be even better than the one in sunlight and I should have no trouble finishing off my basket with a Bunyan Bug No. 2 Yellow Stone Fly.

Paul and I walked nearly the length of the first hole before we could hear each other yell across the river. I knew he hated to be heard yelling, "What were they biting on?" The last two words, "biting on," kept echoing across the water and pleased me.

When the echoes ceased, I yelled back, "Yellow stone flies." These words kept saying themselves until they subsided into sounds of the river. He kept turning his hat round and round in his hands.

I possibly began to get a little ashamed of myself. "I caught them on a Bunyan Bug," I yelled. "Do you want one?"

"No," he yelled before "want one" had time to echo. Then "want one" and "no" passed each other on the back turns.

"I'll wade across with one," I said through the cup of my hands. That's a lot to say across a river, and the first part of it returning met the last part of it just starting. I didn't know whether he had understood what I had said, but the river still answered, "No."

While I was standing in quiet, shady water, I half noticed that no stone flies were hatching, and I should have thought longer about what I saw but instead I found myself thinking about character. It seems somehow natural to start thinking about character when you get ahead of somebody, especially about the character of the one who is behind. I was thinking of how, when things got tough, my brother looked to himself to get himself out of trouble. He never looked for any flies from me. I had a whole round of thoughts on this subject before I returned to reality and yellow stone flies. I started by thinking that, though be was my brother, he was sometimes knot-headed. I pursued this line of thought back to the Greeks who believed that not wanting any help might even get you killed. Then I suddenly remembered that my brother was almost always a winner and often because he didn't borrow flies. So I decided that the response we make to character on any given day depends largely on the response fish are making to character on the same day. And thinking of the response of fish, I shifted rapidly back to reality, and said to myself, "I still have one more hole to go."

I didn't get a strike and I didn't see a stone fly and it was the same river as the one above, where I could have caught my limit a few minutes before if my brother hadn't thrown rocks in it. My prize Bunyan Bug began to look like a fake to me as well as to the fish. To me, it looked like a floating mattress. I cast it upstream and let it drift down naturally as if it had died. Then I popped it into the water as if it had been blown there. Then I made it zigzag while retrieving it, as if it were trying to launch itself into flight. But it evidently retained the appearance of a floating mattress. I took it off, and tried several other flies. There were no flies in the water for me to match, and by the same token there were no fish jumping.

I began to cast glances across the river under my hat brim. Paul wasn't doing much either. I saw him catch one, and he just turned and walked to shore with it, so it couldn't have been much of a fish. I was feeling a little less than more perfect.

Then Paul started doing something he practically never did, at least not since he had been old enough to be cocky. He suddenly started fishing upstream, back over the water he had just fished. That's more like me when I feel I haven't fished the hole right or from the right angle, but, when my brother fished a hole, he assumed nothing was left behind that could be induced to change its mind.

I was so startled I leaned against a big rock to watch.

Almost immediately he started hauling them in. Big ones, and he didn't spend much time landing them either. I thought he gave them too little line and took them in too fast, but I knew what he was up to. He expected to make a killing in this hole, and he wasn't going to let any one fish thrash around in the water until it scared the rest off. He had one on now and he held the line on it so tight he was forcing it high in the air. When it jumped, he leaned back on his rod and knocked the fish into the water again. Full of air now, it streaked across the top of the water with its tail like the propeller of a seaplane until it could get its submarine chambers adjusted and submerge again.

He lost a couple but he must have had ten by the time he got back to the head of the hole.

Then he looked across the river and saw me sitting beside my rod. He started fishing again, stopped, and took another look. He cupped his hands and yelled, "Do you have George's No. 2 Yellow Hackle with a feather not a horsehair wing?" It was fast water and I didn't get all the words immediately. "No. 2" I caught first, because it is a hell of a big hook, and then "George," because he was our fishing pal, and then "Yellow." With that much information I started to look in my box, and let the other words settle into a sentence later.

One bad thing about carrying a box loaded with flies, as I do, is that nearly half the time I still don't have the right one. "No," I admitted across the water, and water keeps repeating your admissions.

"I'll be there," he called back and waded upstream.

"No," I yelled after him, meaning don't stop fishing on my account. You can't convey an implied meaning across a river, or, if you can, it is easy to ignore. My brother walked to the lower end of the first hole where the water was shallow and waded across.

By the time he got to me, I had recovered most of the pieces he must have used to figure out what the fish were biting. From the moment he had started fishing upstream his rod was at such a slant and there was so much slack in his line that he must have been fishing with a wet fly and letting it sink. In fact, the slack was such that he must have been letting the fly sink five or six inches. So when I was fishing this hole as I did the last one—with a cork-body fly that rides on top of the water—I was fighting the last war. "No. 2" hook told me of course it was a hell of a big insect, but "yellow" could mean a lot of things. My big question by the time he got to me was, "Are they biting on some aquatic insect in a larval or nymph stage or are they biting on a drowned fly?"

He gave me a pat on the back and one of George's No. 2 Yellow Hackles with a feather wing. He said, "They are feeding on drowned yellow stone flies."

I asked him, "How did you think that out?"

He thought back on what had happened like a reporter. He started to answer, shook his head when he found he was wrong, and then started out again. "All there is to thinking," he said, "is seeing something noticeable which makes you see something you weren't noticing which makes you see something that isn't even visible."

I said to my brother, "Give me a cigarette and say what you mean."

"Well," he said, "the first thing I noticed about this hole was that my brother wasn't catching any. There's nothing more noticeable to a fisherman than that his partner isn't catching any.

"This made me see that I hadn't seen any stone flies flying around this hole."

Then he asked me, "What's more obvious on earth than sunshine and shadow, but until I really saw that there were no stone flies hatching here I didn't notice that the upper hole where they were hatching was mostly in sunshine and this hole was in shadow."

I was thirsty to start with, and the cigarette made my mouth drier so I flipped the cigarette into the water.

"Then I knew," he said, "if there were flies in this hole they had to come from the hole above that's in the sunlight where there's enough heat to make them hatch.

"After that, I should have seen them dead in the water. Since I couldn't see them dead in the water, I knew they had to be at least six or seven inches under the water where I couldn't see them. So that's where I fished."

He leaned against a big rock with his hands behind his head to make the rock soft "Wade out there and try George's No. 2," he said, pointing at the fly he had given me.

I didn't catch one right away, and I didn't expect to. My side of the river was the quiet water, the right side to be on in the hole above where the stone flies were hatching, but the drowned stone flies were washed down in the powerful water on the other side of this hole. After seven or eight casts, though, a small ring appeared on the surface. A small ring usually means that a small fish has risen to the surface, but it can also mean a big fish has rolled under water. If it is a big fish under water, he won't look so much like a fish as an arch of a rainbow that has appeared and disappeared.

Paul didn't even wait to see if I landed him. He waded out to talk to me. He went on talking as if I had time to listen to him and land a big fish. He said, "I'm going to wade back again and fish the rest of the hole." Sometimes I said, "Yes," and when the fish went out of the water, speech failed me, and when the fish made a long run I said at the end of it, "You'll have to say that over again."

Finally, we understood each other. He was going to wade the river again and fish the other side. We both should fish fairly fast, because Father probably was already waiting for us. Paul threw his cigarette in the water and was gone without seeing whether I landed the fish.

Not only was I on the wrong side of the river to fish with drowned stone flies, but Paul was a good enough roll caster to have already fished most of my side from his own. But I caught two more. They also started as little circles that looked like little fish feeding on the surface but were broken arches of big rainbows under water. After I caught these two, I quit. They made ten, and the last three were the finest fish I ever caught. They weren't the biggest or most spectacular fish I ever caught, but they were three fish I caught because my brother waded across the river to give me the fly that would catch them and because they were the last fish I ever caught fishing with him.

After cleaning my fish, I set these three apart with a layer of grass and wild mint.

Then I lifted the heavy basket, shook myself into the shoulder strap until it didn't cut any more, and thought, "I'm through for the day. I'll go down and sit on the bank by my father and talk." Then I added, "If he doesn't feel like talking, I'll just sit."

I could see the sun ahead. The coming burst of light made it look from the shadows that I and a river inside the earth were about to appear on earth. Although I could as yet see only the sunlight and not anything in it, I knew my father was sitting somewhere on the bank. I knew partly because he and I shared many of the same impulses, even to quitting at about the same time. I was sure without as yet being able to see into what was in front of me that he was sitting somewhere in the sunshine reading the New Testament in Greek. I knew this both from instinct and experience.

Old age had brought him moments of complete peace. Even when we went duck hunting and the roar of the early morning shooting was over, he would sit in the blind wrapped in an old army blanket with his Greek New Testament in one hand

and his shotgun in the other. When a stray duck happened by, he would drop the book and raise the gun, and, after the shooting was over, he would raise the book again, occasionally interrupting his reading to thank his dog for retrieving the duck.

The voices of the subterranean river in the shadows were different from the voices of the sunlit river ahead. In the shadows against the cliff the river was deep and engaged in profundities, circling back on itself now and then to say things over to be sure it had understood itself. But the river ahead came out into the sunny world like a chatterbox, doing its best to be friendly. It bowed to one shore and then to the other so nothing would feel neglected.

By now I could see inside the sunshine and had located my father. He was sitting high on the bank. He wore no hat. Inside the sunlight, his faded red hair was once again ablaze and again in glory. He was reading, although evidently only by sentences because he often looked away from the book. He did not close the book until some time after he saw me.

I scrambled up the bank and asked him, "How many did you get?" He said, "I got all I want." I said, "But how many did you get?" He said, "I got four or five." I asked, "Are they any good?" He said, "They are beautiful."

He was about the only man I ever knew who used the word "beautiful" as a natural form of speech, and I guess I picked up the habit from hanging around him when I was little.

"How many did you catch?" he asked. "I also caught all I want," I told him. He omitted asking me just how many that was, but he did ask me, "Are they any good?" "They are beautiful," I told him, and sat down beside him.

"What have you been reading?" I asked. "A book," he said. It was on the ground on the other side of him. So I would not have to bother to look over his knees to see it, he said, "A good book."

Then he told me, "In the part I was reading it says the Word was in the beginning, and that's right. I used to think water was first, but if you listen carefully you will hear that the words are underneath the water."

"That's because you are a preacher first and then a fisherman," I told him. "If you ask Paul, he will tell you that the words are formed out of water."

"No," my father said, "you are not listening carefully. The water runs over the words. Paul will tell you the same thing. Where is Paul anyway?"

I told him he had gone back to fish the first hole over again. "But he promised to be here soon," I assured him. "He'll be here when he catches his limit," he said. "He'll be here soon," I reassured him, partly because I could already see him in the subterranean shadows.

My father went back to reading and I tried to check what we had said by listening. Paul was fishing fast, picking up one here and there and wasting no time in walking them to shore. When he got directly across from us, he held up a finger on each hand and my father said, "He needs two more for his limit."

I looked to see where the book was left open and knew just enough Greek to recognize λόγος as the Word. I guessed from it and the argument that I was looking at the first verse of John. While I was looking, Father said, "He has one on."

It was hard to believe, because he was fishing in front of us on the other side of the hole that Father had just fished. Father slowly rose, found a good-sized rock and held it behind his back. Paul landed the fish, and waded out again for number twenty and his limit. Just as he was making the first cast, Father threw the rock. He was old enough so that he threw awkwardly and afterward had to rub his shoulder, but the rock landed in the river about where Paul's fly landed and at about the same time, so you can see where my brother learned to throw rocks into his partner's fishing water when he couldn't bear to see his partner catch any more fish.

Paul was startled for only a moment. Then he spotted Father on the bank rubbing his shoulder, and Paul laughed, shook his fist at him, backed to shore and went downstream until he was out of rock range. From there he waded into the water and began to cast again, but now he was far enough away so we couldn't see his line or loops. He was a man with a wand in a river, and whatever happened we had to guess from what the man and the wand and the river did.

As he waded out, his big right arm swung back and forth. Each circle of his arm inflated his chest. Each circle was faster and higher and longer until his arm became defiant and his chest breasted the sky. On shore we were sure, although we could see no line, that the air above him was singing with loops of line that never touched the water but got bigger and bigger each time they passed and sang. And we knew what was in his mind from the lengthening defiance of his arm. He was not going to let his fly touch any water close to shore where the small and middle-sized fish were. We knew from his arm and chest that all parts of him were saying, "No small one for the last one." Everything was going into one big cast for one last big fish.

From our angle high on the bank, my father and I could see where in the distance the wand was going to let the fly first touch water In the middle of the river was a rock iceberg, just its tip exposed above water and underneath it a rock house. It met all the residential requirements for big fish—powerful water carrying food to the front and back doors, and rest and shade behind them.

My father said, "There has to be a big one out there."

I said, "A little one couldn't live out there."

My father said, "The big one wouldn't let it."

My father could tell by the width of Paul's chest that he was going to let the next loop sail. It couldn't get any wider. "I wanted to fish out there," he said, "but I couldn't cast that far."

Paul's body pivoted as if he were going to drive a golf ball three hundred yards, and his arm went high into the great arc and the tip of his wand bent like a spring, and then everything sprang and sang.

Suddenly, there was an end of action. The man was immobile. There was no bend, no power in the wand. It pointed at ten o'clock and ten o'clock pointed at the rock. For a moment the man looked like a teacher with a pointer illustrating something about a rock to a rock. Only water moved. Somewhere above the top of the rock house a fly was swept in water so powerful only a big fish could be there to see it.

Then the universe stepped on its third rail. The wand jumped convulsively as it made contact with the magic current of the world. The wand tried to jump out of the man's right band. His left hand seemed to be frantically waving goodbye to a fish, but actually was trying to throw enough line into the rod to reduce the voltage and ease the shock of what had struck.

Everything seemed electrically charged but electrically unconnected. Electrical sparks appeared here and there on the river. A fish jumped so far downstream that it seemed outside the man's electrical field, but, when the fish had jumped, the man had leaned back on the rod and it was then that the fish had toppled back into the water not guided in its reentry by itself. The connections between the convulsions and the sparks became clearer by repetition. When the man leaned back on the wand and the fish reentered the water not altogether under its own power, the wand recharged with convulsions, the man's hand waved frantically at another departure, and much farther below a fish jumped again. Because of the connections, it became the same fish.

The fish made three such long runs before another act in the performance began. Although the act involved a big man and a big fish, it looked more like children playing. The man's left hand sneakily began recapturing line, and then, as if caught in the act, threw it all back into the rod as the fish got wise and made still another run.

"He'll get him," I assured my father.

"Beyond doubt," my father said. The line going out became shorter than what the left hand took in.

When Paul peered into the water behind him, we knew he was going to start working the fish to shore and didn't want to back into a hole or rock. We could tell he had worked the fish into shallow water because he held the rod higher and higher to keep the fish from bumping into anything on the bottom. Just when we thought the performance was over, the wand convulsed and the man thrashed through the water after some unseen power departing for the deep.

"The son of a bitch still has fight in him," I thought I said to myself, but unmistakably I said it out loud, and was embarrassed for having said it out loud in front of my father. He said nothing.

Two or three more times Paul worked him close to shore, only to have him swirl and return to the deep, but even at that distance my father and I could feel the ebbing of the underwater power. The rod went high in the air, and the man moved backwards swiftly but evenly, motions which when translated into events meant the fish had tried to rest for a moment on top of the water and the man had quickly raised the rod high and skidded him to shore before the fish thought of getting under water again. He skidded him across the rocks clear back to a sandbar before the shocked fish gasped and discovered he could not live in oxygen. In belated despair, he rose in the sand and consumed the rest of momentary life dancing the Dance of Death on his tail.

The man put the wand down, got on his hands and knees in the sand, and, like an animal, circled another animal and waited. Then the shoulder shot straight out, and my brother stood up, faced us, and, with uplifted arm proclaimed himself the victor. Something giant dangled from his list. Had Romans been watching they would have thought that what was dangling had a helmet on it.

"That's his limit," I said to my father.

"He is beautiful," my father said, although my brother had just finished catching his limit in the hole my father had already fished. This was the last fish we were ever to see Paul catch. My father and I talked about this moment several times later, and whatever our other feelings, we always felt it fitting that, when we saw him catch his last fish, we never saw the fish but only the artistry of the fisherman.

While my father was watching my brother, he reached over to pat me, but he missed, so he had to turn his eyes and look for my knee and try again. He must have thought that I felt neglected and that he should tell me he was proud of me also but for other reasons.

It was a little too deep and fast where Paul was trying to wade the river, and he knew it. He was crouched over the water and his arms were spread wide for balance. If you were a wader of big rivers you could have felt with him even at a distance the power of the water making his legs weak and wavy and ready to swim out from under him. He looked downstream to estimate how far it was to an easier place to wade.

My father said, "He won't take the trouble to walk downstream. He'll swim it." At the same time Paul thought the same thing, and put his cigarettes and matches in his hat.

My father and I sat on the bank and laughed at each other. It never occurred to either of us to hurry to the shore in case he needed help with a rod in his right hand and a basket loaded with fish on his left shoulder. In our family it was no great thing for a fisherman to swim a river with matches in his hair. We laughed at each other because we knew he was getting damn good and wet, and we lived in him, and were swept over the rocks with him and held his rod high in one of our hands.

As he moved to shore he caught himself on his feet and then was washed off them, and, when he stood again, more of him showed and he staggered to shore. He never stopped to shake himself. He came charging up the bank showering molecules of water and images of himself to show what was sticking out of his basket, and he dripped all over us, like a young duck dog that in its joy forgets to shake itself before getting close.

"Let's put them all out on the grass and take a picture of them," he said. So we emptied our baskets and arranged them by size and took turns photographing each other admiring them and ourselves. The photographs turned out to be like most amateur snapshots of fishing catches—the fish were white from overexposure and didn't look as big as they actually were and the fishermen looked self-conscious as if some guide had to catch the fish for them.

However, one closeup picture of him at the end of this day remains in my mind, as if fixed by some chemical bath. Usually, just after he finished fishing he had little to say unless he saw he could have fished better. Otherwise, he merely smiled. Now flies danced around his hatband. Large drops of water ran from under his hat on to his face and then into his lips when he smiled.

At the end of this day, then, I remember him both as a distant abstraction in artistry and as a closeup in water and laughter.

My father always felt shy when compelled to praise one of his family, and his family always felt shy when he praised them. My father said, "You are a fine fisherman."

My brother said, "I'm pretty good with a rod, but I need three more years before I can think like a fish."

Remembering that he had caught his limit by switching to George's No. 2 Yellow Hackle with a feather wing, I said without knowing how much I said, "You already know how to think like a dead stone fly."

We sat on the bank and the river went by. As always, it was making sounds to itself, and now it made sounds to us. It would be hard to find three men sitting side by side who knew better what a river was saying.

On Norman Maclean

JOHN MACLEAN

When I was a teenager, finally big enough to keep up with my father on the Big Blackfoot River, he and I spent several summers alone in Montana at our cabin on Seeley Lake. We once fished 31 days in a row, filling the cabin's freezer with milk cartons that had big fishtails sticking out the top. There was no catch-and-release ethic in those days, and our idea of conservation was to catch-and-give-away to the non-fisher folk in the town of Seeley Lake, who appreciated the protein.

My father, Norman Maclean, fished with too many great fly fishermen to think he was the best, though at some aspects of the game he was better than anyone he fished against.

Once he had a fish on, he almost never lost it. He was a careful and patient player of trout: The throb of the fish running through the light wand connected him to the natural world he worshipped even as his own father worshipped the natural and supernatural worlds, mingling the two. As you can tell from his book, *A River Runs Through It*, he fished waters deeper than the river in front of him.

After my father finally slid a fish onto the bank, rushing only at the end when the fish tired and its head could be held out of water, he would muse out loud for a while, especially if it were a big fish. He liked an audience, even if only one teenaged son, though it was clear he addressed a broader public even then.

Standing on the bank with the fish in his hand like a teacher holding out a text, he would recount the details of the battle. Inevitably he turned to what his brother and father would have thought if they had seen the show. His brother, Paul, was one helluva fisherman.

His brother told him, he often said in his muse, that there was nobody as good as Norman Maclean at landing a fish, though Paul criticized him for lacking his, Paul's, aggressiveness in going after fish in difficult spots. Paul became a presence with us on the river, a broad-shouldered figure with a slouch Stetson who would stop for a moment to admire my dad for his artfulness in playing a fish, but who was happy in the knowledge that his creel was heavier and fuller, and always would be.

The old man, my father's father, was a Scottish Presbyterian minister who believed that only God and big fish merited veneration. In his muse, my dad wondered what his father would have thought of him; no answer came back. The old man was an austere presence, watching from atop the high cutbanks as we—dad, Paul and I—cast for a prize.

I am sorry my dad cannot be here tonight to accept this prestigious prize. He has become an old man himself now, and at 86 years of age can no longer climb the high cutbanks. But after many years of musing, he landed the big one in the end: He got all the stories down the right way in one place. He has left his own presence in the remarkable book for which you honor him.

Now instead of being only with me when ghosts arise along the river, he will be among us all, as long as men fish and read books.

George Croonenberghs

JOHN MACLEAN

George Croonenberghs was a giant of a man, a Montana railroad engineer, and a master fly fisherman. He grew up in Missoula, Montana in the early 20th century when the town amounted to two railroad lines, a Forest Service headquarters, and a lot of lumberjacks. George chose the railroad. Missoula also had three great trout streams that joined near the town and then flowed on as the Clark Fork past a plain where Indians still set up teepees for the summer.

The national spotlight had not yet touched Missoula. George, though, was a friend from youth of Norman Maclean, another Missoula native, who immortalized him in his novella *A River Runs Through It*. George and the sturdy flies he tied run like a current through the "little blue book," as Norman often called his novella. The book forever linked George's name to the rhythms of a casting fly rod and the river of the book's title, the Big Blackfoot.

George and the Maclean boys, Norman and Paul, grew up together in Missoula and at Seeley Lake, whose waters flow into the Big Blackfoot and where in the early 1920s their families built cabins side by side. George, the youngest of three Croonenberghs boys, came from a family of giants. You have to cast your mind way back to recreate the impression that the Croonenberghs boys made in those days, when anyone even six feet tall was considered a wonder. George's brothers, Al and Boyd, were respectively six feet seven inches and six feet three inches tall.

George didn't start out at six feet four inches tall, of course. In fact, he was the little kid, the youngest of all the boys. Being the kid, George got left behind when the older guys went off to fish the Blackfoot. Fortune smiled, though, and Norman's father, the Reverend John Norman Maclean, befriended George and taught him to tie flies. The Reverend and the boy would sit on the screened porch of the Maclean cabin and work at a tying vise until it got too windy, and then move inside, where they had to negotiate space with Mrs. Maclean.

"I used to go to see the Reverend, but you had to be careful," George once said. "You had to apply to Mrs. Maclean to see if it was okay. Sometimes she'd say, 'No, the Reverend is taking his nap,' or she'd say, 'No, he's studying, you'll have to come back another time.'"

It's easy to picture the old man instructing the boy: the Reverend, a pipe in his teeth, was an exacting but companionable teacher; George, big for his age and physically adept, was an adoring pupil. But watching George's huge form hunched over a fly tying vise in later life, you had to wonder how someone with those enormous hands could perform tasks of such demanding delicacy, working on a hook no longer than a thumb nail. George was careful, even cautious, in all things, and a gifted craftsman to boot; but part of the answer to that question has to be that he began tying flies early enough to absorb the essential movements into his being. At the age of 87 he could still tie flies that brought joy to the hearts of fisherman and false hopes to brains of fish. Part of the answer, too, is George's essential gentleness; how a six foot four railroad engineer from Missoula managed to convince a World War II draft board that he was a conscientious objector is yet another mystery—the term "reserved occupation" explains part of that one.

The Reverend took George fishing when George was too young to use a rod, but not too young to carry the Reverend's fish basket. The Reverend Maclean was a stylish caster, wearing a glove, using lots of wrist, and beating time with his rod to a four count rhythm, a method that today is considered quaint. Back then it was the norm, however, and today has a classic look when properly performed.

Naturally enough, the other boys took advantage of George, getting him to tie flies for them while making sure he didn't pass them by in other ways. Once George was old enough to fish on his own, Norman's brother Paul, the central figure in *A River Runs Through It*, would hide in the bushes and throw rocks into his fishing holes, trying to fool George into thinking the splashes were fish, and not incidentally spoiling George's chances for a better catch than his. George, the soul of kindness, always said Paul was his best friend.

George soon became skilled enough to tie saleable flies, but making a name in a crowded field proved equally difficult. He solved the problem one day when he caught a magnificent basketful of fish on a secret stretch of river. In those days, Bob

Ward's sporting goods on Broadway would display a fine catch on ice in a glass case on the sidewalk. They put George's fish on exhibition with a note, craftily written by George: "Caught on the Croonenberghs Grasshopper on the Blackfoot River above Clearwater bridge." For weeks afterward the Croonenberghs Grasshopper, which is a big cork thing that works only once in a while, was a sellout, and fishermen lined up basket to basket at the Clearwater bridge, which even back then was fished out water. George wasn't lying: the fish were caught above the Clearwater bridge—miles and miles above it.

Becoming master of the Blackfoot was no small task. For George, it was never enough simply to catch a basketful of fish; he had to figure out why the fish were where they were in the first place. On a hot afternoon as the fish napped, George would wade into holes and chart the bottoms with his feet, and when the fish revived he had them marked. He always fished swiftly, never lingering over a hole or spending much time landing a fish. He fished the hot spots, hauled in the fish—or lost them—and moved on. If a fish broke off, George would instantly cast into the next likely spot: the river was too full of fish to waste time in elegies to lost trout. With his height and strength, George was about the only one in the early days who could cast clear across the Blackfoot without getting his feet wet, which few men can do even today, with graphite rods and weighted lines.

He trained himself to think like a fish in everything from reading water to tying flies. He would test his flies by dropping them into an aquarium suspended on a couple of chairs placed a few feet apart in his back yard. Then he crawled underneath to observe the flies from a trout's distorted perspective. He tied his flies specifically for the Big Blackfoot, and they were as sturdy as they fish they caught. But at least one of them, the Yellow Quill, has attracted fish from New Zealand to Alaska to the rivers of the East Coast.

When I was a boy, my father turned me over to George for instruction. George was happy enough to spend most of the day pulling me along the banks of streams, hammering home a lesson about making the first cast in a hole count the most—fish don't get big by giving second chances—and plucking Gray Quills out of spruce trees where I had snagged them. When I finally graduated to the Blackfoot, George and Norman would sit together on the bank and comment on my abilities, or lack of them. George was firm but kindly, until you let the big one get away. "You muffed him, John, you muffed him," he would say, turn his back, and walk on to the next hole, leaving you feeling as empty as your fish basket.

Toward evening, George often disappeared from view. Off on his own, he could move more swiftly over the slippery rocks, throw line clear across the river, and make perfect first casts into holes whose secret ways he knew by heart. Then toward dark he came back to us as my father and I stood small and wet and tired on the riverbank.

He emerged from the gloaming as a giant shadow, his hair heavy and dark, his face aglow with the joy of being master of the river. He had the grace of an ambling bear. He swung rather than scrambled across the rocks. He stood poised on a big rock until he had figured out a series of steps and then drooped from one to another, with dancing twists and turns. When he stood before us at last and held out his fish basket, a forked tail stuck out one side and the snout of a giant Rainbow out the other.

"If you want to know a secret, I'll tell you one," George once told me. "When I'm sitting beside a stream, trying to see what's driving the fish up, I try to get the flies between me and the sun. Not so much to see their color. That's important, but more important than color is radiance. How do they light up? Radiance is what makes the difference."

During his teaching career at the University of Chicago my father stayed in touch with those back home by writing a Christmas letter—not a single, mass produced letter, but a handwritten one to each person. George was no great correspondent, but he once sent in reply a box of flies with a note that said in entirety, "Substitute for words." My father returned to Seeley Lake each summer with my mother Jessie, my sister Jean, and me, and we mixed in like family with the Croonenberghs clan including George, his wife Jeanne, and daughter Sandy.

Eventually we kids grew up and went our separate ways, but the Croonenberghs-Maclean tie continued. After my father's retirement from teaching, and my mother's too early death, my father went to Seeley Lake earlier in the year and stayed later, sometimes into the snows of November. The Croonenberghs house in Missoula was a welcome rest stop on those trips. When he came out in late spring, he and Jeanne Croonenberghs would hike up Mount Jumbo, which overlooks Missoula, where Jeanne would reintroduce him to wildflowers whose names he had forgotten over the winter in Chicago. In the fall, the cold could become unbearable at the cabin, which isn't insulated and had only a fireplace and later a stove for heat. My dad slept on a thin mattress with newspapers stuffed underneath, in the hope of insulation, and only after years of suffering allowed himself an electric blanket. Then even he could no longer stand the cold, he would head back to Missoula and thaw out at the Croonenberghs'. He kept this up into his eighties.

After my father's death, Jeanne and George became the designated—designated by my father—moral custodians of his memory, when Robert Redford made a movie of *A River Runs Through It*. By then, George was ready to pass along the lore of a lifetime, and did so as fly-fishing consultant for the movie. He and Jeanne loved being part of the film company and spent much time on location, mostly in Paradise Valley near the Yellowstone River. The cast and crew, from Redford down to the prop girls, loved them right back.

As George grew older, he discovered that a rubber boat was an easier way to cover river miles than walking the banks. As he grew older still, it bothered him that he no longer was master of the river. But he took satisfaction in helping others learn to fish, in spinning tales of the old days, and in simply spending a day on the river—he fished other water, but the Big Blackfoot was always THE river.

The Croonenberghs eventually gave up their cabin at the lake, making the Maclean cabin the oldest regional structure continuously occupied by the same family. They were able to enjoy Seeley Lake, though, thanks to their daughter Sandy, who with her husband Heinz bought an all-season home there; being "at the lake" in a warm house *was* a source of joy to George and Jeanne to the end of their days. Now those who were young together and grew old together and are gone belong to Seeley Lake forever.

A Worm's-Eye View of Fishermen

BEATRICE COOK

I am a fishwife—or so it seems after being married over twenty years to a fishin' fool. I married one and raised two and claim to know more about fishermen than a salmon does, which is saying a lot, for fish are smarter than high school girls. I've shared a fisherman's life and therefore know the extremes of unreasonable exultation or blackest despair.

At the altar, I little realized I was pledged to love, honor, and obey three outboard motors, the ways of the river, the whims of the tide, and the wiles of the fish, as well as Bill, the man of my choice Nobody told me I was to rear two babies with fish scales in their curls or that I would learn to change a diaper with one hand while keeping a steady tension on a spool reel with the other. I had to learn—or else.

Before our honeymoon was over, I was faced with a decision: I must become either a fishing-widow or a fishwife. If my husband chased salmon all over the Pacific Northwest without me, I would turn into a sad-eyed, introspective stay-at-home and, in time, resemble Whistler's Mother, who I've always suspected was patiently waiting for some fisherman to come home. So with a prayer in my heart to my new patron saint, Izaak Walton, I chose to become a fishwife, my husband's companion on all his trips. This is a role not to be undertaken lightly, for it requires the touch of a lady, the heart of a lion, and the constitution of a jackass.

Many brides here in the state of Washington have to make up their minds just as I did, for this is the fisherman's Promised Land, overflowing with salmon, bass, trout—and more salmon. Seattle bankers and brokers read the tide charts in the morning paper before turning to the Wall Street listings, and they'll skip dinner when an incoming tide in the evening assures good fishing. It's half an hour from office to rowboat, as Seattle's business section is only a Paul Bunyan fly cast from Elliott Bay, our semi-landlocked harbor, which is teeming with salmon.

In books fishermen are referred to as dreamy, vacant-eyed philosophers who spend more time assembling tackle than they do in stream or boat. But anglers don't dream around here. They fish. The line on one reel or another is damp the year round, except perhaps in early December. At that time, just before the opening of the steelhead season, a kindly Providence planned to have most salmon leave shallow water and stay at sea. It's pure luck that the absence of fish corresponds to the Christmas season when fishermen-family acquaintanceship is renewed and Father is pleased to see how much the children have grown since he last noticed them. This is the time to give Mother the split bamboo rod he himself has wanted so long, and in this land of abundance, hip boots instead of Christmas stockings are hung by the fireplace on Christmas Eve. Chrome and shiny brass spoons make dandy tree ornaments, and a spool of Monel metal line has it all over glass balls.

Of course not everybody out here fishes. There are a few sane and sober merchants, manufacturers, and grocers needed to cater to the fishermen. But at some time during any party or gathering, you'll see a cluster of men hanging on each other's words and there is sure to be a glitter in their eyes. Hands grip an imaginary rod, which suddenly jerks upward to show how that thirty-pounder snapped the leader and made off with all gear. Everybody offers advice and tells how the same thing nearly happened to him—and would have, except for that little trick he knows. The tall tales have started.

All fishermen are liars; it's an occupational disease with them like housemaid's knee or editor's ulcers. Deacons and doctors alike enlarge upon "the one that got away," measuring off with ecclesiastical or surgical fingers the size of the mythical monster. At this point, the uninitiated fishing-widow yawns, but the fishwife nods understandingly. Save face, save the ego at any price—too often it's all a fisherman brings home. I've heard sterling characters swear to the most unlikely stories simply to cover their humiliation. For it is embarrassing to have a wee bass outthink you. I've seen a fifteen-pound salmon make a sucker out of a top-flight executive and a rainbow fool a psychology professor. Those big fish don't get that way by being dumb; a trout that doesn't think two jumps and several runs ahead of the average fisherman is mighty apt to get fried. With light tackle, fish get a fifty-fifty break and you don't need to pity them. The term "poor fish" may be based upon their uninteresting procreative habits, certainly not upon their intelligence.

Before you go with us up the Skagit River for steelhead or to the San Juan Islands for king salmon, I want to let you in on something. Did you know there's a roped-off, high priority section of Heaven exclusively reserved for the wives of fishermen? A celestial retreat uncluttered with leaky gas cans, rusty hooks, flooded motors, kinked wire lines, and mangy fishing hats? Here there will be no mention of incoming tides, three o'clock breakfasts, too much or too little feed. The baked ambrosia will not have to be cleaned and scaled first. In fact, the word "fish" never will be mentioned. This is a well-earned reward for those who, on earth, nursed husbands and sons through all the stages of fishing fever.

The symptoms? You know them well, no matter which creek or coast you fish. There are those moments of grandeur caused by a dozen twelve-inch trout, a mess of silvers or a tremendous king salmon, a string of sea bass or a couple of muskies. This is the time when Father is insufferable, little heeding the words of his wife—or Shakespeare, who reminds him that "Every braggart shall be found an ass." Nearly bursting at the seams, he phones all his cronies and they come on the run, flocking around the dinner table like flies at a Sunday school picnic. Father has his day; Mother, sagging arches; and the cat has the milt.

But days of deepest depression surely will follow when none of the hundred-thousand-dollars' worth of plugs he owns (a fishwife's loose estimate) has any appeal, when frozen herring are so soggy they fall off the hook, or the fish just aren't there anyway. This can drag on for weeks. Sympathy, liver pills, or even benzedrine slipped into coffee does no good. Nothing helps this blue funk but a few pounds of fishy protoplasm on the business-end of a line. However, this treatment must be continued to keep run-of-the-millstream anglers happy during the legal season.

Watch out! Even when lakes or streams are closed by law, a careless whiff of clam chowder will send the inveterate fisherman off again. Way off. Then he gets that mellow, faraway look in his eye which changes to a fanatic gleam as he dashes to the basement. Gear comes rattling out of closets, reels are unwound, and the place becomes an obstacle course with yards of line crisscrossed all over it for inspection. Rusty spark plugs are scraped, oiled—and left to drip on the ironing board. Children are threatened with double hernia as they tug and strain, trying to help Father pull rods apart. The mingled smell of varnish and reel oil acts as a come-on, and feverishly new hooks are tied to hallowed plugs, toothmarked veterans of many battles. These are crooned over while wife and children are forgotten. There's the pungent odor of rubber cement as boots are patched and the sharp ammoniac tingle of brass polish. And you can count on it: there will be a worse stench when Father accidentally—but perennially—drops that half-used jar of spoiled bait eggs or the bottle of home-preserved herring. Both smell higher than an Indian village at sundown. At a time like this, if I mention a social engagement, Father is sure to develop a touch of lumbago, or any other dreamed-up ailment serious enough to keep him home—in the basement. He might as well be fishing!

Just like measles, this sort of thing is expected all over the country in early spring, but it is indigenous to the Puget Sound region where there is no closed season for salmon. At any ungodly moment, winter or summer, a fishwife must be booted and spurred and ready to go. I'm grateful that no fish bites best in total darkness. Now I like to fish, but I'm a convert; I wasn't born that way. However, unlike the addict, I can take it or leave it, and I'd rather leave it at four in the morning when a January gale is strong enough to blow salmon scales backward.

The Pacific Northwest climate is mild and the seasons sort of run together, but an experienced fisherman can tell the time of year by noting what kind of fish tails the cat is chewing on. Winter king salmon are rich, oily, and the best of the year, but they have the nastiest dispositions—not quite so mean, however, as the spring steelhead well downstream and thus still in the full flower of fish-hood, April trout hate to leave home, and summer's silver and king salmon seldom give a novice an even break. Fall brings the mighty hooknose silvers and cutthroat trout. You can see there's never a dull moment for fishermen out here.

Now I didn't know any of this—or suspect lots more—about a quarter of a century ago, when I was a girl and lived in Chicago. The state of Washington was just a half-inch pink square on the map and, like the rest of the Midwest and East, I thought Seattle had virgin forests running between First and Second Avenues. I was headed for a life on the prairie until I met Bill. He changed my plans in a hurry. He breezed in from the West with such a head of steam that I melted in my tracks. He was attending a medical convention and, after one disdainful look at the windy, dirty city, he began telling me about a glorious mountain world where one could go hiking, skiing, or fishing and get home again in time to make the gravy for the pot roast. He told of shooting the rapids in an Indian canoe and about his innumerable camping trips in the San Juan Islands. He spoke of majestic Mount Olympus and Mount Constitution as though they were personal friends, and he promised me a trip through the ice caves of Mount Rainier.

Of course he wedged in stories of fishing trips, so I knew he was a fisherman, but I little guessed all that this implied. He said I'd love it, too, and at the moment I didn't give it a second thought. Bill was so nice and big and brown, I would have been glad to go fishing for the rest of my life on the River Styx. And so, innocently, I rose to the fly and snapped at the lure.

He returned to Seattle. Mother and I followed him west soon after. I little guessed how ill-prepared I was for the life of a fishwife. I had been hand-raised by a widowed mother, definitely a member of the old school whose graduates have a Victorian hangover. To her, fish have intestines, not guts; stomachs, not bellies; and only female dogs are bitches. She thinks paper napkins and horsey women abominations unto the Lord. Well-bred and well-read, she taught me all the niceties of living, which proved slightly inadequate for my role of fishwife.

On the train, I reviewed all I knew about fishing. Terrapin was a member of the social set and salmon always canned. Herring were shirtsleeve fish, caught already smoked or pickled. I thought cod must be easy to catch—any fish would welcome death whose liver smelled so vile. Trout came from streams and whitefish from traps.

I remembered certain gatherings where, with a dab of caviar-smeared toast in one hand and something iced in the other, I innocently had joined in the song that sympathizes with the poor virgin sturgeon which needs no urgin'. Roe was sautéed or canned. In those sheltered pre-fishing days, I would have shuddered to my shoes had I seen "caviar" taken on the hoof. Even today, as an old fishhand, it makes my stomach revolve to watch Indians grasp a ripe, squirming female and hold it a few inches above their upturned mouths. Then they bring the red, gooey eggs directly from producer to consumer, by using a stroking motion of thumb and forefinger along the underside of the belly. Much lip-smacking ensues while they grab another salmon and toss the old one to the squaws. Thanks. I'll take my caviar salted, pickled, spiced, dyed, and spread very thin.

The train rolled on through the wheat belt. Everything I owned was with me. My trousseau frothed with satin and lace numbers such as one sees advertised in Vogue: shimmering bed jackets and cobwebby lingerie. This was the age of pale pink ribbon and I had enough woven in and out of my undies to foul the rudder of a battleship. This was just standard equipment for a bride, I thought. Now I know that the Better Business Bureau should force advertisers to put footnotes on such pages, saying, "Above items of no possible use to a fisherman's bride." Wiser still, there should be a companion page featuring such lovelies as fishwives need: flannel pajamas, wool socks and shirts, blue jeans, hip boots, and long underwear (drop seat).

The prairies stretched out in such vast, endless miles that I had plenty of time for premarital jitters. Bill was a physician by profession, a sports fisherman by preference, and just how would this double-threat deal work out for me? But all my tears were forgotten, magically erased from my mind when the train began to curl and twist through the Cascade Mountains of Washington, We had passed through the Rockies at night so the Cascades were the first mountains I'd ever seen—honest-to-God ones, ripped right out of the National Geographic and practically at my fingertips! The sky was a blue dome over a world of jagged peaks crowned with snow. Misty falls dropped hundreds of feet to the timberline. I was enchanted with the queer little trees that had such sturdy, thick trunks compared with their height. Each mountain fir, with its short, downswept branches to shed the snow, was a miracle of symmetry. Some of them grew right out of crevices in the rock, and I wondered if their struggle for existence gave them that sober chrome green so unlike the frivolous yellow-green of the alders in the valley below, where soil was deep and life was easy.

Now the train was threading its way along a shelf cut from a mountain side, and we were in a great bowl of sky-touching mountains. Everything was sharp and clear: the river that sparkled a thousand feet below us, the snow fields ten miles away, and the track that glinted like silver wires behind us. How did the train ever get up here? There didn't seem to be a single break in the wall of mountains, and I pondered over the vision and skill of those first engineers who had plotted this pass.

The train nosed on, searching its way through a labyrinth of peaks, each curve opening up new wonders. Those thin white threads against the jumble of rocks must be water falls hurtling down through distance and the ages. Near us was a rushing stream, cloudy with glacial silt. It boiled and tumbled down a mile-square façade of naked rock, and its spray nourished rock gardens on either side.

As we worked slowly through the mountains, gradually the train lost altitude. Now we were in another world where everything was size forty-four. Only this time it was trees. I admitted to Mother that Bill's picture-postcards were not fakes—an automobile could drive through a tunneled-out fir. Where these giants thinned to just a scattering of hemlocks and spruce, there was a wild tangle of undergrowth. It was head high and I had a new respect for Lewis and Clark. Oregon is quite similar to Washington, and how could those intrepid explorers ever have cut through this to the coast?

Here a great fir had fallen, thundered to earth generations ago, and its flat, inter-laced root structure stood up as tall as a one-story house. The trees dripped with yards of sage-green beard moss which added a sort of melancholy beauty Everything—forests, mountains, vistas, trees, and sky—was scaled to majestic grandeur, and I wouldn't have been too amazed to see an armored dinosaur or mastodon peek around a cliff.

Regretfully, I said good-bye to my mountains. Then, with little time to get set for such a surprise, we were coasting beside Puget Sound, running just a few feet above high-tide level. Entranced, I gazed over the shimmering Sound toward the Olympic Mountains. They were taller and more splendid than the Cascades—and mine to love forever.

Mountains are good for the ego—they cut one down to size. Man's strivings seem so finite in a land of these proportions; the Empire State Building would look puny backed up against even a minor-league mountain. I didn't realize it then, but at that moment I was beginning to become a Westerner.

The sea gulls flew beside us all the way into Seattle. The cars hitched to a stop, each little bump jerking me back to reality. The depot platform was grimy, gray, and depressing, but suddenly it became a lovely place. Bill was there.

"Mother, Bill's terribly late. And for his own wedding!" . . .

A Defense of Fishermen

GROVER CLEVELAND

By way of introduction and explanation, it should be said that there is no intention at this time, to deal with those who fish for a livelihood. Those sturdy and hard-working people need no vindication or defense. Our concern is with those who fish because they have an occult and mysterious instinct which leads them to love it, because they court the healthful, invigorating exertion it invites, and because its indulgence brings them in close contact and communion with Nature's best and most elevating manifestations. This sort of fishing is pleasure and not work—sport and not money-grabbing. Therefore it is contemptuously regarded in certain quarters as no better than a waste of time. Generous fishermen cannot fail to look with pity upon the benighted persons who have no better conception than this of the uses and benefi- cent objects of rational diversion. In these sad and ominous days of mad fortune-chasing, every patriotic, thoughtful citizen, whether he fishes or not, should lament that we have not among our countrymen more fishermen. There can be no doubt that the promise of industrial peace, of contented labor and of healthful moderation in the pursuit of wealth, in this democratic country of ours, would be infinitely improved if a large share of the time which has been devoted to the concoction of trust and business combinations had been spent in fishing.

The narrow and ill-conditioned people who snarlingly count all fishermen as belonging to the lazy and good-for-nothing class, and who take satisfaction in describing an angler's outfit as a contrivance with a hook at one end and a fool at the other, have been so thoroughly discredited that no one could wish for their more irredeemable submersion. Statesmen, judges, clergymen, lawyers and doctors, as well as thousands of other outspoken members of the fishing fraternity, have so effectively given the lie to these revilers of an honest and conscientious brotherhood that they are glad to find refuge in ignominious silence.

Notwithstanding this, weak, piping voices are still occasionally heard accusing fishermen of certain shortcomings and faults. These are so unsubstantial and unimportant that, as against the high place in the world's esteem claimed by those who love to fish, they might well be regarded as nonessentials, or, in a phrase of the day, as mere matters of detail. But, although it may be true that these charges are unworthy of notice, it cannot be expected that fishermen, proud of the name, will be amiably willing to permit those making such accusations the satisfaction of remaining unchallenged.

At the outset, the fact should be recognized that the community of fishermen constitute a separate class or a sub-race among the inhabitants of the earth. It has sometimes been said that fishermen are born and not made. This is true to the extent that nothing can supply the lack of certain inherent, constitutional and inborn qualities or traits which are absolutely necessary to a fisherman's make-up. Of course there are many who call themselves fishermen and who insist upon their membership in the fraternity who have not in their veins a drop of legitimate fisherman blood. Their self-asserted relationship is nevertheless sometimes seized upon by malicious or ignorant critics as permitting the assumption that the weaknesses and sins of these pretenders are the weaknesses and sins of genuine fishermen; but in truth they are only interlopers who have learned a little fish language, who love to fish only "when they bite," who whine at bad luck, who betray incredulity when they hear a rousing fish story, and who do or leave undone many other things fatal to good and regular standing. They are like certain whites called "squaw-men," who hang about Indian reservations, and gain certain advantages in the tribes by marrying full-blooded Indian women. Surely no just person would for a moment suppose that genuine Indians could be treated fairly by measuring them according to a squaw-man standard. Neither can genuine fishermen be fairly treated by judging them according to the standards presented by squaw-fishermen.

In point of fact, full-blooded fishermen whose title is clear, and whose natural qualifications are undisputed, have ideas, habits of thought and mental tendencies so peculiarly and especially their own, and their beliefs and code of ethics are so exclusively fitted to their needs and surroundings, that an attempt on the part of strangers to speak or write concerning the character or conduct of their approved membership savors of impudent presumption. None but fishermen can properly deal with these delicate matters.

What sense is there in the charge of laziness sometimes made against true fishermen? Laziness has no place in the constitution of a man who starts at sunrise and tramps all day with only a sandwich to eat, floundering through bushes and briers and stumbling over rocks or wading streams in pursuit of elusive trout. Neither can a fisherman who, with rod in hand, sits in a boat or on a bank all day be called lazy—provided he attends to his fishing and is physically and mentally alert in his occupation. This charge may perhaps be truthfully made against squaw-fishermen who become easily discouraged, who "tire and faint" early, and lie down under the shade to sleep, or go in swimming, or who gaze about or read a book while their hooks rest baitless on the bottom; but how false and unfair it is to accuse regular, full-blooded fishermen of laziness, based on such performances as these! And yet this is absurdly done by those who cannot tell a reel from a compass, and who by way of familiarizing themselves with their topic leave their beds at eight o'clock in the morning, ride to an office at ten, sit at a desk until three or perhaps five, with an hour's interval for a hearty luncheon, and go home in the proud belief that they have done an active, hard day's work. Fishermen find no fault with what they do in their own affairs, nor with their conception of work; but they do insist that such people have no right to impute laziness to those who fish.

It is sometimes said that there is such close relationship between mendacity and fishing, that in matters connected with their craft all fishermen are untruthful. It must, of course, be admitted that large stories of fishing adventure are sometimes told by fishermen—and why should this not be so? Beyond all question there is no sphere of human activity so full of strange and wonderful incidents as theirs. Fish are constantly doing the most mysterious and startling things; and no one has yet been wise enough to explain their ways or account for their conduct. The best fishermen do not attempt it; they move and strive in the atmosphere of mystery and uncertainty, constantly aiming to reach results without a clue, and through the cultivation of faculties non-existent or inoperative in the common mind. In these circumstances fishermen necessarily see and do wonderful things. If those not members of the brotherhood are unable to assimilate the recital of these wonders, it is because their believing apparatus has not been properly regulated and stimulated. Such disability falls very far short of justifying doubt as to the truth of the narration. The things narrated have been seen and experienced with a fisherman's eyes and perceptions. This is perfectly understood by listening fishermen; and they, to their enjoyment and edification, are permitted to believe what they hear.

This faculty is one of the safest signs of full-blooded right to membership. If incredulity is intimated by a professed member no injustice will be done if he is at once put under suspicion as a squaw-fisherman. As to non-members who accuse true fishermen of falsehood, it is perfectly clear that they are utterly unfitted to deal with the subject. Upon this theory any story of personal experience told by a fisherman is to the fishing apprehension indubitably true; and, since disbelief in other quarters is owing to the lack of this apprehension, the folly of accusing fishermen of habitual untruthfulness is quite apparent.

The position thus taken by the brotherhood requires that they stand solidly together in all circumstances. Tarpon fishing has added greatly to our responsibilities. Even larger fish than these may, with the extension of American possessions, fall within the treatment of American fishermen. As in all past emergencies, we shall be found sufficient in such future exigencies. All will go well if, without a pretense of benevolent assimilation, we still fish as is our wont, and continue our belief in all our brethren declare they have done or can do. A few thousand years ago the question was impressively asked, "Can'st thou draw out leviathan with a hook?" We must not falter if, upon its repetition in the future, a brother replies: "Yes, with a ten-ounce rod"; nor even if another declares he has already landed one of these monsters. If American institutions are found adequate to the new tasks which Destiny has put upon them in the extension of our lands, the American Chapter of the world's fishermen must not fail to subdue by their time-honored methods and practices, and by continued truthfulness in narration of adventure, any new difficulties presented by the extension of our waters.

Before leaving this branch of our subject, especial reference should be made to one item more conspicuous, perhaps, than any other, among those comprised in the general charge of fishermen's mendacity. It is constantly said that they greatly exaggerate the size of the fish that are lost. This accusation, though most frequently and flippantly made, is in point of fact based upon the most absurd arrogance and a love of slanderous assertion that passes understanding. These are harsh words; but they are abundantly justified.

In the first place, all the presumptions are with the fisherman's contention. It is perfectly plain that large fish are more apt to escape than small ones. Their weight and activity, combined with the increased trickiness and resourcefulness of age and experience, of course, greatly increase their ability to tear out the hook, and enhance the danger that their antics will expose a fatal weakness in hook, leader, line or rod. Another presumption which must be regretfully mentioned arises from the fact that in many cases it is the encounter with a large fish which causes such excitement, and such distraction or perversion of judgment, as leads the fisherman to do the wrong thing or fail to do the right thing at the critical instant—thus actually and effectively contributing to an escape which could not and would not have occurred except in favor of a large fish.

Beyond these presumptions we have the deliberate and simple story of the fisherman himself, giving with the utmost sincerity all the details of his misfortune, and indicating the length of the fish he has lost, or giving in pounds his exact weight. Now why should this statement be discredited? It is made by one who struggled with the escaped fish. Perhaps he saw it. This, however, is not important, for he certainly felt it on his rod, and he knows precisely how his rod behaves in the emergency of every conceivable strain.

All true fishermen who listen to his plain, unvarnished tale accept with absolute faith the declared length and weight of the fish that was almost caught; and with every presumption, besides positive statement, against them, carping outsiders who cannot fish, and who love to accuse fishermen of lying, are exposed in an attempt to originate or perpetuate an envious and malicious libel.

The case of our fraternity on this point of absolute and exact truthfulness is capable of such irrefragable demonstration that anything in the way of confession and avoidance ought to be considered inadmissible. And yet simply for the sake of argument, or by way of curious speculation, it may be interesting to intimate how a variation of a few inches in the exact length or a few ounces in the exact weight of a lost fish, as given by the loser, may be accounted for, without attributing to him intentional falsehood. The theory has been recently started that a trained hunting dog points a bird in the field solely because the bird's scent creates a hypnotic influence on the dog which impels him by a sort of suggestion to direct his nose toward the spot from which such scent emanates. If there is anything worth considering in this theory why may not a struggling fish at the end of a line exert such a hypnotic influence on the intensely excited and receptive nature at the other extremity of the fishing outfit as to suggest an arbitrary and independent statement of the dimensions of the hypnotizer?

With the accusations already mentioned, it would certainly seem that the enmity of those who revile fishermen and their ways should be satisfied. They have not been content, however, in the demonstration of their evil-mindedness without adding to their indictment against the brotherhood the charge of profanity. Of course, they have not the hardihood to allege that our profanity is of that habitual and low sort which characterizes the coarse and ill-bred, who offend all decent people by constantly interlarding their speech with fearful and irrelevant oaths. They, nevertheless, find sufficient excuse for their accusation in the sudden ejaculations, outwardly resembling profanity, which are occasionally wrung from fishermen in trying crises and in moments of soul-straining unkindness of Fate.

Now this question of profanity is largely one of intention and deliberation. The man who, intending what he says, coolly indulges in imprecation, is guilty of an offense that admits of no excuse or extenuation; but a fisherman can hardly be called profane who, when overtaken without warning by disaster, and abruptly hurled from the exhilarating heights of delightful anticipation to the depths of dire disappointment, impulsively gives vent to his pent-up emotion by the use of a word which, though found in the list of oaths, is spoken without intentional imprecation and because nothing else seems to suit the occasion. It is by no means to be admitted that fishing tends even to this semblance of profanity. On the contrary, it imposes a self-restraint and patient forbearance upon its advanced devotees which tend to prevent sudden outbursts of feeling.

It must in frankness be admitted, however, by fishermen of every degree, that when the largest trout of the day winds the leader about a snag and escapes after a long struggle, or when a large salmon or bass, apparently fatigued to the point of non-resistance, suddenly, by an unexpected and vicious leap, frees himself from the hook, the fisherman's code of morals will not condemn beyond forgiveness the holder of the straightened rod if he impulsively, but with all the gentility at his command, exclaims: "Damn that fish!" It is probably better not to speak at all; but if strong words are to be used perhaps these will serve as well as any that can do justice to the occasion.

Uncle Toby, overcome with tender sympathy, swore with an unctuous, rotund oath, that his sick friend should not die; and we are told that "the accusing spirit which flew up to Heaven's chancery with the oath blushed as he gave it in; and the recording angel as he wrote it down dropped a tear upon the word and blotted it out forever."

The defense of the fishing fraternity which has been here attempted is by no means as completely stated as it should be. Nor should the world be allowed to overlook the admirable affirmative qualities which exist among genuine members of the brotherhood, and the useful traits which an indulgence in the gentle art cultivates and fosters. A recital of these, with a description of the personal peculiarities found in the ranks of fishermen and the influence of these peculiarities on success or failure, are necessary to a thorough vindication of those who worthily illustrate the virtues of our clan.

A Single Step

GEORGE REIGER

Once, while poking along the recently flood-ravaged banks of Rock Creek in the District of Columbia, I came across two men and a boy fishing by the dam below Oakhill Cemetery. When I asked the age-old question, "How's fishing?" their replies were sufficiently evasive to encourage me to linger.

Sure enough, first the boy, then one of the men, got bites. They flicked their rod tips as nonchalantly as possible, but the resulting liveliness of their lines made further subterfuge futile. Each landed a channel catfish of about a pound and a half. When I asked whether they'd caught others, pride overcame discretion, and each angler hoisted a stringer of channel cats, bullheads, and sunfishes.

Meanwhile, not many yards away, car-imprisoned commuters crawled by, unaware of our presence, eyes fixed on the bumpers and tail-lights of the vehicles ahead of them. If and when Washington commuters go fishing, most drive to the trout streams of western Maryland and Pennsylvania; or down to the salty waters bracketing the Delmarva peninsula. Although many of their children become fishermen in their own right, who's to say they're more worthy anglers than those who learn their craft by the less than pristine waters of Rock Creek?

Non-anglers assume that fishing is entirely about catching fish. Catching is important, of course. It's all that matters to beginners, and if veteran anglers didn't at least occasionally find their quarry in a feeding mood, they'd take up some related pastime, like the study of plasma physics. But veterans also know that as we grow older, fishing becomes as much about ritual and memory as putting new notches on the reel.

Many non-anglers, especially those who've come of age in the past quarter-century, think fishing is a spectator sport dominated by tournaments and dependant on high-tech equipment. Yet even competition fishermen know that angling means participation, not voyeurism, and that the most successful anglers have knowledge and special skills superceding gadgetry. Ultimately, each and every fishing trip begins with the individual making a single step from the shore into the water, or from the dock onto a boat, where he or she hopes and expects the anxieties of ordinary life to seep away on the current and tides, allowing him or her to become someone better.

Herbert Hoover observed that all men are equal before fish, and surely the boy with a menial summer job, casting into the dawn, believes that something wonderful is about to happen; the woman whose reality has not quite matched the bright expectations of college is renewed by the sight of birds far out over the waves; and for the troubled man, each moment of fishing dilutes his old sins and fresh suffering.

Philip Wylie once wrote that all anglers are philosophers, not because of our alleged patience—the usual explanation—but because we understand, even as children, that angling is lifelong recreation. Whitewater kayaking and mountaineering are sports for youth alone. Time may alter the kind or quantity of angling we do, but it never ends our opportunity. The old man casting over a darkening pool and the white-haired lady watching her sand-spiked rod nod to the surf are only variations on the little boy who once chased suckers in the shallows or the little girl who collected shells along the beach. The ghosts of who we were commune over increasing seasons with whom we are today. We're humbled by this, and some are even made wiser by the eternal nature of the fact that angling—like every epic journey—begins with but a single step.

The Even-Tempered Angler (selection)

LOUIS RUBIN

The real test of which kind of fishing one prefers above all other forms is probably that of the association of ideas. When you hear the word "fishing," what image comes into your mind? Doubtless for the trout or salmon fisherman the picture that "fishing" conveys involves standing, feet braced against the current, in a stream of cold rushing water, up to one's waist and with the water swirling outside one's waders, while expertly dropping a dry fly across fifty feet of water so that it settles without a ripple upon the surface where a trout has been feeding.

For the black-bass fisherman, the image that is summoned by the word "fishing" must be the exploding force of a huge largemouth—a lunker or hawg, the B.A.S.S. Masters call it— as it breaks the surface of the lake to grab a plug tossed skillfully to within a foot of the bank, and the tautness of the monofilament as the rod is lifted to halt it.

The offshore fisherman, moving along the edge of the Gulf Stream in a powerful boat and taking the light swells easily, must surely dream of the leap, high above the spray, of the billfish while the fisherman strains to hold the bending rod in its socket. For the inshore fisherman trolling for kings and big blues, there is the moment when the rod bends in a wide bow, the click mechanism on the reel rasps and the drag hisses as the line is stripped from the reel, followed by the rush to pick up the rod and to feel, transmitted along its length, the plunging weight of a big fish.

For myself, however much I enjoy those kinds of fishing, and however much I crave going after flounder with live shrimp in the tidal creeks of the coastal salt marsh that I have watched and loved watching since my boyhood, the word "fishing," uttered abruptly and without particular context, means something else.

It is the month of August, in Gloucester County, Virginia. I am anchored in a motorboat in twenty feet of water, inshore from the red nun buoy opposite the Naval Weapons Station just upstream from Yorktown on the York River. An hour earlier the buoy was slanted upstream from the force of the incoming tide; now it floats upright. I have caught a half-dozen good gray trout, and I am waiting for another, but there has been a hiatus in the fishing. I know that other fish will come along presently and am content to wait.

Everything is still. The gulls are at rest. They are perched on the stakes of an old fish trap in toward shore. The grass of the tidal marsh, the foliage of the trees on the shoreline beyond them, a quarter mile away, are in full green. Yet there seems in that greenness shading that is too fulfilled for the green growth of the spring and earlier summer, a ripening beyond the point of greatest strength and beginning to shade into decline.

There is the sound of a boat, a gasoline engine over across the way. A white boat, low and slender, is easing downstream—a crab boat heading home after working upriver. So far away on the water is it that it seems to have no wake, no waves, sliding across the water as if in a tableau. The sky overhead is remote and endless, a blue canopy with indifferent clouds.

A breeze picks up, lightly patterns the surface of the river into lines and shapes. The slight waves come slapping against the sides of the boat, making a low, hollow tapping sound. A gull lifts itself from its fellows and swings off in a wide arc; its white wings propel it across the river toward the shore. Its sharp cry interrupts the silence as it trails off, disappears. There is crying among the remaining gulls, but not one rises to follow.

The calling subsides, the gulls sit quietly and wait. The breeze falls off. The surface of the water is still. The crab boat is so far away that its engine makes no sound at all. All things are at rest.

It cannot last. It must not. The tide must change, the wind pick up, to blow away the stillness, the gulls rise to their scavenging, the world get on with its affairs. Soon we will be leaving for home, and the green of the marsh and trees will turn yellow as the summer sun recedes and autumn comes.

Not once does the season stop, for all that it seems now to suspend itself. It was passing by all the time, and what seems rest is only the momentary consciousness of its movement on its regular, methodical course. As surely as the gull rises into the air and swerves away, the tide is flowing and the earth tilting away from the sun.

Yet they seem to have stopped this day, as if the summer, and the season, and the sun were like a steel ball rolling up an incline, propelled by its own momentum, further and further—until the force of inertia moves to equalize the momentum, and asserts itself, and prevails.

For a moment, before the downward plummet, at the very top of the ultimate forward ascent, the one force is countered by the other, and summer seems, here on the river, to have stopped in midflight.

It is then, just then, that another fish bites.

What's in a Name?

HOWARD FRANK MOSHER

"Name children some names and see what you do."—"Maple," Robert Frost

It was the summer of 1969, and I had just made a monumentally foolish mistake. Imagining that there were shortcuts to learning how to write and publish fiction, I accepted a creative writing fellowship at the University of California at Irvine and lit out with my wife, from our home in Vermont, for the Pacific coast. Along the way, we fished. We fished in the Upper Peninsula of Hemingway's Michigan, in Norman Maclean's Montana, up in the mountains of Alberta. We fished in Washington and Oregon, and then we hit southern California, where there were no trout, just automobiles and palm trees.

One afternoon a week or so after we'd arrived, I stopped at the intersection of Hollywood and Vine, where a man in a gorilla suit was busily directing traffic. A guy in a phone company truck pulled up beside me. He must have noticed my green license plate because he rolled down his window and called out, in a deadly serious voice, "I'm from Vermont, too. Go home while you still can."

So, missing the mountains, the farms and the woods I'd begun to write about, and, not least of all, the fishing, that's exactly what we did. Three days later we were back in northern

Vermont. I had no writing degree, no job, no prospects. There were two small consolations. We'd gotten home just in time for the fall brown trout run, and the brook trout fishing in the beaver bogs was just starting to pick up again.

"What have you done for work before?" Jake Blodgett asked me on the morning after my somewhat less than triumphal return to New England.

Standing on the falling-in door stoop of the tall, white-haired logger and former whiskey runner, feeling his pale-blue stare cut through me like a chainsaw, I admitted that all I'd ever done was to teach school, but hearing that he needed a helper, I was hoping to get some "real-life" experience.

Jake thought about this proposition. Then he said, "Well, schoolteacher. How much would you want for pay?"

Now it was my turn to think. Finally, I said that I'd never worked in the woods before, and suggested that Jake try me out for a few days, then pay me what I was worth to him.

"That wouldn't be much," he said, and it wasn't. But for the rest of that fall and on into the winter, I worked with Jake, up in the mountains near the Canadian border, skidding the logs he cut out to a clearing with his ancient lumbering horse.

After work and on Sundays, we fished the brooks and rivers of the border country. When the lakes froze, we went ice fishing. Over lunch in the woods, and on our fishing expeditions, Jake told me stories of his wild, Prohibition-era days, running Canadian booze, making moonshine, outwitting game wardens. He was the best fisherman I'd ever known, with a sixth sense of where trout lay and how to entice them to strike, and a sixth sense, too, for telling a good story. During the course of that fall and winter, the Vermont woods became my graduate school, Jake Blodgett my literary mentor.

One day in a snowstorm he asked me if I'd ever write about his life. I told him yes. Jake nodded. "Well, schoolteacher," he said, "then you better get on with it."

I love Labrador. I love its big, wild lakes, its unexplored whitewater rivers, its northern lights flaring up pink and silver and blue across the entire night sky. Most of all, I love its brook trout. In 1992, my 20-year-old son, Jake, and I stood by a nameless Labrador river we'd walked over a nameless mountain to reach. I was upstream from Jake a hundred yards or so, and we were both catching brookies from three to five pounds, as fast as we could land them.

"What have you got on there?" I called out to Jake over the rapids. "A whale?"

"No, a two-pound brook trout," he called back.

"That's no brook trout. That fish you're fighting is huge."

"Oh, that," Jake said. "That's the twenty-pound lake trout that has my two-pound brook trout in its mouth and won't let go."

Thinking how much my son's logger-whiskeyrunner-fisherman namesake would have enjoyed being here to see this, I began to laugh. Jake, in the meantime, handed me his fly rod, walked into the river, wrapped his arms about that monstrous laker and picked it up out of the rushing water, with the brook trout still in its jaws.

At that moment, I had a father's, and a fisherman's, epiphany. I realized, standing in the last wilderness of eastern North America, one hundred miles from the nearest settlement, that like his namesake, my son was attuned and connected to big woods and wild rivers, and the wild animals and fish that lived in them, in a way I could only marvel at. That, too, would have delighted my old bootlegger friend, and so would Jake's reply when I asked him what he was going to do with his unusual two-for-one catch.

"Put them back where they belong and fish some more," Jake said, and that, of course, is just what we proceeded to do.

The Solitary and Friendly Sport

R. PALMER BAKER, JR.

In this story three fishermen stop their car at a crossroad and ask a woodsman the way to Beaver Creek.

"What you fellers lookin' for?"

They say they are going fishing. Trout fishing.

In due course the backwoodsman tells them the way. "You fellers got any whiskey with you?"

They say no.

"How about a little 'baccy?" They say they don't smoke.

"Well, now," says the backwoodsman, "I thought you fellers said you was goin' fishin'.'

There is something to this story. Trout fishing is the most solitary yet the most companionable of sports. It can be very elegant and very disreputable. One of my companions was equally devoted to dry fly fishing and bridge. His idea of a successful trip was to play cards most of the night, fish in the morning, sleep away the afternoon, and then fish the evening rise. When he died, at a sadly early age, his friends knew that this was his idea of heaven. He used to admire and not just laugh at Webster's wonderful cartoon of the four salmon fishermen playing bridge in a hut near the river. Outside, another member of the party staggers under the weight of an enormous fish and calls for attention. "George, you're dummy," says one of the players, "you go look at the damn fish."

On a Thursday before Decoration Day, the bridge master and I left the city with two other friends to fish the New York waters of the Battenkill. One member of our party did not have a license, so we looked for file office of the town clerk at the county seat. Misdirected, we entered a lawyer's office. After learning of our mistake and apologizing to his secretary, we said—three of the party being lawyers—that we should like to meet him. This was not possible; she told us. This was the month of May, and every Thursday afternoon he went fishing.

The afternoon was a fine one, and we got out on the stream as quickly as we could, knowing that a long evening of bridge lay ahead of us. Cahills were coming off the water in numbers, and the trout were taking them with regularity. Our bridge master was in his element. He caught and released one fish after another. Downstream, a worm fisherman could contain himself no longer He came up along the bank, just as another trout was landed.

"Hey, mister! What bait you usin'? The bridge master drew himself up.

"My dear fellow," he said, "this is a dry fly." Then retribution followed. Turning toward shore, he stepped into a hole. Quietly the bridge master went under, holding his Leonard aloft like Excalibur. His fishing hat gently floated downstream, and a moment later, walruslike, he emerged.

This companionable kind of fishing is one of the happiest aspects of the sport. Yet it is also rewarding now and then to fish by yourself. Solitude, particularly for the city man, is at the heart of fishing for trout.

The best times for this are days stolen from work, the beginnings of vacations, the end of some sustained endeavor. I remember one day at the close of college, when I was released—how temporarily!—from intellectual bondage. It was on the Vermont–New York line, and I did not have a care in the world. Early in the morning a big trout kept rising at the center of the biggest pool in the river. I almost drowned trying to reach him with the fly, but he was much too far out for me. At that time I eschewed the wearing of waders, and when I came out of the water I was numb with cold; but neither this nor the failure to catch the trout diminished the pleasure of the morning.

In the afternoon I fished a meadow tributary. The best pools were open and without cover, so it was necessary to cast while lying almost prone. If the fly landed properly, the trout jumped when they took it.

After the war I returned to the river again, staying with my wife's sister, who was opening her country house for the summer. At six o'clock the June morning was glorious. Since I did not have my license, I had to wait until after breakfast before fishing, so I dressed and walked through the village and across the fields to look at the stream before the household was awake.

The nearest pool was bordered on one side by hayfields and on the other by the slope of a wooded hill. Seated on a tree root at the head of the pool, comfortably smoking his pipe, was a local fisherman of great repute. He had been fishing with minnows and was through for the day. Together, the two trout in his basket weighed at least five pounds. I admired them with envy and delight.

The rest of the day was like standing at the gates of paradise. In the morning we bought the license, did the shopping, and got the house ready for the summer. At noon neighbors insisted on having us for lunch. In the afternoon we had to follow a golf tournament. But then my hostess took pity.

After the tournament, we ate an early supper and drove quickly back to the house. While we were passing a graveyard I was told to hold my breath and make a wish. "Now," she said, as I drew my breath, "you will catch your trout."

There were two good hours of daylight ahead of me. Off I went, through the village and across the fields, with my rod.

At dusk the swallows began to dive and circle, feeding on the mayflies that were coming off the water. The little trout started splashing at the flies on the surface.

Then two bigger fish began to rise steadily in a little bay at the head of the pool. The current swirled there against a high grassy bank where two Guernsey cows were feeding, now and then lifting their heads to look with curiosity at the fisherman below them. Each time a mayfly drifted along this bank there was a dimple on the surface and the insect disappeared.

Kneeling on a gravel bar, I was able to get very close to this location and, for once, to float my fly, a Cahill, without drag to one of the rising trout. He took it with a dimple, followed the pressure of the line, and allowed himself to be landed in the pool below the gravel bar. He was a brook trout, not too common in this part of the river, June-fat and a foot long.

The second trout along the bank took the fly in the same way. It was a brown trout, almost identical in size, and so I had a good brace. Having been defeated by this river more than once, I placed the fish in my bag and walked back to the house with satisfaction.

My hostess and her husband were standing in the kitchen. When I held the two fish out to her, one in each hand, she said, "My goodness, they're still alive; they're quivering."

"No," I said. "That's me." And I thanked her for the graveyard wish and what had turned out to be a perfect day.

When you are fishing alone, you had better bring your fish home if you want your friends and family to believe you. On the other hand, the return of a large trout to the stream without a witness can result in a fine sense of moral superiority.

The fact is that the fly-fisherman is likely to raise his biggest and most difficult trout when he is on the stream alone, concentrating and undisturbed. One spring morning, when I looked from the office window, the sun was sparkling on the waters of the North River, the city plane trees were green, and the pigeons were wheeling on a fresh west wind. The thought of that day wasted in the city was intolerable. I closed my desk and left.

Two hours later I was on one of the streams in the Croton watershed. Although heavily fished at the beginning of the season, some of these are good brown trout waters. They have a cool and constant flow from the reservoir outlets and their banks are shaded and protected from siltation. Most of the fish are stocked, but now and then the fly-fisherman takes a wild trout, and once in a while a big one comes up from the reservoir below.

This was one of those occasions—an escape from the city—when solitude is a joy. I walked upstream for fifteen minutes before making the first cast. Violets were blooming along the edge of the woods. The red-winged blackbirds called to each other as they nested at the edges of the swamp. Presently I was walking in a grove of hemlocks, approaching the first pool.

The first attempt was made with a dun variant, a smoky-gray fly with a long hackle. Immediately two little trout splashed and jumped over it. At about the same time, a hatch of small red-gray flies was seen coming off the water. When the fly was changed to a Red Quill, one of the little trout took it at once. He was returned to his family and I proceeded upstream.

None of the rising fish was of any size, but one came up in virtually every pool. When I came to one of the larger pools I fished the lower end carefully, but there was no response. This was odd. There should have been several small trout at the tail of the pool. Then I looked upstream, to the very head of the pool, where the current flowed between two big rocks. There was a tiny splash in the current.

On another occasion I had seen a splash like this and later had been able to iden-tify it. The splash was caused not by a little fish but by the flick of a big trout's tail as it turned in the current. Suddenly I was convinced that this was a similar occasion, particularly since the absence of small fish at the tail indicated that a big one might have driven them off.

The Red Quill was dried, oiled, and dipped in the stream to wash off the excess dressing. I got it into the air and began lengthening the cast. Back and forth went the line, along the side of the pool so as not to throw its shadow over the trout. In a moment all was in readiness for the final delivery when the back cast hung solidly up in a hemlock branch.

Good-bye, Red Quill; good-bye, leader. At this point I was not going to move from my position and disturb the pool. After drawing the line tight and cursing a little, I broke off the fly and the first tippet of the leader With shaking hands I finally succeeded in tying on a new tippet and another Red Quill.

This time more care was used with the back cast. The fly landed in the current between the rocks, floated two inches, and simply disappeared.

If I had not already been sure, I would have known this was a big fish when I tightened on the line. For a moment he did not move. Then he jumped. He jumped six times. He was certainly fifteen inches long—a monster for the stream. He began to run up and down the pool, powerfully, frantically. Because I was now standing at the tail, he turned each time he saw me. He wanted badly to go downstream toward the reservoir from which he no doubt had recently come.

Now he raced upstream, into the current between the rocks where he had taken the fly, and in an instant he was fighting in the pool above me. Then I made the mistake of stepping out on the bank to follow I am convinced that he saw me. He came back downstream with a leap, raced through the pool, and was into the fast water below me. When I stripped in line and snubbed him he jumped one more time and was gone

There is a catharsis in this kind of experience. The next day I was again prepared for work. My angling friends who know the stream nod their heads and say they believe me when I tell the story. I think some do. And some may not.

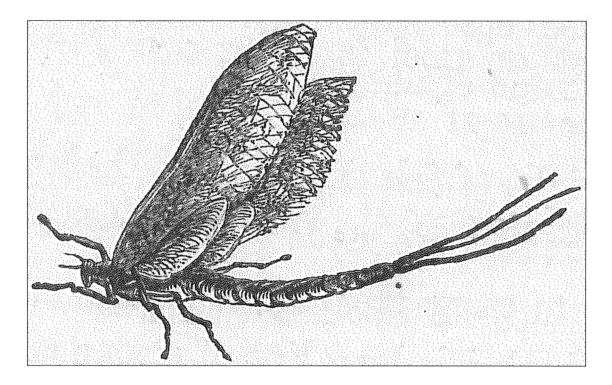

Midstream Crisis

LAMAR UNDERWOOD

As the year began, I decided to embrace the advice of my friend Sparse Grey Hackle, who told me: "Let the wolf out!" He was dead right. It was the only way to go. No more Mister Nice Guy!

My New Year's resolution was a notice served on all creatures, great and small, that in the open seasons ahead I was going to fill my hand. I was fed up with two-trout days, three-bass weekends and no-deer vacations. I'd had it with calling to bird dogs that wouldn't stand still and turkeys that would (two ridges away!). I didn't want to see another pheasant getting up 200 yards away down a corn row or another bay full of ducks and geese rafted up and preening their feathers under skies that had flown in from Palm Springs.

Government wags told me that in the previous season some 2.5 million hunters had shot 12 million ducks. The calculator that lives beside my checkbook told me that works out to five or six ducks per hunter. I didn't get any five ducks! Who the hell shot my ducks?

All around, the previous year had not just been bad; it had been a disaster. I zigged when they zagged. The northeasters and I booked into the same places at the same times. I frightened the spots off brown trout while bass slept through my offerings. The deer left the mountain country I hunt, but those from the woods alongside my house found my tulips and peas in the spring, then shredded two young pines during rubtime in the fall. Plenty of geese crossed the pit blinds I hunkered in all season, but they were so high they were a menace to aviation—and they held express tickets.

My dismal performances afield forced me to face what the late John Foster Dulles called "an agonizing reappraisal." Clearly, my tactics were lousy; my timing stank, my equipment belonged in a museum.

I knew better than to seek some all-embracing formula as my game plan. Each subject would have to be tackled separately, tactics and gear made precise. The geese, I felt, would be the simplest problem to deal with. I began squirreling away the bucks to purchase a 10-gauge magnum automatic, with which I intended to wreak havoc on the Eastern Shore. My more immediate problem—and infinitely more complex—was what to do about those trout.

Since the Romans knew nothing about splitcane rods and matching the hatch, they invented a calendar that starts the new year off from the pit of winter. For me and millions of other fishermen the real new year begins on the opening day of trout season. My usual opening-day scenario looked like this:

An already-pudgy figure, bulked further by enough clothes to outfit the Klondike gold rush, stands hip-deep in a flow of black water torn into sudsy rips by protruding rocks and bearing of the countryside what the winter snows have been holding in storage: sticks, leaves, tires, a bloated cat, the occasional beer can. Overhead the sky is a glowering mass of putty, against which the bare branches of the trees snap and creak with iron-hard stiffness as blasts of wind arrive from Siberia. For hours our man alternates making casts, peering intently at the jaunty little flies that ride the current like miniature galleons, and fumbling stiff fingers through his flybox in search of new offerings. To find a greater fool, you would have to look inside an ice fishing shanty.

The bottom of a trout stream is its food factory, and on this day it will not be violated by anything except the soles of el piscator's waders. Although he will soon abandon his dry flies (how quickly the credo fades: "I'd rather catch one on top than five down deep"), our man will make only tentative probes into the depths. His wet flies, streamers and nymphs will sweep harmlessly over the heads of the stone-hugging trout. Troutless by 3 o'clock, he will seek the solace of the lodge where fire, firewater and kindred snake-bit companions will be waiting with tales of woe and livers in various stages of distress.

Long before opening day dawned last season, I was determined to never again be a part of this demented tableau.

For weeks I hit the books with an intensity seldom mounted in my professional life. Schwiebert, Whitlock, Marinaro, Swisher-Richards, Cucci-Nastasi—the great masters of flyfishing for trout were devoured. Their instruction manifested itself in a barrage of catalogs and small packages of flies arriving daily from every comer of troutdom. My wading vest bulged with trinkets. Latin names of bugs came trippingly off the tongue.

Opening day, I stood thigh-deep at the head of a pool of black water, frigid and swollen with runoff. Coming to the stream, I had received the usual assortment of reports that the fish were in a coma. The voice on the car radio had said something about snow. None of these things intimidated me at all. This year I was ready.

To meet this early and elemental trouting condition, I pried open a box of nymphs. These were not ordinary nymphs, but masterpieces of illusion—caterpillar-like, hairy-leggy-juicy-looking. Each was weighted with enough piano wire to outfit a Steinway. Never mind that they would hit the water with the finesse of a slam-dunk. They would go down, my friend, down, down to the very noses of these frozen wisenheimers. I would fish these creations with a leader hacked to three feet. (Long leaders, I had learned, rise in the pushing and swelling of the current.) The whole outfit would ride down with high-density sinking line topped by a fluorescent strike indicator to tell me when I had a customer.

You don't cast such a rig. What you do is sort of heave the whole mess out and to one side, paying close attention that a hook in the ear is not the immediate result of the effort.

I watched the curls of line and leader straighten downstream toward a boulder that slashed the smooth flow. I tried to form a mental image of what the nymph was doing—sinking, tumbling, ticking over rocks. The line straightened past the boulder. I paid out three more long pulls from the reel, watching the strike indicator bob on downstream.

Suddenly I thought I saw it dart forward. I came back with rod and line and felt the weight of a trout. As the brown—a lovely 15-incher—darted and splashed on the way to the net, my elation soared. My patience and virtue and hard study were to be rewarded. The masters of the game were indeed wise and learned men.

After that, you can imagine my heart-hammering excitement when the next 30 minutes yielded two more fish, about the same size as the first.

Then the devil sent his disciples to descend upon me, like a plague of locusts. First one, then two, then three other anglers were crowding into my stretch of water. Not one asked what I was using. They simply assumed I had found "The Place."

Never mind, I told myself. You can afford to be generous. I waded from the stream and pointed up toward uninhabited water. In a few minutes I was sloshing, much too fast, through a bouldery run of pocket water when I felt my right foot sliding down an eel-slick ledge. I lurched hard to the left, but that leg would not bear the burden. I went down into the water on my back with a teeth-jarring crash. Totally submerged for a second, I stood up and cursed my luck and the worn felt soles of my waders. I was drenched, achingly cold, and clearly out of action for the rest of the day.

As I waded to the edge of the stream, I discovered another result of my accident with dramatic suddenness. As I made a little sideways move with my left leg to step around a rock, I felt a nauseating wave of pain. I did not want to feel such a shock again, ever, so now I picked my way gingerly along, trying to protect the knee.

Yuk! Yuk! See the man all soaking wet and limping toward his car. Fat-ass must've fallen in. Yuk! Yuk!

A prominent physician whom I trust sentenced the knee to six weeks of healing. Because I could not wade the stream, I could not fish for trout. The great fly hatches of early spring for which I had prepared myself so diligently came and went: the Blue Quills, the Hendericksons, the Grannon caddis, the March Browns.

My mood was foul and depressed. Without my jogging program, with which I had successfully been losing weight, I quickly regained ten pounds. Going to work in New York on the train one day I was struck by a thought as morbid as any I've ever had: The obituary page of the *New York Times* named very few males in their 90s. No, the ages of the boys getting their names in the paper were in the 70s and 80s. At age 45 I had the startling realization that in all likelihood I was more than halfway to the barn. Life begins at 80? Give me a break!

Okay, my somber mood told me, so you've lost some of your good moves and speed. You can't hit a 60-yard mallard or sink a three-foot putt. On the tennis court children who can't get into an R-rated film have you gasping like a beached whale. The guide can show you a tarpon at 60 feet, and you may or may not be able to get the fly to it (probably not, given any kind of wind). But relax, buster. For the years have given you wisdom. Look at what you did with those opening-day trout!

I was still clinging to this slightly uplifting notion when I finally got back to the river in late May. One of the year's best hatches remained. According to the grapevine, the Sulphurs had arrived in tentative numbers two days earlier, and all signs pointed to their major emergence late that evening.

The hatch of *Ephemerella dorothea*, which goes on with diminishing consistency for about six weeks on good eastern streams, ranks as a favorite because it stirs smart, self-respecting trout into an unusual orgy of gluttony. Unlike some mayfly hatches, which deliver more sizzle than steak, the appearance of the No. 16 yellow-and-dun flies in the last hour before darkness produces fishing so fast and exciting that it is the stuff for cool hands and stout hearts.

My favorite slick-water was flat empty that evening. My recent misfortune was all forgotten as I waded into position and made a few desultory casts while waiting for the hatch to begin. The air was heavy with humidity, and low clouds on the ridges promised that darkness would come early and perhaps a thunderstorm with it.

The time that passed seemed interminable. Nothing came off the darkening water, not even caddis. A kingfisher flew upstream, scolding my presence. I heard a great homed owl up on the mountain and an answering cry from nearby. Then I saw the first delicate yellow mayfly climbing steeply toward the trees. In a few moments there was another, then another, then another, and then I actually saw one in the instant it left the water—and beyond it the swirl of a trout.

My line arched through the growing dusk. I saw my artificial Sulphur begin its jaunty ride down the feeding lane where the trout had swirled. It floated on downstream unharmed. There were other rises all over the pool now—not splashy water-throwing slaps, but subtle bulges and swirls.

I really started worrying when my bogus Sulphur made three more rides through the melee without interesting a trout. What was wrong? The fly? The leader? My thoughts screamed as I watched the hatch and rises go on: You've been out of action so long you don't know what you're doing.

In the middle of this burst of self-condemnation I saw something—flashes of darting trout just beneath the surface. That was it! The trout were not taking the surface duns! They were nymphing, gulping the insects as they rose to the surface and in the film as they emerged into winged shape.

I was prepared for this, but my hands trembled as I opened the flybox and got out a floating nymph. The light was going fast, but I managed to tie on the fly without digging out my night light. In my excitement, however, I dropped my reading half-glasses into the stream. Klutz! Fool! I should have had them on a cord around my neck.

No matter. I had the right ammo now, and the fish were still going strong as I roll-cast the nymph to the top of the pool. Instantly a trout was on, and I felt a flush of ultimate satisfaction.

The fish was a strong pulsating weight as it struggled upstream for a few seconds. Then the line went slack as the trout bolted downstream almost past my legs, a momentary shadow that caused me to gasp: I was into my largest trout ever.

The reel screamed appropriately as the fish bolted downstream. He reached the lip of the falls that terminated the pool and turned to face the current. The steady pressure on the 5X felt unbelievable. I had the feeling of the fish backing up, backing to the edge of the tumbling water. He was going to be washed over the lip! I had to do something! I palmed the flange of the reel, increasing the drag, and thereby succeeded in instantly breaking off the trout as surely as though I'd been trying to.

I reeled in the sickeningly slack line and looked at the 5X tippet. So many trout were still taking the sulphur nymphs all over the pool that the excitement smothered the loss of the big fish. I quickly had another floating nymph out, ready to tie on. I felt my shirt pocket for my reading glasses and remembered where they had gone. I held the fly at arm's length against the gloom of the darkening sky. No way. I could not thread the eye of the hook in that dimness.

No problem. My night light had a magnifying glass that fit over the top of the light. No sweat, just stay cool.

I was deeply aware of the rises continuing all over the pool as I pulled the light out and draped its cord around my neck. I felt deeper into the pocket for the magnifying glass. It wasn't there! I flipped the switch on the light. Nothing! *Click, click. Click, click.* Still nothing! Okay, the batteries are dead. You're on your own. Now just hold the fly very still against what is left of the sky and tie it on.

My panic rose as I tried unsuccessfully to tie on the No. 16 Sulphur. I tied a No. 14. It would not go. In a final burst of madness and inspiration, I dug out a No. 10 Blonde Wulff, the biggest fly in my vest. Maybe it would work on these feeding fish.

Perhaps it would have. I don't know. I never got the Wulff tied on. My vision is 20-20, but at age 45 I could not see close up well enough to tie on a fly and resume fishing a hatch that I had waited for all winter.

I reeled in slowly, felt the end of the leader reach the reel, then broke down my rod. The splashes of feeding trout popped out from the darkness. I could not see the rises now, but they were distinctive above the murmur the current made as it tailed from the pool downstream.

Slowly the disappointment drained away. The easy moves, the good speed. Going, going with the years. Yet it was true: You were wiser, vastly richer in the things you knew. Such as realizing right now that what made fishing so great was that on any given outing, things could happen that you would remember all of your days. Few other times in life could offer that. That is the easy part of change—the knowing, the feeling. The other side is that you have left something precious behind—something you had used up and would have to go on without.

Flashes of lightning came across the ridgetop, then the roll of advancing thunder. The feeding grew quieter, then died out completely. The bursts of lightning helped me find my way up the hillside to the lane that led back to the car.

I did not know if I had reached the end of something or the beginning.

The wind blew on the high ridges, gusting along the slopes, coming down to the river.

Blue Dun

FRANK MELE

It is natural, I think, for beginnings to be arbitrary. Even human lives, it seems, can begin somewhat capriciously. Any account of inceptions is therefore apt to be treacherous, or at best, unreliable—especially so, if one seeks for causes to satisfy the human prerequisite to Effect. How to enter into even the merest thumbnail history of an attitude compounded from flowing waters, bankside dawdlers, bamboo, cock's hackles, and a certain color of indeterminate hue, and to give some intimation of their genesis, is a task for wiser heads than mine.

I suppose I could say, for example, that the glowing vision of a Blue Dun cape materialized one night as my pregnant mother knelt at prayer before her little Madonna. But this would be sheer fabrication, and even worse, an affront to the quality of her fervor, for she wanted her unborn son to be a violinist. In her frame of mind, the Blue Dun cape would have been taken for some harping angel in miniature, or a biblical dove with Blue Dun feathers appropriate to the sky of Heaven.

Now, all this might ingratiate me to the good folks of the world, but I would be answerable to the few who know that it is from just such compromises that many a potent myth has had its start. Caught thus, between the half-truths of our salty worthies and the gem-hard unpleasantries of the few, I could try to salvage some of my peace of mind by affirming that since myths appear to be as necessary as breathing to the run-of-the-mill of the species, I shall not try to discredit them, since, by acquiescing to that grand old custom, there is the chance of an absolution of anglers. In other words, if what is sauce for the goose, et cetera, there is no longer ground for casting aspersions on anglers. And no need to take their redemption any farther. For all that anglers' myths tend to fragility, they are still a good deal less vulnerable than the contrivances of ordinary men. I trust that now I can get on with the narrative without ransacking my racial memory for some specious cause—say, an angling ancestor who might justify the events to follow.

There was little in my childhood that might have cast any significant shadows before, unless it was a predilection for puddles. Later, in boyhood, when great and sudden rainstorms magically transformed the city streets into brooks, an unexplainable ecstasy would drive me out of doors to hover dreamy-eyed about the curbstone banks of the new rivulets. To this day, when a muskrat clambers out to some riverbank, I am reminded of the rats that scrambled out of the flooded sewer drains and went scurrying over the great cobblestones of the street.

Some years later, done with early studies, well past the intermediate stage, and reeking with the faint, musty odor of the mud, weeds, and pickerel of the farmland streams near my native Rochester, I went to Syracuse to find new ways for scaling the higher reaches of violin playing. That I had already been one of the youngest members of the Rochester Philharmonic Orchestra did not seem to me as impressive, honorable, or profitable as to have the inner beauty of a musical phrase revealed to me by a gaunt and profane master, Andre Polah, my teacher, an artist of stature—one of the elect, whose career had been stifled by an ironic accident.

An ominous silence had settled over the nation. And when in its deepest recesses, a cataclysmic bomb exploded, shattering the national economy, the country reeled and staggered in a state of shock. Life went on, but with empty pockets and, quite often, an empty belly—that is, among the laboring classes and those of us in the arts. And when, against the protestations and vilifications of outraged Pilgrims, who had acquired affluence presumably without the help of God, a crippled and compassionate President decreed the Work Projects, we musicians filed due notice of bona fide indigence, cut the fringes from our trouser cuffs, and began to use our professional skills as members of the new symphony orchestra. It was held to be one of the more contemptible projects, in that men were getting paid, however minimally, for merely making great music.

Andre was a gifted conductor as well, and when he was appointed director of the orchestra he set about reconciling his passion for a high standard of performance, as much as his choleric nature would permit, with the inevitable quota of mediocrities that were better suited to vaudeville than to Mozart, Brahms, Debussy, and yes, even Stravinsky. There was now relief from want, but not from the humiliation that attended its formalities; and what shreds of dignity had survived the stigma attached to the projects were annihilated by a jibing press and the indignation of the good burghers of upper New York State. Those were gloomy days, scarcely relieved by the pall of grime that hung over the scabrous public buildings. The drabness of that city was exceeded only by a pervasive meanness of spirit. But redemption could be found in the beauty of its countryside. Out beyond the green drumlins, among the valleys to the northeast and south, beautiful streams with Indian names beckoned, inviting heavy hearts to lightness, and corroded hopes to a good burnishing at the hands of waterside alders.

Andre was a fly-fisher, and when this mad Dutchman adopted me as his fishing companion, my hopes began to soar as an early zeal for bait casting got transposed to the fly rod. As in violin playing, I sought out the masters, ransacking the shelves of the university and public libraries for books on flyfishing. In the stacks I found Emlyn Gill, Bergman, Hewitt, Southard, Lord Grey. I saved enough to send to Paul Young for his *Making and Using the Fly and Leader*. And then I began to tie flies, buying hooks by the dozen when I could afford them. Certain exotic materials could only be purchased. Others I begged. And many I borrowed from an environment that had taken on a new depth. A rich world of texture and color had opened to me. For the first time I saw the extraordinary range of color in dogs, cats, pet and wild rabbits, monkeys, mice, squirrels, ducks, geese, and fowl of all kinds. My visits to the zoo now had a vibrant urgency that gave pause to children and made the keepers nervous. And when the orchestra played at a county fair that was famous for its yearly exhibit of rare fowl, and I found the attendant away for lunch, my head swam. In the operation that followed, a dizziness nearly overcame me, fearing that at any moment the uproar would fetch a guard.

One morning at rehearsal a new man came in dragging a cello by the scruff of the neck. Andre had briefed me about him over the previous day's intermission coffee. In the excitement Andre's English, normally unpredictable, had slipped a few cogs and was being ground up by Dutch, French, and German accents. Under those great eyebrows of Holland straw his blue eyes were gleaming wolfishly. In a gravelly bass he told me the news. "This man is un maker of rodts! Un goddamt specialiste von fly rodts! Dry-fly rodts!" I could not have been more impressed had Andre announced the entry of Pablo Casals into our ranks. Our rods were of poor quality, soft as willow. Andre's treasured rods and reels by Hardy had been stolen from his car years ago.

Andre's words were still reverberating in my ear as Brenan took his place at the rear of the cello section. As he began to tune his cello he looked so unprofessional that I began to get faintly sick. But shortly I saw something that made me close my eyes in blessed relief. There would not be, could not be, any repercussion from the podium. Hopelessly out of practice after years of rodmaking, Brenan had sacked valor for a plausible discretion. It would have been difficult for him to have made an audible mistake. He was bowing away impassively, in step with the others, the bow hair hovering over the treacherous rapids then settling down agreeably in the more navigable runs, glides, and pools. It was a stroke of true wisdom, appreciated none the less by Andre than by me. One day, Brenan invited me to his shop.

Coming in to the warmth of a little world of bamboo out of the whiplashing snows and icy sidewalks of Syracuse was no less than a bit of parochial magic, bringing easement and balm to a troubled soul. The shop's mood was a mélange of violinmaker's shop and tackle store, sources both for repose and wonder. There I saw and fondled my first dry-fly rods. Had Brenan had an apprenticeship or a family tradition there would not have been any flaw of workmanship. If imperfect, they were superb in action; I have had a few in hand since then that were comparable to his best rods, and many that were inferior. However prudent a cellist, Dan was an adventurous rod-maker; and in the matter of rod design for the dry fly he was ahead of his time.

A blackboard with the chalked heading, "Days to Opening Day" read "63," awaiting the first of the coterie to come in to roost out of the waning afternoon, leaving the gloom, chill, and snow to the defeated day. By five-thirty the blackboard read "62." I basked in the warmth of talk that diverted the winter stream to its summer course on the shop's floor. Rods sprang to life. Lines darted and looped under the soiled sky of the ceiling. At a bench to one side sat Bill, Dan's son, at his afterwork vise, contriving a better bivisible fly than the last. Flies whisked about. A great trout rose to McBride's fly of last summer, then plunged downward to sulk in the depths of the floor below. It was the rite of the Waiting Men enduring their season of work with invocations to a reluctant spring—not a whit less primitive than the crude and basic formalities of their remote ancestors. From a judicial chamber, from a locomotive's cab, from symphony hall, office, machine shop, barroom, laboratory, they had come to improvise upon their truth, which was the Dry Fly.

Later, at a nearby tavern, Dan, mellowing in whisky, would hold forth for the hardier few. A gifted writer on many aspects of the sport, Dan had an extensive correspondence with leading figures in the field. His knowledge of angling history of the Catskill and Adirondack mountains was imposing and intimate; and the names I culled out of those benign extemporizations sounded like a roll call of latter-day saints: Theodore Gordon, La Branche, Hewitt, Holden, of the "Idyll of the Split Bamboo," Izaak Walton (no less a figure than Dante), Halford, the English Prince of the True Faith, and then the glorious school of Catskill fly-tyers who had received Gordon's afflatus at death: Rueben Cross, Herman Christian, the Darbees, Walt Dette. By now Dan had become for me the arbiter of all things piscatorial, and an inexhaustible source of fishing lore.

One afternoon at the tavern Dan had soared to really admirable form, and was weaving in and out of the key of Dry Fly Major with the skill of an Irish Bach when, at once, he struck an arresting chord. "The Quill Gordon fly," said Dan, "was the great turning point in American dry-fly fishing. Gordon's creativity in his choice of materials and his ingenuity in determining a just style for our waters set the pattern that was to become our tradition. After an extensive correspondence with the mighty Halford, and a cordial exchange of flies, he departed once and for all from the English tradition, retaining only that which could be adapted to his concept of a fly that could dance on our broken waters, and which, on our long glides and pools, looked like a newly hatched dun. It is therefore *de rigueur*, mandatory, that this fly be tied with the natural Blue Dun hackle! Else it is not a true Quill Gordon fly!" By now Dan's voice had the ring of One Hundred Proof. "For that matter," he added, "no fly could rightfully bear the name Dun unless it was tied in the natural color!"

There it was. With four words Dan had wakened me out of a deep sleep, only to plunge me into a nightmare of frustration at the thought of all those Quill Gordon flies I had tied from a very well dyed cock's neck of excellent quality. I had traded a Pernambuco violin bow for it to a greedy dealer in fly-tying materials. The fact that the bow was not a true Pernambuco was small consolation. The neck was not a true Blue Dun. Dan's words resolved all doubts that I had had from time to time about those flies. Their color was inert. They reminded me of ash. Dan's incantation had at once set me before the Veil that concealed a great Mystery. What the revelation could conceivably be was as yet only a strange stirring of blood in my head. This color, Blue Dun, would I know it were I to come suddenly face to face with it? What could there be about it which had set it apart so remotely yet compellingly on a mountain peak in my mind?

"Well, Frankie," said Dan. "I can only say that there is nothing quite like it. I don't know how to describe it. One simply has to see the natural Blue Dun for himself, with his own eyes. Only then can he understand. It is one of Nature's rare moods. It is color and light making their ways out of chaos and darkness." For the moment I had to content myself with this Hibernian tune from the Prophet. Had Dan had access then to Gordon's letters to the great English angler, G. E. M. Skues, he would have quoted:

"My farmer friend and I have been trying to breed good dun hackles, but the cocks are turning out poorly."

Later: "I found a blue cock of the year yesterday and hope that I will succeed in buying the bird—the neck is of such a lovely color—"

And six years later: "It seems too bad when we consider how rarely one finds a cock with blue dun hackles." Even then, it seems, the natural color was painfully scarce.

Dan, I am sure, was not aware of what was happening to me, else he would have modified his dictum from unalterable law to permissible deviation. He had a deep respect for my skill as a violinist, and a personal liking that probably set me only a cut or two below Theodore Gordon, for Dan adored great music. But I do believe that had he altered his pronunciamento out of care for my peace of mind, and that of my family's, I doubt that it would have greatly diverted the course of the future. Blue Dun was now a fever in my brain.

The violence of my reaction and its later consequences cannot be entirely ascribed to Dan, with all due respect to his eloquence and imagery. Later events tend to suggest that the occasion triggered something deep within, well beyond normal reach, well to the other side of any intimation, even, of its existence; for I had yet to see a single feather of natural Blue Dun.

Then, streambound early one Sunday morning, as the car was hurtling over the road, the irascible Marcel gave me what appears now to be the first lucid description of the color Blue Dun. This taut but amiable Frenchman, a hairdresser, was a passionate angler whose fly casting was a model of elegance and precision. He was singing obscene French songs, by way, I thought, of exorcising the previous day's ordeal with fat and fretful matrons. When he had finished still another classic of the latrine I put the question to him. He was a knowledgeable and meticulous fly-tyer.

"Marcel. What is the real Blue Dun like? The natural—you know-"

"Ah, mon cher," he replied. "That? What can I say? It is like nothing else, and everything. It is not blue, like the flag blue. It is something that is always—How shall I say? Becoming?"

Late that afternoon at Marcel's home I saw my first natural Blue Dun neck. I was silent a long time. It was real, and it was there. But it was unreal; and it was somewhere else. Marcel was right. It was in the act of becoming. I raised my eyes at last and spoke.

"Marcel. Where is Blue Dun?"

"Ah." Marcel canted his head a bit to one side. "That is a difficult question. How shall I tell you? That it is where you find it? Yes. To find it. Until then it is like the—like the smoke—"

"In search of the sky."

"Yes! Exactly!" Marcel nodded sharply, then suddenly fixed me with a curious look followed by an expression of bewilderment, as of a spirit scurrying through the ages.

"But how did you know?" he asked, from a great distance.

"I'm not sure," I said, my words sounding from afar. "You may have said it once before, and I remembered it."

Hairdressers, I believe, are masters of applied psychology. Marcel had read something in my face that was unintentional, of which I was not aware. "What size do you tie the Quill Gordon?" he asked.

"Twelve."

He riffled affectionately through the quivering hackles, then carefully plucked out two and gave them to me. It was an act of superlative generosity, well beyond friendship. I had heard it said that the French were stingy. I say that they are selectively extravagant. On that occasion it was nothing less than a minor sacrifice, which only a cynic can make without pomp. "Bon!" concluded Marcel. "You are now fit to enter the Beaverkill. You are going next week with Dan?"

"Yes. Dan is taking three of us. It will be my very first time. I have never seen it, except in dreams."

"Ah," sighed Marcel. "It is a dream within a dream."

On a fresh summer morning a week later, as Blue Dun was rising in the east, a Ford went wheezing toward the valleys where the sacred rivers ran. Under the wise and gentle guidance of Dan, the Prophet, three of us were to have our baptism at last in the Beaverkill River.

Hours later, when the southern hills had greatened to Catskill massiveness, we descended a long, winding grade and the Ford stopped, heaving and burbling in exhaustion at the bank of a majestic pool. We alighted. The Prophet turned to us, intoned the keynote and conducted an impromptu cantata, the hymn, "Praise God from Whom All Blessings Flow." It was an unlikely chorus: a nominal Protestant, a fled Catholic, a remoted Jew, and an atheist. But it was in time, and fervent. In a many-celled fly box, squatting in its own special compartment, the fly with the mystical color listened, awaiting its first flight over the holy waters.

If memory serves me, and often it doesn't, we camped near to the Mountain Pool. Darkness was nigh, and wood was fetched at Dan's request for a fire big enough to conjure up the Spirits of the River, that he might transpose the secrets that passed back and forth from the distant rapids to the crackling flames. As the night deepened, the thin, reedy chords of a harmonica floated in and out of the conversational murmur. It was a nostalgic whimper before the fact of smallness beneath a firmament of stars—the Aeolian harp of the Catskills singing of humility and peace, and gratitude to the great Unknown.

Later, two figures materialized from the outer world of darkness and entered the glow of the fire to bring their hands to Dan's. Gladness and surprise were in the Prophet's greetings, and through their fullness there ran a finely gleaming thread of respect. One of them was Reuben Cross, the greathearted and improvident master of fly-making who was already a legend, and with him was Alfred W. Miller, the Sparse Grey Hackle of the genial writings that were enriching Beaverkill lore.

In the early morning I entered the waters, rod in hand. I do not remember how many trout rose to my fly—or whether, indeed, any did. But I shall not forget that I moved as in a dream, hearing the voices of the river rising and falling with mysterious clarity through the hovering mists. And I remember the crystalline water that seemed to magnify the purity of the rocks, and the cool green darkness of the ferns, a profusion of frail, lush arches in the shadowed banks; and as the mist began to rise, a doe and her fawn crossed the pool below.

In the ensuing years, my work as a symphonist took me to various parts of the country for the fall, winter, and spring months. As each music season rounded its peak, and spring was faintly visible in the distant valley, the voice of a wakened obsession would begin loudening to a command to action. The trail was faint, often washed out. But, like a stubborn hound, I would return to certain crossways, hoping for a cold scent that would lead miraculously to a Blue Dun cape of quality that had fallen asleep in mid-flight. When the orchestra played The Moldau, a tone poem which the Bohemian Smetana had distilled from the sounds of a great river, my left-hand fingers would scurry agreeably with the riffles at its headwaters, but the bow had become a fly rod in the other hand. The fly was, appropriately, a Blue Dun, since I had long ago formulated the theory that the natural Dun-hackled fly would take trout anywhere in the world at one time or another.

On nights off, a few of us would meet to play chamber music. The music we made, mostly for ourselves, was the most rewarding of all in terms of personal fulfillment. And if a pianist and a bassist were present, no great persuasion was needed for them to join us in a reading of Schubert's "Trout" Quintet, a tribute to that noble fish by the Austrian genius. As in the song that had inspired the Quintet, the measured, buoyant cheer of its theme would have been perfect incidental music to the ballet of a stately brown swirling at his feast of mayfly nymphs aspiring to dunhood. Later, in the quiet of the Pittsburgh night, I would write another of those ritual letters—this time to a house in England: "Gentlemen, would you by chance have a cock's cape of natural Blue Dun of good quality to offer? I am aware of the rarity of this color and am, accordingly, prepared to consider the payment of a premium. I would be most grateful—"

I suppose it was inevitable that I should one day settle in the Catskills. I had had as much as I wanted of the unquiet life, and one year I returned, not merely for the summer, but to stay, in a village within twenty minutes' drive of the Esopus, a river proud and mighty still, its spirit unbroken after years of torment by water-greedy Manhattan. My community had a rich and highly respected tradition of the arts, offering scope for playing in a summer series of distinction and a likely potential for students of the violin and viola. Then, within one to two hours' reach there flowed the great rivers of angling history, allegedly tired, but still alluring and productive in their classically temperamental fashion. These were the Schoharie, the Delawares, East and West, the Willowemoc, and the Neversink and Beaverkill rivers.

My decision, however, had come at a time when, for perhaps too many reasons, mind and body had wandered off into a twilight world. There is a withering hostility in the winter Catskills, a taut suspension of life outdoors that can drive men's backs against their own walls. There is beauty, too; and joy may be found or contrived. But the gnawings of a marginal life can dispose a man toward the consolations of the jug. The cheapness and goodness of native applejack made it possible to appease a growing congenital thirst, transporting me to an inner island so beguiling that I did not want to leave. I was unable to. Years drifted by. Then, shambling one day through the familiar vapors, I stumbled over my persistent little man again, the one I had ignored and even insulted so often in the past. This time I heard him out; I believed him, and together we managed to stop it once and for all. I did not know it then, but he was congenital, too.

As I improved I began reconstituting the sport, and shortly began to hear the distant crowing of Blue Dun roosters again. The awakening was owing in part to the interest and kindness of Preston Jennings, who had recently retired to nearby Bearsville. His classic *A Book of Trout Flies* was, for me, the first truly significant work on angling entomology and dry-fly design for Eastern streams. It brought order to the chaos of a still rather wayward tradition of American dry-fly fishing and carried it to solid ground. It was issued in a limited edition by a private press in elegant format and was, ironically, remaindered. Its cost at the time was one factor. The other may have been the cool objectivity of a style uninviting to those American anglers who were still disposed toward boyish writings on fishing. However, by now the book had reemerged as a rare find, commanding premium prices—and it was very scarce. All told, it amounted very nearly to a conspiracy. Accordingly, Jennings was not awarded the honor due him in his lifetime. His genius is reflected in another work, the *Streamside Guide*, by Arthur Flick; and Jennings may be said to have been godfather to this indispensable little book.

Curiously, I found that Jennings' passion for the stream had also entered a state of suspension, although unlike mine, his was marked by sobriety, tinged however, with disillusion. Some causes for the latter have been implied. Then, too. Bobby was a man of sensibility, intelligence, and aesthetic awareness, all of which together can incline one to vulnerability. Such persons must stand on reserve or perish, at risk of incurring a judgment of pride. But such was not the case, and I like to think that I may have played a small part in his reconciliation to the Catskill streams, for which I think he was glad, or so it seemed as I watched him flexing his beloved Payne rod over a rifflehead, proving the potency of his Blue Dun Variant in conjuring a fifteen-inch brown out of its depths.

At his home one evening, Bobby brought out a small box and opened it with a reverence. Suggestive of a collector opening to some fabulous diamond. In it were dry flies which had been tied by Herman Christian and Theodore Gordon. I could not imagine them more perfect had they been tied that morning. One of the original models for the Quill Gordon fly was among them. Its form and color engraved themselves in my mind and thereafter became the model for my own imitations. I have since seen other flies allegedly by Gordon, but none had the finesse or the buoyant elegance.

As a tyer, Bobby was a superior artist, and his materials were the finest I had ever seen, or have ever seen since. Among his necks were Blue Duns as fine as I ever hope to see. Jennings was also inclined to the artist's brush and palette, and I believe that this, together with a related color-study, in which he had been absorbed for some time, had drawn him and his gracious wife to an artistic environment. His experience with salmon flies while fishing the great coastal rivers of the East had led to an inquiry into the reasons for the effectiveness of the many-hued salmon fly; and that to a study of the prismatic effect given off by the tiny bubbles of air formed about the microscopic filaments or hairs on the body of a rising nymph. Further inquiry had suggested that the salmon's memory held an indelible association of these colors with the food nymphs of its grilsehood. All told, his efforts had begun to yield up a logical case for the salmon fly and its seemingly irrational gaudiness.

I felt pleased, even honored by Jennings' friendship, but in a rather vague, disembodied way. For those were difficult days—days in which the slow withdrawal of the alcohol had brought to view the shambles of a once productive life, and of a collective fruitfulness reduced to abject singleness. Vaguely aware of trudging forward, I was mostly conscious of a mouthful of ashes, of a battered spirit which had barely averted bankruptcy. But, as I have since gathered, my outer aspect was one of calm bordering on indifference, occasionally rising to arrogance. How far this was from the actual inward state would be a volume in itself, a compact little book, some of whose contents Bobby may have discerned; for one evening, in his studio, as he was delving into a drawer, he turned suddenly to me with a smile. In his outstretched hand was a superb cape of natural Blue Dun. For reasons that have never been clear, I declined it, with a thick murmur of thanks. I doubt whether I could have offended him more. I had virtually spit into the face of a noble gesture, one prompted by the purest motive of intuitive sensibility. Apparently, my reconstruction still had a long way to go. It is not surprising then, that after an unfortunate misunderstanding, we never saw each other again.

An offer came from an orchestra in Texas. Glad for the opportunity of relief from the aftermath of recent history, I accepted. Far from the Catskills, far from trout, my bewildered fly rods huddling in a friend's closet, I entered into the symphonic world again under the benevolent auspices of a mild Texas winter. But when the last Norther had subsided to spring, the old song of the quest began humming in

my head again—and the voices of the rivers that flowed under the distant silhou-
ettes of my mountains. I began to write letters that were utterly incongruous with
that flat and surly land: "Gentlemen, would you by chance—Blue Dun? I would be
most grateful—"

Returned to a comparatively tranquil and ordered life in the Catskills, I found it
necessary from time to time to suspend the attrition of the long, bitter winters with
occasional jaunts to Jerusalem. Together with my angling companions of some years
we found respite from the winter jitters by observing, from time to time, one of a
number of what may be called "Darbee Days." I suppose that, given other circumstances, they may have been called "Walt Dette," "Bill Kelly," or "Roy Steenrod"
Days, for they, too, were a part of the angling-conservation custodianship at the banks
of the great tradition. They were the Keepers of the Gate. But the Darbees were
friends of long standing; and then—well, yes, there was also the little matter of their
Blue Dun fowl, a strain of their own breeding that glared peevishly out the many
cages in the back yard. Inside, we basked in the homemade sunlight of hackles,
hooks, furs, rods, reels, lines, leaders, nets, selecting materials with which to tie flies
at home later, by way of preserving our sanities during the deserted time of the year.
There was talk of flies, of streams, of the men who lived for them, of books in which
the waters ran, and where now and then one found a superior music which had been
inspired by the trout, a simple vertebrate, but with this difference: That it stirred a
mystery in the deepest recess of our beings, a primal nostalgia that quickened in the
sight of its brilliant spots and bands of iridescence where gulps of moonlight had con-
gealed to color. Padding in with feminine unobtrusiveness, the First Lady of
American fly-tying gave greeting and passed to some other phase of sorting. Held by
some to be, craftwise, the better half of the Darbee legend, Elsie would have dis-
dained and Harry confirmed it. Actually, the difference, if any, was beyond the ken
of niggling amateurs. Above the genial drone of Harry's voice on the trail of a point
of conservation there sounded the faint, rhythmical fanfare of Blue Dun cocks, proud
in their little beaked trumpets.

Later, on the long drive home, fly life hatched and surfaced in the murmuring
car, and the unheard litanies to a reluctant spring that sang under our words must
surely have been noted under the thick ice of Pepacton Reservoir and commented
upon with frigid bubbles by the huge trout which had greatened in it within a few
miles of its source, the self-renouncing Delaware.

Came the fall of another year, and Fate took one of us for a disastrous ride. For
two weeks Jim Mulligan lay in a coma. Waking, he was to lie for two years in a veterans hospital bed until the one half of his body could support the paralyzed half.
How many connivances and fabrications that ,Joe Nazzaro and I dreamed up en route
to the hospital I cannot remember; nor how many precious days of liberty that Joe,

and I, too, gave up that we might bring the stream to the distant bedside where our shattered friend lay.

But mercy, however capricious, will also have its say; and in having regained the use of one half of his body, Jim, a distinguished cartoonist, set himself the formidable task of transferring the skill of a now inert hand to the strong but untrained one. There came a winter's day at last when the inroads of "cabin fever" decreed a Darbee Day. Once again, with our valiant but unsteady Jim, we set off on wings of Blue Dun.

At Margaretville we crossed the upper Delaware and shortly were following the shoreline road of the severely beautiful Pepacton. Later, turning away from the reservoir, we began the long ascent, then down to Roscoe; and when we crossed the upper Beaverkill I doffed the only hat for the three of us. Shortly beyond the village, on the Manor road, we skirted the Willowemoc, greenbubbling at its icy lips and winter-dark in the upper pool. In the riffles above, a cold fire flared under a shaft of brilliant sunlight from a rift in the gray clouds.

Time has not perceptibly dimmed my memory of Darbee's greeting to the man whom destiny had banged on the brain; nor the implication that it had done so ineffectively. Out the candor of his blue eyes, out the heart of a rich experience, came the blessing of man's humanity to man: a beckoning to Jim to search and find a wholeness of his own. Before we left he gave Jim the token that would articulate his wish for many a year. It was in a paper sack.

As the car was cantering home along the Pepacton road Jim opened the paper sack with his good hand. In the waning light of the afternoon we saw the Blue Dun cape glowing. As he turned it we saw the component glints in the light from the reflecting whiteness of the reservoir. Visibly moved by his great good fortune, Jim's speech, till now painfully laborious, made a curious modulation and he said, slowly but clearly, "It seems to have other meanings."

In my cabinet of fly materials there is a special drawer. Lying in it is a small number of Blue Dun capes of varying shades nestling about each other in all the glory of their muted iridescence. They were all acquired more or less honorably: that is, in the sense that legitimacy and honesty are terms subject to parochial rules, and that it takes a good deal of imagination to transcend our little moral geographies.

I will not say how many there are, because I want to be surprised each time I count them. And when I do so, it is less to affirm my possessiveness than the privilege of their custody. That they are only a small part of countless numbers of shades and attitudes of color piques me, but it does not disturb me, for the ones allotted to me all have their special meaning. Each is a memento of a particular quest. They invite, of course, to other quests, but I really need not undertake them, because each day the colors are a little bit different, as each day is different; and thus they multiply in my mind's eye. Through their difference, as in the multicolored variants of Bach's great "Chaconne," there runs the somber strain of the fact that I grow older, and soon the fiddle strings will fray out and their sound must fade. But the colors will not, for Blue Dun waits upon other questions, whose answers, even more than mine, will disavow finality. As for instance, "Why is Blue Dun?"

One could as well ask: "Why is Love?" Or, indeed, "Why is Life?"

PART VII

Classic
Fishing Stories

Storytelling on the Thames

JEROME K. JEROME

The neighborhood of Streatley and Goring is a great fishing center. There is some excellent fishing to be had here. The river abounds in pike, roach, dace, gudgeon, and eels, just here; and you can sit and fish for them all day.

Some people do. They never catch them. I never knew anybody catch anything, up the Thames, except minnows and dead cats, but that has nothing to do, of course, with fishing! The local fisherman's guide doesn't say a word about catching anything. All it says is the place is "a good station for fishing"; and, from what I have seen of the district, I am quite prepared to bear out this statement.

There is no spot in the world where you can get more fishing, or where you can fish for a longer period. Some fishermen come here and fish for a day, and others stop and fish for a month. You can hang on and fish for a year, if you want to: it will be all the same.

The *Angler's Guide to the Thames* says that "jack and perch are also to be had about here," but there the *Angler's Guide* is wrong. Jack and perch may be about there. Indeed, I know for a fact that they are. You can see them there in shoals, when you are out for a walk along the banks: they come and stand half out of the water with their mouths open for biscuits. And, if you go for a bathe, they crowd round, and get in your way, and irritate you. But they are not to be "had" by a bit of worm on the end of a hook, nor anything like it—not they!

I am not a good fisherman myself. I devoted a considerable amount of attention to the subject at one time, and was getting on, as I thought, fairly well; but the old hands told me that I should never be any real good at it, and advised me to give it up. They said that I was an extremely neat thrower, and that I seemed to have plenty of gumption for the thing, and quite enough constitutional laziness. But they were sure I should never make anything of a fisherman. I had not got sufficient imagination.

They said that as a poet, or a shilling shocker, or a reporter, or anything of that kind, I might be satisfactory, but that, to gain any position as a Thames angler, would require more play of fancy, more power of invention than I appeared to possess.

Some people are under the impression that all that is required to make a good fisherman is the ability to tell lies easily and without blushing; but this is a mistake. Mere bald fabrication is useless; the veriest tyro can manage that. It is in the circumstantial detail, the embellishing touches of probability, the general air of scrupulous—almost of pedantic—veracity, that the experienced angler is seen.

Anybody can come in and say, "Oh, I caught fifteen dozen perch yesterday evening," or "Last 'Monday I landed a gudgeon, weighing eighteen pounds, and measuring three feet from the tip to the tail."

There is no art, no skill, required for that sort of thing. It shows pluck, but that is all.

No; your accomplished angler would scorn to tell a lie, that way. His method is a study in itself.

He comes in quietly with his hat on, appropriates the most comfortable chair, lights his pipe, and commences to puff in silence. He lets the youngsters brag away for a while, and then, during a momentary lull, he removes the pipe from his mouth, and remarks, as he knocks the ashes out against the bars:

"Well, I had a haul on Tuesday evening that it's not much good my telling anybody about."

"Oh! why's that?" they ask.

"Because I don't expect anybody would believe me if I did," replies the old fellow calmly, and without even a tinge of bitterness in his tone, as he refills his pipe, and requests the landlord to bring him three of Scotch—cold.

There is a pause after this, nobody feeling sufficiently sure of himself to contradict the old gentleman. So he has to go on by himself without any encouragement.

"No," he continues thoughtfully; "I shouldn't believe it myself if anybody told it to me, but it's a fact, for all that. I had been sitting there all the afternoon and had caught literally nothing—except a few dozen dace and a score of jack; and I was just about giving it up as a bad job when I suddenly felt a rather smart pull at the line. I thought it was another little one, and I went to jerk it up. Hang me, if I could move the rod! It took me half an hour—half an hour, sir!—to land that fish; and every moment I thought the line was going to snap! I reached him at last, and what do you think it was? A sturgeon! A forty-pound sturgeon! Taken on a line, sir! Yes, you may well look surprised—I'll have another three of Scotch, landlord, please."

And then he goes on to tell of the astonishment of everybody who saw it; and what his wife said, when he got home, and of what Joe Buggles thought about it.

I asked the landlord of an inn up the river once, if it did not injure him, sometimes, listening to the tales that the fishermen about there told him; and he said:

"Oh, no; not now, sir. It did used to knock me over a bit at first, but, lor love you! me and the missus we listens to 'em all day now. It's what you're used to, you know. It's what you're used to."

I knew a young man once, he was a most conscientious fellow, and, when he took to fly fishing, he determined never to exaggerate his hauls by more than twenty-five per cent.

"When I have caught forty fish," said he, "then I will tell people that I have caught fifty, and so on. But I will not lie any more than that, because it is sinful to lie."

But the twenty-five per cent plan did not work well at all. He never was able to use it. The greatest number of fish he ever caught in one day was three, and you can't add twenty-five per cent to three—at least, not in fish.

So he increased his percentage to thirty-three and a third; but that, again, was awkward, when he had caught only one or two; so, to simplify matters, he made up his mind to just double the quantity.

He stuck to this arrangement for a couple of months, and then he grew dissatisfied with it. Nobody believed him when he told them that he only doubled, and he, therefore, gained no credit that way whatever, while his moderation put him at a disadvantage among the other anglers. When he had really caught three small fish, and said he had six, it used to make him quite jealous to hear a man, who he knew for a fact had caught only one, going about telling people he had landed two dozen.

So, eventually, he made one final arrangement with himself, which he has religiously held to ever since, and that was to count each fish that he caught as ten, and to assume ten to begin with. For example, if he did not catch any fish at all, then he said he had caught ten fish—you could never catch less than ten fish by his system; that was the foundation of it. Then, if by any chance he really did catch one fish, he called it twenty, while two fish would count thirty, three forty, and so on.

It is a simple and easily worked plan, and there has been some talk lately of its being made use of by the angling fraternity in general. Indeed, the Committee of the Thames Anglers' Association did recommend its adoption about two years ago, but some of the older members opposed it. They said they would consider the idea if the number were doubled, and each fish counted as twenty.

If ever you have an evening to spare, up the river, I should advise you to drop into one of the little village inns, and take a seat in the taproom. You will be nearly sure to meet one or two old rodmen, sipping their toddy there, and they will tell you enough fishy stories, in half an hour, to give you indigestion for a month.

George and I—I don't know what had become of Harris; he had gone out and had a shave, early in the afternoon, and had then come back and spent full forty minutes in pipe-claying his shoes, we had not seen him since—George and I, therefore, and the dog, left to ourselves, went for a walk to Wallingford on the second evening, and, coming home, we called in at a little riverside inn, for a rest and other things.

We went into the parlor and sat down. There was an old fellow there, smoking a long clay pipe, and we naturally began chatting.

He told us that it had been a fine day today, and we told him that it had been a fine day yesterday, and then we all told each other that we thought it would be a fine day tomorrow; and George said the crops seemed to be coming up nicely.

After that it came out, somehow or other, that we were strangers in the neighborhood, and that we were going away the next morning. Then a pause ensued in the conversation, during which our eyes wandered round the room. They finally rested upon a dusty old glass case, fixed very high up above the chimney piece, and containing a trout. It rather fascinated me, that trout; it was such a monstrous fish. In fact, at first glance, I thought it was a cod.

"Ah!" said the old gentleman, following the direction of my gaze, "fine fellow that, ain't he?"

"Quite uncommon," I murmured; and George asked the old man how much he thought it weighed.

"Eighteen pounds six ounces," said our friend, rising and taking down his coat. "Yes," he continued, "it wur sixteen year ago, come the third o' next month, that I landed him. I caught him just below the bridge with a minnow. They told me he wur in the river, and I said I'd have him, and so I did. You don't see many fish that size about here now, I'm thinking. Good night, gentlemen, good night."

And out he went, and left us alone.

We could not take our eyes off the fish after that. It really was a remarkably fine fish. We were still looking at it, when the local carrier, who had just stopped at the inn, came to the door of the room with a pot of beer in his hand, and he also looked at the fish.

"Good-sized trout, that," said George, turning round to him.

"Ah! you may well say that, sir," replied the man; and then, after a pull at his beer, he added, "Maybe you wasn't here, sir, when that fish was caught?"

"No," we told him. We were strangers in the neighborhood.

"Ah !" said the carrier, "then, of course, how should you? It was nearly five years ago that I caught that trout."

"Oh! was it you who caught it, then?" said I.

"Yes, sir," replied the genial old fellow. "I caught him just below the lock—least-ways, what was the lock then—one Friday afternoon; and the remarkable thing about it is that I caught him with a fly. I'd gone out pike fishing, bless you, never thinking of a trout, and when I saw that whopper on the end of my line, blest if it didn't quite take me aback. Well, you see, he weighed twenty-six pound. Good night, gentlemen, good night."

Five minutes afterward, a third man came in, and described how he had caught it early one morning, with bleak; and then he left, and a stolid, solemn-looking, middle-aged individual came in, and sat down over by the window.

None of us spoke for a while; but at length, George turned to the newcomer and said:

"I big your pardon, I hope you will forgive the liberty that we—perfect strangers in the neighborhood—are taking, but my friend here and myself would be much obliged if you would tell us how you caught that trout."

"Why, who told you I caught that trout!" was the surprised query. We said that nobody had told us so, but somehow or other we felt instinctively that it was he who had done it.

"Well, it's a most remarkable thing—most remarkable," answered the stolid stranger, laughing: "because, as a matter of fact, you are quite right. I did catch it. But fancy your guessing it like that. Dear me, it's really a most remarkable thing."

And then he went on, and told us how it had taken him half an hour to land it, and how it had broken his rod. He said he had weighed it carefully when he reached home, and it had turned the scale at thirty-four pounds.

He went in his turn, and when he was gone, the landlord came in to us. We told him the various histories we had heard about his trout, and he was immensely amused, and we all laughed very heartily.

"Fancy Jim Bates and Joe Muggles and Mr. Jones and old Billy Maunders all telling you that they had caught it. Ha! ha! ha! Well, that is good," said the honest old fellow, laughing heartily. "Yes, they are the sort to give it me, to put up in my parlor, if they had caught it, they are! Ha! ha! ha!"

And then he told us the real history of the fish. It seemed that he had caught it himself, years ago, when he was quite a lad; not by any art or skill, but by that unaccountable luck that appears to always wait upon a boy when he plays the wag from school, and goes 'way out fishing on a sunny afternoon, with a bit of string tied onto the end of a tree.

He said that bringing home that trout had saved him from a whacking, and that even his schoolmaster had said it was worth the rule of three and practice put together.

He was called out of the room at this point, and George and I again turned our gaze upon the fish.

It really was a most astonishing trout. The more we looked at it, the more we marveled at it.

It excited George so much that he climbed up on the back of a chair to get a better view of it.

And then the chair slipped, and George clutched wildly at the trout case to save himself, and down it came with a crash, George and the chair on top of it.

"You haven't injured the fish, have you?" I cried in alarm, rushing up.

"I hope not," said George, rising cautiously and looking about.

But he had. That trout lay shattered into a thousand fragments—I say a thousand, but they may have been only nine hundred. I did not count them.

We thought it strange and unaccountable that a stuffed trout should break up into little pieces like that.

And so it would have been strange and unaccountable, if it had been a stuffed trout, but it was not.

That trout was plaster of Paris.

On the Loch

WILLIAM BLACK

A considerable wind arose during the night; Mr. Hodson did not sleep very well; and, lying awake toward morning, he came to the conclusion that he had been befooled, or rather that he had befooled himself, with regard to that prodigy of a gamekeeper. He argued with himself that his mental faculties must have been dulled by the long day's travel; he had come into the inn jaded and tired; and then, finding himself face to face with an ordinarily alert and intrepid intellect, he had no doubt exaggerated the young man's abilities, and made a wonder of him where no wonder was needed. That he was a person of considerable information and showed common sense was likely enough. Mr. Hodson, in his studies of men and things, had heard something of the intelligence and education to be found among the working classes in Scotland. He had heard of the hand-loom weavers who were learned botanists; of the stonemasons who were great geologists; of the village poets who, if most of their efforts were but imitations of Ferguson and Burns and Tannahill, would here and there, in some chance moment of inspiration, sing out some true and pathetic song, to be taken to the hearts of their countrymen, and added to a treasure store of rustic minstrelsy such as no other nation in the world has ever produced. At the same time he was rather anxious to meet Strang again, the better to get the measure of him. And as he was also curious to see what this neighborhood into which he had penetrated looked like, he rose betimes in the morning—indeed, before the day was fully declared.

The wind still moaned about the house, but outside there was no sign of any storm; on the contrary, everything was strangely calm. The lake lay a dark lurid purple in the hollow of the encircling hills; and these, along the eastern heavens, were of the deepest and softest olive green; just over them was a line of gleaming salmon rod, keen and resplendent as if molten from a furnace; and over that again soft saffron-dusky clouds, deepening in tone the higher they hung in the clear pale steel hues of the overhead sky. There was no sign of life anywhere—nothing but the birch woods sloping down to the shore; the moorland wastes of the lower hills; and above these the giant bulk and solemn shadows of Ben Clebrig,[1] dark against the dawn. It was a lovely sight; he began to think he had never before in his life felt himself so much alone. But whence came the sound of the wind that seemed to go moaning down the strath toward the purple lake?

Well, he made no doubt that it was up toward the north and west that the storm was brewing; and he remembered that a window in the sitting room below looked in that direction; there he would be able to ascertain whether any fishing was practicable. He finished his dressing and went down. The breakfast table was laid; a mighty mass of peats was blazing cheerfully in the spacious fireplace. And the storm? Why, all the wide strath on this northern side of the house was one glow of yellow light in the now spreading sunrise; and still farther away in the north the great shoulders of Ben Loyal[2] had caught a faint roseate tinge; and the same pale and beautiful color seemed to transfuse a large and fleecy cloud that clung around the snow-scarred peak. So he came to the conclusion that in this corner of the glen the wind said more than it meant; and that they might adventure on the loch without risk of being swamped or blown ashore.

The, slim tall Highland lass made her appearance with further plenishings for the table, and "Good moarning!" she said, in her pretty way, in answer to his greeting.

"Say, now, has that man come down from Tongue yet?"

"No, sir," said Nelly, "he wass no come down yet." And then she looked up with a demure smile. "They would be keeping the New Year at Tongue last night."

"Keeping the New Year on the fourteenth of January?"

"It's the twelfth is the usual day, sir," she explained, "but that was Saturday, and they do not like a Saturday night, for they have to stop at twelve o'clock, and so most of them were keeping it last night."

"Oh, indeed. Then the festive gentleman won't show up today?"

"But it is of no matter whateffer whether he comes or no; for I am sure that Ronald will be willing to lend a hand. Oh, I am sure of it. I will ask him myself."

---

[1]That is, the Hill of the Playing Trout.
[2]More properly Ben Laoghal, the Hill of the Calves.

"You will ask him?" was Mr. Hodson's internal soliloquy. "It is to you he will grant a favor. Indeed!"

He fixed his eyes on her.

"He is a good-looking young fellow, that Ronald."

She did not answer that; she was putting the marmalade, and the honey, and the cream on the table.

"He is not married?"

"No, sir."

"Well, now, when he thinks about getting married, I suppose he'll pretty well have his choice about here?"

"Indeed there iss others besides him," said Nelly rather proudly, but her face was red as she opened the door.

Well, whether it was owing to the intervention of Nelly or not, as soon as Mr. Hodson was ready to start he found Ronald waiting for him without; and not only that, but he had already assumed command of the expedition, having sent the one gillie who had arrived down to bale the boat. And then he would overhaul Mr. Hodson's fishing gear—examining the rods, testing the lines and traces, and rejecting all the spoon baits, angels, sand eels, and what not, that had been supplied by the London tackle maker, for two or three of the familiar phantom minnows. Mr. Hodson could scarcely believe that this was the same man who last night had been discussing the disestablishment of state churches and the policy of protecting native industries. He had not a word for anything but the business before him; and the bold fashion in which he handled those minnows, all bristling with hooks, or drew the catgut traces through his fingers (Mr. Hodson shivered and seemed to feel his own fingers being cut to the bone), showed that he was as familiar with the loch as with the hillside or the kennel.

"I'm not much on salmon-fishing myself," the American remarked modestly.

"It's rather early in the season, sir, I'm afraid," was the answer. "But we might get a fish after all; and if we do it'll be the first caught in Scotland this year, I warrant."

They set out and walked down to the shore of the loch, and there Mr. Hodson seated himself on the gunwale of the flat-bottomed coble and watched the two men putting the rods together and fixing the traces. The day had now declared itself; wild and stormy in appearance, but fair on the whole; great floods of sunshine falling suddenly on the yellow slopes and the russet birch woods; and shadows coming as rapidly across the far heights of Clebrig, steeping the mountains in gloom. As for the gillie who had been proof against the seductions of keeping the New Year, and who was now down on one knee, biting catgut with his teeth, he was a man as tall and as sallow as Mr. Hodson himself, but with an added expression of intense melancholy and hopelessness. Or was that but temporary?

"Duncan doesna like that boat," Ronald said, glancing at Mr. Hodson.

The melancholy man did not speak, but shook his head gloomily.

"Why?"

As the gillie did not answer, Ronald said, "He thinks there is no luck with that boat."

"That boat?" the gillie said, with an angry look toward the hapless coble. "She has the worst luck of any boat in Sutherland—tam her!" he added, under his breath.

"In my country," the American said, in his slow way, "we don't mind luck much; we find perseverance about as good a horse to win with in the end."

He was soon to have his perseverance tried. Everything being ready, they pushed off from the shore, Ronald taking stroke oar, the gillie at the bow, Mr. Hodson left to pay out the lines of the two rods, and fix these in the stern, when about five-and-thirty yards had gone forth. At first, it is true, he waited and watched with a trifle of anxiety. He wanted to catch a salmon; it would be something to write about to his daughter; it would be a new experience for himself. But when time passed and the boat was slowly rowed along the loch at a measured distance from the shore, without any touch of anything coming to make the point of either rod tremble, he rather gave up his hope in that direction, and took to talking with Ronald. After all, it was not salmon fishing alone that had brought him into these wilds.

"I suppose it is really too early in the season," he observed, without much chagrin.

"Rayther," said Ronald.

"Rawther," said the melancholy gillie.

But at that instant something happened that startled every one of them out of their apathy. The top of one of the rods was violently pulled at, and then there was a long shrill yell of the reel.

"There he is, sir! there he is, sir!" Ronald called.

Mr. Hodson made a grab blindly—for he had been looking at the scenery around—at one of the rods. It was the wrong one. But before he knew where he was, Ronald had got hold of the other and raised the top so as to keep a strain on the fish. The exchange of the rods was effected in a moment. Then when Ronald had wound in the other line and put the rod at the bow, he took to his oar again, leaving Mr. Hodson to fight his unknown enemy as best he might, but giving him a few words of direction from time to time, quietly, as if it were all a matter of course.

"Reel in, sir, reel in—keep an even strain on him—let him go—let him go if he wants—"

Well, the fish was not a fierce fighter; after the first long rush he scarcely did anything; he kept boring downward, with a dull, heavy weight. It seemed easy work; and Mr. Hodson—triumphant in the hope of catching his first salmon—was tempted to call aloud to the melancholy gillie, "Well, Duncan, how about luck now?"

"I think it's a kelt," the man answered morosely.

But the sinister meaning of this reply was not understood.

"I don't know what you call him," said Mr. Hodson, holding on with both hands to the long, lithe grilse rod that was bent almost double. "Celt or Saxon, I don't know; but I seem to have got a good grip of him."

Then he heard Ronald say, in an undertone, to the gillie, "A kelt? No fears. The first rush was too heavy for that."

And the gillie responded sullenly, "He's following the boat like a cow."

"What is a kelt, anyway?" the American called out. "Something that swims, I suppose? It ain't a man?"

"I hope it's no a kelt, sir," said Ronald—but doubtfully. "But what is a kelt, then, when he's at home?"

"A salmon, sir, that hasna been down to the sea; we'll have to put him back if he is."

Whirr! went the reel again; the fish, kelt or clean salmon, had struck deep down. But the melancholy creature at the bow was taking no further interest in the fight. He was sure it was a kelt. Most likely the minnow would be destroyed. Maybe he would break the trace. But a kelt it was. He knew the luck of this "tammed" boat.

The struggle was a tedious one. The beast kept boring down with the mere force of its weight, but following the coble steadily; and even Ronald, who had been combating his own doubts, at length gave in: he was afraid it was a kelt. Presently the last suspicion of hope was banished. With a tight strain on him, the now exhausted animal began to show near the surface of the water—his long eel-like shape and black back revealing too obviously what manner of creature he was. But this revelation had no effect on the amateur fisherman, who at last beheld the enemy he had been fighting with so long. He grew quite excited. A kelt?—he was a beautiful fine fish! If he could not be eaten he could be stuffed! Twenty pounds he was, if an ounce!—would he throw back such a trophy into the loch?

Ronald was crouching in the stern of the boat, the big landing net in his hand, watching the slow circling of the kelt as it was being hauled nearer and nearer. His sentiments were of a different kind.

"Ah, you ugly brute!—ah, you rascal—ah—ah!"—and then there was a deep scoop of the landing net; and the next minute the huge eel-like beast was in the bottom of the boat, Duncan holding on to its tail, and Ronald gripping it by the gills, while he set to work to get the minnow out of its jaws. And then without further ado—and without stopping to discuss the question of stuffing—the creature was heaved into the water again, with a parting benediction of "Bah, you brute!" It took its leave rapidly.

"Well, it's a pity, sir," Ronald said; "that would have been a twenty-four-pound salmon if he had been down to the sea."

"It's the luck of this tammed boat," Duncan said gloomily.

But Mr. Hodson could not confess to any such keen sense of disappointment. He had never played so big a fish before, and was rather proud that so slight a grilse rod and so slender a line should (of course, with some discretion and careful nursing on his part) have overmastered so big a beast. Then, he did not eat salmon; there was no loss in that direction. And as he had not injured the kelt in any way, he reflected that he had enjoyed half an hour's excitement without doing harm to anything or anybody, and he was well content. So he paid out the two lines again, and set the rods, and began to renew his talk with Ronald touching the customs connected with the keeping of the New Year.

After all, it was a picturesque kind of occupation, kelts or no kelts. Look at the scene around them—the lapping waters of the loch, a vivid and brilliant blue when the skies were shining fair, or black and stormy again when the clouds were heavy in the heavens; and always the permanent features of the landscape—the soft yellows of the lower straths, where the withered grass was mixed with the orange bracken; the soft russet of the leafless birch woods fringing the shores of the lake; the deep-violet shadows of Ben Clebrig stretching up into the long swaths of mist; and then the fair amphitheater of hills—Ben Hee, and Ben Hope, and Ben Loyal—with sunlight and shade intermingling their ethereal tints, but leaving the snow streaks always sparkling and clear. He got used to the monotony of the slow circling of the upper waters of the lake. He forgot to watch the points of the rods. He was asking all kinds of questions about the stags and the hinds, about ptarmigan, and white hare, and roe, about the price of sheep, the rents of crofts, the comparative wages of gillies, and shepherds, and foresters, and keepers, and stalkers, and the habits and customs of land agents and factors. And at length, when it came to lunchtime, and when they landed and found for him a sheltered place under the lee of a big rock, and when Ronald pointed out to him a grassy bank, and said rather ruefully—

"I dinna like to see that place empty, sir. That's where the gentlemen have the salmon laid out, that they may look at them at lunchtime—" Mr. Hodson, as he opened the little basket that had been provided for him, answered cheerfully enough—

"My good friend, don't you imagine that I feel like giving it up yet. I'm not finished with this lake, and I'll back perseverance against luck any day. Seems to me we've done very well so far; I'm content."

By and by they went back into the coble again and resumed their patient pursuit; and there is little doubt that by this time Ronald had come to the conclusion that this stranger who had come among them was a singularly odd and whimsical person.

It was remarkable enough that he should have undertaken this long and solitary journey in order to fish for salmon, and then show himself quite indifferent as to whether he got any or not; and it was scarcely human for anyone to betray no disappointment whatever when the first fish caught proved to be a kelt; but it was still stranger than man rich enough to talk about renting a deer forest should busy himself with the petty affairs of the very poorest people around. Why, he wanted to know how much Nelly the housemaid could possibly save on her year's wages; whether she was supposed to lay by something as against her wedding day; or whether any of the lads about would marry her for her pretty face alone. And when he discovered that Mr. Murray, the innkeeper, was about to give a New Year supper and dance to the lads and lasses of the neighborhood, he made no scruple about hinting plainly that he would be glad of an invitation to join that festive party.

"Not if I'm going to be anything of a wet blanket," he said candidly. "My dancing days are over, and I'm not much in the way of singing; but I'll tell them an American story; or I'll present them with a barrel of whisky—if that will keep the fun going."

"I'm sure they'll be very glad, sir," Ronald said, "if ye just come and look on. When there's gentlemen at the Lodge, they generally come down to hear the pipes, and the young gentlemen have a dance too."

"What night did you say?"

"Monday next, sir."

Well, he had only intended remaining here for a day or two, to see what the place was like; but this temptation was too great. Here was a famous opportunity for the pursuit of his favorite study the study of life and manners. This, had Ronald but known it, was the constant and engrossing occupation that enabled this contented traveler to accept with equanimity the ill luck of kelt catching; it was a hobby he could carry about with him everywhere; it gave a continuous interest to every hour of his life. He cared little for the analyses of science; he cared less for philosophical systems; metaphysics he laughed at; but men and women—the problems of their lives and surroundings, their diverse fortunes and aspirations and dealings with each other—that was the one and constant subject that engrossed his interest. No doubt there was a little more than this; it was not merely as an abstract study that he was so fond of getting to know how people lived. The fact was that, even after having made ample provision for his family, he still remained possessed of a large fortune; his own expenditure was moderate; and he liked to go about with the consciousness that here or there, as occasion served, he could play the part of a little Providence. It was a harmless vanity; moreover, he was a shrewd man, not likely to be deceived by spurious appeals for charity. Many was the young artist whom he had introduced to buyers; many the young clerk whom he had helped to a better situation; more than one young woman in the humblest of circumstances had suddenly found herself enabled to purchase her wedding outfit (with a trifle over, toward the giving her greater value in her lover's eyes), through the mysterious benevolence of some unknown benefactor. This man had been brought up in a country where everyone is restlessly pushing forward; and being possessed of abundant means, and a friendly disposition, it seemed the most natural thing in the world that here or there, at a fitting opportunity, he should lend a helping hand. And there was always this possibility present to him—this sense of power—as he made those minute inquiries of his into the conditions of the lives of those among whom he chanced to be living.

The short winter day was drawing to a close; the brilliant steely blue of the driven water had given place to a livid gray; and the faint gleams of saffron yellow were dying out in the western skies.

"Suppose we'd better be going home now," Mr. Hodson remarked at a venture, and with no great disappointment in his tone.

"I'm afraid, sir, there's no much chance now," Ronald said.

"We must call again; they're not at home today," the other remarked, and began with much complacency to reel in one of the lines. He was doing so slowly, and the men were as slowly pulling in for the shore in the gathering dusk, when whirr! went the other reel. The loud and sudden shriek in this silence was a startling thing; and no less so was the springing into the air—at apparently an immense distance away— of some creature, kelt or salmon, that fell into the water again with a mighty splash. Instinctively Mr. Hodson had gripped this rod and passed the other one he had been reeling in to Strang. It was an anxious moment. Whirr! went another dozen yards of line; and again the fish sprang into the air—this time plainly visible.

"A clean fish, sir! a clean fish!" was the welcome cry.

But there was no time to hazard doubts or ask questions; this sudden visitor at the end of the line had not at all made up his mind to be easily captured. First of all he came sailing in quietly toward the boat, giving the fisherman all he could do to reel in and keep a strain on him; then he whirled out the line so suddenly that the rod was nearly bent double; and then, in deep water, he kept persistently sulking and boring, refusing to yield an inch. This was a temporary respite.

"Well, now, is this one all right?" Mr. Hodson called out—but he was rather bewildered, for he knew not what this violent beast might not be after next, and the gathering darkness looked strange, the shadows of Clebrig overhead seeming to blot out the sky.

"A clean fish, sir," was the confident answer.

"No doubt o' that, sir," even the melancholy Duncan admitted; for he foresaw a dram now, if not a tip in actual money.

Then slowly and slowly the salmon began to yield to the strain on him—which was considerable, for this was the heavier of the two rods—and quickly the line was got in, the pliant curve of the rod remaining always the same; while Mr. Hodson flattered himself that he was doing very well now, and that he was surely becoming the master of the situation. But the next instant something happened that his mind was not rapid enough to comprehend: something dreadful and horrible and sudden: there was a whirring out of the reel so rapid that he had to lower the point of the rod almost to the water; then the fish made one flashing spring along the surface—and this time he saw the creature, a gleam of silver in the dusk—and then, to his unspeakable dismay and mortification, he felt the line quite slack. He did utter a little monosyllable.

"He's off, sir," the melancholy gillie said in a tone of sad resignation. "Not a bit, sir, not a bit! Reel in, quick!" Ronald called to him; and the fisherman had sense enough to throw the rod as far back as he could to see if there was yet some strain on it. Undoubtedly the fish was still there. Moreover, this last cantrip seemed to have taken the spirit out of him. By and by, with a strong, steady strain on him, he suffered himself to be guided more and more toward the boat, until, now and again, they could see a faint gleam in the dark water; and now Ronald had relinquished his oar and was crouching down in the stern—this time not with the landing net in his hand, but with the bright steel clip just resting on the gunwale.

"He's showing the white feather now, sir; give him a little more of the butt."

However, he had not quite given in yet; each time he came in sight of the boat he would make another ineffectual rush, but never getting down deeper than three or four yards. And then, with a short line and the butt well toward him, he began to make slow semicircles this way and that; and always he was being steadily hauled nearer the coble; until with one quick dip and powerful upward pull Ronald had got him transfixed on the gaff and landed—the huge, gleaming, beautiful silver creature!—in the bottom of the boat.

"Well done, sir!—a clean fish—a beauty—the first caught in Scotland this year, I know!"—these were the exclamations he heard now; but he scarcely knew how it had all happened, for he had been more excited than he was aware of. He felt a vague and general sense of satisfaction; wanted to give the men a glass of whisky, and had none to give them; thought that the capture of a salmon was a noble thing; would have liked his daughter Carry to hear the tidings at once; and had a kind of general purpose to devote the rest of that year to salmon fishing in the Highlands. From this entrancement he was awakened by a dispute between the two men as to the size of the fish.

"He's twelve pounds, and no more," the melancholy Duncan said, eying him all over.

"Look at his shoulders, man," Ronald rejoined. "Fourteen pounds if he's an ounce. Duncan, lad, ye've been put off your guessing by the sight of the kelt."

"He's a good fish whateffer," Duncan was constrained to admit—for he still foresaw that prospect of a dram when they returned to the inn, with perhaps a more substantial handseling of good luck.

Of course, they could do no more fishing that afternoon, for it was nearly dark; but it was wonderful how the capture of this single salmon seemed to raise the spirits of the little party as they got ashore and walked home. There was a kind of excitement in the evening air. They talked in a rapid and eager way—about what the fish had done, what were the chances of such and such a rush, the probable length of time it had been up from the sea, the beauty of its shape, the smallness of its head, the freshness of its color, and so forth—and there was a kind of jubilation abroad. The first fish caught in Scotland that year!—of course, it must be packed forthwith and sent south to his daughter Carry and her friends. And Mr. Hodson was quite facetious with the pretty Nelly when she came in to lay the table for dinner, and would have her say whether she had not yet fixed her mind on one or other of these young fellows around. As for the small hamlet of Inver-Mudal, it was about as solitary and forlorn a habitation as any to be found in the wilds of northern Scotland; and he was there all by himself; but with the blazing peat fire, and the brilliant white cloth on the dinner table, and the consciousness that the firm, stout-shouldered, clean-run fourteen-pounder was lying in the dairy on a slab of cold stone, he considered that Inver-Mudal was a most enjoyable and sociable and comfortable place, and that he had not felt himself so snug and so much at home for many and many a day.

Three Bottles of Claret

W. C. PRIME

It had been a delicious afternoon on Profile Lake; one of those days when the very glory of the other country seems to come down among our mountains. The little lake had presented, as usual on such evenings, a gay and brilliant scene. It was a lake of Paradise. A dozen boats were out with parties of ladies or with anglers, some of the latter fishing with floats and worms, some casting flies, and now and then getting up fair trout. I had passed the time after a fashion that is somewhat lazy and luxurious, lying at full length in the bottom of my boat, drifting idly around while I read an old book, occasionally sinking into a doze and dreaming. As evening came down the various parties left the lake, and at last in the twilight Dupont came up in his boat alongside of mine, and we found ourselves, as often before, alone on the lake.

Among all my memories of trout fishing there are none more pleasant than the memories of those evenings on Profile Lake, when my friend and I, with our boats at anchor a few rods apart, have cast our flies long after the darkness prevented our seeing their fall, and whether we got rises or not were content to see the stars come over the mountains, or the moonlight descend into the ravine and silver the surface of the lake.

This evening was profoundly still; not a breath of air disturbed the leaf of a tree. One could hardly hope to find a Profile Lake trout so foolish as to take a fly on such a glassy surface. I was lazy and indolent, but Dupont was making long and steady casts, always graceful, and as sure as graceful. I paused and watched him. I could just see in the twilight the fall of his tail fly, some fifty feet away from his hand, as it touched the water close inshore under a great rock, and I felt in my own arm the thrill which was in his as I saw the slightest commotion on the surface, and knew that a good fish had risen and "sucked in" the fly without striking it. It was a very pretty contest then, with his light Norris rod and a fish that would weigh over a pound. The silence was profound. No sound on water or land or in the air. Few night birds are heard in our forests thereabouts, and in the cool evenings the insects are still. So I looked on while he patiently wearied and landed his fish—a good size for this overfished lake, where the trout have little chance to grow large. It is in some respects the most wonderful trout pond I have ever known. In the rush of travel hundreds of men and boys, and many ladies, take trout here every summer. Few days in July and August see less than ten or fifteen rods on the lake. We have estimated an annual catch of at least three thousand trout in this small pond, and the supply seems equally great each year. This is largely due to the protection of the smaller pond above the lake, which is the breeding place, and where no fishing is permitted.

I had taken nothing. In fact, I had not made a dozen casts. But now I began to work, laying the flies away in the shoal water near the inlet. It is the advantage of fly fishing that one can cover so large a space of water without moving position. It is an easy matter in still weather to whip every inch of a circle of a hundred and fifty feet diameter.

The fisherman who tries the water of a new lake, uncertain whether there be any trout in it, should, if possible, cast at evening near an inlet. He will often find the largest trout in water not over six inches deep. It is probable that at this hour of the day the large trout are on the feed, and seek near the inlet the smaller fish as well as insects. I remember an evening in Northern New Hampshire, when Dupont and myself took twenty-seven trout between sunset and an hour after dark, every one of which weighed over two pounds, and every one took the fly in water about ten inches deep. There was a brilliant full moon that night, and they rose later than usual. An old Adirondack guide has frequently told me that in those waters large trout rise freely to the fly between one and three o'clock in the morning. I have never been able to verify his saying, for I have never loved fishing well enough to toil all night at it as did the apostles, nor to get out of bed very long before day. I have, however, not infrequently cast for a half hour before the dawn on water where trout were abundant, and I never got a rise until day was fairly shining. But I am not willing to place my limited experience against the assertion of the guide, backed as it was by the statement of sportsmen that they had known him to go out of camp at midnight and return before daylight with a load of trout. In some of the streams of the Pacific coast I have been told trout are taken with bait at all hours of the night in streams where one is seldom taken in daylight. All this goes to the question whether fish sleep, a question not yet satisfactorily answered.

I could not provoke a rise, and it grew dark apace. I threw my line back for a long cast. It was very near being a case of broken rod, for there was a sharp jerk as the flies went through the air, the line came in all in a heap, and something fell into the water close to the boat. I picked up the slack and hauled in—a bat. The wretch had taken a small black gnat, and the hook was in his throat. So much for casting a fly in the dark. It was the last cast I made that evening. We went. ashore and strolled up the dark road to the hotel.

The windows blazed their light into the gloom of the Notch, making a strange contrast to the darkness of the forest road from which we emerged. The sound of the music in the drawing room drove all forest ideas out of one's head. It was nine o'clock, and the dancing had begun. The Profile House is a small world in the midst of the mountain solitudes. Including guests and persons employed about the house, there were nearly eight hundred men, women, and children there that night, and every station in life was represented.

Have I anywhere in these sketches mentioned my old friend, Major Wilson? He was sometimes one of our group at the Rookery in years past, but since he had grown to full age he seldom ventured far from his own dinner table. Why should he, since he esteemed it the main luxury of life? Do not imagine him a useless man, a mere bon vivant. He was a hearty old man, a patron of art, and very generous withal. A man is none the worse for loving a good dinner. Gastronomy is as much one of the fine arts as trout-fishing or sculpture. It is very depraved taste which despises good cookery. Table decoration, furniture, and provision form almost the only safe standard by which to estimate national or individual civilization; for civilization is not, as some people imagine, a question of morals or religion. Christianity is not synonymous with civilization; neither does its introduction civilize a nation. It deals with the individual man, not with communities. Men call New York a Christian city, England a Christian country, the people of the United States a Christian people. This is pure nonsense. There are not more than one in ten, perhaps not more than one in a hundred, of the people who are in any proper sense Christians; whose morals, manners, or characters have been directly touched by the refining influences of personal Christianity. Obviously the influence and example of the Christian has its effect on his companions, but that is no reason for calling a people Christian who have only a small sprinkling of Christians among them. Nor can we stand a comparison with some heathen nations. Christianity cannot afford to be saddled with the absurd and barbarous customs of our social life, or with the manners and customs of so-called Christian peoples, especially when it appears that the civilization of Japan is in many respects in advance of that of England or America. We have innumerable habits and manners which are barbarous. The dress of a gentleman or of a lady in New York in this year 1873 is barbarous, whether regarded by standards of taste, comfort, or usefulness. A dress coat was no more absurd a costume on the West Coast African, who wore nothing else, than it is on the diner-out of New York. A stovepipe hat is so thoroughly ridiculous that no barbarous nation has ever invented anything remotely resembling it.

Seek a standard where you will, and, after all, it will be found that the manner and matter of feeding is a tolerably safe one by which to measure comparative civilization.

The Major had been a week or two at the Profile House, living at his ease, and rather content with the table, which was not by any means a poor one, and solaced for any minor failures by his own wine. He did not wander much among the mountains, but contented himself, book in hand, with the sunshine on the broad piazza, and evenings in his own rooms, where his man John, who had been his personal servant more than thirty years, took care to make him comfortable. His rooms were near mine, and that evening after Dupont and myself had dined—for I make it dinner however late the coming home occurs—I went to see the Major.

One can be very comfortable in a summer hotel if he will take a little trouble and go to a little expense. One cannot be comfortable at any summer hotel in America or the world without these. The rooms of my friend were two ordinary bedrooms, one of which he used as a salon; and by a very little exertion it had been made into a cozy and rather brilliant room. The table was literally covered with books and periodicals, for the Major had a hunger for reading which could never be satisfied, and every mail brought him packages. He was tearing off the envelope from an Innsbruck book catalogue as I entered the room, and I recognized the label of an old acquaintance.

"So you get catalogues from Carl Pfaundler, do you? I have picked up some good things in his shop."

"Yes. I have a pretty extensive list of booksellers sending me their catalogues, but it's getting to be rather a nuisance. I've about done with buying old books. Come in; find a chair—John, a chair—help yourself to the claret. You dined late, I fancy. Did you get me a good trout for breakfast?"

"Not a trout. I took a bat on the wing. Did you ever eat bat?"

"Never. I suppose it would be about the same thing as mice. Mice are not good; the flavor is musky. Rats are much better, and very decent eating, if they are properly fed. I don't know why bats might not be made eatable. They are carnivorous; but dogs are good food, if well cooked. However, we don't need to try experiments in this land, where the markets are better than in any other country on earth."

"I'm glad to hear you say that, Major. I have said it often, and it's pleasant to be backed by a man of your gastronomic taste."

"Who disputes it? Surely no one who knows anything about eating. There are articles, of course, which are to be found in other countries superior to the same article here; but America is the only land for general good eating. One gets fearfully tired of a European kitchen, even with all the resources of Paris in the palmiest days of the Brothers. But here the varieties of fish and flesh are inexhaustible; and fruit—nowhere in the world is there a fruit market comparable with that of New York. An English sole is not equal in flavor to a flounder taken in clear water at Stonington, and a turbot is no better than a tautog. Shad, sheepshead, Spanish mackerel, red snappers, bass, bluefish—a fresh bluefish is glorious—where will you stop in the list of fish that abound on our coast, every one of which is better than any salt-water fish known on the other side of the Atlantic?"

"Excepting sardines."

"Well, I may perhaps except sardines."

"May? None of your prejudices, old fellow. There's no dish of fish to be invented equal to sardines, fried and served as they used to do it in the old San Marco at Leghorn. I lament the closing of that house with profound regret. I have gone down from Florence more than once to pass a night there just for the sake of the delicious breakfast I used to get on those sardines. No one else cooked or served them so in any town on the French or Italian coast."

"I remember fifty years ago seeing them catch sardines along the shore at Naples."

"Yes, I have sat many a morning in the window at the old Vittoria, looking out on the sea and watching the sardine nets come in, glittering with diamonds; and I have taken them with a rod at Leghorn." "I never found trout south of the Alps. Why is that?"

"Simply because you never looked for them yourself. The hotels rarely furnish them; but you can get them in Lombardy if you want them. I have taken trout in the Izak above Trent, and at Botzen."

"My dear boy, what a muddle your brain must be in about historic places. The idea of talking about trout fishing at Trent, a place with which one never associated any idea but of profound ecclesiastical and theological significance."

"There's a charm in trout fishing, Major, which you would have appreciated if your education had not been neglected. It has never failed me; and I have studied no small amount of history as I strolled along the bank of a trout stream. Were you ever at Salzburg?"

"There several times, and always fared well at the Hotel de l'Europe."

"Ah yes, you think first of the hotel. So do many old travelers. So I confess do I sometimes. A poor inn is a fearful obstacle to the enjoyment of art or antiquity. But there are trout streams around Salzburg, and some fine trout in them; and I have passed some of the pleasantest days along those streams, looking up at the grand pile of the Untersberg, in whose caverns the two emperors sit face to face, sleeping, but now nearly ready to wake. I was fishing there in June, 1871, and wondering what could happen to rouse the mighty Charles, and a month later the thunders of Weissembourg must have shaken the imperial slumbers. But Ischl, Major, Ischl— were you ever at Ischl? It is the most lovely spot in Europe. Go there before you die, and don't go to the Hotel Bauer on the hill, but to Sarsteiner's, the Kreutz, a capital inn, with old books in the halls, and pictures of all sorts of places, and large bedrooms and saloons, and a kitchen that is not to be surpassed in or out of the Tyrol. It will suit you. The valley of the Traun is a glorious place, and the river is the only river my eyes ever saw which is indisputably superior in beauty of water to our White Mountain streams. The delicate apple-green tint does not harm its transparency. You can see bottom in twenty feet of water. It flows like a liquid chrysoprase, and the trout and grayling in it are superb. Mr. Sarsteiner controls all the fishing in the valley, and is himself an angler, a man of reading and extensive travel, and is interested in fish breeding. The fishing is close at hand too. I went out of the house one evening about seven o'clock, and walked in five minutes to the other side of the Traun, just above the bridge and opposite the promenade, where the river glides swiftly down over a pebble bottom. It was nearly dark, but in fifteen minutes I had a half-dozen good trout which the boy stowed safely in a barrel; for in Switzerland and the Tyrol, when you go afishing, you have always with you a boy who carries a small barrel in which it is his duty to keep the fish alive until they are transferred to the tank which every inn keeps stocked with plenty of trout. It had gotten to be quite dark, and I was casting a large white moth across the swift current, when I got the heaviest strike, with one exception, that I ever felt from a trout in Europe. He made a splendid struggle; but the little Norris rod did its duty, and I brought him to barrel in a few minutes—that is to say, I landed and unhooked him, and handed him to the boy while I hurried to cast again. I had made only one cast when the boy shouted, 'He's too big for the barrel'; and I turned to laugh at his vain endeavors to crowd his tail into the hole. He was, in fact, two inches longer than the barrel, which had not been made in expectation of such fish. So I slipped him into his short quarters, and gave up the sport, and in five minutes he was the admiration of a crowd in the kitchen of the Golden Cross, swimming around in a small tank into which cold spring water poured a steady stream. He weighed only two and three quarter pounds English; but Mr. Sarsteiner told me that, though he had seen larger trout there, he was one of the largest, if not the largest, that he had ever known taken with a fly in the Tyrol. All the way up the river to Lake Haldstadt there are plenty of fine trout, and I have enjoyed many a day's sport along the beautiful stream."

"Now for the exception."

"What exception?"

"You said it was the heaviest strike, with one exception, that you ever felt in Europe."

"I'm a little ashamed of that other. You remember the Rhine above the falls, from Schaffhausen to the Chateau Laufen? I was fishing it one evening, years ago, in a boat, with a strong German boy to row. I had to keep a sharp lookout, for the current is wild, and it is not quite sure that, if you are careless, you may not go over the falls. By the by, Major, with all our boasting, we haven't many cataracts in America as fine as the Rhine Falls. It's a grand piece of scenery. It looks better from below than above, however, if you happen to be in a heavy boat with a stupid boy as oarsman. We were just on the edge of the swift water, and I told him to hold on by the bushes and keep the craft steady while I cast. He obeyed, until a tremendous swirl and swash startled him as a trout struck the fly. The rush was so sudden that the boy was absolutely scared, so that he let go the bushes, and the boat swept right across the line at the same instant that the trout went down. My second joint broke close to the butt ferrule, and we went like lightning toward the falls. I dropped my rod to seize an oar, and threw my whole weight on it. The boat yielded, took the cant I intended, and plunged bow on into the bank, where I seized the bushes and held on till the young Teuton came to his senses. Meantime the second joint and tip had gone overboard, and the reel was paying out. I brought in line very gently, and grasping the lower end of the second joint, dropped the butt, and proceeded to try an old and difficult plan of using the hand instead of a reel. As soon as I got in slack enough I felt the fish. He was at the bottom, and made a rush when he felt the first steady pressure of the tip. It took me twenty minutes, with second joint and tip, to kill that trout, well on to four pounds' weight, and the largest I ever killed east of the Atlantic. That same evening I took twenty more trout, and no one of them went over four ounces."

"I am one of the few," said the Major, sipping his claret appreciatively, and then tossing the full glass down his capacious throat, as if to wash a way out for talk—"I am one of the few who once loved angling, but have lost their taste for it. I've been latterly thinking the matter over, and—can you justify yourself in it? Isn't it cruelty to animals? You know these are days in which men are getting to have notions on that subject."

"I've no objection to their notions, and I have the highest opinion of the Society for the Prevention of Cruelty to Animals; but we must guard our sympathies that they do not go too far. No man of decency will be guilty of wanton cruelty to a beast. I have a warm love for some beasts. My dogs, my horses, have I not loved them? But there is much nonsense afloat on the subject. I rate the life of a beast somewhat lower than that of a man, and his comfort in the same ratio. I must often work even when I am sick. Rheumatism bothers me, and I have frequently to walk and even run when I am lame. Yes, perhaps it is gout. We won't discuss that; but lame or not I must work. Business requires it. I would drive a lame horse for the same reason. A poor carman can not afford to let his horse rest, any more than he can afford to rest himself, on account of a slight ailment. It's an error therefore to suppose it always wrong to get work out of a suffering animal. So, too, I would kill a horse to accomplish a result which I valued at a higher rate than the life of the horse, if I could not accomplish it in any other way. Some philanthropists, good men, but thoughtless, who would never dream of blaming a man for earning his bread and that of his children when he was sick and suffering, but would rather commend him, would fine and imprison him for working his sick horse with the same necessity impelling him.

"They should try to make a reasonable distinction in these matters between wanton cruelty and the necessary work that we must get out of a sick animal. I never saw a nobler beast, or one to which I was more thoroughly attached than my bay horse Mohammed; but great as he was and much as I loved him, do you not believe I would have ridden him through fire and tempest till he fell down dead, if it were necessary to save his mistress, who loved him as well as I, a pain or a sorrow? Should I let her suffer to save a horse from suffering? Does your notion of charity extend so far as that? Mine does not. I might give myself pain to save him pain; but her?—Never. Mohammed would have said so too if he could have spoken. I know he would.

"In war this whole subject is understood well, and no one thinks of finding fault with the destruction of the lives of beasts to accomplish the purposes of men; for in war human life is freely expended to purchase results. Who would blame an officer for using his lame, sick, dying mules and horses to the last moment to accomplish an object in the face of the enemy? It is then a mere question with beasts and with men, how much must be sacrificed to do the work. Would you require them to let sick mules rest in hospital, if they had no others?"

"Then you don't approve of stopping cars and omnibuses in New York, and compelling the passengers to dismount and find other conveyances, because the horses are lame?"

"Not at all. It is well meant, but it is bad in principle, and injures the society which does it. It would be right and proper to take a note of the horses and their owners and drivers, and make the necessary complaint in the police court, and if the animals were treated with wanton cruelty punish the guilty. But the time of a passenger is often worth thousands of dollars per minute, and the probability of such value outweighs all considerations of comfort to horses. In the days of the horse disease, when all the cities were suffering, it was both necessary and proper to use sick horses for transportation. It was a pure question of money value then. Shall a merchant allow ten thousand dollars' worth of perishable goods to decay for the sake of saving the health or the comfort of a cart horse? Yet the absurd proposition was forced on the public that it was their duty to sacrifice their own comfort, property, and health to the comfort of the horses. Nonsense. If you had a sick child, would you hesitate to kill a horse if necessary to get a surgeon or a physician in time to save the child's life? If you had a loaded wagon full of perishable articles of great value, would you hesitate to use your lame horses, or kill them if necessary to save your property? Let us teach kindness to animals, men and beasts, and make it infamous to treat them with unnecessary or wanton cruelty; but don't let us get our ideas mixed up on the subject, so that we place the comfort of the beasts above that of the men. For all our purposes the comfort and the life of a beast have a measurable value. The owner is the judge of that value to him."

"But how about killing fish for sport?"

"In the name of sense, man, if God made fish to be eaten, what difference does it make if I enjoy the killing of them before I eat them? You would have none but a fisherman by trade do it, and then you would have him utter a sigh, a prayer, and a pious ejaculation at each cod or haddock that he killed; and if by chance the old fellow, sitting in the boat at his work, should for a moment think there was, after all, a little fun and a little pleasure in his business, you would have him take a round turn with his line, and drop on his knees to ask forgiveness for the sin of thinking there was sport in fishing.

"I can imagine the sad-faced, melancholy-eyed man, who makes it his business to supply game for the market as you would have him, sober as the sexton in Hamlet, and forever moralizing over the gloomy necessity that has doomed him to a life of murder! Why, sir, he would frighten respectable fish, and the market would soon be destitute.

"The keenest day's sport in my journal of a great many years of sport was when, in company with some other gentlemen, I took three hundred bluefish in three hours' fishing off Block Island, and those fish were eaten the same night or the next morning in Stonington, and supplied from fifty to a hundred different tables, as we threw them up on the dock for anyone to help himself. I am unable to perceive that I committed any sin in taking them, or any sin in the excitement and pleasure of taking them.

"It is time moralists had done with this mistaken morality. If you eschew animal food entirely, then you may argue against killing animals, and I will not argue with you. But the logic of this business is simply this: The Creator made fish and flesh for the food of man, and as we can't eat them alive, or if we do we can't digest them alive, the result is we must kill them first, and (see the old rule for cooking a dolphin) it is sometimes a further necessity, since they won't come to be killed when we call them, that we must first catch them. Show first, then, that it is a painful necessity—a necessity to be avoided if possible—which a good man must shrink from and abhor, unless starved into it, to take fish or birds, and which he must do when he does it with regret, and with sobriety and seriousness, as he would whip his child, or shave himself when his beard is three days old, and you have your case. But till you show this, I will continue to think it great sport to supply my market with fish.

"Between ourselves, Major, I am of opinion that Peter himself chuckled a little when he took an extra-large specimen of the Galilee carp, and I have no doubt that he and James, and even the gentle and beloved John, pulled with a will on the miraculous draught of fishes."

"Probably you are right; but I have lost my love for the sport. I can hardly say how it came about with me. I think it was the result of a long illness which I had in my middle life, and from which I recovered slowly, and in such strict confinement that the love of reading grew on me, and other employments lost the zest which I once found in them. I sometimes wonder now how you can read all winter and go afishing all summer as you do. I can't separate myself from my books."

"You are growing quite too bookish of late years, if you will pardon me for saying so, my old friend."

"As how?"

"I mean that you are getting to be dreamy in your manner, and you don't seem to realize the common events of life. You live so much among thoughts and imaginations that you're getting to be quite useless as a companion, except when one wants to talk or listen."

"I haven't lost my appreciation of claret."

"So I perceive."

"Your glass is empty. Help yourself."

"Thanks; I'm doing very well."

"Talking of books and fishing, Effendi, did you ever come across the *Dyalogus Creaturarum*?"

"Yes, I have the Gouda edition of Leeu, 1482 I believe is the date."

"There's a comical little picture of a fisherman in it, illustrating a fabled talk between two fish. I don't know whether there is any older picture of the gentle art in existence, but that is worth noting as a historical illustration, for the angler there uses a float."

"The literature of angling is abundant, and art has always found ample range in its illustration. I have seen a score of pictures of fishing on ancient Egyptian monuments. Many modern artists are enthusiastic anglers. And in what kind of life could they find more of the beautiful? Look at a trout. Is there any object more exquisitely beautiful?"

"Yes, a small rattlesnake."

"Gaudy, Major, and brilliant, but the brilliance of the diamond and ruby compared with the soft glow of the pearl. Do you know these little Pemigewasset trout are so exquisite in their pearl and rose colors that I didn't wonder the other day at the exclamation of a very pretty girl in the chariot on the way to the Flume, when they pulled up by me down the river and asked to see my basket. 'Oh, I want to kiss them,' she said."

"You didn't know her?"

"Never saw her before, or since."

"It was a fresh remark. I like it. I wonder who she was. It's a pleasant thing now and then to hear a bit of nature out of red lips."

"Your experience in the utterances of red lips is rather limited, Major. I was telling you just now that you live too much on books and too little on realities."

"On red lips, for instance?"

"Exactly. An old bachelor like you has great opportunities in life. You might take to fishing even, and perhaps some day, when you have a full basket, a pretty girl may ask you to let her look at the speckled beauties, and then—what might not happen as a consequence?"

"Bah! I've been through it all."

"You?"

"I."

"Fishing and—"

"Red lips—yes. Redder than this blood of the grape, and a thousand times as maddening. What do you boys of these late years fancy you can teach me, either in sports of the forest or loves of the town? I had drunk all the wine of that life up, and the cup was empty before you were born."

The Major was excited, and his dates were evidently confused. But it was refreshing to be called a boy, and I urged him on. He told stories of old sporting days, which proved that he was no idle boaster when he said he had gone through all that. He grew fairly brilliant as he talked.

"I remember," said he, "the very last night I ever passed in the forest. It had been some years then since I had given up my rifle and rod, but an old companion persuaded me to join him in November in Sullivan County, in New York, and I went up the Erie Railroad to Narrowsburg, and struck out into the woods for a ten-mile tramp to our appointed place of meeting. I knew the country as well as you know these mountains, but at evening I had loitered so that instead of being near the cabin of our old guide I was three miles away; darkness was setting down fast, and a heavy snowstorm was evidently coming on. I, who had often said I would never camp out again so long as roofs remained among the inhabitants of earth, found myself wishing for the darkest hole in a rock or a hollow tree. Is it that the ground is not so soft a bed as it used to be, or have we grown harder?

"Night and gloom thickened around me. My eyes, from watching the clouds, retained vision of them longer than one who opened his suddenly at the place and time would have believed possible. The trees had passed through the various shapes and shadows which they assume in the twilight and first darkness. They were grim, tall giants, some standing, some leaning, some fallen prone and lying as they fell, dead and still; and some had gone to dust that lay in long mounds, like the graves of old kings. I kept on, pushing my way steadily, for there was no spot that I could find fit for a resting place, and I had hope of reaching a good point for the night halt by proceeding. I hit on it at length. There was a hill down which I went, tripping at every fourth step, and plunging into indescribable heaps of brush and leaves and stones, until I came out suddenly on the edge of a piece of burnt land, which a fire had gone over last summer. A pile of fallen trees lay on the very border of the unburned forest, and I sought shelter among them from a driving blast, which now brought snow with it in quantities. I faced the tempest a moment, and thought of that passage in which Festus described the angels thronging to Eden and 'alighting like to snowflakes.' I wished that there were more similarity, and that the flakes were fewer and farther between. But there was a terrible reality in the night and storm, which drove poetry from my brain. At this moment I discovered a pile of hemlock bark, gathered by someone to be carried to the tanneries. It was the first indication of this being an inhabited part of the world; but it was no proof that inhabitants were near, for these piles of bark are often gathered in remote parts of the forest. But it was a great discovery. There was enough of it to roof the City Hall; and in fifteen minutes there was as neat a cabin built among the fallen timber as any man could desire under the circumstances. It was artistically built too, for I had built such before; and, by the by, I recollect one which Joe Willis once constructed, in which the chimney arrangements proved unsafe, and we awoke at about daylight among the flames of our entire establishment. True, he laid it to my restlessness in the night, and actually charged me with getting my feet into the fire and scattering the coals, while I dreamed of the immortal—who was it that won immortality by setting fire to the Temple of Diana? But it was false, atrociously false. I was dreaming of—, but let that pass.

"The wind grew furious, and the snow came thicker, finer, and faster, but none reached me as I sat in my shelter, open indeed on one side, but fully protected there by a fire built at a safe distance, which blazed as a pile should blaze that was the funeral pyre of more than one of the forest giants.

"And now the sound of the wind in the forest grew terrible in the grandeur of its harmonies. A lonesome man, far from my fellows, the sole human companion of the storm, the sole human witness of the fury of the tempest, I sat, or lay, half reclined on the heap of brush that I had gathered for a bed, and with my hand screening my face from the intense heat of the fire, looked out into the abyss of darkness, and watched the snowflakes driving from far up down toward the flames, as if they sought instantaneous and glad relief from cold and wretched wanderings; and I wondered whether, of intelligent creatures, I was alone in that wild, grand, and magnificent scene.

"Sometimes I thought I could hear human voices in the lull of the storm; but oftener I imagined that the inhabitants of other worlds were near, and that they were unearthly sounds which were so strange and abrupt and startling; and when I closed my eyes I was certain that, among all the confusion, I could hear the rushing wings of more than ten legions of angels; and in a moment of still calm, one of those awful pauses that occur in furious storms, in the deep, solemn silence I heard a cry, a faint but wild and mournful cry, and it seemed far off, farther than the forest, farther than the opposite mountain, beyond the confines of the world, and the cry grew into a wail—a wail of unutterable anguish, agony, and woe—such a wail as might have been Eve's when the flaming sword flashed between her and Abel; and it came nearer, nearer, nearer, and it filled the air, the sky, the universe it seemed, and thrilled through my soul till I sprang to my feet, and dashed out into the blinding, mad tempest. It was so long since I had heard it, that I had forgotten that voice of the mountain wind; but now I remembered it as the blasts swept by me, wailing, shouting, laughing, shrieking, and I retired to my warm nook, and laughed back at the storm, and slept and dreamed. I never slept better.

"I awoke at daybreak, and the storm was over. A blue break in the clouds let through the light of a November moon, clear, soft, and exceedingly beautiful. Dawn drove the moonlight out of the forest, and I pushed on then and got my breakfast with old Steven in his cabin. I have never slept in the forest since that night. Help yourself to the claret, Effendi. It seems to me it's growing cold. Yes; I have led that life, and liked it well enough once."

"You've told me of your forest experiences, Major, but you rather fight shy of the subject of the red lips."

"I tell you I have tasted the wine of red lips to intoxication; but there were lips that I never touched whose utterances were more intoxicating."

The Major sat looking into the fire; for though it was August we had bright wood fires in the evenings, as we often do at the Profile House. He looked very steadily at the coals on the hearth, shivered once as if he were cold, bolted two glasses of claret in quick succession, and I waited, confident that I should hear his story at last. Soon he began to talk.

"Draw your chair close up. Light another pipe, and fill your glass. It is a cold night. My old bones shudder when I hear the wind wail over the house and through the trees. Capital claret, that! John, come in here. Open another bottle of claret, John. What, not another! Certainly, man, I must have it. This is only the second, and Mr. —— has drank half, of course. Not drank any! You don't mean to say that he has been drinking nothing all the blessed evening? Effendi, I thought you knew my rules better than that. But you always would have your own way.

"One more bottle, John—but one. It shall be the last; and, John, get some Maraschino—one of the thick, black bottles with the small necks, and open it. But you know how, old fellow, and just do your best to make us comfortable.

"How the wind howls! My boy, I am seventy-three years old, and seven days over. My birthday was a week ago today.

"An old bachelor! Yea, verily. One of the oldest kind. But what is age? What is the paltry sum of seventy years? Do you think I am any older in my soul than I was half a century ago? Do you think, because my blood flows slower, that my mind thinks more slowly, my feelings spring up less freely, my hopes are less buoyant, less cheerful, if they look forward only weeks instead of years? I tell you, boy, that seventy years are a day in the sweep of memory; and 'Once young forever young' is the motto of an immortal soul. I know I am what men call old; I know my cheeks are wrinkled like parchment, and my lips are thin, and my head gray even to silver. But in my soul I feel that I am young, and I shall be young till the earthly ceases and the unearthly and eternal begins.

"I have not grown one day older than I was at thirty-two. I have never advanced a day since then. All my life long since that has been one day—one short day; no night, no rest, no succession of hours, events, or thoughts has marked any advance.

"I have been living forty years by the light of one memory—by the side of one grave.

"John, set the bottle down on the hearth. You may go. You need not sit up for me. We will see each other to bed tonight. Go, old fellow, and sleep soundly.

"She was the purest angel that flesh ever imprisoned, the most beautiful child of Eve. I can see her now. Her eyes raying the light of heaven—her brow white, calm, and holy—her lips wreathed with the blessing of her smile. She was as graceful as a form seen in dreams, and she moved through the scenes around her as you have seen the angelic visitors of your slumber move through crowded assemblies, without effort, apparently with some superhuman aid.

"She was fitted to adorn the splendid house in which she was born and grew to womanhood. It was a grand old place, built in the midst of a growth of oaks that might have been there when Columbus discovered America, and seemed likely to stand a century longer. They are standing yet, and the wind tonight makes a wild lament through their branches.

"I recall the scenery of the familiar spot. There was a stream of water that dashed down the rocks a hundred yards from the house, and which kept always full and fresh an acre of pond, over which hung willows and maples and other trees, while on the surface the white blossom of the lotus nodded lazily on the ripples with Egyptian sleepiness and languor.

"The old house was built of dark stone, and had a massive appearance, not relieved by the somber shade in which it stood. The sunshine seldom penetrated to the ground in the summer months, except in one spot, just in front of the library windows, where it used to lie and sleep in the grass, as if it loved the old place. And if sunshine loved it, why should not I?"

The Major's voice faded, his head slowly fell forward.

I left him sitting there, his head bowed on his breast, his eyes closed, his breathing heavy. My own eyes were misty. The mood might never come again. I would never know this story.

In the hall I found John, sitting bolt upright in a large chair. "Why, John, I thought the Major sent you to bed long ago."

"Yes, sir; the Major always sends me to bed at the third bottle, sir, and I always doesn't go. He's been telling the old story, now hasn't he, sir?"

"Yes."

John laid his long black finger knowingly up by the side of his nose and looked at me.

"That story never gets telled."

"Why, John—you don't mean to say—eh?"

"All the claret, sir?"

"John, my man, go in and take care of him. He is either asleep or drunk. Curious, that! Why didn't I think that a man was hardly to be believed after the second bottle, and perfectly incredible on the third."

It would be difficult to describe all that I dreamed about that night.

Ol' Settler of Deep Hole

IRVING BACHELLER

Uncle Eb was a born lover of fun. But he had a solemn way of fishing that was no credit to a cheerful man. It was the same when he played the bass viol, but that was also a kind of fishing at which he tried his luck in a roaring torrent of sound. Both forms of dissipation gave him a serious look and manner, that came near severity. They brought on his face only the light of hope and anticipation the shadow of disappointment.

We had finished our stent early the day of which I am writing. When we had dug our worms and were on our way to the brook with pole and line a squint of elation hold of Uncle Eb's face. Long wrinkles deepened as he looked into the sky for a sign of the weather, and then relaxed a bit as he turned his eyes upon the smooth sward. It was no time for idle talk. We tiptoed over the leafy carpet of the woods. Soon as I spoke he lifted his hand with a warning "Sh-h!" The murmur of the stream was in our ears. Kneeling on a mossy knoll we baited the hooks; then Uncle Eb beckoned to me.

I came to him on tiptoe.

"See thet there foam 'long side o' the big log?" he whispered, pointing with his finger.

I nodded.

"Cre-e-ep up jest as ca-a-areful as ye can," he went on whispering. "Drop in a leetle above an' let 'er float down."

Then he went on, below me, lifting his feet in slow and stealthy strides.

He halted by a bit of drift wood and cautiously threw in, his arm extended, his finger alert. The squint on his face took a firmer grip. Suddenly his pole gave a leap, the water splashed, his line sang in the air and fish went up like a rocket. As we were looking into the tree tops it thumped the shore beside him, quivered a moment and flopped down the bank. He scrambled after it and went to his knees in the brook coming up empty handed. The water was slopping out of his boot legs.

"Whew!" said he, panting with excitement as I came over to him. "Reg'lar ol' he one," he added, looking down at his boots. "Got away from me—consarn him! Hed a leetle too much power in the arm."

He emptied his boots, baited up and went back to his fishing. As I looked up at him he stood leaning over the stream jiggling his hook. In a moment I saw a tug at the line. The end of his pole went under water like a flash. It bent double as Uncle Eb gave it a lift. The fish began to dive and rush. The line cut the water in a broad semicircle and then went far and near with long, quick slashes. The pole nodded and writhed like a thing of life. Then Uncle Eb had a look on him that is one of the treasures of my memory. In a moment the fish went away with such a violent rush, to save him, he had to throw his pole into the water.

"Heavens an' airth!" he shouted, "the ol' settler!"

The pole turned quickly and went lengthwise into the rapids. He ran down the bank and I after him. The pole was speeding through the swift water. We scrambled over logs and through bushes, but the pole went faster than we. Presently it stopped and swung around. Uncle Eb went splashing into the brook. Almost within reach of the pole he dashed his foot upon a stone falling headlong in the current. I was close upon his heels and gave him a hand. He rose hatless, dripping from head to foot and pressed on. He lifted his pole. The line clung to a snag and then gave way; the tackle was missing. He looked at it silently, tilting his head. We walked slowly to the shore. Neither spoke for a moment.

"Must have been a big fish," I remarked.

"Powerful!" said he, chewing vigorously on his quid of tobacco as he shook his head and looked down at his wet clothing. "In a desp'rit fix ain't I?"

"Too bad!" I exclaimed.

"Seldom ever hed sech a disapp'intment," he said. "Ruther counted on ketchin' thet fish—he was s' well hooked!"

He looked longingly at the water a moment. "If I don't go hum," said he, "an' keep my mouth shet I'll say sumthin' I'll be sorry fer."

He was never quite the same after that. He told often of his struggle with this unseen, mysterious fish and I imagined he was a bit more given to reflection. He had had hold of the "ol' settler of Deep Hole,"—a fish of great influence and renown there in Faraway. Most of the local fishermen had felt him tug at the line one time or another. No man had ever seen him for the water was black in Deep Hole. No fish had ever exerted a greater influence on the thought, the imagination, the manners or the moral character of his contemporaries. Tip Taylor always took off his hat and sighed when he spoke of the "ol' settler." Ransom Walker said he had once seen his top fin and thought it longer than a razor. Ransom took to idleness and chewing tobacco immediately after his encounter with the big fish, and both vices stuck to him as long as he lived. Everyone had his theory of the "ol' settler." Most agreed he was a very heavy trout. Tip Taylor used to say that in his opinion " 'Twas nuthin' more'n a plain, overgrown, common sucker," but Tip came from the Sucker Brook country where suckers lived in colder water and were more entitled to respect.

Mose Tupper had never had his hook in the "ol' settler" and would believe none of the many stories of adventure at Deep Hole that had thrilled the township.

"Thet fish hes made s' many liars 'round here ye dunno who t' b'lieve," he had said at the corners one day, after Uncle Eb had told his story of the big fish. "Somebody 't knows how t' fish hed oughter go 'n ketch him fer the good o' the town—thet's what I think."

Now Mr. Tupper was an excellent man but his incredulity was always too bluntly put. It had even led to some ill feeling.

He came in at our place one evening with a big hook and line from "down east"—the kind of tackle used in salt water.

"What ye goin' t' dew with it?" Uncle Eb inquired. "Ketch thet fish ye talk s' much about—goin' t' put him out o' the way."

" 'Taint fair," said Uncle Eb, "it's leading a pup with a log chain."

"Don't care," said Mose, "I'm goin' t' go fishin' t'morer. If there reely is any sech fish—which I don't believe there is—I'm goin' t' rassle with him an' mebbe tek him out o' the river. Thet fish is sp'ilin' the moral character o' this town. He oughter be rode on a rail—thet fish hed."

How he would punish a trout in that manner Mr. Tupper failed to explain, but his metaphor was always a worse fit than his trousers and that was bad enough.

It was just before haying and, there being little to do, we had also planned to try our luck in the morning. When, at sunrise, we were walking down the cow path to the woods I saw Uncle Eb had a coil of bed cord on his shoulder.

"What's that for?" I asked.

"Wall," said he, "goin' t' hev fun anyway. If we can't ketch one thing we'll try another."

We had great luck that morning and when our basket as near full we came to Deep Hole and made ready for a swim in the water above it. Uncle Eb had looped an end of bed cord and tied a few pebbles on it with bits of string.

"Now," said he presently, "I want t' sink this loop t' the bottom an' pass the end o' the cord under the drift wood t we can fetch it 'crost under water."

There was a big stump, just opposite, with roots running down the bank into the stream. I shoved the line under the drift with a pole and then hauled it across where Uncle Eb drew it up the bank under the stump roots.

"In 'bout half an hour I cal'late Mose Tupper 'll be 'long," he whispered. "Wisht ye'd put on yer clo's an' lay here back o' the stump an' hold on t' the cord. When ye feel a bite give a yank er two an' haul in like Sam Hill—fifteen feet er more quicker'n scat. Snatch his pole right away from him. Then lay still."

Uncle Eb left me, shortly, going up stream. It was near an hour before I heard them coming. Uncle Eb was talking in a low tone as they came down the other bank.

"Drop right in there," he was saying, "an' let her drag down, through the deep water, deliberate like. Git clus t' the bottom."

Peering through a screen of bushes I could see an eager look on the unlovely face of Moses. He stood leaning toward the water and jiggling his hook along the bottom. Suddenly I saw Mose jerk and felt the cord move. I gave it a double twitch and began to pull. He held hard for a jiffy and then stumbled and let go yelling like mad. The pole hit the water with a splash and went out of sight like a diving frog. I brought it well under the foam and drift wood. Deep Hole resumed its calm, unruffled aspect. Mose went running toward Uncle Eb.

"'S a whale!" he shouted. "Ripped the pole away quicker'n lightnin'."

"Where is it?" Uncle Eb asked.

"Tuk it away f' me," said Moses. "Grabbed it jes' like thet," he added with a violent jerk of his hand.

"What d' he dew with it?" Uncle Eb inquired.

Mose looked thoughtfully at the water and scratched his head, his features all a tremble.

"Dunno," said he. "Swallered it mebbe."

"Mean t' say ye lost hook, line, sinker 'n pole?"

"Hook, line, sinker 'n pole," he answered mournfully. "Come nigh haulin' me in tew."

"'Taint possible," said Uncle Eb.

Mose expectorated, his hands upon his hips, looking down at the water.

"Wouldn't eggzac'ly say 'twas possible," he drawled, "but 'twas a fact."

"Yer mistaken," said Uncle Eb.

"No I haint," was the answer, "I tell ye I see it."

"Then if ye see it the nex' thing ye orter see 's a doctor. There's sumthin' wrong with you sumwheres."

"Only one thing the matter o' me," said Mose with a little twinge of remorse. "I'm jest a natural born perfect durn fool. Never c'u'd b'lieve there was any sech fish."

"Nobody ever said there was any sech fish," said Uncle Eb. "He's done more t' you 'n he ever done t' me. Never served me no sech trick as thet. If I was you I'd never ask nobody t' b'lieve it. 'S a leetle tew much."

Mose went slowly and picked up his hat. Then he returned to the bank and looked regretfully at the water.

"Never see the beat o' thet," he went on. "Never see sech power 'n a fish. Knocks the spots off any fish I ever hearn of."

"Ye riled him with that big tackle o' yourn," said Uncle Eb. "He wouldn't stan' it."

"Feel jest as if I'd hed holt uv a wil' cat," said Mose. "Tuk the hull thing—pole an' all—quicker 'n lightnin'. Nice a bit o' hickory as a man ever see. Gol' durned if I ever heern o' the like o' that, ever."

He sat down a moment on the bank.

"Got t' rest a minute," he remarked. "Feel kind o' wopsy after thet squabble."

They soon went away. And when Mose told the story of "the swallered pole" he got the same sort of reputation he had given to others. Only it was real and large and lasting.

"What d' ye think uv it?" he asked, when he had finished.

"Wall," said Ransom Walker, "wouldn't want t' right out plain t' yer face."

"'Twouldn't be p'lite," said Uncle Eb soberly.

"Sound a leetle ha'sh," Tip Taylor added.

"Thet fish has jerked the fear o' God out he way it looks t' me," said Carlyle Barber.

"Yer up 'n the air, Mose," said another. "Need a sinker on ye."

They bullied him—they talked him down, demurring mildly, but firmly.

"Tell ye what I'll do," said Mose sheepishly, "I'll b'lieve you fellers if you'll b'lieve me."

"What, swop even? Not much!" said one, with emphasis. "'Twouldn't be fair. Ye've ast us t' b'lieve a genuwine out 'n out impossibility."

Mose lifted his hat and scratched his head thoughtfully. There was a look of embarrassment in his face.

"Might a ben dreamin'," said he slowly. "I swear it's gittin' so here 'n this town a feller can't hardly b'lieve himself."

"Fur's my experience goes," said Ransom Walker, "he'd a fool 'f he did."

"'Minds me o' the time I went fishin' with Ab Thomas," said Uncle Eb. "He ketched an ol' socker the fust thing. I went off by myself 'n got a good sized fish, but 'twant s' big 's hisn. So I tuk 'n opened his mouth 'n poured in a lot o' fine shot. When I come back Ab he looked at my fish 'n begun t' brag. When we weighed 'em mine was leetle heavier.

"'What!' says he. ' 'Tain't possible thet leetle cuss uv a trout 's heavier 'n mine."

"' 'Tis sartin,' I said.

"'Dummed deceivin' business,' said he as he hefted 'em both. 'Gittin so ye can't hardly b'lieve the stillyurds.'"

The Lucy Coffin

W. D. WETHERELL

My father, so long a distinguished member of the Philadelphia bar, was totally incapable of making up a story. His clients were expected to tell him in simple words what had happened, and then he would try to shape the plain words, the unadorned facts, into an argument a jury would find compelling. Imagination, exaggeration, hyperbole—he actively disapproved of all three. This was bad luck for me, since I was born with an oversupply of each, something he blamed on heredity, a great-uncle who wrote advertisements for Florida real estate back in the Twenties, and, before me, was the closest thing to a writer the family had.

So the one story Dad told me I listened to very closely. It was a fish story of course. Fly fishing was Dad's one vulnerability, the only thing we could tease him about, or theme his birthday presents around, or, on great occasions, actually share with him out on the water.

He was good at it, he fished all over the world, and his eyes came alive on a river in a way they didn't even in the courtroom. He never had the usual fisherman's virtue of patience . . . he despised patience, considered it the most mediocre of virtues . . . but what he had instead was endurance, getting out on the water before anyone else in camp and coming back far later. And he looked the part, too, once he started putting some years on. Wrinkles made him more handsome, not less. People always imagined him with a pipe in his mouth, squinting toward the sunset, though the truth is he never smoked.

That this passion was fueled in part by a rather dry, stiff, passionless marriage should perhaps come as no surprise. There were lots of dry, stiff, passionless marriages in the Philadelphia of those years. My parents didn't divorce, they had old-fashioned notions about what was owed their children, and I don't remember any particular arguments. Mother went her way, Dad went his, at least until her last years, when there was a softening, a drawing together, that surprised no one more than them.

I'm not sure when I first heard Dad's one and only story—there doesn't seem to be a place in memory where I didn't know it. He was just old enough to have served in the last days of the war, and it wasn't until almost a year after it ended that he was discharged. He went back to law school and graduated quickly—which means the story begins in the late spring of 1948.

He decided that before starting his practice he would treat himself to one grand fishing expedition. He would take a train to Vermont, then spend the summer hiking and hitchhiking through the hills, fishing every single stream and pond he came upon, boarding at farmhouses where he could find them, or camping rough in the woods. For three months, he would care about nothing except fishing, think about nothing except fishing, press the summer so deep in his memory it would never shake loose.

And that's pretty much the way it turned out. He traveled north along the Connecticut River, and when he came to a tributary, he would fish upstream toward the west, then strike out cross-country and follow the next tributary downstream to its junction with the big river—a back and forth, weaving kind of progression that meant there was very little water he missed. The days of the log drives were over, but there were plenty of old-time rivermen left who were more than happy to tell him where the big trout were hiding—and they weren't often wrong.

Back in the Depression, tramps and hobos had been distrusted, even feared here, but once the farm wives realized Dad was just fishing, a veteran, he was often given a room free of charge. In the morning, there would be chores he could help out with, and afternoons he would spend chasing the browns and rainbows that lived in the deep pools, or fishing for wild brook trout in the beaver ponds where most of these rivers had their starts, wading in the muck if he had to, sometimes taking all day to build a raft.

Thanks to his zigzag pattern, his getting stuck on rivers he loved best, it took him June and a good part of July to advance northwards sixty miles. There was still a lot of Vermont left to go before he hit Canada, but suddenly, between one tributary and the next, the landscape dramatically changed. The Connecticut veered away into New Hampshire, and the rivers flowed north towards Quebec and the St. Lawrence. The forest, instead of being dominated by maple and pine, was now mostly spruce, with boreal swamps and undulating sheets of pewter-colored rock. The farms were few and far between and mostly failed—this was a land of empty farmhouses where ghostly curtains blew out through shattered glass.

The first part of the story, the background, my father told quickly, with a lawyer's fine sense for how much he could ask of a jury's patience. But he would always hesitate here, take his glasses off and put them back on again, look out the nearest window, smile ruefully, then turn back again, his voice pitched now to a lower key.

"And then something odd happened, something I hadn't counted on. You have to understand that I was pretty cocky in those days. I thought, when it came to fly fishing, I was the hottest thing to ever hit Vermont. But once I got into the deep woods, the lonely country, things changed. I couldn't catch a fish, no matter how hard I tried. Not a trout, not a sucker, not even a chub. They all had locks on their jaws and for the life of me I couldn't find the key."

It was late August now, hot, with low water in all the streams. He slept in the woods most nights, though when it rained he found shelter in abandoned logging camps set in pockets against the ridges. On one nameless stream, fishing through a tunnel of alders, his leather wallet of flies, his best flies, dropped into the water and floated away, so he was down now to his rejects and spares.

"For the first time all summer, I began feeling sorry for myself. A thunderstorm hit me that night, so I was a pretty sorry sight once morning came. The only thing keeping me from heading to the train station and home was that the terrain was growing gentle again, with those beautiful open hillsides similar to what I had seen further south. I'll fish one more river, I decided. Just one more and then I'm done."

He was walking along, drying out in the sunshine, when he came upon an iron bridge with unusually elaborate scrollwork, and past it, a tree with a crudely-painted sign. *Hand Tied Flies!* It read. In that lonely countryside, it startled him; it could have said *Hand Cut Diamonds* and he wouldn't have been more surprised. There was an arrow pointing uphill along a road so rough a mule would have turned around in disgust. Figuring he had nothing to lose, he started up it—and that's when he had his second surprise.

On the top of the hill, set under a grove of ancient maple, was a small white farmhouse with an attached red barn. It wasn't derelict or abandoned like so many of the highest places but well-cared for, neat, even prim. Holsteins had trampled the yard up, but there was a garden surrounded by a picket fence, and it wasn't a vegetable garden either, but a flower garden, with tall showy gladiolas that were obviously meant to be cut and brought inside.

There was no one around, at least not at first, but when my father circled behind the barn he came upon a tool shed where a husky young man sat on a wicker chair listening to the Red Sox game on the radio. On the workbench beside him were piles of chicken feathers and Christmas tinsel and small black hooks. It was as if, my father said, the man knew he was coming and wanted to get right down to business.

"I saw your sign," my father said.

The young man looked Dad over. "Fly fisherman?"

"I try to be."

"Then you'll want six of these."

He handed over a Prince Albert tobacco tin. Inside were half a dozen of the rattiest looking, most outlandish flies Dad had ever seen. There looked to be muskrat fur in it, and duck quill, and a huge shank of rooster hackle—and Dad's first temptation was to laugh out loud.

"How much?" he asked carefully, not wanting to offend him.

"A dollar for the six."

"Does it have a name?"

"No. Well, sure. The Lucy Coffin. There, I just named it. You try that, fish it up on top slathered in fly dope, and if you use anything else you ain't as smart as you look."

Those of you who know fish stories can sense where this is headed. Dad stuffed those flies in his pocket, then forgot all about them. The last river he fished in Vermont was the Willoughby. As with all the other places he fished in August, he couldn't find a way to get the trout to rise—until, desperate, he remembered the Lucy Coffin. Tying one on, he threw it out there with a why-not kind of cast—and promptly rose a three-pound brown that fought him stubbornly for a good half hour. Six more fish followed, each almost as big, and when he finally gave up because of darkness, trout were still jumping toward it out of the black. For the last week of his trip, he fished nothing else—and everywhere it immediately resulted in the same kind of triumphs.

That was Dad's story, his one and only. Even as a kid, I wondered about it, not so much whether it was true or not . . . since Dad didn't make anything up, I knew it was true . . . but at the sweetness that would come into his tone, especially during the last part about that lonely, forgotten farm. It seemed more wistfulness than the summer really warranted, though obviously, being alone like that, at a time when a place was at its most beautiful and forgotten, had left an enduring impression.

I'd like to say, as a kid, I never tired of hearing him tell this story, but the truth is, I did get tired, particularly when I reached my teens. A magic fly? A fly that worked miracles? Sure, Dad. Right. Anything you say.

And then, from a storyteller's point of view, he made a smart move. The summer I was sixteen, driving me back from a camp counselor job I had in Maine, he detoured over to show me Vermont. We fly fished several of the streams he discovered in 1948; Dad, unlike most men who are experts at something, was more than willing to let me go off and learn on my own, playing dumber than he really was, knowing I would either fall in love with it on my own or it wouldn't take.

We only had four days. On the third, I suddenly woke up to the fact we were now doing more driving than fishing, going off on dirt roads that led away from the rivers uphill. All these detours seemed of the same pattern. "We're low on flies," Dad would announce, then suddenly swerve the wheel to the right. We would drive to the top of the hill where the road gave out into ruts, Dad would get out, look over the abandoned field going back to brush, maybe take a few steps toward what remained of a farmhouse . . . a cellar hole, a blackened chimney . . . then come back to the car shaking his head.

"Well, it was around here somewhere. Things have changed, all this forest. I was on foot, never bothered with maps. Half the streams I didn't even know what their names were. Being lost was part of the adventure."

I tried to be helpful. "Maybe it was over by that river we fished yesterday? I saw a lot of old farms."

My father considered this, then shook his head. "Well, maybe, but I don't think so, Paul. I searched there pretty thoroughly last time."

"Last time?"

He smiled, shyly. "Oh, I had a business trip to Boston a couple years back. Came over here for a few days, looked around. It wasn't fishing season. Mud season, so I couldn't get very far." He raised himself up on tiptoes, put his hands around his eyes like binoculars. 'See that open meadow over there? Let's see if we can find a road, then, if it's not there, we'll do some fishing."

He was quiet driving home. It was by far the best four days together we ever had, it got me started fly fishing, but I was confused at how silent he seemed, how disappointed. If we hadn't found his fly shop, that was okay by me. The Lucy Coffin? Hell, we caught plenty of trout without it—which is what I wanted to tell him, but he had his lawyer's face on now, his *losing* lawyer's face, and I knew that was something I couldn't dent.

When my mother died three years ago, Dad took it harder than any of us would have expected. As I said, during her last years their dependence on each other kept growing as their friends and colleagues one by one disappeared. Passion Dad had missed out on in life, but at least he found a quiet warmth, and losing that, at his age, hurt him deeply.

When I first broached the idea of a fishing trip, Dad was hesitant. He still fished, but mostly in ponds now, trolling streamers from a rowboat. I made it sound like I was the one who badly needed to get away . . . I had just finished a book; I was worn out, in need of a change . . . and, though he could see right through my stratagems, Dad wasn't immune to what June was doing to the air, even in suburban Philadelphia.

But he still hesitated; there was a meeting at his retirement community he was supposed to chair, and I had to come out with the argument I'd been saving as my clincher.

"We'll go and see if we can find the old place where you bought the Lucy Coffin. Maybe even find the same man."

"Dead," Dad grunted.

"How do you know that? You said he was about your own age, didn't you? He could still be tying flies. And even if he's gone, we'll make a real effort to locate where that farm was, that shouldn't be impossible."

"It's vanished. I couldn't find it last time."

"You had me in tow."

"Well no. The time after that, I searched pretty hard."

"You went back again?"

"Four or five times now."

"Four or five times?"

I'd been on the lookout for signs of dotage, but still this surprised me—he said it in a sly, secretive way, like he'd admitted sneaking off to Las Vegas. I didn't know the story had such a hold on him still. For me, it was nostalgic, going back up there, and I suppose I expected it was merely that for him, a story that sleeps wherever stories sleep in men his age, not something that actively burned.

He was waiting for me in the parking lot when I got there Thursday morning—the leathery, craggy-looking version of Dad, a rod tube sticking out from his ancient duffel bag, his waders slung around his shoulders like a bandolier.

Our drive north was on the quiet side—except for grandkids, none of the subjects we came up with seemed to take hold. Always before we could fall back on politics, me kidding him about being a Republican, him teasing me about being a Democrat, but that kind of teasing isn't possible anymore. Only once did he broach anything even remotely serious. We were up in Massachusetts, we had just gone through a long stretch of malls, and he waved his hand around, as if indicating, not just what we could see out the window, but the deeper, more essential part we could only sense.

"Countries are like old men, Paul. They get ugly when they get old . . ." and the truth of that, the doubled truth, kept things pretty quiet until we hit Vermont.

It was much better after that. The long evening shadows cut across the interstate, there were caddis flies dancing like flames around the top of the highest birches, and when we got out of the car at our motel the smell of late-blooming lilac made us look at each other and smile. Next morning, up early, we drove into the mountains, and the farther we drove the younger and fresher the land seemed. I got Dad to tell his story again, not the end he always rushed toward, but the earlier part, those June weeks when he had wandered around the foothills with no motive in live other than catching rainbows, brookies and browns.

We fished some of the same streams. Dad took forever stringing up his rod and pulling on his waders, but once in the river he did fine, not shuffling along like an old man in slippers, but high-stepping like a stork. We both caught trout. They weren't the natives he remembered, they were probably two weeks off the stock truck, but the rivers rushed the same way they always rushed, the willows danced the same dance in the wind, and there were afternoon hatches of mayflies we did very well with, fishing deep into dark. If anything, Dad seemed to have more energy and pep at the end of the day than he had when we began.

"Rhubarb pie," he said, taking a deep sniff of evening air. "I can still smell it. All these farm wives baked great rhubarb pies."

We spent the next day on a little tributary that wasn't on the map. I had to peel the alders back so Dad could enter the best pool, but when he did he caught three wild brookies, the last, for that water, a real monster, pushing fifteen inches. We admired it for the few seconds he took to let it slip back from his hand to the water. "One to quit on," I said, not really thinking about my words. "Yes, one to quit on," Dad said softly, thinking about them hard.

That night we found an old tourist home, the kind you wouldn't think existed anymore. *Titus Takes Tourists* read the sign out front—and Titus turned out to be even older than my father, with a thick mountain accent I could barely understand. But Dad could understand—he and Titus sat up talking half the night. "Twenty bucks!" his wife said, when it was time to leave. She acted embarrassed to ask so much, so, at least in this respect, we were back in 1948 at last.

But it was time to go home now. I had a book signing scheduled in Washington and Dad still wanted to chair his meeting. I had big ideas about driving it all in one day, so we left early, when the fog still lay clotted on the river. We crossed on an old iron bridge, and instead of a regular paved roadbed, there were thick old beams that made it bumpy. Something about the bumps, or the smell of creosote, or the lacy pattern of the metal got Dad thinking.

"Is there a road up here to the right?" he asked, before we were all the way over.

"It doesn't look like much of a road, Dad." I pointed in the vague direction of Philadelphia. "We've got a long drive ahead of us."

"Is there an old barn? Small, like it was made for miniature cows? Two gables, crazy windows?"

He was looking directly at me when he asked this—he was testing himself by not looking out the window.

"What's left of a barn, yes. There, you look yourself. Underneath all that poison ivy."

Dad nodded without looking, as if I were telling him nothing he didn't already know. "Turn right," he said, with a strange tremor in his voice—and then he closed his eyes, as if only by doing so could he find the right way. "There should be a bog in half a mile, then an apple orchard, then a small wooden dam."

Maybe there were those things—the washouts and ruts kept my attention fixed on the driving. A switchback got us onto an easier grade, and the upper part went under a tunnel of purple lilacs that must have been the last to bloom in the entire state. They don't grow wild, someone had once planted them, so maybe we were on the right track after all—and yet no mental effort I was capable of making could make that thick forest disappear, picture this as ever having been open.

The road ended in at a washout that could have swallowed a tank. I parked on its lip. Dad, without saying anything, opened his door and started striding through the trees. Certainty—his whole posture was shaped to it—and though I was a long way from feeling this myself, I started after him.

I caught up pretty fast. There were some spruce, then a band of dying birch, and I remembered that birch were the trees that grew first on abandoned land, and just when I was trying to figure out how many years this could take, I came into a little clearing in the middle of which stood a house.

It was standing, I'll say that much for it. The tin roof seemed pinned by rusty lightning rods to the simple Cape that stood beneath. The siding had long ago been weathered into bone color, hunters had riddled much of it with bullets, and the windows were starred with broken glass. In front was a porch that had once faced the road, but its supports had collapsed and the gingerbread trim, algae-covered and blistered, lay in pieces in the tall grass that licked the sides.

Dad stood staring down at something, and when I came up to him he pointed, bent stiffly, reached out his hand. Below a broken window the planks had been replaced with fresh, clean pine, making it look as if someone had chosen this spot to begin their renovations. Had they started, then, faced with the enormity of the job, given up? Except for that and a deflated soccer ball we found near the pyramid-heaped ruins of the barn, there were no signs of recent life.

Some of the debris had been pulled over to where an enormous apple tree had muscled out its own clearing. Dad reached down to turn through the planks. The third or fourth had purple lettering burned into its side like an old tattoo—he held it up to the light so we could read it—but it seemed an advertisement for seed or fertilizer, and didn't say anything about hand-tied flies.

"Is this it?" I asked.

I stood there staring toward the farmhouse, trying to imagine paint on it, a shiny new roof, curtains, flowers. I don't know what Dad saw. Again, as with the forest, the hand of time was too heavy for me to lift.

Dad's voice, when he started, was pitched very soft, like the voice a gentle man uses when someone is sleeping in the next room. And he touched the apple tree while he talked. That seemed important to him, the simple rough contact.

"What I'll never forget is how she was standing there waiting at the top of the road. Not waiting for me—waiting for anyone, their life was so lonely. I remember thinking how the sign for flies was their way of luring strangers just so they could have a little talk with someone besides themselves. If so, it was a good lure—it caught me easily enough."

A brown and shriveled apple, last year's, clung to the branch. He reached his hand toward it, and the motion alone was enough to make it fall.

"There was just the two of them. Her brother was seventeen—heavy, strong, and so round-shouldered he was nearly humpbacked. He could take care of cows all right, and winter he worked with the loggers. Their father had gone off to a defense plant after Pearl Harbor and that's the last they ever saw of him. Their mother died of cervical cancer a few years later. Lucy had the care of her, there was no one else. The parents or grandparents were either very brave or very stupid to have made a farm so high. The boy's name was Ira and her name was Lucy. Lucy Coffin."

The name, which I expected and didn't expect, seemed to come out of him hard. He coughed, or pretended to, and I followed his eyes back to the road.

He remembered what she looked like that first evening, he said. A young woman his own age standing there with an apron on, staring intently toward the dusk, wiping, with a wonderfully impatient gesture, the curly red hair that fell down across her eyes. She was beautiful, of course, though not in a way he had ever learned to see as beautiful before. He thought first of a tomboy, someone freckled and athletic, but she was past that stage now, and the chores hadn't yet roughened her skin. In the brief interval of grace that lay between he saw a girl so fresh and brave and natural it took his breath away, right from that first moment.

"I ended up staying with them for two weeks—they were absurdly grateful for my company. It was like they lived on an island and I had brought them news of the outside world. It was incredibly hard, the life they led, especially during the war years. It was thirty-five miles to the nearest movie house, and they told me how they would use horses to get down their road, then shovel out their old Ford from the snow, push and shove it to get it going, putting on chains when they got to macadam, then drive all that way just to see a double feature, getting back after midnight so they could tend to the cows. Ira liked fishing, so we hit it off pretty quick. He tied flies, sold a few now and then down in town, but they were cheap, gaudy things, nothing special. He really didn't understand what was happening between Lucy and me. Her bedroom faced the barn, and I remember waking up with her, getting out of bed quietly, pulling on my sweater, walking over to the window and seeing Ira stripped to the waist chopping away at five in the morning, and then at night he still wouldn't be finished, all the work he had."

Neither one of them knew much about anything except work. Once a month there were those expeditions to go see Clark Gable or Bette Davis, but except for these their life had few ornaments. Dad explained how he found an old kite in the barn leftover from when they were little, but neither one remembered how to fly it, and when he tied a tail on, got it up in the air, they thought he was a magician. And a picnic—they had never thought it possible, to go somewhere pretty and eat outside just for fun. At night, the three of them sat by the radio listening to the Red Sox and then Jack Benny. When Ira trudged off exhausted to bed, he and Lucy would walk outside together with a blanket and lie under the stars.

Neither one of them was a hick, he wanted to make sure I understood that. Lucy had an energy and directness nothing could stop, except for the one great bafflement that had her in its grip—how to be brave and deal with what life had brought her without her bravery digging a trap for her, making the loneliness even worse. For all the harshness in her life, she had a wonderful laugh and once started it would run away with her, set him laughing, too—laughing so much they cried. And silence— how many other girls her age knew how to make silence say everything? If he could teach her about kites and picnics, she could teach him about sweetness . . . never before had he suspected life was capable of being so sweet . . . and, in the end, what sadness was, too.

One afternoon they helped Ira finish his chores so they could all go fishing. Ira fished hard, but without much skill, and spent most of the time admiring my father's little Payne fly rod. After their picnic, he and Lucy walked upstream toward a water- fall. She had borrowed Ira's hat for the sun, a battered old porkpie with flies tucked in the band, and before long, that's pretty much all she was wearing, that floppy red hat. He laughed over that, and she laughed, too, bending over a little pool where the water was so thin it acted like a mirror.

My father explained all this while holding onto the apple tree, but now he stepped away, seemed actually to break that invisible cord, and walked slowly back to where I stood in the center of those rotting old planks. He looked old . . . I was startled at how old he suddenly looked . . . and maybe it was the dark evening shadows doing that, or maybe it was the contrast with the young man I followed so intently in his story. Time had stopped while he was telling it, but it was ticking again, and, judging by the way he closed his eyes, Dad felt the rush of those minutes even more than I did.

"I thought about asking her to come away with me—I thought about nothing else that last week. Would she have come? It would have broken her brother's heart. Still, I think if I had pressed her she would have come. Our worlds were so different. When I asked her about her future, she wouldn't tell me about any dreams or plans, but then right toward the end she did. 'I'd like to be in pictures,' she said. Out of all her loneliness, she could come up with nothing else."

My father's voice deepened—it was like he was struggling to recapture his lawyer's tone, get back into that safety zone where words expressed simple, incontrovertible facts.

"Lucy is one day younger than I am. She was born on October sixth and I was born on October seventh, and I teased her about how much younger she was, how much wiser I was. Every single birthday since I've thought about where she might be, what life has brought her. I've always wondered if we kept pace somehow, she in her world, me in mine . . . I got up in the middle of the night, being careful not to wake her. I didn't leave a note for her, but I left one for Ira on the kitchen table, along with that little Payne fly rod. I walked down the road in the moonlight, and never before had I seen anything so beautiful, and yet every step was torture. I can feel this even now, understand that Paul? Arthritis, that young doctor of mine says whenever I got for my checkup. But that's not what a man my age feels in his knees. It's all those times you walked away from someone you should never have walked away from."

I went over and took his arm, since he actually seemed faltering now, and there were those roots and rocks to navigate before we got back to the car.

"So there wasn't a fly?" I said. "No Lucy Coffin?"

"Oh, there was a fly all right." He reached into his pocket, brought out his leather fly book, the one he used for his very best flies. He opened it, held it toward the keyhole of light still visible in the west.

"Ira could tie in a clumsy, self-taught way. He gave me some Black Gnats before I left. Six of them. Years when the memory hurt worst, I would take one out and tie it on. I have one left. Here, open your hand."

I felt something sharp and tickly against my palm; I folded my fist tight to make sure it stayed there, that it didn't drop loose. *Mine now.* I didn't say it, but, like a small child accepting a present, that's what I felt.

"Yours now," my father said, reading my thoughts. He smiled—not a happy smile, not a sad smile either, but one that seemed pressed into the thin, permeable layer that lies in between. I could see him stare toward the first stars, sensed him using the silence to set up a line to go out on, like an old experienced storyteller from way back when, not someone who just had the one.

"I fished Ira's fly pretty hard all those two weeks, and never caught a thing on it, but for once in my life I didn't care."

Crocker's Hole

R. D. BLACKMORE

The Culm, which rises in Somersetshire, and hastening into a fairer land (as the border waters wisely do) falls into the Exe near Killerton, formerly was a lovely trout stream, such as perverts the Devonshire angler from due respect toward Father Thames and the other canals round London. In the Devonshire valleys it is sweet to see how soon a spring becomes a rill, and a rill runs on into a rivulet and a rivulet swells into a brook; and before one has time to say, "What are you at?"—before the first tree it ever spoke to is a dummy, or the first hill it ever ran down has turned blue, here we have all the airs and graces, demands and assertions of a full-grown river.

But what is the test of a river? Who shall say? "The power to drown a man," replies the river darkly. But rudeness is not argument. Rather shall we say that the power to work a good undershot wheel, without being dammed up all night in a pond, and leaving a tidy back stream to spare at the bottom of the orchard, is a fair certificate of river-hood. If so, many Devonshire streams attain that rank within five miles of their spring; aye, and rapidly add to it. At every turn they gather aid, from ash-clad dingle and aldered meadow, mossy rock and ferny wall, hedge-trough-roofed with bramble netting, where the baby water lurks, and lanes that coming down to ford bring suicidal tribute. Arrogant, all-engrossing river, now it has claimed a great valley of its own; and whatever falls within the hill scoop sooner or later belongs to itself. Even the crystal "shutt" that crosses the farmyard by the woodrick, and glides down an aqueduct of last year's bark for Mary to fill the kettle from; and even the tricklets that have no organs for telling or knowing their business, but only get into unwary oozings in and among the water grass, and there make moss and forget themselves among it—one and all, they come to the same thing at last, and that is the river.

The Culm used to be a good river at Culmstock, tormented already by a factory, but not strangled as yet by a railroad. How is it now the present writer does not know, and is afraid to ask, having heard of a vile "Culm Valley Line." But Culmstock bridge was a very pretty place to stand and contemplate the ways of trout; which is easier work than to catch them. When I was just big enough to peep above the rim, or to lie upon it with one leg inside for fear of tumbling over, what a mighty river it used to seem, for it takes a treat there and spreads itself. Above the bridge the factory stream falls in again, having done its business, and washing its hands in the innocent half that has strayed down the meadows. Then under the arches they both rejoice and come to a slide of about two feet, and make a short, wide pool below, and indulge themselves in perhaps two islands, through which a little river always magnifies itself and maintains a mysterious middle. But after that, all of it used to come together, and make off in one body for the meadows, intent upon nurturing trout with rapid stickles, and buttercuppy corners where fat flies may tumble in. And here you may find in the very first meadow, or at any rate you might have found, forty years ago, the celebrated "Crocker's Hole."

The story of Crocker is unknown to me, and interesting as it doubtless was, I do not deal with him, but with his Hole. Tradition said that he was a baker's boy who, during his basket rounds, fell in love with a maiden who received the cottage loaf, or perhaps good "Households" for her master's use. No doubt she was charming, as a girl should be, but whether she encouraged the youthful baker and then betrayed him with false role, or whether she "consisted" throughout—as our cousins across the water express it—is known to their *manes* only. Enough that she would not have the floury lad; and that he, after giving in his books and money. sought an untimely grave among the trout. And this was the first pool below the bread walk deep enough to drown a five-foot baker boy. Sad it was; but such things must be, and bread must still be delivered daily.

A truce to such reflections—as our foremost writers always say, when they do not see how to go on with them—but it is a serious thing to know what Crocker's Hole was like; because at a time when (if he had only persevered, and married the maid, and succeeded to the oven, and reared a large family of short-weight bakers) he might have been leaning on his crutch beside the pool, and teaching his grandson to swim by precept (that beautiful proxy for practice)—at such a time, I say there lived a remarkable fine trout in that hole. Anglers are notoriously truthful, especially as to what they catch, or even more frequently have not caught. Though I may have written fiction, among many other sins—as a nice old lady told me once—now I have to deal with facts; and foul scorn would I count it ever to make believe that I caught that fish. My length at that time was not more than the butt of a four-jointed rod, and all I could catch was a minnow with a pin, which our cook Lydia would not cook, but used to say, "Oh, what a shame, Master Richard! They would have been trout in the summer, please God! if you would only a' let 'em grow on." She is living now and will bear me out in this.

But upon every great occasion there arises a great man; or to put it more accurately, in the present instance, a mighty and distinguished boy. My father, being the parson of the parish, and getting, need it be said, small pay, took sundry pupils, very pleasant fellows, about to adorn the universities. Among them was the original "Bude Light," as he was satirically called at Cambridge, for he came from Bude, and there was no light in him. Among them also was John Pike, a born Zebedee if ever there was one.

John Pike was a thickset younker, with a large and bushy head, keen blue eyes that could see through water, and the proper slouch of shoulder into which great anglers ripen; but greater still are born with it; and of these was Master John. It mattered little what the weather was, and scarcely more as to the time of year, John Pike must have his fishing every day, and on Sundays he read about it, and made flies. All the rest of the time he was thinking about it.

My father was coaching him in the fourth book of *The Aeneid* and all those wonderful species of Dido, where passion disdains construction; but the only line Pike cared for was of horsehair. "I fear, Mr. Pike, that you are not giving me your entire attention," my father used to say in his mild dry way; and once when Pike was more than usually abroad, his tutor begged to share his meditations. "Well, sir," said Pike, who was very truthful, "I can see a green drake by the strawberry tree, the first of the season, and your derivation of 'barbamus' put me in mind of my barberry dye." In those days it was a very nice point to get the right tint for the mallard's feather.

No sooner was lesson done than Pike, whose rod was ready upon the lawn, dashed away always for the river, rushing headlong down the hill, and away to the left through a private yard, where "No Thoroughfare" was put up and a big dog stationed to enforce it. But Cerberus himself could not have stopped John Pike; his conscience backed him up in trespass the most sinful when his heart was inditing of a trout upon the rise.

All this, however, is preliminary, as the boy said when he put his father's coat upon his grandfather's tenterhooks, with felonious intent upon his grandmother's apples; the main point to be understood in this, that nothing—neither brazen tower, hundred-eyed Argus, nor Cretan Minotaur—could stop John Pike from getting at a good stickle. But, even as the world knows nothing of its greatest men, its greatest men know nothing of the world beneath their very nose, till fortune sneezes dexter. For two years John Pike must have been whipping the water as hard as Xerxes, without having ever once dreamed of the glorious trout that lived in Crocker's Hole. But why, when he ought to have been at least on bowing terms with every fish as long as his middle finger, why had he failed to know this champion? The answer is simple—because of his short cuts. Flying as he did like an arrow from a bow, Pike used to hit his beloved river at an elbow, some furlong below Crocker's Hole, where a sweet little stickle sailed away downstream, whereas for the length of a meadow upward the water lay smooth, clear, and shallow; therefore the youth, with so little time to spare, rushed into the downward joy.

And here it may be noted that the leading maxim of the present period, that man can discharge his duty only by going counter to the stream, was scarcely mooted in those days. My grandfather (who was a wonderful man, if he was accustomed to fill a cart in two days of fly fishing on the Barle) regularly fished downstream; and what more than a cartload need anyone put into his basket?

And surely it is more genial and pleasant to behold our friend the river growing and thriving as we go on, strengthening its voice and enlarging its bosom, and sparkling through each successive meadow with richer plenitude of silver, than to trace it against its own grain and good will toward weakness, and littleness, and imma-ture conceptions.

However, you will say that if John Pike had fished upstream, he would have found this trout much sooner. And that is true; but still, as it was, the trout had more time to grow into such a prize. And the way in which John found him out was this. For some days he had been tormented with a very painful tooth, which even poi-soned all the joys of fishing. Therefore he resolved to have it out and sturdily entered the shop of John Sweetland, the village blacksmith, and there paid his sixpence. Sweetland extracted the teeth of the village, whenever they required it, in the sim-plest and most effectual way. A piece of fine wire was fastened round the tooth, and the other end round the anvil's nose, then the sturdy blacksmith shut the lower half of his shop door, which was about breast-high, with the patient outside and the anvil within; a strong push of the foot upset the anvil, and the tooth flew out like a well-thrown fly.

When John Pike had suffered this very bravely, "Ah, Master Pike:' said the blacksmith, with a grin, "I reckon you won't pull out thic there big vish"—the smithy commanded a view of the river—"clever as you be, quite so peart as thiccy."

"What big fish?" asked the boy, with deepest interest, though his mouth was bleeding fearfully.

"Why, that girt mortial of a vish as hath his hover in Crocker's Hole. Zum on 'em saith as a' must be a zammon."

Off went Pike with his handkerchief to his mouth, and after him ran Alec Bolt, one of his fellow pupils, who had come to the shop to enjoy the extraction.

"Oh, my!" was all that Pike could utter, when by craftily posting himself he had obtained a good view of this grand fish.

"I'll lay you a crown you don't catch him!" cried Bolt, an impatient youth, who scorned angling.

"How long will you give me?" asked the wary Pike, who never made rash wagers.

"Oh! till the holidays if you like; or, if that won't do, till Michaelmas?"

Now the midsummer holidays were six weeks off—boys used not to talk of "vacations" then, still less of "recesses."

"I think I'll bet you," said Pike, in his slow way, bending forward carefully, with his keen eyes on this monster, "but it would not be fair to take till Michaelmas. I'll bet you a crown that I catch him before the holidays—at least, unless some other fellow does?"

The day of that most momentous interview must have been the 14th day of May. Of the year I will not be so sure; for children take more note of days than of years, for which the latter have their full revenge thereafter. It must have been the 14th, because the morrow was our holiday, given upon the 15th of May, in honor of a birthday.

Now, John Pike was beyond his years wary as well as enterprising, calm as well as ardent, quite as rich in patience as in promptitude and vigor. But Alec Bolt was a headlong youth, volatile, hot, and hasty, fit only to fish the Maelstrom, or a torrent of new lava. And the moment he had laid that wager he expected his crown piece; though time, as the lawyers phrase it, was "expressly of the essence of the contract." And now he demanded that Pike should spend the holiday in trying to catch that trout.

"I shall not go near him:' that lad replied, "until I have got a new collar." No piece of personal adornment was it, without which he would not act, but rather that which now is called the fly cast, or the gut cast, or the trace, or what it may be. "And another thing," continued Pike; "the bet is off if you go near him, either now or at any other time, without asking my leave first, and then only going as I tell you."

"What do I want with the great slimy beggar?" the arrogant Bolt made answer. "A good rat is worth fifty of him. No fear of my going near him, Pike. You shan't get out of it that way."

Pike showed his remarkable qualities that day, by fishing exactly as he would have fished without having heard of the great Crockerite. He was upon and away upon the millstream before breakfast; and the forenoon he devoted to his favorite course—first down the Craddock stream, a very pretty confluent of the Culm, and from its junction, down the pleasant hams, where the river winds toward Uffculme. It was my privilege to accompany this hero, as his humble Sancho; while Bolt and the faster race went up the river ratting. We were back in time to have Pike's trout (which ranged between two ounces and one half pound) fried for the early dinner; and here it may be lawful to remark that the trout of the Culm are of the very purest excellence, by reason of the flinty bottom, at any rate in these the upper regions. For the valley is the western outlet of the Black Down range, with the Beacon hill upon the north, and the Hackpen long ridge to the south; and beyond that again the Whetstone hill, upon whose western end wark portholes scarped with white grit mark the pits. But flint is the staple of the broad Culm Valley under good, well-pastured loam; and here are chalcedonies and agate stones.

At dinner everybody had a brace of trout—large for the larger folk, little for the little ones, with coughing and some patting on the back for bones. What of equal purport could the fierce rat hunter show? Pike explained many points in the history of each fish, seeming to know them none the worse, and love them all the better, for being fried. We banqueted, neither a whit did soul get stinted of banquet impartial. Then the wielder of the magic rod very modestly sought leave of absence at the teatime.

"Fishing again, Mr. Pike, I suppose," my father answered pleasantly; "I used to be fond of it at your age; but never so entirely wrapped up in it as you are."

"No, sir; I am not going fishing again. I want to walk to Wellington, to get some things at Cherry's."

"Books, Mr. Pike? Ah! I am very glad of that. But I fear it can only be fly books."

"I want a little Horace for eighteenpence—the Cambridge one just published, to carry in my pocket—and a new hank of gut."

"Which of the two is more important? Put that into Latin, and answer it."

"*Utrurn pluris facio? Placcurn flocd. Viscera magni.*" With this vast effort Pike turned as red as any trout.

"After that who could refuse you?" said my father. "You always tell the truth, my boy, in Latin or in English."

Although it was a long walk, some fourteen miles to Wellington and back, I got permission to go with Pike; and as we crossed the bridge and saw the tree that overhung Crocker's Hole, I begged him to show me that mighty fish.

"Not a bit of it," he replied. "It would bring the blackguards. If the blackguards once find him out, it is all over with him."

"The blackguards are all in factory now, and I am sure they cannot see us from the windows. They won't be out till five o'clock."

With the true liberality of young England, which abides even now as large and glorious as ever, we always called the free and enlightened operatives of the period by the courteous name above set down, and it must be acknowledged that some of them deserved it, although perhaps they poached with less of science than their sons. But the cowardly murder of fish by liming the water was already prevalent.

Yielding to my request and perhaps his own desire—manfully kept in check that morning—Pike very carefully approached that pool, commanding me to sit down while he reconnoitered from the meadow upon the right bank of the stream. And the place which had so sadly quenched the fire of the poor baker's love filled my childish heart with dread and deep wonder at the cruelty of women. But as for John Pike, all he thought of was the fish and the best way to get at him.

Very likely that hole is "holed out" now, as the Yankees well express it, or at any rate changed out of knowledge. Even in my time a very heavy flood entirely altered its character; but to the eager eye of Pike it seemed pretty much as follows, and possibly it may have come to such a form again:

The river, after passing through a hurdle fence at the head of the meadow, takes a little turn or two of bright and shallow indifference, then gathers itself into a good strong slide, as if going down a slope instead of steps. The right bank is high and beetles over with yellow loam and grassy fringe; but the other side is of flinty shingle, low and bare and washed by floods. At the end of this rapid, the stream turns sharply under an ancient alder tree into a large, deep, calm repose, cool, unruffled, and sheltered front the sun by branch and leaf—and that is the hole of poor Crocker.

At the head of the pool (where the hasty current rushes in so eagerly, with noisy excitement and much ado) the quieter waters from below, having rested and enlarged themselves, come lapping up round either curve, with some recollection of their past career, the hoary experience of foam. And sidling toward the new arrival of the impulsive column, where they meet it, things go on which no man can describe without his mouth being full of water. A *V* is formed, a fancy letter *V*, beyond any designer's tracery and even beyond his imagination, a perpetually fluctuating limpid wedge, perpetually creneled and rippled into by little ups and downs that try to make an impress but can only glide away upon either side or sink in dimples under it. And here a gray bough of the ancient alder stretches across, like a thirsty giant's arm, and makes it a very ticklish place to throw a fly. Yet this was the very spot our John Pike must put his fly into, or lose his crown.

Because the great tenant of Crocker's Hole, who allowed no other fish to wag a fin there, and from strict monopoly had grown so fat, kept his victualing yard—if so low an expression can be used concerning him—without above a square yard of this spot. He had a sweet hover, both for rest and recreation, under the bank, in a placid antre, where the water made no noise, but tickled his belly in digestive ease. The loftier the character is of any being, the slower and more dignified his movements are. No true psychologist could have believed—as Sweetland the blacksmith did, and Ms. Pook the tinman—that this trout could ever be the embodiment of Crocker. For this was the last trout in the universal world to drown himself for love; if truly any trout has done so.

"You may come now, and try to look along my back," John Pike, with a reverential whisper, said to me. "Now, don't be in a hurry, young stupid; kneel down. He is not to be disturbed at his dinner, mind. You keep behind me, and look along my back; I never clapped eyes on such a whopper."

I had to kneel down in a tender reminiscence of pastureland and gaze carefully; and not having eyes like those of our Zebedee (who offered his spine for a camera, as he crawled on all fours in front of me), it took me a long time to descry an object most distinct to all who have that special gift of piercing with their eyes the water. See what is said upon this subject in that delicious book, *The Gamekeeper at Home.*

"You are no better than a muff," said Pike, and it was not in my power to deny it.

"If the sun would only leave off," I said. But the sun, who was having a very pleasant play with the sparkle of the water and the twinkle of the leaves, had no inclination to leave off yet, but kept the rippling crystal in a dance of flashing facets, and the quivering verdure in a steady flush of gold.

But suddenly a May fly, a luscious gray drake, richer and more delicate than canvasback or woodcock, with a dart and a leap and a merry zigzag, began to enjoy a little game above the stream. Rising and falling like a gnat, thrilling her gauzy wings, and arching her elegant pellucid frame, every now and then she almost dipped her three long tapering whisks into the dimples of the water.

"He sees her! He'll have her as sure as a gun!" cried Pike, with a gulp, as if he himself were "rising." "Now can you see him, stupid?"

"Crikey, crokums!" I exclaimed, with classic elegance; "I have seen that long thing for five minutes; but I took it for a tree."

"You little"—animal quite early in the alphabet—"now don't you stir a peg, or I'll dig my elbow into you."

The great trout was stationary almost as a stone, in the middle of the *V* above described. He was gently fanning with his large clear fins, but holding his own against the current mainly by the wagging of his broad-fluked tail. As soon as my slow eyes had once defined him, he grew upon them mightily, molding himself in the matrix of the water, as a thing put into jelly does. And I doubt whether even John Pike saw him more accurately than I did. His size was such, or seemed to be such, that I fear to say a word about it; not because language does not contain the word, but from dread of exaggeration. But his shape and color may be reasonably told without wounding the feeling of an age whose incredulity springs from self-knowledge.

His head was truly small, his shoulders vast; the spring of his back was like a rainbow when the sun is southing; the generous sweep of his deep elastic belly, nobly pulped out with rich nurture, showed what the power of his brain must be, and seemed to undulate, time for time, with the vibrant vigilance of his large wise eyes. His latter end was consistent also. An elegant taper run of counter, coming almost to a cylinder, as a mackerel does, boldly developed with a hugeous spread to a glorious amplitude of swallowtail. His color was all that can well be desired, but ill described by any poor word palette. Enough that he seemed to tone away from olive and umber, with carmine stars, to glowing gold and soft pure silver, mantled with a subtle flush of rose and fawn and opal.

Swoop came a swallow, as we gazed, and was gone with a flick, having missed the May fly. But the wind of his passage, or the skit of wing, struck the merry dancer down, so that he fluttered for one instant on the wave, and that instant was enough. Swift as the swallow, and more true of aim, the great trout made one dart, and a sound, deeper than a tinkle, but as silvery as a bell, rang the poor ephemerid's knell. The rapid water scarcely showed a break; but a bubble sailed down the pool, and the dark hollow echoed with the music of a rise.

"He knows how to take a fly," said Pike; "he has had too many to be tricked with mine. Have him I must; but how ever shall I do it?"

All the way to Wellington he uttered not a word, but shambled along with a mind full of care. When I ventured to look up now and then, to surmise what was going on beneath his hat, deeply set eyes and a wrinkled forehead, relieved at long intervals by a solid shake, proved that there are meditations deeper than those of philosopher or statesman.

Surely no trout could have been misled by the artificial May fly of that time, unless he were either a very young fish, quite new to entomology; or else one afflicted with a combination of myopy and bulimy. Even now there is room for plenty of improvement in our counterfeit presentment; but in those days the body was made with yellow mohair, ribbed with red silk and gold twist and as thick as a fertile bumblebee. John Pike perceived that to offer such a thing to Crocker's trout would probably consign him—even if his great stamina should overget the horror—to an uneatable death, through just and natural indignation. On the other hand, while the May fly lasted, a trout so cultured, so highly refined, so full of light and sweetness, would never demean himself to low bait, or any coarse son of a maggot.

Meanwhile, Alec Bolt allowed poor Pike no peaceful thought, no calm absorption of high mind into the world of flies, no placid period of cobbler's wax, floss silk, turned hackles, and dubbing. For in making of flies John Pike had his special moments of inspiration, times of clearer insight into the everlasting verities, times of brighter conception and more subtle execution, tails of more elastic grace and heads of a neater and nattier expression. As a poet labors at one immortal line, compressing worlds of wisdom into the music of ten syllables, so toiled the patient Pike about the fabric of a fly comprising all the excellence that ever sprang from maggot. Yet Bolt rejoiced to jerk his elbow at the moment of sublimest art. And a swarm of flies was blighted thus.

Peaceful, therefore, and long-suffering, and full of resignation as he was, John Pike came slowly to the sad perception that arts avail not without arms. The elbow, so often jerked, at last took a voluntary jerk from the shoulder, and Alec Bolt lay prostrate, with his right eye full of cobbler's wax. This put a desirable check upon his energies for a week or more, and by that time Pike had flown his fly.

When the honeymoon of spring and summer (which they are now too fashionable to celebrate in this country), the heyday of the whole year marked by the budding of the wild rose, the start of the wheat ear from its sheath, the feathering of the lesser plantain, and flowering of the meadowsweet, and, foremost for the angler's joy, the caracole of May flies—when these things are to be seen and felt (which has not happened at all this year), then rivers should be mild and bright, skies blue and white with fleecy cloud, the west wind blowing softly, and the trout in charming appetite.

On such a day came Pike to the bank of Culm, with a loudly beating heart. A fly there is, not ignominious, or of cowdab origin, neither gross and heavy-bodied, from cradlehood of slimy stones, nor yet of menacing aspect and suggesting deeds of poison, but elegant, bland, and of sunny nature, and obviously good to eat. Him or her—why quest we which?—the shepherd of the dale, contemptuous of gender, except in his own species, has called, and as long as they two coexist will call, the Yellow Sally. A fly that does not waste the day in giddy dances and the fervid waltz, but undergoes family incidents with decorum and discretion. He or she, as the case may be—for the natural history of the riverbank is a book to come hereafter, and of fifty men who make flies not one knows the name of the fly he is making—in the early morning of June, or else in the second quarter of the afternoon, this Yellow Sally fares aboard, with a nice well-ordered flutter.

Despairing of the May fly, as it still may be despaired of, Pike came down to the river with his masterpiece of portraiture. The artificial Yellow Sally is generally always—as they say in Cheshire—a mile or more too yellow. On the other hand, the Yellow Dun conveys no idea of any Sally. But Pike had made a very decent Sally, not perfect (for he was young as well as wise), but far above any counterfeit to be had in fishing-tackle shops. How he made it, he told nobody. But if he lives now, as I hope he does, any of my readers may ask him through the G. P. O. and hope to get an answer.

It fluttered beautifully on the breeze, and in such living form that a brother or sister Sally came up to see it, and went away sadder and wiser. Then Pike said: "Get away, you young wretch," to your humble servant who tells this tale; yet, being better than his words, allowed that pious follower to lie down upon his digestive organs and with deep attention watch. There must have been great things to see, but to see them so was difficult. And if I huddle up what happened, excitement also shares the blame.

Pike had fashioned well the time and manner of this overture. He knew that the giant Crockerite was satiate now with May flies, or began to find their flavor failing, as happens to us with asparagus, marrow-fat peas, or strawberries, when we have had a month of them. And he thought that the first Yellow Sally of the season, inferior though it were, night have the special charm of novelty. With the skill of a Zulu, he stole up through the branches over the lower pool till he came to a spot where a yard-wide opening gave just space for spring of rod. Then he saw his desirable friend at dinner, wagging his tail, as a hungry gentleman dining with the Lord Mayor agitates his coat. With one dexterous whirl, untaught by any of the many books upon the subject, John Pike laid his Yellow Sally (for he cast with one fly only) as lightly as gossamer upon the rapid, about a yard in front of the big trout's head. A moment's pause, and then too quick for words was the thing that happened.

A heavy plunge was followed by a fearful rush. Forgetful of the current the river was ridged, as if with a plow driven under it; the strong line, though given out as fast as might be, twanged like a harp string as it cut the wave, and then Pike stood up, like a ship dismasted, with the butt of his rod snapped below the ferrule. He had one of those foolish things, just invented, a hollow butt of hickory; and the finial ring of his spare top looked out, to ask what had happened to the rest of it. "Bad luck!" cried the fisherman; "but never mind, I shall have him next time, to a certainty."

When this great issue came to be considered, the cause of it was sadly obvious. The fish, being hooked, had made off with the rush of a shark for the bottom of the pool. A thicket of saplings below the alder tree had stopped the judicious hooker from all possibility of following; and when he strove to turn him by elastic pliance, his rod broke at the breach of pliability. "I have learned a sad lesson," said John Pike, looking sadly.

How many fellows would have given up this matter, and glorified themselves for having hooked so grand a fish, while explaining that they must have caught him, if they could have done it! But Pike only told me not to say a word about it, and began to make ready for another tug of war. He made himself a splice rod, short and handy, of well-seasoned ash, with a stout top of bamboo, tapered so discreetly, and so balanced in its spring, that verily it formed an arc, with any pressure on it, as perfect as a leaf poplar in a stormy summer. "Now break it if you can," he said, "by any amount of rushes; I'll hook you by your jacket collar; you cut away now, and I'll land you."

This was highly skillful, and he did it many times; and whenever I was landed well, I got a lollipop, so that I was careful not to break his tackle. Moreover he made him a landing net, with a kidney-bean stick, a ring of wire, and his own best nightcap of strong cotton net. Then he got the farmer's leave, and lopped obnoxious bushes; and now the chiefest question was: What bait, and when to offer it? In spite of his sad rebuff, the spirit of John Pike had been equable. The genuine angling mind is steadfast, large, and self-supported, and to the vapid, ignominious chaff; tossed by swine upon the idle wind, it pays as much heed as a big trout does to a dance of midges. People put their fingers to their noses and said: "Master Pike, have you caught him yet?" and Pike only answered: "Wait a bit." If ever this fortitude and perseverance is to be recovered as the English Brand (the one thing that has made us what we are, and may yet redeem us from niddering shame), a degenerate age should encourage the habit of fishing and never despairing. And the brightest sign yet for our future is the increasing demand for hooks and gut.

Pike fished in a manlier age, when nobody would dream of cowering from a savage because he was clever at skulking; and when, if a big fish broke the rod, a stronger rod was made for him, according to the usage of Great Britain. And though the young angler had been defeated, he did not sit down and have a good cry over it.

About the second week in June, when the May fly had danced its day and died—for the season was an early one—and Crocker's trout had recovered from the wound to his feelings and philanthropy, there came a night of gentle rain, of pleasant tinkling upon window ledges, and a soothing patter among young leaves, and the Culm was yellow in the morning. "I mean to do it this afternoon," Pike whispered to me, as he came back panting. "When the water clears there will be a splendid time."

The lover of the rose knows well a gay voluptuous beetle, whose pleasure is to lie embedded in a fount of beauty. Deep among the incurving petals of the blushing fragrance, he loses himself in his joys sometimes, till a breezy waft reveals him. And when the sunlight breaks upon his luscious dissipation, few would have the heart to oust him, such a gem from such a setting. All his back is emerald sparkles, all his front red Indian gold, and here and there he grows white spots to save the eye from aching. Pike put his finger in and fetched him out, and offered him a little change of joys, by putting a Limerick hook through his thorax, and bringing it out between his elytra. *Cetonia aurata* liked it not, but pawed the air very naturally, and fluttered with his wings attractively.

"I meant to have tried with a fern web," said the angler; "until I saw one of these beggars this morning. If he works like that upon the water, he will do. It was hopeless to try artificials again. What a lovely color the water is! Only three days now to the holidays. I have run it very close. You be ready, younker."

With these words he stepped upon a branch of the alder, for the tone of the waters allowed approach, being soft and sublustrous, without any mud. Also Master Pike's own tone was such as becomes the fisherman, calm, deliberate, free from nerve, but fall of eye and muscle. He stepped upon the alder bough to get as near as might be to the fish, for he could not cast this beetle like a fly; it must be dropped gently and allowed to play. "You may come and look," he said to me; "when the water is so, they have no eyes in their tails."

The rose beetle trod upon the water prettily, under a lively vibration, and he looked quite as happy and considerably more active, than when he had been cradled in the anthers of the rose. To the eye of a fish he was a strong individual, fighting courageously with the current, but sure to be beaten through lack of fins; and mercy suggested, as well as appetite, that the proper solution was to gulp him.

"Hooked him in the gullet. He can't get off!" cried John Pike, laboring to keep his nerves under. "Every inch of tackle is as strong as a bell pull. Now, if I don't land him, I will never fish again!"

Providence, which had constructed Pike, foremost of all things, for lofty angling—disdainful of worm and even minnow—Providence, I say, at this adjuration, pronounced that Pike must catch that trout. Not many anglers are heaven-born; and for one to drop off the hook halfway through his teens would be infinitely worse than to slay the champion trout. Pike felt the force of this, and rushing through the rushes, shouted: "I am sure to have him, Dick! Be ready with my nightcap."

Rod in a bow like a springle riser; line on the hum, like the string of Paganini; winch on the gallop, like a harpoon wheel, Pike, the headcenter of everything, dashing through thick and thin, and once taken overhead—for he jumped into the hole, when he must have lost him else, but the fish too impetuously towed him out, and made off in passion for another pool, when, if he had only retired to his hover, the angler might have shared the baker's fate—all these things (I tell you, for they all come upon again, as if the day were yesterday) so scared me of my never very stead-fist wits, that I could only holloa! But one thing I did, I kept the nightcap ready.

Plain Fishing

FRANK R. STOCKTON

"Well, sir," said old Peter, as he came out on the porch with his pipe, "so you came here to go fishin'?"

Peter Gruse was the owner of the farm-house where I had arrived that day, just before supper-time. He was a short, strong-built old man, with a pair of pretty daughters, and little gold rings in his ears. Two things distinguished him from the farmers in the country round about: one was the rings in his ears, and the other was the large and comfortable house in which he kept his pretty daughters. The other farmers in that region had fine large barns for their cattle and horses, but very poor houses for their daughters. Old Peter's ear-rings were indirectly connected with his house. He had not always lived among those mountains. He had been on the sea, where his ears were decorated, and he had traveled a good deal on land, where he had ornamented his mind with many ideas which were not in general use in the part of his State in which he was born. His house stood a little back from the high road, and if a traveler wished to be entertained, Peter was generally willing to take him in, provided he had left his wife and family at home. The old man himself had no objection to wives and children, but his two pretty daughters had.

These young women had waited on their father and myself at supper-time, one continually bringing hot griddle cakes, and the other giving me every opportunity to test the relative merits of the seven different kinds of preserved fruit which, in little glass plates, covered the otherwise unoccupied spaces on the tablecloth. The latter, when she found that there was no further possible way of serving us, presumed to sit down at the corner of the table and begin her supper. But in spite of this apparent humility, which was only a custom of the country, there was that in the general air of the pretty daughters which left no doubt in the mind of the intelligent observer that they stood at the wheel in that house. There was a son of fourteen, who sat at table with us, but he did not appear to count as a member of the family.

"Yes," I answered, "I understood that there was good fishing hereabout, and, at any rate, I should like to spend a few days among these hills and mountains."

"Well," said Peter, "there's trout in some of our streams, though not as many as there used to be, and there's hills a plenty, and mountains too, if you choose to walk fur enough. They're a good deal furder off than they look. What did you bring with you to fish with?"

"Nothing at all," I answered. "I was told in the town that you were a great fisherman, and that you could let me have all the tackle I would need."

"Upon my word," said old Peter, resting his pipe-hand on his knee and looking steadfastly at me, "you're the queerest fisherman I've see'd yet. Nigh every year, some two or three of 'em stop here in the fishin' season, and there was never a man who didn't bring his jinted pole, and his reels, and his lines, and his hooks, and his dry-goods flies, and his whiskey-flask with a long strap to it. Now, if you want all these things, I haven't got 'em."

"Whatever you use yourself will suit me," I answered.

"All right, then," said he. "I'll do the best I can for you in the mornin'. But it's plain enough to me that you're not a game fisherman, or you wouldn't come here without your tools."

To this remark I made answer to the effect that, though I was very fond of fishing, my pleasure in it did not depend upon the possession of all the appliances of professional sport.

"Perhaps you think," said the old man, "from the way I spoke, that I don't believe them fellers with the jinted poles can ketch fish, but that ain't so. That old story about the little boy with the pin-hook who ketched all the fish, while the gentleman with the modern improvements, who stood alongside of him, kep' throwin' out his beautiful flies and never got nothin', is a pure lie. The fancy chaps, who must have ev'rythin' jist so, gen'rally gits fish. But for all that, I don't like their way of fishin', and I take no stock in it myself. I've been fishin', on and off, ever since I was a little boy, and I've caught nigh every kind there is, from the big jew-fish and cavalyoes down South, to the trout and minnies round about here. But when I ketch a fish, the first thing I do is to try to git him on the hook, and the next thing is to git him out of the water jist as soon as I kin. I don't put in no time worryin' him. There's only two animals in the world that likes to worry smaller creeturs a good while afore they kill 'em; one is the cat, and the other is what they call the game fisherman. This kind of a feller never goes after no fish that don't mind being ketched. He goes fur them kinds that loves their home in the water and hates most to leave it, and he makes it jist as hard fur 'em as he kin. What the game fisher likes is the smallest kind of a hook, the thinnest line, and a fish that it takes a good while to weaken. The longer the weak'nin' business kin be spun out, the more the sport. The idee is to let the fish think there's a chance fur him to git away. That's jist like the cat with her mouse. She lets the little creetur hop off, but the minnit he gits fur enough away, she jumps on him and jabs him with her claws, and then, if there's any game left in him, she lets him try again. Of course the game fisher could have a strong line and a stout pole and git his fish in a good sight quicker, if he wanted to, but that wouldn't be sport. He couldn't give him the butt and spin him out, and reel him in, and let him jump and run till his pluck is clean worn out. Now, I likes to git my fish ashore with all the pluck in 'em. It makes 'em taste better. And as fur fun, I'll be bound I've had jist as much of that, and more, too, than most of these fellers who are so dreadful anxious to have everythin' jist right, and think they can't go fishin' till they've spent enough money to buy a suit of Sunday clothes. As a gen'ral rule they're a solemn lot, and work pretty hard at their fun. When I work I want to be paid fur it, and when I go in fur fun I want to take it easy and cheerful. Now I wouldn't say so much agen these fellers," said old Peter, as he arose and put his empty pipe on a little shelf under the porch-roof, "if it wasn't for one thing, and that is, that they think that their kind of fishin' is the only kind worth considerin'. The way they look down upon plain Christian fishin' is enough to rile a hitchin'-post. I don't want to say nothin' agen no man's way of attendin' to his own affairs, whether it's kitchen-gardenin', or whether it's fishin', if he says nothin' agen my way; but when he looks down on me, and grins at me, I want to haul myself up, and grin at him, if I kin. And in this case, I kin. I s'pose the house-cat and the cat-fisher (by which I don't mean the man who fishes for cat-fish) was both made as they is, and they can't help it; but that don't give 'em no right to put on airs before other bein's, who gits their meat with a square kill. Good-night. And sence I've talked so much about it, I've a mind to go fishin' with you to-morrow myself."

The next morning found old Peter of the same mind, and after breakfast he proceeded to fit me out for a day of what he called "plain Christian trout-fishin'." He gave me a reed rod, about nine feet long, light, strong, and nicely balanced. The tackle he produced was not of the fancy order, but his lines were of fine strong linen, and his hooks were of good shape, clean and sharp, and snooded to the lines with a neatness that indicated the hand of a man who had been where he learned to wear little gold rings in his ears.

"Here are some of these feather insects," he said, "which you kin take along if you like." And he handed me a paper containing a few artificial flies. "They're pretty nat'ral," he said, "and the hooks is good. A man who came here fishin' gave 'em to me, but I shan't want 'em to-day. At this time of year grasshoppers is the best bait in the kind of place where we're goin' to fish. The stream, after it comes down from the mountain, runs through half a mile of medder land before it strikes into the woods agen. A grasshopper is a little creetur that's got as much conceit as if his jinted legs was fish-poles, and he thinks he kin jump over this narrer run of water whenever he pleases; but he don't always do it, and then if he doesn't git snapped up by the trout that lie along the banks in the medder, he is floated along into the woods, where there's always fish enough to come to the second table."

Having got me ready, Peter took his own particular pole, which he assured me he had used for eleven years, and hooking on his left arm a good-sized basket, which his elder pretty daughter had packed with cold meat, bread, butter, and preserves, we started forth for a three-mile walk to the fishing-ground. The day was a favorable one for our purpose, the sky being sometimes over-clouded, which was good for fishing, and also for walking on a highroad; and sometimes bright, which was good for effects of mountain-scenery. Not far from the spot where old Peter proposed to begin our sport, a small frame-house stood by the roadside, and here the old man halted and entered the open door without knocking or giving so much as a premonitory stamp. I followed, imitating my companion in leaving my pole outside, which appeared to be the only ceremony that the etiquette of those parts required of visitors. In the room we entered, a small man in his shirt-sleeves sat mending a basket-handle. He nodded to Peter, and Peter nodded to him.

"We've come up a-fishin'," said the old man. "Kin your boys give us some grasshoppers?"

"I don't know that they've got any ready ketched," said he, "for I reckon I used what they had this mornin'. But they kin git you some. Here, Dan, you and Sile go and ketch Mr. Gruse and this young man some grasshoppers. Take that mustard-box, and see that you git it full."

Peter and I now took seats, and the conversation began about a black cow which Peter had to sell, and which the other was willing to buy if the old man would trade for sheep, which animals, however, the basket-mender did not appear just at that time to have in his possession. As I was not very much interested in this subject, I walked to the back-door and watched two small boys in scanty shirts and trousers, and ragged straw hats, who were darting about in the grass catching grasshoppers, of which insects, judging by the frequent pounces of the boys, there seemed a plentiful supply.

"Got it full?" said their father, when the boys came in.

"Crammed," said Dan.

Old Peter took the little can, pressed the top firmly on, put it in his coat-tail pocket, and rose to go. "You'd better think about that cow, Barney," said he. He said nothing to the boys about the box of bait; but I could not let them catch grasshoppers for us for nothing, and I took a dime from my pocket, and gave it to Dan. Dan grinned, and Sile looked sheepishly happy, and at the sight of the piece of silver an expression of interest came over the face of the father. "Wait a minute," said he, and he went into a little room that seemed to be a kitchen. Returning, he brought with him a small string of trout. "Do you want to buy some fish?" he said. "These is nice fresh ones. I ketched 'em this mornin'."

To offer to sell fish to a man who is just about to go out to catch them for himself might, in most cases, be considered an insult, but it was quite evident that nothing of the kind was intended by Barney. He probably thought that if I bought grasshoppers, I might buy fish. "You kin have 'em for a quarter," he said.

It was derogatory to my pride to buy fish at such a moment, but the man looked very poor, and there was a shade of anxiety on his face which touched me. Old Peter stood by without saying a word. "It might be well," I said, turning to him, "to buy these fish, for we may not catch enough for supper."

"Such things do happen," said the old man.

"Well," said I, "if we have these we shall feel safe in any case." And I took the fish and gave the man a quarter. It was not, perhaps, a professional act, but the trout were well worth the money, and I felt that I was doing a deed of charity.

Old Peter and I now took our rods, and crossed the road into an enclosed field, and thence into a wide stretch of grass land, bounded by hills in front of us and to the right, while a thick forest lay to the left. We had walked but a short distance, when Peter said: "I'll go down into the woods, and try my luck there, and you'd better go along up stream, about a quarter of a mile, to where it's rocky. P'raps you ain't used to fishin' in the woods, and you might git your line cotched. You'll find the trout'll bite in the rough water."

"Where is the stream?" I asked.

"This is it," he said, pointing to a little brook, which was scarcely too wide for me to step across, "and there's fish right here, but they're hard to ketch, fur they git plenty of good livin' and are mighty sassy about their eatin'. But you kin ketch 'em up there."

Old Peter now went down toward the woods, while I walked up the little stream. I had seen trout-brooks before, but never one so diminutive as this. However, when I came nearer to the point where the stream issued from between two of the foot-hills of the mountains, which lifted their forest-covered heights in the distance, I found it wider and shallower, breaking over its rocky bottom in sparkling little cascades.

Fishing in such a jolly little stream, surrounded by this mountain scenery, and with the privileges of the beautiful situation all to myself, would have been a joy to me if I had had never a bite. But no such ill-luck befell me. Peter had given me the can of grasshoppers after putting half of them into his own bait-box, and these I used with much success. It was grasshopper season, and the trout were evidently on the lookout for them. I fished in the ripples under the little waterfalls; and every now and then I drew out a lively trout. Most of these were of moderate size, and some of them might have been called small. The large ones probably fancied the forest shades, where old Peter went. But all I caught were fit for the table, and I was very well satisfied with the result of my sport.

About noon I began to feel hungry, and thought it time to look up the old man, who had the lunch-basket. I walked down the bank of the brook, and some time before I reached the woods I came to a place where it expanded to a width of about ten feet. The water here was very clear, and the motion quiet, so that I could easily see to the bottom, which did not appear to be more than a foot below the surface. Gazing into this transparent water, as I walked, I saw a large trout glide across the stream, and disappear under the grassy bank which overhung the opposite side. I instantly stopped. This was a much larger fish than any I had caught, and I determined to try for him.

I stepped back from the bank, so as to be out of sight, and put a fine grasshopper on my hook; then I lay, face downward, on the grass, and worked myself slowly forward until I could see the middle of the stream; then quietly raising my pole, I gave my grasshopper a good swing, as if he had made a wager to jump over the stream at its widest part. But as he certainly would have failed in such an ambitious endeavor, especially if he had been caught by a puff of wind, I let him come down upon the surface of the water, a little beyond the middle of the brook. Grasshoppers do not sink when they fall into the water, and so I kept this fellow upon the surface, and gently moved him along, as if, with all the conceit taken out of him by the result of his ill-considered leap, he was ignominiously endeavoring to swim to shore. As I did this, I saw the trout come out from under the bank, move slowly toward the grasshopper, and stop directly under him. Trembling with anxiety and eager expectation, I endeavored to make the movements of the insect still more natural, and, as far as I was able, I threw into him a sudden perception of his danger, and a frenzied desire to get away. But, either the trout had had all the grasshoppers he wanted, or he was able, from long experience, to perceive the difference between a natural exhibition of emotion and a histrionic imitation of it, for he slowly turned, and, with a few slight movements of his tail, glided back under the bank. In vain did the grasshopper continue his frantic efforts to reach the shore; in vain did he occasionally become exhausted, and sink a short distance below the surface; in vain did he do everything that he knew, to show that he appreciated what a juicy and delicious morsel he was, and how he feared that the trout might yet be tempted to seize him; the fish did not come out again.

Then I withdrew my line, and moved back from the stream. I now determined to try Mr. Trout with a fly, and I took out the paper old Peter Gruse had given me. I did not know exactly what kind of winged insects were in order at this time of the year, but I was sure that yellow butterflies were not particular about just what month it was, so long as the sun shone warmly. I therefore chose that one of Peter's flies which was made of the yellowest feathers, and, removing the snood and hook from my line, I hastily attached this fly, which was provided with a hook quite suitable for my desired prize. Crouching on the grass, I again approached the brook. Gaily flitting above the glassy surface of the water, in all the fancied security of tender youth and innocence, came my yellow fly. Backward and forward over the water he gracefully flew, sometimes rising a little into the air, as if to view the varied scenery of the woods and mountains, and then settling for a moment close to the surface, to better inspect his glittering image as it came up from below, and showing in his every movement his intense enjoyment of summer-time and life.

Out from his dark retreat now came the trout, and settling quietly at the bottom of the brook, he appeared to regard the venturesome insect with a certain interest. But he must have detected the iron-barb of vice beneath the mask of blitheful innocence, for, after a short deliberation, the trout turned and disappeared under the bank. As he slowly moved away, he seemed to be bigger than ever. I must catch that fish! Surely he would bite at something. It was quite evident that his mind was not wholly unsusceptible to emotions emanating from an awakening appetite, and I believed that if he saw exactly what he wanted, he would not neglect an opportunity of availing himself of it. But what did he want? I must certainly find out. Drawing myself back again, I took off the yellow fly, and put on another. This was a white one, with black blotches, like a big miller moth which had fallen into an ink-pot. It was surely a conspicuous creature, and as I crept forward and sent it swooping over the stream, I could not see how any trout, with a single insectivorous tooth in his head, could fail to rise to such an occasion. But this trout did not rise. He would not even come out from under his bank to look at the swiftly flitting creature. He probably could see it well enough from where he was.

But I was not to be discouraged. I put on another fly; a green one with a red tail. It did not look like any insect that I had ever seen, but I thought that the trout might know more about such things than I. He did come out to look at it, but probably considering it a product of that modern aestheticism which sacrifices natural beauty to medieval crudeness of color and form, he retired without evincing any disposition to countenance this style of art.

It was evident that it would be useless to put on any other flies, for the two I had left were a good deal bedraggled, and not nearly so attractive as those I had used. Just before leaving the house that morning, Peter's son had given me a wooden matchbox filled with worms for bait, which, although I did not expect to need, I put in my pocket. As a last resort I determined to try the trout with a worm. I selected the plumpest and most comely of the lot; I put a new hook on my line; I looped him about it in graceful coils, and cautiously approached the water, as before. Now a worm never attempts to wildly leap across a flowing brook, nor does he flit in thoughtless innocence through the sunny air, and over the bright transparent stream. If he happens to fall into the water, he sinks to the bottom; and if he be of a kind not subject to drowning, he generally endeavors to secrete himself under a stone, or to burrow in the soft mud. With this knowledge of his nature I gently dropped my worm upon the surface of the stream, and then allowed him slowly to sink. Out sailed the trout from under the bank, but stopped before reaching the sinking worm. There was a certain something in his action which seemed to indicate a disgust at the sight of such plebeian food, and a fear seized me that he might now swim off, and pay no further attention to my varied baits. Suddenly there was a ripple in the water, and I felt a pull on the line. Instantly I struck; and then there was a tug. My blood boiled through every vein and artery, and I sprang to my feet. I did not give him the butt; I did not let him run with yards of line down the brook; nor reel him in, and let him make another mad course up stream; I did not turn him over as he jumped into the air; nor endeavor, in any way, to show him that I understood those tricks, which his depraved nature prompted him to play upon the angler. With an absolute dependence upon the strength of old Peter's tackle, I lifted the fish. Out he came from the water, which held him with a gentle suction as if unwilling to let him go, and then he whirled through the air like a meteor flecked with rosy fire, and landed on the fresh green grass a dozen feet behind me. Down on my knees I dropped before him as he tossed and rolled, his beautiful spots and colors glistening in the sun. He was truly a splendid trout, fully a foot long, round and heavy. Carefully seizing him, I easily removed the hook from the bony roof of his capacious mouth thickly set with sparkling teeth, and then I tenderly killed him, with all his pluck, as old Peter would have said, still in him.

I covered the rest of the fish in my basket with wet plantain leaves, and laid my trout king on this cool green bed. Then I hurried off to the old man, whom I saw coming out of the woods. When I opened my basket and showed him what I had caught, Peter looked surprised, and, taking up the trout, examined it.

"Why, this is a big fellow," he said. "At first I thought it was Barney Sloat's boss trout, but it isn't long enough for him. Barney showed me his trout, that gen'rally keeps in a deep pool, where a tree has fallen over the stream down there. Barney tells me he often sees him, and he's been tryin' fur two years to ketch him, but he never has, and I say he never will, fur them big trout's got too much sense to fool round any kind of victuals that's got a string to it. They let a little fish eat all he wants, and then they eat him. How did you ketch this one?"

I gave an account of the manner of the capture, to which Peter listened with interest and approval.

"If you'd a stood off and made a cast at that feller, you'd either have caught him at the first flip, which isn't likely, as he didn't seem to want no feather flies, or else you'd a skeered him away. That's all well enough in the tumblin' water, where you gen'rally go fur trout, but the man that's got the true feelin' fur fish will try to suit his idees to theirs, and if he keeps on doin' that, he's like to learn a thing or two that may do him good. That's a fine fish, and you ketched him well. I've got a lot of 'em, but nothin' of that heft."

After luncheon we fished for an hour or two with no result worth recording, and then we started for home. A couple of partridges ran across the road some distance ahead of us, and these gave Peter an idea.

"Do you know," said he, "if things go on as they're goin' on now, that there'll come a time when it won't be considered high-toned sport to shoot a bird slam-bang dead. The game gunners will pop 'em with little harpoons, with long threads tied to 'em, and the feller that can tire out his bird, and haul him in with the longest and thinnest piece of spool thread, will be the crackest sportsman."

At this point I remarked to my companion that perhaps he was a little hard on the game fishermen.

"Well," said old Peter, with a smile on his corrugated visage, "I reckon I'd have to do a lot of talkin' before I'd git even with 'em, fur the way they give me the butt for my style of fishin'. What I say behind their backs I say to their faces. I seed one of these fellers once with a fish on his hook, that he was runnin' up an' down the stream like a chased chicken. 'Why don't you pull him in?' says I. 'And break my rod an' line?' says he. 'Why don't you have a stronger line and pole?' says I. 'There wouldn't be no science in that,' says he. 'If it's your science you want to show off,' says I, 'you ought to fish for mud eels. There's more game in 'em than there is in any other fish round here, and as they're mighty lively out of water you might play one of 'em fur half an hour after you got him on shore, and it would take all your science to keep him from reelin' up his end of the line faster than you could yourn.'"

When we reached the farm the old man went into the barn, and I took the fish into the house. I found the two pretty daughters in the large room, where the eating and some of the cooking was done. I opened my basket, and with great pride showed them the big trout I had caught. They evidently thought it was a large fish, but they looked at each other, and smiled in a way that I did not understand. I had expected from them, at least, as much admiration for my prize and my skill as their father had shown.

"You don't seem to think much of this fine trout that I took such trouble to catch," I remarked.

"You mean," said the elder girl, with a laugh, "that you bought of Barney Sloat."
I looked at her in astonishment.

"Barney was along here to-day," she said, "and he told about your buying your fish of him."

"Bought of him!" I exclaimed, indignantly. "A little string of fish at the bottom of the basket I bought of him, but all the others, and this big one, I caught myself."

"Oh, of course," said the pretty daughter, "bought the little ones and caught all the big ones!"

"Barney Sloat ought to have kept his mouth shut," said the younger pretty daughter, looking at me with an expression of pity. "He'd got his money, and he hadn't no business to go telling on people. Nobody likes that sort of thing. But this big fish is a real nice one, and you shall have it for your supper."

"Thank you," I said, with dignity, and left the room.

I did not intend to have any further words with these young women on this subject, but I cannot deny that I was annoyed and mortified. This was the result of a charitable action. I think I was never more proud of anything than of catching that trout; and it was a good deal of a downfall to suddenly find myself regarded as a mere city man fishing with a silver hook. But, after all, what did it matter?

The boy who did not seem to be accounted a member of the family came into the house, and as he passed me he smiled good-humoredly, and said: "Buyed 'em!"

I felt like throwing a chair at him, but refrained out of respect to my host. Before supper the old man came out on to the porch where I was sitting. "It seems," said he, "that my gals has got it inter their heads that you bought that big fish of Barney Sloat, and as I can't say I seed you ketch it, they're not willin' to give in, 'specially as I didn't git no such big one. 'Tain't wise to buy fish when you're goin' fishin' yourself. It's pretty certain to tell agen you."

"You ought to have given me that advice before," I said, somewhat shortly. "You saw me buy the fish."

"You don't s'pose," said old Peter, "that I'm goin' to say anythin' to keep money out of my neighbor's pockets. We don't do that way in these parts. But I've told the gals they're not to speak another word about it, so you needn't give your mind no worry on that score. And now let's go in to supper. If you're as hungry as I am, there won't be many of them fish left fur breakfast."

That evening, as we were sitting smoking on the porch, old Peter's mind reverted to the subject of the unfounded charge against me. "It goes pretty hard," he remarked, "to have to stand up and take a thing you don' like when there's no call fur it. It's bad enough when there is a call fur it. That matter about your fish buyin' reminds me of what happened two summers ago to my sister, or ruther to her two little boys—or, more correct yit, to one of 'em. Them was two cur'ous little boys.

They was allus tradin' with each other. Their father deals mostly in horses, and they must have got it from him. At the time I'm tellin' of they'd traded everythin' they had, and when they hadn't nothin' else left to swap they traded names. Joe he took Johnny's name, and Johnny he took Joe's. Jist about when they'd done this, they both got sick with sumthin' or other, the oldest one pretty bad, the other not much. Now there ain't no doctor inside of twenty miles of where my sister lives. But there's one who sometimes has a call to go through that part of the country, and the people about there is allus very glad when they chance to be sick when he comes along. Now this good luck happened to my sister, fur the doctor come by jist at this time. He looks into the state of the boys, and while their mother has gone downstairs he mixes some medicine he has along with him. 'What's your name?' he says to the oldest boy when he'd done it. Now as he'd traded names with his brother, fair and square, he wasn't goin' back on the trade, and he said, 'Joe.' 'And my name's Johnny,' up and says the other one. Then the doctor he goes and gives the bottle of medicine to their mother, and says he: 'This medicine is fur Joe. You must give him a tablespoonful every two hours. Keep up the treatment, and he'll be all right. As fur Johnny, there's nothin' much the matter with him. He don't need no medicine.' And then he went away. Every two hours after that Joe, who wasn't sick worth mentionin', had to swallow a dose of horrid stuff, and pretty soon he took to his bed, and Johnny he jist played round and got well in the nat'ral way. Joe's mother kept up the treatment, gittin' up in the night to feed that stuff to him; but the poor little boy got wuss and wuss, and one mornin' he says to his mother, says he: 'Mother, I guess I'm goin' to die, and I'd ruther do that than take any more of that medicine, and I wish you'd call Johnny and we'll trade names back agen, and if he don't want to come and do it, you kin tell him he kin keep the old minkskin I gave him to boot, on account of his name havin' a Wesley in it.' 'Trade names,' says his mother, 'what do you mean by that?' And then he told her what he and Johnny had done. 'And did you ever tell anybody about this?' says she. 'Nobody but Dr. Barnes,' says he. 'After that I got sick and forgot it.' When my sister heard that, an idee struck into her like you put a fork into an apple dumplin'. Traded names, and told the doctor! She'd all along thought it strange that the boy that seemed wuss should be turned out, and the other one put under treatment; but it wasn't fur her to set up her opinion agen that of a man like Dr. Barnes. Down she went, in about seventeen jumps, to where Eli Timmins, the hired man, was ploughin' in the corn. 'Take that horse out of that,' she hollers, 'and you may kill him if you have to, but git Dr. Barnes here before my little boy dies.' When the doctor come he heard the story, and looked at the sick youngster, and then says he: 'If he'd kept his minkskin, and not hankered after a Wesley to his name, he'd a had a better time of it. Stop the treatment, and he'll be all right.' Which she did; and he was. Now it seems to me that this is a good deal like your case. You've had to take a lot of medicine that didn't belong to you, and I guess it's made you feel pretty bad; but I've told my gals to stop the treatment, and you'll be all right in the mornin'. Good-night. Your candlestick is on the kitchen table."

For two days longer I remained in this neighborhood, wandering alone over the hills, and up the mountain-sides, and by the brooks, which tumbled and gurgled through the lonely forest. Each evening I brought home a goodly supply of trout, but never a great one like the noble fellow for which I angled in the meadow stream.

On the morning of my departure I stood on the porch with old Peter waiting for the arrival of the mail driver, who was to take me to the nearest railroad town.

"I don't want to say nothin'," remarked the old man, "that would keep them fellers with the jinted poles from stoppin' at my house when they comes to these parts a-fishin'. I ain't got no objections to their poles; 'tain't that. And I don't mind nuther their standin' off, and throwin' their flies as fur as they've a mind to; that's not it. And it ain't even the way they have of worryin' their fish. I wouldn't do it myself, but if they like it, that's their business. But what does rile me is the cheeky way in which they stand up and say that there isn't no decent way of fishin' but their way. And that to a man that's ketched more fish, of more different kinds, with more game in 'em, and had more fun at it, with a lot less money, and less tomfoolin' than any fishin' feller that ever come here and talked to me like an old cat tryin' to teach a dog to ketch rabbits. No, sir; agen I say that I don't take no money fur entertainin' the only man that ever come out here to go a-fishin' in a plain, Christian way. But if you feel tetchy about not payin' nothin', you kin send me one of them poles in three pieces, a good strong one, that'll lift Barney Sloat's trout, if ever I hook him."

I sent him the rod; and next summer I am going out to see him use it.

Owen's Adventure

ROBERT ALLEN

I cannot tell whether dyspeptic people ever become fishermen, or whether fishermen can ever become dyspeptic; but it would be as hard a trial as any I can conceive—even to one of the guards who finished at the battle of Waterloo the tender discipline of the Peninsular war—to drink whisky punch all night in a cabin, and set forth at daybreak, for the enlivening purpose of traversing a bog, of twenty miles extent, saturated with rain. If the powers of digestion are a little irregular and fastidious, perhaps this would be an occasion to call forth some of these extraordinary antics their defective subordination so frequently suggests.

Owen's face looked, if possible, more lengthy than ever; and I thought I could discover in the major's eye somewhat of the golden tinge, which, though in the main rather a pretty color, is not highly esteemed even by gentlemen from India, who come to drink Epsom salt water at the pleasant vortex for invalids—Cheltenham. But I was afraid to venture an observation, fully impressed with the convictions that the Tu quoque would form a just rejoinder. I won't say that I was quite well, or that a good bed, with a nice clean-capped chambermaid lighting me hitherto, and fumbling about the clothes with an old frying-pan, with holes in the lid, would not have o'ertopped the hopes of the fresh in the river. But here was nothing but the wild heath, the resounded river, now charged to its banks' edge, bursting through the chasms of solid granite, and in the stillness of the dawn roaring through the glens. The mists still covered the tops of the mountains, and showed forth the dreariness and desolation of an unexplored expanse.

Nature had made some little confusion in what philosopher Square calls, "the external fitness of things"; the heat without is by no means in a proper ratio of that within the body; for, though both the major and myself had taken especial care and used considerable diligence in fortifying the inner man with all the warmth which new whisky could possibly excite, it is a curious fact in physics, for which I am wholly incompetent to account, that the exterior man did shiver most intolerably. There was a disinclination to parlance also—at other times little to be charged on the major; and I believe, friends as we were, nothing would have been more easy at the moment than to have concocted a very nice quarrel. None of us were quarrelsome, but the discourse was monosyllabic, and our words were chilled; but neither dared confess the discomfort under which we all three labored.

I thought of nothing but the twenty miles, and continued to occupy myself in ratiocinative deductions, arising from the fact that a man had been known to achieve the distance even without once throwing himself horizontally on a wet bog—an inclination, however, which, ever and anon, assumed considerable force. Not unfrequently did I persuade myself that I could walk, and sustain the dignity of the *ad sidera vultus*, with my eyes shut. Nothing could be seen; the bog was level; nor was I roused from the favorable view I had been induced to take of this very pernicious fallacy but by the practical squash into the morass, which generally invited the other foot to the rescue of the offending member, which it was not then exactly convenient to amputate. There was no inequality of wretchedness, therefore, both feet being well saturated with the porterlike overflowing of the bog.

As to Owen, I had conceived hopes that he at least would break down, and give me some color for following his example. The imperturbable villain had secured a piece of lighted turf, and, as I looked behind to observe how he got on, I had the mortification of witnessing a countenance of the utmost complacency, in the principle feature of which was stuck a short black pipe, and out of which very principal feature issued long volumes of detestable-looking smoke. There was no chance from him. There was nothing for it but to push on.

The river was swollen to a flood; but, as the rain had now ceased and the fall was rapid, we anticipated a good cast by midday. The major grumbled at the disappointment, as he had determined to carry into the town the wherewith of a good dinner. I found in this state of the water the roe useless—the fish were scattered by the extended volume of the stream. We were at least three hours too early, as the major ventured to observe after a few casts.

"It's a glorious morning, however," said he.

"Splendid."

"The fresh morning air is very refreshing."

"I daresay it is."

"This is a grand specimen of the fisherman's life. Now, I just observe to you that nothing gives a greater relish to a breakfast than the mountain air—it's perfectly astonishing what it will do for the health."

"And the comfort too."

"Why, I was thinking that the smallest drop of whisky might do no great hurt, and help us onward."

This was the point the gallant officer had been aiming at ever since our departure. I could not resist the temptation of assuring him that it was, of all things in the world, the proper thing: the stimulus should be kept up when there was no sport to enliven the labors. The major's draught was not loud but deep; and there was a manifestation of enterprise almost simultaneously engendered.

"Huzza for the lob-trouts this day!—the thick water will be off in an hour. It was just after such a day that I grabbed fifty of the best salmon I ever saw—all fresh run from the sea."

"What is the process of grabbling?"

"After a fresh flood, the salmon come up in shoals to the falls, and there rest till they are sufficiently recovered to make the leap. They are then sulky—will take neither bait nor fly, but stick like logs under the fall. I then quietly take a dozen large cod hooks, tie them back to back, and, with a stout stick, a strong cord, and heavy lead sinker, let down to the bottom, every now and then twitch to the right, then to the left, then upward, and inwise, and outward. Fifty of the silvery villains fell victim to my industry, till the proprietor of the fall came personally to pay me a visit, and had the audacity to question both my right to fish and the fairness of the style of it. As to the fairness of it, said I, all is fair in love, war, and fishing; and as to the right, you'll particularly honor me by the acceptance of this card, where my name and rank are neatly engraved for the satisfaction of all gentlemen who may render themselves worthy of my notice. Will you believe that the spalpeen refused to fight, and talked something about the law? I wished him good day—regretted I had mistaken his calling—the mistake being exactly the converse of Hamlet's, as I had conceived a fishmonger was a gentleman. I gave him no chance for his law, as I pushed on beyond his district before he had obtained the summons. But the fifty salmon were capital. I distributed them among all the poor cottagers as I passed along. Faith, it was many a day since any of them had seen such a meal, although living on the very banks of the river.—Did you see that rise?"

The intimidation was enough. The fish had begun to stir, and the water was now clearing. We were within four miles of the town, which the major represented as bad enough at all times, but worse without notice. It was arranged, therefore, that Owen should push forward to apprise the landlord of our coming, and give the necessary orders. He was especially enjoined, if possible, to take with him a salmon, which was to be ready on our arrival. Owen pocketed his black pipe, and, charged by so important a mission, in which his skill as an angler was to be put to the test, with an air of offended dignity at the doubt implied, strutted over the bog, while the major and myself prepared our tackle.

The major's first throw instantly rose a fish, but he rose short. The same fish rose again at my fly, still short. Down went the major's rod, and, regardless of the recent rains, he proceeded to seat himself on the grass.

"Now, what fly do the willful vermin want? A flood, and a light yellow golden pheasant not do for the epicurean villains?"

We produced the books, and, after a long examination and due balancing of probabilities, we selected a light-blue hackle and gray wing. We were right; the first cast produced a salmon firmly hooked; he was my prize. In a minute, the major was fast linked to another. In the hilarity of the moment, the major hurled up his hat, as his fish steadily pushed up the stream.

I was not less exulting; but the moment of conflict I knew had not yet arrived. In due course, my fish conceived it more agreeable to travel downward—a disposition I had no means of restraining—and, favored by the strong current, had though proper to adopt the railroad rate of traveling; I mean that rate expressed in the splendid schedules, about arriving here and there at such particular hours, but which schedules, and the columns they contain, have no further effect than that of disappointing elderly gentlemen who look for a hot dinner at 3:30, and get it cold at 5:20. My salmon had none of this irregularity; he pushed downward in earnest, and not according to any schedule. In doing so—I could not help it, whatever my gallant colleague may say when he reads these pages—he crossed the major's line, whose fish was traveling upward at the slow coach pace, checked the lines, and, I grieve to say, with such violence as to smash both. The remnants came up without trouble. The major looked at me, and I looked at the major.

* * * * * *

These asterisks express a pause—it was a long one. It is altogether wrong, and very wicked, to ejaculate,—and so it is to write down apostrophes that have immediate reference to a state of misfortune not quite applicable to sublunary matters, but which exclusively belong to a particular extent of heat hereafter, and, therefore, I refrain. But I must record the fact that my gallant companion in arms did throw down his white hat—that he did stamp upon it, notwithstanding its intrinsic value as a hat—that he did commit devastation on the very small proportion of hair which remained at the back of his head, regardless of its inestimable beauty—and that he did then and there declare that I had no right—that it was wholly against the common law of angling, and, as he believed on his soul, against a particular act of parliament—to allow my fish to run down while his was taking the opposite direction!

There was nothing to be said; I had no excuse to offer; the fish was pertinacious, and the act of parliament referred to did not extend to him, however applicable to me. That was all I could urge; but if it had not happened that the major had some respect for me on other accounts, I verily believe our friendship had been form that moment at an end.

"That was the right color," I observed, after some time, and looking cautiously at the major as he gazed on the stream in a certain inert state of intellect and bodily function. He looked toward me peeringly, as though he was examining the extent of my grief, expecting, doubtlessly, to observe a height of mental anguish which equaled or exceeded his own.

"It was a tolerable color, by St. Patrick!" and he began to mend the disposition of his hat, by thrusting his hand rather energetically into the crown, and using other persuasives to a resumption of its original form. "You may say that; it was a tolerable color."

I like to see a man recovering form a violent passion, the cause of which is irremediable. The indignation evaporates, but a strong pride remains, which will not allow the possessor to acknowledge that the cause was irremediable. The major had been unhappy but for the opportunity of casting all blame on me; and I ventured, therefore, to hint that the statute to which he had so learnedly referred really applied to himself, as it strictly forbade any person or persons whatever, under a penalty thereinafter named, holding, playing, drowning, or following any fish, whensoever it shall or may happen that another person, &c. The recitation of this act did not convince him; but it sufficiently soothed him to endure the renovation of the tackle with some coolness, although the knots were completed with some jerks, each being accompanied by a consignment direct to inferior regions.

We were presently surprised by a succession of leaps; four or five salmon at once cleared the surface. Our surprise and curiosity were soon satisfied; the nose of an otter was elevated, then another, and another. We were up in a moment; the rifle had been left with Owen. It was a brood.

"Pelt them with stones!" cried the major.

This I did with all imaginable industry, and succeeded in separating the young ones from the parents. The latter had gone down the stream, while the three whelps, unable to sustain themselves under water for so great a length of time, popped up their heads in exactly the most inconvenient places. The chase now began; as the young ones had started up the stream, we had no difficulty in keeping them in that direction. At length the three perched on a rock, and began to cry with the small voice of a cat; they were obviously in the wrong, and had missed the old ones, who were doubtless not far off.

The skill of the major was now in requisition; he had hastily tied to his line all the large salmon flies he could find, and, at the distance of twenty yards, ere I was informed of his intention, covered the three whelps by a foot; they immediately started, and the major as immediately drew.

"Here's one at least," exclaimed he.

It was true; he had one of the otters fast; but the difficulty of holding him was not trifling. The fight was exactly in the style of a large and heavy fish; first he was down to the bottom of the pool, then, with the rapidity of lightning, he rose at another part where he was least expected. The contest was one of most singular dexterity on one part, and strength and agility on the other. At length, the smaller of the two fishermen began to yield, and, in a few minutes, he was dragged by main force to the shore. I now assisted in the fight, but warily, as the little animal bit ferociously at everything that was put toward him. He died the death of honor; he was stoned to death, and crammed into the creel as the most remarkable trophy of expert angling.

It was hopeless to expect any success, at least within a considerable range on the river, the otters having taken down the stream; and I was by no means unwilling to dismount the flies, and go in search of comfort, a very attenuated portion of which had, for the last twenty-four hours, been our lot. In the triumph of his skill, my companion had forgotten the contretemps in which he affected to believe me so deeply implicated, and we improved in good humor and courtesy as we shortened the distance to Castlebar.

The road was indeed a rough and boggy one; but, after the difficulties we had encountered by the riverside, even this seemed tolerably direct; every second step did not, as before, give us one foot in the bog.

At length the turfy smoke of Castlebar met our view, and the exhilaration I immediately felt at the near prospect of food, raiment, and lodging, would not be repressed; strength returned to my previously tottering limbs, and my companion's heavy stump became more energetic.

On our entrance into Castlebar, and on inquiring for the inn, we found that the town was really in a hubbub. It happened to be market-day, and groups of persons surrounded us. At last we were accosted by one of the country people, who seemed more capable of addressing the strangers than the rest, who informed us that our attendant, Owen, was in trouble—in truth, at that moment, in durance—for an offense of rather an extraordinary character. The landlord, who was of the roughest order, received us at the door.

"If it's your honor's man that's taken up, he has sent a dozen times to inquire for you, to clear him before the magistrate."

The major, who had contracted a real friendship for our humble attendant, was on fire.

"Who is the magistrate that dares to take up my man, without first informing myself? Oh, it's myself will settle the matter without the law at all at all."

I could perceive, without much difficulty, that my friend was in an unlikely mood to become just then a very successful advocate. Leaving him, therefore, to the pocketbook from which he was selecting a card, with no very friendly intention toward the magistrate, I proceeded to make further inquiries, and learned that our Achates had been exhibiting himself in a state that would have even offended the ladies of the Connemara wilds—in fact, that he had been stopped in a state of entire nudity, running like a madman among all the people coming to market—that he had been seized, covered, and brought before the magistrate, to whom he gave so lame an account of our honors, that he had been consigned to durance till our arrival.

Our astonishment was immeasurable, and could only be appeased by the supposition that Owen's peculiarity of character had at length subsided into absolute madness. We forthwith proceeded to the rescue, the major burning with indignation, and determined to get up a fight with someone on this score. I succeeded, however, in prevailing on him to allow me to be the manager of the business; and, having sent up my name to the magistrate, we were immediately admitted. His account was that our companion had really been taken as described in the road; and that the people were fully impressed with the notion that he was deranged—a conviction to which he himself had arrived upon hearing the facts. For our satisfaction, he would send again for him, to enable him to give what explanation he pleased on the matter.

Owen was soon produced. At sight of us he forthwith brightened up.

"Och, and it's all right now, anyway! Your honors have got the salmon; I left him to be dressed; and is it myself would go to disappoint your honors of a breakfast along with a few spalpeen market people! I wonder what divil of a country this, that a man mayn't catch a salmon, because the river runs by the side of the road. But your honors will spake for me, and explain it, anyhow, to his nobleness of justice."

I requested permission to ask Owen for his own version, which being readily granted, the prisoner began:—

"It's clear, your honors will remember ordering me to catch a salmon, and go on before to the inn. Well, burn the rise I'd get, your honor, till I came within half a mile of the town; there I sees as fair a rise at the nathural as ever my eyes was blest with. Oh! Be aisy, sis, I—is it there you are, and I wanting ye for my master's breakfast? With that, I makes a clane cast, and covered the beauty to an inch. Up he came—

away went my winch, and I thought of my sowl he'd niver done running till my line was smashed. Into the river I pitches my rod—away run the fish, and way run I—and, faith, I'd enough to do to keep up, anyway, for the stones and the bogs bothered my speed intirely. At last he tops; oh! sis I, it's my turn now, and with that I goes up toward my rod; off boults the fish to the other side of the stream. There was nothing but a swimming or a ducking for it, and, to keep all clane and go dacent into the town like, I pulls off my bits of things, and swims over the river to the place where the wild brute had carried my rod. The divil a bit he stand a minute. Off went the salmon again; and it was then I had a run for it after the river, so, seeing my rod going doubts tide, and, finding the road alongside the river far best for running, to the road I went; and it's a pity your honors weren't there to see the sport—run salmon, run I, for a good half mile—there I caught my rod; and it's a good to the heart to see the way he played. But I soon landed my fish, and what do your honors think? In a fine country like this, a lot of spalpeens, without with your leave, or by your leave, or any politeness at all, seized hould of me, crams an ould frieze or two over me, and brings me to be put to prison. 'Oh!' sis I, 'but I'm a freeborn Irishman,' sis I; 'and there are two rale gintlemen that'll see me righted,' sis I. 'And what have I done?' sis I.—'Done?' sis they. 'Haven't ye been running stark naked among the people, and them women?' sis they.—'The divil a woman or man,' sis I, 'did I see at all at all'; and if your nobleness and honor will give me the book, I'll swear the same on my Bible oath this moment. What do they tell his honor, but that there were lots of women coming to market, and his honor believes 'em, maybe because I'm a Catholic. I saw nobody all the time but the rod, and that was running swately."

I assured the magistrate of my entire conviction that Owen was innocent of any intentional wrong; and such was, I believe, the ardor with which he pursued the sport, that I did not doubt his declaration that he had seen nobody.

The magistrate was pleased to find that the affair was of no further consequence, and ordered Owen to be discharged, assuring him, however, that his being a Catholic had had nothing whatever to do with his detention or discharge, and in this declaration I joined; but the major, seizing the hand of Owen, and in the presence of the magistrate, declared his entire approval of the fisherman's whole course of conduct. "And, for myself, I'd follow a salmon into the very palace rather than lose him, anyway. So, say nothing of being a trifle deficient in the cut of your surtout."

The major was now about to wax wroth in approval of Owen's conduct; and just as he was fumbling about for the card, on which was neatly engraved "Major ——, ——th Regiment," I thrust my arm within his, bowed to the man of authority, and we were at our inn before the gallant officer could determine in what way the proper insult ought to be conveyed to a magistrate. Owen was admitted to dine with us off the salmon which had been the cause of all his distress and degradation.

We were indeed weary, but had acquired in our peregrinations a perfect knowledge of what will be reasonably expected in a night up the mountains by the sportsman in Ireland.

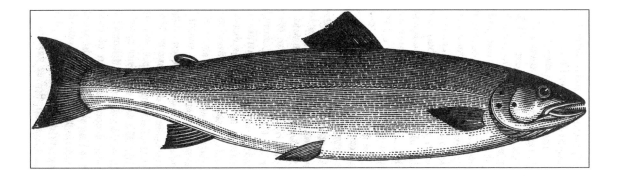

A Fatal Salmon

FRANK FORESTER

It was as fair a morning of July as ever dawned in the blue summer sky; the sun as yet had risen but a little way above the waves of fresh green foliage which formed the horizon of the woodland scenery surrounding Widecomb Manor; and his heat, which promised ere mid-day to become excessive, was tempered now by the exhalations of the copious night-dews, and by the cool breath of the western breeze, which came down through he leafy gorges, in long, soft swells from the open moorlands.

All nature was alive and joyous; the air was vocal with the piping melody of the blackbirds and thrushes, caroling in every brake and bosky dingle; the smooth, green lawn before the windows of the old hall was peopled with whole tribes of fat, lazy hares, limping about among the dewy herbage, fearless, as it would seem, of man's aggression; and to complete the picture, above, a score of splendid peacocks were strutting to and fro on the paved terraces, or perched upon the carved stone balustrades, displaying their gorgeous plumage to the early sunshine.

The shadowy mists of the first morning twilight had not been dispersed from the lower regions, and were suspended still in the middle air in broad fleecy masses, though melting rapidly away in the increasing warmth and brightness of the day.

And still a fain blue line hovered over the bed of the long rocky gorge, which divided the chase from the open country, floating about it like the steam of a seething caldron, and rising here and there into tall smoke-like columns, probably where some steeper cataract of the mountain-stream sent its foam skyward.

So early, indeed, was the hour, that had my tale been recited of these degenerate days, there would have been no gentle eyes awake to look upon the loneliness of a new-awakened nature.

In the good days of old, however, when daylight was still deemed to be the fitting time for labor and for pastime, and night the appointed time for natural and healthful sleep, the dawn was wont to brighten beheld by other eyes than those of clowns and milkmaids, and the gay songs of the matutinal birds were listened to be ears that could appreciate their untaught melodies.

And now, just as the stable clock was striking four, the great oaken door of the old Hall was thrown open with a vigorous swing that made it rattle on its hinges, and Jasper St. Aubyn came bounding out into the fresh morning air, with a foot as elastic as that of the mountain roe, singing a snatch of some quaint old ballad.

He was dressed simply in a close-fitting jacket and tight hose of dark-green cloth, without any lace or embroidery, light boots of untanned leather, and a broad-leafed hat, with a single eagle's feather thrust carelessly through the band. He wore neither cloak nor sword, though it was a period at which gentlemen rarely went abroad without these, their distinctive attributes; but in the broad black belt which girt his rounded waist he carried a stout wood-knife with a buckhorn hilt; and over his shoulder there swung from a leathern thong a large wicker fishing-basket.

Nothing, indeed, could be simpler or less indicative of any particular rank or station in society than young St. Aubyn's garb, yet it would have been a very dull and unobservant eye which should take him for aught less than a high-born and high-bred gentleman.

His fine intellectual face, his bearing erect before heaven, the graceful ease of his every motion, as he hurried down the flagged steps of the terrace, and planted his light foot on the dewy greensward, all betokened gentle birth and gentle associations.

But he thought nothing of himself, nor cared for his advantages, acquired or natural. The long and heavy salmon-rod which he carried in his right hand, in three pieces as yet unconnected, did not more clearly indicate his purpose than the quick marking glance which he cast toward the half-veiled sun and hazy sky, scanning the signs of the weather.

"It will do, it will do," he said to himself, thinking as it were aloud, "for three or four hours at least; the sun will not shake off those vapors before eight o'clock at the earliest, and if he do come out than hot and strong, I don't know but the water is dark enough after the late rains to serve my turn a while longer. It will blow up, too, I think, from the westward and there will be a brisk curl on the pools. But come, I must be moving, if I would reach Darringford to breakfast."

And as he spoke he strode out rapidly across the park toward the deep chasm of the stream, crushing a thousand aromatic perfumes from the dewy wild-flowers with his heedless foot, and thinking little of the beauties of nature, as he hastened to the scene of his loved exercise.

It was not long, accordingly, before he reached the brink of the steep rocky bank above the stream, which he proposed to fish that morning, and paused to select the best place for descending to the water's edge.

It was, indeed, as striking and romantic a scene as ever met the eye of painter or of poet. On the farther side of the gorge, scarcely a hundred yards distant, the dark limestone rocks rose sheer and precipitous from the very brink of the stream, rifted and broken into angular blocks and tall, columnar masses, from the clefts of which, wherever they could find oil enough support their scanty growth, a few stunted oaks shot out almost horizontally with their gnarled arms and dark-green foliage, and here and there the silvery bark and quivering tresses of the birch relieved the monotony of color by their gay brightness. Above, the cliffs were crowned with the beautiful purple heather, now in its very glow of summer bloom, about which were buzzing myriads of wild bees, sipping their nectar from its cups of amethyst.

The hither side, though rough and steep and broken, was not, in the place where Jasper stood, precipitous; indeed it seemed as if at some distant period a sort of land-slip had occurred, by which the summit of the rocky wall had been broken into massive garments, and hurled down in an inclined plane into the bed of the stream, on which it had encroached with its shattered blocks and rounded boulders.

Time, however, had covered all this abrupt and broken slope with a beautiful growth of oak and hazel coppice, among which, only at distant intervals, could the dun weather-beaten flanks of the great stones by discovered.

At the base of this descent, a hundred and fifty feet perhaps below the stand of the young sportsman, flowed the dark arrowy stream—a wild and perilous water. As clear as crystal, yet as dark as the brown cairngorm, it came pouring down among the broken rocks with a rapidity and force which showed what must be its fury when swollen by a storm among the mountains, here breaking into wreaths of rippling foam where some unseen ledge chafed its current, there roaring and surging white as December's snow among the great round-headed rocks, and there again wheeling in sullen eddies, dark and deceitful, round and round some deep rock-rimmed basin.

Here and there, indeed, it spread out into wide, shallow, rippling rapids, filling the whole bottom of the ravine from side to side, but more generally it did not occupy above the fourth part of the space below, leaving sometimes on this margin, sometimes on that, broad pebbly banks, or slaty ledges, affording an easy footing and a clear path to the angler in its troubled waters.

After a rapid glance over the well-know scene, Jasper plunged into the coppice, and following a faint track worn by the feet of the wild-deer in the first instance, and widened by his own bolder tread, soon reached the bottom of the chasm, though not until he had flushed from the dense oak covert two noble black cocks with their superb forked tails, and glossy purple-lustered plumage, which soared away, crowing their bold defiance, over the heathery moorlands.

Once at the water's edge, the young man's tackle was speedily made ready, and in a few minutes his long line went whistling through the air, as he wielded the powerful two-handed rod, as easily as if it had been a stripling reed, and the large gaudy peacock-fly alighted on the wheeling eddies, at the tail of a long arrowy shoot, as gently as it if had settled form too long a flight. Delicately, deftly, it was made to dance and skim the clear, brown surface, until it had crossed the pool and neared the hither bank; then again, obedient to the pliant wrist, it arose on glittering wing, circled half around the angler's head, and was sent fifteen yards aloof, straight as a wild bee's flight, into the little mimic whirlpool, scarce larger than the hat of the skilful fisherman, which spun around and round just leeward of a gray ledge of limestone. Scarce had it reached its mark before the water broke all round it, and the gray deceit vanished, the heavy swirl of the surface, as the break was closing, indicating the great size of the fish which had risen. Just as the swirl was subsiding, and the forked tail of the monarch of the stream was half seen as he descended, that indescribably but well-know turn of the angler's wrist fixed the barded hook and taught the scaly victim the nature of the prey he had gorged so heedlessly.

With a wild bound he threw himself three feet out of the water, showing his silver sides, with the sea-lice yet clinging to his scales, a fresh sea-run fish of fifteen, ay, eighteen pounds, and perhaps over.

On his broad back he strikes the water, but not as he meant the tightened line; for as he leaped the practiced hand had lowered the rod's tip, that it fell in a loose bight below him. Again! again! again! And yet a fourth time he bounded into the air with desperate and vigorous *soubresaults*, like an unbroken steed that would dismount his rider, lashing the eddies of the dark stream into the bright bubbling streaks, and making the heart of his captor beat high with anticipations of the desperate struggle that should follow, before the monster should lie panting and exhausted on the yellow sand or moist greensward.

Away! with the rush of an eagle through the air, he is gone like an arrow down the rapids—how the reel rings, and the line whistles from the swift working wheel; he is too swift, too headstrong to be checked as yet; tenfold the strength of that slender tackle might not control him in his first fiery rush.

But Jasper, although young in years, was old in the art, and skilful as the craftiest of the gentle craftsmen. He gives him the butt of his rod steadily, trying the strength of his tackle with a delicate and gentle finger, giving him line at every rush, yet firmly, cautiously, feeling his mouth all the while, and moderating his speed even while he yields to his fury.

Meanwhile, with the eye of intuition, and the nerve of iron, he bounds along the difficult shore, he leaps from rock to rock, alighting on their slippery tops with the firm agility of the rope-dancer, he splashes knee-deep through the slippery shallows, keeping his line ever taught, inclining his rod over his shoulder, bearing in his fish ever with a killing pull, steering him clear of every rock or stump against which he would fain smash the tackle, and landing him at length in a fine open roomy pool, at the foot of a long stretch of white and foamy rapids, down which he has just piloted him with the eye of faith, and the foot of instinct.

And now the great Salmon has turned sulky; like a piece of lead he has sunk to the bottom of the deep black pool, and lies on the gravel bottom in the sullenness of despair.

Jasper stooped, gathered up in his left hand a heavy pebble, and pitched it into the pool, as nearly as he could guess to the whereabout of his game—another—and another! Aha! that last has roused him. Again he throws himself clear out of water, and again foiled in his attempt to smash the tackle, dashes away down stream impetuous.

But his strength is departing—the vigor of his rush is broken. The angler gives him the butt abundantly, strains on him with a heavier pull, yet ever yields a little as he exerts his failing powers; see, his broad, silver side has thrice turned up, even to the surface, and though each time he was recovered himself, each time it has been with a heavier and more sickly motion.

Brave fellow! his last race is run, his last spring sprung—no more shall he disport himself in the bright reaches of the Tamar; no more shall the Naiads wreathe his clear silver scales with river-greens and flowery rushes.

The cruel gaff is in his side—his cold blood stains the eddies for a moment—he flaps out his death-pang on the hard limestone.

"Who-whoop! a nineteen-pounder!"

Meantime the morning had worn onward, and ere the great fish was brought to the basket, the sun had soared clear above the mist-wreaths, and had risen so high into the summer heaven that his slant rays poured down into the gorge of the stream, and lighted up the clear depths with a luster so transparent that ever pebble at the bottom might have been discerned, with the large fish here and there floating mid-depth, with their heads upstream, their gills working with a quick motion, and their broad tails vibrating at short intervals slowly but powerfully, as they lay motionless in opposition to the very strongest of the swift current.

The breeze had died away, there was no curl upon the water, and the heat was oppressive.

Under such circumstances, to whip the stream was little better than mere loss of time, yet as he hurried with a fleet foot down the gorge, perhaps with some ulterior object, beyond the mere love of sport, Jasper at times cast his fly across the stream, and drew it neatly, and, as he thought, irresistibly, right over the recusant fish; but though once or twice a large lazy Salmon would sail up slowly from the depths, and almost touch the fly with his nose he either sunk down slowly in disgust, without breaking the water, or flapped his broad tail over the shining fraud as if to mark his contempt.

It had now got to be near noon, for, in the ardor of his success, the angler had forgotten all about his intended breakfast; and, his first fish captured, had contented himself with a slender meal furnished from out his fishing-basket and his leathern bottle.

Jasper had traversed by this time some ten miles in length, following the sinuosities of the stream, and had reached a favorite pool at the head of along, straight, narrow trench, cut by the waters themselves in the course of time, through the hard schistous rock which walls the torrent on each hand, not leaving the slightest ledge or margin between the rapids and the precipice.

Through his wild gorge of some fifty yards in length, the river shoots like an arrow over a steep inclined plane of limestone rock, the surface of which is polished by the action of the water, till it is as slippery as ice, and at the extremity of leaps, down a sheer descent of some twelve feet into a large, wide basin, surrounded by softly swelling banks of greensward, and a fair amphitheater of woodland.

At the upper end this pool is so deep as to be vulgarly deemed unfathomable; below, however, it expands yet wider into a shallow rippling ford, where it is crossed by the high-road, down stream of which again there is another long, sharp rapid, and another fall, over the last steps of the hills; after which the nature of the stream becomes changed, and it murmurs gently onward through a green pastoral country, unrippled and uninterrupted.

Just in the inner angle of the high-road, on the right hand of the stream, there stood an old-fashioned, low-browed, thatch-covered stone cottage, with a rude portico of rustic woodwork overrun with jasmine and virgin-bower, and a pretty flower-garden sloping down in successive terraces to the edge of the basin. Beside this, there was no other house in sight, unless it were part of the roof of a mill which stood in the low ground on the brink of the second fall, surrounded with a mass of willows. But the tall steeple of a country church, raising itself heavenward above the brow of the hill, seemed to show that, although concealed by the undulations of the ground, a village was hard at hand.

The morning had changed a second time, a hazy film had crept up to the zenith, and the sun was now covered with a pale golden veil, and a slight current of air down the gorge ruffled the water.

It was a capital pool, famous for being the temporary haunt of the very finest fish, which were wont to lie there awhile, as if to recruit themselves after the exertions of leaping the two falls and stemming the double rapid, before attempting to ascend the stream farther.

Few, however, even of the best and boldest fishermen, cared to wet a line in its waters, in consequence of the supposed impossibility of following a heavy fish through the gorge below, or checking him at the brink of the fall. It is true, that throughout the length of the pass, the current was broken by bare, slippery rocks peering above the waters, at intervals, which might be cleared by an active cragsman; and it had been in fact reconnoitered by Jasper and others in cool blood, but the result of the examination was that it was deemed impassable.

Thinking, however, little of striking a large fish, and perhaps desiring to waste a little time before scaling the banks and merging on the high-road, Jasper threw a favorite fly of peacock's hurl and gold tinsel lightly across the water; and, almost before he had time to think, had hooked a monstrous fish, which, at the very first leap, he set down as weighing at least thirty pounds.

Thereupon followed a splendid display of piscatory skill. Well knowing that his fish must be lost if he once should succeed in getting his head down the rapid, Jasper exerted every nerve, and exhausted every art to humor, to meet, to retrain, to check him. Four times the fish rushed for the pass, and four times Jasper met him so stoutly with the butt, trying his tackles to the very utmost, that he succeeded in forcing him from the perilous spot. Round and round the pool he had piloted him, and had taken post at length, hoping that the worst was already over, close to the opening of the rocky chasm.

He was gone—but Jasper's blood was up, and thinking of nothing but his sport, he dashed forward, and embarked, with a fearless foot, into the terrible descent.

Leap after leap he took with beautiful precision, alighting firm and erect on the centre of each slippery block, and bounding thence to the next with unerring instinct, guiding his fish the while with consummate skill through the intricacies of the pass.

There were now but three more leaps to be taken before he would reach the flat table-rock above the fall, which once attained, he would have firm foothold and a fair field; already he rejoiced, triumphant in the success of his bold attainment, and confident in victory, when a shrill female shriek reached his ears from the pretty flower-garden; caught by the sound, he diverted his eyes, just as he leaped, toward the place thence it came; his foot slipped and the next instant he was flat on his back in the swift stream, where it shot the most furiously over the glassy rock. He struggled manfully, but in vain. The smooth, slippery surface afforded no purchase to his gripping fingers, no hold to his laboring feet. One fearful, agonizing conflict with the wild waters, and he was swept helplessly over the edge of the fall, his head, as he glanced down foot foremost, striking the rocky brink with fearful violence.

He was plunged into the deep pool, and whirled round and round by the dark eddies long before he rose, but still, though stunned and half-disabled, he strove terribly to support himself, but it was all in vain.

Again he sunk and rose once more, and as he rose that wild shriek again reached his ears, and his last glance fell upon a female form wringing her hands in despair on the bank, and a young man rushing down in wild haste from the cottage on the hill.

He felt that aid was at hand, and struck out again for life—for dear life!

But the water seemed to fail beneath him.

A slight flash sprang across his eyes, his brain reeled, and all was blackness.

He sunk to the bottom, spurned it with his feet, and rose once more, but not to the surface.

His quivering blue hands emerged alone above the relentless waters, grasped for a little moment at empty space, and then disappeared.

The circling ripples closed over him, and subsided into stillness.

He felt, know, suffered nothing more.

His young, warm heart was cold and lifeless—his soul had lost its consciousness—the vital spark had faded into darkness—perhaps was quenched forever.

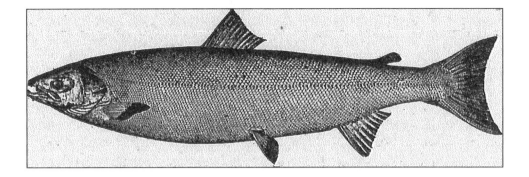

A Gallant Poacher

JOHN BUCHAN

When the Hispana crossed the Bridge of Larrig His Majesty's late Attorney-General was modestly concealed in a bush of broom on the Crask side, from which he could watch the sullen stretches of the Lang Whang. He was carefully dressed for the part in a pair of Wattie Lithgow's old trousers much too short for him, a waistcoat and jacket which belonged to Sime the butler and which had been made about the year 1890, and a vulgar flannel shirt borrowed from Shapp. He was innocent of a collar, he had not shaved for two days, and as he had forgotten to have his hair cut before leaving London his locks were of a disreputable length. Last, he had a shocking old hat of Sir Archie's from which the lining had long since gone. His hands were sun-burned and grubby, and he had removed his signet-ring. A light ten-foot greenheart rod lay beside him, already put up, and to the tapered line was fixed a tapered cast ending in a strange little cocked fly. As he waited he was busy oiling fly and line.

His glass showed him an empty haugh, save for the figure of Jimsie at the far end close to the Wood of Larrigmore. The sun-warmed waters of the river drowsed in the long dead stretches, curled at rare intervals by the faintest western breeze. The banks were crisp green turf, scarcely broken by a boulder, but five yards from them the moss began—a wilderness of hags and tussocks. Somewhere in its depths he knew that Benjie lay coiled like an adder, waiting on events.

Leithen's plan, like all great strategy, was simple. Everything depended on having Jimsie out of sight of the Lang Whang for half an hour. Given that, he believed he might kill a salmon. He had marked out a pool where in the evening fish were usually stirring, one of those irrational haunts which no piscatorial psychologist has ever explained. If he could fish fine and far, he might cover it from a spot below a high bank where only the top of his rod would be visible to watchers at a distance. Unfortunately, that spot was on the other side of the stream. With such tackle, landing a salmon would be a critical business, but there was one chance in ten that it might be accomplished; Benjie would be at hand to conceal the fish, and he himself would disappear silently into the Crask thickets. But every step bristled with horrid dangers. Jimsie might be faithful to his post—in which case it was hopeless; he might find the salmon dour, or a fish might break him in the landing, or Jimsie might return to find him brazenly tethered to forbidden game. It was no good thinking about it. On one thing he was decided: if he were caught, he would not try to escape. That would mean retreat in the direction of Crask, and an exploration of the Crask coverts would assuredly reveal what must at all costs be concealed. No. He would go quietly into captivity, and trust to his base appearance to be let off with a drubbing.

As he waited, watching the pools turn from gold to bronze, as the sun sank behind the Glenraden peaks, he suffered the inevitable reaction. The absurdities seemed huge as mountains, the difficulties innumerable as the waves of the sea. There remained less than an hour in which there would be sufficient light to fish—Jimsie was immovable (he had just lit his pipe and was sitting in meditation on a big stone)—every moment the Larrig waters were cooling with the chill of evening. Leithen consulted his watch, and found it half-past eight. He had lost his wrist-watch, and had brought his hunter, attached to a thin gold chain. That was foolish, so he slipped the chain from his button-hole and drew it through the arm-hole of his waistcoat.

Suddenly he rose to his feet, for things were happening at the far side of the haugh. Jimsie stood in an attitude of expectation—he seemed to be hearing something far upstream. Leithen heard it too, the cry of excited men . . . Jimsie stood on one foot for a moment in doubt; then he turned and doubled towards the Wood of Larrigmore . . . The gallant Crossby had got to business and was playing hare to the hounds inside the park wall. If human nature had not changed, Leithen thought, the whole force would presently join the chase—Angus and Lennox and Jimsie and Dave and doubtless many volunteers. Heaven send fleetness and wind to the South London Harrier, for it was his duty to occupy the interest of every male in Strathlarrig till such time as he subsided with angry expostulation into captivity.

The road was empty, the valley was deserted, when Leithen raced across the bridge and up the south side of the river. It was not two hundred yards to his chosen stand, a spit of gravel below a high bank at the tail of a long pool. Close to the other bank, nearly thirty yards off, was the shelf where fish lay of an evening. He tested the water with his hand, and its temperature was at least 60 degrees. His theory, which he had learned long ago from the aged Bostonian, was that under such conditions some subconscious memory revived in salmon of their early days as parr when they fed on surface insects, and that they could be made to take a dry fly.

He got out his line to the required length with half a dozen casts in the air, and ten put his fly three feet above the spot where a salmon was wont to lie. It was a curious type of cast, which he had been practicing lately in the early morning, for by an adroit check he made the fly alight in a curl, so that it floated for a second or two with the leader in a straight line away from it. In this way he believed that the most suspicious fish would see nothing to alarm him, nothing but a hapless insect derelict on the water.

Sir Archie had spoken truth in describing Leithen to Wattie Lithgow as an artist. His long, straight, delicate casts were art indeed. Like thistledown the fly dropped, like thistledown it floated over the head of the salmon, but like thistledown it was disregarded. There was indeed a faint stirring of curiosity. From where he stood Leithen could see that slight ruffling of the surface which means an observant fish . . .

Already ten minutes had been spent in this barren art. The crisis craved other measures.

His new policy meant a short line, so with infinite stealth and care Leithen waded up the side of the water, sometimes treading precarious ledges of peat, sometimes waist deep in mud and pond-weed, till he was within twenty feet of the fishing-ground. Here he had not the high bank for a shelter, and would have been sadly conspicuous to Jimsie, had that sentinel remained at his post. He crouched low and cast as before with the same curl just ahead of the chosen spot.

But now his tactics were different. So soon as the fly had floated past where he believed the fish to be, he sank it with a dexterous twist of the rod-point, possible only with a short line. The fly was no longer a winged thing; drawn away under water, it roused in the salmon early memories of succulent nymphs . . . At the first cast there was a slight swirl, which meant that a fish near the surface had turned to follow the lure. The second cast the line straightened and moved swiftly up-stream.

Leithen had killed in his day many hundreds of salmon—once in Norway a notable beast of fifty-five pounds. But no salmon he had ever hooked had stirred in his breast such excitement as this modest fellow of eight pounds. "'Tis not so wide as a church-door,'" he reflected with Mercutio, "'but 'twill suffice'—if I can only land him." But a dry-fly cast and a ten-foot rod are a frail wherewithal for killing a fish against time. With his ordinary fifteen-footer and gut of moderate strength he could have brought the little salmon to grass in five minutes, but now there was immense risk of a break, and a break would mean that the whole enterprise had failed. He dared not exert pressure; on the other hand, he could not follow the fish except by making himself conspicuous on the greensward. Worst of all, he had at the best ten minutes of the job.

Thirty yards off an otter slid into the water. Leithen wished he was King of the Otters, as in the Highland tale, to summon the brute to his aid.

The ten minutes had lengthened to fifteen—nine hundred seconds of heart-disease—when, wet to the waist, he got his pocket-gaff into the salmon's side and drew it on to the spit of gravel where he had started fishing. A dozen times he thought he had lost, and once when the fish ran straight up the pool his line was carried out to its last yard of backing. He gave thanks to high Heaven, when, as he landed it, he observed that the fly had all but lost its hold and in another minute would have been free. By such narrow margins are great deeds accomplished.

He snapped the cast from the line and buried it in mud. Then cautiously he raised his head above the bank. The gloaming was gathering fast, and so far as he could see the haugh was still empty. Pushing his rod along the ground, he scrambled on to the turf.

There he had a grievous shock. Jimsie had reappeared, and he was in full view of him. Moreover, there were two men on bicycles coming up the road, who, with the deplorable instinct of human nature, would be certain to join in any pursuit. He was on turf as short as a lawn, cumbered with a tell-tale rod and a poached salmon. The friendly hags were a dozen yards off, and before he could reach them his damning baggage would be noted.

At this supreme moment he had an inspiration, derived from the memory of the otter. To get out his knife, cut a ragged wedge from the fish, and roll it in his handkerchief was the work of five seconds. To tilt the rod over the bank so that it lay in the deep shadow was the work of three more . . . Jimsie had seen him, for a wild cry came down the stream, a cry which brought the cyclists off their machines and set them staring in his direction. Leithen dropped his gaff after the rod, and began running towards the Larrig bridge—slowly, limpingly, like a frightened man with no resolute purpose of escape. And as he ran he prayed that Benjie from the deeps of the moss had seen what had been done and drawn the proper inference.

It was a bold bluff, for he had decided to make the salmon evidence for, not against him. He hobbled down the bank, looking over his shoulder often as if in terror, and almost ran into the arms of the cyclists, who, warned by Jimsie's yells, were waiting to intercept him. He dodged them, however, and cut across to the road, for he had seen that Jimsie had paused and had noted the salmon lying blatantly on the sward, a silver splash in the twilight. Leithen doubled up the road as if going towards Strathlarrig, and Jimsie, the fleet of foot, did not catch up with him till almost on the edge of the Wood of Larrigmore. The cyclists, who had remounted, arrived at the same moment to find a wretched muddy tramp in the grip of a stalwart but breathless gillie.

"I tell ye I was daein' nae harm,' the tramp whined. "I was walkin' up the waterside—there's nae law to keep a body frae walkin' up a water-side when there's nae fence—and I seen an auld otter killin' a saumon. The fish is there still to prove I'm no leein'."

"There is a fush, but you wass thinkin' to steal the fush, and you would have had it in your breeks if I hadna seen you. That is poachin' ma man, and you will come up to Strathlarrig. The master said that anyone goin' near the watter was to be lockit up, and you will be lockit up. You can tell all the lees you like in the mornin'."

Then a thought struck Jimsie. He wanted the salmon, for the subject of otters in the Larrig had been a matter of dispute between him and Angus, and here was evidence for his own view.

"Would you two gentlemen oblige me by watchin' this man while I rin back and get the fush? Bash him on the head if he offers to rin."

The cyclists, who were journalists out to enjoy the evening air, willingly agreed, but Leithen showed no wish to escape. He begged a fag in a beggar's whine, and, since he seemed peaceable, the two kept a good distance for fear of infection. He stood making damp streaks in the dusty road, a pitiable specimen of humanity, for his original get-up was not improved by the liquefaction of his clothes and a generous legacy of slimy peat. He seemed to be nervous, which indeed he was, for if Benjie had not seized his chance he was utterly done, and if Jimsie should light upon his rod he was gravely compromised.

But when Jimsie returned in a matter of ten minutes he was empty-handed.

"I never kenned the like," he proclaimed. "That otter has come back and gotten the fush. Ach, the maleecious brute!"

The rest of Leithen's progress was not triumphant. He was conducted to the Strathlarrig lodge, where Angus, whose temper and wind had alike been ruined by the pursuit of Crossby, laid savage hands upon him, and frog-marched him to the back premises. The head-keeper scarcely heeded Jimsie's tale. "Ach, ye poachin' va-aga-bond. It is the jyle ye'll get," he roared, for Angus was in a mood which could only be relieved by violence of speech and action. Rumbling Gaelic imprecations, he hustled his prisoner into an outhouse, which had once been a larder and was now a supplementary garage, slammed and locked the door, and, as a final warning, kicked it viciously with his foot, as if to signify what awaited the culprit when the time came to sit on his case.

Early next morning, when the great door of Strathlarrig House was opened and the maids had begun their work, Oliphant, the butler—a stately man who had been trained in a ducal family—crossed the hall to connoiter the outer world. There he found an under-housemaid, nursing a strange package which she averred she had found on the doorstep. It was some two feet long, swathed in brown paper, and attached to its string was a letter inscribed to Mr. Junius Bandicott.

The parcel was clammy and Oliphant handled it gingerly. He cut the cord, disentangled the letter, and revealed an oblong of green rushes bound with string. The wrapping must have been insecure, for something forthwith slipped from the rushes and flopped on the marble floor, revealing to Oliphant's disgusted eyes a small salmon, blue and stiff in death.

At that moment Junius, always an early bird, came whistling downstairs. So completely was he convinced of the inviolability of the Strathlarrig waters that the spectacle caused him no foreboding.

"What are you flinging fish about for, Oliphant?" he asked cheerfully.

The butler presented him with the envelope. He opened it and extracted a dirty half-sheet of notepaper, on which was printed in capitals, "With the compliments of John Macnab."

Amazement, chagrin, amusement followed each other on Junius's open countenance. Then he picked up the fish and marched out of doors shouting "Angus" at the top of a notably powerful voice. The sound brought the scared face of Professor Babwater to his bedroom window.

Angus, who had been up since four, appeared from Lady Maisie's Pool, where he had been contemplating the waters. His vigil had not improved his appearance or his temper, for his eye was red and choleric and his beard was wild as a mountain goat's. He cast one look at the salmon, surmised the truth, and held up imploring hands to Heaven.

"John Macnab!" said Junius sternly. "What have you got to say to that."

Angus had nothing audible to say. He was handling the fish with feverish hands and peering at its jaws, and presently under his fingers a segment fell out.

"That fush was cleekit," observed Lennox, who had come up. "It was never catched with a flee."

"Ye're a leear," Angus roared. "Just tak a look at the mouth of it. There's the mark of the huke, ye gommeril. The fush was took wi' a rod and line."

"You may reckon it was," observed Junius. "I trust John Macnab to abide by the rules of the game."

Suddenly light seemed to break in on Angus's soul. He bellowed for Jimsie, who was placidly making his way towards the group at the door, lighting his pipe as he went.

"Look at that, James Mackenzie. Aye, look at it. Feast your een on it. You wass tellin' me there wass otters in the Larrig and I said there wass not. You wass tellin' me there wass an otter had a fush last night at the Lang Whang. There's your otter and be damned to ye!"

Jimsie, slow of comprehension, rubbed his eyes. "Where wass you findin' the fush? Aye, it's the one I seen last night. That otter must be wrang in the heid."

"It is not wrang in the heid. It's you that are wrang in the heid, James Mackenzie. The otter is a ver-ra clever man, and its name will be John Macnab." Slowly enlightenment dawned on Jimsie's mind.

"He wass the tramp," he ingeminated. "He wass the tramp."

"And he's still lockit up," Angus cried joyfully. "Wait till I get my hands on him." He was striding off for the garage when a word from Junius held him back.

"You won't find him there. I gave orders last night to let him go. You know, Angus, you told me he was only a tramp that had been seen walking up the river."

"We will catch him yet!" cried the vindictive head-keeper. "Get you on your bicycle, Jimsie, and away after him. He'll be on the Muirtown road . . . There's just the one road he can travel."

"No, you don't," said Junius. "I don't want him here. He has beaten us fairly in a match of wits, and the business is finished."

"But the thing's no possible," Jimsie moaned. "The skeeliest fisher would not take a saumon in the Lang Whang with a flee . . . And I wasna away many meenutes . . . And the tramp was a poor shilpit body—not like a fisher or any kind of gentleman at all—at all . . . And he hadna a rod . . . The thing's no possible.

"I think it was the Deevil."

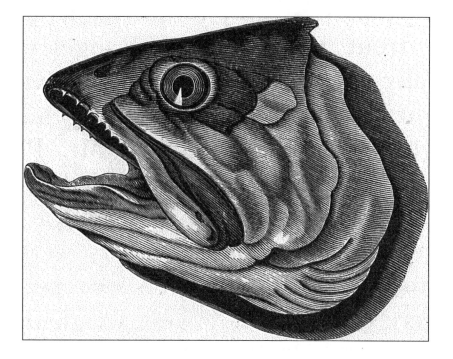

Brannigan's Trout

NICK LYONS

After the crack up, he was hospitalized for six months. Twice the doctors warned Jane that they might lose him. Then, when they saved him, they warned that there was probably brain damage. When he was released, in November, they told him he'd be paralyzed on his right side for life. Four doctors confirmed the verdict.

There was nothing for it.

Perhaps there was a slight chance, but not likely, that regular exercise, steady exercise over a period of several years, might restore some small portion of his mobility. Not much. Possibly none. Frankly, Brannigan was not inclined to try. Why go through all the effort? So he sat silent and sullen in the wheelchair that grey afternoon and allowed the men in white to push him to the car, lift and place him into the front seat, collapse the chair and put it in the back, then tell Jane how he was to get in and out, how she was to rig the contraption and place it for him. Like a baby.

He said not a word on the long trip through the sere, dead countryside. Jane told him about the boys, and which friends had called; Mike Novak might come over that evening. He didn't even nod. His great black-haired head thrown back and tilted to one side, he watched with dead eyes the fleeting fields of withered cornstalks, leafless trees, dark scudding clouds. There was nothing for it. He was forty-six and it was over. He couldn't sell books or anything else anymore; he didn't know whether he could drink beer with his friends, chop wood, tend his garden, drive, smoke, sing, read, write; and certainly the fishing season was over for him. Permanently.

The crash in all its stark detail, the fluky chance of it, kept flashing through his brain: Johnny Wohl driving, across the seat from him saying, seconds before, "Well, Billy, we made a day of it, didn't we? I never saw the river so alive." And Mike in the back. Laughing wildly and about to say something about having caught three Hendricksons. Then the rasp of brakes, the black car coming just that moment smoothly out of the side road, the jolt of fear, his hands flying up, his back thrusting backward against the seat, the hurtling forward—and darkness, and stabbing, raw pain in his shoulders, his head. Then nothing. Johnny Wohl and the two teenagers in the black car had been killed instantly. Mike came out of it with his right pinky broken. Well, good for him. Good for old Mike.

As for himself, it would have been better to have had it over then, right then when it happened. Quick. No more pain to die than to live, then. He need merely not have come out of the coma. After that first, searing pain, poof. For good. And they all said he's only lived because he wanted to live. So he lived—like a half-squashed worm.

He saw suddenly in his mind the 20-guage shotgun in the cabinet in his den. Would Jane have removed it? This was no time to ask. That night, when the boys were doing their homework, he'd wheel in by himself and just take a look-see. He'd take it out, break it open . . . take a look-see.

At dinner, Jane talked constantly—about the Murphy's new Brittany spaniel; the good batch of slab wood Frank had hauled from the lumber yard, piece by piece, and cut himself; the threat of an early snow. Brannigan looked up now and then from his plate, spread his lips slightly in the best he could do for a smile, and nodded. He said nothing. He was still not sure what the cracked, alien sound of his voice—what remained of speech—would be to these people, whether he could put together all the words needed for one whole sentence. Whenever he raised his head and looked toward one of his sons, Frank to his right, fifteen, Junior on his left, a year older and dark-haired too, rebellious, they were looking at their own plates. They knew every-thing. When he looked back at his own plate and prepared his next strategy to get a piece of meat to his mouth, he thought he saw, peripherally, their heads raise slightly and turn toward him. He didn't think he could bear it. Not that. He'd come through Normandy without a scratch; he'd never been seriously ill in his life.

Working diligently with the fork in his left hand, like they'd taught him in the hospital, he speared a piece of the steak Jane had cut for him, shifted the fork carefully in his hand, and brought it to his mouth. He chewed the meat slowly for a few moments, then lowered the fork to get another. But the prongs pressed against the gristle, slipped, and flicked the chunk of meat onto the floor. Brannigan looked after it, heard Jane say, "I'll pick it up later, dear," then slammed the fork down on his plate. Frank and Junior raised their hunched shoulders and looked up sharply. Jane took a deep breath.

"Nuff," muttered Brannigan. "Nuff." He pushed the wheelchair away, turning it, and, his hand on the wheel-rail, glided into the living and toward his den—hearing Frank say something low that ended with "like that," and Junior's heavier voice, and then Jane telling them in a normal voice to finish quickly and go upstairs: they'd talk of it later.

He negotiated the living room and came to the door of his den. His room. The door was closed but he came against it sideways, took his left hand from the wheel-rail and reached out for the knob. As he did so, the chair slipped back a few inches and he was only able to touch a bit of the knob. He gritted his teeth, pounded his left hand down on the armrest, wheeled himself close again, and tried another time. Again the chair slipped back a bit and he couldn't, hard as he strained, even touch the knob. *Damned. Damned.* He sat in the chair, breathing heavily for a few moment, then tried again, got it, flung the door open, gave the wheel-rail a sharp thrust forward, and was in his room. *His* room.

God, how many good hours he'd spent there. The soft old armchair. His own mount of the four-pound brook trout he's caught in Canada that summer with Mike and Johnny. The humidor with those long black dago-ropes he loved so much. Fireplace. Little fly-tying table—just like he'd left it. Silver rod cases in the cabinet he'd built himself. The old black-bear rug he'd bought, over Jane's hilarious objections. *His room.*

It was a room to which he slunk after a knockdown argument with Jane, a lousy road trip; he went there to plan his selling strategies, realign the world, read quietly in the evening or tie flies. He'd had most of his serious talks with his boys in this room; and he'd laughed and drunk beer and told stories half the night with Johnny and Mike here. Useless now. There was not one thing in the room, as he looked around, that he wanted.

The shotgun.

His eyes shifted sharply to the oak cabinet with the V-back that fitted into the corner so snugly. It was there. He went to his fly-tying table, opened the middle drawer, and felt with his hand among the capes and bobbins until his fingers found and closed tightly around the long brass key. Then, holding the key in the palm of his left hand, he used his fingers to push the chair over to the cabinet.

He had only that one gun, a beautiful 20-gauge with polished walnut stock, grey shoulder cushion, twin slate-grey barrels. He liked the feel of it in his hands, the power with which it jerked back when he shot. He'd gotten his first grouse with it last winter. Sam, Johnny's Brittany, had frozen on point, Johnny had called for the flush, and the grouse, a single, had exploded with a whirr from the underbrush. "Yours!" shouted Mike, and he'd swung, led, and watched the bird pause, sputter, and fall. He remembered the deep satisfaction he'd felt from that connection, that force which shot out from him and dropped that bird.

The shotgun.

Another moment and he'd have it in his hands, feel its sleek powerful lines, its smooth stock. The gun held power, energy, force; merely to have it in your hands was to feel some electrical current, some charge of strength shot into your veins, your body. "Look-see," he said, flinching at the cracked, strange sound of his voice, inserting the key into the lock and turning, then opening the cabinet door slowly.

It was not there. The cabinet was empty.

His eyes blazed and he slammed the door shut. It was not there. She had taken it. Grasping the wheel-rail he thrust downward and began to roll across the carpet toward the closed door to the living room. She had taken it. "Gun," he said, his voice a rasping growl. "Gun. Gun." Then, opening the door, he let his head fall, and he muttered, "Did she . . . really . . . think . . ."

"So the point is that *I* asked Jane for your goddamn shotgun because mine is at the gunsmith and I ain't got one to use next week," Mike said ten minutes later when they were alone in the den. "She didn't want to let me have it. Nope. 'Mike,' she says, 'Billy loves that rifle.' That's what she called it, a rifle, 'and I don't think I can let you have it.'"

Brannigan frowned. He looked intently at the bronze, hearty face of his friend, that bullish chest above toothpick legs, the straight black, always greasy and carefully combed hair, the mechanic's hands, stained black.

"I says: 'Look, Janie, he may not be out until after Christmas and I know he'd want me to put a few notches on it for him. One thing about Billy, he don't like a good rod or shotgun lying around. Offends his Scotch-Irish blood.'"

"Lie."

"I was going to take it out to the range, test it on some clays, but if you'd like it back, got some special use for it, I'll . . ." He broke off, lowered his voice, and said: "It's been rough, ain't it, kiddo?"

"Ruh-uf."

"Yeah, said Mike, turning his back and walking across the room to look at the big, bright male brook trout on the wall. "Remember when you got that one, Billy?" he said without turning around. "You'd cast that big funny fly from New Zealand, the Red Setter, looked like a whore's hairdo, into the swirls below the falls. I was behind you. I'd gotten one about three pounds that morning and you was burning mad.

Didn't even speak to me at lunch. Well, maybe I was being a bit rotten about it." He came and sat down in the soft old armchair. "I must've turned and the next thing I know your rod's bent like a crescent moon and you're yelling like a banshee. Johnny thinks you've fallen in or got bit by a snake, so he comes running up, and by this time there's the goddamnedest smug look on your face! You've got the fish well hooked, you've seen him roll, and you know the size of him—and you know you got the greatest audience any mug ever had."

He watched Brannigan's eyes. They changed as he told the story.

"You're using this ten-pound-test leader and can't possibly lose that fish unless it gets into the rapids, and you're acting just as cockeyed cool as a cock of the roost. Johnny and me, we may be a little green around the gills but we're sitting polite as you please, murmuring a few friendly words of praise now and then—like, 'Did *that* lemon have to get it?'—and you keep playing him gently, making maybe a bit too much of a show of fear when it heads downstream. Cool. Very cool, Billy. And when Johnny wants to net him for you, with the big net, what do you do? Wave him away, and fuss with that minnow net you carry."

The faintest trace of a smile began to struggle around the corners of Brannigan's twisted mouth and eyes.

"So this absolute monster of a brookie, the biggest trout any of us has ever seen, is beat, and over on its side, and you're swiping at it with your net—probably trying to get it to rush off so's the show can go on—and first you get the tail in, right?"

Brannigan nodded.

"Then when it flops out, you try to bend it in, from the middle, but the monster won't be bent, so you go for the head, which barely fits into that guppy net, and then you've got it head first to about the gills and sort of clamp your hand down on the rest and come yelping out of the water, the line and rod and net and you all tangled together, and you fall on it. God, that fish was gorgeous—and there he is. That the way it happened, Billy? Something like that?"

Brannigan raised his left hand in a little shrug. "Ha-pinned . . . like . . . that."

"So the point is, you got one. You got one bigger than any of us ever got, even Johnny, God rest his soul, and now you figure, 'The big bird's crapped on me. I've caught my last big fish and shot my last grouse.' That it?"

"That-z-it."

"Johnny doesn't make it and you ain't satisfied to be here. Instead of being pleased I come tonight, passing up some very possible quail, you're going to stew in your own bile, right?"

"Rrr-ight."

"There's no one in particular to hate for it, so you figure you'll spread the hate around, to Jane and the boys, and especially yourself, and maybe you'll get lucky and not be around too much longer to be a burden to anyone. Well, I see your point, Brannigan. Lot of logic to it. Then say maybe there's a chance in a couple hundred thousand that you get anything back on that right side, so you say, 'Bad odds.'" He walked to the fly-tying table, picked up one of the capes, a pale ginger, and bent back the hackle of one feather. "A good one, Billy. First-rate dry-fly neck. Good small size, too." Then he went to the humidor and drew out one of the twisted black cigars. "You don't mind?" Brannigan, watching him closely, did not change his expression. Mike put the cigar in the center of his mouth, struck a match, and got the tip of the cigar glowing like a little coal. "Good cigar, Billy." He puckered his lips, held the cigar in three fingers, and took a long puff.

Brannigan kept watching him. He had not moved his chair from the moment Mike had come in. *Quail. Big trout. A grouse or two. Lives for that. Two wives, maybe have ten more. Funny guy. The way he holds that cigar—like he owned the world, all of it. Shotgun. Ask.*

"So the point is, it would break my sweet heart if you wasn't around, kiddo. Know what I mean? You know what I did when they told me you was"—he put out his hand, palm down, and rocked it slightly—"maybe not going to make it? I prayed. Me. Prayed. I said, 'Oh, God, let old Billy come through with *anything*, any goddamnit thing at all, so long as he's here and I can brag to him now and then about what quail I'm snatching—anything, God, just so long as he's here where I can see his ugly black-haired head now and then'"—he puffed hard at the cigar—"when the quail ain't flying and the trout is down. It's rough, right?"

Ask about shotgun.

"Suddenly the rules is all changed."

The gun.

"So the point is," he said, puffing hard, exhaling three times in rapid succession—"Hell, I don't know what the point is, Billy, but it will be awfully lonely next May when the Hendricksons start popping not to . . . Here, catch this"—and he tossed a softball, underhand, directly at Brannigan's chest. The left hand went up and forced the ball against the right shoulder. The right shoulder, limp and loose, twitched ever so slightly toward the ball. Brannigan held the ball for a moment, then took it in his left hand and tossed it back. Then he left his right shoulder and slowly dug his fingers into the muscle. "Not . . . much left."

"You'll cast lefty," said Mike. "Once knew an old poacher name of Sven who had to learn because there was bad brush on the right side. Dry-fly purist of a poacher." And the story went on for twenty minutes, and included a patrol dog named Wolf, five pound rainbows, two delicious young women, the true origin of "Sven's left curve drop cast," which only lefties could use, and then, just before the point of it all, Mike simply said, "It's eleven. The quail will have flown. I'll bring the 20-gauge tomorrow, eh?"

Brannigan smiled, a slow, deep smile that spread into his cheeks and eyes, and stayed, even when the twitch started. He nudged his right hand out with his left, so Mike could take and hold it, and Mike took it and held it in both of his own, rubbing the lifeless thing vigorously, then turning quickly for the door. Before he got there, Brannigan said: "The gun . . . yours."

The limbs remember, he thought, working the rake lightly across the soil he'd just fitted with seed, *and so does the earth. It remembers what it must do to these seeds, and the seeds, someplace deep within them, knew what they must do.*

Back and forth he moved the rake, holding it firmly in his left hand, using his nearly useless right to steady it. The May sun was warm but not bright, and kneaded his broad naked shoulders. He could walk without the cane now—somewhat. With that bizarre arc. His hair had gone snow white, which he liked, but otherwise, if he didn't move and didn't talk, he looked nearly the same.

Everyone else had planted a week or two ago but he'd worked more slowly, as he had to—long patient hours, setting his fertilizer, running the hand plow steadily across the small garden he'd staked out last spring, seeding the soil. This would be a good year. He could feel it. He's learned how to coax green from the brown soil, how important it was, always, to be patient—to lay the proper foundation, however long that took, before you could expect anything to grow. Tomatoes, cucumbers, carrots, radishes, onions—he'd had these last year; now he added kale, zucchini, tarragon, other herbs. Each day now he would work on his garden for several hours, bending down to it, plucking, feeling, watering, watching. It all mattered. Even the watching. Every day. He'd increased the size of his garden by a third this year. It would require more work but he could do it. He still forgot many things—names, events, people he had known; but he forgot nothing connected to his garden. It would be a good garden this year, as fruitful as anyone's garden. Maybe better.

Got it all now, he thought, leaning against the rake, *and Mike will be here soon to take us a-fishing.* It would be good to be in the car, on a trip, listening to Mike's excited patter, it would be good to try the river again. Mike had said the Hendricksons had started.

Three years. Days, weeks, months had ticked by, minute by minute, and imperceptibly the changes had come. The insurance had kept them from bankruptcy, Jane had begun to work for a real-estate agent in town—and had blossomed with it. Junior was earning his way in college, his own man, and Frank was a senior in high school and working part-time at Mike's garage. They didn't need what he'd once earned; he knew that what they needed most he could give them only after he had given it to himself.

He had done the exercises the men in white advised, with barbells and bicycle—over and over and again; he hated to do them and stopped when it came time to work in his garden. Several times last spring Mike had taken him to the West Branch, which they'd often fished together, before he got wracked. At first he merely found a rock, sat down, and watched. But he had not been able to resist the tug, deep inside him, to be on the stream, part of it, fishing. Wasn't that *really* why he'd done all those endless, tedious exercises, up and down, back and forth, hour after hour, all those months?

It had been impossible at first, after nearly two years. He had slipped twice on the rocks before he even reached the river. Even with the cane his right leg would not hold on broken terrain. Then he slipped again when he took his first tentative step into the water, careening badly, catching himself on his left arm. "No help, no help," he'd said when Mike stepped toward him. Then he'd been unable to strip line an cast left-handed, and finally, after several mad minutes he had given it up and fallen again on his way out, slamming his chin into a rock, cutting it sharply. No. It was not possible. He could not do it.

But it was a warm May morning and Mike would be there soon and it would be better this year. He'd earned it. Perhaps he'd even take his first trout since the crash.

Mike came promptly at twelve, and in a few minutes they were in the car racing toward the West Branch. "Magnificent day, Billy," Mike said, pushing the pedal harder. "The Hendricksons will be on in all their glory. They'll be popping out and the birds will be working, and we're going to get us a few. The cornfield run. I can feel a certain fat old brownie just waiting for you there today."

Mike parked along a small dirt turnoff and they got out and began to rig their rods, put on the waders. Mike was suited up and ready before Brannigan had worked on leg into his hip boots. "Go on, Mike. I'll be there . . . when I'm there."

"So you're tired of my company. Fine. I'm going upstream, you take the middle of the run. Where the current slows. Take your time: we're a half hour early. Lousy luck, kiddo."

Brannigan watched him stride off, his bull back bouncing even in waders. Then he finished raising his boots, strapped them to his belt, and got out his vest. He could use his right hand as a support now, to hold on section of the rod firmly enough for his left to insert the other section; he managed it, with guides aligned, on only the second try. Then he strung the line slowly through the guides until the end of the fly line and all of the leader were outside the tip top. It was well he had practiced all winter.

He got out a Hendrickson he'd tied before the crash, kept in mothballs, and held it as firmly as he could with his right fingers. Then he tried to insert the point of the leader. It would not go. He kept shoving it off to the side, or shaking the fly. Finally he dropped the fly in the grass and had to bend down, slowly, to look for it. When he found it, he stayed on the ground in the shadow of the car and held the fly up to the sky so that the light-blue would show through the hole and he could better fit in the leader. The operation took him five minutes.

As he began to walk along the edge of the cornfield toward the river, his right leg came up in a large, jerky arc, and then down again, one step after the other. Slowly. There was no rush. There was plenty of time. Mike had coaxed him out several more times last summer and fall, and each time he fell but there was some slight improvement. Not much. Not enough for him to know he could do it, like he could garden, not enough to get a line out far enough to tempt a trout—but some. You had to connive. You had to be cunning and crafty, and to forget how it once was. You had to remember always that it would not all come back, not ever. You had to work within the fixed knowledge that you continue to improve, always, and that this counted, but that even at your very best, some day, you would be, by the world's standards, a lemon.

Perhaps he'd get one today. His first. It would be wonderful if he could get into a really large trout, perhaps seventeen or eighteen inches. You didn't have to make many casts, just the right one at the right time. He'd practiced on the lawn and he knew he now could get enough distance to reach the lip of the current in the cornfield pool. He'd once fished it many times. There was room for a decent backcast, and the shallow bar on his side of the run was hard earth and rubble, with only a few rocks that might trip him up. Mike had made a good choice; he'd be fishing upstream, in the fast water where the Hendricksons hatched, but there'd be plenty of fish falling back into the pool to pick up the duns as they floated down, especially once the hatch really got going

One step at a time—the right leg out first, and down, out and down. No hurry. You couldn't rush a walk anymore than you could a garden. You couldn't rush anything. Anyway, you saw more when you walked this slow—those crows pecking at corn seeds, that huge growth of skunk cabbage, lush and green and purple, the fuzzy green on the boughs of the willows. A gorgeous day, only slightly overcast now, perfect for Hendricksons.

As he neared the row of trees that bordered the river, he could see Mike upstream, wading deep; his rod was held high and had a sharp arc. *Good old Mike. Got one already.* Up and out, then down. Then again. And again. He worked his way through the alders to the edge of the river. The water was perfect—dark and alive, flecked with bubbles and eddies where the current widened and slowed. Like he'd dreamed it all winter. Yes, that was a fish. And another. He looked to the sky and saw four or five tan flies flutter and angle off into the trees. *Yes. Yes.*

He took a tentative step into the water and felt a touch of fear as he left the firmness of the earth. No matter. It would pass. All the old feeling was there; he could still feel, deep within him, something in him reaching out to the life of the river—its quick faceted run above the long flat pool below; its translucent dark green and gliding shadows. Flowing, always moving. Changing. The same and not the same. He picked out a dun and watched it bound, like a tiny tan sailboat, over the tail of the riffle, then swirl and float into slower water where it vanished in a sudden pinching of the surface.

Yes, they were moving today. He could see six, seven fish in fixed feeding positions, rising steadily. There was plenty of time. *Don't rush. Do it very, very slowly.* They'd be going good for another hour; he wanted to pick out one good fish, near enough for him to reach with his short cast. Only one good fish. He didn't want a creelful. Only one.

Upstream, Mike was into another trout, and a few minutes later while Brannigan still eased slowly, steadily into deeper water, inch by inch, Mike had another. *We've caught one of those magical days*, he thought. *Another foot or so . . .* At last, deep as he dared go, he stood on firm hard rubble in water up to his thighs. He stripped line deliberately by raising and lowering his right hand; then, holding the loose line as best he could, he made an extremely short cast. *Good. Much better this year.* Then he stood, rod poised, watching the spreading circles of feeding fish. There were two twelve-inchers in the middle current lane, feeding freely, and two small fish back ten feet; he couldn't reach any of those anymore, though they'd once have been easy enough casts. He could never have finished to that rise in the far eddy, though: the currents were too tricky, the cast too long. Too bad. That was a large fish.

Then he saw the steady sipping rise directly upstream from him, not thirty feet away. Sometimes the largest fish rose like that, but so did fingerlings. It was time to try. He could reach that fish.

His first cast was too short and too hard. His next was off to the right and too hard. The next two were not bad but the fish both times rose to a natural a second before his fly floated past. On his next cast, the trout rose freely, took, and, gripping line and handle with his left hand, as he'd practiced, he struck and had the fish on. A good one. A bright, large leaper that came out, shaking its spots at him and falling back, and then streaking up into the current, across to the far bank, boring deep, and then leaping again.

"Mike!" He usually didn't talk while he fished but he wanted his friend to see this. He hadn't shouted very loud and above him, Mike, busy with still another fish, did not hear. Again the fish came out. "A beauty," he said audibly. "A fine brown." Again the fish raced across the current, stripping line from the reel, arching the rod sharply. *Got to get it. Can't lose this one.*

In ten minutes he could tell the trout was tiring. But it was still on the opposite side of the current. As he began to retrieve the line slowly, the fish came into the current and allowed itself to be carried downstream. Then, suddenly, it bolted directly toward him and the like went slack. "No, no," he said, struggling but unable to strip back line quickly enough.

When he regained control, the fish was gone. He drew the line back slowly until he could see the bedraggled fly. The fish had merely pulled out on the slack line—because of his goddam right arm. His right arm—which might as well not be there.

He was sitting in the car, all his equipment packed away, when Mike came back. Mike had caught seven fish, all of size but none as large as the one Brannigan had lost, and said it was the best day he could remember, except of course the day he'd gotten the three-pound brookie in Canada and Brannigan that lucky male. Brannigan offered a weak smile but said nothing, and Mike looked at him and then said nothing as he took off his vest and waders.

In the car, heading home, he turned to Brannigan and asked quietly, "How'd you do, Billy? Take any?"

"I lost one . . . Mike. Pretty good fish. Then I decided I'd better quit because at least I hadn't fallen in. Like every other time. So I headed . . . out. Slowly. Praising myself all the time . . . that at least I hadn't taken . . . a bath this time."

"You took some bad ones last year, Billy."

"I'd lost a good one, a really good fish, and that didn't make . . . me feel too cheery . . . Yet I'd hooked it and played it a long time . . . which I . . . never did before, not since I got wrecked, and I figured . . . if I could get out without a spill, I'd . . . still be ahead."

"Was it really a good fish, Billy?"

"Big. Very big brown."

"Sixteen inches."

"More."

"That's a big fish."

"So I was one step or two from the bank, smiling and praising myself . . . that I . . . hadn't fallen, when . . . I went into a pothole."

"Hell!"

"So I went down and over, ass . . . over teakettle. Almost drowned."

"Billy!"

"Almost. My head went under . . . and I was on my right side and couldn't . . . get leverage, and sort of forced my head out, and went under again, and gagged. Know I was going to die. I felt the grasp of brakes . . . in my brain. I suddenly . . . did not want to die. They water was shallow . . . but it was deep enough. Deep enough. Mike. I did not want to die," he said quietly. "So finally I managed to twist over onto my left side. Broke my rod. Slammed my bone badly. Barely . . . got out of it."

Mike looked over at this friend who had lost his fish, nearly ended it all. He had not one word to cheer him with. Brannigan was sitting in the same seat he'd been in when the accident smashed him, and there was a curious grin on his face. "Maybe we

. . . really shouldn't go anymore, Billy," Mike said soberly. "Know what I mean?" He had hoped desperately that Brannigan would get one good trout, that this day might be a new beginning. He had for three years said everything he knew to say. He had no words left.

Faintly, as a slight pressure first and then a firm grip, Mike felt his friend's left hand on his shoulder. "No," he heard Brannigan say. And when he turned: "We're going . . . to keep going . . . back."

A Fatal Success

HENRY VAN DYKE

Beekman De Peyster was probably the most passionate and triumphant fisherman in the Petrine Club. He angled with the same dash and confidence that he threw into his operations in the stock-market. He was sure to be the first man to get his flies on the water at the opening of the season. And when we came together for our fall meeting, to compare notes of our wanderings on various streams and make up the fish-stories for the year, Beekman was almost always "high hook." We expected, as a matter of course, to hear that he had taken the most and the largest fish.

It was so with everything that he undertook, he was a masterful man. If there was an unusually large trout in a river, Beekman knew about it before any one else, and got there first, and came home with the fish. It did not make him unduly proud, because there was nothing uncommon about it. It was his habit to succeed, and all the rest of us were hardened to it.

When he married Cornelia Cochrane, we were consoled for our partial loss by the apparent fitness and brilliancy of the match. If Beekman was a masterful man, Cornelia was certainly what you might call a mistressful woman. She had been the head of her house since she was eighteen years old. She carried her good looks like the family plate; and when she came into the breakfast-room and said good-morning, it was with an air as if she presented every one with a check for a thousand dollars. Her tastes were accepted as judgments, and her preferences had the force of laws. Wherever she wanted to go in the summertime, there the finger of household destiny pointed. At Newport, at Bar Harbor, at Lenox, at Southampton, she made a record. When she was joined in holy wedlock to Beekman De Peyster, her father and mother heaved a sigh of satisfaction, and settled down for a quiet vacation in Cherry Valley.

It was in the second summer after the wedding that Beekman admitted to a few of his ancient Petrine cronies, in moments of confidence (unjustifiable, but natural), that his wife had one fault.

"It is not exactly a fault," he said, "not a positive fault, you know. It is just a kind of a defect, due to her education, of course. In everything else she's magnificent. But she doesn't care for fishing. She says it's stupid,—can't see why any one should like the woods,—calls camping out the lunatic's diversion. It's rather awkward for a man with my habits to have his wife take such a view. But it can be changed by training. I intend to educate her and convert her. I shall make an angler of her yet."

And so he did.

The new education was begun in the Adirondacks, and the first lesson was given at Paul Smith's. It was a complete failure.

Beekman persuaded her to come out with him for a day on Meacham River, and promised to convince her of the charm of angling. She wore a new gown, fawn-color and violet, with a picture-hat, very taking. But the Meacham River trout was shy that day; not even Beekman could induce him to rise to the fly. What the trout lacked in confidence the mosquitoes more than made up. Mrs. De Peyster came home much sunburned, and expressed a highly unfavorable opinion of fishing as an amusement and of Meacham River as a resort.

"The nice people don't come to the Adirondacks to fish," said she; "they come to talk about the fishing twenty years ago. Besides, what do you want to catch that trout for? If you do, the other men will say you bought it, and the hotel will have to put in a new one for the rest of the season."

The following year Beekman tried Moosehead Lake. Here he found an atmosphere more favorable to his plan of education. There were a good many people who really fished, and short expeditions in the woods were quite fashionable. Cornelia had a camping-costume of the most approved style made by Dewlap on Fifth Avenue,—pearl-gray with linings of rose-silk,—and consented to go with her husband on a trip up Moose River. They pitched their tent the first evening at the mouth of Misery Stream, and a storm came on. The rain sifted through the canvas in a fine spray, and Mrs. De Peyster sat up all night in a waterproof cloak, holding an umbrella. The next day they were back at the hotel in time for lunch.

"It was horrid," she told her most intimate friend, "perfectly horrid. The idea of sleeping in a shower-bath, and eating your breakfast from a tin plate, just for sake of catching a few silly fish! Why not send your guides out to get them for you?"

But, in spite of this profession of obstinate heresy, Beekman observed with secret joy that there were signs, before the end of the season, that Cornelia was drifting a little, a very little but still perceptibly, in the direction of a change of heart. She began to take an interest, as the big trout came along in September, in the reports of the catches made by the different anglers. She would saunter out with the other people to the corner of the porch to see the fish weighed and spread out on the grass. Several times she went with Beekman in the canoe to Hardscrabble Point, and showed distinct evidences of pleasure when he caught large trout. The last day of the season, when he returned from a successful expedition to Roach River and Lily Bay, she inquired with some particularity about the results of his sport; and in the evening, as the company sat before the great open fire in the hall of the hotel, she was heard to use this information with considerable skill in putting down Mrs. Minot Peabody of Boston, who was recounting the details of her husband's catch at Spencer Pond. Cornelia was not a person to be contented with the back seat, even in fish-stories.

When Beekman observed these indications he was much encouraged, and resolved to push his educational experiment briskly forward to his customary goal of success.

"Some things can be done, as well as others," he said in his masterful way, as three of us were walking home together after the autumnal dinner of the Petrine Club, which he always attended as a graduate member. "A real fisherman never gives up. I told you I'd make an angler out of my wife; and so I will. It has been rather difficult. She is 'dour' in rising. But she's beginning to take notice of the fly now. Give me another season, and I'll have her landed."

Good old Beekman! Little did he think—But I must not interrupt the story with moral reflections.

The preparations that be made for his final effort at conversion were thorough and prudent. He had a private interview with Dewlap in regard to the construction of a practical fishing-costume for a lady, which resulted in something more reasonable and workmanlike than had ever been turned out by that famous artist. He ordered from Hook & Catchett a lady's angling-outfit of the most enticing description,—a split-bamboo rod, light as a girl's wish, and strong as a matron's will; an oxidized silver reel, with a monogram on one side, and a sapphire set in the handle for good luck; a book of flies, of all sizes and colors, with the correct names inscribed in gilt letters on each page. He surrounded his favorite sport with an aureole of elegance and beauty. And then he took Cornelia in September to the Upper Dam at Rangeley.

She went reluctant. She arrived disgusted. She stayed incredulous. She returned—Wait a bit, and you shall hear how she returned.

The Upper Dam at Rangeley is the place, of all others in the world, where the lunacy of angling may be seen in its incurable stage. There is a cozy little inn, called a camp, at the foot of a big lake. In front of the inn is a huge dam of gray stone, over which the river plunges into a great oval pool, where the trout assemble in the early fall to perpetuate their race. From the tenth of September to the thirtieth, there is not an hour of the day or night when there are no boats floating on that pool, and no anglers trailing the fly across its waters. Before the late fishermen are ready to come in at midnight, the early fishermen may be seen creeping down to the shore with lanterns in order to begin before cock-crow. The number of fish taken is not large,— perhaps five or six for the whole company on an average day,—but the size is sometimes enormous,—nothing under three pounds is counted, and they pervade thought and conversation at the Upper Dam to the exclusion of every other subject. There is no driving, no dancing, no golf, no tennis. There is nothing to do but fish or die.

At first, Cornelia thought she would choose the latter alternative. But a remark of that skilful and morose old angler, McTurk, which she overheard on the verandah after supper, changed her mind.

"Women have no sporting instinct," said he. "They only fish because they see men doing it. They are imitative animals."

That same night she told Beekman, in the subdued tone which the architectural construction of the house imposes upon all confidential communications in the bedrooms, but with resolution in every accent, that she proposed to go fishing with him on the morrow.

"But not on that pool, right in front of the house, you understand. There must be some other place, out on the lake, where we can fish for three or four days, until I get the trick of this wobbly rod. Then I'll show that old bear, McTurk, what kind of an animal woman is."

Beekman was simply delighted. Five days of diligent practice at the mouth of Mill Brook brought his pupil to the point where he pronounced her safe.

"Of course," he said patronizingly, "you haven't learned all about it yet. That will take years. But you can get your fly out thirty feet, and you can keep the tip of your rod up. If you do that, the trout will hook himself, in rapid water, eight times out of ten. For playing him, if you follow my directions, you'll be all right. We will try the pool tonight, and hope for a medium-sized fish."

Cornelia said nothing, but smiled and nodded. She had her own thoughts.

At about nine o'clock Saturday night, they anchored their boat on the edge of the shoal where the big eddy swings around, put out the lantern and began to fish. Beekman sat in the bow of the boat, with his rod over the left side; Cornelia in the stern, with her rod over the right side. The night was cloudy and very black. Each of them had put on the largest possible fly, one a "Bee-Pond" and the other a "Dragon;"

but even these were invisible. They measured out the right length of line, and let the flies drift back until they hung over the shoal, in the curly water where the two currents meet.

There were three other boats to the left of them. McTurk was their only neighbor in the darkness on the right. Once they heard him swearing softly to himself, and knew that he had hooked and lost a fish.

Away down at the tail of the pool, dimly visible through the gloom, the furtive fisherman, Parsons, had anchored his boat. No noise ever came from that craft. If he wished to change his position, he did not pull up the anchor and let it down again with a bump. He simply lengthened or shortened his anchor rope. There was no click of the reel when he played a fish. He drew in and paid out the line through the rings by hand, without a sound. What he thought when a fish got away, no one knew, for he never said it. He concealed his angling as if it had been a conspiracy. Twice that night they heard a faint splash in the water near his boat, and twice they saw him put his arm over the side in the darkness and bring it back again very quietly.

"That's the second fish for Parsons," whispered Beekman, "what a secretive old Fortunatus he is! He knows more about fishing than any man on the pool, and talks less."

Cornelia did not answer. Her thoughts were all on the tip of her own rod. About eleven o'clock a fine, drizzling rain set in. The fishing was very slack. All the other boats gave it up in despair; but Cornelia said she wanted to stay out a little longer, they might as well finish up the week.

At precisely fifty minutes past eleven, Beekman reeled up his line, and remarked with firmness that the holy Sabbath day was almost at hand and they ought to go in.

"Not till I've landed this trout," said Cornelia.

"What? A trout! Have you got one?"

"Certainly; I've had him on for at least fifteen minutes. I'm playing him Mr. Parsons' way. You might as well light the lantern and get the net ready; he's coming in towards the boat now."

Beekman broke three matches before he made the lantern burn; and when he held it up over the gunwale, there was the trout sure enough, gleaming ghostly pale in the dark water, close to the boat, and quite tired out. He slipped the net over the fish and drew it in—a monster.

"I'll carry that trout, if you please," said Cornelia, as they stepped out of the boat; and she walked into the camp, on the last stroke of midnight, with the fish in her hand, and quietly asked for the steelyard.

Eight pounds and fourteen ounces,—that was the weight. Everybody was amazed. It was the "best fish" of the year. Cornelia showed no sign of exultation, until just as John was carrying the trout to the ice-house. Then she flashed out:

"Quite a fair imitation, Mr. McTurk,—isn't it?"

Now McTurk's best record for the last fifteen years was seven pounds and twelve ounces.

So far as McTurk is concerned, this is the end of the story. But not for the De Peysters. I wish it were. Beekman went to sleep that night with a contented spirit. He felt that his experiment in education had been a success. He had made his wife an angler.

He had indeed, and to an extent which he little suspected. That Upper Dam trout was to her like the first taste of blood to the tiger. It seemed to change, at once, not so much her character as the direction of her vital energy. She yielded to the lunacy of angling, not by slow degrees, (as first a transient delusion, then a fixed idea, then a chronic infirmity, finally a mild insanity,) but by a sudden plunge into the most violent mania. So far from being ready to die at Upper Dam, her desire now was to live there and to live solely for the sake of fishing—as long as the season was open.

There were two hundred and forty hours left to midnight on the thirtieth of September. At least two hundred of these she spent on the pool; and when Beekman was too exhausted to manage the boat and the net and the lantern for her, she engaged a trustworthy guide to take Beekman's place while he slept. At the end of the last day her score was twenty-three, with an average of five pounds and a quarter. His score was nine, with an average of four pounds. He had succeeded far beyond his wildest hopes.

The next year his success became even more astonishing. They went to the Titan Club in Canada. The ugliest and most inaccessible sheet of water in that territory is Lake Pharaoh. But it is famous for the extraordinary fishing at a certain spot near the outlet, where there is just room enough for one canoe. They camped on Lake Pharaoh for six weeks, by Mrs. De Peyster's command; and her canoe was always the first to reach the fishing-ground in the morning, and the last to leave it in the evening.

Some one asked him, when he returned to the city, whether he had good luck.

"Quite fair," he tossed off in a careless way; "we took over three hundred pounds."

"To your own rod?" asked the inquirer, in admiration.

"No-o-o," said Beekman, "there were two of us."

There were two of them, also, the following year, when they joined the Natasheebo Salmon Club and fished that celebrated river in Labrador. The custom of drawing lots every night for the water that each member was to angle over the next day, seemed to be especially designed to fit the situation. Mrs. De Peyster could fish her own pool and her husband's too. The result of that year's fishing was something phenomenal. She had a score that made a paragraph in the newspapers and called out editorial comment. One editor was so inadequate to the situation as to entitle the article in which he described her triumph "The Equivalence of Woman." It was well-meant, but she was not at all pleased with it.

She was now not merely an angler, but a "record" angler of the most virulent type. Wherever they went, she wanted, and she got, the pick of the water. She seemed to be equally at home on all kinds of streams, large and small. She would pursue the little mountain-brook trout in the early spring, and the Labrador salmon in July, and the huge speckled trout of the northern lakes in September, with the same avidity and resolution. All that she cared for was to get the best and the most of the fishing at each place where she angled. This she always did.

And Beekman,—well, for him there were no more long separations from the partner of his life while he went off to fish some favorite stream. There were no more home-comings after a good day's sport to find her clad in cool and dainty raiment on the verandah, ready to welcome him with friendly badinage. There was not even any casting of the fly around Hardscrabble Point while she sat in the canoe reading a novel, looking up with mild and pleasant interest when he caught a larger fish than usual, as an older and wiser person looks at a child playing some innocent game. Those days of a divided interest between man and wife were gone. She was now fully converted, and more. Beekman and Cornelia were one; and she was the one.

The last time I saw the De Peysters he was following, her along the Beaverkill, carrying a landing-net and a basket, but no rod. She paused for a moment to exchange greetings, and then strode on down the stream. He lingered for a few minutes longer to light a pipe.

"Well, old man," I said, "you certainly have succeeded in making an angler of Mrs. De Peyster."

"Yes, indeed," he answered,—"haven't I?" Then he continued, after a few thoughtful puffs of smoke, "Do you know, I'm not quite so sure as I used to be that fishing is the best of all sports. I sometimes think of giving it up and going in for croquet."

On Dry-Cow Fishing as a Fine Art

RUDYARD KIPLING

It must be clearly understood that I am not at all proud of this performance. In Florida men sometimes hook and land, on rod and tackle a little finer than a steam-crane and chain, a mackerel-like fish called "tarpon," which sometime run to 120 pounds. Those men stuff their captures and exhibit them in glass cases and become puffed up. On the Columbia River sturgeon of 150 pounds weight are taken with the line. When the sturgeon is hooked the line is fixed to the nearest pine tree or steamboat-wharf, and after some hours or days the sturgeon surrenders himself, if the pine or the line do not give way. The owner of the line then states on oath that he has caught a sturgeon, and he, too, becomes proud.

These things are mentioned to show how light a creel will fill the soul of a man with vanity. I am not proud. It is nothing to me that I have hooked and played seven hundred pounds weight of quarry. All my desire is to place the little affair on record before the mists of memory breed the miasma of exaggeration.

The minnow cost eighteenpence. It was a beautiful quill minnow, and the tackle-maker said that it could be thrown as a fly. He guaranteed further in respect to the triangles—it glittered with triangles—that, if necessary, the minnow would hold a horse. A man who speaks too much truth is just as offensive as a man who speaks too little. None the less, owing to the defective condition of the present law of libel, the tackle-master's name must be withheld.

The minnow and I and a rod went down to a brook to attend to a small jack who lived between two clumps of flags in the most cramped swim that he could select. As a proof that my intentions were strictly honorable, I may mention that I was using a light split-cane rod—very dangerous if the line runs through the weeds, but very satisfactory in clean water, inasmuch as it keeps a steady strain on the fish and prevents him from taking liberties. I had an old score against the jack. He owed me two live-bait already, and I had reason to suspect him of coming up-stream and interfering with a little bleak-pool under a horse-bridge which lay entirely beyond his sphere of legitimate influence. Observe, therefore, that my tackle and my motives pointed clearly to jack, and jack alone; though I knew that there were monstrous big perch in the brook.

The minnow was thrown as a fly several times, and, owing to my peculiar, and hitherto unpublished, methods of fly throwing, nearly six pennyworth of the triangles came off, either in my coat-collar, or my thumb, or the back of my hand. Fly fishing is a very gory amusement.

The jack was not interested in the minnow, but towards twilight a boy opened a gate of the field and let in some twenty or thirty cows and half-a-dozen cart-horses, and they were all very much interested. The horses galloped up and down the field and shook the banks, but the cows walked solidly and breathed heavily, as people breathe who appreciate the Fine Arts.

By this time I had given up all hope of catching my jack fairly, but I wanted the live-bait and bleak-account settled before I had quite made up my mind to borrow a tin of chloride of lime from the farm-house—another triangle had fixed itself in my fingers—I made a cast which for pure skill, exact judgment of distance, and perfect coincidence of hand and eye and brain, would have taken every prize at a bait-casting tournament. That was the first half of the cast. The second was postponed because the quill minnow would not return to its proper place, which was under the lobe of my left ear. It had done thus before, and I supposed it was in collision with a grass tuft, till I turned around and saw a large red and white bald faced cow tying to rub what would be withers in a horse with her nose. She looked at me reproachfully, and her look said as plainly as words: "The season is too far advanced for gadflies. What is this strange disease?"

I replied, "Madam, I must apologize for an unwarrantable liberty on the part of my minnow, but if you will have the goodness to keep still until I can reel in, we will adjust this little difficulty."

I reeled in very swiftly and cautiously, but she would not wait. She put her tail in the air and ran away. It was a purely involuntary motion on my part: I struck. Other anglers may contradict me, but I firmly believe that if a man had foul-hooked his best friend through the nose, and that friend ran, the man would strike by instinct. I struck, therefore, and the reel began to sing just as merrily as though I had caught my jack. But had it been a jack, the minnow would have come away. I told the tackle-maker this much afterwards, and he laughed and made allusions to the guarantee about holding a horse.

Because it was a fat innocent she-cow that had done me no harm the minnow held—held like an anchor-fluke in coral moorings—and I was forced to dance up and down an interminable field very largely used by cattle. It was like salmon fishing in a nightmare. I took gigantic strides, and every stride found me up to my knees in marsh. But the cow seemed to skate along the squashy greens by the brook, to skim over the miry backwaters, and to float like a mist through the patches of rush that squirted black filth over my face. Sometimes we whirled through a mob of her friends—there were no friends to help me—and they looked scandalized; and some-times a young and frivolous cart-horse would join in the chase for a few miles, and kick solid pieces of mud into my eyes; and through all the mud, the milky smell of kine, the rush and the smother, I was aware of my own voice crying: "Pussy, pussy, pussy! Pretty pussy! Come along then, puss-cat!" You see it is so hard to speak to a cow properly, and she would not listen—no, she would not listen.

Then she stopped, and the moon got up behind the pollards to tell the cows to lie down; but they were all on their feet, and they came trooping to see. And she said, "I haven't had my supper, and I want to go to bed, and please don't worry me." And I said, "The matter has passed beyond any apology. There are three courses open to you, my dear lady. If you'll the common sense to walk up to my creel I'll get my knife and you shall have all the minnow. Or, again, if you'll let me move across to your near side, instead of keeping me so coldly on your off side, the thing will come away in one tweak. I can't pull it out over your withers. Better still, go to a post and rub it out, dear. It won't hurt much, but if you think I'm going to lose my rod to please you, you are mistaken." And she said, "I don't understand what you are saying. I am very, very unhappy." And I said, "It's your fault for trying to fish. Do go to the nearest gate-post, you nice fat thing, and rub it out."

For a moment I fancied she was taking my advice. She ran away and I followed. But all the other cows came with us in a bunch, and I thought of Phaeton trying to drive the Chariot of the Sun, and Texan cowboys killed by stampeding cattle, and "Green Grow the Rushes, O!" and Solomon and Job, and "loosing the bands of Orion," and hooking Behemoth, and Wordsworth who talks about whirling around with stones and rocks and trees, and "Here we go round the Mulberry bush," and "Pippin Hill," and "Hey Diddle Diddle," and most especially the top joint of my rod. Again she stopped—but now where in the neighborhood of my knife—and her sis-ters stood moonfaced round her. It seemed that she might, now, run towards me, and I looked for a tree, because cows are very different from salmon, who only jump against the line, and never molest the fisherman. What followed was worse than any direct attack. She began to buck-jump, to stand on her head and her tail alternately, to leap to the sky, all four feet together, and to dance on her hind legs. It was so violent and improper, so desperately unladylike, that I was inclined to blush, as one would blush at the sight of a prominent statesman sliding down a dire escape, or a duchess chasing her cook with a skillet. That flop-some abandon might go on all night in the lonely meadow among the mists, and if it went on all night—this was pure inspiration—I might be able to worry through the fishing line with my teeth.

Those who desire an entirely new sensation should chew with all their teeth, and against time, through a best waterproofed silk line, one end of which belongs to a mad cow dancing fairy rings in the moonlight; at the same time keeping one eye on the cow and the other on the top joint of a split-cane rod. She buck-jumped and I bit on the slack just in front of the reel; and I am in a position to state that that line was cored with steel wire throughout the particular section which I attacked. This had been formally denied by the tackle-maker, who is not to be believed.

The wheep of the broken line running through the rings told me that henceforth the cow and I might be strangers. I had already bidden good-bye to some tooth or teeth; but not price is too great for freedom of the soul.

"Madam," I said, "the minnow and twenty feet of very superior line are your alimony without reservation. For the wrong I have unwittingly done to you I express my sincere regret. At the same time, may I hope that Nature, the kindest of nurses, will in due season—"

She or one of her companions must have stepped on her spare end of the line in the dark, for she bellowed wildly and ran away, followed by all the cows. I hoped the minnow was disengaged at last; and before I went away looked at my watch, fearing to find it nearly midnight. My last cast for the jack was made at 6:23 P.M. There lacked still three and a-half minutes of the half-hour; and I would have sworn that the moon was paling before the dawn!

"Simminly someone were chasing they cows down to bottom o' Ten Acre," said the farmer that evening. "'Twasn't you, sir?"

"Now under what earthly circumstances do you suppose I should chase your cows? I wasn't fishing for them, was I?"

Then all the farmer's family gave themselves up to jam-smeared laughter for the rest of the evening, because that was a rare and precious jest, and it was repeated for months, and the fame of it spread from the farm to another, and yet another at least three miles away, and it will be used again for the benefit of visitors when the freshets come down in spring.

But to the greater establishment of my honor and glory I submit in print this bald statement of fact, that I may not, through forgetfulness, be tempted later to tell how I hooked a bull on a Marlow Buzz, how he ran up a tree and took to water, and how I played him along the London-road for thirty miles, and gaffed him at Smithfield. Errors of this kind may creep in with the lapse of years, and it is my ambition ever to be a worthy member of that fraternity who pride themselves on never deviating by one hair's breadth from the absolute and literal truth.

The Hole

GUY DE MAUPASSANT

"Cuts and wound that caused death"—That was the heading of the charge which brought Leopold Renard, upholsterer, before the Assize Court.

Round him were the principal witnesses, Madame Flameche, widow of the victim, Louis Ladureau, cabinetmaker, and Jean Durdent, plumber.

Near the criminal was his wife, dressed in black, a little ugly woman, who looked like a monkey dressed as a lady.

This is how Renard described the drama:

"Good heavens, it is a misfortune of which I am the first and last victim, and with which my will has nothing to do. The facts are their own commentary, Monsieur le President. I am an honest man, a hard-working man, an upholsterer in the same street for the last sixteen years, known, liked, respected, and esteemed by all, as my neighbors have testified, even the porter, who is not folatre every day. I am fond of work, I am fond of saving, I like honest men, and respectable pleasures. That is what has ruined me, so much the worse for me; but as my will had nothing to do with it, I continue to respect myself.

"Every Sunday for the last five years, my wife and I have spent the day at Passy. We get fresh air, not to say that we are fond of fishing—as fond of it as we are of small onions. Melie inspired me with that passion, the jade; she is more enthusiastic than I am, the scold, and all the mischief in this business is her fault, as you will see immediately.

"I am strong and mild-tempered, without a pennyworth of malice in me. But she, oh la la! She looks insignificant, she is short and thin, but she does more mischief than a weasel. I do not deny that she has some good qualities; she has some, and those very important to a man in business. But her character! Just ask about it in the neighborhood; even the porter's wife, who has just sent me about my business—she will tell you something about it.

"Every day she used to find fault with my mild temper: 'I would not put up with this! I would not put up with that.' If I had listened to her, Monsieur le President, I should have had at least three bouts of fisticuffs a month."

Madame Renard interrupted him: "And for good reasons too; they laugh best who laugh last."

He turned toward her frankly: "Oh! very well, I can blame you, since you were the cause of it."

Then, facing the President again he said:

"I will continue. We used to go to Passy every Saturday evening, so as to be able to begin fishing at daybreak the next morning. It is a habit which has become second nature with us, as the saying is. Three years ago this summer I discovered a place, oh! such a spot! There, in the shade, were eight feet of water at least and perhaps ten, a hole with a retour under the bank, a regular retreat for fish and a paradise for any fisherman. I might look upon that hole as my property, Monsieur le President, as I was its Christopher Columbus. Everybody in the neighborhood knew it, without making any opposition. They used to say: 'That is Renard's place'; and nobody would have gone to it, not even Monsieur Plumsay, who is renowned, be it said without any offense, for appropriating other people's places.

"Well, I went as usual to that place, of which I felt as certain as if I had owned it. I had scarcely got there on Saturday, when I got into Delila, with my wife. Delila is my Norwegian boat, which I had built by Fourmaise, and which is light and safe. Well, as I said, we got into the boat and we were going to bait, and for baiting there is nobody to be compared with me, and they all know it. You want to know with what I bait? I cannot answer that question; it has nothing to do with the accident; I cannot answer, that is my secret. There are more than three hundred people who have asked me; I have been offered glasses of brandy and liquors, fried fish, matelotes, to make me tell! But just go and try whether the chub will come. Ah! they have patted my stomach to get at my secret, my recipe. Only my wife knows, and she will not tell it, any more than I shall! Is not that so, Melie?"

The President of the Court interrupted him:

"Just get to the facts as soon as you can."

The accused continued: "I am getting to them; I am getting to them. Well, on Saturday. July 8, we left by the five twenty-five train, and before dinner we went to ground-bait as usual. The weather promised to keep fine, and I said to Melie: 'All right for to-morrow!' And she replied: 'It looks like it.' We never talk more than that together.

"And then we returned to dinner. I was happy and thirsty, and that was the cause of everything. I said to Melie: 'Look here Melie, it is fine weather, so suppose I drink a bottle of Casque a meche. That is a little white wine which we have christened so, because if you drink too much of it prevents you from sleeping and is the opposite of a nightcap. Do you understand me?

"She replied: 'You can do as you please, but you will be ill again, and will not be able to get up to-morrow.' That was true, sensible, prudent, and clear-sighted, I must confess. Nevertheless, I could not withstand it, and I drank my bottle. It all comes from that.

"Well, I could not sleep. By Jove! It kept me awake till two o'clock in the morning, and then I went to sleep so soundly that I should not have heard the angel shouting at the Last Judgment.

"In short, my wife woke me at six o'clock and I jumped out of bed, hastily put on my trousers and jersey, washed my face and jumped on board Delila. But it was too late, for when I arrived at my hole it was already taken! Such a thing had never happened to me in three years, and it made me feel as if I were being robbed under my own eyes. I said to myself, Confound it all! confound it! And then my wife began to nag at me. 'Eh! What about your Casque a meche! Get along, you drunkard! Are you satisfied, you great fool?' I could say nothing, because it was all quite true, and so I landed all the same near the spot and tried to profit by what was left. Perhaps after all the fellow might catch nothing, and go away.

"He was a little thin man, in white linen coat and waistcoat, and with a large straw hat, and his wife, a fat woman who was doing embroidery, was behind him.

"When she saw us take up our position close to their place, she murmured: 'I suppose there are no other places on the river!' And my wife, who was furious, replied: 'People who know how to behave make inquiries about the habits of the neighborhood before occupying reserved spots.'

"As I did not want a fuss, I said to her: 'Hold your tongue, Melie. Let them go on, let them go on; we shall see.'

"Well, we had fastened Delila under the willow-trees, and had landed and were fishing side by side, Melie and I, close to the two others; but here, Monsieur, I must enter into details.

"We had only been there about five minutes when our male neighbor's float began to go down two or three times, and then he pulled out a chub as thick as my thigh, rather less, perhaps, but nearly as big! My heart beat, and the perspiration stood on my forehead, and Melie said to me: 'Well, you sot, did you see that?'

"Just then, Monsieur Bru, the grocer of Poissy, who was fond of gudgeon fishing, passed in a boat, and called out to me: So somebody has taken your usual place, Monsieur Renard? And I replied: 'Yes, Monsieur Bru, there are some people in this world who do not know the usages of common politeness.'

"The little man in linen pretended not to hear, nor his fat lump of a wife, either."

Here the President interrupted him a second time: "Take care, you are insulting the widow, Madame Flameche, who is present.

Renard made his excuses: "I beg your pardon, I beg your pardon, my anger carried me away . . . Well, not a quarter of an hour had passed when the little man caught another chub and another almost immediately, and another five minutes later.

"The tears were in my eyes, and then I knew that Madame Renard was boiling with rage, for she kept on nagging at me: 'Oh! how horrid! Don't you see that he is robbing you of your fish? Do you think that you will catch anything? Not even a frog, nothing whatever. Why, my hands are burning, just to think of it.'

"But I said to myself: 'Let us wait until twelve o clock. Then this poaching fellow will go to lunch, and I shall get my place again. As for me, Monsieur le President, I lunch on the spot every Sunday; we bring our provisions in 'Delila.' But there! At twelve o'clock, the wretch produced a fowl out of a newspaper, and while he was eating, actually he caught another chub!

"Melie and I had a morsel also, just a mouthful, a mere nothing, for our heart was not in it.

"Then I took up my newspaper, to aid my digestion. Every Sunday I read the Gil Blas in the shade like that, by the side of the water. It is Columbine's day, you know, Columbine who writes the articles in the Gil Blas. I generally put Madame Renard into a passion by pretending to know this Columbine. It is not true, for I do not know her, and have never seen her, but that does not matter; she writes very well, and then she says things straight out for a woman. She suits me, and there are not many of her sort.

"Well, I began to tease my wife, but she got angry immediately, and very angry, and so I held my tongue. At that moment our two witnesses, who are present here, Monsieur Ladureau and Monsieur Durdent, appeared on the other side of the river. We knew each other by sight. The little man began to fish again, and he caught so many that I trembled with vexation, and his wife said: 'It is an uncommonly good spot, and we will come here always, Desire.' As for me, a cold shiver ran down my back, and Madame Renard kept repeating: 'You are not a man; you have the blood of a chicken in your veins'; and suddenly I said to her: 'Look here, I would rather go away, or I shall only be doing something foolish.'

"And she whispered to me as if she had put a red-hot iron under my nose: 'You are not a man. Now you are going to run away, and surrender your place! Off you go, Bazaine!'

"Well, I felt that, but yet I did not move, while the other fellow pulled out a bream, Oh! I never saw such a large one before, never! And then my wife began to talk aloud, as if she were thinking, and you can see her trickery. She said: 'That is what one might call stolen fish, seeing that we baited the place ourselves. At any rate, they ought to give us back the money we have spent on bait.'

"Then the fat woman in the cotton dress said in turn: 'Do you mean to call us thieves, Madame?' And they began to explain, and then they came to words. Oh! Lord! those creatures know some good ones. They shouted so loud, that our two witnesses, who were on the other bank, began to call out by way of a joke: 'Less noise over there; you will prevent your husbands from fishing.'

"The fact is that neither of us moved any more than if we had been two tree-stumps. We remained there, with our noses over the water, as if we had heard nothing, but by Jove, we heard all the same. 'You are a mere liar.'

"'You are nothing better than a street-walker.'

"'You are only a trollop.'

"'You are a regular strumpet.'

"And so on, and so on; a sailor could not have said more.

"Suddenly I heard a noise behind me, and turned round. It was the other one, the fat woman who had fallen on to my wife with her parasol. Whack! Whack! Melie got two of them, but she was furious, and she hits hard when she is in a rage, so she caught the fat woman by the hair and then, thump, thump. Slaps in the face rained down like ripe plums. I should have let them go on—women among themselves, men among themselves—it does not do to mix the blows, but the little man in the linen jacket jumped up like a devil and was going to rush at my wife. Ah! no, no, not that, my friend! I caught the gentleman with the end of my fist, crash, crash, one on the nose, the other in the stomach. He threw up his arms and legs and fell on his back into the river, just into the hole.

"I should have fished him out most certainly, Monsieur le President, if I had had the time. But unfortunately the fat woman got the better of it, and she was drubbing Melie terribly. I know that I ought not to have assisted her while the man was drinking his fill, but I never thought that he would drown, and said to myself: 'Bah, it will cool him.'

"I therefore ran up to the women to separate them, and all I received was scratches and bites. Good Lord, what creatures! Well, it took me five minutes, and perhaps ten, to separate those two viragoes. When I turned round, there was nothing to be seen, and the water was as smooth as a lake. The others yonder kept shouting: 'Fish him out!' It was all very well to say that, but I cannot swim and still less dive!

"At last the man from the dam came, and two gentlemen with boat-hooks, but it had taken over a quarter of an hour. He was found at the bottom of the hole in eight feet of water, as I have said, but he was dead, the poor little man in his linen suit! There are the facts, such as I have sworn to. I am innocent, on my honor."

The witnesses having deposed to the same effect, the accused was acquitted.

The Lady or the Salmon?

ANDREW LANG

The circumstances which attended and caused the death of the Hon. Houghton Grannom have not long been known to me, and it is only now that, by the decease of his father, Lord Whitchurch, and the extinction of his noble family, I am permitted to divulge the facts. That the true tale of my unhappy friend will touch different chords in different breasts, I am well aware. The sportsman, I think, will hesitate to approve him; the fair, I hope, will absolve. Who are we, to scrutinize human motives, and to award our blame to actions which, perhaps, might have been our own, had opportunity beset and temptation beguiled us? There is a certain point at which the keenest sense of honor, the most chivalrous affection and devotion, cannot bear the strain, but break like a salmon line under a masterful stress. That my friend succumbed, I admit; that he was his own judge, the severest, and passed and executed sentence on himself, I have now to show.

I shall never forget the shock with which I read in the "Scotsman," under "Angling," the following paragraph:

"Tweed.—Strange Death of an Angler.—An unfortunate event has cast a gloom over fishers in this district. As Mr. K-, the keeper on the B- water, was busy angling yesterday, his attention was caught by some object floating on the stream. He cast his flies over it, and landed a soft felt hat, the ribbon stuck full of salmon-flies. Mr. K- at once hurried up-stream, filled with the most lively apprehensions. These were soon justified. In a shallow, below the narrow, deep and dangerous rapids called "The Trows," Mr. K- saw a salmon leaping in a very curious manner. On a closer examination, he found that the fish was attached to a line. About seventy yards higher he found, in shallow water, the body of a man, the hand still grasping in death the butt of the rod, to which the salmon was fast, all the line being run out. Mr. K- at once rushed into the stream, and dragged out the body, in which he recognized with horror the Hon. Houghton Grannom, to whom the water was lately let. Life had been for some minutes extinct, and though Mr. K- instantly hurried for Dr. -, that gentleman could only attest the melancholy fact. The wading in "The Trows" is extremely dangerous and difficult, and Mr. Grannom, who was fond of fishing without an attendant, must have lost his balance, slipped, and been dragged down by the weight of his waders. The recent breaking off of the hon. gentleman's contemplated marriage on the very wedding-day will be fresh in the memory of our readers."

This was the story which I read in the newspaper during breakfast one morning in November. I was deeply grieved, rather than astonished, for I have often remonstrated with poor Grannom on the recklessness of his wading. It was with some surprise that I received, in the course of the day, a letter from him, in which he spoke only of indifferent matters, of the fishing which he had taken, and so forth. The letter was accompanied, however, by a parcel. Tearing off the outer cover, I found a sealed document addressed to me, with the superscription, "Not to be opened until after my father's decease." This injunction, of course, I have scrupulously obeyed. The death of Lord Whitchurch, the last of the Grannoms, now gives me liberty to publish my friend's *Apologia pro morte et vita sua.*

"Dear Smith" (the document begins), "Before you read this—long before, I hope—I shall have solved the great mystery—if, indeed, we solve it. If the water runs down to-morrow, and there is every prospect that it will do so, I must have the opportunity of making such an end as even malignity cannot suspect of being voluntary. There are plenty of fish in the water; if I hook one in "The Trows," I shall let myself go whither the current takes me. Life has for weeks been odious to me; for what is life without honor, without love, and coupled with shame and remorse? Repentance I cannot call the emotion which gnaws me at the heart, for in similar circumstances (unlikely as these are to occur) I feel that I would do the same thing again.

"Are we but automata, worked by springs, moved by the stronger impulse, and unable to choose for ourselves which impulse that shall be? Even now, in decreeing my own destruction, do I exercise free-will, or am I the sport of hereditary tendencies, of mistaken views of honor, of a seeming self-sacrifice, which, perhaps, is but selfishness in disguise? I blight my unfortunate father's old age; I destroy the last of an ancient house; but I remove from the path of Olive Dunne the shadow that must rest upon the sunshine of what will eventually, I trust, be a happy life, unvexed by memories of one who loved her passionately. Dear Olive! how pure, how ardent was my devotion to her none knows better than you. But Olive had, I will not say a fault, though I suffer from it, but a quality, or rather two qualities, which have completed my misery. Lightly as she floats on the stream of society, the most casual observer, and even the enamored beholder, can see that Olive Dunne has great pride, and no sense of humor. Her dignity is her idol. What makes her, even for a moment, the possible theme of ridicule is in her eyes an unpardonable sin. This sin, I must with penitence confess, I did indeed commit. Another woman might have forgiven me. I know not how that may be; I throw myself on the mercy of the court. But, if another could pity and pardon, to Olive this was impossible. I have never seen her since that fatal moment when, paler than her orange blossoms, she swept through the porch of the church, while I, disheveled, mud-stained, half-drowned—ah! that memory will torture me if memory at all remains. And yet, fool, maniac, that I was, I could not resist the wild, mad impulse to laugh which shook the rustic spectators, and which in my case was due, I trust, to hysterical but NOT unmanly emotion. If any woman, any bride, could forgive such an apparent but most unintentional insult, Olive Dunne, I knew, was not that woman. My abject letters of explanation, my appeals for mercy, were returned unopened. Her parents pitied me, perhaps had reasons for being on my side, but Olive was of marble. It is not only myself that she cannot pardon, she will never, I know, forgive herself while my existence reminds her of what she had to endure. When she receives the intelligence of my demise, no suspicion will occur to her; she will not say "He is fitly punished;" but her peace of mind will gradually return.

It is for this, mainly, that I sacrifice myself, but also because I cannot endure the dishonor of a laggard in love and a recreant bridegroom.

So much for my motives: now to my tale.

"The day before our wedding-day had been the happiest in my life. Never had I felt so certain of Olive's affections, never so fortunate in my own. We parted in the soft moonlight; she, no doubt, to finish her nuptial preparations; I, to seek my couch in the little rural inn above the roaring waters of the Budon.

Move eastward, happy earth, and leave
Yon orange sunset fading slow;
From fringes of the faded eve
Oh, happy planet, eastward go,

I murmured, though the atmospheric conditions were not really those described by the poet.

Ah, bear me with thee, smoothly borne,
Dip forward under starry light,
And move me to my marriage morn,
And round again to—

"River in grand order, sir," said the voice of Robins, the keeper, who recognized me in the moonlight. "There's a regular monster in the Ashweil," he added, naming a favorite cast; "never saw nor heard of such a fish in the water before."

"Mr. Dick must catch him, Robins," I answered; "no fishing for me tomorrow."

"No, sir," said Robins, affably. "Wish you joy, sir, and Miss Olive, too. It's a pity, though! Master Dick, he throws a fine fly, but he gets flurried with a big fish, being young. And this one is a topper."

With that he gave me good-night, and I went to bed, but not to sleep. I was fevered with happiness; the past and future reeled before my wakeful vision. I heard every clock strike; the sounds of morning were astir, and still I could not sleep. The ceremony, for reasons connected with our long journey to my father's place in Hampshire, was to be early—half-past ten was the hour. I looked at my watch; it was seven of the clock, and then I looked out of the window: it was a fine, soft grey morning, with a south wind tossing the yellowing boughs. I got up, dressed in a hasty way, and thought I would just take a look at the river. It was, indeed, in glorious order, lapping over the top of the sharp stone which we regarded as a measure of the due size of water.

The morning was young, sleep was out of the question; I could not settle my mind to read. Why should I not take a farewell cast, alone, of course? I always disliked the attendance of a gillie. I took my salmon rod out of its case, rigged it up, and started for the stream, which flowed within a couple of hundred yards of my quarters. There it raced under the ash tree, a pale delicate brown, perhaps a little thing too colored. I therefore put on a large Silver Doctor, and began steadily fishing down the ash-tree cast. What if I should wipe Dick's eye, I thought, when, just where the rough and smooth water meet, there boiled up a head and shoulders such as I had never seen on any fish. My heart leaped and stood still, but there came no sensation from the rod, and I finished the cast, my knees actually trembling beneath me. Then I gently lifted the line, and very elaborately tested every link of the powerful casting-line. Then I gave him ten minutes by my watch; next, with unspeakable emotion, I stepped into the stream and repeated the cast. Just at the same spot he came up again; the huge rod bent like a switch, and the salmon rushed straight down the pool, as if he meant to make for the sea. I staggered on to dry land to follow him the easier, and dragged at my watch to time the fish; a quarter to eight. But the slim chain had broken, and the watch, as I hastily thrust it back, missed my pocket and fell into the water. There was no time to stoop for it; the fish started afresh, tore up the pool as fast as he had gone down it, and, rushing behind the torrent, into the eddy at the top, leaped clean out of the water. He was 70 lbs. if he was an ounce. Here he slackened a little, dropping back, and I got in some line. Now he sulked so intensely that I thought he had got the line round a rock. It might be broken, might be holding fast to a sunken stone, for aught that I could tell; and the time was passing, I knew not how rapidly. I tried all known methods, tugging at him, tapping the butt, and slackening line on him. At last the top of the rod was slightly agitated, and then, back flew the long line in my face. Gone! I reeled up with a sigh, but the line tightened again. He had made a sudden rush under my bank, but there he lay again like a stone. How long? Ah! I cannot tell how long! I heard the church clock strike, but missed the number of the strokes. Soon he started again down-stream into the shallows, leaping at the end of his rush—the monster. Then he came slowly up, and "jiggered" savagely at the line. It seemed impossible that any tackle could stand these short violent jerks. Soon he showed signs of weakening. Once his huge silver side appeared for a moment near the surface, but he retreated to his old fastness. I was in a tremor of delight and despair. I should have thrown down my rod, and flown on the wings of love to Olive and the altar. But I hoped that there was time still—that it was not so very late! At length he was failing. I heard ten o'clock strike. He came up and lumbered on the surface of the pool. Gradually I drew him, plunging ponderously, to the graveled beach, where I meant to "tail" him. He yielded to the strain, he was in the shallows, the line was shortened. I stooped to seize him. The frayed and overworn gut broke at a knot, and with a loose roll he dropped back towards the deep. I sprang at him, stumbled, fell on him, struggled with him, but he slipped from my arms. In that moment I knew more than the anguish of Orpheus. Orpheus! Had I, too, lost my Eurydice? I rushed from the stream, up the steep bank, along to my rooms. I passed the church door. Olive, pale as her orange-blossoms, was issuing from the porch. The clock pointed to 10.45. I was ruined, I knew it, and I laughed. I laughed like a lost spirit. She swept past me, and, amidst the amazement of the gentle and simple, I sped wildly away. Ask me no more. The rest is silence."

Thus ends my hapless friend's narrative. I leave it to the judgment of women and of men. Ladies, would you have acted as Olive Dunne acted? Would pride, or pardon, or mirth have ridden sparkling in your eyes? Men, my brethren, would ye have deserted the salmon for the lady, or the lady for the salmon? I know what I would have done had I been fair Olive Dunne. What I would have done had I been Houghton Grannom I may not venture to divulge. For this narrative, then, as for another, "Let every man read it as he will, and every woman as the gods have given her wit."

Fish Are Such Liars!

ROLAND PERTWEE

There had been a fuss in the pool beneath the alders, and the small rainbow trout, with a skitter of his tail, flashed upstream, a hurt and angry fish. For three consecutive mornings he had taken the rise in that pool, and it injured his pride to be jostled from his drift just when the May fly was coming up in numbers. If his opponent had been a half-pounder like himself, he would have stayed and fought, but when an old hen fish, weighing fully three pounds, with a mouth like a rat hole and a carnivorous, cannibalistic eye rises from the reed beds and occupies the place, flight is the only effective argument.

But Rainbow was very much provoked. He had chosen his place with care. Now the May fly was up, the little French chalk stream was full of rising fish, and he knew by experience that strangers are unpopular in that season. To do one's self justice during a hatch, one must find a place where the fly drifts nicely overhead with the run of the stream, and natural drifts are scarce even in a chalk stream. He was not content to leap at the fly like a hysterical youngster who measured his weight in ounces and his wits in milligrams. He had reached that time of life which demanded that he should feed off the surface by suction rather than exertion. No living thing is more particular about his table manners than a trout, and Rainbow was no exception.

"It's a sickening thing," he said to himself, "and a hard shame." He added: "Get out of my way," to a couple of fat young chug with big mouths who were bubbling the surface in the silly, senseless fashion of their kind.

"Chub indeed!"

But even the chub has a home and he had none—and the life of a homeless river dweller is precarious.

"I will not and shall not be forced back to midstream," he said.

For, save at eventide or in very special circumstances, trout of personality do not frequent open water where they must compete for every insect with the wind, the lightning-swift sweep of swallows and martins, and even the laborious pursuit of predatory dragon-flies with their bronze wings and bodies like rods of colored glass. Even as he spoke he saw a three-ouncer leap at a dapping May fly which was scooped out of his jaws by a passing swallow. Rainbow heard that tiny click as the May fly's body cracked against the bird's beak. A single wing of yellowy gossamer floated downward and settled upon the water. Under the shelving banks to right and left, where the fly, discarding its nymph and still too damp for its virgin flight, drifted downstream, a dozen heavy trout were feeding thoughtfully and selectively.

"If only some angler would catch one of them, I might slip in and occupy the place before it gets known there's a vacancy."

But this uncharitable hope was fulfilled, and with another whisk of his tail he propelled himself into the unknown waters upstream. A couple of strands of rusty barbed wire, relic of the war, spanned the shallows from band to bank. Passing beneath them he came to a narrow reach shaded by willows, to the first of which was nailed a board bearing the words Pêche Réservée. He had passed out of the communal into private water—water running languidly over manes of emerald weed between clumps of alder, willow herb, tall crimson sorrel and masses of yellow iris. Ahead, like an apple-green rampart, rose the wooded heights of a forest; on either side were flat meadows of yellowing hay. Overhead, the vast expanse of blue June sky was tufted with rambling clouds. "My scales!" said Rainbow. "Here's water!"

But it was vain to expect any of the best places in such a reach would be vacant, and to avoid a recurrence of his unhappy encounter earlier in the morning, Rainbow continued his journey until he came to a spot where the river took one of those unaccountable right-angle bends which result in a pool, shallow on the one side, but slanting into deeps on the other. Above it was a water break, a swirl, smoothing, as it reached the pool, into a sleek, swift run, with an eddy which bore all the lighter floating things of the river over the calm surface of the little backwater, sheltered from above by a high shelving bank and a tangle of bramble of herb. Here is this backwater the twig, the broken reed, the leaf, the cork, the fly floated in suspended activity for a few instants until drawn back by invisible magnetism to the main current.

Rainbow paused in admiration. At the tail of the pool two sound fish were rising with regularity, but in the backwater beyond the eddy the surface was still and unbroken. Watching open-eyed, Rainbow saw not one but a dozen May flies, fat, juicy, and damp from the nymph, drift in, pause, and carried away untouched. It was beyond the bounds of possibility that such a place could be vacant, but there was the evidence of his eyes to prove it; and nothing if not a tryer, Rainbow darted across the stream and parked himself six inches below the water to await events.

It so happened that at the time of his arrival the hatch of fly was temporarily suspended, which gave Rainbow leisure to make a survey of his new abode. Beyond the eddy was a submerged snag—the branch of an apple tree borne there by heavy rains, water-logged, anchored, and intricate—an excellent place to break an angler's line. The river bank on his right was riddled under water with old rat holes, than which there is not better sanctuary. Below him and to the left was a dense bed of weeds brushed flat by the flow of the stream.

"If it comes to the worst," said Rainbow, "a smart fish could do a get-away here with very little ingenuity, even from a cannibalistic old hen like—hullo!"

The exclamation was excited by the apparition of a gauzy shadow on the water, which is what a May fly seen from below looks like. Resisting a vulgar inclination to leap at it with the violence of a youngster, Rainbow backed into the correct position which would allow the stream to present the morsel, so to speak, upon a tray. Which it did—and scarcely a dimple on the surface to tell what had happened.

"Very nicely taken, if you will accept the praise of a complete stranger," said a low, soft voice, one inch behind his line of sight.

Without turning to see by whom he had been addressed, Rainbow flicked a yard upstream and came back with the current four feet away. In the spot he had occupied an instant before lay a great old trout of the most benign aspect, who could not have weighed less than four pounds.

"I beg your pardon," said Rainbow, "but I had no idea that any one—that is, I just dropped in en passant, and finding an empty house, I made so bold—"

"There is no occasion to apologize," said Old Trout seductively. "I did not come up from the bottom as early to-day as is my usual habit at this season. Yesterday's hatch was singularly bountiful and it is possible I did myself too liberally."

"Yes, but a gentleman of your weight and seniority can hardly fail to be offended at finding—"

"Not at all," Old Trout broke in. "I perceive you are a well-conducted fish who does not advertise his appetite in a loud and splashing fashion."

Overcome by the charm of Old Trout's manner and address, Rainbow reduced the distance separating them to a matter of inches.

"Then you do not want me to go?" he asked.

"On the contrary, dear young sir, stay by all means and take the rise. You are, I perceive, of the rainbow or, as they say here in France, of the Arc-en-ciel family. As a youngster I had the impression that I should turn out a rainbow, but events proved it was no more than the bloom, the natural sheen of youth."

"To speak the truth, sir," said Rainbow, "unless you had told me to the contrary, I would surely have thought you one of us."

Old Trout shook his tail. "You are wrong," he said. "I am from Dulverton, an English trout farm on the Exe, of which you will have heard. You are doubtless surprised to find an English fish in French waters."

"I am indeed," Rainbow replied, sucking in a passing May fly with such excellent good manners that it was hard to believe he was feeding. "Then you, sir," he added, "must know all about the habits of men."

"I may justly admit that I do," Old Trout agreed. "Apart from being hand-reared, I have in my twelve years of life studied the species in moods of activity, passivity, duplicity, and violence."

Rainbow remarked that such must doubtless have proved of invaluable service. It did not, however, explain the mystery of his presence on a French river.

"For, sir," he added, "Dulverton, as once I heard when enjoying 'A Chat about Rivers,' delivered by a much-traveled sea trout, is situated in the west of England, and without crossing the Channel I am unable to explain how you arrived here. Had you belonged to the salmon family, with which, sir, it is evident you have no connection, the explanation would be simple, but in the circumstances it baffles my understanding."

Old Trout waved one of his fins airily. "Yet cross the Channel I certainly did," said he, "and at a period in history which I venture to state will not readily be forgotten. It was during the war, my dear young friend, and I was brought in a can, in company with a hundred yearlings, to this river, or rather the upper reaches of this river, by a young officer who wished to further an entente between English and French fish even as the war was doing with the mankind of these two nations."

Old Trout sighed a couple of bubbles and arched his body this way and that.

"There was a gentleman and a sportsman," he said. "A man who was acquainted with our people as I dare to say very few are acquainted. Had it ever been my lot to fall victim to a lover of the rod, I could have done so without regret to his. If you will take a look at my tail, you will observe that the letter W is perforated on the upper side. He presented me with this distinguishing mark before committing me, with his blessing, to the water."

"I have seldom seen a tail more becomingly decorated," said Rainbow. "But what happened to your benefactor?"

Old Trout's expression became infinitely sad. "If I could answer that," said he, "I were indeed a happy trout. For many weeks after he put me into the river I used to watch him in what little spare time he was able to obtain, casting a dry fly with the exquisite precision and likeness to nature in all the likely pools and runs and eddies near his battery position. Oh, minnows! It was a pleasure to watch that man, even as it was his pleasure to watch us. His bravery, too! I call to mind a dozen times when he fished unmoved and un-startled while bullets from machine guns were packing at the water like herons and thudding into the mud banks upon which he stood."

"An angler!" remarked Rainbow. "It would be no lie to say I like him the less on that account."

Old Trout became unexpectedly stern.

"Why so?" he retorted severely. "Have I not said he was also a gentleman and a sportsman? My officer was neither a pot-hunter nor a beast of prey. He was a purist—a man who took delight in pitting his knowledge of nature against the subtlest and most suspicious intellectual forces of the wild. Are you so young as not yet to have learned the exquisite enjoyment of escaping disaster and avoiding error by the exercise of personal ingenuity? Pray, do not reply, for I would hate to think so hard a thing of any trout. We as a race exist by virtue of our brilliant intellectuality and hypersensitive selectivity. In waters where there are no pike and only an occasional otter, but for the machinations of men, where should we turn to school our wits? Danger is our mainstay, for I tell you, Rainbow, that trout are composed of two senses—appetite, which makes of us fools, and suspicion, which teaches us to be wise."

Greatly chastened not alone by what Old Trout had said but by the forensic quality of his speech, Rainbow rose short and put a promising May fly onto the wing.

"I am glad to observe," said Old Trout, "that you are not without conscience."

"To tell you the truth, sir," Rainbow replied apologetically, "my nerve this morning has been rudely shaken, but for which I should not have shown such want of good sportsmanship."

And with becoming brevity he told the tale of his eviction form the pool downstream. Old Trout listened gravely, only once moving, and that to absorb a small blue dun, an insect which he keenly relished.

"A regrettable affair," he admitted, "but as I have often observed, women, who are the gentlest creatures under water in adversity, are a thought lacking in moderation in times of abundance. They are apt to snatch."

"But for a turn of speed, she would certainly have snatched me," said Rainbow.

"Very shocking," said Old Trout. "Cannibals are disgusting. They destroy the social amenities of the river. We fish have but little family life and should therefore aim to cultivate a freemasonry of good-fellowship among ourselves. For my part, I am happy to line up with other well-conducted trout and content myself with what happens along with my own particular drift. Pardon me!" he added, breasting Rainbow to one side. "I invited you to take the rise of May fly, but I must ask you to leave the duns alone." Then, fearing this remark might be construed to reflect adversely upon his hospitality, he proceeded: "I have a reason which I will explain later. For the moment we are discussing the circumstances that led to my presence in this river."

"To be sure—your officer. He never succeeded in deluding you with his skill?"

"That would have been impossible," said Old Trout, "for I had taken up a position under the far bank where he could only have reached me with a fly by wading in a part of the river which was in view of a German sniper."

"Wily!" Rainbow chuckled. "Cunning work, sir."

"Perhaps," Old Trout admitted, "although I have since reproached myself with cowardice. However, I was at the time a very small fish and a certain amount of nervousness is forgivable in the young."

At this gracious acknowledgement the rose-colored hue in Rainbow's rainbow increased noticeably—in short, he blushed.

"From where I lay," Old Trout went on, "I was able to observe the maneuvers of my officer and greatly profit thereby."

"But excuse me, sir," said Rainbow, "I have heard it said that an angler of the first class is invisible from the river."

"He is invisible to the fish he is trying to catch," Old Trout admitted, "but it must be obvious that he is not invisible to the fish who lie beside or below him. I would also remind you that during the war every tree, every scrap of vegetation, and every vestige of natural cover had been torn up, trampled down, razed. The river banks were as smooth as the top of your head. Even the buttercup, that very humorous flower that tangles up the back cast of so many industrious anglers, was absent. Those who fished on the Western Front had little help from nature."

Young Rainbow sighed, for, only a few days before, his tongue had been badly scratched by an artificial alder which had every appearance of reality.

"It would seem," he said, "that this war had its merits."

"My young friend," said Old Trout, "you never made a greater mistake. A desire on the part of our soldiery to vary a monotonous diet of bully beef and biscuit often drove them to resort to villainous methods of assault against our kind."

"Nets?" gasped Rainbow in horror.

"Worse than nets—bombs," Old Trout replied. "A small oval black thing called a Mills bomb, which the shameless fellows flung into deep pools."

"But surely the chances of being hit by such a—"

"You reveal a pathetic ignorance," said Old Trout. "There is no question of being hit. The wretched machine exploded under water and burst our people's insides or stunned us so that we floated dead to the surface. I well remember my officer coming upon such a group of marauders one evening—yes, and laying about him with his fists in defiance of King's Regulations and the Manual of Military Law. Two of them he seized by the collar and the pants and flung into the river. Spinning minnow, that was a sight worth seeing! 'You low swine,' I heard him say; 'you trash, you muck! Isn't there enough carnage without this sort of thing?' Afterward he sat on the bank with the two dripping men and talked to them for their soul's sake.

"'Look ahead, boys. Ask yourselves what are we fighting for? Decent homes to live in at peace with one another, fields to till and forests and rivers to give us a day's sport and fun. It's our rotten job to massacre each other, but, by gosh, don't let's massacre the harmless rest of nature as well. At least, let's give 'em a running chance. Boys, in the years ahead, when all the mess is cleared up, I look forward to coming back to this old spot, when there is alder growing by the banks, and willow herb and all reeds and the drone of insects instead of the rumble of those guns. I don't want to come back to a dead river that I helped to kill, but to a river ringed with rising fish—some of whom were old comrades of the war.' He went on to tell of us hundred Dulverton trout that he had marked with the letter W. 'Give 'em their chance," he said, 'and in the years to come those beggars will reward us a hundred times over. They'll give us a finer thrill and put up a cleaner fight than old Jerry ever contrived.' Those were emotional times, and though you may be reluctant to believe me, one of those two very wet men dripped water from his eyes as well as his clothing.

"'Many's the 'appy afternoon I've 'ad with a roach pole on Brentford Canal,' he sniffed, 'though I've never yet tried m' hand against a trout.' 'You shall do it now,' said my officer, and during the half-hour that was left of daylight that dripping soldier had his first lesson in the most delicate art in the world. I can see them now—the clumsy, wet fellow and my officer timing him, timing him—"one and two, and one and two, and—' The action of my officer's wrist with its persuasive flick was the prettiest thing I have ever seen."

"Did he carry out his intention and come back after the war?" Rainbow asked.

"I shall never know," Old Trout replied. "I do not even know if he survived it. There was a great battle—a German drive. For hours they shelled the river front, and many falling short exploded in our midst with terrible results. My own bank was torn to shreds and our people suffered. How they suffered! About noon the infantry came over—hordes in field gray. There were pontoons, rope bridges and hand-to-hand fights on both banks and even in the stream itself."

"And your officer?"

"I saw him once, before the water was stamped dense into liquid mud and dyed by the blood of men. He was in the thick of it, unarmed, and a German officer called on him to surrender. For answer he struck him in the face with a light cane. Ah, that wrist action! Then a shell burst, smothering the water with clods of fallen earth and other things."

"Then you never knew?"

"I never knew, although that night I searched among the dead. Next day I went downstream, for the water in that place was polluted with death. The bottom of the pool in which I had my place was chocked with strange and mangled tenants that were not good to look upon. We trout are a clean people that will not readily abide in dirty houses. I am a Dulverton trout, where the water is filtered by the hills and runs cool over stones."

"And you have stayed here ever since?"

Old Trout shrugged a fin. "I have moved with the times. Choosing a place according to the needs of my weight."

"And you have never been caught, sir, by any other angler?"

"Am I not here?" Old Trout answered with dignity.

"Oh, quite, sir. I had only thought, perhaps, as a younger fish enthusiasm might have resulted to your disadvantage, but that, nevertheless, you had been returned."

"Returned! Returned!" echoed Old Trout. "Returned to the frying-pan! Where on earth did you pick up that expression? We are in France, my young friend; we are not on the Test, the Itchen, or the Kennet. In this country it is not the practice of anglers to return anything, however miserable in size."

"But nowadays," Rainbow protested, "there are Englishmen and Americans on the river who show us more consideration."

"They may show you more consideration," said Old Trout, "but I am of an importance that neither asks for nor expects it. Oblige me by being a little more discreet with your plurals. In the impossible event of my being deceived and caught, I should be introduced to a glass case with an appropriate background of rocks and reeds."

"But, sir, with respect, how can you be so confident of our unassailability?" Rainbow demanded, edging into position to accept an attractive May fly with yellow wings that was drifting downstream toward him.

"How?" Old Trout responded. "Because—" Then suddenly: "Leave it, you fool!"

Rainbow had just broken the surface when the warning came. They yellow-winged May fly was wrenched off the water with a wet squeak. A tangle of limp cast lapped itself round the upper branches of a willow far upstream and a raw voice exclaimed something venomous in French. By common consent the two fish went down.

"Well, really," expostulated Old Trout, "I hoped you were above that kind of thing! Nearly to fall victim to a downstream angler. It's a little too much! And think of the effect it will have on my prestige. Why, that incompetent fool will go about boasting that he rose me. Me!"

For some minutes Rainbow was too crestfallen even to apologize. At last: "I am afraid," he said, "I was paying more heed to what you were saying than to my own conduct. I never expected to be fished from above. The fly was on uncommonly good imitation and it is a rare thing for a Frenchman to use Four-X gut."

"Rubbish," said Old Trout testily. "These are mere half-pound arguments. Four-X gut, when associated with a fourteen-stone shadow, should deceive nothing over two ounces. I saved your life, but it is all very provoking. If that is a sample of your general demeanor, it is improbable that you will ever reach a pound."

"At this season we are apt to be careless," Rainbow wailed. "And nowadays it is so hard, sir, to distinguish the artificial fly from the real."

"No one expects you to do so," was the answer, "but common prudence demands that you should pay some attention to the manner in which it is presented. A May fly does not hit the water with a splash, neither is it able to sustain itself in midstream against the current. Have you ever seen a natural insect leave a broadening wake of cutwater behind its tail? Never mind the fly, my dear boy, but watch the manner of its presentation. Failure to do that has cost many of our people their lives."

"You speak," said Rainbow, a bit sulkily, "as though it were a disgrace for a trout ever to suffer defeat at the hands of an angler."

"Which indeed it is, save in exceptional circumstances," Old Trout answered. "I do not say that a perfect upstream cast from a well-concealed angler, when the fly alights dry and cocked and dances at even speed with the current, may not deceive us to our fall. And I would be the last to say that a grasshopper skillfully dapped on the surface through the branches of an overhanging tree will inevitably bring about our destruction. But I do most emphatically say that in such a spot as this, where the slightest defect in presentation is multiplied a hundred-fold by the varying water speeds, a careless rise is unpardonable. There is only one spot—and that a matter of twelve yards downstream—from which a fly can be drifted over me with any semblance to nature. Even so, there is not one angler in a thousand who can make that cast with success, by reason of a willow which cramps the back cast and the manner in which these alders on our left sprawl across the pool."

Rainbow did not turn about to verify these statements because it is bad form for a trout to face downstream. He contented himself by replying, with a touch of acerbity: "I should have thought, sir, with the feelings you expressed regarding sportsmanship, you would have found such a sanctuary too dull for your entertainment."

"Every remark you make serves to aggravate the impression of your ignorance," Old Trout replied. "Would you expect a trout of my intelligence to put myself in some place where I am exposed to the vulgar assaults of every amateur upon the bank? Of the green boy who lashes the water into foam, of the purblind peasant who slings his fly at me with a clod of earth or a tail of weed attached to the hood? In this place I invite attention from none but the best people—the expert, the purist."

"I understood you to say that there were none such in these parts," grumbled Rainbow.

"There are none who have succeeded in deceiving me," was the answer. "As a fact, for the last few days I have been vastly entranced by an angler who, by any standard, is deserving of praise. His presentation is flawless and the only fault I can detect in him is a tendency to overlook piscine psychology. He will be with us in a few minutes, since he knows it is my habit to lunch at noon."

"Pardon the interruption," said Rainbow, "but there is a gallant hatch of fly going down. I can hear your two neighbors at the tail of the pool rising steadily."

Old Trout assumed an indulgent air. "We will go up if you wish," said he, "but you will be well advised to observe my counsel before taking the rise, because if my angler keeps his appointment you will most assuredly be meunièred before nightfall."

At this unpleasant prophecy Rainbow shivered. "Let us keep to weed," he suggested.

But Old Trout only laughed, so that bubbles from the river bed rose and burst upon the surface.

"Courage," said he; "it will be an opportunity for you to learn the finer points of the game. If you are nervous, lie nearer to the bank. The natural fly does not drift there so abundantly, but you will be secure from the artificial. Presently I will treat you to an exhibition of playing with death you will not fail to appreciate." He broke off and pointed with his eyes. "Over you and to the left."

Rainbow made a neat double rise and drifted back into line. "Very mellow," he said—"very mellow and choice. Never tasted better. May I ask, sir, what do you mean by piscine psychology?"

"I imply that my angler does not appreciate the subtle possibilities of our intellect. Now, my officer concerned himself as vitally with what we were thinking as with what we were feeding upon. This fellow, secure in the knowledge that this presentation is well-nigh perfect, is content to offer me the same variety of flies day after day, irrespective of that fact that I have learned them all by heart. I have, however, adopted the practice of rising ever now and then to encourage him."

"Rising? At an artificial fly? I never heard such temerity in all my life," gasped Rainbow.

Old Trout moved his body luxuriously. "I should have said, appearing to rise," he amended. "You may have noticed that I have exhibited a predilection for small duns in preference to the larger Ephemeridae. My procedure is as follows: I wait until a natural dun and his artificial May fly are drifting downstream with the smallest possible distance separating them. Then I rise and take the dun. Assuming I have risen to him, he strikes, misses, and is at once greatly flattered and greatly provoked. By this device I sometimes occupy his attention for over an hour and thus render a substantial service to others of my kind who would certainly have fallen victim to his skill."

"The river is greatly in your debt, sir," said Young Rainbow, with deliberate satire.

He knew by experience that fish as well as anglers are notorious liars, but the exploit his host recounted was a trifle too strong. Taking a sidelong glance, he was surprised to see that Old Trout did not appear to have appreciated the subtle ridicule of his remark. The long, lithe body had become almost rigid and the great round eyes were focused upon the surface with an expression of fixed concentration.

Looking up, Rainbow saw a small white-winged May fly with red legs and a body the color of straw swing out from the main stream and describe a slow circle over the clam surface above Old Trout's head. Scarcely an inch away a tiny blue dun, its wings folded as closely as the pages of a book, floated attendant. An upward rush, a sucking kerr-rop, and when the broken water had calmed, the dun had disappeared and the May fly was dancing away downstream.

"Well," said Old Trout, "how's that, my youthful skeptic? Pretty work, eh?"

"I saw nothing in it," was the impertinent reply. "There is not a trout on the river who could not have done likewise."

"Even when one of those two flies was artificial?" Old Trout queried tolerantly.

"But neither of them was artificial," Rainbow retorted. "Had it been so, the angler would have struck. They always do."

"Of course he struck," Old Trout replied.

"But he didn't," Rainbow protested. "I saw the May fly go down with the current."

"My poor fish!" Old Trout replied. "Do you presume to suggest that I am unable to distinguish an artificial from a natural fly? Are you so blind that you failed to see the prismatic colors in the water from the paraffin in which the fly had been dipped? Here you are! Here it is again!"

Once more the white-winged insect drifted across the backwater, but this time there was no attendant dun.

"If that's a fake I'll eat my tail," said Rainbow.

"If you question my judgment," Old Trout answered, "you are at liberty to rise. I dare say, in spite of a shortage of brain, that you would eat comparatively well."

But Rainbow, in common with his kind, was not disposed to take chances.

"We may expect two or three more casts from this fly and then he will change it for a bigger. It is the same program every day without a variation. How differently my officer would have acted. By now he would have discovered my little joke and turned the tables against me. Aye me, but some men will never learn! Your mental outfit, dear Rainbow, is singularly like a man's," he added. "It lacks elasticity."

Rainbow made no retort and was glad of his forbearance, for every word Old Trout had spoken was borne out by subsequent events. Four times the white-winged May fly described an arc over the backwater, but in the absence of duns Old Trout did not rise again. Then came a pause, during which, through a lull in the hatch, even the natural insect was absent from the river.

"He is changing his fly," said Old Trout, "but he will not float it until the hatch starts again. He is casting beautifully this morning and I hope circumstances will permit me to give him another rise."

"But suppose," said Rainbow breathlessly, "you played this game once too often and were foul hooked as a result?"

Old Trout expanded his gills broadly. "Why, then," he replied, "I should break him. Once round a limb of that submerged apple bough and the thing would be done. I should never allow myself to be caught and no angler could gather up the slack and haul me into midstream in time to prevent me reaching the bough. Stand by."

The shadow of a large, dark May fly floated cockily over the backwater and had almost returned to the main stream when a small iron-blue dun settled like a puff of thistledown in its wake.

The two insects were a foot nearer the fast water than the spot where Old Trout was accustomed to take the rise. But for the presence of a spectator, it is doubtful whether he would have done so, but Young Rainbow's want of appreciation had excited his vanity, and with a rolling swoop he swallowed the dun and bore it downward.

And then an amazing thing happened. Instead of drifting back to his place as was expected, Old Trout's head was jerked sideways by an invisible force. A thin translucent thread upcut the water's surface and tightened irresistibly. A second later Old Trout was fighting, fighting, fighting to reach the submerged apple bough with the full weight of the running water and the full strength of the finest Japanese gut strained against him.

Watching, wide-eyed and aghast, form one of the underwater rat holes into which he has hastily withdrawn, Rainbow saw the figure of a man rise out of a bed of irises downstream and scramble upon the bank. In his right hand, with the wrist well back, he held a light split-cane rod whose upper joint was curved to a half-circle. The man left hand was detaching a collapsible landing net from the ring of his belt. Every attitude and movement was expressive of perfectly organized activity. His mouth was shut as tightly as a steel trap, but a light of happy excitement danced in his eyes.

"No, you don't, my fellar," Rainbow heard him say. "No, you don't. I knew all about that apple bough before ever I put a fly over your pool. And the weed bed on the right," he added, as Old Trout made a sudden swerve half down and half across stream.

Tucking the net under his arm the man whipped up the slack with a lightning-like action. The maneuver cost Old Trout dear, for when, despairing of reaching the weed and burrowing into it, he tried to regain his old position, he found himself six feet farther away from the apple bough than when the battle began.

Instinctively Old Trout knew it was useless to dash downstream, for a man who could take up slack with the speed his adversary had shown would profit by the expedient to come more quickly to term with him. Besides, lower down there was broken water to knock the breath out of his lungs even where he lay straining and slugging this way and that, the water was pouring so fast into his open mouth as nearly to drown him. His only chance of effecting a smash was by a series of jumps, followed by quick dives. Once before, although he had not confessed it to Rainbow, Old Trout had saved his life by resorting to this expedient. It takes the strain off the line and returns it so quickly that even the finest gut is apt to sunder.

Meanwhile, the man was slowly approaching, winding up as he came. Old Trout, boring in the depths, could hear the click of the check reel with increasing distinctness. Looking up, he saw that the cast was almost vertical above his head, which meant that the moment to make the attempt was at hand. The tension was appalling, for ever since the fight began his adversary had given him the butt unremittingly. Aware of his own weight and power, Old Trout was amazed that any tackle could stand the strain.

"Now's my time," he thought, and jumped.

It was no ordinary jump, but an aerial rush three feet out of the water, with a twist at its apex and a cutting lash of the tail designed to break the cast. But his adversary was no ordinary angler, and at the first hint of what was happening he dropped the point of the rod flush with the surface.

Once and once more Old Trout flung himself into the air, but after each attempt he found himself with diminishing strength and with less line to play with.

"It looks to me," said Rainbow mournfully, "as if my unhappy host will lose this battle and finish up in that glass case to which he was referring a few minutes ago." And greatly affected, he burrowed his nose in the mud and wondered, in the event of this dismal prophecy coming true, whether he would be able to take possession of the pool without molestation.

In consequence of these reflections he failed to witness the last phase of the battle when, as will sometimes happen with big fish, all the fight went out of Old Trout, and rolling wearily over and over, he abandoned himself to the clinging embraces of the net. He never saw the big man proudly carry Old Trout back into the hayfield, where, before proceeding to remove the fly, he sat down beside a shallow dike and lit a cigarette and smiled largely. Then, with an affectionate and professional touch, he picked up Old Trout by the back of the neck, his forefinger and thumb sunk firmly in the gills.

"You're a fine fellar," he said, extracting the fly; "a good sportsman and a funny fish. You fooled me properly for three days, but I think you'll own I outwitted you in the end."

Rummaging in his creel for a small rod of hard wood that he carried for the purpose of administering the quietus, he became aware of something that arrested the action. Leaning forward, he stared with open eyes at a tiny W perforated in the upper part of Old Trout's tail.

"Shades of the war! Dulverton!" he exclaimed. Then with a sudden warmth: "Old chap, old chap, is it really you? This is red-letter stuff. If you're not too far gone to take another lease of life, have it with me."

And with the tenderness of a woman, he slipped Old Trout into the dike and in a tremble of excitement hurried off to the auberge where the fishermen lodged, to tell a tale no one even pretended to believe.

For the best part of an hour Old Trout lay in the shallow waters of the dike before slowly cruising back to his own place beneath the overhanging bank. The alarming experience through which he had passed had made him a shade forgetful, and he was not prepared for the sight of Young Rainbow rising steadily at the hatch of fly.

"Pardon me, but a little more to your right," he said, with heavy courtesy.

"Diving otters!" cried Young Rainbow, leaping a foot clear of the water. "You, sir! You!"

"And why not?" Old Trout replied. "Your memory must be short if you have already forgotten that this is my place."

"Yes, but—" Rainbow began and stopped.

"You are referring to that little circus of a few minutes ago," said Old Trout. "It is possible you failed to appreciate the significance of the affair? I knew at once it was my dear officer when he dropped the artificial dun behind the natural May fly. In the circumstances I could hardly do less than accept his invitation. Nothing is more delightful than a reunion of comrades of the war." He paused and added: "We had a charming talk, he and I, and I do not know which of us was the more affected. It is a tragedy that such friendship and such intellect as we share cannot exist in common element."

And so great was his emotion that Old Trout dived and buried his head in the weeds. Whereby Rainbow did uncommonly well during the midday hatch.

A Wedding Gift

JOHN TAINTOR FOOTE

George Baldwin Potter is a purist. That is to say, he either takes trout on a dry fly or he does not take them at all. He belongs to a number of fishing clubs, any member of which might acquire his neighbor's wife, beat his children, or poison a dog and still cast a fly, in all serenity, upon club waters; but should he impale on a hook a lowly though succulent worm and immerse the creature in those same waters it would be better that he send in his resignation at once, sooner than face the shaken committee that would presently wait upon him.

George had become fixed in my mind as a bachelor. This, or course, was a mistake. I am continually forgetting that purists rush into marriage when approaching or having just passed the age of forty. The psychology of this is clear.

For twenty years, let us say, a purist's life is completely filled by his efforts to convert all reasonable men to his own particular method of taking trout. He thinks, for example, that a man should not concern himself with more than a dozen types of standard flies. The manner of presenting them is the main consideration. Take any one of these flies, then, and place, by means of an eight-foot rod, a light, tapered line, and a mist-colored leader of reasonable length, on fast water—if you want trout. Of course, if you want to listen to the birds and look at the scenery, fish the pools with a long line and an eight-foot leader. Why, it stands to reason that—

The years go by as he explains these vital facts patiently, again and again, to Smith and Brown and Jones. One wet, cold spring, after fighting a muddy stream all day, he re-explains for the better part of an evening and takes himself, somewhat wearily upstairs. The damp and chill of the room at whatever club he may be fishing is positively tomblike. He can hear the rain drumming on the roof and swishing against the windows. The water will be higher than ever tomorrow, he reflects, as he puts out the lights and slides between the icy sheets. Steeped to the soul in cheerless dark, he recalls numbly that when he first met Smith and Brown and Jones they were fishing the pools with a long line. That was, let's see—fifteen—eighteen—twenty years ago. Then he must be forty. It isn't possible! Yes, it is a fact that Smith and Brown and Jones are still fishing the pools with a long line.

In the first faint light of dawn he falls into an uneasy, muttering slumber. The dark hours between have been devoted to intense thought and a variety of wiggles which have not succeeded in keeping the bedclothes against his shoulder blades.

Some time within the next six months you will remember that you have forgotten to send him a wedding present.

George, therefore, having arrived at his fortieth birthday, announced his engagement shortly thereafter. Quite by chance I ran across his bride-to-be and himself a few days before the ceremony, and joined them at lunch. She was a blonde in the early twenties, with wide blue eyes and a typical rose-and-white complexion. A rushing, almost breathless account of herself, which she began the moment we were seated, was curious, I thought. It was as though she feared an interruption at any moment. I learned that she was an only child, born and reared in Greater New York; that her family had recently moved to New Rochell; that she had been shopping madly for the past two weeks; that she was nearly dead, but that she had some adorable things.

At this point George informed me that they would spend their honeymoon at a certain fishing club in Maine. He then proceeded to describe the streams and lakes in that section at some length-during the rest of the luncheon, as a matter of fact. His fiancée, who had fallen into a wordless abstraction, only broke her silence with a vague murmur as we parted.

Owing to this meeting I did not forget to send a wedding present. I determined that my choice should please both George and his wife through the happy years to come.

If I had had George to consider, I could have settled the business in two minutes at a sporting-goods store. Barred from these for obvious reasons, I spent a long day in a thoroughly exhausting search. Late in the afternoon I decided to abandon my hopeless task. I had made a tremendous effort and failed. I would simply buy a silver doodad and let it go at that.

As I staggered into a store with the above purpose in view, I passed a show case devoted to fine china, and halted as my eyes fell on a row of fish plates backed by artfully rumpled blue velvet. The plates proved to be hand painted. On each plate was one of the different varieties of trout, curving up through green depths to an artificial fly just dropping on the surface of the water.

In an automatic fashion I indicated the plates to a clerk, paid for them, gave him my card and the address, and fled from the store. Some time during the next twenty-four hours it came to me that George Potter was not among my nearest and dearest. Yet the unbelievable sum I had left with that clerk in exchange for those fish plates could be justified in no other way.

I thought this fact accounted for the sort of frenzy with which George flung himself upon me when next we met, some two months later. I had been weekending in the country and encountered him in the Grand Central Station as I emerged from the lower level. For a long moment he wrung my hand in silence, gazing almost feverishly into my face. At last he spoke:

"Have you got an hour to spare?"

It occurred to me that it would take George an hour at least to describe his amazed delight at the splendor of my gift. The clock above Information showed that it was 12:45. I therefore suggested that we lunch together.

He, too, glanced at the clock, verified its correctness by his watch, and seized me by the arm.

"All right," he agreed, and was urging me toward the well-filled and somewhat noisy station café before I grasped his intention and tried to suggest that we go elsewhere. His hand only tightened on my arm.

"It's all right," he said; "good food, quick service—you'll like it."

He all but dragged me into the café and steered me to a table in the corner. I lifted my voice above an earnest clatter of gastronomical utensils and made a last effort.

"The Biltmore's just across the street."

George pressed me into my chair, shoved a menu card at me and addressed the waiter.

"Take his order." Here he jerked out his watch and consulted it again. "We have forty-eight minutes. Service for one. I shan't be eating anything; or, no—bring me some coffee—large cup—black."

Having ordered mechanically, I frankly stared at George. He was dressed, I now observed, with unusual care. He wore a rather dashing gray suit. His tie, which was an exquisite shade of gray-blue, was embellished by a handsome pearl. The handkerchief, appearing above his breast pocket, was of the same delicate gray-blue shade as the tie. His face had been recently and closely shaven, also powdered; but above that smooth whiteness of jowl was a pair of curiously glittering eyes and a damp, beaded brow. This he now mopped with his napkin.

"Good God," said I, "what is it, George?"

His reply was to extract a letter from his inside coat pocket and pass it across the table, his haunted eyes on mine. I took in its few lines at a glance:

"Father has persuaded me to listen to what you call your explanation. I arrive Grand Central 2:45, daylight saving, Monday." Isabelle.

Poor old George, I thought; some bachelor indiscretion; and now, with his honeymoon scarcely over, blackmail, a lawsuit, heaven only knows what.

"Who," I asked, returning the letter, "is Isabelle?"

To my distress, George again resorted to his napkin. Then, "My wife," he said.

"Your wife!"

George nodded.

"Been living wither people for the last month. Wish he'd bring that coffee. You don't happen to have a flask with you?"

"Yes, I have a flask." George brightened. "But it's empty. Do you want to tell me about your trouble? Is that why you brought me here?"

"Well, yes," George admitted. "But the point is—will you stand by me? That's the main thing. She gets in"—here he consulted his watch—"in forty-five minutes, if the train's on time." A sudden panic seemed to seize him. His hand shot across the table and grasped my wrist. "You've got to stand by me, old man—act as if you knew nothing. Say you ran into me here and stayed to meet her. I'll tell you what—say I didn't' seem to want you to stay. Kid me about wanting her all to myself, or something like that. Get the point? It'll give me a chance to sort of—well, you understand."

"I see what you mean, of course," I admitted. "Here's your coffee. Suppose you have some and then tell me what this is all about—if you care to, that is."

"No sugar, no cream," said George to the waiter; "just pour it. Don't stand there waving it about—pour it, pour it!" He attempted to swallow a mouthful of steaming coffee, gurgled frightfully and grabbed his water glass. "Great jumping Jehoshaphat!" he gasped, when he could speak, and glared at the waiter, who promptly moved out into the sea of diners and disappeared among a dozen of his kind.

"Steady, George," I advised as I transferred a small lump of ice from my glass to his coffee cup.

George watched the ice dissolve, murmured "Idiot" several times, and presently swallowed the contents of the cup in two gulps.

"I had told her," he said suddenly, "exactly where we were going. She mentioned Narragansett several times—I'll admit that. Imagine—Narragansett! Of course I bought her fishing things myself. I didn't buy knickers or woolens or flannel shirts—naturally. You don't go around buying a girl breeches and underwear before you're married. It wouldn't be—well, it isn't done, that's all. I got her the sweetest three-ounce rod you ever held in your hand. I'll bet I could put out sixty feet of line with it against the wind. I got her a pair of English waders that didn't weigh a pound. They cost me forty-five dollars. The rest of the outfit was just as good. Why, her fly box was a Truxton. I could have bought an American imitation for eight dollars. I know a lot of men who'll buy leaders for themselves at two dollars apiece and let their wives fish with any kind of tackle. I'll give you my word I'd have used anything I got for her myself. I sent it all out to be packed with her things. I wanted her to feel that it was her own—not mine. I know a lot of men who give their wives a high-class rod or an imported reel and then fish with it themselves. What time is it?"

"Clock right up there," I said. But George consulted his watch and used his napkin distressingly again.

"Where was I?"

"You were telling me why you sent her fishing things out to her."

"Oh, yes! That's all of that. I simply wanted to show you that from the first I did all any man could do. Ever been in the Cuddiwink district?"

I said that I had not.

"You go in from Buck's Landing. A lumber tug takes you up to the head of Lake Owonga. Club guides meet you there and put you through in one day—twenty miles by canoe and portage up the west branch of the Penobscot; then nine miles by trail to Lost Pond. The club's on Lost Pond. Separate cabins, with a main dining and loafing camp, and the best squaretail fishing on earth—both lake and stream. Of course, I don't fish the lakes. A dry fly belongs on a stream and nowhere else. Let me make it perfectly clear."

George's manner suddenly changed. He hunched himself closer to the table, dropped an elbow upon it and lifted an expository finger.

"The dry fly," he stated, with a new almost combative ring in his voice, "is designed primarily to simulate not only the appearance of the natural insect but its action as well. This action is arrived at through the flow of the current. The moment you move a fly by means of leader you destroy the—

I saw that an interruption was imperative.

"Yes, of course," I said; "but your wife will be here in—"

It was pitiful to observe George. His new-found assurance did not flee—flee suggests a withdrawal, however swift—it was immediately and totally annihilated. He attempted to pour himself some coffee, take out his watch, look at the clock, and mop his brow with his napkin at one and the same instant.

"You were telling me how to get to Lost Pond," I suggested.

"Yes, to be sure," said George. "Naturally you go in light. The things you absolutely have to have—rods, tackle, waders, wading shoes, and so forth, are about all a guide can manage at the portages in addition to the canoe. You pack in extras yourself—change of underclothes, a couple of pairs of socks, and a few toilet articles. You leave a bag or trunk at Buck's Landing. I explained this to her. I explained it carefully. I told her either a week-end bag or one small trunk. Herb Trescott was my best man. I left everything to him. He saw us on the train and handed me tickets and reservations just before we pulled out. I didn't notice in the excitement of getting away that he'd given me three trunk checks all stamped 'Excess.' I didn't notice it till the conductor showed up, as a matter of fact. Then I said, 'Darling, what in heaven's name have you brought three trunks for?' She said—I can remember her exact words—'Then you're not going to Narragansett?'

"I simply looked at her. I was too dumbfounded to speak. At last I pulled myself together and told her in three days we'd be whipping the best squaretail water in the world. I took her hand, I remember, and said, 'You and I together, sweetheart,' or something like that."

George sighed and lapsed into a silence which remained unbroken until his eye happened to encounter the face of the clock. He started and went on:

"We got to Buck's Landing, but way of Bangor, at six in the evening of the following day. Buck's Landing is a railroad station with grass growing between the ties, a general store and hotel combined, and a lumber wharf. The store keeps canned peas, pink-and-white candy, and felt boots. The hotel part is—well, it doesn't matter except that I don't think I ever saw so many deer heads; a few stuffed trout but mostly deer heads. After supper the proprietor and I got the three trunks up to the largest room: We just go them in and that was all. The tug left for the head of the lake at seven next morning. I explained this to Isabelle. I said we'd leave the trunks there until we came out, and offered to help her unpack the one her fishing things were in. She said, 'Please go away!' So I went away. I got out a rod and went down to the wharf. No trout there, I knew; but I thought I'd limber up my wrist. I put on a Cahill Number Fourteen—or was it Sixteen—"

George knitted his brows and stared intently but unseeingly at me for some little time.

"Call it a Sixteen," I suggested.

George shook his head impatiently and remained concentrated in thought.

"I'm inclined to think it was a Fourteen," he said at last. "But let it go; it'll come to me later. At any rate, the place was alive with big chub—a foot long, some of 'em. I'll bet I took fifty—threw 'em back, of course. They kept on rising after it got dark. I'd tell myself I'd go after one more cast. Each time I'd hook a big chub, and—well, you know how the time slips away.

"When I got back to the hotel all the lights were out. I lit matches until I got upstairs and found the door to the room. I'll never forget what I saw when I opened that door—never! Do you happen to know how many of the kind of things they wear a woman can get into one trunk? Well, she had three and she'd unpacked them all. She had used the bed for the gowns alone. It was piled with them—literally piled; but that wasn't a starter. Everywhere you looked was a stack of things with ribbons in 'em. There were enough shoes and stockings for a girl's school; silk stockings, mind you, and high-heeled shoes and slippers." Here George consulted clock and watch. "I wonder if that train's on time," he wanted to know.

"You have thirty-five minutes, even if it is," I told him; "go right ahead."

"Well, I could see something was wrong from her face. I didn't know what, but I started right in to cheer her up. I told her all about the chub fishing I'd been having. At last she burst into tears. I won't go into the scene that followed. I'd ask her what was the matter and she'd say, 'Nothing,' and cry frightfully. I know a lot of men who would have lost their tempers under the circumstances, but I didn't; I give you my word. I simply said, 'There, there,' until she quieted down. And that isn't all. After a while she began to show me her gowns. Imagine—at eleven o'clock at night, at Buck's Landing! She'd hold up a dress and look over the top of it at me and ask me how I liked it, and I'd say it was all right. I know a lot of men who wouldn't have sat there two minutes.

"At last I said, 'They're all all right, darling,' and yawned. She was holding up a pink dress covered with shiny dingle-dangles, and she threw the dress on the bed and all but had hysterics. It was terrible. In trying to think of some way to quiet her it occurred to me that I'd put her rod together and let her feel the balance of it with the feel I'd bought her—a genuine Fleetwood, mind you—attached. I looked around for her fishing things and couldn't find them. I'll tell you why I couldn't find them." George paused for an impressive instant to give his next words the full significance due them. "They weren't there!"

"No?" I murmured weakly.

"No," said George. "And what do you suppose she said when I questioned her? I can give you her exact words—I'll never forget them. She said, 'There wasn't any room for them.'" Again George paused. "I ask you," he inquired at last, "I ask you as man to man; what do you think of that?"

I found no adequate reply to this question and George, now thoroughly warmed up, rushed on.

"You'd swear I lost my temper then, wouldn't you? Will, I didn't. I did say something to her later, but I'll let you be the judge when we come to that. I'll ask you to consider the circumstances. I'll ask you to get Old Faithful in your mind's eye."

"Old Faithful?" I repeated. "Then you went to the Yellowstone later?"

"Yellowstone! Of course not! Haven't I told you we were already at the best trout water in America? Old Faithful was a squaretail. He'd been in the pool below Horseshoe Falls for twenty years, as a matter of record. We'll come to that presently. How are we off for time?"

"Thirty-one minutes," I told him. "I'm the watching the clock—go ahead."

"Well, there she was, on a fishing trip with nothing to fish with. There was only one answer to that—she couldn't fish. But I went over everything she'd brought in three trunks and I'll give you my word she didn't have a garment of any sort you couldn't see through.

"Something had to be done and done quick, that was for sure. I fitted her out from my own things with a sweater, a flannel shirt, and a pair of knickerbockers. Then I got the proprietor up and explained the situation. He got me some heavy underwear and two pairs of woolen stockings that belonged to his wife. When it came to shoes it looked hopeless, but the proprietor's wife, who had got up, too, by this time, thought of a pair of boy's moccasin's that were in the store and they turned out to be about the right size. I made arrangements to rent the room we had until we came out again to keep her stuff in, and took another room for the night—what was left of it after she'd repacked what could stay in the trunks and arranged what couldn't so it wouldn't be wrinkled.

"I got up early, dressed, and took my duffle down to the landing. I wakened her when I left the room. When breakfast was ready I went to see why she hadn't come down. She was all dressed, sitting on the edge of the bed. I said, 'Breakfast is ready, darling,' but I saw by her face that something was wrong again. It turned out to be my knickers. They fitted her perfectly—a little tight in spots—except in the waist. They would simply have fallen off if she hadn't held them up.

"Well, I was going in so light that I only had one belt. The proprietor didn't have any—he used suspenders. Neither did his wife—she used—well, whatever they use. He got me a piece of clothesline and I knotted it at each and ran it through the what-you-may-call-'ems of the knickers and tied it in front. The knickers sort of puckered all the way around, but they couldn't come down—that was the main thing. I said, 'There you are, darling.' She walked over and tilted the mirror of the bureau so that she could see herself from head to foot. She said, 'Who are going to be at this place where we are going?' I said, 'Some of the very best dry-fly men in the country.' She said, 'I don't mean them; I mean the women. Will there be any women there?'

"I told her, certainly there would be women. I asked her if she thought I would take her into a camp with nothing but men. I named some of the women: Mrs. Fred Beal and Mrs. Brooks Carter and Talcott Ranning's sister and several more.

"She turned around slowly in front of the mirror, staring into it for a minute. Then she said, 'Please go out and close the door.' I said, 'All right, darling; but come right down. The tug will be here in fifteen minutes.'

"I went downstairs and waited for ten minutes, then I heard the tug whistle for the landing and ran upstairs again. I knocked at the door. When she didn't answer I went in. Where do you suppose she was?"

I gave it up.

"In bed!" said George in an awe-struck voice. "In bed with her face turned to the wall; and listen, I didn't lose my temper as God is my judge. I rushed down to the wharf and told the tug captain I'd give him twenty-five dollars extra if he'd hold the boat till we came. He said all right and I went back to the room.

"The breeches had done it. She simply wouldn't wear them. I told her that at a fishing camp in Maine clothes were never thought of. I said, 'No one thinks of anything but trout, darling.' She said, 'I wouldn't let a fish see me looking like that.'" George's brow beaded suddenly. His hands dived searchingly into various pockets. "Got a cigarette? I left my case in my other suit."

He took a cigarette from me, lighted it with shaking fingers and inhaled deeply.

"It went on like that for thirty minutes. She was crying all the time, of course. I had started down to tell the tug captain it was all off, and I saw a woman's raincoat hanging in the hall. It belonged to someone up in one of the camps, the proprietor told me. I gave him seventy-five dollars to give to whoever owned it when he came out, and took it upstairs. In about ten minutes I persuaded her to wear it over the rest of her outfit until we got to camp. I told her one of the women would be able to fix her up all right when we got there. I didn't believe it, of course. The women at camp were all old-timers; they'd gone in as light as the men, but I had to say something.

"We had quite a trip going in. The guides were at the head of the lake all right—Indian Joe and new a man I'd never seen, called Charlie. I told Joe to take Isabelle—he's one of the best canoemen I ever saw. I was going to paddle bow for my man, but I'd have to bet a cookie Indian Joe could stay with us on any kind of water. We had to beat it right through to make camp by night. It's a good stiff trip, but it can be done. I looked back at the other canoe now and then we struck about a mile of white water that took all I had. When we were through the other canoe wasn't in sight. The river made a bend there, and I thought it was just behind and would show up any minute.

"Well, it didn't show up and I began to wonder. We hit our first portage about ten o'clock and landed. I watched downstream for twenty minutes, expecting to sight the other canoe every instant. Then Charlie, who hadn't opened his head, said, 'Better go back,' and put the canoe in again. We paddled downstream for all that was in it. I was stiff with fright. We saw 'em coming about three miles lower down and back-paddled till they came up. Isabelle was more cheerful-looking than she'd been since we left New York, but Joe had that stony face an Indian gets when he's sore.

"I said, 'Anything wrong?' Joe just grunted and drove the canoe past us. Then I saw it was filled with wild flowers. Isabelle said she'd been picking them right off the banks all the way long. She said she'd only had to get out of the boat once, for the blue ones. Now, you can't beat that—not in a thousand years. I leave it to you if you can. Twenty miles of stiff current, with five portages ahead of us and a nine-mile hike at the end of that. I gave that Indian the devil for letting her do such a thing, and tipped the flowers into the Penobscot when we unloaded for the first portage. She didn't speak to me on the portage, and she got into her canoe without a word.

"Nothing more happened going in, except this flower business had lost us two hours, and it was so dark when we struck the swamp at Loon Lake that we couldn't follow the trail well and kept stumbling over down timber and stepping into bog holes. She was about fagged out by then, and the mosquitoes were pretty thick through there. Without any warning she sat down in the trail. She did it so suddenly I nearly fell over her. I asked her what was the matter and she said, 'This is the end'—just like that—'this is the end!' I said, 'The end of what, darling?' She said, 'Of everything!' I told her if she sat there all wet and muddy she'd catch her death. She said she hoped so. I said, 'It's only two miles more, darling. Just think, tomorrow we'll be on the best trout water in the world!' With that she said, 'I want my mother, my darling mother,' and bowed her head in her hands. Think if over, please; and remember, I didn't lose my temper. You're sure there's nothing left in your flask?"

"Not a drop more, George," I assured him. "Go ahead; we've only twenty-five minutes."

George looked wildly at the clock, then at his watch.

"A man never has it when he wants it most. Have you noticed that? Where was I?"

"You were in the swamp."

"Oh, yes! Well, she didn't speak after that, and nothing I could say would budge her. The mosquitoes had got wind of us when we stopped and were coming in swarms. We'd be eaten alive in another ten minutes. So I told Joe to give his pack to Charlie and help me pick her up and carry her. Joe said, 'No, by damn!' and folded his arms. When an Indian gets sore he stays sore, and when he's sore he's stubborn. The mosquitoes were working on him good and plenty, though, and at last he said, 'Me carry packs. Charlie help carry—that.' He flipped his hand over in the direction of Isabelle and took the pack from Charlie.

"It was black as your hat by now, and the trail through there was only about a foot wide with swamp on each side. It was going to be some job getting her out of there. I thought Charlie and I would make a chair of our arms and stumble along with her some way; but when I started to lift her up she said, 'Don't touch me!' and got up and went on. A blessing if there ever was one. We got to camp at ten that night.

"She was stiff and sore the next morning—you expect it after a trip like that—besides, she'd caught a little cold. I asked her how she felt, and she said she was going to die and asked me to send for a doctor and her mother. The nearest doctor was at Bangor and her mother was in New Rochelle. I carried her breakfast over from the dining camp to our cabin. She said she couldn't eat any breakfast, but she did drink a cup of coffee, telling me between sips how awful it was to die alone in a place like that.

"After she'd had the coffee she seemed to feel better. I went to the camp library and got The Dry Fly on American Waters, by Charles Darty. I considered him the soundest man in the country. He's better than Pell or Fawcett. My chief criticism of him is that in his chapter on Streams East of the Alleghenies—east of the Alleghenies, mind you—he recommends the Royal Coachman. I consider the Lead-Wing Coachman a serviceable fly on clear, hard-fished water; but the Royal—never! I wouldn't give it a shade over the Professor or the Montreal. Just consider the body alone of the Royal Coachman—never mind the wings and hackle—the body of the Royal is—"

"Yes, I know, George," I said; "but—"

I glanced significantly at the clock. George started, sighed, and resumed his narrative.

"I went back to the cabin and said, 'Darling, here is one of the most intensely interesting books ever written. I'm going to read it aloud to you. I think I can finish it to-day. Would you like to sit up in bed while I read?' She said she hadn't strength enough to sit up in bed, so I sat down beside her and started reading. I had read about an hour, I suppose, when she did sit up in bed quite suddenly. I saw she was staring at me in a queer, wild way that was really startling. I said, 'What is it, darling?' She said, 'I'm going to get up. I'm going to get up this instant.'

"Well, I was delighted, naturally. I thought the book would get her by the time I'd read it through. But there she was, as keen as mustard before I'd got well into it. I'll tell you what I made up my mind to do, right there. I made up my mind to let her use my rod that day. Yes, sir—my three-ounce Spinoza, and what's more, I did it."

George looked at me triumphantly, then lapsed into reflection for a moment.

"If ever a man did everything possible to—well, let it go. The main thing is, I have nothing to reproach myself with—nothing. Except—but we'll come to that presently. Of course, she wasn't ready for dry flies yet. I borrowed some wet flies from the club steward, got some cushions for the canoe and put my rod together. She had no waders, so a stream was out of the question. The lake was better, anyway, that first day; she'd have all the room she wanted for her back cast.

"I stood there on the landing with her before we got into the canoe and showed her just how to put out a fly and recover it. Then she tried it." A sort of horror came into George's face. "You wouldn't believe any one could handle a rod like that," he said huskily. "You couldn't believe it unless you'd seen it. Gimme a cigarette.

"I worked with her a half hour or so and saw no improvement—none whatever. At last she said, 'The string is too long. I can't do anything with such a long string on a pole.' I told her gently—gently, mind you—that the string was an eighteen-dollar double-tapered Hurdman line, attached to a Gebhardt reel on a three-ounce Spinoza rod. I said, 'We'll go out on the lake now. If you can manage to get a rise, perhaps it will come to you instinctively.'

"I paddled her out on the lake and she went at it. She'd spat the flies down and yank them up and spat them down again. She hooked me several times with her back cast and got tangled up in the line herself again and again. All this time I was speaking quietly to her, telling her what to do. I give you my word I never raised my voice—not once—and I thought she'd break the tip every moment.

"Finally she said her arm was tired and lowered the rod. She'd got everything messed up with her last cast and the flies were trailing just over the side of the canoe. I said, 'Recover your cast and reel in, darling.' Instead of using her rod, she took hold of the leader close to the flies and started to pull them into the canoe. At that instant a little trout—couldn't have been over six inches—took the tail fly. I don't know exactly what happened, it was all over so quickly. I think she just screamed and let go of everything. At any rate, I saw my Spinoza bounce off the gunwale of the canoe and disappear. There was fifty feet of water just there. And now listen carefully: not one word did I utter—not one. I simply turned the canoe and paddled to the landing in absolute silence. No reproaches of any sort. Think that over!"

I did. My thoughts left me speechless. George proceeded:

"I took out a guide and tried dragging for the rod with a gang hook and heavy sinker all the rest of the day. But the gangs would only foul on the bottom. I gave up at dusk and paddled in. I said to the guide—it was Charlie—I said, 'Well, it's all over, Charlie.' Charlie said, 'I brought Mr. Carter in and he had an extra rod. Maybe you could borrow it. It's a four-ounce Meecham.' I smiled. I actually smiled. I turned and looked at the lake. 'Charlie,' I said, 'somewhere out there in that dark water, where the eye of man will never behold it again, is a three-ounce Spinoza—and you speak of a Meecham.' Charlie said, 'Well, I just thought I'd tell you.' I said, 'That's all right, Charlie. That's all right.' I went to the main camp, saw Jean, the head guide and made arrangements to leave the next day. Then I went to our cabin and sat down before the fire. I heard Isabelle say something about being sorry. I said, 'I'd rather not talk about it, darling. If you don't mind, we'll never mention it again.' We sat there in silence, then, until dinner.

"As we got up from dinner, Nate Griswold and his wife asked us to play bridge with them that evening. I'd told no one what had happened, and Nate didn't know, of course. I simply thanked him and said we were tired, and we went back to our cabin. I sat down before the fire again. Isabelle seemed restless. At least she said,

'George.' I said, 'What is it, darling?' She said, 'Would you like to read to me from that book?' I said, 'I'm sorry, darling; if you don't mind I'll just sit here quietly by the fire.'

"Somebody knocked at the door after a while. I said, 'Come in.' It was Charlie. I said, 'What is it, Charlie?' Then he told me that Bob Frazer had been called back to New York and was going out the next morning. I said, 'Well, what of it?' Charlie said, 'I just thought you could maybe borrow his rod.' I said, 'I thought you understood about that, Charlie.' Charlie said, 'Well, that's it. Mr. Frazer's rod is a three-ounce Spinoza.'

"I got up and shook hands with Charlie and gave him five dollars. But when he'd gone I began to realize what was before me. I'd brought in a pint flask of prewar Scotch. Prewar—get that! I put this in my pocket and went over to Bob's cabin. Just as I was going to knock I lost my nerve. I sneaked away from the door and went down to the lake and sat on the steps of the canoe landing. I sat there for quite a while and took several nips. At last I thought I'd jut go and tell Bob of my loss and see what he said. I went back to his cabin and this time I knocked. Bob was putting a few odds and ends in a shoulder pack. His rod was in its case, standing against the wall.

"I said, 'I hear you're going out in the morning.' He said, 'Yes, curse it, my wife's mother has to have some sort of damned operation or other.' I said, 'How would a little drink strike you, Bob?' He said, 'Strike me! Wait a minute! What kind of drink?' I took out the flask and handed it to him. He unscrewed the cap and held the flask to his nose. He said, 'Great heavens above, it smells like—' I said, 'It is.' He said, 'It can't be!' I said, 'Yes, it is.' He said, 'There's a trick in it somewhere.' I said, 'No, there isn't—I give you my word.' He tasted what was in the flask carefully. Then he said, 'I call this white of you, George,' and took a good stiff snort. When he was handing back the flask he said, 'I'll do as much for you some day, if I ever get the chance.' I took a snifter myself.

"Then I said, 'Bob, something awful has happened to me. I came here to tell you about it.' He said, 'Is that so? Sit down.' I sat down and told him. He said, 'What kind of rod was it?' I said, 'A three-ounce Spinoza.' He came over and gripped my hand without a word. I said, 'Of course, I can't use anything else.' He nodded, and I saw his eyes flicker toward the corner of the room where his own rod was standing. I said, 'Have another drink, Bob.' But he just sat down and stared at me. I took a good stiff drink myself. Then I said, 'Under ordinary circumstances, nothing on earth could hire me to ask a man to—' I stopped right there.

"Bob got up suddenly and began to walk up and down the room. I said, 'Bob, I'm not considering myself—not for a minute. If it was last season, I'd simply have gone back to-morrow without a word. But I'm not alone any more. I've got the little girl to consider. She's never seen a trout taken in her life—think of it, Bob! And here she is, on her honeymoon, at the best water I know of. On her honeymoon, Bob!' I waited for him to say something, but he went to the window and stared out, with his back to me. I got up and said good-night and started for the door. Just as I reached it he turned from the window and rushed over and picked up his rod. He said, 'Here, take it,' and put the rod case in my hands. I started to try to thank him, but he said, 'Just go ahead with it,' and pushed me out the door."

The waiter was suddenly hovering above us with his eyes on the dishes.

"Now what do you want?" said George.

"Never mind clearing here," I said. "Just bring me the check. Go ahead, George."

"Well, of course, I can't any more than skim what happened finally, but you'll understand. It turned out that Ernie Payton's wife had an extra pair of knickers and she loaned them to Isabelle. I was waiting outside the cabin while she dressed next morning, and she called out to me, 'Oh, George, they fit!' Then I heard her begin to sing. She was a different girl when she came out to go to breakfast. She was almost smiling. She'd done nothing but slink about the day before. Isn't it extraordinary what will seem important to a woman? Gimme a cigarette."

"Fifteen minutes, George," I said as I supplied him.

"Yes, yes, I know. I fished the Cuddiwink that day. Grand stream, grand. I used a Pink Lady—first day on a stream with Isabelle—little touch of sentiment—and it's a darn good fly. I fished it steadily all day. Or did I try a Seth Green about noon? It seems to me I did, now that I recall it. It seems to me that where the Katahdin brook comes in I—"

"It doesn't really matter, does it, George?" I ventured.

"Of course, it matters!" said George decisively. "A man wants to be exact about such things. The precise details of what happens in a day's work on a stream are of real value to yourself and others. Except in the case of a record fish, it isn't important that you took a trout; it's exactly how you took him that's important."

"But the time, George," I protested.

He glanced at the clock, swore softly, mopped his brow—this time with the blue-gray handkerchief—and proceeded.

"Isabelle couldn't get into the stream without waders, so I told her to work along the bank a little behind me. It was pretty thick along there, second growth and vines mostly; but I was putting that Pink Lady on every foot of good water and she kept up with me easily enough. She didn't see me take many trout, though. I'd look for her, after landing one, to see what she thought of the way I'd handled the fish, and almost invariably she was picking the ferns or blueberries, or getting herself untangled from something. Curious things, women. Like children, when you stop to think of it."

George stared at me unseeingly for a moment.

"And you never heard of Old Faithful?" he asked suddenly. "Evidently not, from what you said a while ago. Well, a lot of people have, believe me. Men have gone to Cuddiwink district just to see him. As I've already told you, he lay beside a ledge in the pool below Horseshoe Falls. Almost nothing else in the pool. He kept it cleaned out. Worst sort of cannibal, of course—all big trout are. That was the trouble—he wanted something that would stick to his ribs. No flies for him. Did his feeding at night.

"You could see him dimly if you crawled out on a rock that jutted above the pool and looked over. Hey lay in about ten feet of water, right by his ledge. If he saw you he'd back under the ledge, slowly, like a submarine going into dock. Think of the biggest thing you've ever seen, and that's the way Old Faithful looked, just laying there as still as the ledge. He never seemed to move anything, not even his gills. When he backed in out of sight he seemed to be drawn under the ledge by some invisible force.

"Ridgway—R. Campbell Ridgway—you may have read his stuff. Brethren of the Wild, that sort of thing—claimed to have seen him move. He told me about it one night. He said he was lying with just his eyes over the edge of the rock, watching the trout. Said he'd been there an hour, when down over the falls came a young red squirrel. I had fallen in above and been carried over. The squirrel was half drowned, but struck out feebly for shore. Well, so Ridgway said—Old Faithful came up and took Mister Squirrel into camp. No hurry; just came drifting up, sort of inhaled the squirrel and sank down to the ledge again. Never made a ripple, Ridgway said; just business.

"I'm telling you all this because it's necessary that you get an idea of that trout in your mind. You'll see why in a minute. No one ever had hold of him. But it was customary, if you fished the Cuddiwink, to make a few casts over him before you left the stream. Not that you ever expected him to rise. It was just a sort of gesture. Everybody did it.

"Knowing that Isabelle had never seen trout taken before, I made a day of it—naturally. The trail to camp leaves the stream just at the falls. It was pretty late when we got to it. Isabelle had her arms full of—heaven knows what—flowers and grass and ferns and fir branches and colored leaves. She'd lugged the stuff for hours. I remember once that day I was fighting a fourteen-inch blackberry—I think it was—she'd found. How does that strike you? And listen! I said, 'It's a beauty, darling.' That's what I said—or something like that . . . Here, don't you pay that check! Bring it here, waiter!"

"Go on, George!" I said. "We haven't time to argue about the check. You'd come to the trail for camp at the falls."

"I told Isabelle to wait at the trail for a few minutes, while I went below the falls and did the customary thing for the edification of Old Faithful. I only intended to make three or four casts with the Number Twelve Fly and the hair-fine leader I had on, but in getting down to the pool I hooked the fly in a bush. In trying to loosen it I stumbled over something and fell. I snapped the leader like a thread, and since I had to put on another, I tied on a fairly heavy one as a matter of form.

"I had reached for my box for a regulation fly of some sort when I remembered a fool thing that Billy Roach had given me up on the Beaverkill the season before. It was fully two inches long; I forget what he called it. He said you fished it dry for bass or large trout. He said you worked the tip of your rod and made it wiggle like a dying minnow. I didn't want the contraption, but he'd borrowed some fly oil from me and insisted on my taking it. I'd stuck it in the breast pocket of my fishing jacket and forgotten it until then.

"Well, I felt in the pocket and there it was. I tried it on and went down to the pool. Now let me show you the exact situation." George seized a fork. "This is the pool." The fork traced an oblong figure on the tablecloth. "Here is Old Faithful's ledge." The fork deeply marked this impressive spot. "Here are the falls, with white water running to here. You can only wade to this point here, and then you have an abrupt six-foot depth. 'But you can put a fly from here to here with a long line,' you say. No, you can't. You've forgotten to allow for your back cast. Notice this bend here? That tells the story. You're not more than twenty feet from a lot of birch and whatnot, when you can no longer wade. 'Well then, it's impossible to put a decent fly on the water above the sunken ledge,' you say. It looks like it, but this is how it'd done: right here is a narrow point running to here, where it dwindles off to a single fat rock. If you work out on the point you can jump across to this rock—situated right here—and there you are, with about a thirty-foot cast to the sunken ledge. Deep water all around you, of course, and the rock is slippery; but—there you are. Now notice this small cove, right here. The water from the falls rushes past it in a froth, but in the cove it forms a deep eddy, with the current moving round and round like this." George made a slow circular motion with the fork. "You know what I mean?"

I nodded.

"I got out on the point and jumped to the rock; got myself balanced, worked out the right amount of line and cast the dungaree Bill had forced on me, just above the sunken ledge. I didn't take the water lightly and I cast again, but I couldn't put it down decently. It would just flop in—too much weight and too many feathers. I suppose I cast it a dozen times, trying to make it settle like a fly. I wasn't thinking of trout—there would be nothing in there except Old Faithful—I was just monkeying with this doodle-bug thing, now that I had it on.

"I gave up at last and let it lie out where I had cast it. I was standing there looking at the falls roaring down, when I remembered Isabelle, waiting up on the trail. I raised my rod preparatory to reeling in and the what-you-may-call-'em made a kind of dive and wiggle out there on the surface. I reached for my reel handle. Then I realized that the thingamajig wasn't on the water. I didn't see it disappear, exactly; I was looking at it, and then it wasn't there. 'That's funny,' I thought, and struck instinctively. Well, I was fast—so it seemed—and no snags in there. I gave it the butt three or four times, but the rod only bowed and nothing budged. I tried to figure it out. I thought perhaps a water-logged timber had come diving over the falls and upended right there. Then I noticed the rod take more of a bend and the line began to move through the water. It moved out slowly, very slowly, into the middle of the pool. It was exactly as though I was hooked on to a freight train just getting under way.

"I knew what I had hold of then, and yet I didn't believe it. I couldn't believe it. I kept thinking it was a dream, I remember. Of course, he could have gone away with everything I had any minute if he'd wanted to, but he didn't. He just kept moving slowly, round and round the pool. I gave him what pressure the tackle would stand, but he never noticed a little thing like that; just kept moving around the pool for hours, it seemed to me. I'd forgotten Isabelle; I admit that. I'd forgotten everything on earth. There didn't seem to be anything else on earth, as a matter of fact, except the falls and the pool and Old Faithful and me. At last Isabelle showed up on the bank above me, still lugging her ferns and whatnot. She called down to me above the noise of the falls. She asked me how long I expected her to wait alone in the woods, with night coming on.

"I hadn't had the faintest idea how I was going to try to land the fish until then. The water was boiling past the rock I was standing on, and I couldn't jump back to the point without giving him slack and perhaps falling in. I began to look around and figure. Isabelle said, 'What on earth are you doing?' I took off my landing net and tossed it to the bank. I yelled, 'Drop that junk quick and pick up that net!' She said, 'What for, George?' I said, 'Do as I tell you and don't ask questions!' She laid down what she had and picked up the net and I told her to go to the cove and stand ready.

"She said, 'Ready for what?' I said, 'You'll see what presently. Just stand there.' I'll admit I wasn't talking quietly. There was the noise of the falls to begin with, and—well, naturally, I wasn't.

"I went to work on the fish again. I began to educate him to the lead. I thought if I could lead him into the cove he would swing right past Isabelle and she could net him. It was slow work—a three-ounce rod—imagine! Isabelle called, 'Do you know what time it is?' I told her to keep still and stand where she was. She didn't say anything more than that.

"At last the fish began to come. He wasn't tired—he'd never done any fighting, as a matter of fact—but he'd take a suggestion as to where to go from the rod. I kept swinging him nearer and nearer the cove each time he came around. When I saw he was about ready to come I yelled to Isabelle. I said, 'I'm going to bring him right past you, close to the top. All you have to do is to net him.'

"When the fish came round again I steered him into the cove. Just as he was swinging past Isabelle the stuff she'd been lugging began to roll down the bank. She dropped the landing net on top of the fish and made a dive for those leaves and grasses and things. Fortunately the net handle lodged against the bank, and after she'd put her stuff in a nice safe place she came back and picked up the net again. I never uttered a syllable. I deserve no credit for that. The trout had made a surge and shot out into the pool and I was too busy just then to give her any idea of what I thought.

"I had a harder job getting him to swing in again. He was a little leery of the cove, but at last he came. I steered him toward Isabelle and lifted him all I dared. He came up nicely, clear to the top. I yelled, 'Here he comes! For God's sake, don't miss him!' I put everything on the tackle it would stand and managed to check the fish for an instant right in front of Isabelle.

"And this is what she did: it doesn't seem credible—it doesn't seem humanly possible; but it's a fact that you'll have to take my word for. She lifted the landing net above her head with both hands and brought it down on top of the fish with all her might!"

George ceased speaking. Despite its coating of talcum powder, I was able to detect an additional pallor in his countenance.

"Will I ever forget it as long as I live?" he inquired at last.

"No, George," I said, "but we've just exactly eleven minutes left."

George made a noticeable effort and went on.

"By some miracle the fish stayed on the hook; but I got a faint idea of what would have happened if he's taken a real notion to fight. He went around the pool so fast it must have made him dizzy. I heard Isabelle say, 'I didn't miss him, George'; and then—well, I didn't lose my temper; you wouldn't call it that exactly. I hardly knew what I said. I'll admit I shouldn't have said it. But I did say it; no doubt of that; no doubt of that whatever."

"What was it you said?" I asked.

George looked at me uneasily.

"Oh, the sort of thing a man would say impulsively—under the circumstances."

"Was it something disparaging about her?" I inquired.

"Oh, no," said George, "nothing about her. I simply intimated—in a somewhat brutal way, I suppose—that's she'd better get away from the pool—er—not bother me any more is what I meant to imply."

For the first time since George had chosen me for a confidant I felt a lack of frankness on his part.

"Just what did you say, George?" I insisted.

"Well, it wasn't altogether my words," he evaded. "It was the tone I used, as much as anything. Of course, the circumstances would excuse—Still, I regret it. I admit that. I've told you so plainly."

There was no time in which to press him further.

"Well, what happened then?" I asked.

"Isabelle just disappeared. She went up the bank, of course, but I didn't see her go. Old Faithful was still nervous and I had to keep my eye on the line. He quieted down in a little while and continued to promenade slowly around the pool. I suppose this kept up for half an hour more. Then I made up my mind that something had to be done. I turned very carefully on the rock, lowered the tip until it was on the line with the fish, turned the rod under my arm until it was pointing behind me and jumped.

"Of course, I had to give him slack; but I kept my balance on the point by the skin of my teeth, and when I raised the rod he was still on. I worked to the bank, giving out line, and crawled under some bushes and things and got around to the cove at last. Then I started to work again to swing him into the cove, but absolutely nothing doing. I could lead him anywhere except into the cove. He'd had enough of that; I didn't blame him, either.

"To make a long story short, I stayed with him for two hours. For a while it was pretty dark; but there was a good-sized moon that night, and when it rose it shone right down on the pool through a gap in the trees fortunately. My wrist was gone completely, but I managed to keep some pressure on him all the time, and at last he forgot about what had happened to him in the cove. I swung him in and the current brought him past me. He was on his side by now. I don't think he was tired even then—just discouraged. I let him drift over the net, heaved him out on the bank and sank down beside him, absolutely all in. I couldn't have got to my feet on a bet. I just sat there in a sort of daze and looked at Old Faithful, gleaming in the moonlight.

"After a half-hour's rest I was able to get up and go to camp. I planned what I was going to do on the way. There was always a crowd in the main camp living room after dinner. I simply walked into the living room without a word and laid Old Faithful on the center table.

"Well, you can imagine faintly what happened. I never got any dinner—couldn't have eaten any, as a matter of fact. I didn't even get a chance to take off my waders. By the time I'd told just how I'd done it to one crowd, more would come in and look at Old Faithful; and then stand and look at me for a while; and then make me tell it all over again. At last everybody began to dig up anything they had with a kick in it. Almost every one had a bottle he'd been hoarding. There was Scotch and gin and brandy and rye and a lot of experimental stuff. Art Bascom got a tin dish pan from the kitchen and put in on the table beside Old Faithful. He said, 'Pour your contributions right in here, men.' So each man dumped whatever he had into the dish pan and everybody helped himself.

"It was great, of course. The biggest night of my life, but I hope I'll never be so dog-tired again. I felt as though I'd taken a beating. After they'd weighed Old Faithful—nine pounds five and a half ounces; and he'd been out of water two hours—I said I had to go to bed, and went.

"Isabelle wasn't in the cabin. I thought, in a hazy way, that she was with some of the women, somewhere. Don't get the idea I was stewed. But I hadn't had anything to eat, and the mixture in that dish pan was plain TNT.

"I fell asleep as soon as I hit the bed; slept like a log till daylight. Then I half woke up, feeling that something terrific had happened. For a minute I didn't know what; then I remember what it was. I had landed Old Faithful on a three-ounce rod!

"I lay there and went over the whole thing from the beginning, until I came to Isabelle with the landing net. That made me look at where her head should have been on the pillow. It was there. She wasn't in the cabin. I thought perhaps she'd got up early and gone out to look at the lake or the sunrise or something. But I got up in a hurry and dressed.

"Well, I could see no signs of Isabelle about camp. I ran into Jean just coming from the head guide's cabin and he said, 'Too bad about your wife's mother.' I said, 'What's that?' He repeated what he'd said, and added, 'She must be an awful sick woman.' Well, I got out of him finally that Isabelle had come straight up from the stream the evening before, taken two guides and started for Buck's Landing. Jean had urged her to wait until morning, naturally; but she'd told him she must get to her mother at once, and took on so, as Jean put it, that he had to let her go.

"I said, 'Let me have Indian Joe, stern, and a good man, bow. Have 'em ready in ten minutes.' I rushed to the kitchen, drank two cups of coffee and started for Buck's Landing. We made the trip down in seven hours, but Isabelle had left with her trunks on the 10:40 train.

"I haven't seen her since. Went to her home once. She wouldn't see me; neither would her mother. Her father advised not forcing things—just waiting. He said he'd do what he could. We'll, he's done it—you read the letter. Now you know the whole business. You'll stick, of course, and see me through just the first of it, old man. Of course, you'll do that, won't you? We'd better get down to the train now. Track nineteen."

"George," I said, "one thing more: just what did you say to her when she—"

"Oh, I don't know," George began vaguely.

"George," I interrupted, "no more beating about the bush. What did you say?"

I saw his face grow even more haggard, if possible. Then it mottled into a shade resembling the brick on an old colonial mansion.

"I told her—" he began in a low voice.

"Yes?" I encouraged.

"I told her to get the hell out of there."

And now a vision was presented to my mind's eye; a vision of twelve fish plates, each depicting a trout curving up through green waters to an artificial fly. The vision extended on through the years. I saw Mrs. George Baldwin Potter ever gazing upon those rising trout and recalling the name on the card which had accompanied them to her door.

I turned and made rapidly for the main entrance of the Grand Central Station. In doing so I passed the clock above Information and saw that I still had two minutes in which to be conveyed by a taxicab far, far from the entrance to Track Nineteen.

I remember hearing the word "quitter" hurled after me by a hoarse, despairing voice.

Mr. Theodore Castwell

G. E. M. SKUES

Mr. Theodore Castwell, having devoted a long, strenuous and not unenjoyable life to hunting to their doom innumerable salmon, trout, and grayling in many quarters of the globe, and having gained much credit among his fellows for his many ingenious improvements in rods, flies, and tackle employed for that end, in the fullness of time died and was taken to his own place.

St. Peter looked up from a draft balance sheet at the entry of the attendant angel.

"A gentleman giving the name of Castwell. Says he is a fisherman, your Holiness, and has 'Fly-Fishers' Club, London' on his card."

"Hm-hm," says St. Peter. "Fetch me the ledger with his account." St. Peter perused it.

"Hm-hm," said St. Peter. "Show him in."

Mr. Castwell entered cheerfully and offered a cordial right hand to St. Peter.

"As a brother of the angle—" he began.

"Hm-hm," said St. Peter. "I have been looking at your account from below."

"I am sure I shall not appeal to you in vain for special consideration in connection with the quarters to be assigned to me here."

"Hm-hm," said St. Peter.

"Well, I've seen worse accounts," said St. Peter. "What sort of quarters would you like?"

"Do you think you could manage something in the way of a country cottage of the Test Valley type, with modern conveniences and, say, three quarters of a mile of one of those pleasant chalk streams, clear as crystal, which proceed from out the throne, attached?"

"Why, yes," said St. Peter. "I think we can manage that for you. Then what about your gear? You must have left your fly rods and tackle down below. I see you prefer a light split cane of nine foot or so, with appropriate fittings. I will indent upon the Works Department for what you require, including a supply of flies. I think you will approve of our dresser's productions. Then you will want a keeper to attend you."

"Thanks awfully, your Holiness," said Mr. Castwell. "That will be first-rate. To tell you the truth, from the Revelations I read, I was inclined to fear that I might be just a teeny-weeny bit bored in heaven."

"In h-hm-hm," said St. Peter, checking himself.

It was not long before Mr. Castwell found himself alongside an enchantingly beautiful clear chalk stream, some fifteen yards wide, swarming with fine trout feeding greedily: and presently the attendant angel assigned to him had handed him the daintiest, most exquisite, light split-cane rod conceivable—perfectly balanced with the reel and line—with a beautifully damped tapered cast of incredible fineness and strength, and a box of flies of such marvelous tying as to be almost mistakable for the natural insects they were to simulate.

Mr. Castwell scooped up a natural fly from the water, matched it perfectly from the fly box, and knelt down to cast to a riser putting up just under a tussock ten yards or so above him. The fly lit like gossamer, six inches above the last ring; and next moment the rod was making the curve of beauty. Presently, after an exciting battle, the keeper netted out a beauty of about two and a half pounds.

"Heavens," cried Mr. Castwell. "This is something like."

"I am sure his Holiness will be pleased to hear it," said the keeper.

Mr. Castwell prepared to move upstream to the next riser when he noticed that another trout had taken up the position of that which he had just landed, and was rising. "Just look at that," he said, dropping instantaneously to his knee and drawing off some line. A moment later an accurate fly fell just above the neb of the fish, and instantly Mr. Castwell engaged in battle with another lusty fish. All went well, and presently the landing net received its two and a half pounds.

"A very pretty brace," said Mr. Castwell, preparing to move on to the next string of busy nebs which he had observed putting up around the bend. As he approached the tussock, however, he became aware that the place from which he had just extracted so satisfactory a brace was already occupied by another busy feeder.

"Well, I'm damned," said Mr. Castwell. "Do you see that?"

"Yes, sir," said the keeper.

The chance of extracting three successive trout from the same spot was too attractive to be forgone, and once more Mr. Castwell knelt down and delivered a perfect cast to the spot. Instantly it was accepted and battle was joined. All held, and presently a third gleaming trout joined his brethren in the creel.

Mr. Castwell turned joyfully to approach the next riser round the bend. Judge, however, his surprise to find that once more the pit beneath the tussock was occupied by a rising trout, apparently of much the same size as the others.

"Heavens," exclaimed Mr. Castwell. "Was there ever anything like it?"

"No, sir," said the keeper.

"Look here," said he to the keeper, "I think I really must give this chap a miss and pass on to the next."

"Sorry, it can't be done, sir. His Holiness would not like it."

"Well, if that's really so," said Mr. Castwell, and knelt rather reluctantly to his task.

Several hours later he was still casting to the same tussock.

"How long is this confounded rise going to last?" inquired Mr. Castwell. "I suppose it will stop soon."

"No, sir," said the keeper.

"What, isn't there a slack hour in the afternoon?"

"No afternoon, sir."

"What? Then what about the evening rise?"

"No evening rise, sir," said the keeper.

"Well, I shall knock off now. I must have had about thirty brace from that corner."

"Beg pardon, sir, but his Holiness would not like that."

"What?" said Mr. Castwell. "Mayn't I even stop at night?"

"No night here, sir," said the keeper.

"Then do you mean that I have got to go on catching these damned two-and-a-half-pounders at this corner forever and ever?"

The keeper nodded.

"Hell!" said Mr. Castwell.

"Yes," said his keeper.

ACKNOWLEDGMENTS

All the excerpts used in this book are used by permission of the author, the author's estate, or by statute unless otherwise noted.

Where works have been reprinted recently, the last known edition is indicated for the reader's benefit.

"The Primitive Fish-Hook" by Barnet Phillips. From *The Century*. "Ælian—The Macedonian Invention, or the First Mention of an Artificial Fly" by William Radcliffe. From *Fishing from the Earliest Times* (Ares Publishers Inc., 1974). "The Compleat Angler" by Izaak Walton and Charles Cotton. From *The Compleat Angler: Or, The Contemplative Man's Recreation* (Modern Library, 1998.) "'Ktaadn Trout' and 'The Ponds' (Selections)" by Henry David Thoreau (1846). "Trout: Meeting Them on the 'June Rise'" by "Nessmuk." From *Fishing with a Fly*, eds. Charles F. Orvis and A. Nelson Cheney (Book Sales, 1990). "Trout Fishing on Long Island" by Frank Forester. From the Appendix of Walton and Cotton's *Compleat Angler*. "Reuben Wood: My First Fish" by Fred Mather. From *Men I Have Fished With* (Forest and Stream Publishing Co., 1897). "Trouting Along the Catasauqua" by Frank Forester. From *Frank Forester's Fugitive Sporting Sketches*. "The Boy and the Angle" by Rowland E. Robinson. From *Silver Fields and Other Sketches of a Farmer-Sportsman* (Houghton Mifflin Company). "The Boy and the Brook" by Lathan A. Crandall. From *Days in the Open* (Fleming H. Revell Company). "A Little Miss and a Big Fish" by Ruth Mae Lawrence. From *Tragic Fishing Moments*, ed. Will H. Dilg (The Reilly & Lee Company, 1922). "Some Memories of Early Days" by Lord Grey of Falloden. From *Fly Fishing* (The Lyons Press, 1985). "Fishing with My Daddy" by Jimmy Carter. From *An Outdoor Journal* (University of Arkansas Press, 1988). "The River God" by Roland Pertwee. From *The Saturday Evening Post* (July 7, 1928). "They're in the River" by John McPhee. From *The Founding Fish* (Farrar, Straus & Giroux, 2002). "The Black Bass as a Game Fish" by James A. Henshall. From *Book of the Black Bass* (Kensinger Publishing, 2006). "Red, White, and Bluegill" by Ted Leeson. From

Field & Stream (July 2004). "Sacred Eels" by James Prosek. "Colors that Attract Bass" by Ozark Ripley. From *Bass and Bass Fishing* (Sportsman's Digest Publishing Co., 1924). "The Leopard of the Lake" by Leonard Hulit. From *Fishing with a Boy: The Tale of a Rejuvenation* (Stewart Kidd Co., 1921). "A Big Fish, S-o-o-o-o Long" by W. N. Hull. From *Fishing Across the Continent: Short True Stories for Boys* (Kensinger Publishing, 2005). "The 'Lunge" by Stewart Edward White. From *The Forest* (Kensinger Publishing, 2005). "Slasher and the Shad" by Hart Stilwell. From *Outdoor Life Anthology of Fishing Adventures: The World's Best Stories of Fishing Adventures* (Popular Science Publishing Co., Inc., 1945). "Carp Fishing" by Frank Forester. From *Frank Forester's Fish and Fishing of the United States, and British Provinces of North America* by Frank Forester (Arno Publishing, 1970). "Bow-fin Fishing in the South Slang" by Rowland E. Robinson. From *Thomas H. Chubb's Catalogue of Anglers' Supplies*. "The Mascalonge" by James A. Henshall. From *Bass, Pike, Perch, and Other Game Fishes of North America* (Stewart Kidd Co., 1923). "A Pickerel Yarn" by Fred Mather. From *Forest and Stream*, September 4, 1897. "A Big Muskellunge" by W. N. Hull. From *Fishing Across the Continent* by W. N. Hull (A. Flanagan Co., 1905). "The Shanty" by Jerry Gibbs. "Fishing in the Ohio," John James Audubon. From *Delineations of American Scenery and Character* (Kensinger Publishing, 2006). "Down to the Sea!" by Charles Kingsley. From *The Water-Babies* (Puffin Classics, 1995). "Tale of a Bonefish" by C. Blackburn Miller. From *Outdoor Life Anthology of Fishing Adventures: The World's Best Stories of Fishing Adventures* (Popular Science Publishing Co., Inc., 1945). "The Angler and the Weakfish" by Charles Bradford. From *The Angler's Secret* (G. P. Putman's Sons, 1904). "Sea-Fishing in Simon's Bay" by Sir George Aston. From *Mostly About Trout* (George Allen & Unwin Ltd., 1921). "Sharks on the Shell Bars" by Vereen Bell. From *Outdoor Life Anthology of Fishing Adventures: The World's Best Stories of Fishing Adventures* (Popular Science Publishing Co., Inc., 1945). "The Saga of the Yellowfin" by Mark Sosin. "Keeping Busy When Not on the Casting Deck" by Lefty Kreh. "The Angler's Battle Royal: The Taking of the Tarpon" by Charles F. W. Mielatz. From *The Outing* Magazine (1903). "The Tarpon of Turner's River" by A. W. Dimock. From *The Book of the Tarpon* (Meadow Run Press, 2004). "The King of the Mackerel" by Charles F. Holder. From *Big Game Fishes* (The Macmillan Company, 1924). "The Island" by Margot Page. From *Little Rivers* (The Lyons Press, 1995). "Trailing the Sea-Bat" by Charles Frederick Holder. From *The Outing Magazine* (April 1900). "Byme-by-Tarpon" by Zane Grey. From *Tales of Fishes* (Amereon Limited, 1976). "Skelton's Party" (selection) by Thomas McGuane. From *The Armchair Angler* (Galahad Books, 1996). "The Lakes at Inhluzane" by Tom Sutcliffe. From *Hunting Trout* (2003). "2000 Words of Heartfelt Advice" by Verlyn Klinkenborg. "About the Brown Trout" by Samuel G. Camp. From *Field & Stream* Magazine (March 1907). "The Trout and the Indian" by General John McNulta.

From *Field & Stream* Magazine (May 1900). "First of April" by William Senior. From *Near and Far* (Sampson Low, Marston, & Co. 1888. "Practical Dry-Fly Fishing for Beginners" by Emlyn M. Gill. From *Practical Dry-Fly Fishing* (Easton Press, 1996). "The Evolution of a Flyfisher" by Joan Salvato Wulff. "Pied Beauty" by Gerard Manley Hopkins. From *An Angler's Garland of Fields, Rivers and Many Other Country Contentments* compiled by Eric Parker (Carroll & Nicholson, 1952). "A Bit of Luck" by Harry Plunket-Greene. From *Where the Bright Waters Meet* (Excellent Press, 2006). "Fishing with a Worm" by Bliss Perry. From *Fishing With a Worm* (Houghton Mifflin, 1916). "Nuptial Dress and Etiquette" by O. W. Smith. From *Trout Lore* (Frederick A. Stokes Company, 1917). "The Value of Observation" by George M. LaBranche. From *The Dry Fly and Fast Water* (Greycliffe Publishing, 1998). "The Demon of the Foam" by H. Prescott Beach. From *The Best of Sports Afield* (Atlantic Monthly Press, 1996). "Salmon-Fishing" by A. G. Wilkinson. From *Sport With Gun and Rod in American Woods and Waters*, ed. Alfred M. Mayer (The Century Co., 1883). "Empty Baskets Change the Tune" by Alexander Mackie. From *An Angler's Anthology*, ed. Eugene Burns (The Telegraph Press, 1952). "Two Old Trout of the Pools, and the Little Dry-Fly that Finally Accomplished Their Ruin" by Emlyn M. Gill. From *Practical Dry-Fly Fishing* (Easton Press, 1996). "The Big Trout of the Hog-Back" by O. W. Smith. From *The Best of Sports Afield* (Atlantic Monthly Press, 1996). "The Finest Trout in the River" by Harry Plunket-Greene. From *Where the Bright Waters Meet* (Excellent Press, 2006). "Winter Angling" by Frank S. Pinckney. From *Fishing With a Fly*, eds. Charles F. Orvis and A. Nelson Cheney (Book Sales, 1990). "Nothing Fishy About Trout" by Dave Barry. From *The Miami Herald* (September 19, 2004). "In Praise of Trout—And Also Me" by Paul O'Neil. Copyright © 1964 by Life Inc. Reprinted with permission. All rights reserved. "The Miramichi it ain't, so all right, it's 116th St." by John Bryan. From *Sports Illustrated* (October 17, 1977). "An Exploring Expedition" by W. C. Prime. From *I Go A-Fishing* (Harper & Brothers, 1915). "A Furcoated Fish" by B. F. Wilder. From *Tragic Fishing Moments*, ed. Will H. Dilg (The Reilly & Lee Co., 1922). "The Sportsman Tourist" by John A. Lant. From *The Best of Field & Stream* (The Lyons Press, 2002). "Memories of Mahseer" by P. R. Bairnsfather. From *A Book of Fishing Stories*, ed. F. G. Aflalo (Dent & Sons, Ltd., 1913). "The One That Got Away" (selection) by Howell Raines. From *The One That Got Away: A Memoir* (Scribner, 2006). "The Man Who Lived Two Lives in One: Zane Grey" by Robert H. Boyle. From *Sports Illustrated* (April 29, 1960). "Thaddeus Norris" by Fred Mather. From *My Angling Friends* (Forest and Stream Publishing Co., 1901). "The Angler" by Washington Irving. From *Roger Caras' Treasury of Great Fishing Stories* (Galahad Books, 1999). "What and Who Is an Angler?" by Thaddeus Norris. From *The Armchair Angler*, eds. Terry Brykcyznski and David Reuther (BBS Publishing Corporation, 1994). "The Fisherman's Song" by Thomas D'Urfey. "The

Devout Angler" by Collin D. B. Ellis. "Observations on the Practice of Angling" by John J. Brown. From *The American Angler's Guide* (Derrydale, 1993). "Note to *Don Juan* Canto XIII" by Lord Byron (1818). "Fishin' Jimmy" by Annie Trumbull Slosson. From *Fishin' Jimmy* (Books for Libraries Press, 1969). "A Painter, an Angler, and Some Others" by William Scrope. From *Days and Nights of Salmon Fishing in the Tweed* (The Mercat Press, 1975). "Fishing" by Reverend Thomas Bastard (1498). "Crazy for Rivers" (selection) by Bill Barich (The Lyons Press, 1999). "A River Runs Through It" (selection) by Norman Maclean (University of Chicago Press, 1976). "On Norman Maclean" by John Maclean (from *Fly Rod & Reel*, 1990). "George Croonenberghs" by John Maclean. From an introduction for George Croonenberghs at a meeting of a Chicago chapter of Trout Unlimited and from a eulogy given in October, 2005. "A Worm's-Eye View of Fishermen" by Beatrice Cook. From *The Armchair Angler*, eds. Terry Brykcyznski and David Reuther (BBS Publishing Corporation, 1994). "A Defense of Fishermen," Grover Cleveland. From *A Creelful of Fishing Stories*, ed. Henry van Dyke (Charles Scribner's Sons, 1932). "A Single Step" by George Reiger. From *The Washington Post*. "The Even-Tempered Angler" (selection) by Louis Rubin (Winchester Press, 1983). "What's in a Name?" by Howard Frank Mosher. "The Solitary and Friendly Sport" by R. Palmer Baker Jr. From *The Armchair Angler*, eds. Terry Brykcyznski and David Reuther (BBS Publishing Corporation, 1994). "Midstream Crisis" by Lamar Underwood. From *Editors in the Stream* (Halo Books, 1992). "Blue Dun" by Frank Mele. From *Small in the Eye of a River* (Paul Pursell, 1988). "Storytelling on the Thames" by Jerome K. Jerome. From *Three Men in a Boat* (Viking, 1978). "Ol' Settler of Deep Hole" by Irving Bacheller. From *Eben Holden: A Tale of the North Country* (Dodo Press, 2006). "The Lucy Coffin" by W.D. Wetherell. "A Fatal Salmon," Frank Forester. From *A Creelful of Fishing Stories: A Pastime Book*, ed. Henry van Dyke (Charles Scribner's Sons, 1932). "A Gallant Poacher" by John Buchan. From *John Mcnab* (The Houghton Mifflin Company, 1925). "Brannigan's Trout" by Nick Lyons. From *Full Creel* (Grove Atlantic, 2001). "A Fatal Success" by Henry van Dyke. From *Fisherman's Luck* (Indypublish.com, 2002). "On Dry-Cow Fishing as a Fine Art" by Rudyard Kipling. From *The Fishing Gazette* (December 1890). "The Hole" by Guy de Maupassant. From *Selected Short Stories* (Penguin, 1987). "The Lady or the Salmon?" by Andrew Lang. From *Angling Sketches* (Kensing Publishing, 2006). "Fish Are Such Liars!" (selection) by Roland Pertwee. From *Fish are Such Liars!* (Livingston Publishers, 1972). "A Wedding Gift" by John Taintor Foote. From *A Wedding Gift* (The Lyons Press, 1992). "Mr. Theodore Castwell" by G. E. M. Skues. From *Side-Lines, Side-Lights & Reflections* (Seeley Service & Co., Ltd., 1932).